Contents

Additional resources available for instructors:

Benjamin/Cummings Digital Library for Introductory Chemistry, 2nd edition (0-321-04637-4)

This cross-platform CD-ROM features all of the visuals from the Russo/Silver text. The CD-ROM provides instructors with a complete set of illustrations for incorporation into lecture presentations, study materials, and tests.

Printed Test Bank (0-321-05326-5)

By Paris Svoronos and Soraya Svoronos of Queensborough Community College of the City University of New York

This printed test bank includes over 1700 questions that correspond to the major topics in the text.

Computerized Test Bank (0-321-05328-1)

By Paris Svoronos and Soraya Svoronos of Queensborough Community College of the City University of New York

This dual-platform CD-ROM includes over 1700 questions that correspond to the major topics in the text.

Benjamin/Cummings Custom Laboratory Program

Create a custom laboratory manual by selecting labs and reorganizing experiments from our existing library, or by adding your own.

Study Guide and Selected Solutions (0-321-05327-3)

By Saundra Yancy McGuire of Louisiana State University

Features examples from each chapter, learning objectives, review of key concepts from the text, and additional problems for student practice. Also provides comprehensive answers and explanations to selected end-of-chapter problems from the text.

Instructor's Manual for the Introductory Chemistry Laboratory Manual (0-321-05330-3)

By Doris Kimbrough of University of Colorado at Denver and Wendy Gloffke of Cedar Crest College

For each lab, the manual provides teaching instructions, variations on experiments, thought-provoking discussion questions, and postlab suggestions.

Color Acetates (0-321-05329-X)

Includes 150 full-color acetates.

Additional resources available for students:

Problem Solving Guide and Workbook (0-321-06866-1)

By Saundra Yancy McGuire of Louisiana State University

Provides over 200 worked examples and more than 550 practice problems and quiz questions to help students develop and practice their problem-solving skills.

The Chemistry of Life CD-ROM for Introductory Chemistry (0-8053-3109-3)

By Robert M. Thornton, University of California, Davis

Through high-quality animations and interactive simulations, this CD-ROM helps students master crucial chemistry concepts. Simulated lessons, complete with interactive quizzes, cover: atomic structure, reactions and equilibrium, properties of water, acids and bases, and the structure and function of macromolecules. It also includes an illustrated glossary and topics correlated with the text.

Special Edition of The Chemistry Place (http://www.aw.com/chemplace/)

This special edition of **The Chemistry Place** engages students in interactive exploration of chemistry concepts and provides a wealth of tutorial support. Tailored to Russo/Silver Second Edition, the site includes detailed objectives for each chapter of the text, interactive tutorials featuring simulations, animations, and 3-D visualization tools, multiple-choice and short-answer quizzes, an extensive set of Web links, and a mathematics review. For instructors, a **Syllabus Manager** makes it easy to create an online syllabus complete with weekly assignments, projects, and test dates that students may access on the ChemPlace site.

Complete Solutions Manual

for

Introductory Chemistry

Second Edition

by

Steve Russo
Cornell University

Mike Silver
Hope College

Saundra Yancy McGuire

Louisiana State University

Benjamin
Cummings

San Francisco • Boston • New York
Cape Town • Hong Kong • London • Madrid • Mexico City
Montreal • Munich • Paris • Singapore • Sydney • Tokyo • Toronto

Executive Editor:	Ben Roberts
Senior Developmental Editor:	Margot Otway
Developmental Editor:	Irene Nunes
Marketing Manager:	Christy Lawrence
Director of Marketing:	Stacy Treco
Associate Project Editor:	Lisa Leung
Production Coordination:	Joan Marsh
Production Management:	Joan Keyes, Dovetail Publishing Services
Text illustrations:	Dovetail Publishing Services
Cover Image:	Quade Paul, fiVth.com
Cover Design:	Tony Asaro
Manufacturing:	Vivian McDougal
Printer and Binder:	Pearson Education

ISBN 0-321-05331-1

2 3 4 5 6 7 8 9 10—DPC—04 03 02 01
www.aw.com/bc

Acknowledgments

I extend my heartfelt gratitude to the many individuals who have worked tirelessly to produce this solutions manual.

My most sincere thanks go to Melissa Bailey Crawford, my writing assistant who checked many of the solutions; and to Irene Nunes, who significantly edited the solutions to make them most useful for beginning students. My thanks also go to Steve Russo and Mike Silver, authors of the textbook, for including me on this project. I also wish to thank Ben Roberts, executive editor, for his continuous support, and Lisa Leung, assistant editor, for her helpful assistance throughout the project. Very special thanks go to Joan Keyes of Dovetail Publishing Services for the meticulous manner in which she produced the final copy.

Last, but certainly not least, I want to thank my husband, Steve, for his understanding and patience for the many long hours of family time I spent solving introductory chemistry problems.

Saundra Y. McGuire, Ph.D.
Director, Center for Academic Success
Adjunct Professor, Department of Chemistry
Louisiana State University
Baton Rouge, LA 70809
smcgui1@lsu.edu

CHAPTER
1

What Is Chemistry?

1.1 See solution in textbook.

1.2 Milk is a heterogeneous mixture. If you could use a microscopic spoon to take samples from different locations in a container of milk, the spoon would pick up fat globules from some locations and watery liquid from other locations.

1.3 Fog is a heterogeneous mixture. A microscopic spoon used to take samples would pick up water in some spots and air in others.

1.4 See solution in textbook.

1.5 (d) and (e) are compounds. (a) is an elemental substance, (b) is a heterogeneous mixture, and (c) is a homogeneous mixture.

1.6 True. All compounds are pure substances, but a pure substance can also be an elemental substance. Example: O_2, N_2, and Fe are pure substances but are not compounds (they are elemental substances).

1.7 See solution in textbook.

1.8 (c) This change in state is an example of freezing—a liquid changes to a solid.

1.9 False. It is ethanol in the gas state but still ethanol.

1.10 Heat the metal until it just begins to melt. Then measure the temperature of the liquid to see if it is the same as the melting point of gold. Melting point is a characteristic property of pure substances and therefore can be used to determine the identity of a substance.

1.11 See solution in textbook.

1.12 Methane and oxygen are the reactants; water and carbon dioxide are the products.

1.13 (b) Both products contain hydrogen, H, an element not present in either reactant.

1.14 See solution in textbook.

1.15 A law summarizes experimental data and states an experimentally proved relationship between natural phenomena.

1.16 If the theory is used to predict the results of proposed experiments and then the data from those experiments agree with the prediction, this is good evidence the theory is correct.

1.17 Science is the experimental investigation and explanation of natural phenomena. Technology is the application of scientific knowledge. Example: scientists', through experiments, discovered microwave radiation. The development of the microwave oven is a technological application of this discovery.

1.18 Chemistry is the study of matter and the transformations it undergoes.

1.19 Numerous answers possible. Example: insecticides were developed in chemical laboratories to help control agricultural pests (positive result), but they pollute lakes and streams (negative result).

1.20 Numerous answers possible. One is that the chemical industry may be reluctant to fund basic research because of the possibility there will be no immediate financial profit from the work.

1.21 Numerous answers possible.

1.22 Matter is anything that has mass and occupies space.

1.23 Yes, because every compound is a pure substance and a mixture is defined as two or more pure substances intermingled. Example: salt water is a mixture of the two compounds $NaCl$ and H_2O.

1.24 A solution is a *homogeneous* mixture, which means the composition is the same in every part of the mixture. A heterogeneous mixture has variable composition.

1.25 It is a heterogeneous mixture. A microscopic spoon would be able to extract either flour or sugar, depending on where in the mixture the spoon was placed. No amount of mechanical grinding of two solids can ever produce a solution (which, remember, is just another name for homogeneous mixture).

1.26 (a) It is a heterogeneous mixture, as in Problem 1.25.
(b) It is a solution. Once the mixture becomes liquid (molten), the composition is constant throughout because the Cu and Zn atoms mix completely.
(c) It is a solution. When the liquid freezes, all the Cu and Zn atoms are still completely intermingled and the composition is the same throughout the solid.

1.27 Air (once we have filtered out all the pollution particles!) is a solution because the atoms and molecules of which it is composed are evenly dispersed throughout, resulting in a constant composition throughout.

1.28 An element is one of the basic building blocks of matter. There are 113 known elements today.

1.29 Na comes from *natrium* , the Latin word meaning "sodium," and Fe comes from *ferrum,* the Latin word meaning "iron." With only 26 letters in the English alphabet and 113 known elements, there are not enough letters for each element to have a one-letter symbol.

1.30 The smallest possible piece of an element is an atom. There are a few elemental substances whose smallest unit is a diatomic (two-atom) molecule. You should memorize all the diatomic elemental substances. They are hydrogen, H_2, nitrogen, N_2, oxygen, O_2, fluorine, F_2, chlorine, Cl_2, bromine, Br_2, and iodine, I_2.

1.31 Lead, Pb; molybdenum, Mo; tungsten, W; chromium, Cr; mercury, Hg.

1.32 Sulfur, S; chlorine, Cl; phosphorus, P; magnesium, Mg; manganese, Mn.

1.33 Ti, titanium; Zn, zinc; Sn, tin; He, helium; Xe, xenon; Li, lithium.

1.34 U, uranium; Pu, plutonium; Cs, cesium; Ba, barium; F, fluorine; Si, silicon.

1.35 An elemental substance contains only one type of atom, and a compound contains two or more different types of atoms. Example: nitrogen gas, N_2, and lead, Pb, are elemental substances; water, H_2O, and carbon dioxide, CO_2, are compounds.

1.36 The chemical formula tells how many of each type of atom are present in the smallest possible piece of a pure substance.

1.37 Numerous answers possible. Example: the elements hydrogen and oxygen, both gases at room temperature, combine to form the compound water, a liquid at room temperature.

1.38 F_2, P_4, Ar, and Al are elemental substances because each contains atoms of only one element; $BrCl_3$, C_2H_2, HCl, and Al_2O_3 are compounds because each contains atoms of more than one element.

1.39 Chlorine, Cl_2, sulfur, S_8, and neon, Ne, are elemental substances (atoms of only one element); octane, C_8H_{18}, is a compound (atoms of more than one element).

1.40 The chemical formula for hydrogen peroxide is H_2O_2.

1.41 The chemical formula for nonane is C_9H_{20}.

1.42 The chemical formula for glucose is $C_6H_{12}O_6$.

1.43 (a) Knowing the chemical formula N_2, you can say that the smallest possible piece of nitrogen gas contains two nitrogen atoms.

(b) Nitrogen gas is not a compound. It is an elemental substance because it contains only one type of atom.

1.44 The three most common states of matter are solid, liquid, and gas.

1.45 Sublimation is the process whereby matter changes directly from the solid state to the gas state.

1.46 Condensation (gas state to liquid state) is the opposite of evaporation (liquid state to gas state).

1.47 The propane would be a gas, and the hexane would be a liquid.

1.48 The melting point is $-117.3°C$ because melting point and freezing point are the same temperature.

1.49 Sublimation is occurring. The compound the mothballs are made of is going directly from the solid state to the gas state.

1.50 The melting point is $0°C$ or $32°F$, and the boiling point is $100°C$ or $212°F$.

1.51 O_2 and O_3 are completely different substances and therefore have completely different physical and chemical properties. When determining chemical and physical properties, the *number* of atoms in a molecule is as important as *which* atoms are present.

1.52 Because H_2O and H_2O_2 are different compounds, they have different properties.

1.53 The sugar has undergone a physical change because its chemical composition is not changed when it dissolves in the water. The sugar can be recovered by evaporating the water.

1.54 The ethanol has undergone a chemical change because its chemical composition has been changed. New compounds have been formed.

1.55 A chemical reaction represents the chemical transformation of one or more substances (the reactants) to one or more different substances (the products).

1.56 This is a description of a chemical property because it tells you how white phosphorus behaves when combined with another substance.

1.57 This is a chemical change because the pure substance Ag is transformed into the different pure substance Ag_2S.

1.58 A chemical transformation has taken place because a new compound has been formed. Any compound formed in a chemical transformation usually has properties very different from the properties of the substances from which it was made, and that is certainly the case here.

1.59 A law is a statement that summarizes experimental data. A theory is a statement that proposes an explanation of why a law is true.

1.60 The scientific method requires that experiments be run to test a theory. If a theory is false, experimental data will yield results that are different from those predicted by the theory.

1.61 Numerous answers possible.

1.62 Numerous answers possible. Four factors that might account for the "failure" of the scientific method are human error, faulty experimental equipment, biased scientists who do not accurately report results, and incomplete data.

1.63 C, Na, and Hg are elemental substances; $NaHCO_3$ and CO_2 are compounds.

1.64 $C(s)$, $N_2(g)$, and $N_2(l)$, are elemental substances; $H_2O(l)$ and $HNO_3(l)$ are compounds.

1.65 (a) Science.   (b) Science.   (c) Technology.   (d) Science.   (e) Technology.

1.66 Sulfuric acid is the compound. Ozone is an elemental substance, and stainless steel and coffee are mixtures.

1.67 This process is a chemical reaction because a new substance is formed.

1.68 (a) Mixture.   (b) Mixture.   (c) Compound.   (d) Compound.
(e) Elemental substance.

1.69 Evaporation.

1.70 (a) Sodium.   (b) Iron.   (c) Cobalt.   (d) Tin.   (e) Manganese.

1.71 (a) Gold.   (b) Mercury.   (c) Potassium.   (d) Phosphorus.   (e) Silver.

1.72 This is a chemical change because iron, Fe, is transformed into Fe_2O_3, iron oxide, a/k/a rust.

1.73 This is the definition of a scientific law.

1.74 The salt and sugar can form homogeneous mixtures with water. Because their particles can never intermingle completely with water, sand and gold form heterogeneous mixtures with water.

1.75 The sugar dissolved in water is a liquid that is a mixture, and the melted sugar is a liquid that is a pure substance.

1.76 Numerous answers possible. One is alcohol and water.

1.77 Numerous answers possible. One is carbon dioxide gas in a carbonated soft drink.

1.78 The copper and zinc must be melted, mixed to form a homogeneous liquid solution, and then cooled to form brass, a solid solution.

1.79 Numerous answers possible. One is oxygen gas dissolved in nitrogen gas, which is a homogeneous mixture because one substance *dissolved* in another forms a *solution*, which is another name for homogeneous mixture.

1.80 Sublimation.

1.81 A chemical change; a change in color generally indicates that a new substance is formed.

1.82 A chemical change; all combustion (explosive combustion in this case) requires oxygen, and there the explosive powder in the dynamite reacted with oxygen from the air.

1.83 You would use a magnet to separate the iron filings from the sand.

1.84 You would first add water to the mixture, dissolving the salt. Once all the salt was dissolved, you would filter the liquid–sand mixture. The sand would remain on the filter paper, and evaporating the filtered water would leave you with the salt isolated.

1.85 This separation cannot be done physically because pure water is a compound and the components of a compound can be separated only by *chemical* means.

1.86 N_2 is the only elemental substance in this list.

1.87 This is a scientific theory because it offers an explanation ("because they all have a single electron . . . ") for some experimentally observed behavior (that these metals react with water).

1.88 The substances to the left of the arrow, $C_6H_{12}O_6$ and O_2, are the reactants; those to the right of the arrow, CO_2 and H_2O, are products. The equation represents a chemical change because new substances are formed.

1.89 The 14-karat gold is the homogeneous mixture made by melting gold and other metals together and then letting the solution solidify.

1.90 Fog is the heterogeneous mixture because it is made of numerous components and its composition varies from one place to another in a sample.

1.91 True.

1.92 Ozone, O_3, is the elemental substance in this list.

1.93 Bronze, which is a solid solution of copper metal and tin metal.

1.94 True.

1.95 NaCl is the only compound in the list, being made of two types of atoms. Ozone and liquid nitrogen are elemental substances, 18-karat gold is a homogeneous mixture of gold and other metals, and iced tea is a heterogeneous mixture of a tea solution and solid H_2O.

CHAPTER
2

The Numerical Side of Chemistry

2.1 See solution in textbook.

2.2 Ike is more accurate. Mike's average value is 262, which is higher than the actual value; Ike's average value is 260, which is equal to the actual value. However, Mike is more precise because his values have a spread of 10 (266 − 256) and Ike's have a spread of 36 (278 − 242).

2.3 Jack will be more accurate. If he completely fills the half-quart container twice, the total volume will be very close to 1 quart. However, Jill needs to estimate 1/40 of the 10-gallon container, which is difficult to do with much accuracy (1/40 because 1 gallon = 4 quarts).

2.4 See solution in textbook.

2.5 The uncertainty is ±0.05 gallon because the last digit in the measured volume, 16.0 gallons, is in the tenths column.

2.6 The uncertainty is ±0.005 volt because the tenths value can be read from the dial (each shorter mark on the dial is 0.1 volt). Thus the first digit that must be estimated is the one in the hundredths place. You get the uncertainty by putting a 1 in the uncertain position and dividing by 2: 0.01 ÷ 2 = 0.005.

2.7 See solution in textbook.

2.8 You would express the uncertainty ±0.5 inch in the measured value 600 inches by using a decimal point—600.—to indicate that both zeros are significant.

2.9

	Number of significant figures	Uncertainty
10.0	3	0.1 ÷ 2 = ±0.05
0.004 60	3	0.000 01 ÷ 2 = ±0.000 005
123	3	1 ÷ 2 = ±0.5

2.10 See solution in textbook.

2.11 0.473 (the negative exponent means the number gets smaller).

2.12 47,325 (the positive exponent means the number gets larger).

2.13 See solution in textbook.

2.14 0.002 35

2.15 6000

2.16 See solution in textbook.

2.17 $4.710\,000\,0 \times 10^{13}$. The fact that the uncertainty is ±0.5 million tells you the final significant digit is in the 1-million column (because 1 million ÷ 2 = 0.5 million), which in this number is the fifth zero from the left.

2.18 $4.710\,000 \times 10^{13}$. The uncertainty of ±5 million tells you the last significant digit is in the 10-millions column, the fourth zero from the left.

2.19 See solution in textbook.

2.20 44 miles². The answer can have only two significant figures because of the 2.0 miles.

2.21 660. hours. The exact 3 has an infinite number of significant figures, meaning the number of significant figures in the answer is determined by the value 220. hours. The decimal point following the zero tells you this number has three significant figures, and that is how many the answer must have.

2.22 See solution in textbook.

2.23 See solution in textbook.

2.24 (a) 6.1×10^2 pounds/inch. The answer can have only two significant figures because of the 2.0 inches.

    (b) 6.11×10^2 or 611 pounds/inch. The answer can have only three significant figures because of the 2.00 inches.

    (c) 86.88 cm because the 4 you multiply by is an exact number, assumed to have an infinite number of signficant figures. Thus the product of 21.72 × 4 should contain the same number of digits as there are in 21.72.

2.25 See solution in textbook.

2.26
$$
\begin{array}{r}
1555 \text{ cm} \\
+ \quad 0.001 \text{ cm} \\
+ \quad 0.8 \text{ cm} \\
\hline
1555.801 \text{ cm}
\end{array}
$$
, which rounded off to the correct number of significant figures is 1556 cm.

2.27
$$
\begin{array}{r}
142 \text{ cm} \\
- \quad 0.48 \text{ cm} \\
\hline
141.52 \text{ cm}
\end{array}
$$
, which rounded off to the correct number of significant figures is 142 cm.

2.28 See solution in textbook.

2.29 4.736 km. The fact that 1 km is the same as 1000 m means that 4.736 km is the same as 4.736×1000 m = 4736 m.

2.30 25 mm. The fact that 1 mm is the same as 0.001 m means that 25 mm is the same as 25×0.001 m = 0.025 m.

2.31 See solution in textbook.

2.32 Because 1 mL is 1/1000 of a liter, multiply the given number of liters by 0.001 to get milliliters.

2.33 $1 \text{ cm}^3 = 1$ mL, which means that $246.7 \text{ cm}^3 = 246.7$ mL.

2.34 K = °C + 273.15; therefore °C = K − 273.15; 263.5 K − 273.15 = − 9.7°C.

$$°F = 32 + \frac{9}{5}°C = 14.5°F$$

2.35 See solution in textbook.

2.36 The volume of the cube is 10.0 mm × 10.0 mm × 10.0 mm = 1000 mm³. Because the problem asks for grams per milliliter, you must convert this volume to milliliters. The easiest way to do this is to first change mm³ to cm³. Note that 10.0 mm = 1.00 cm; thus $(10.00 \text{ mm})^3 = (1.00 \text{ cm})^3$, or 1000 mm³ = 1.00 cm³. The density of the cube is therefore 4.70 g/1.00 cm³ = 4.70 g/cm³. Because 1.00 cm³ = 1.00 mL, the density is 4.70 g/mL.

2.37 $\dfrac{500.0 \text{ g}}{150.5 \text{ mL}} = 3.322 \text{ g} / \text{mL}$

2.38 See solution in textbook.

2.39 $\dfrac{1 \text{ day}}{24 \text{ h}} \qquad \dfrac{24 \text{ h}}{1 \text{ day}}$

2.40 $50.0 \text{ miles} \times \dfrac{1 \text{ h}}{600.0 \text{ miles}} = 0.0833 \text{ h}$

2.41 $\dfrac{600.0 \text{ miles}}{1 \text{ h}} \times 50.0 \text{ h} = 3.00 \times 10^4 \text{ miles}$

2.42 See solution in textbook.

2.43 $500.0 \text{ L} \times \dfrac{1000 \text{ mL}}{1 \text{ L}} \times \dfrac{0.001\,30 \text{ g}}{1 \text{ mL}} = 650. \text{ g} = 6.50 \times 10^2 \text{ g}$

$650. \text{ g} \times \dfrac{1 \text{ kg}}{1000 \text{ g}} = 0.650 \text{ kg}$

2.44 $1.50 \text{ lb} \times \dfrac{453.6 \text{ g}}{1 \text{ lb}} \times \dfrac{1 \text{ mL}}{11.4 \text{ g}} = 59.7 \text{ mL}$

2.45 Conversion factors: $\dfrac{6 \text{ cups flour}}{1 \text{ cake}} \qquad \dfrac{1 \text{ cup flour}}{120.0 \text{ g flour}}$

$6955 \text{ g flour} \times \dfrac{1 \text{ cup flour}}{120.0 \text{ g flour}} \times \dfrac{1 \text{ cake}}{6 \text{ cups flour}} = 9.660 \text{ cakes}$

You can bake nine cakes (it's not possible to bake a partial cake).

2.46 Your time conversion is easy enough—hours to minutes—but going from meters squared to feet squared knowing only the conversion factors given in the chapter means several multiplications plus squaring the factors:

$250.0 \dfrac{\text{m}^2}{\text{h}} \times \dfrac{1 \text{ h}}{60 \text{ min}} \times \left(\dfrac{1 \text{ ft}}{12 \text{ in.}} \right)^2 \times \left(\dfrac{1 \text{ in.}}{2.54 \text{ cm}} \right)^2 \times \left(\dfrac{100 \text{ cm}}{1 \text{ m}} \right)^2 = 44.85 \text{ ft}^2/\text{min}$

The answer has four significant digits because 2.54 cm in the centimeter–inch conversion factor is an exact number.

2.47 See solution in textbook.

2.48 See solution in textbook.

2.49 See solution in textbook.

2.50 See solution in textbook.

2.51 See solution in textbook.

2.52 Convert volume in milliliters to mass in grams:

$50.0 \text{ mL} \times \dfrac{0.785 \text{ g}}{\text{mL}} = 39.3 \text{ g ethanol}$

The temperature change is $60.0°\text{C} - 22.0°\text{C} = 38.0 \text{ C}°$. Now get the specific heat of ethanol from Table 2.5 of the textbook and use the heat equation:

$2.43 \dfrac{\text{J}}{\text{g} \cdot \text{C}°} \times 39.3 \text{ g} \times 38.0 \text{ C}° \times \dfrac{1 \text{ kJ}}{1000 \text{ J}} = 3.63 \text{ kJ}$

2.53 $3.63 \text{ kJ} \times \dfrac{1000 \text{ J}}{1 \text{ kJ}} = 3630 \text{ J}$

$3.63 \text{ kJ} \times \dfrac{1 \text{ Cal}}{4.184 \text{ kJ}} = 0.868 \text{ Cal}$

$3.63 \text{ kJ} \times \dfrac{1 \text{ cal}}{4.184 \text{ J}} = \dfrac{1000 \text{ J}}{1 \text{ kJ}} = 868 \text{ cal}$

2.54 The temperature change is $35.5°\text{C} - 22.0°\text{C} = 13.5 \text{ C}°$. Thus

$1.000 \dfrac{\text{cal}}{\text{g water} \cdot \text{C}°} \times 1.00 \text{ kg water} \times \dfrac{1000 \text{ g water}}{1 \text{ kg water}} \times 13.5 \text{ C}° = 1.35 \times 10^4 \text{ cal}$

This is the calorie count for only 0.1000 g of the candy. Because the problem asks for big-C Calories per gram of candy, you have one more step:

$\dfrac{1.35 \times 10^4 \text{ cal}}{0.100 \text{ g candy}} \times \dfrac{1 \text{ Cal}}{1000 \text{ cal}} = 1.35 \times 10^2 \text{ Cal/g candy}$

2.55 The 3 in "3 feet in a yard" is an exact number and therefore is really 3.0000 . . . with an unlimited number of significant figures. The 3 in "a certain piece of wood is 3 feet long" comes from a measurement and therefore has some uncertainty associated with it.

2.56 Precision refers to how close to one another various measurements of the same quantity are. Accuracy refers to how close a measured result is to the true value. Although a set of measurements can be both accurate *and* precise, the two terms never mean the same thing.

2.57 You should choose the accurate result because a precise value that is not accurate is useless. An accurate value that is not precise usually gets you at least close to the true value. For instance, for a true value of 583, the precise but inaccurate measurements 520, 520, 519 are useless but the accurate but imprecise measurements 573, 588, 594 are of value.

2.58 The measurements are neither accurate nor precise. The average of the three measurements is 2.7 miles, far from the true value of 1.6 miles. The range between the largest and smallest measurements is 0.8 mile, half the true distance!

2.59 The person with the tape measure. He or she needs to make only one measurement, but the person with the ruler has to make at least 200 measurements and add them to get the length. There would be uncertainty associated with each measurement, resulting in a significant loss of accuracy in the result.

2.60 ±1/16 inch. The uncertain digit is the one that is estimated as lying somewhere between the markings. The ruler is marked in eighths, and therefore the estimating is done in the sixteenths place.

2.61 The convention is that the last digit written is assumed to be uncertain, and the uncertainty is determined by putting a 1 in the place of the uncertain digit and dividing by 2. Some examples:
15.2 $0.1 \div 2 = 0.05 \Rightarrow 15.2 \pm 0.05$
1534 $1 \div 2 = 0.5 \Rightarrow 1534 \pm 0.5$
0.00987 $0.00001 \div 2 = 0.000005 \Rightarrow 0.00987 \pm 0.000005$

2.62 Because no measuring tool has an infinite number of markings. The last digit written in a reported measured value is always an estimate between the markings.

2.63 (a) $0.01 \div 2 = 0.005 \Rightarrow 12.60 \pm 0.005 \text{ cm}$
(b) $0.1 \div 2 = 0.05 \Rightarrow 12.6 \pm 0.05 \text{ cm}$
(c) $0.000\,000\,01 \div 2 = 0.000\,000\,005 \Rightarrow 0.000\,000\,03 \pm 0.000\,000\,005 \text{ inch}$
(d) $1 \div 2 = 0.5 \Rightarrow 125 \pm 0.5 \text{ feet}$

2.64 (a) Four.   (b) Three.   (c) One.   (d) Three.

2.65 Replacing the uncertain digit, 5, by 1 gives 0.1 million years. Dividing this value by 2 gives an uncertainty of 0.05 million years, which is 50,000 years.

2.66 (a) No trailing zeros.   (b) No trailing zeros.   (c) No trailing zeros.   (d) 0.01$\underline{0}$

2.67 (a) 12.2$\underline{02}$ (b) No significant zeros.   (c) 2$\underline{05}$ (d) 0.01$\underline{0}$

2.68 (a) 12.202 ±0.0005 km   (b) 0.01 ±0.005 mL   (c) 205 ±0.5°C   (d) 0.010 ±0.0005 g

2.69 It is not clear whether 30 has one or two significant figures because the zero may or may not be significant. Adding the decimal point at the end of the number indicates that the trailing zero is significant, meaning 30. has two significant digits.

2.70 The measurement 2200 feet can be interpreted as having four, three, or two significant digits. Without more information, you cannot tell.

2.71 (a) 56.0 kg (three significant figures).
(b) 0.000 25 m (two significant figures).
(c) 5,600,000 miles (four significant figures, but you cannot tell that by looking at this normal notation).
(d) 2 feet (one significant figure).

2.72 (a) 56.0 ±0.05 kg
(b) 0.000 25 ±0.000 005 m
(c) 5,600,000 ±500 miles. Remember, this measured value has only four significant figures, which means the uncertain digit is in the thousands position: 1000 ÷ 2 = 500.
(d) 2 ±0.5 feet

2.73 (a) An uncertainty of ±5 feet means the number divided by 2 to calculate the uncertainty was in the tens position. Therefore only the 3 in 30 is significant. This is indicated in scientific notation by writing 3×10^1 feet.
(b) ±0.5 feet came from having the 1 for the uncertainty calculation in the ones place, meaning both 3 and 0 are significant: 3.0×10^1 feet.
(c) ±0.05 feet came from having the 1 for the uncertainty calculation in the tenths place, meaning you are entitled to one more significant figure: 3.00×10^1 feet.

2.74 2.2×10^3 feet, because ±50 feet means the uncertain digit is in the hundreds place. Therefore only the two 2's in 2200 are significant.

2.75 (a) 2.26×10^2 (b) 2.260×10^2 (c) 5.0×10^{-10} (d) 3×10^{-1} (e) 3.0×10^{-1}
(f) 9.00×10^8. The ±0.5 million means the uncertain digit is in the millions place, which is the second zero to the right of the 9.
(g) $9.000 006 \times 10^8$. The ±50 means the uncertain digit is in the hundredths place, which is the 5. Because the first digit to be dropped is 7, you must round the retained 5 up to 6.

2.76 (a) One significant figure. Uncertainty is 0.001 ÷ 2 = ±0.0005 kg.
(b) Two significant figures. Uncertainty is 0.000 01 ÷ 2 = ±0.5 m.
(c) Three significant figures. Uncertainty is 1 ÷ 2 = ±0.5 L.
(d) Four significant figures. Uncertainty is 0.000 001 ÷ 2 = ±0.000 000 5 m.
(e) Two significant figures. Uncertainty is 100,000 ÷ 2 = ±50,000 km.

2.77 102 inches because the least certain measured value, either 100. or 2, has its uncertain digit in the ones position, which means the answer has its uncertain digit in the ones position. The uncertainty is ±0.5 inch.

2.78 (a) 4.6 cm   (b) 4.6 m^2
(c) 1.000×10^4 J if all zeros in the 1000 are significant, 1×10^4 J if none of them are significant.
(d) Because of the 0.1, your answer can have only one significant figure. Thus even though your calculator displays 12.4, all you are allowed to report is 10 mm^2 or, better, 1×10^1 mm^2.

2.79 $20,450.2 \text{ feet} \times \dfrac{1 \text{ mile}}{5280 \text{ feet}} = 3.873\,14 \text{ miles}$ (six significant figures because 5280 is an exact number).

2.80 (a) 2.55×10^5 km. The 33,300 has its uncertain digit in the hundreds position; the 222,000 has its uncertain digit in the thousands position and so is the less certain value. Therefore the answer must have its uncertain digit in the thousands position: 255,300 becomes 2.55×10^5.

(b) 1.000×10^{18} J. Your display was 1exp18, but both values in this division have four significant figures, meaning the answer should also have four.

(c) 2.11×10^2 m. The uncertain digit is in the ones position in 234 and in the tenths position in 23.4. The subtraction rule tells you the answer must therefore be uncertain in the ones position: 210.6 becomes 2.11×10^2.

(d) 4.00×10^4 L. The uncertain digit is in the hundreds position in $4.00 \times 10^4 = 40,000$ and in the thousandths position in $6.00 \times 10^{-1} = 0.600$. The answer must therefore be uncertain in the hundreds position: 40,000.600 becomes 4.00×10^4.

2.81 Length, meter; volume, cubic meter.

2.82 Liter (L) and milliliter (mL). These units are used more often than the cubic meter because they are more commonly encountered in everyday situations and in the laboratory.

2.83 It is always correct to use cm^3 instead of mL. The two units are exactly equivalent.

2.84 To eliminate the confusion caused by having different sets of nonuniform measuring scales.

2.85 (a) 2.31×10^9 m (b) 5.00×10^{-6} m (c) 1.004×10^0 m (d) 5.00×10^{-12} m (e) 2.5×10^2 m

2.86 A Celsius degree is larger. There are only 100 Celsius degree between the freezing point and boiling point of water. However, there are 180 Fahrenheit degrees in this same temperature range. Therefore a Fahrenheit degree is only 5/9 the size of a Celsius degree ($100/180 = 5/9$).

2.87 The Celsius and Fahrenheit scales can have negative temperature values. The Kelvin scale cannot because the zero point on the Kelvin scale is absolute zero. There is no colder temperature possible than absolute zero, 0 K.

2.88 (a) $(22.5°C \times 9/5) + 32 = 72.5°F$; $22.5°C + 273.15 = 295.65\text{ K} = 295.6\text{ K}$

(b) $(-3.0°F - 32)(5/9) = -19.4°C$; $-19.4°C + 273.15 = 253.75\text{ K} = 253.8\text{ K}$

(c) $0.0\text{ K} - 273.15 = -273.15°C = -273.2°C$; $(-273.2°C \times 9/5) + 32 = -459.8°F$

(d) $(65.1°C \times 9/5) + 32 = 149°F$; $65.1°C + 273.15 = 338.15\text{ K} = 338.2\text{ K}$

2.89 32°F; 0°C; 273 K

2.90 There are 180 F° for every 100 C°, and 180 F°/100 C° = 9 F°/5 C°.

2.91 (a) In the left cylinder, each shorter mark is 0.1 mL, which means the uncertain digit in a volume measurement must be in the hundredths position. The uncertainty is thus $0.01 \div 2 = \pm 0.005$ mL. In the right cylinder, each shorter mark is 10 mL, which means the uncertain digit in a volume measurement is in the ones position and the uncertainty is $1 \div 2 = \pm 0.5$ mL.

(b) The left cylinder contains 1.18 ±0.005 mL. The right cylinder contains 98 ±0.5 mL. Adding the two numbers yields 98 mL + 1.18 mL = 99.18 mL, which must be reported as 99 mL because the 98 value restricts your answer to being uncertain in the ones position. The uncertainty in this value is $1 \div 2 = \pm 0.5$ mL.

2.92 $V = 1.6 \text{ cm} \times 1.6 \text{ cm} \times 1.6 \text{ cm} = 4.096 \text{ cm}^3 = 4.1 \text{ cm}^3$.

2.93 The student who reports 1.5 cm used the ruler incorrectly. The ruler is marked in millimeters, which is tenths of centimeters. The uncertainty therefore lies in the hundredths place, and the measurement should be reported to the hundredths place—1.50 cm.

2.94 The radius is $\dfrac{2.55 \text{ cm}}{2} = 1.275 \text{ cm} = 1.28 \text{ cm}$.

2.95 Density is the amount of mass in a given volume of a material. It is called a derived unit because it is a combination of one SI base unit, mass, and one SI derived unit, volume.

2.96 From Table 2.4, you know that the density of water at 25°C is 0.997 g/mL. Therefore

$$1000.0 \text{ mL} \times 0.997 \frac{g}{mL} = 997 \text{ g}$$

2.97 From Table 2.4, you know that the density of mercury at 25°C is 13.6 g/mL. Therefore

$$2.0 \text{ L} \times \frac{1000 \text{ mL}}{1 \text{ L}} \times 13.6 \frac{g}{mL} = 27{,}200 \text{ g} = 2.7 \times 10^4 \text{ g}$$

2.98 The volume of the stick is 10.0 cm × 10.0 cm × 10.0 cm = 1.00×10^3 cm^3 = 1.00×10^3 mL. Therefore

$$1.00 \times 10^3 \text{ mL} \times \frac{0.9 \text{ g}}{mL} = 9 \times 10^2 \text{ g}$$

2.99 First determine the mass of the pumpkin. Then place the pumpkin in a container completely filled with water and collect the water the pumpkin displaces in a calibrated container. The volume of the pumpkin is equal to the volume of the water displaced by the pumpkin. Calculate density by dividing the mass by the volume.

2.100 The two students measure the same density, 19.3 g/mL. The student who works with the 200-g bar finds that it occupies twice the volume of the 100-g bar. Because density is an intensive property, its value does not depend on the size of the sample.

2.101 Place a chunk of each metal in a container of liquid mercury, which has a density of 13.6 g/mL. The lead, with a density of 11.4 g/mL, is less dense than the mercury and therefore floats. Gold, with a density of 19.3 g/mL, is denser than the mercury and therefore sinks.

2.102 $1.25 \text{ days} \times \frac{24 \text{ h}}{1 \text{ day}} \times \frac{60 \text{ min}}{1 \text{ h}} \times \frac{60 \text{ s}}{1 \text{ min}} = 1.08 \times 10^5 \text{ s}$

2.103 $100.0 \text{ miles} \times \frac{1 \text{ h}}{45.0 \text{ miles}} \times \frac{60 \text{ min}}{1 \text{ h}} = 133 \text{ min}$

2.104 $\frac{25.50 \text{ dollars}}{h} \times \frac{1 \text{ h}}{60 \text{ min}} \times \frac{1 \text{ min}}{60 \text{ s}} = 7.083 \times 10^{-3} \text{ dollars/s}$

2.105 $100.0 \text{ glonkins} \times \frac{0.911 \text{ ounce}}{1 \text{ glonkin}} \times \frac{28.35 \text{ g}}{1 \text{ ounce}} \times \frac{1 \text{ mL}}{19.3 \text{ g}} \times \frac{1 \text{ L}}{1000 \text{ mL}} = 0.134 \text{ L}$

2.106 $1.000 \times 10^3 \text{ cm}^3 \times \frac{1 \text{ mL}}{1 \text{ cm}^3} \times \frac{1 \text{ L}}{1000 \text{ mL}} \times \frac{0.264 \text{ gallon}}{1 \text{ L}} = 0.264 \text{ gallon}$

2.107 Volume = 10.2 cm × 43.7 cm × 95.6 cm = 4.26×10^4 cm^3 = 4.26×10^4 mL

$$4.26 \times 10^4 \text{ mL} \times \frac{1 \text{ L}}{1000 \text{ mL}} = 42.6 \text{ L}$$

2.108 The mass in grams is

$$2.43 \times 10^2 \text{ kg} \times \frac{1000 \text{ g}}{1 \text{ kg}} = 2.43 \times 10^5 \text{ g}$$

The volume is 4.26×10^4 mL (from Problem 2.113), making the density

$$\text{Density} = \frac{\text{Mass}}{\text{Volume}} = \frac{2.43 \times 10^5 \text{ g}}{4.26 \times 10^4 \text{ mL}} = 5.70 \text{ g / mL}$$

2.109 (a) The length of the edge is = 100.0 cm + 1.40 cm = 101.4 cm. You must report the answer to the tenths place because a sum cannot be more certain than the least certain measurement, which in this case is the 100.0 cm.

(b) Volume = $(101.4 \text{ cm})^3 = 1.043 \times 10^6 \text{ cm}^3 = 1.043 \times 10^6 \text{ mL}$

(c) Density $= \dfrac{111 \text{ kg}}{1.043 \times 10^6 \text{ mL}} \times \dfrac{1000 \text{ g}}{1 \text{ kg}} = 0.106 \text{ g / mL}$

2.110 The volume in cubic inches is 6.00 inches × 7.00 inches × 8.00 inches = 336 inches^3. Because the given conversion factor is for inches, you must cube it:

$$336 \text{ inches}^3 \times \left(\frac{2.54 \text{ cm}}{1 \text{ inch}}\right)^3 \times \frac{1 \text{ mL}}{1 \text{ cm}^3} \times \frac{1 \text{ L}}{1000 \text{ mL}} = 5.51 \text{ L}$$

2.111 You must convert both units of the given speed, and that means many conversion factors. Just take things one step at a time. Start with the numerator, meters to miles; then continue with the denominators, seconds to hours:

$$80.0 \frac{\text{m}}{\text{s}} \times \frac{3.28 \text{ ft}}{1 \text{ m}} \times \frac{1 \text{ mile}}{5280 \text{ ft}} \times \frac{60 \text{ s}}{1 \text{ min}} \times \frac{60 \text{ min}}{1 \text{ h}} = 179 \text{ miles / h}$$

2.112 In an equation, the two sides are equal to each other and must remain equal in order not to change the meaning of the equation. For the sides to remain equal, whatever is done to one side must also be done to the other. In this case, both sides must be multiplied by the same amount.

2.113 To solve for x means to get x alone on one side of the equals sign—in other words, to *isolate* x. For $y = z/x$, a good first step is to get x out of the denominator and onto the left side, accomplished by multiplying both sides by x.

$$x \times y = \frac{z}{x} \times x \Rightarrow xy = z$$

Dividing both sides by y isolates x:

$$\frac{xy}{y} = \frac{z}{y} \Rightarrow x = \frac{z}{y}$$

2.114 Adding x to both sides gives $y + x = z$. Then subtracting y from both sides gives the value of x:

$$y + x = z - x + x \Rightarrow y + x = z$$

$$y + x - y = z - y \Rightarrow x = z - y$$

2.115 First get the term containing x alone by subtracting 2 from both sides. Doing this leaves you with $y - 2 = z/x$. To get x out of the denominator, multiply both sides by x, getting the term $(y - 2)x$ on the left. Do not bother to do this multiplication because you want x by itself. Simply divide both sides by $y - 2$.

$$y - 2 = \frac{z}{x} + 2 - 2 \Rightarrow y - 2 = \frac{z}{x}$$

$$(y - 2) \times x = \frac{z}{x} \times x \Rightarrow (y - 2)x = z$$

$$\frac{(y - 2)x}{y - 2} = \frac{z}{y - 2} \Rightarrow x = \frac{z}{y - 2}$$

2.116 Using algebraic manipulation means solving the density equation for mass:

$$\text{Density} = \frac{\text{Mass}}{\text{Volume}}$$

$$\text{Volume} \times \text{Density} = \cancel{\text{Volume}} \times \frac{\text{Mass}}{\cancel{\text{Volume}}}$$

$$\text{Volume} \times \text{Density} = \text{Mass}$$

Substituting in the given values gives

50.00 mL × 1.15 g/mL = 57.5 g

2.117 With unit analysis, start with the information given and multiply by the appropriate conversion factor:

$$\frac{1.15 \text{ g}}{\cancel{\text{mL}}} \times 50.00 \cancel{\text{ mL}} = 57.5 \text{ g}$$

The answer is the same as in Problem 2.116.

2.118 Energy is the capacity for doing work.

2.119 1 cal is the amount of heat energy necessary to warm 1 g of water from 25°C to 26°C.

2.120 (a) $4.50 \cancel{\text{ Cal}} \times \dfrac{1000 \text{ cal}}{1 \cancel{\text{ Cal}}} = 4500 \text{ cal} = 4.50 \times 10^3 \text{ cal}$

(b) $600.0 \cancel{\text{ Cal}} \times \dfrac{4.184 \text{ kJ}}{1 \cancel{\text{ Cal}}} = 2510. \text{ kJ}$

(c) $1.000 \cancel{\text{ J}} \times \dfrac{1 \text{ cal}}{4.184 \cancel{\text{ J}}} = 0.2390 \text{ cal}$

(d) $50.0 \cancel{\text{ Cal}} \times \dfrac{4.184 \cancel{\text{ kJ}}}{1 \cancel{\text{ Cal}}} \times \dfrac{1000 \text{ J}}{1 \cancel{\text{ kJ}}} = 2.09 \times 10^5 \text{ J}$

2.121 The specific heat for any substance is the amount of heat energy necessary to increase the temperature of 1 g of the substance by 1 C°.

2.122 The specific heats are 0.901 J/g·C° for aluminum and 0.449 J/g·C° for iron. The aluminum block needs more heat energy because aluminum has the larger specific heat. It needs

$$\frac{0.901 \text{ J} / \text{g} \cdot \text{C}°}{0.449 \text{ J} / \text{g} \cdot \text{C}°} = 2.01 \text{ times as much heat energy}$$

Another way to say the same thing is that the aluminum block needs 0.901 J − 0.449 J = 0.452 J more heat per gram per Celsium degree increase in temperature.

2.123 $\underbrace{2.00 \cancel{\text{ L}} \times \dfrac{1000 \cancel{\text{ mL}}}{1 \cancel{\text{ L}}} \times \dfrac{1.00 \text{ g}}{\cancel{\text{ mL}}}}_{\text{Water mass}} \times \underbrace{\dfrac{4.184 \text{ J}}{\text{g} \cdot \cancel{\text{C}°}}}_{\substack{\text{Water} \\ \text{specific} \\ \text{heat}}} \times \underbrace{18.0 \cancel{\text{ C}°}}_{\substack{\text{Temp.} \\ \text{increase}}} = 1.51 \times 10^5 \text{ J}$

$$1.51 \times 10^5 \cancel{\text{ J}} \times \frac{1 \text{ kJ}}{1000 \cancel{\text{ J}}} = 151 \text{ kJ}$$

2.124 To keep all the generated heat inside the unit so that it can warm the water and thereby be measured.

2.125 $0.200 \text{ kg water} \times \dfrac{1000 \text{ g}}{1 \text{ kg}} \times \dfrac{4.184 \text{ J}}{\text{g} \cdot \text{C}^\circ} \times 6.6 \text{ C}^\circ = 5.5 \times 10^3 \text{ J}$ released when 2.50 g of wood burned

$$\dfrac{5.5 \times 10^3 \text{ J}}{2.50 \text{ g}} = 2.2 \times 10^3 \text{ J per gram of wood}$$

2.126 $2.00 \text{ lb} \times \dfrac{453.6 \text{ g}}{1 \text{ lb}} \times \dfrac{0.449 \text{ J}}{\text{g} \cdot \text{C}^\circ} \times 60.0 \text{ C}^\circ = 2.44 \times 10^4 \text{ J}$

2.127 You need 2.44×10^4 J of heat energy, and each gram of wood supplies 2.2×10^3 J. Therefore the mass of wood you need is

$$2.44 \times 10^4 \text{ J} \times \dfrac{1 \text{ g wood}}{2.2 \times 10^3 \text{ J}} = 11 \text{ g wood}$$

2.128 Manipulate the heat equation to solve for change in temperature and then insert the given data. Because the manipulated equation has a fraction on one side, things get a bit complex, and for this reason it's a good idea to do unit conversions first. Because specific heats are given in the textbook Table 2.5 in J/g·C°, convert to grams and joules:

$$2.000 \text{ ton} \times \dfrac{2000 \text{ lb}}{1 \text{ ton}} \times \dfrac{453.6 \text{ g}}{1 \text{ lb}} = 1.8144 \times 10^6 \text{ g}$$

(carry the extra significant figure until your final step)

$$8.000 \times 10^6 \text{ kJ} \times \dfrac{1000 \text{ J}}{1 \text{ kJ}} = 8.000 \times 10^9 \text{ J}$$

These values give a temperature change of

$$\dfrac{8.000 \times 10^9 \text{ J}}{(0.901 \text{ J} / \text{g} \cdot \text{C}^\circ) \times 1.8144 \times 10^6 \text{ g}} = 4894 \text{ C}^\circ$$

Because the initial temperature of the block was 22.0°C, the block reaches a temperature of 22.0°C + 4894°C = 4916°C. Ouch, hot!

2.129 (c). 1230.0 m has five significant digits, and the converted value must also have five:

$$1230.0 \text{ m} \times \dfrac{1 \text{ km}}{1000 \text{ m}} = 1.2300 \text{ km}$$

Answer (d) has the correct number of significant digits but the wrong prefix on the unit:

$$1230.0 \text{ m} \times \dfrac{1000 \text{ mm}}{1 \text{ m}} = 1.2300 \times 10^6 \text{ mm} \neq 1.2300 \text{ mm}$$

2.130 (a) $(7.98 \times 10^{23} \, \mu\text{L}) \times \dfrac{1 \text{ L}}{1 \times 10^6 \, \mu\text{L}} = 7.98 \times 10^{17} \text{ L}$

(b) $(3.00 \times 10^{-3} \text{ mg}) \times \dfrac{1 \text{ g}}{1000 \text{ mg}} = 3.00 \times 10^{-6} \text{ g}$

(c) $(4.21 \times 10^8 \text{ mL}) \times \dfrac{1 \text{ cm}^3}{1 \text{ mL}} \times \left(\dfrac{1 \text{ m}}{100 \text{ cm}}\right)^3 \times \dfrac{264 \text{ gallons}}{1 \text{ m}^3} = 1.11 \times 10^5 \text{ gallons}$

2.131 $V = (4/3) \, \pi r^3 = (4/3) \times 3.14159 \times (4.00 \text{ cm})^3 = 268 \text{ cm}^3$

2.132 Because the answer must have grams in it, first convert the given mass to grams:

$$2.5 \text{ kg} \times \frac{1000 \text{ g}}{1 \text{ kg}} = 2.5 \times 10^3 \text{ g}$$

$$\text{Density} = \frac{\text{Mass}}{\text{Volume}} = \frac{2.5 \times 10^3 \text{ g}}{268 \text{ cm}^3} = 9.3 \text{ g/cm}^3$$

2.133 (b). 0.000 0003 L has only one significant figure, meaning the converted value can have only one. Answer (a) has the correct number of significant figures but the wrong prefix on the unit:

$$3 \times 10^{-6} \text{ L} \times \frac{1000 \text{ mL}}{1 \text{ L}} = 0.003 \text{ mL} \neq 3 \text{ mL}$$

2.134 $\dfrac{60.0 \text{ mi}}{\text{h}} \times \dfrac{1.61 \text{ km}}{1 \text{ mi}} \times \dfrac{1000 \text{ m}}{1 \text{ km}} \times \dfrac{1 \text{ h}}{60 \text{ min}} \times \dfrac{1 \text{ min}}{60 \text{ s}} = 26.8 \text{ m / s}$

2.135 $\dfrac{11.0 \text{ km}}{\text{L}} \times \dfrac{1 \text{ mi}}{1.61 \text{ km}} \times \dfrac{3.79 \text{ L}}{1 \text{ gallon}} = 25.9 \text{ mi/gallon}$

2.136 (a) °C = (5/9)(72°F − 32) = 22°C
　　　 K = 22°C + 273.15 = 295 K
　　　(b) °F = 32 + (9/5)(−12°C) = 10.4°F
　　　 K = −12°C + 273.15 = 261 K
　　　(c) °C = 178 K − 273.15 = −95°C
　　　 °F = 32 + (9/5)(−95°C) = −139°F

2.137 1 Calorie = 1000 calories = 1 kilocalorie; 1 calorie = 0.001 Calorie = 1 milliCalorie.

2.138 The volume of the stopper is 37.42 mL − 25.46 mL = 11.96 mL

$$\text{Density} = \frac{\text{Mass}}{\text{Volume}} = \frac{16.74 \text{ g}}{11.96 \text{ mL}} = 1.400 \text{ g/mL}$$

2.139 (a) Subtract 32 from both sides and then multiply both sides by 5/9:

$$°F - 32 = \frac{9}{5}°C + 32 - 32 \Rightarrow °F - 32 = \frac{9}{5}°C$$

$$\frac{5}{9} \times (°F - 32) = \frac{5}{9} \times \left(\frac{9}{5}°C\right) \Rightarrow \frac{5}{9} \times (°F - 32) = °C$$

(b) Divide both sides by nR:

$$\frac{PV}{nR} = \frac{nRT}{nR} \Rightarrow \frac{PV}{nR} = T$$

(c) Multiply both sides by λ and divide both sides by E:

$$E \times \lambda = \frac{hc}{\lambda} \times \lambda \Rightarrow E \times \lambda = hc$$

$$\frac{E\lambda}{E} = \frac{hc}{E} \Rightarrow \lambda = \frac{hc}{E}$$

2.140 (a) $2.37 \times 10^2 \text{ L} \times \dfrac{1000 \text{ mL}}{1 \text{ L}} = 2.7 \times 10^5 \text{ mL}$

(b) $800 \text{ kg} \times \dfrac{1000 \text{ g}}{1 \text{ kg}} = 8 \times 10^5 \text{ g}$

2.140 (c) $0.592 \ \text{mm} \times \dfrac{1 \ \text{m}}{1000 \ \text{mm}} = 5.92 \times 10^{-4} \ \text{m}$

(d) $8.31 \ \text{g} \times \dfrac{1 \ \text{kg}}{1000 \ \text{g}} = 8.31 \times 10^{-3} \ \text{kg}$

(e) $9.62 \times 10^{-6} \ \text{L} \times \dfrac{1 \times 10^6 \ \mu\text{L}}{1 \ \text{L}} = 9.62 \ \mu\text{L}$

(f) $8000 \ \text{m} \times \dfrac{1 \ \text{km}}{1000 \ \text{m}} = 8 \ \text{km}$

(g) $19.3 \ \text{mg} \times \dfrac{1 \ \text{g}}{1000 \ \text{mg}} = 1.93 \times 10^{-2} \ \text{g}$

(h) $0.003 \ 45 \ \text{mL} \times \dfrac{1 \ \text{L}}{1000 \ \text{mL}} = 3.45 \times 10^{-6} \ \text{L}$

2.141 (a) $\dfrac{1.34 \ \text{g}}{\text{L}} \times \dfrac{1 \ \text{L}}{1000 \ \text{mL}} = 1.34 \times 10^{-3} \ \text{g/mL}$

(b) $\dfrac{1.34 \ \text{g}}{\text{L}} \times \dfrac{1 \ \text{kg}}{1000 \ \text{g}} = 1.34 \times 10^{-3} \ \text{kg/mL}$

(c) $\dfrac{1.34 \ \text{g}}{\text{L}} \times \dfrac{1 \ \text{kg}}{1000 \ \text{g}} \times \dfrac{1 \ \text{L}}{1000 \ \text{mL}} = 1.34 \times 10^{-6} \ \text{kg/mL}$

2.142 Solve the heat equation for mass by dividing both sides by specific heat and by change in temperature:

Heat = Specific heat × Mass × Change in temperature

$$\text{Mass} = \dfrac{\text{Heat}}{\text{Specific heat} \times \text{Change in temperature}} = \dfrac{8.8 \times 10^3 \ \text{J}}{2.20 \ \text{J}/ \text{g} \cdot \text{C}^\circ \times 15 \ \text{C}^\circ} = 2.7 \times 10^2 \ \text{g}$$

2.143 Multiplying or dividing: the number of significant figures in the answer is determined by which multiplied/divided number has the fewest significant figures. Examples: 725 × 2.6352 = 1.91 × 10³, 427.45 ÷ 3.0 = 1.4 × 10². Adding or subtracting: the number of significant figures in the answer is determined by which added/subtracted number is least certain. Examples: 72_5 + 2.6352 = 72_8, 427.45 − 3._0 = 424._5.

2.144 (a) 23.0°C + 273.15 = 296.2 K
(b) (5/9)(98.6°F − 32) = 37.0°C
(c) Because there is no direct Fahrenheit/Kelvin relationship given in the textbook, you must convert to °C first:
296 K − 273.15 = 23°C
32 + (9/5)(23°C) = 73°F
(d) Again convert to °C first, then to kelvins:
(5/9)(32°F − 32) = 0°C
0°C + 273.15 = 273 K
(e) 523 K − 273.15 = 250°C
(f) 32 + (9/5)(38°C) = 100°F

2.145 (a) Neither accurate nor precise. The large spread between the highest and lowest values means the set is not precise. The average value (6.38 g + 9.23 g + 4.36 g) ÷ 3 = 6.66 g tells you the set is not accurate.
(b) Both accurate (the average value is 8.56 g) and precise (very small spread in the three values).

(c) Accurate (the average is 8.54 g) but not precise (large spread).

(d) Precise (very small spread) but not accurate (average 6.26 g).

2.146 The calorie content is a measure of the heat energy contained in the bread, and that contained heat energy is equal to the heat energy absorbed by the water. The change in temperature of the water is $33.0°C - 25.0°C = 8.0°C$. Therefore after you have converted the water mass to grams, you have

Heat energy absorbed by water =
Specific heat of water × Mass of water × Change in temperature

$$\frac{1.00 \text{ cal}}{g \cdot C°} \times 1000 \text{ g} \times 80 \text{ } C° = 8.0 \times 10^3 \text{ cal}$$

The bread's Calorie content is

$$8.0 \times 10^3 \text{ cal} \times \frac{1 \text{ Cal}}{1000 \text{ cal}} = 8.0 \text{ Cal}$$

2.147 $\text{Density} = \dfrac{\text{Mass}}{\text{Volume}}$

$\text{Volume} = 3.0 \text{ cm} \times 4.0 \text{ cm} \times 5.0 \text{ cm} = 60. \text{ cm}^3$

$\text{Density} = \dfrac{470.0 \text{ g}}{60. \text{ cm}^3} = 7.8 \text{ g/cm}^3$

2.148 (a) The student is accurate but not precise. The average of her three numbers is 235 g, making her accurate, but the large high-low spread makes her imprecise (but lucky!).

2.149 $\text{Density} = \dfrac{\text{Mass}}{\text{Volume}}$

$\text{Volume} = 28.10 \text{ mL} - 25.00 \text{ mL} = 3.10 \text{ mL}$

$\text{Density} = \dfrac{8.34 \text{ g}}{3.10 \text{ mL}} = 2.69 \text{ g/mL}$

2.150 Heat energy = Specific heat × Mass × Change in temperature

Change in temperature = $75.0°C - 40.0°C = 35.0°C$

$$\text{Heat energy} = \frac{0.385 \text{ J}}{g \cdot C°} \times 454 \text{ g} \times 35.0 \text{ } C° = 6.12 \times 10^3 \text{ J}$$

$$(6.12 \times 10^3 \text{ J}) \times \frac{1 \text{ kJ}}{1000 \text{ J}} = 6.12 \text{ kJ}$$

2.151 The conversion equation is $°F = 32 + (9/5)°C$. Make approximations the quick way by adding 30 instead of 32 and multiplying by 2 instead of 9/5. Because 9/5 (1.8) is only a little less than 2 and 32 is only a little more than 30, the errors introduced by making these two approximations tend to cancel, giving a result close to the actual value. As an example, convert 80.5°C:

Quick way $80.5 \times 2 = 161$
              $161 - 16 = 145$
              $145 + 30 = 175°F$

Equation $32 + \dfrac{9}{5}(80.5°C) = 177°F$

2.152 (a) 2.3×10^7 (b) 2.30×10^7 (c) 2.3000×10^7 (d) $2.30\,000 \times 10^7$ (e) $2.3\,000\,000 \times 10^7$

2.153 Although water contains no calories, the body must expend ("burn") energy to raise the temperature of the ice-cold water from approximately 0°C to the body temperature of 37°C.

2.154 With markings every 0.01 mL, the estimated (uncertain) digit is in the thousandths position, making the uncertainty $0.001 \div 2 = \pm0.0005$.

2.155 Density = Mass/Volume

Density of A = 200.0 g/25.64 mL = 7.800 g/ml
Density of B = 200.0 g/10.36 mL = 19.31 g/ml
Density of C = 200.0 g/17.54 mL = 11.40 g/ml

Therefore A is iron, B is gold, and C is lead.

2.156 Solve the heat equation for change in termperature and then insert the given values, remembering to first convert kilojoules to joules to agree with the specific heat units of J/g·C°:

$$\text{Change in temperature} = \frac{\text{Heat}}{\text{Specific heat} \times \text{Mass}}$$

$$= \frac{10,000\,J}{4.184\,J/g \cdot C° \times 250\,g} = 9.6\ C°$$

Final temperature of water = 23.0°C + 9.6 C° = 32.6°C

2.157 (a) The uncertain digit, 8, is in the tenths position, making the uncertainty 0.1 m $\div$ 2 = ±0.05 m.

(b) The uncertain digit, 6, is in the ten-thousandths position, making the uncertainty 0.0001 g $\div$ 2 = ±0.00005 g.

(c) $(0.001 \times 10^3\ L) \div 2 = \pm0.0005 \times 10^3 = \pm0.5$ L

(d) 1 cm $\div$ 2 = ±0.5 cm

(e) No uncertainty because 18 here is an exact number.

2.158 (a) 5.93×10^{-1} (b) 4.39×10^5 (c) 7.40×10^{-5}
(d) 2.35×10^{-1} (e) 8.26×10^1 (f) 5.30×10^2

2.159 A Calorie is 1000 calories.

2.160 Precision refers to the closeness to one another of a series of measurements, and therefore the word can never be used to describe a single measurement.

2.161 (a) When adding/subtracting numbers written in scientific notation, first change all numbers to the same power of 10:

$$
\begin{array}{cc}
5.03 \times 10^2 & 50.3 \times 10^1 \\
\underline{+\ 0.81 \times 10^2} \quad \text{or} & \underline{+\ \ 8.1 \times 10^1} \\
5.84 \times 10^2 & 58.4 \times 10^1 = 5.84 \times 10^2
\end{array}
$$

(b) 4.4×10^{-1}; only two significant digits because of the 0.53.

(c) 2.01×10^{23}; three significant digits because the 3 is exact, meaning the number of significant digits is determined by the 6.02.

(d) As in part (a), change all numbers to the same power of 10:

$$
\begin{array}{cc}
3.960 \times 10^3 & 39.60 \times 10^2 \\
\underline{-\ 0.462 \times 10^3} \quad \text{or} & \underline{-\ 4.62 \times 10^2} \\
3.498 \times 10^3 & 34.98 \times 10^2 = 3.498 \times 10^3
\end{array}
$$

2.162 The volume is length $\times$ width $\times$ height: 6.0 cm $\times$ 6.0 cm $\times$ 6.0 cm = 216 cm³.
The answer can have only two significant digits, but keep the 216 from your calculator display as you do the unit conversion and then round off:

$$216\ cm^3 \times \left(\frac{1\ m}{100\ cm} \right)^3 = 2.16 \times 10^{-4}\,m^3 = 2.2 \times 10^{-4}\,m^3$$

2.163 (a) $20 \text{ atoms} \times \dfrac{20.2 \text{ atomic mass units}}{1 \text{ atom}} = 404 \text{ atomic mass units}$

(b) $20 \text{ atoms} \times \dfrac{20.2 \text{ atomic mass units}}{1 \text{ atom}} \times \dfrac{1.66 \times 10^{-24} \text{g}}{1 \text{ atomic mass units}} = 6.71 \times 10^{-22} \text{g}$

(c) $6.022 \times 10^{23} \text{ atoms} \times \dfrac{20.2 \text{ atomic mass units}}{1 \text{ atom}} \times \dfrac{1.66 \times 10^{-24} \text{g}}{1 \text{ atomic mass units}} = 20.2 \text{ g}$

or

$$6.022 \times 10^{23} \text{ atoms} \times \dfrac{6.71 \times 10^{-22} \text{g}}{20 \text{ atoms}} = 20.2 \text{ g}$$

2.164 Ethanol because its specific heat is smaller than that of water. The smaller the specific heat, the greater the temperature rise for a given amount of heat energy added.

2.165 Solve the density equation for volume and then insert the data:

$$\text{Density} = \frac{\text{Mass}}{\text{Volume}} \qquad \text{Volume} = \frac{\text{Mass}}{\text{Density}}$$

(a) $\dfrac{15.0 \text{ g}}{0.997 \text{ g/mL}} = 15.0 \text{ mL}$

(b) $\dfrac{15.0 \text{ g}}{0.917 \text{ g/mL}} = 16.4 \text{ mL}$

(c) $\dfrac{15.0 \text{ g}}{0.7 \text{ g/mL}} = 21.4 \text{ mL} = 2 \times 10^{1} \text{mL}$ (only one significant figure allowed)

(d) $\dfrac{15.0 \text{ g}}{11.4 \text{ g/mL}} = 1.32 \text{ mL}$

(e) $\dfrac{15.0 \text{ g}}{13.6 \text{ g/mL}} = 1.10 \text{ mL}$

(f) $\dfrac{15.0 \text{ g}}{0.000\ 18 \text{ g/mL}} = 8.3 \times 10^{4} \text{mL}$

2.166 (a) Significant. The uncertainty ± 0.5 tells you the uncertain digit is in the ones position ($1 \div 2 = 0.5$), and this uncertain digit is significant.

(b) Not significant. The uncertainty ± 5 tells you the uncertain digit is in the tens position ($10 \div 2 = 5$). Therefore this trailing zero in the ones position is a placeholder for locating the decimal point.

(c) Significant because it comes after the decimal point.

(d) Significant because it comes after the decimal point.

(e) Possibly significant, no way to tell. This number could be normal notation for either 5.4×10^2 (trailing zero not significant) or 5.40×10^2 (trailing zero significant).

2.167 (a) Six. Both trailing zeros are significant because they follow the decimal point.

(b) Three. The uncertainty ± 5 means the uncertain digit is in the tens position ($10 \div 2 = 5$). The rightmost zero is only a placeholder and not significant.

(c) Two. The uncertainty ± 50 means the uncertain digit is in the hundreds position ($100 \div 2 = 50$). The second and third zeros are therefore placeholders and not significant.

(d) Four. The uncertainty ±0.5 means the uncertain digit is in the ones position
(1 ÷ 2 = 0.5). All three trailing zeros are therefore significant.

(e) Four

2.168 Because it is densest, the mercury is at the bottom. Because it is least dense, the gasoline is at the top.

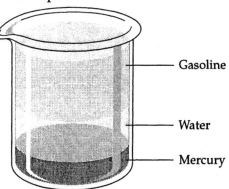

Gasoline

Water

Mercury

2.169 (a) True.

(b) False. When adding or subtracting a series of measured values, the number of significant figures in the answer is limited by the least certain measured value.
Example: 3724 + 3.2 = 3727. The 3.2 has the fewest significant figures but is certain to the tenths position. The 3724 is certain only to the ones position, and therefore is the measured value that determines the number of significant figures in the answer—the answer must be uncertain in the ones position. In this example, that restriction means four significant figures are allowed in the answer despite the 3.2.

2.170 (a) $\dfrac{1.04\,J}{g\cdot C°}\times\dfrac{1\ cal}{4.184\,J}=0.249\ cal/g\cdot C°$

(b) $\dfrac{0.84\,J}{g\cdot C°}\times\dfrac{1\ cal}{4.184\,J}=0.20\ cal/g\cdot C°$

2.171 $15\ weeks\times\dfrac{3\,h}{week}\times\dfrac{60\ min}{1\,h}\times\dfrac{60\,s}{1\ min}\times\dfrac{1000\ ms}{1\,s}=1.6\times10^{8}\ ms$

2.172 In any measured value, the last digit written is the uncertain digit, and the uncertainty of the measured value is calculated by placing a 1 in the position of the uncertain digit and dividing by 2.

2.173 (a) 5.02×10^{5} (b) 3.8402×10^{-5} (c) 4.36×10^{8}
(d) 8.47×10^{3} (e) 5.91×10^{-3} (f) 6.58×10^{-1}

2.174 $800\ ft^{2}\times\left(\dfrac{12\ inches}{1\ ft}\right)^{2}\times\left(\dfrac{1\ m}{39.37\ inches}\right)^{2}=74.3\ m^{2}$

2.175 $350\ Canadian\ dollars\times\dfrac{1\ U.S.\ dollar}{1.54\ Canadian\ dollars}=227\ U.S.\ dollars$

2.176 The two blocks contain the same amount of matter. The gram is a unit of mass, and therefore the two blocks have the same mass. *Matter* was defined in Chapter 1 of the textbook as anything that has mass (and occupies space). Thus the two blocks contain the same amount of matter because they have the same mass. (Because lead and gold have different densities, the blocks occupy different *volumes*, but that point is not asked about in the problem.)

2.177 (a) Two.   (b) Two.   (c) None.   (d) Cannot tell.   (e) Three.

2.178 (a) 0.189   (b) 793.2   (c) 10^{-14} (d) 0.346

2.179 No. In 580., the decimal point indicates that the trailing zero is significant. In 580, the trailing zero may or may not be significant; there is no way to tell with the value written this way.

2.180 These two temperature units are equal in size because on both the Kelvin scale and the Celsius scale there are 100 units between the freezing point and boiling point of water.

2.181 It is more likely that the student's laboratory technique is bad because his measurements vary widely.

2.182 (a) 0.0179   (b) 0.000 000 008 76   (c) 48,800,000,000   (d) 75.2   (e) 8.37   (f) 4184

2.183 (a) Density = Mass/Volume = 195 g/25.0 cm^3 = 7.80 g/cm^3
(b) Volume = Mass/Density = 500.0 g/7.80 g/cm^3 = 64.1 cm^3
(c) The substance floats in mercury because it is less dense than mercury.

2.184 (a) $536 \text{ mg} \times \dfrac{1 \text{ g}}{1000 \text{ mg}} = 0.536 \text{ g} = 5.36 \times 10^{-1} \text{g}$

(b) $8.26 \text{ dg} \times \dfrac{1 \text{ g}}{10 \text{ dg}} = 0.826 \text{ g} = 8.26 \times 10^{-1} \text{g}$

(c) $0.0057 \text{ } \mu\text{g} \times \dfrac{1 \text{ g}}{1 \times 10^{6} \text{ } \mu\text{g}} = 0.000 \text{ } 000 \text{ } 005 \text{ } 7 \text{ g} = 5.7 \times 10^{-9} \text{g}$

(d) $139 \text{ kg} \times \dfrac{1 \text{ g}}{1 \times 10^{-3} \text{kg}} = 139{,}000 \text{ g} = 1.39 \times 10^{5} \text{g}$

(e) $836 \text{ ng} \times \dfrac{1 \text{ g}}{1 \times 10^{9} \text{ng}} = 0.000 \text{ } 000 \text{ } 836 \text{ g} = 8.36 \times 10^{-7} \text{g}$

(f) $0.073 \text{ Mg} \times \dfrac{1 \text{ g}}{1 \times 10^{-6} \text{Mg}} = 73{,}000 \text{ g} = 7.3 \times 10^{4} \text{g}$

2.185 (a) $\dfrac{1.3 \times 10^{-3} \text{g}}{\text{mL}} \times \dfrac{1 \text{ kg}}{1000 \text{ g}} \times \dfrac{1000 \text{ mL}}{1 \text{ L}} = 1.3 \times 10^{-3} \text{kg} / \text{L}$

(b) $\dfrac{1.3 \times 10^{-3} \text{g}}{\text{mL}} \times \dfrac{1 \text{ kg}}{1000 \text{ g}} \times \dfrac{2.204 \text{ lb}}{1 \text{ kg}} \times \dfrac{1000 \text{ mL}}{1 \text{ L}} \times \dfrac{1 \text{ L}}{1.057 \text{ qt}} \times \dfrac{4 \text{ qt}}{1 \text{ gallon}} = 1.1 \times 10^{-2} \text{lb} / \text{gallon}$

2.186 The lemonade in the glass containing the aluminum is cooler because more heat energy has flowed out of the liquid and into the block to change the block's temperature. The block masses are the same, and the block temperature changes are the same. Therefore it's a matter of looking at the joules that leave each liquid to heat up the blocks. The specific heat of aluminum, 0.901 J/g·C°, is approximately twice that of iron, 0.449 J/g·C°. Thus the amount of heat energy that had to flow from the liquid to heat the aluminum block by 20 C° is approximately twice the amount that had to flow from the liquid to heat the iron block by 20 C°. Having lost twice as much heat energy, the liquid in the glass containing the aluminum is cooler than the liquid in the glass containing the iron.

2.187 (a) 1.0726×10^{4}. Changing both numbers in the sum from scientific notation to normal notation shows that both are uncertain in the ones position. Therefore their sum has its uncertainty in the ones position: 9865 + 861 = 10726.
(b) 4.42×10^{-19}. Only three significant figures allowed because of the 3.00 and/or 4.50.
(c) 1.471×10^{-18}. The 3.821 restricts the answer to four significant figures.

(d) 9.0618×10^2. Because the 5 is exact, the number of significant figures in the answer is determined by the two numbers of the subtraction. Normal notation shows that both numbers are uncertain in the tenths position, and therefore their difference has five significant figures: $4560.0 - 29.1 = 4530.9$. Dividing this value by the exact number 5 gives an answer having five significant figures.

2.188 $\text{Density} = \dfrac{\text{Mass}}{\text{Volume}}$

$\text{Mass} = \text{Density} \times \text{Volume}$

(a) $\dfrac{11.4 \text{ g}}{\text{mL}} \times 50.0 \text{ mL} = 570. \text{ g}$

(b) $\dfrac{0.785 \text{ g}}{\text{mL}} \times 50.0 \text{ mL} = 39.3 \text{ g}$

(c) $\dfrac{1.4 \times 10^{-3} \text{ g}}{\text{mL}} \times 50.0 \text{ mL} = 0.070 \text{ g}$

(d) $\dfrac{8.4 \times 10^{-5} \text{ g}}{\text{mL}} \times 50.0 \text{ mL} = 0.0042 \text{ g}$

(e) $\dfrac{13.6 \text{ g}}{\text{mL}} \times 50.0 \text{ mL} = 680. \text{ g}$

(f) $\dfrac{19.3 \text{ g}}{\text{mL}} \times 50.0 \text{ mL} = 965 \text{ g}$

2.189 (a) $\dfrac{1 \text{ kg}}{1000 \text{ g}}$ $\dfrac{1000 \text{ g}}{1 \text{ kg}}$

(b) $\dfrac{1 \text{ g}}{0.001 \text{ kg}}$ $\dfrac{0.001 \text{ kg}}{1 \text{ g}}$

(c) $\dfrac{1 \text{ yd}}{3 \text{ ft}}$ $\dfrac{3 \text{ ft}}{1 \text{ yd}}$

(d) $\dfrac{1 \text{ m}}{100 \text{ cm}}$ $\dfrac{100 \text{ cm}}{1 \text{ m}}$

(e) $\dfrac{1 \text{ cm}}{0.01 \text{ m}}$ $\dfrac{0.01 \text{ m}}{1 \text{ cm}}$

2.190 $125 \text{ lb/in}^2 \times \dfrac{1 \text{ atm}}{14.70 \text{ lb/in}^2} = 8.50 \text{ atm}$

2.191 (a) 4×10^3 (b) 0.37

(c) 10.12. The product of 6.23 and 0.042 is 0.26, only two significant digits but certain to the hundredths position. Add this to 9.86 and you get a sum certain to the hundredths position—legitimately gaining a significant digit.

2.192 Incorrect because 1 ft equals exactly 12 inches by definition. There is no uncertainty.

2.193 (a) Two, determined by the 0.0080.

(b) Three. The $22.1 \times 10^2 = 2210$ is uncertain in the tens position, meaning the sum must also be: $530 + 2210 = 2740 = 274 \times 10^3$.

(c) Five. The $5.830 \times 10^2 = 583.0$ is uncertain in the tenths position, and the same is true for the $22.100 \times 10^2 = 2210.0$. Therefore the sum is also uncertain in the tenths position: $583.0 + 2210.0 = 2793.0 = 2.7930 \times 10^3$.

(d) Four, determined by 100.0 and 0.1500.

(e) Two, determined by 0.15.

2.194 $350 \text{ pounds} \times \dfrac{1 \text{ U.S. dollar}}{0.690 \text{ pound}} = 507 \text{ U.S. dollars}$

2.195 More likely to be precise. Her good laboratory technique will yield measurements that are close to one another (high precision), but the volumes she reads will all be 5 mL higher than the true volume (low accuracy) because of the incorrect markings.

2.196 Because ice is less dense than liquid water, the ice that forms in a lake floats on the liquid water, forming a layer of ice above the liquid water. If ice were denser than liquid water, any ice that formed in a lake would sink to the bottom, and the lake would freeze solid, from the bottom up. It is the fact that ice floats on top that allows a liquid-water environment for fish below, making ice-fishing possible.

2.197 (a) Four.   (b) Two.   (c) Three.   (d) Eight.   (e) Four.

2.198 (a) $\dfrac{70 \text{ mi}}{h} \times \dfrac{1.6 \text{ km}}{1 \text{ mi}} = 1.1 \times 10^2 \text{ km} / \text{h}$

(b) $\dfrac{70 \text{ mi}}{1 \text{ h}} \times \dfrac{1.6 \text{ km}}{1 \text{ mi}} \times \dfrac{1 \text{ h}}{60 \text{ min}} \times \dfrac{1 \text{ min}}{60 \text{ s}} = 0.031 \text{ km} / \text{s}$

or

$\dfrac{1.1 \times 10^2 \text{ km}}{h} \times \dfrac{1 \text{ h}}{3600 \text{ s}} = 0.031 \text{ km} / \text{s}$

(c) $\dfrac{70 \text{ mi}}{1 \text{ h}} \times \dfrac{1.6 \text{ km}}{1 \text{ mi}} \times \dfrac{1000 \text{ m}}{1 \text{ km}} = 1.1 \times 10^5 \text{ m} / \text{h}$

or

$\dfrac{1.1 \times 10^2 \text{ km}}{h} \times \dfrac{1000 \text{ m}}{1 \text{ km}} = 1.1 \times 10^5 \text{ m} / \text{h}$

(d) $\dfrac{70 \text{ mi}}{1 \text{ h}} \times \dfrac{1.6 \text{ km}}{1 \text{ mi}} \times \dfrac{1000 \text{ m}}{1 \text{ km}} \times \dfrac{1 \text{ h}}{60 \text{ min}} \times \dfrac{1 \text{ min}}{60 \text{ s}} = 3.1 \times 10^1 \text{ m} / \text{s}$

or

$\dfrac{1.1 \times 10^5 \text{ m}}{h} \times \dfrac{1 \text{ h}}{3600 \text{ s}} = 3.1 \times 10^1 \text{ m} / \text{s}$

2.199 To compress the gas means to squeeze a given mass of it into a smaller volume. Compressing therefore increases the density of the gas because a given mass is forced to occupy a smaller volume. The relationship density = mass/volume tells you that, when mass stays constant, density must go up when volume goes down.

2.200 Heat = Specific heat × Mass × Change in temperature
The change in temperature is 37.0°C − 25.0°C = 12.0 C°.

(a) $\dfrac{0.449\text{ J}}{g \cdot C°} \times 50.0\text{ }g \times 12.0\text{ }C° = 269\text{ J}$

(b) $\dfrac{0.901\text{ J}}{g \cdot C°} \times 50.0\text{ }g \times 12.0\text{ }C° = 541\text{ J}$

(c) $\dfrac{0.14\text{ J}}{g \cdot C°} \times 50.0\text{ }g \times 12.0\text{ }C° = 84\text{ J}$

(d) $\dfrac{4.18\text{ J}}{g \cdot C°} \times 50.0\text{ }g \times 12.0\text{ }C° = 2.51 \times 10^3\text{ J}$

2.201 Water undergoes the most gradual temperature change because it has the highest specific heat. Mercury undergoes the fastest temperature change because it has the lowest specific heat.

CHAPTER
3

The Evolution of Atomic Theory

3.1 See solution in textbook.

3.2 See solution in textbook.

3.3 See solution in textbook.

3.4 See solution in textbook.

3.5 The law of conservation of matter requires that the total mass of the substances produced equal the total mass of coal plus oxygen. The coal seems to disappear because it is converted to carbon dioxide, which is a colorless, odorless gas. If you were to capture the carbon dioxide and determine its mass, you would find that mass to be equal to the combined mass of reacting coal and oxygen.

3.6

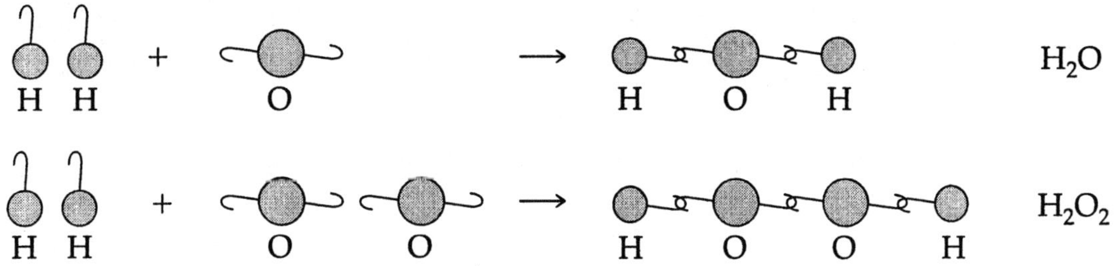

3.7 See solution in textbook.

3.8 The atomic number of Br is 35, which is also the number of protons in the nucleus. The mass number equals protons plus neutrons. Therefore the Br isotope with 44 neutrons has a mass number of 79, and the Br isotope with 46 neutrons has a mass number of 81. The full atomic symbols are $^{79}_{35}\text{Br}$ and $^{81}_{35}\text{Br}$.

3.9 The atoms of both isotopes have 35 electrons. In all neutral atoms, the number of electrons equals the number of protons.

3.10	$^{14}_{7}\text{N}$	$^{24}_{12}\text{Mg}$	$^{23}_{11}\text{Na}$	$^{59}_{26}\text{Fe}$
Mass number	14	24	23	59
Atomic number	7	12	11	26
Number of protons	7	12	11	26
Number of neutrons	7	12	12	33
Number of electrons	7	12	11	26

3.11 See solution in textbook.

3.12 The atomic mass of ^{24}Mg is the mass of one atom ^{24}Mg. Therefore

$$\frac{23.9850 \text{ amu}}{1 \text{ atom } ^{24}\text{Mg}} \times (1 \times 10^{18} \text{ atoms } ^{24}\text{Mg}) \times \frac{1.660\,54 \times 10^{-24} \text{ g}}{1 \text{ amu}} = 3.982\,81 \times 10^{-5}\,\text{g}$$

3.13 (a) The abundance of the $^{37}_{17}\text{Cl}$ isotope is $100\% - 75.77\% = 24.23\%$. (The 100 is taken to be an exact number.)

(b) Weighted average =

$$\left(\text{Atomic mass isotope 1} \times \frac{\% \text{ isotope 1}}{100}\right) + \left(\text{Atomic mass isotope 2} \times \frac{\% \text{ isotope 2}}{100}\right) + \dots$$

The weighted average for chlorine is therefore

$$\left(34.969 \text{ amu} \times \frac{75.77}{100}\right) + \left(36.966 \text{ amu} \times \frac{24.23}{100}\right) = 35.45 \text{ amu}$$

(c) $^{37}_{17}\text{Cl}$ is $\dfrac{36.966}{34.969} = 1.0571$ times heavier than $^{35}_{17}\text{Cl}$.

3.14 See solution in textbook.

3.15 No. The metal–nonmetal boundary passes only through the representative-elements region of the periodic table.

3.16 The elements in a group have similar physical and chemical properties.

3.17 See solution in textbook.

3.18 Elements expected to have properties similar to those of Br are elements in the same group, which is group 17. The group 17 elements having atomic number greater than 40 are iodine, atomic number 53, and astatine, atomic number 85. Iodine is in period 5, which contains 18 elements, giving iodine a periodicity of 18. Astatine is in period 6, which contains 32 elements, giving astatine a periodicity of 32.

3.19 If these three classes of elements were removed, the periodic table would be eight columns wide. Except for the first period, which would keep its periodicity of 2, the periodicity would be 8 in every period instead of the 2, 8, 8, 18, 18, 32, 32, periodicity that actually exists.

3.20 See solution in textbook.

3.21 Atomic size decreases from left to right in the periodic table and increases from top to bottom. Therefore the order (smallest to largest) is O < S < Mg < Sr < Rb.

3.22 26 protons means the atomic number is 26, making the element iron, Fe; 30 neutrons means the mass number is $26 + 30 = 56$. Only 23 electrons to go with 26 protons means an unbalanced electrical charge of $26 - 23 = 3$, and this charge is positive because protons outnumber electrons. The symbol is therefore $^{56}_{26}\text{Fe}^{3+}$ for this group 8 element.

3.23 Eight protons means the atomic number is 8, making the element oxygen, O; eight neutrons means the mass number is $8 + 8 = 16$. Ten electrons means an unbalanced electrical charge of $10 - 8 = 2$, which is negative because electrons outnumber protons. The symbol is $^{16}_{8}O^{2-}$, and the group name is chalcogen.

3.24 When wood burns, in addition to the ash left as residue, gases are produced. The sum of the masses of all gases produced plus the mass of the ash equals the mass of the wood (plus the oxygen) burned.

3.25 (a) $\dfrac{94.08 \text{ g S}}{100.00 \text{ g sample}} \times 100\% = 94.08\% \text{ S}$

$\dfrac{(100.00 \text{ g} - 94.08 \text{ g})\text{H}}{100.00 \text{ g sample}} \times 100\% = 5.92\% \text{ H}$

Because the sample contains only sulfur and hydrogen, the sum of their percentages must add up to 100%. Therefore another way to calculate the percent H is to subtract the percent S from 100: $100\% - 94.08\% = 5.92\%$ H (the 100% is an exact number).

(b) The law of constant composition.

3.26 Because of the law of constant composition, all samples of any substance made up of more than one element must have the same relative amounts of the elements and therefore the same formula. In terms of Dalton's theory, all samples of hydrogen sulfide have the same formula H_2S because one sulfur atom always "hooks up with" two hydrogen atoms.

3.27 (a) The mass of A is 126.9 g + 35.45 g = 162.4 g. The percentages are therefore

$\dfrac{126.9 \text{ g I}}{162.4 \text{ g A}} \times 100\% = 78.14\% \text{ I in A}$

$100\% - 78.14\% = 21.86\% \text{ Cl in A}$

(b) The mass of B is 126.9 g + 106.4 g = 233.3 g.

$\dfrac{126.9 \text{ g I}}{233.3 \text{ g B}} \times 100\% = 54.39\% \text{ I in B}$

$100\% - 54.39\% = 45.61\% \text{ Cl in B}$

3.28 $12.0 \text{ g C} + 70.0 \text{ g S} \longrightarrow 76.0 \text{ g CS}_2 + x \text{ g of unused S}$

(a) To obey the law of conservation of matter, the total mass on the right side of this equation must equal the total mass on the left side, which is 82.0 grams. Solve for x by subtracting 76.0 g CS_2 from both sides:

$12.0 \text{ g C} + 70.0 \text{ g S} - 76.0 \text{ g CS}_2 \longrightarrow \cancel{76.0 \text{ g CS}_2} + x \text{ g} - \cancel{76.0 \text{ g CS}_2}$

$x = 12.0 \text{ g} + 70.0 \text{ g} - 76.0 \text{ g} = 60.0 \text{ g unused S}$

(b) Because all the carbon was used to make the 76.0 g of carbon disulfide, the percent C is

$\dfrac{12.0 \text{ g C}}{76.0 \text{ g CS}_2} \times 100\% = 15.8\% \text{ C}$

(c) Although 70.0 g of sulfur was mixed with the carbon, 6.0 g of that sulfur did not react. Therefore only 70.0 g − 6.0 g = 64.0 g of the sulfur was incorporated into the 76.0 g of CS_2. The percent S is

$\dfrac{64.0 \text{ g S}}{76.0 \text{ g CS}_2} \times 100\% = 84.2\% \text{ S}$

(d) 15.8% + 84.2% = 100.0%

3.29 The nitrogen atom in NH_3 would have three hooks, one for each H atom:

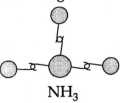

NH_3

3.30 (a) Because each compound contains only Na and O, any mass of the compound that is not O must be Na. Therefore the Na mass in A is 19.50 g − 8.00 g = 11.50 g, and the Na mass in B is 61.98 g − 16.00 g = 45.98 g.

(b) Compound A:

$$\%Na = \frac{11.50 \text{ g Na}}{19.50 \text{ g sample}} \times 100\% = 59.0\%$$

$$\%O = \frac{8.00 \text{ g O}}{19.50 \text{ g sample}} \times 100\% = 41.0\%$$

Compound B:

$$\%Na = \frac{45.98 \text{ g Na}}{61.98 \text{ g sample}} \times 100\% = 74.19\%$$

$$\%O = \frac{16.00 \text{ g O}}{61.98 \text{ g sample}} \times 100\% = 25.81\%$$

3.31 Rutherford reasoned that an atom must be mostly empty space (which is why most alpha particles passed straight through) but must have somewhere inside it an extremely tiny but massive part that carried a positive electrical charge (which is why a few alpha particles are deflected).

3.32 By the fact that the central area on the detecting screen was where the great majority of green flashes occurred. Only a very few of the green flashes were far from the central area.

3.33 The physics of Rutherford's time predicted that any changed particle (such as an electron) moving in a circular path (as it was in Rutherford's model) must continuously radiate energy. This meant that Rutherford's moving electrons would continuously lose energy, slow down, and eventually spiral into the nucleus. Thus all atoms would collapse.

3.34 It would imply that the positive charges in the atom were evenly distributed throughout the atom and not present in a tiny area in the center. This would mean either that the structure of the atom was consistent with Thomson's plum-pudding model or that there were no charged particles in an atom.

3.35 An atom's mass number is the sum of its protons and neutrons. An atom's identity depends solely on the number of protons. You would not be able to determine the number of protons from the mass number alone because the mass number varies with different numbers of neutrons in different isotopes of an element.

3.36 Yes. In a neutral atom, the number of electrons is equal to the number of protons. Knowing the number of protons allows you to determine the elemental identity.

3.37 The diameter of an atom's nucleus is about 1/10,000 the diameter of the atom. Therefore most of the atom is empty space occupied by the extremely tiny electrons.

3.38 In any full atomic symbol, the mass number (protons plus neutrons) is the top number and the atomic number (protons only) is the bottom number. In any neutral atoms, the proton number and electron number must be the same.

	$^{15}_{8}O$	$^{16}_{8}O$	$^{37}_{17}Cl$	$^{23}_{11}Na$
Mass number	15	16	37	23
Atomic number	8	8	17	11
Number of protons	8	8	17	11
Number of neutrons	7	8	20	12
Number of electrons	8	8	17	11

3.39 $^{235}_{92}U$ and $^{238}_{92}U$.

3.40 The atomic number and the symbol do not agree. Carbon has an atomic number of 6, not 7. The element whose atomic number is 7 is nitrogen.

3.41 The number of protons tells you the atomic number is 79. Add the proton number and neutron number to get the mass number: $79 + 118 = 197$. The symbol therefore is $^{197}_{79}Au$.

3.42 A mass number equal to a proton number means the atom contains no neutrons. The only atom that qualifies is $^{1}_{1}H$.

3.43 Because gold, Au, has 79 protons and lead, Pb, has 82, you would have to remove three protons from the lead nucleus.

3.44 Atomic mass is the weighted average of the masses of all the naturally occurring isotopes of an element. Mass number is the sum of the protons and neutrons in an atom of the element.

3.45 Because all masses are given relative to the mass of the isotope $^{12}_{6}C$.

3.46 $^{12}_{6}C$ is the only isotope whose atomic mass and mass number are equal. This is true because chemists have assigned $^{12}_{6}C$ an atomic mass of exactly 12 amu.

3.47 The atomic mass given for oxygen in the periodic table, 15.999 amu, is the weighted average of all naturally occurring oxygen isotopes. The atomic mass of carbon-12 is exactly 12 amu. Therefore an "average" oxygen atom is:

$$\frac{15.999 \text{ amu}}{12.0000 \text{ amu}} = 1.3333$$

times more massive than a carbon-12 atom.

3.48 The atomic mass of titanium, Ti, is 47.88 amu, making an "average" titanium atom 47.88 amu/12 amu = 3.990 times more massive than a $^{12}_{6}C$ atom.

3.49 The atomic mass of oxygen, O, is 15.999 amu, and that of helium, He, is 4.003 amu, making an "average" oxygen atom 15.999 amu/4.003 amu = 3.997 times more massive than a helium atom.

3.50 Only the isotope $^{12}_{6}C$ has a defined mass of exactly 12 amu. However, $^{12}_{6}C$ is not the only isotope of carbon. The atomic mass of 12.011 in the periodic table is the weighted average of all the naturally occurring isotopes of carbon.

3.51 (a) Exactly 235 amu.
(b) With uranium-235 as the standard reference, the atomic masses of all the lighter elements would be a very small fraction of 235. Dealing with such small numbers would be an unnecessary nuisance.

3.52 (a) Because only these two isotopes make up the total amount of bromine, the abundance of bromine-81 must be 100% − 50.69% = 49.31%

(b) The atomic mass of the isotope mixture is calculated by weighting the two individual atomic masses according to their abundance:

$$\text{Atomic mass of Br} = \left(78.918\,336 \text{ amu} \times \frac{50.69}{100}\right) + \left(80.916\,289 \text{ amu} \times \frac{49.31}{100}\right) = 79.90 \text{ amu}$$

3.53 Atomic mass is the weighted average of the atomic masses of all isotopes of an element. An atomic mass of 1.2000 amu, because it is higher than the Earth value of 1.0079 amu, means that the percentage of the higher-mass ^2H must be greater on the other planet than it is on Earth.

3.54 (d) Because uranium-238, with an atomic mass of 238.0508 amu, represents 99.27% of the uranium found in nature, the atomic mass should be very close to 238.0508 amu. However, because 0.72% of the element is uranium-235, the atomic mass will be a little less than 238.05 amu. Thus, 238.03 amu is the best estimate.

3.55 (a) Mendeleev ordered the elements according to atomic mass, and he stacked all elements having similar properties in the same vertical column.

(b) He discovered that his ordering gave eight columns; the properties repeated themselves every eight elements. This repeating behavior is called either chemical periodicity or periodic behavior.

(c) Mendeleev's ordering was by atomic mass; the modern ordering is by atomic number.

3.56 When Mendeleev arranged the 70 elements known to him, there were holes in the table, but the properties of the missing elements could be predicted. Because chemists knew what they were looking for, this led to the rapid discovery of the "missing" elements.

3.57 Chemical periodicity refers to the fact that the chemical properties repeat themselves every 8, 18, or 32 elements.

3.58 Eight groups—1, 2, 13, 14, 15, 16, 17, and 18.

3.59 Considering just the 44 representative elements:
% Metals = (20/44) × 100% = 45.45%
% Nonmetals = (17/44) × 100% = 38.64%
% Metalloids = (7/44) × 100% = 15.91%

Using the entire periodic table:

% Metals = (88/112) × 100% = 78.57%
% Nonmetals = (17/112) × 100% = 15.18%
% Metalloids = (7/112) × 100% = 6.25%

Notice that the percentage of metals is much higher when you use the entire periodic table.

3.60 IA (1), alkali metals; IIA (2), alkaline earth metals; VIA (16), chalcogens; VIIA (17), halogens; VIIIA (18), noble gases.

3.61 Hydrogen, because it is the only gas in the group and is not a metal. All of the other elements in group 1 are metals.

3.62 A group is a vertical column of elements having similar chemical properties. A period is a horizontal row of elements.

3.63 One electron and one proton.

3.64 (a) $BeCl_2$, $CaCl_2$, $SrCl_2$, $BaCl_2$, $RaCl_2$.

(b) $BeBr_2$, $MgBr_2$, $CaBr_2$, $SrBr_2$, $BaBr_2$, $RaBr_2$.

(c) The principle that elements in the same group exhibit similar chemical behavior.

3.65 They are among the most unreactive substances known, and they are the only group in the periodic table that contains only gases.

3.66 Numerous answers possible. The transition metals are elements 21–30, 39–48, 57, 72–80, 89, and 104–112.

3.67 The transition metal portion is 10 elements wide; the lanthanide/actinide portion is 14 elements wide.

3.68 The change from 8 to 18, which begins in period 4, is caused by the ten columns of transition metals (8 + 10 = 18). The change from 18 to 32, which begins in period 6, is caused by the 14 columns of lanthanides/actinides (18 + 14 = 32).

3.69 Because Si is a metalloid, its properties are intermediate between those of metals and those of nonmetals.

3.70 One proton is added to the nucleus in each block you cross, and one more electron is added outside the nucleus. The added positive nuclear charge pulls the electrons in closer to the nucleus, causing the size of the atoms to decrease.

3.71 Fe < Ti < Hf < Cs.

3.72 F < S < Se < Ca.

3.73 No, student X correctly constructed the model, but student Y did not. Only the number of electrons can be changed to produce an ion. If the number of protons is changed, the elemental identity of the substance changes. Student X made $^{14}_{6}C^{2+}$; by adding two protons, student Y made $^{14}_{8}O^{2+}$.

3.74 All species in the table carry a charge, which means the proton number is different from the electron number. When the charge is positive, the ion has more protons than electrons. When the charge is negative, the ion has more electrons than protons. Mass number, which is protons plus neutrons, is the top number in the symbol, atomic number is the bottom number.

	$^{15}_{8}O^{+}$	$^{27}_{13}Al^{3+}$	$^{31}_{15}P^{3-}$	$^{58}_{28}Ni^{+}$
Mass number	15	27	31	58
Atomic number	8	13	15	28
Number of protons	8	13	15	28
Number of neutrons	7	14	16	30
Number of electrons	7	10	18	27
Charge on ion	+1	+3	−3	+1

3.75 First ionization energy is the minimum amount of energy required to completely remove one electron from an atom.

3.76 True. Because the negatively charged electron is being pulled away from the positively charged nucleus, energy is required to make the separation.

3.77 First ionization energy decreases as you go down a group and increases as you go across a period.

3.78 As you go down a group, the size of the atom increases and the outermost electrons are farther away from the nucleus. Because these outer electrons are farther away, each one feels less pull from the nucleus and is easier to remove. Therefore its separation requires less energy. As you go across a period, the atomic size decreases, and an outermost electron is closer to the positively charged nucleus. More energy is therefore needed to remove the electron.

3.79 Aluminum, Al, should be the most difficult to ionize because it is the smallest of the three atoms. Sodium, Na, should have the smallest first ionization energy because it is the largest of the three atoms. The smallest atom is the hardest to ionize because its electrons are closest to the positively charged nucleus.

3.80 Magnesium, Mg, should be the most difficult to ionize because it is the smallest of the three atoms. Its electrons are closest to the nucleus and hardest to remove. Potassium, K, should have the smallest first ionization energy because it is the largest of the three atoms.

3.81 Yes, the halogens (group 17) do follow the expected trend. The ionization energies decrease going down the halogen group, as the atomic size increases.

3.82 (a) Each sodium atom easily loses an electron to form the cation Na^+, and each Cl atom in Cl_2 easily gains an electron to form the anion Cl^-. Therefore an electron transfer from sodium to chlorine is very favorable.

(b) Being a group 1 metal, lithium has a low first ionization energy and easily loses one electron to become a Li^+ ion (just as Na easily becomes Na^+). Being a group 17 nonmetal, each bromine atom in Br_2 tends to gain one electron to become a Br^- ion (just as Cl becomes Cl^-). The result is formation of lithium bromide, LiBr, a compound similar to sodium chloride, NaCl.

3.83 (a) The nitrogen gains three electrons. Nitrogen is to the right of lithium on the periodic table and therefore has a higher first ionization energy than lithium. The lithium, with a smaller first ionization energy, has a tendency to lose electrons and loses them to nitrogen.

(b) An anion because it acquires a negative charge after gaining electrons.

(c) $^{14}_{7}N^{3-}$

3.84 In a *continuous* spectrum, there are no regions of darkness. Each color blends smoothly into the next.

3.85 A line spectrum is made up of specific discrete colors separated by regions of darkness. A continuous spectrum consists of all colors, with adjacent colors blending smoothly into each other and no regions of darkness separating the colors.

3.86 (a) Percent by mass oxygen

$$\frac{32.00 \text{ g O}}{34.01 \text{ g sample}} \times 100\% = 94.09\% \text{ O}$$

Percent by mass hydrogen

$$\frac{(34.01 \text{ g} - 32.00 \text{ g}) \text{ H}}{34.01 \text{ g sample}} \times 100\% = 5.910\% \text{ H}$$

or
$100\% - 94.09\% = 5.910\% \text{ H}$

(b) The second company's product must also be 94.09% O and 5.910% H because the law of constant compostion states that all samples of a pure compound always contain the same percent by mass of the elements making up the compound.

(c) Being pure hydrogen peroxide, it must contain 94.09% O; which means every 100.00 g of sample contains 94.09 g O and you therefore have the conversion factor you need:

$$91.83 \text{ g sample} \times \frac{94.094 \text{ g O}}{100.00 \text{ g sample}} = 86.40 \text{ g O}$$

3.87 Both compounds contain only Sn and O. Because the mass percents of all parts of a whole must add up to 100%, the mass percents of oxygen are
Oxide A $100\% - 78.77\%$ Sn = 21.23% O
Oxide B $100\% - 88.12\%$ Sn = 11.88% O

3.88 You would have to measure the mass of the wood before burning and the mass of the oxygen consumed, and sum these two masses. You would also have to measure the mass of the ash, carbon dioxide, and water vapor produced, and sum these three masses. The two sums would be equal, indicating that the total amount of mass did not change during the reaction.

3.89 The results from Rutherford's alpha-particle experiment. That some of the particles were deflected instead of passing right through the gold atoms is evidence that there must be something massive in each atom. That only a very few of the particles were deflected is evidence that this massive something must occupy a relatively tiny part of each atom.

3.90 The law of conservation of matter tells you that the amount of matter after the reaction must be equal to the amount before the reaction. Because you start with 5 g of A and end up with 7 g of C, the amount of B reacting must be 7 g − 5 g = 2 g.

3.91 She is correct. Isotopes of an element differ only in the number of neutrons in their nuclei.

3.92 He is incorrect. Different numbers of protons in two nuclei mean two different elements.

3.93 By adding two electrons to the neutral atom.

3.94 Adding a proton to an atom's nucleus does not create a cation. Rather it changes the elemental identity of the atom. Here, adding a proton to a sodium atom (atomic number 11) changes it to a magnesium atom (atomic number 12). (The way to create cations is to strip electrons away from a neutral atom.)

3.95 Number of protons = atomic number = 9 protons.
Number of electrons = number of protons = 9 electrons.
Number of neutrons = mass number − atomic number = 19 − 9 = 10 neutrons.

3.96 Number of protons = atomic number = 26 protons.
Number of electrons = number of protons − one electron for each positive charge on ion = 26 − 2 = 24 electrons.
Number of neutrons = mass number − atomic number = 56 − 26 = 30 neutrons.

3.97 (a) Protons = atomic number = 35 protons.
Electrons = number of protons = 35 electrons.
Neutrons = mass number − atomic number = 79 − 35 = 44 neutrons.
(b) Protons = atomic number = 35 protons.
Electrons = number of protons + one electron for each negative charge on ion = 35 + 1 = 36 electrons.
Neutrons = mass number − atomic number = 81 − 35 = 46 neutrons.
(c) Protons = atomic number = 11 protons.
Electrons = number of protons − one electron for each positive charge on ion = 11 − 1 = 10 electrons.
Neutrons = mass number − atomic number = 23 − 11 = 12 neutrons.
(d) Protons = atomic number = 1 proton.
Electrons = number of protons − one electron for each positive charge on ion = 1 − 1 = 0 electrons.
Neutrons = mass number − atomic number = 3 − 1 = 2 neutrons.

3.98 $\left(14.00308 \text{ amu} \times \dfrac{99.635}{100}\right) + \left(15.00011 \text{ amu} \times \dfrac{0.3650}{100}\right) = 14.01 \text{ amu}$

3.99 Because there are only two isotopes, the abundance of ^{109}Ag must be 100% − 51.84% = 48.16%.

$\left(106.90509 \text{ amu} \times \dfrac{51.84}{100}\right) + \left(108.9047 \text{ amu} \times \dfrac{48.16}{100}\right) = 107.9 \text{ amu}$

3.100 All the elements in a given group had to have similar chemical properties.

3.101 There are 44 known main-group elements. All of them are representative elements because *main group* and *representative* are different names for the same group of elements.

3.102 (a) Cl < S < Na < Cs.   (b) Cs < Na < S < Cl.

3.103 (b) Cl < Br < As < Ca < Sr.   (b) Sr < Ca < As < Br < Cl.

3.104 Zirconium, Zr, has atomic number 40, meaning a neutral Zr atom contains 40 electrons. Therefore the Zr^{4+} cation must contain 40 − 4 = 36 electrons. To be a 2+ cation and contain 36 electrons, an atom must contain 38 protons, making it the element whose atomic number is 38—strontium, Sr. The cation is Sr^{2+}.

3.105 Bromine, Br, has atomic number 35, meaning a neutral Br atom contains 35 electrons. Therefore the Br⁻ anion must contain $35 + 1 = 36$ electrons. To be a 1+ cation and contain 36 electrons, an atom must contain 37 protons, making it the element whose atomic number is 37—rubidium, Rb. The cation is Rb^+.

3.106 A 2+ charge means the number of protons in the cation exceeds the number of electrons by two. Element X therefore contains $10 + 2 = 12$ protons, which makes it magnesium, Mg.

3.107 Potassium, K, has the largest radius because, of the four atoms listed, it lies farthest to the left and lowest in the periodic table. Chlorine, Cl, has the largest first ionization energy because it lies farthest to the right and in the highest position.

3.108

Name of group or classification	Period	Group	Elemental Symbol	Atomic Number	Atomic Mass (amu)	Metal, metalloid, or nonmetal?
Transition metal	4	VIIIB (8)	Fe	26	55.845	Metal
Noble gas	1	VIIIA (18)	He	2	4.003	Nonmetal
Halogen	5	VIIA (17)	I	53	126.905	Nonmetal
Alkali metal	4	IA (1)	K	19	39.098	Metal
Halogen	3	VIIA (17)	Cl	17	35.453	Nonmetal
Noble gas	2	VIIIA (18)	Ne	10	20.180	Nonmetal
Chalcogen	2	VIA (16)	O	8	15.999	Nonmetal
——	3	IVA (14)	Si	14	28.086	Metalloid
Actinide	7	——	U	92	238.029	Metal

3.109 (a) g Cl = 110.99 g − 40.98 g = 70.01 g Cl

(b) $\% \, Ca = \dfrac{40.98 \text{ g}}{110.99 \text{ g}} \times 100\% = 36.92\% \text{ Ca}$

(c) $\% \, Cl = \dfrac{70.01 \text{ g}}{110.99 \text{ g}} \times 100\% = 63.08\% \text{ Cl}$

3.110 In Thomson's plum-pudding model, the atom is a cloud of positive electricity with electrons embedded throughout. In Rutherford's model, the atom is mostly empty space but contains a tiny, massive, positively charged nucleus in the center and electrons occupying the region outside the nucleus.

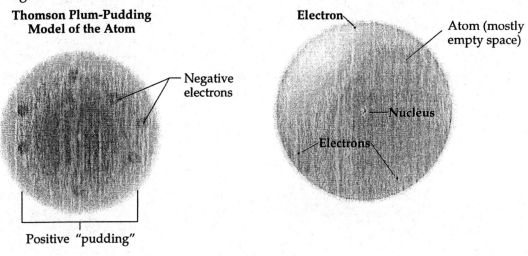

3.111 Rb < Ca < Se < S < F

3.112 In the modern periodic table the elements are arranged in order of increasing atomic number. In Mendeleev's periodic table the elements were arranged in order of increasing atomic mass.

3.113 N, Si, P, K, Au

3.114 Atomic number is the bottom number in the symbol; mass number is the top number. Atomic number tells you number of protons, number of neutrons is mass number minus atomic number, and number of electrons equals number of protons because these are neutral atoms.

	Atomic number	Mass number	Protons	Neutrons	Electrons
$^{27}_{13}Al$	13	27	13	14	13
$^{60}_{27}Co$	27	60	27	33	27
$^{200}_{79}Au$	79	200	79	121	79
$^{238}_{92}U$	92	238	92	146	92
$^{127}_{53}I$	53	127	53	74	53

3.115 Properties of metals: shiny, good conductors of electricity and heat, malleable. Properties of nonmetals: brittle, poor conductors of electricity and heat. Metalloids can behave as metals or as nonmetals and generally have properties intermediate between those of metals and nonmetals.

3.116 Rutherford accepted the plum pudding model of the atom, with its positive charges and negative electrons spread throughout the atom. The massive, fast-moving alpha particles should have passed through the thin gold foil just as a bullet would be expected to pass through tissue paper.

3.117 (a) Alkali metals   (b) Alkaline earth metals   (c) Halogens   (d) Noble gases or rare gases

3.118

$$2\,H \quad + \quad S \quad \longrightarrow \quad H_2S$$

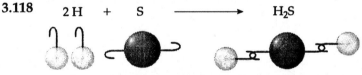

3.119 (a) $^{17}_{8}O$ (b) $^{119}_{50}Sn$ (c) $^{23}_{11}Na$ (d) $^{58}_{28}Ni$ (e) $^{137}_{56}Ba$

3.120 (a) Positively   (b) Protons, neutrons   (c) Nucleus   (d) Protons, electrons

3.121 The larger an atom, the smaller its first ionization energy.

3.122 The table of first ionization energies in section 3.7 of the textbook tells you the value for calcium is 6.1 eV and that for fluorine is 17.4 eV. Therefore calcium atoms give up electrons much more easily than fluorine atoms do.
(a) Fluorine atoms gain electrons.
(b) Calcium atoms lose electrons.
(c) Gaining one electron gives each fluorine a 1− charge.
(d) Losing two electrons gives each calcium a 2+ charge.
(e) $^{40}_{20}Ca^{2+}$ $^{19}_{9}F^{-}$

3.123 Chemical periodicity refers to the regular way in which the chemical properties of the elements repeat as you move in order of atomic number through the periodic table. The properties of lithium, for example, repeat in sodium, and you get from lithium to sodium by moving across period 2. The same properties repeat again in potassium, and you get from sodium to potassium by moving across period 3.

3.124

	Atomic number	Mass number	Protons	Neutrons	Electrons	Symbol
Protium	1	1	1	0	1	^1_1H
Deuterium	1	2	1	1	1	^2_1H
Tritium	1	3	1	2	1	^3_1H

3.125 The tendency to lose electrons is measured by ionization energy. The element with the lowest first ionization energy has the most metallic character, therefore, and the element with the highest first ionization energy has the least metallic character: Ne < Be < Li < Na < Cs.

3.126 The atom with the lower first ionization energy loses an electron more easily.
(a) K   (b) Na   (c) Rb   (d) S   (e) Br

3.127 Mass number is the number of protons plus neutrons in an atom; it is always a whole number. Atomic mass is the weighted average of the masses of all of the isotopes of an element; it is usually not a whole number but is numerically very close to the mass number.

3.128 (a) % Copper-65 = 100% − 69.17% = 30.83%

(b) $\left(62.94 \text{ amu} \times \dfrac{69.17}{100} \right) + \left(64.93 \text{ amu} \times \dfrac{30.83}{100} \right) = 63.55 \text{ amu}$

3.129 The elements in a group have similar characteristics, much as members of the same family do.

3.130 The first statement is not exactly true because atoms are not indivisible, fundamental particles; they are composed of protons, neutrons, and electrons. The second statement is not exactly true because atoms can be created and destroyed in nuclear reactions.

3.131 (a) Beryllium   (b) Magnesium   (c) Iron   (d) Sulfur   (e) Argon   (f) Copper

CHAPTER
4

The Modern Model of the Atom

4.1 See solution in textbook.

4.2 $E = \dfrac{hc}{\lambda}$, where $h = 6.626 \times 10^{-34}$ J·s, $c = 3.00 \times 10^8$ m/s, and λ is wavelength:

$$E = \frac{(6.626 \times 10^{-34} \text{ J·s}) \times (3.00 \times 10^8 \text{ m/s})}{660.5 \text{ nm} \times (1 \times 10^{-9} \text{ m/nm})} = 3.01 \times 10^{-19} \text{ J}$$

4.3 $E = \dfrac{hc}{\lambda}$, where $h = 6.626 \times 10^{-34}$ J·s, $c = 3.00 \times 10^8$ m/s, and λ is wavelength:

$$\lambda = \frac{hc}{E} = \frac{(6.626 \times 10^{-34} \text{ J·s}) \times (3.00 \times 10^8 \text{ m/s})}{3.50 \times 10^{-19} \text{ J}} = 5.68 \times 10^{-7} \text{ m}$$

$$5.68 \times 10^{-7} \text{ m} \times \frac{1 \times 10^9 \text{ nm}}{1 \text{ m}} = 568 \text{ nm}$$

Light of this wavelength is yellow.

4.4 The average height of an adult person is about 6 ft = 1.8 m = 1.8×10^0 m. Radiation of this wavelength is in the radio and television region of the electromagnetic spectrum. This is very-low-energy electromagnetic radiation.

4.5 See solution in textbook.

4.6 Sulfur has 16 protons and therefore 16 electrons:

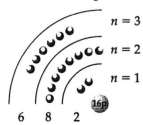

Two more electrons can go in the $n = 3$ shell because its capacity is eight electrons.

4.7 Because the electron in the low-n shell is closer to the nucleus than the electron in the high-n shell is and feels a stronger attraction to the nucleus.

4.8 $2n^2 = 2 \times 5^2 = 50$ electrons.

4.9 See solution in textbook.

4.10 The highest-energy state is the one that requires the greatest amount of energy to move an electron. Problem 4.9 tells you the move $2 \longrightarrow 3$ takes 1.25 eV and the move $1 \longrightarrow 2$ takes 6.75 eV. The move $1 \longrightarrow 3$ takes 9.00 eV $-$ 1.00 eV $=$ 8.00 eV, and therefore this move creates the highest-energy state:

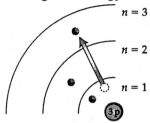

4.11 A Li$^+$ ion has lost one electron, and for the ion to be in the ground state, the two remaining electrons must be in the lowest shell:

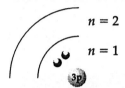

4.12 (a) Atomic number 6 identifies this atom as carbon.
(b) Because it has six protons (atomic number 6) and eight electrons, this is an anion carrying a 2$-$ charge.
(c)

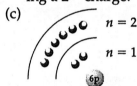

4.13 The $n = 1$ shell has three electrons in this diagram; the maximum is two electrons for this shell. The $n = 2$ shell has only six electrons; the maximum is eight for this shell, and it should be filled before an electron is placed in the $n = 3$ shell. The correct Bohr model for the F$^-$ anion is

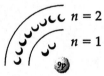

4.14 See solution in textbook.

4.15 Arsenic, As, has 33 electrons, making the electron configuration $1s^2 2s^2 2p^6 3s^2 3p^6 3d^{10} 4s^2 4p^3$. There are five valence electrons (the $4s$ and $4p$ electrons), and the roman-numeral group number is VA. The number of valence electrons does agree with the group number.

4.16 Scandium, Sc, has 21 electrons; therefore the electron configuration is $1s^2 2s^2 2p^6 3s^2 3p^6 4s^2 3d^1$. Remember, the $4s$ subshell usually gets filled before the $3d$ subshell.

4.17 See solution in textbook.

4.18 Kr has 36 electrons. The first 20 go in order, $1s$, $2s$, $2p$, $3s$, $3p$, $4s$, but when you get to the first d subshell, subtract 1 from the period number to end up with $3d$. Then go back to 4 when you re-enter the p block: $1s^22s^22p^63s^23p^64s^23d^{10}4p^6$. It is proper for Kr to be in group VIIIA because it has eight valence electrons, two in $4s$ and six in $4p$.

4.19 Pd has 46 electrons. When you subtract 1 from the period number each time you enter the d block, you get the configuration $1s^22s^22p^63s^23p^64s^23d^{10}4p^65s^24d^8$.

4.20 See solution in textbook.

4.21 Ra has 88 electrons. The first 54 go in the usual positions, giving the configuration $1s^22s^22p^63s^23p^64s^23d^{10}4p^65s^24d^{10}5p^6$. Then begin period 6 with $6s^2$, go one deep into $6d$ for $6 - 1 = 5d^1$, then go through the whole $6f$ row for $6 - 2 = 4f^{14}$. Now go back to $6 - 1 = 5d^1$ for nine more. Then $6p^6$ and end with $7s^2$. The configuration is therefore $1s^22s^22p^63s^23p^64s^23d^{10}4p^65s^24d^{10}5p^66s^24f^{14}5d^{10}6p^67s^2$. The first noble-gas element preceding radium is radon, Rn, making the abbreviated notation $[Rn]7s^2$.

4.22 U has 92 electrons. When you detour to $6 - 2 = 4f^{14}$ after passing La and detour to $7 - 2 = 5f^3$ after passing Ac, the configuration you get is $1s^22s^22p^63s^23p^64s^23d^{10}4p^65s^24d^{10}5p^66s^24f^{14}5d^{10}6p^67s^26d^15f^3$. The first noble-gas element preceding uranium is radon, Rn, making the abbreviated notation $[Rn]7s^26d^15f^3$.

4.23 See solution in textbook.

4.24 Rewriting the configuration to emphasize the valence electrons gives: $1s^22s^22p^63s^23p^63d^34s^2$. The highest value of n is 4, meaning this is a period 4 element. The $4s^2$ outermost occupiedd shell tells you this element has two valence electrons, meaning it "should" be Ca in period 4. It is not Ca, however, and to see why, count the electrons. Calcium, atomic number 20, has 20, but this element has 23, making it the transition metal vanadium, V, a group VB (5) element. The rule about number of valence electrons works only for the representative (A group) elements.

4.25 In $[Xe]6s^1$ the highest value of n is 6, making this a period 6 element. Because the element has only one valence electron, it is in group IA. The element is cesium, Cs. To be sure this is not a group B element masquerading as a group A element (see solution 4.24), count the electrons: 54 to Xe + 1 = 55. Cesium is correct.

4.26 See solution in textbook.

4.27

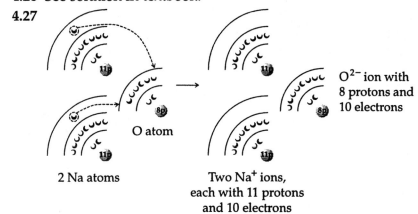

2 Na atoms   O atom   Two Na⁺ ions, each with 11 protons and 10 electrons   O²⁻ ion with 8 protons and 10 electrons

4.28 Ba is a group IIA metal and thus loses two electrons to become Ba^{2+}; F is a group VIIA non-metal and so gains one electron to become F^-. To have charge neutrality, the formula must be BaF_2.

4.29 Al is a group IIIA metal and thus loses three electrons to become Al^{3+}; O is a group VIA non-metal and so gains two electrons to become O^{2-}. To have charge neutrality, the formula must be Al_2O_3.

4.30 The wavelength of green light is in the range of 500 nm = 500 × 10⁻⁹ m = 5000 × 10⁻¹⁰ m. The wavelength of X rays is in the range of 1 × 10⁻¹⁰ m, meaning X-ray wavelengths are much shorter than green-light wavelengths:

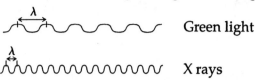

Green light

X rays

4.31 Because radiation energy is inversely related to wavelength, the shorter the wavelength, the higher the energy. Therefore the X rays, with shorter wavelength, have higher energy.

4.32 They are at the high-energy end of the electromagnetic radiation spectrum and can cause damage to cells and tissues.

4.33 $30 \text{ miles} \times \dfrac{1.61 \text{ km}}{1 \text{ mile}} \times \dfrac{1000 \text{ m}}{1 \text{ km}} \times \dfrac{1 \text{ s}}{3.00 \times 10^8 \text{ m}} = 1.6 \times 10^{-4} \text{ s}$

4.34 The visible light takes

$$9.3 \times 10^7 \text{ miles} \times \frac{1.6093 \text{ km}}{1 \text{ mile}} \times \frac{1000 \text{ m}}{1 \text{ km}} \times \frac{1 \text{ s}}{3.00 \times 10^8 \text{ m}} \times \frac{1 \text{ min}}{60 \text{ s}} = 8.3 \text{ min}$$

The gamma rays also take 8.3 min because all electromagnetic radiation travels at the same speed, regardless of its energy or wavelength.

4.35 (2) is true. According to the equation $E = hc/\lambda$, the energy of light decreases as its wavelength increases. The equation indicates that the energy and wavelength are *inversely* related to each other because λ is in the denominator.

4.36 Table 2.3 of the textbook tells you that *nano-* is the prefix for 10^{-9}. Therefore 1.00 nm is

$$1.00 \text{ nm} \times \frac{1.00 \times 10^{-9} \text{ m}}{1 \text{ nm}} = 1.00 \times 10^{-9} \text{ m}$$

The inches conversion is

$$1.00 \text{ nm} \times \frac{1.00 \times 10^{-9} \text{ m}}{1 \text{ nm}} \times \frac{100 \text{ cm}}{1 \text{ m}} \times \frac{1 \text{ inch}}{2.54 \text{ cm}} = 3.94 \times 10^{-8} \text{ inch}$$

4.37 Gamma rays are much higher in energy and will damage cells and tissues. Radio waves do not have enough energy to cause damage to cells and tissues.

4.38 $E = hc/\lambda$, where $h = 6.63 \times 10^{-34} \text{ J} \cdot \text{s}$, $c = 3.00 \times 10^8 \text{ m/s}$, and λ is wavelength.

$$E = \frac{(6.63 \times 10^{-34} \text{ J} \cdot \text{s}) \times (3.00 \times 10^8 \text{ m/s})}{10 \text{ m}} = 1.99 \times 10^{-26} \text{ J}$$

4.39 $E = \dfrac{(6.63 \times 10^{-34} \text{ J} \cdot \text{s}) \times (3.00 \times 10^8 \text{ m/s})}{10 \text{ pm}} \times \dfrac{1 \times 10^{12} \text{ pm}}{1 \text{ m}} = 1.99 \times 10^{-14} \text{ J}$

The X ray is

$$\frac{1.99 \times 10^{-14}}{1.99 \times 10^{-26}} = 1 \times 10^{12}$$

times more energetic than the radio wave of problem 4.38.

4.40 Indigo line, $\lambda = 410.1$ nm:

$$E = \frac{hc}{\lambda} = \frac{(6.63 \times 10^{-34} \text{ J} \cdot \text{s}) \times (3.00 \times 10^8 \text{ m/s})}{410.1 \times 10^{-9} \text{ m}} = 4.85 \times 10^{-19} \text{ J}$$

Blue line, $\lambda = 434$ nm

$$E = \frac{(6.63 \times 10^{-34} \text{ J} \cdot \text{s}) \times (3.00 \times 10^8 \text{ m/s})}{434 \times 10^{-9} \text{ m}} = 4.58 \times 10^{-19} \text{ J}$$

Blue-green line, $\lambda = 486$ nm

$$E = \frac{(6.63 \times 10^{-34} \text{ J} \cdot \text{s}) \times (3.00 \times 10^8 \text{ m/s})}{486 \times 10^{-9} \text{ m}} = 4.09 \times 10^{-19} \text{ J}$$

Red line, $\lambda = 656.3$ nm

$$E = \frac{(6.63 \times 10^{-34} \text{ J} \cdot \text{s}) \times (3.00 \times 10^8 \text{ m/s})}{656.3 \times 10^{-9} \text{ m}} = 3.03 \times 10^{-19} \text{ J}$$

Notice that as the wavelength increases from indigo to red, the energy decreases.

4.41 You would appear first at the starting line, then a certain time later you would instantaneously appear some distance ahead, and later still some farther distance ahead, until finally you would appear instantaneously at the finish line.

4.42 In the movement of everyday objects, the difference in energy levels is much too small to be observed or measured.

4.43 *Quantized energy* means that the energy any object possesses can have only certain allowable values and no in-between values.

4.44 Quantum physics is more general because both large and small particles obey its laws. Classical physics deals only with large objects, and in large objects quantization cannot be observed because differences in allowed energy levels are too small to be noticed.

4.45 That something inside the atom is allowed to possess only certain energies, as opposed to any energy. Thus the atom can release only light energy of specific (quantized) energies rather than a continuous range of energies.

4.46 Energy and stability are inversely related. The higher the energy of an object, the less stable it is; the lower the energy, the more stable.

4.47 (a) is more stable because unlike charges—such as an electron and an atomic nucleus—attract each other and are stable when close to each other; (b) is less stable because like charges repel each other and are less stable when close to each other.

4.48 (a) is most stable, and (c) is least stable. Unlike charges attract each other, and the closer the two are, the more stable the situation. An example is an electron in an atom. The closer the electron is to the nucleus, the lower the energy of the electron. Because energy content and stability are inversely related, the closer to the nucleus the electron is, the more stable the situation.

4.49 The *n* value for an electron dictates which shell the electron occupies. As *n* increases for an electron, both its energy and its distance from the nucleus increase.

4.50 Because the energy would not be quantized, classical physics could be used to describe the behavior of the electron.

4.51 Electron shell.

4.52 Energy must be added to an atom to move an electron farther from the nucleus because the attractive forces holding the negative electron near the positive nucleus must be overcome.

4.53 The *n* value for an electron dictates which shell the electron occupies. An increase in *n* value means the electron moves farther from the nucleus, and as a result of the move the electron's energy increases.

4.54 $2n^2$ electrons, where *n* is the orbit's principal quantum number.

4.55 The lower shells are of lower energy; the electrons go into lower-energy positions before going into higher-energy (less stable) positions.

4.56 An excited state because the $n = 2$ energy shell is not filled, yet there is an electron in the $n = 3$ shell. This means an $n = 2$ electron was excited into the $n = 3$ shell.

4.57 Bohr's rules say that inner shells are filled first. The atom of Problem 4.56 would have its lowest-energy (most stable) configuration if the electron in the $n = 3$ shell were moved to the $n = 2$ shell:

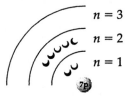

4.58 Because the electrons cannot have any energy values between orbits. These intermediate energies are not allowed in a quantized atom.

4.59 The energy of an electron depends on its distance from the nucleus. The Bohr model says each allowed distance from the nucleus has its own discrete, characteristic energy value. Therefore saying an electron can be only at certain distances from the nucleus means the electron can have only certain energy values.

4.60 An atom's valence shell is the outermost shell containing electrons.

4.61 Because atoms in the same group have identical valence-shell configurations.

4.62 A line spectrum is a record of someting giving off discrete amounts of energy. The Bohr model says electrons in atoms give off discrete amounts of energy as they change orbits, which means the atomic spectra they produce are line spectra.

4.63 A ground-state configuration is the lowest-energy configuration possible, in which all electrons are in the shells having the lowest-energy values consistent with the restriction that $2n^2$ is the maximum number of electrons allowed in any shell. An excited-state configuration is one in which one or more electrons are boosted into higher-energy shells when the atom absorbs energy.

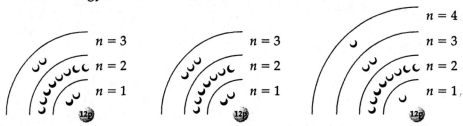

Mg ground state   Mg excited states

4.64 True. The H^+ cation has no electrons because the one valence electron in the neutral H atom was lost to form the cation. The definition of excited state is that one or more electrons are in a high-energy shell when there is room available in a lower-energy shell.

4.65

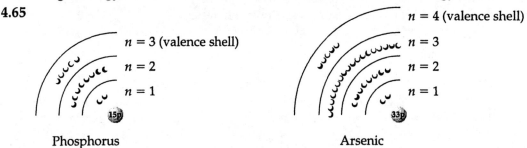

Phosphorus   Arsenic

These two elements have similar chemical properties because both have five electrons in the valence shell.

4.66 (a) 12.1 eV would be needed to go from $n = 1$ (1.0 eV) to $n = 3$ (13.1 eV).

(b) 12.1 eV. As this light was emitted, the electron would fall from $n = 3$ (13.1 eV) to $n = 1$ (1.0 eV).

(c) 12.1 eV light is ultraviolet.

4.67 Nothing. The electron would remain in the ground state because it needs more than 5.1 eV to be excited into the $n = 2$ shell. It needs 10.2 eV to be excited from $n = 1$ (1.0 eV) to $n = 2$ (11.2 eV).

4.68 The energy of the shells would have to be continuous, not quantized.

4.69 (a) 1: Nothing wrong. Seven protons but only six electrons means it is a cation. No shell filled beyond maximum capacity.

2: Nothing wrong. Same number of protons and electrons. No shell filled beyond maximum capacity.

3: Too many electrons in $n = 1$ shell, which holds a maximum of $2 \times 1^2 = 2$.

(b) 1: $^{14}_{7}N^+$ 2: $^{14}_{7}N$

(c) 1: Ground state because every electron has the lowest energy possible consistent with the $2n^2$ limit.

2: Excited state because one electron is in the $n = 3$ shell when the $n = 2$ shell is not filled to capacity.

4.70 The number of valence electrons is equal to the roman-numeral group number.

4.71 〰〰〰〰〰〰 Red light

𝗔𝗔𝗔𝗔𝗔𝗔𝗔𝗔 Blue light

Because it has the shorter wavelength, blue light has the higher energy. The blue light would therefore be associated with relaxation from a higher state, meaning in this case the relaxation from $n = 4$ to $n = 2$.

4.72 The energy of the $n = 5$ shell is 14.1 eV, and that of the $n = 3$ shell is 13.1 eV. The energy of the emitted light is therefore 14.1 eV − 13.1 eV = 1.0 eV.

$$E = \frac{hc}{\lambda}$$

$$\lambda = \frac{hc}{E} = \frac{(6.626 \times 10^{-34}\,J \cdot s) \times (3.00 \times 10^8\,m/s)}{1.0\,eV} \times \frac{1\,eV}{1.602 \times 10^{-19}\,J} = 1.24 \times 10^{-6}\,m$$

$$1.24 \times 10^{-6}\,m \times \frac{1 \times 10^9\,nm}{1\,m} = 1.24 \times 10^3\,nm$$

4.73 Because Planck's constant h is given in joule-seconds in the textbook, convert the given wavelength to meters before using the energy equation:

$$1772.6\,nm \times \frac{1\,m}{1 \times 10^9\,nm} = 1.7726 \times 10^{-6}\,m$$

$$E = \frac{(6.626 \times 10^{-34}\,J \cdot s) \times (3.00 \times 10^8\,m/s)}{1.7726 \times 10^{-6}\,m} = 1.12 \times 10^{-19}\,J$$

$$1.12 \times 10^{-19}\,J \times \frac{1\,eV}{1.602 \times 10^{-19}\,J} = 0.700\,eV$$

The energy-level diagram on page 129 of the textbook tells you the energy of the $n = 4$ shell is 13.8 eV. Subtract the emitted 0.700 eV from this value and you get 13.1 eV, which is the energy of the $n = 3$ shell. Therefore the electron relaxed to the $n = 3$ shell.

4.74 The simple Bohr model predicts nine electrons in the $n = 3$ shell of potassium. However, the chemical behavior of this element suggests that it has 1 valence electron in the $n = 4$ shell.

4.75 The experimental evidence was that line spectra contained a number of closely spaced lines of nearly identical energy. Because the lines were of nearly identical energy, they must be in the same shell. Therefore the small differences in energy suggested that the lines were the result of separations within a shell.

4.76 (a) $n = 1, 2, 3, 4, 5 \ldots$, with 1 representing the lowest-energy shell.

(b) s, p, d, f with s representing the lowest-energy subshell.

(c) The number of subshells in a given shell is equal to the n number of the shell. There is one subshell in the $n = 1$ shell, two subshells in the $n = 2$ shell, and so on.

4.77 The s subshell holds a maximum of 2 electrons, the p holds 6, the d holds 10, and the f holds 14.

4.78 Bohr put the nineteenth electron in the $4s$ subshell instead of in the $3d$ subshell. He justified this placement by reasoning that potassium is in group IA, which means it must have one valence electron. Placing the nineteenth electron in the $4s$ subshell is the only arrangement consistent with this fact.

4.79 Drawing the diagram this way implies that the $3d$ subshell is larger than the $4s$ subshell. That is *not* so! An electron in the $4s$ subshell of an atom is, on average, farther from the nucleus than an electron in the $3d$ subshell is.

4.80 (a) Boron has 5 electrons: $1s^2 2s^2 2p^1$

(b) Scandium has 21 electrons: $1s^2 2s^2 2p^6 3s^2 3p^6 4s^2 3d^1$

(c) Cobalt has 27 electrons: $1s^2 2s^2 2p^6 3s^2 3p^6 4s^2 3d^7$

(d) Selenium has 34 electrons: $1s^2 2s^2 2p^6 3s^2 3p^6 4s^2 3d^{10} 4p^4$

(e) Ruthenium has 44 electrons: $1s^2 2s^2 2p^6 3s^2 3p^6 4s^2 3d^{10} 4p^6 5s^2 4d^6$

4.81 (a) $[\text{He}]2s^2 2p^1$

(b) $[\text{Ar}]4s^2 3d^1$

(c) $[\text{Ar}]4s^2 3d^7$

(d) $[\text{Ar}]4s^2 3d^{10} 4p^4$

(e) $[\text{Kr}]5s^2 4d^6$

4.82 (a) Barium (56 electrons): $1s^2 2s^2 2p^6 3s^2 3p^6 4s^2 3d^{10} 4p^6 5s^2 4d^{10} 5p^6 6s^2$

(b) Tungsten (74 electrons): $1s^2 2s^2 2p^6 3s^2 3p^6 4s^2 3d^{10} 4p^6 5s^2 4d^{10} 5p^6 6s^2 4f^{14} 5d^4$

(c) Lead (82 electrons): $1s^2 2s^2 2p^6 3s^2 3p^6 4s^2 3d^{10} 4p^6 5s^2 4d^{10} 5p^6 6s^2 4f^{14} 5d^{10} 6p^2$

(d) Praseodymium (59 electrons): $1s^2 2s^2 2p^6 3s^2 3p^6 4s^2 3d^{10} 4p^6 5s^2 4d^{10} 5p^6 6s^2 5d^1 4f^2$

(e) Protactinium (91 electrons): $1s^2 2s^2 2p^6 3s^2 3p^6 4s^2 3d^{10} 4p^6 5s^2 4d^{10} 5p^6 6s^2 4f^{14} 5d^{10} 6p^6 7s^2 6d^1 5f^2$

4.83 (a) $[\text{Xe}]6s^2$

(b) $[\text{Xe}]6s^2 4f^{14} 5d^4$

(c) $[\text{Xe}]6s^2 4f^{14} 5d^{10} 6p^2$

(d) $[\text{Xe}]6s^2 5d^1 4f^2$

(e) $[\text{Rn}]7s^2 6d^1 5f^2$

4.84 The highest n value tells you the period. The total number of electrons having that n value tells you the number of valence electrons, which for the representative elements equals the roman-numeral group number.

(a) Period 2, group VA—nitrogen.

(b) Period 3, group IA—sodium.

(c) Period 4, group VIIA—bromine.

4.85 (a) Incorrect; $2s$ should come after $1s$.

(b) Incorrect; $2s$ subshell holds a maximum of two electrons and should be followed by $2p$ subshell.

(c) Incorrect; $1s$ subshell must come first in a ground-state configuration.

(d) Incorrect; $2p$ subshell holds a maximum of six electrons.

(e) Incorrect; $2p$ subshell should have six electrons before any electrons go into $3s$ subshell.
(f) Correct.

4.86 Valence electrons are those in the outermost occupied shell. Therefore look for the highest principal quantum number and add all electrons in all subshells having that highest n value: (a) five, (b) one, (c) two, (d) eight, (e) two.

4.87 The period tells you the shell in which the valence electrons are placed—in other words, the n value of the valence shell.

4.88 O: $1s^22s^22p^4$; O^{2+}: $1s^22s^22p^2$; O^{2-}: $1s^22s^22p^6$. You would expect to find O^{2-} in most compounds of oxygen because the octet rule is satisfied in this anion. (There are eight valence electrons.)

4.89 In the d block, the n level that is filling is 1 less than the period. For example, the $3d$ electrons are being added in the fourth period. In the f block, the n level that is filling is 2 less than the period. For example, the $4f$ electrons are being added in the sixth period.

4.90 The s block is 2 elements wide because each s subshell holds 2 electrons. The p block is 6 elements wide because each p subshell holds 6 electrons. The d block is 10 elements wide because each d subshell holds 10 electrons. The f block is 14 elements wide because each f subshell holds 14 electrons.

4.91 The octet rule states that atoms react in such a way as to put eight electrons in the valence shell. Having eight valence electrons gives an atom a noble gas valence electron configuration and makes them exceptionally stable, just as the noble gases are.

4.92 By losing their valence electron(s).

4.93 By gaining enough electrons to have eight in the outermost occupied shell.

4.94

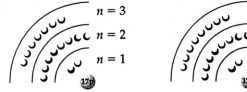

Cl neutral atom   Cl$^-$ ion

There are seven electrons in the valence shell in Cl and eight in Cl$^-$.

4.95

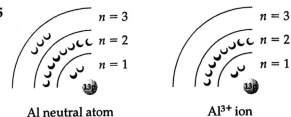

Al neutral atom   Al^{3+} ion

There are three electrons in the valence shell in Al and eight in Al^{3+}.

4.96 Each sodium atom has one valence electron, which it loses to obtain an octet. Each sulfur atom has six valence electrons and gains two to have an octet. Thus each sulfur atom needs two sodium atoms, and the formula of the compound is Na$_2$S.

4.97 Each lithium atom has one valence electron, which it loses to obtain an octet. Each nitrogen atom has five valence electrons, and gains three to have an octet. Thus each nitrogen atom needs three lithium atoms, and the formula of the compound is Li$_3$N.

4.98 Because it is the same as the number of valence electrons, the roman-numeral group number allows us to predict how many electrons are gained or lost to form an octet. Elements with fewer than four valence electrons lose electrons to form an octet. Elements with more valence electrons gain electrons to form an octet. For example, elements in group IIA lose two electrons; elements in group VA gain three electrons.

4.99 (a) No charge on either drawing means these are two neutral atoms. The number of protons tells you the atomic number, and knowing the number of neutrons allows you to calculate the mass number. The elements are $^{23}_{11}$Na and $^{31}_{15}$P.

(b) The sodium needs to lose one electron to have an octet in its valence shell, and phosphorus needs to gain three electrons to have an octet in its valence shell. Therefore sodium is the metal and phosphorus is the nonmetal.

(c) Each P atom, needing three electrons, reacts with three Na atoms. The formula of the resulting compound is Na_3P.

(d)

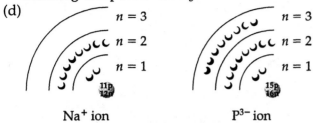

4.100 XY_2. The group IIA element loses two electrons, and the group VIIA element gains one electron. Therefore two Y atoms are needed for each X atom.

4.101 Hydrogen generally loses its one electron, similar to what the other elements in group IA do to obtain an octet. However, when hydrogen loses its electron, it does not obtain an octet; it is left with no electrons.

4.102 Aluminum has three valence electrons, which it loses to form a 3+ cation. Both oxygen and sulfur have six valence electrons and gain two to form a 2− anion. Because Al needs to lose three electrons and oxygen and sulfur need to gain two, each compound contains two Al^{3+} cations and three anions. The formulas are similar because both oxygen and sulfur have the same number of valence electrons.

4.103 True.

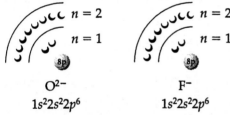

4.104 It is true that Mg^{2+} and Na^+ have identical electron configurations; it is false that they have similar properties. The two ions have different charges, different sizes, and different chemical reactivities.

4.105 A representative metal will lose all of its valence electrons. Because the roman-numeral group number is equal to the number of valence electrons, you can tell how many electrons a metal atom will lose by looking at its roman-numeral group number. The charge on the metal cation will be a positive number equal to the roman-numeral group number.

4.106 A representative nonmetal will gain enough electrons to have a total of eight in its valence shell. Because the roman-numeral group number is equal to the number of valence electrons, you can tell how may electrons it will gain by subtracting the number of valence electrons from 8. The charge on the nonmetal anion will be a negative number equal to 8 minus the roman-numeral group number.

4.107 The charges on the cation and anion tell how many electrons are lost and gained, respectively, to form the ions. The formula of the compound is simply the minimum number of each ion needed to have an equal number of electrons transferred. For example, if Mg *loses* two electrons to form Mg^{2+} and Cl *gains* one electron to form Cl^-, a minimum of two electrons must be transferred in the reaction. Therefore one Mg^{2+} will combine with two Cl^- to form $MgCl_2$.

4.108 (a) Because the one additional electron for each element is placed in the same valence shell across an entire period, one might expect the atom size to stay the same.

(b) Atomic size decreases from left to right across a period because one electron is added to the valence shell *and* one proton is added to the nucleus. The added proton makes the nucleus more positive, which causes it to more strongly attract the surrounding electrons. The increased pull on the electrons shrinks the atom.

4.109 Going down a group, the valence electrons are placed in successively larger shells, increasing the size of the atom.

4.110 Beryllium has the smaller $1s$ subshell. The nuclear charge in Be is $+4$, and the nuclear charge in Li is $+3$. The greater charge in Be pulls the electrons in closer to the nucleus, shrinking the subshells.

4.111 Lithium has the smaller valence shell. The Li valence shell is the $n = 1$ shell. The Na valence shell is the $n = 2$ shell. In general, shells increase in size as n increases.

4.112 Lithium is larger because atomic size decreases as you go from left to right in a period.

4.113 Sodium is larger because atomic size increases going down a group.

4.114 Si < Mg < Na < Rb

4.115 By placing an atom's electrons in various subshells, Bohr's model places each electron in a particular location that we can, in theory, describe exactly. According to modern quantum mechanical theory, you cannot know precisely both (1) where an electron is at a given moment and (2) where it will be at any future moment. The more precisely you know one, the less precisely you know the other. Therefore, the Bohr concept of electrons traveling in exact orbits around the nucleus is incorrect.

4.116 The phenomenon whereby an electron is able to penetrate a barrier even though it does not have enough energy to do so.

4.117 An orbital is a region of space around the nucleus of an atom in which it is most probable that an electron will be found.

4.118 *s* orbital   *p* orbital   *d* orbital

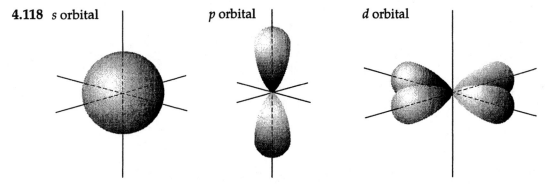

4.119 The picture would be very fuzzy, indicating that the camera cannot record your exact position at any moment. The only thing it can record is the probability that you are in a certain region of the photograph.

4.120 Heisenberg's uncertainty principle, by stating that it is impossible to exactly locate an electron. If an electron couldn't be exactly located in a volume of space, Schrödinger reasoned, it could be thought of as being everywhere in that volume at once, filling it like a cloud.

4.121 The speed at which light travels is 3.00×10^8 m/s. The time needed to travel the distance is

$$3.00 \times 10^3 \text{ miles} \times \frac{1.61 \text{ km}}{1 \text{ mile}} \times \frac{1000 \text{ m}}{1 \text{ km}} \times \frac{1 \text{ s}}{3.00 \times 10^8 \text{ m}} = 1.61 \times 10^{-2} \text{ s}$$

4.122 $5.00 \times 10^{-5} \text{ cm} \times \dfrac{1 \text{ m}}{100 \text{ cm}} \times \dfrac{1 \times 10^9 \text{ nm}}{1 \text{ m}} = 5.00 \times 10^2 \text{ nm}$

4.123 Because λ stands for wavelength, this is a simple conversion:

$$2.50\times10^{-5}\,\text{m}\times\frac{1\times10^{9}\,\text{nm}}{1\,\text{m}}=2.50\times10^{4}\,\text{nm}$$

$$\frac{2.50\times10^{4}\,\text{nm infrared}}{750\,\text{nm red}}=33.3$$

The infrared wavelength is 33.3 times longer than the red wavelength.

4.124 (a) No. Table 4.1 of the textbook tells you that a wavelength below 380 nm is ultraviolet light, and the human eye cannot see ultraviolet light.

(b) $E=\dfrac{hc}{\lambda}=\dfrac{(6.626\times10^{-34}\,\text{J·s})\times(3.00\times10^{8}\,\text{m/s})}{2.852\times10^{-7}\,\text{m}}=6.97\times10^{-19}\,\text{J}$

4.125 Use the energy equation, in the form $\lambda = hc/E$ for the first row and in the form $E = hc/\lambda$ for the second and third rows.

Wavelength (m)	Wavelength (nm)	Energy (J)
3.52×10^{-8} m	35.2 nm	5.65×10^{-18} J
2.6020×10^{-6} m	2602.0 nm	7.64×10^{-20} J
7.85×10^{-12} m	7.85×10^{-3} nm	2.53×10^{-14} J

4.126 It would require the absorption of light energy. Moving an electron away from the nucleus requires energy to overcome the attraction the nucleus has for the electron.

4.127 Energy is released. An electron initially in a shell having a higher n value needs less energy once it is in a shell having a lower n value. The electron releases the energy it no longer needs.

4.128 The energy it takes to move the electron is equal to the difference in the energy levels of the two shells.

4.129 The ground state has a filled $n = 1$ shell and the rest of the electrons are in the $n = 2$ shell. Thus relaxing only one of the electrons in the $n = 3$ shell gives a configuration that has lower energy than the original configuration but still is not the ground state:

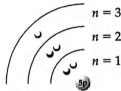

(a) Lower-energy excited state   (b) Ground state

4.130 The number and arrangement of electrons in the valence shell give an atom its chemical properties.

4.131 You can get the energy of the emitted light from the energy-level diagram on page 129 of the textbook:
(14.2 eV in $n = 6$) − (1.0 eV in $n = 1$) = 13.2 eV emitted

$$13.2\,\text{eV}\times\frac{1.602\times10^{-19}\,\text{J}}{1\,\text{eV}}=2.11\times10^{-18}\,\text{J}$$

The wavelength of light having this energy is

$$\lambda=\frac{hc}{E}=\frac{(6.626\times10^{-34}\,\text{J·s})\times(3.00\times10^{8}\,\text{m/s})}{2.11\times10^{-18}\,\text{J}}=9.42\times10^{-8}\,\text{m}\times\frac{1\times10^{9}\,\text{nm}}{1\,\text{m}}=94.2\,\text{nm}$$

4.132 Gallium and aluminum both have three valence electrons (shown below in grey):

Al $1s^2 2s^2 2p^6 3s^2 3p^1$ Ga $1s^2 2s^2 2p^6 3s^2 3p^6 3d^{10} 4s^2 4p^1$

The ten d electrons in gallium are not in the valence shell and therefore do not influence chemical properties.

4.133 (a) Ground state. All 26 electrons are in the subshells assigned to them by the four-block periodic table guide.

(b) Incorrect. The $4s$ subshell, because it is lower in energy than the $3d$ subshell, should be filled before any electrons are put in the $3d$ subshell.

(c) Incorrect. The $2p$ subshell has more than its maximum allowable number of electrons.

4.134 (a) 14 electrons means this neutral atom is silicon. The valence shell is $n = 3$ and contains four valence electrons.

(b) Neon has 10 electrons, meaning this neutral atom has 11 and is therefore sodium. It has one valence electron.

(c) Argon has 18 electrons, meaning this neutral atom has $18 + 15 = 33$ and is arsenic. The valence electrons are only those in the shell having the highest n value, which is $n = 4$. Therefore this atom has five valence electrons.

4.135 The d subshell is being filled. It fills *after* the s subshell having the next highest principal quantum number n has been filled.

4.136 Argon has 18 electrons, and therefore so does this anion. Carrying a $2-$ charge means the number of electrons in the anion must exceed the number of protons by 2. The number of protons, which defines the element, is therefore $18 - 2 = 16$, making the element sulfur and the ion S^{2-}.

4.137 They have the same electron configuration: $1s^2 2s^2 2p^6$.

4.138 Calcium, a metal with two valence electrons, loses two electrons to achieve a valence-shell octet. This loss gives calcium a $2+$ charge. Sulfur, a nonmetal with six valence electrons, gains two electrons to achive a valence-shell octet. This gain gives sulfur a $2-$ charge. Only one $2+$ calcium is needed to combine with a $2-$ sulfide to yield a neutral compound.

4.139 (a) N. Nitrogen has a nuclear charge of $+7$; flourine has a nuclear charge of $+9$; and these two elements are in the same period and so have the same number of electron shells. The more positive F nucleus pulls more on the electrons, making N electrons easier to break away.

(b) Ba. The outermost electrons in magnesium are in the $n = 3$ shell. Those in barium are in the $n = 6$ shell. The farther electrons feel less nuclear pull and are thus easier to break away.

(c) Ca. The outermost electrons in nitrogen are in the $n = 2$ shell. Those in calcium are in the $n = 3$ shell. Being farther from the nucleus, calcium valence electrons break away more easily.

4.140 The ionization energy of the alkali metal is much lower than that of the halogen. Therefore, when they react with each other, the alkali metal easily loses its valence electron and the halogen resists losing any of its valence electrons (it tends to gain one valence electron instead).

4.141 Li_3N. Nitrogen, a group VA nonmetal with five valence electrons, gains three electrons to achieve a valence-shell octet and become N^{3-}. Lithium, a group IA metal with one valence electron, loses that electron to achieve a valence-shell octet and become Li^+. It takes three Li^+ ions to combine with one N^{3-} ion to achieve a neutral compound.

4.142 The $4s$ electron, being a larger electron cloud, spends more time, on average, farther from the nucleus. This increases its energy.

4.143 $\lambda = \dfrac{hc}{E} = \dfrac{(6.626 \times 10^{-34}\,J \cdot s) \times (3.00 \times 10^8\,m/s)}{1.00 \times 10^{-15}\,J} = 1.99 \times 10^{-10}\,m \times \dfrac{1 \times 10^9\,nm}{1\,m} = 0.199\,nm$

4.144 The waves are more energetic than visible light because their wavelength is shorter.

4.145 (c) Gamma rays, because they are the most energetic and therefore can most easily damage cells and tissues.

4.146 (a) Ca^+: $1s^2 2s^2 2p^6 3s^2 3p^6 4s^1$ (b) Li: $1s^2 2s^1$ (c) P^{3-}: $1s^2 2s^2 2p^6 3s^2 3p^6$
(d) Ar^+: $1s^2 2s^2 2p^6 3s^2 3p^5$ (e) Si^{2+}: $1s^2 2s^2 2p^6 3s^2$
P^{3-} is the only one that has a valence-shell octet.

4.147 (a)

4.148 (a) Ar: $1s^2 2s^2 2p^6 3s^2 3p^6$ (b) Na^+: $1s^2 2s^2 2p^6$ (c) C^{2-}: $1s^2 2s^2 2p^4$
(d) O^{2-}: $1s^2 2s^2 2p^6$ (e) Ca^{2+}: $1s^2 2s^2 2p^6 3s^2 3p^6$
Every atom/ion except C^{2-} has a valence shell octet.

4.149 (e) The shell having the lowest principal quantum number has the lowest energy. Within a shell, the s subshell is the lowest-energy subshell.

4.150 (b). Antimony, atomic number 51, has 51 electrons in the neutral atom, and therefore (c), (d) and (e) are obviously wrong because they show 52, 41, and 41, respectively. (a) is wrong because it has electrons going into the $5d$ subshell while leaving the lower-energy $5p$ subshell empty.

4.151 $E = \dfrac{(6.63 \times 10^{-34}\,\text{J} \cdot \text{s}) \times (3.00 \times 10^8\,\text{m}/\text{s})}{5.00 \times 10^{-7}\,\text{m}} = 3.98 \times 10^{-19}\,\text{J}$

4.152 To be quantized means that only a certain set amount of something is available. Thus (a) is quantized because if you want to, say, move the water from one place to another, you can move 16 oz or 32 oz or 48 oz and so forth but never any volumes between these. (b) is not quantized because there is a continuous flow of water from the fountain and you can get any volume you want. By the same reasoning, (c) is not quantized and (d) is.

4.153 (a) Calcium, group IIA metal, loses two valence electrons to have an $n = 3$ octet. Bromine, group VIIA nonmetal, gains one electron to have an $n = 4$ octet. One Ca^{2+} combines with two Br^-: $CaBr_2$.
(b) Potassium, group IA metal, loses one valence electron. Nitrogen, group VA nonmetal, gains three electrons. Three K^+ combine with one N^{3-}: K_3N.
(c) Aluminum, group IIIA metal, loses three electrons to form Al^{3+} ion. Sulfur, group VIA nonmetal, gains two electrons to form S^{2-} ion. To form a compound that is electrically neutral, these two ions must combine in a 2:3 ratio: Al_2S_3.
(d) Sodium, group IA metal, loses one electron. Iodine, group VIIA nonmetal, gains one electron. One Na^+ combines with one I^-: NaI.
(e) Magnesium, group IIA metal, loses two electrons. Oxygen, group VIA nonmetal, gains two electrons. One Mg^{2+} combines with one O^{2-}: MgO.

4.154 Be < Mg < Ca < Sr < Ba.

4.155 Table 4.1 of the textbook tells you that red light has an average wavelength of 700 nm and an average energy of 1.85 eV and that indigo/violet light has an average wavelength of 410 nm and an average energy of 3.2 eV. The colors in ROY G. BIV are therefore arranged in order of decreasing wavelength and increasing energy.

4.156 (a) Quantized.   (b) Classical, quantum.

4.157 (a) Al: $1s^2 2s^2 2p^6 3s^2 3p^1$
[Ne] $3s^2 3p^1$
Three valence electrons
(b) I: $1s^2 2s^2 2p^6 3s^2 3p^6 4s^2 3d^{10} 4p^6 5s^2 4d^{10} 5p^5$
[Kr] $5s^2 4d^{10} 5p^5$
Seven valence electrons
(c) Rb: $1s^2 2s^2 2p^6 3s^2 3p^6 4s^2 3d^{10} 4p^6 5s^1$
[Kr] $5s^1$
One valence electron

(d) Ar: $1s^2 2s^2 2p^6 3s^2 3p^6$
[Ar]
Eight valence electrons
(e) Mg: $1s^2 2s^2 2p^6 3s^2$
[Ne] $3s^2$
Two valence electrons

4.158 lose, gain

4.159 The valence shell is the occupied shell having the highest principal quantum number n. The value of n corresponds to the element's period. The valence shells are therefore $n = 3$ for Mg, $n = 4$ for Ge, $n = 6$ for W, $n = 3$ for Cl, and $n = 6$ for Cs.

4.160 $$E = \frac{(6.63 \times 10^{-34}\,\text{J} \cdot \text{s}) \times (3.00 \times 10^8\,\text{m}/\text{s})}{1.00 \times 10^{-12}\,\text{m}} = 1.99 \times 10^{-13}\,\text{J}$$

4.161 The maximum number of electrons in a shell is equal to $2n^2$, where n represents the shell number. The maximum in the $n = 2$ shell is $2 \times 2^2 = 8$ electrons. The maximum in the $n = 6$ shell is $2 \times 6^2 = 72$ electrons.

4.162 That there are 32 electrons in this neutral atom tells you the atomic number is 32, making the element germanium, Ge. It is in group IVA (14) and period 4. Another way to see period and group number is from the way the electrons are configured. The highest occupied shell is $n = 4$, making this a period 4 element. The four valence electrons in this shell ($4s^2$ and $4p^2$) make it a group IVA element.

4.163 (a) Mg loses 2.
(b) Se gains 3.
(c) Al loses 3.
(d) Sr loses 2.
(e) Br gains 1.
(f) P gains 3.

4.164 It is impossible to know with certainty both the position of an electron and where the electron is going. The more accurately one of these two details is known, the less accurately the other is known. This means that electrons must be viewed not as particles, but rather as probability clouds of negatively charged matter.

4.165 $$1000 \text{ miles} \times \frac{5280 \text{ ft}}{1 \text{ mile}} \times \frac{12 \text{ in.}}{1 \text{ ft}} \times \frac{2.54 \text{ cm}}{1 \text{ in.}} \times \frac{1 \text{ m}}{100 \text{ cm}} \times \frac{1 \text{ s}}{3.00 \times 10^8 \text{ m}} = 5.36 \times 10^{-3}\,\text{s}$$

4.166 Lower in energy. The negative electrons are attracted to the positive nucleus, and you can model the attraction as a spring connecting the two. When the electron is in a close shell, the spring is relaxed and the electron has low energy. Just as you must put energy into a real-life spring to stretch it, you must put energy into the electron to "stretch" it to some shell farther from the nucleus.

4.167 Use the ground-state electron configurations:
P: $1s^2 2s^2 2p^6 3s^2 3p^3$, 9 p electrons.
Mg: $1s^2 2s^2 2p^6 3s^2$, 6 p electrons.
Se: $1s^2 2s^2 2p^6 3s^2 3p^6 4s^2 3d^{10} 4p^4$, 16 p electrons.
Zn: $1s^2 2s^2 2p^6 3s^2 3p^6 4s^2 3d^{10}$, 12 p electrons.

4.168 The configuration is $1s^2 2s^2 2p^6 3s^2 3p^6$ for all four species. Ca^{2+} has lost two electrons to achieve the Ar noble gas configuration. K^+ has lost one electron to achieve it, and S^{2-} has gained two electrons.

4.169 The electromagnetic spectrum on page 121 of the textbook shows the wavelengths and relative energies.

(a) Increasing wavelength: gamma rays < X rays < ultraviolet light < visible light < infrared radiation < radio/television waves.

(b) Increasing energy: radio/television waves < infrared radiation < visible light < ultraviolet light < X rays < gamma rays.

4.170

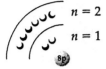

$n = 2$

$n = 1$

There are six electrons in the valence shell, and this shell can accept two more electrons to achieve a valence-shell octet.

4.171 Because the configurations are all for neutral atoms, counting electrons lets you know the atomic number. The elements are (a) Br (b) B (c) Rb (d) U (e) Ca.

4.172 The orbits in the Bohr atom are fixed paths in which electrons move. Orbitals are regions of space within which a negatively charged cloud of electrons has a certain probability of being found.

4.173 The highest n value for any element is numerically equal to the period of the element. Therefore (a) cobalt, period 4, $n = 4$; (b) arsenic, period 4, $n = 4$; (c) strontium, period 5, $n = 5$; (d) polonium, period 6, $n = 6$.

CHAPTER

5

Chemical Bonding and Nomenclature

5.1 See solution in textbook.

5.2 Table 5.1 of the textbook tells you phosphorus usually forms three bonds and hydrogen usually forms one bond. The formula is therefore PH_3.

5.3 Table 5.1 of the textbook tells you silicon usually forms four bonds and bromine usually forms one bond. The formula is therefore $SiBr_4$.

5.4 See solution in textbook.

5.5 F, group VIIA, has seven valence electrons and therefore needs to form one bond to achieve an octet. H, group IA, has one valence electron and needs to form one bond to obtain its duet. (Remember that hydrogen is stable with two valence electrons because its valence shell is $n = 1$.) The formula of the compound formed is therefore HF. The dot structure is $H\!:\!\ddot{\underset{..}{F}}\!:$.

5.6 Oxygen has six valence electrons and therefore needs to form two bonds to achieve an octet. Because hydrogen forms one bond, the formula is H_2O. The dot structure is $H\!:\!\ddot{\underset{..}{O}}\!:\!H$.

5.7 See solution in textbook.

5.8 H needs one electron to complete its valence duet, Cl needs one electron to complete its valence octet, and O needs two. The Lewis dot diagrams are

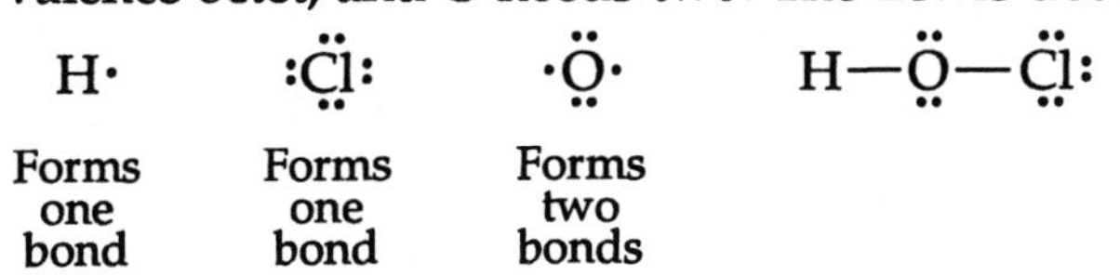

$H\cdot$ $:\!\ddot{\underset{..}{Cl}}\!:$ $\cdot\ddot{\underset{..}{O}}\cdot$ $H—\ddot{\underset{..}{O}}—\ddot{\underset{..}{Cl}}\!:$

Forms   Forms   Forms
one   one   two
bond   bond   bonds

5.9 Each carbon atom has four valence electrons and therefore forms four bonds, either with H or with another C. Each hydrogen atom forms one bond:

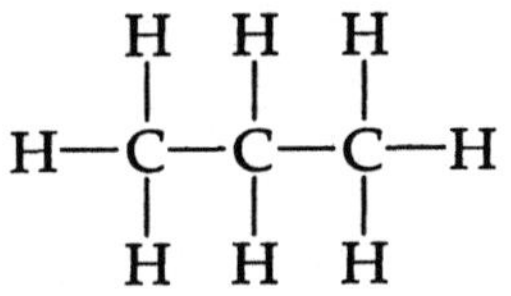

```
      H   H   H
      |   |   |
  H—C — C — C—H
      |   |   |
      H   H   H
```

5.10 See solution in textbook.

5.11 Begin by drawing the individual dot diagrams with the atoms positioned as described in the problem. As a general rule, any C that has no H bonded to it is in the middle of the molecule:

$$\text{H·}$$
$$\text{H· ·}\overset{\displaystyle\cdot}{\underset{\displaystyle\cdot}{\text{C}}}\text{· ·}\overset{\displaystyle\cdot}{\text{C}}\text{· ·}\overset{\displaystyle\cdot}{\text{C}}\text{· ·H}$$
$$\text{H·}$$

Pairing electrons to form single bonds gives

$$\begin{array}{c} \text{H} \\ | \\ \text{H}-\text{C}-\overset{\displaystyle\cdot}{\underset{\displaystyle\cdot}{\text{C}}}-\overset{\displaystyle\cdot}{\underset{\displaystyle\cdot}{\text{C}}}-\text{H} \\ | \\ \text{H} \end{array}$$

Let the two carbons that still have unpaired electrons form a multiple bond and you are done:

$$\begin{array}{c} \text{H} \\ | \\ \text{H}-\text{C}-\text{C}\equiv\text{C}-\text{H} \\ | \\ \text{H} \end{array}$$

5.12 The dot diagrams with atoms positioned as described:

$$\text{H· ·}\overset{\displaystyle\cdot}{\underset{\displaystyle\cdot}{\text{C}}}\text{· ·}\overset{\displaystyle\cdot}{\text{N}}\text{:}$$

Form single bonds:

$$\text{H}-\overset{\displaystyle\cdot}{\underset{\displaystyle\cdot}{\text{C}}}-\overset{\displaystyle\cdot}{\text{N}}\text{:}$$

Form multiple bonds with the remaining *unpaired* electrons (the N does not bond via its paired electrons):

$$\text{H}-\text{C}\equiv\text{N:}$$

5.13 Draw the atoms positioned as described, following the general rule that C bonded to no H is usually in the middle of the molecule:

$$\text{·H :}\overset{\displaystyle\cdot\cdot}{\text{O}}\text{· H·}$$
$$\text{H· ·}\overset{\displaystyle\cdot}{\underset{\displaystyle\cdot}{\text{C}}}\text{· ·}\overset{\displaystyle\cdot}{\underset{\displaystyle\cdot}{\text{C}}}\text{· ·}\overset{\displaystyle\cdot}{\underset{\displaystyle\cdot}{\text{C}}}\text{· ·H}$$
$$\text{H·} \qquad \text{H·}$$

Form single bonds:

$$\begin{array}{ccc} \text{H} & \overset{\displaystyle\cdot\cdot}{\text{O}}\text{·} & \text{H} \\ | & | & | \\ \text{H}-\text{C}-\overset{\displaystyle\cdot}{\text{C}}-\text{C}-\text{H} \\ | & & | \\ \text{H} & & \text{H} \end{array}$$

Form a multiple bond with the remaining *unpaired* electrons:

$$\begin{array}{ccc} \text{H} & \overset{\displaystyle\cdot\cdot}{\underset{\displaystyle\cdot\cdot}{\text{O}}} & \text{H} \\ | & \| & | \\ \text{H}-\text{C}-\text{C}-\text{C}-\text{H} \\ | & & | \\ \text{H} & & \text{H} \end{array}$$

5.14 See solution in textbook.

5.15 Step 1: SO_3 has 24 valence electrons: 6 from S and $3 \times 6 = 18$ from O.

Step 2: Make first atom in formula central and connect atoms via single bonds:

$$\begin{array}{c} O \\ | \\ O-S-O \end{array} \quad \text{6 electrons assigned}$$

Step 3: Add remaining electrons ($24 - 6 = 18$) as lone pairs. Begin with the terminal atoms and complete the octet on one atom before going on to the next:

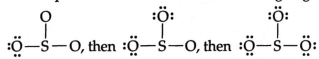

| One octet done, 12 electrons assigned | Two octets done, 18 electrons assigned | One octet done, all 24 electrons assigned |

Step 4: You are not done because all 24 electrons have been assigned but S does not have an octet. To fix things, form an O=S double bond with any O atom. The three possible structures are all equally good because they all obey the octet rule:

$$:\ddot{O}-\overset{\overset{\displaystyle :O:}{\|}}{S}-\ddot{O}: \quad \text{or} \quad :\ddot{O}=\overset{\overset{\displaystyle :\ddot{O}:}{|}}{S}-\ddot{O}: \quad \text{or} \quad :\ddot{O}-\overset{\overset{\displaystyle :\ddot{O}:}{|}}{S}=\ddot{O}:$$

5.16 Step 1: $SO_3{}^{2-}$ has 26 valence electrons: 6 from S, $3 \times 6 = 18$ from O, and add 2 for the 2− charge.

Step 2: $\begin{array}{c} O \\ | \\ O-S-O \end{array}$ 6 electrons assigned

Step 3: Add remaining 20 electrons, completing one atom's octet before moving on to another atom:

$$:\ddot{O}-\overset{\overset{\displaystyle O}{|}}{S}-O, \text{ then } :\ddot{O}-\overset{\overset{\displaystyle :\ddot{O}:}{|}}{S}-O, \text{ then } :\ddot{O}-\overset{\overset{\displaystyle :\ddot{O}:}{|}}{S}-\ddot{O}:, \text{ then } \left[:\ddot{O}-\overset{\overset{\displaystyle :\ddot{O}:}{|}}{S}-\ddot{O}:\right]^{2-}$$

| One octet done, 12 electrons assigned | Two octets done, 18 electrons assigned | Three octets done, 24 electrons assigned | Four octets done, all 26 electrons assigned |

5.17 Step 1: NO^+ has 10 valence electrons: 5 from N, 6 from O, and subtract 1 for the 1+ charge.

Step 2: $N-O$ 2 electrons assigned

Step 3: $:\ddot{N}-O,$ then $:\ddot{N}-\ddot{O}$

| One octet done, 8 electrons assigned | Still only one octet done, but all 10 electrons assigned |

Step 4: Use lone pairs to complete O octet (moving the O lone pair doesn't work):

$$:\ddot{N}-\ddot{O}: \quad \text{becomes} \quad [:N\equiv O:]^+$$

Both octets done, all 10 electrons assigned

5.18 No. Resonance forms differ only in the placement of electrons. Because the atoms are arranged differently in the two structures, they are not resonance forms.

5.19 See solution in textbook.

5.20 Because the three atoms in O_3 are identical, $\Delta EN = 0$ and the bonds in the molecule are pure covalent bonds.

5.21 EN for Si = 1.8 and EN for O = 3.5; therefore $\Delta EN = 1.7$. Because $\Delta EN > 0$ and the two atoms are both nonmetals, the bond is polar covalent. (At $\Delta EN = 1.7$, this same bond would, by convention, be called ionic if the molecule were a metal/nonmetal combination.)

5.22 Because Be is at the top of group 2 and Ba is much farther down in the same group, she knows that Be is more electronegative than Ba. Therefore ΔEN for Ba/Cl is greater than ΔEN for Be/Cl, making $BaCl_2$ more ionic than $BeCl_2$.

5.23 See solution in textbook.

5.24

Formula	Cation	Anion	Name
CaF_2	Ca^{2+}	F^-	Calcium fluoride
$CsBr$	Cs^+	Br^-	Cesium bromide
Al_2S_3	Al^{3+}	S^{2-}	Aluminum sulfide
K_2O	K^+	O^{2-}	Potassium oxide

5.25 They all contain two bromide ions because group IIA metals form 2+ cations and Br forms a 1− anion.

5.26 See solution in textbook.

5.27 Because there are three Cl^- anions in the formula, titanium must have a 3+ charge to maintain electrical neutrality. $TiCl_3$ is therefore titanium(III) chloride.

5.28 The II tells you the tin cation carries a 2+ charge. Because the fluoride anion carries a 1− charge, the formula is SnF_2.

5.29 See solution in textbook.

5.30 Nitrogen monoxide.

5.31 Phosphorus pentachloride.

5.32 P_4S_{10}

5.33 See solution in textbook.

5.34 Na_2CO_3 because the carbonate ion carries a 2− charge.

5.35 Calcium hypochlorite

5.36 $Mg(HCO_3)_2$ because the hydrogen carbonate ion (also called the bicarbonate ion) carries a 1− charge.

5.37 A molecule is a stable collection of atoms that are bound together.

5.38 No. Molecules that contain atoms of the same element are called elemental substances, not compounds. Examples of molecules that are elemental substances are O_2, N_2, and P_4.

5.39 The properties of molecules can be very different from the properties of the elements in the molecules. Some molecules have healing powers, such as aspirin and tetracycline; others have the ability to alter the taste of food, such as sodium chloride and aspartame. Many other examples are possible.

5.40 Diatomic molecules in the atmosphere are nitrogen, N_2, and oxygen, O_2. Triatomic molecules in the atmosphere are ozone, O_3, water vapor, H_2O, carbon dioxide, CO_2, and nitrogen dioxide, NO_2.

5.41 Because C_2H_6O and CH_4O have different numbers of carbon and hydrogen atoms, the chemical properties of the two compounds differ. The two molecules are metabolized differently in the human body. In this case, one is toxic, the other is not.

5.42 Yes, a molecule is an elemental substance if all atoms it contains are of the same element. Examples are Cl_2, O_3, and S_8.

5.43 Numerous answers possible. Basically, a covalent bond is an attractive force created between atoms when the atoms share electrons.

5.44 A covalent bond is not the shared electrons per se. Rather it is *the attractive force* created by the sharing.

5.45 Because the shared electrons are attracted to both nuclei. This positive–negative attractive force is what bonds the atoms to each other.

5.46 For any two systems that contain different amounts of energy, the system with less energy is more stable. The H_2 molecule is more stable than two separate H atoms because the energy of the H_2 molecule is less than the combined energy of the two separate atoms.

5.47 The two separate H atoms are attracted to each other because each negative electron is attracted to the positive nucleus of the other atom. When the two mutually attracted atoms are held apart, the system has high energy and therefore low stability. When the atoms get close enough to share electrons—in other words, form H_2—the H_2 system has lower energy and therefore greater stability.

5.48 The H_2 bond distance is not shorter than 0.74 Å because if the atoms were closer than 0.74 Å to each other, the repulsion between the two positive nuclei and the repulsion between the two negative electrons would push the atoms apart. The bond distance is not longer than 0.74 Å because the atoms feel the greatest attractive force (and are therefore most stable) when they are 0.74 Å from each other.

5.49 Released. A covalent bond forms when two atoms can create a more stable system by combining. The way to create a more stable system is to release energy.

5.50 Because the inner electrons are too close to the atom's nucleus to be shared with other atoms.

5.51 Because there would no longer be an attraction between two electrons and two nuclei.

5.52 Boiling water will not produce hydrogen gas and oxygen gas because the energy required to break the covalent bonds in water is much more than the energy required to boil water.

5.53 We mean that the two electrons shared by two atoms (the bonding electrons) are both counted as valence electrons for both atom sharing them.

5.54 A straight line.

5.55 Typically one.

5.56 The nitrogen atom is correct. The oxygen atom should be $\cdot \ddot{\text{O}} \colon$ because one electron must be placed on each of the four sides before any electrons are paired. Fluorine should have seven valence electrons, not six, and should be $\cdot \ddot{\text{F}} \colon$.

5.57 The number of dots will equal the roman-numeral group number.

5.58 (a) Sulfur, VIA, $\cdot \ddot{\text{S}} \colon$ (b) Iodine, VIIA, $\cdot \ddot{\text{I}} \colon$

(c) Helium, noble gas, $\text{He} \colon$ (d) Boron, IIIA, $\cdot \dot{\text{B}} \cdot$

5.59 Chlorine is diatomic because it has seven valence electrons and needs one more to achieve an octet. It gains this electron by forming a covalent bond with another Cl atom, forming Cl_2. Both Ne and He have a full valence shell and therefore do not bond with another atom. Alternatively, you can say that because the Cl atom has an unshared electron, it forms one bond (in this case to another Cl atom). Because Ne and He have no unshared electrons, they do not form any bonds.

5.60 As paired electrons or as unpaired electrons.

5.61 Oxygen has six valence electrons, making it necessary for it to form two bonds to achieve an octet. Hence it combines with two hydrogens to form H_2O. Forming the molecule HO would leave the oxygen one electron short of an octet:

H—$\ddot{\text{O}}$—H   H—$\ddot{\text{O}}\cdot$

5.62 The diagram $\cdot \ddot{\text{S}} \colon$ tells you sulfur needs to form two bonds to have an octet, and the diagram H$\cdot$ tells you hydrogen needs to form one bond to have a duet. Therefore the compound formed is H_2S, H—$\ddot{\text{S}}$—H.

5.63 The diagrams $\cdot \overset{\cdot\cdot}{\underset{\cdot}{P}} \cdot$ and $\cdot \overset{\cdot\cdot}{\underset{\cdot\cdot}{Br}} \colon$ tell you phosphorus forms three bonds and bromine forms one bond, making the compound PBr$_3$,

$$\colon\!\overset{\cdot\cdot}{\underset{\cdot\cdot}{Br}}\!-\!\overset{\cdot\cdot}{\underset{\vert}{P}}\!-\!\overset{\cdot\cdot}{\underset{\cdot\cdot}{Br}}\!\colon$$
$$\colon\!\overset{\cdot\cdot}{\underset{\cdot\cdot}{Br}}\!\colon$$

5.64 Three Br atoms combine with N, just as three Br atom combine with P. Because N and P are both in group VA, they have the same number of valence electrons (five), and need to form the same number of bonds (three) to achieve an octet.

5.65 Step 1: The dot diagrams are $\cdot \overset{\cdot}{\underset{\cdot}{C}} \cdot$ $\cdot \overset{\cdot\cdot}{\underset{\cdot\cdot}{O}} \cdot$ H$\cdot$. Because the molecule contains two C, six H, and one O, there are $(2 \times 4) + (6 \times 1) + 6 = 20$ electrons to be assigned.

Step 2: The only way to have O attached to both C and no O–H bonds is

$$\begin{array}{ccccccc} & H & & & H & \\ & | & & & | & \\ H\!-\!\!&C&\!\!-\!O\!-\!\!&C&\!\!-\!H \\ & | & & & | & \\ & H & & & H & \end{array} \qquad \text{16 electrons assigned}$$

Step 3:
$$\begin{array}{ccccccc} & H & & & H & \\ & | & & & | & \\ H\!-\!\!&C&\!\!-\!\overset{\cdot\cdot}{\underset{\cdot\cdot}{O}}\!-\!\!&C&\!\!-\!H \\ & | & & & | & \\ & H & & & H & \end{array}$$

All octets (or duets) formed,
all 20 electrons assigned

There are eight bonding pairs of electrons in the molecule and two lone pairs.

5.66 Step 1: The dot diagrams are $\cdot \overset{\cdot}{\underset{\cdot}{C}} \cdot$ $\cdot \overset{\cdot\cdot}{\underset{\cdot\cdot}{O}} \cdot$ H$\cdot$. Because the molecule contains two C, six H, and one O, there are 20 electrons to be assigned.

Step 2: With only one C bonded to O, you can guess that O must also bond to at least one H:

$$\begin{array}{cccccc} & H & H & & \\ & | & | & & \\ H\!-\!\!&C&\!\!-\!\!&C&\!\!-\!O\!-\!H \\ & | & | & & \\ & H & H & & \end{array} \qquad \text{16 electrons assigned}$$

Step 3:
$$\begin{array}{cccccc} & H & H & & \\ & | & | & & \\ H\!-\!\!&C&\!\!-\!\!&C&\!\!-\!\overset{\cdot\cdot}{\underset{\cdot\cdot}{O}}\!-\!H \\ & | & | & & \\ & H & H & & \end{array}$$

All octets (or duets) formed,
all 20 electrons assigned

There are eight bonding pairs and two lone pairs in the molecule. Because the beverage ethanol and the solvent ether have very different properties, it is evident that the arrangement of the atoms in a molecule is an important determinant of chemical properties.

5.67 The H atom has one valence electron and therefore tends to form one covalent bond with other atoms, in that way filling it $n = 1$ valence shell with the full complement of two electrons. The He atom has two valence electrons in its $n = 1$ valence shell and therefore does not bond with other atoms because its valence shell is filled.

5.68 Because He has a full $n = 1$ valence shell, it forms no bonds. Drawing the two electrons as unshared electrons would imply that the He could form two bonds; this is incorrect.

5.69 Oxygen has six electrons in its valence shell, arranged as two electron pairs and two unpaired electrons. The two unpaired electrons will form two bonds, allowing the oxygen atom to achieve an octet of valence-shell electrons.

5.70 Three bonds. The atom has five valence electrons and needs three more to achieve an octet.

5.71 Step 1: C_2H_4 has 12 valence electrons, $2 \times 4 = 8$ from $\cdot \overset{\cdot}{C} \cdot$ and $4 \times 1 = 4$ from $\cdot H$.

Step 2: Carbons are usually connected to other carbons in a molecule, and therefore the skeleton structure is probably

$$H—\underset{\underset{H}{|}}{C}—\underset{\underset{H}{|}}{C}—H \qquad \text{Ten electrons assigned}$$

Step 3: Add remaining valence electrons as a lone pair on C:

$$H—\underset{\underset{H}{|}}{\overset{\cdot\cdot}{C}}—\underset{\underset{H}{|}}{C}—H$$

One octet done, all
12 electrons assigned

Step 4: The C on the right does not have an octet, meaning you need to convert the lone pair to a double bond:

$$H—\underset{\underset{H}{|}}{C}=\underset{\underset{H}{|}}{C}—H$$

5.72 The ethylene bond is weaker because it is only a double bond, whereas the bond in acetylene is a triple bond. The more shared electrons, the stronger the bond.

5.73 Resonance forms are valid dot diagrams for a given molecule that differ from one another only in the position of the electrons.

5.74 Step 1: SO_2 contains 18 valence electrons: 6 from $\cdot \overset{\cdot\cdot}{\underset{\cdot\cdot}{S}} \cdot$ and $(2 \times 6) = 12$ from $\cdot \overset{\cdot\cdot}{\underset{\cdot\cdot}{O}} \cdot$.

Step 2: $O—S—O$ 4 electrons assigned

Step 3: $:\overset{\cdot\cdot}{\underset{\cdot\cdot}{O}}—S—O$, then $:\overset{\cdot\cdot}{\underset{\cdot\cdot}{O}}—S—\overset{\cdot\cdot}{\underset{\cdot\cdot}{O}}:$, then $:\overset{\cdot\cdot}{\underset{\cdot\cdot}{O}}—\overset{\cdot\cdot}{S}—\overset{\cdot\cdot}{\underset{\cdot\cdot}{O}}:$

One octet done,	Two octets done,	Still only two
10 electrons	16 electrons	octets done, all
assigned	assigned	18 electrons assigned

Step 4: Convert lone pairs to double bonds to complete the octet for S. There are two resonance forms here:

$$:\overset{\cdot\cdot}{\underset{\cdot\cdot}{O}}—\overset{\cdot\cdot}{S}=\overset{\cdot\cdot}{O}: \quad \text{and} \quad :\overset{\cdot\cdot}{O}=\overset{\cdot\cdot}{S}—\overset{\cdot\cdot}{\underset{\cdot\cdot}{O}}:$$

5.75 Step 1: O_3 contains $(6 \times 3) = 18$ valence from the three $\cdot \overset{\cdot\cdot}{\underset{\cdot}{O}}:$.

Step 2: $O—O—O$ 4 electrons assigned

Step 3: $:\overset{\cdot\cdot}{\underset{\cdot\cdot}{O}}—O—O$, then $:\overset{\cdot\cdot}{\underset{\cdot\cdot}{O}}—O—\overset{\cdot\cdot}{\underset{\cdot\cdot}{O}}:$, then $:\overset{\cdot\cdot}{\underset{\cdot\cdot}{O}}—\overset{\cdot\cdot}{O}—\overset{\cdot\cdot}{\underset{\cdot\cdot}{O}}:$

One octet done,	Two octets done,	Still only two
10 electrons	16 electrons	octets done, all
assigned	assigned	18 electrons assigned

Step 4: Convert lone pairs to double bonds to complete the octet for the middle O. There are two resonance forms here:

$$:\overset{\cdot\cdot}{\underset{\cdot\cdot}{O}}—\overset{\cdot\cdot}{O}=\overset{\cdot\cdot}{O}: \quad \text{and} \quad :\overset{\cdot\cdot}{O}=\overset{\cdot\cdot}{O}—\overset{\cdot\cdot}{\underset{\cdot\cdot}{O}}:$$

5.76 Yes, there should be similarities because both compounds have the same number of valence electrons and both contain only atoms from group VIA.

5.77 There are two resonance forms for ozone (see Problem 5.75). Because the actual molecule is an average of the two resonance structures, each bond is an average of a single bond and a double bond. Therefore each bond is more accurately thought of as a 1.5 bond.

5.78 Because the bond between oxygen atoms in O_2 is a full double bond and the bonds in O_3 are 1.5 bonds, the O_2 bond is stronger and therefore more energy input is required to break it.

5.79 The diagram is wrong. CO has 10 valence electrons, 4 from $\cdot\overset{\displaystyle\cdot}{C}\cdot$, and 6 from $\cdot\overset{\displaystyle\cdot}{\underset{\displaystyle\cdot}{O}}:$, but the diagram shows 14. The correct structure is: $:C\equiv O:$.

5.80 C_3H_6O has 24 valence electrons, $3 \times 4 = 12$ from $\cdot\overset{\displaystyle\cdot}{C}\cdot$, $6 \times 1 = 6$ from $\cdot H$, and 6 from $\cdot\overset{\displaystyle\cdot}{\underset{\displaystyle\cdot}{O}}:$, which is the number shown in the drawing. The error in the drawing is that the central carbon has only six electrons. Complete its octet by changing one of the O lone pairs to a double bond.

$$
\begin{array}{c}
\text{H} \quad :\!\overset{\displaystyle}{O}\!: \quad \text{H} \\
| \qquad \| \qquad | \\
\text{H}-\overset{\displaystyle|}{\underset{\displaystyle|}{C}}-\overset{\displaystyle}{C}-\overset{\displaystyle|}{\underset{\displaystyle|}{C}}-\text{H} \\
| \qquad\qquad | \\
\text{H} \qquad\quad \text{H}
\end{array}
$$

5.81 There should be three covalent bonds between the phosphorus atoms. Each $\cdot\overset{\displaystyle\cdot}{P}\cdot$ atom has five valence electrons and therefore needs to form three bonds to achieve an octet: $\overset{\displaystyle\cdot\cdot}{P}\!\equiv\!\overset{\displaystyle\cdot\cdot}{P}$.

5.82 Step 1: NO_3^- contains 24 valence electrons: 5 from $\cdot\overset{\displaystyle\cdot}{\underset{\displaystyle\cdot}{N}}\cdot$, $3 \times 6 = 18$ from $\cdot\overset{\displaystyle\cdot}{\underset{\displaystyle\cdot}{O}}:$, and one to give the ion its $1-$ charge.

Step 2: O—N—O   6 electrons assigned
$$\qquad\qquad\quad |$$
$$\qquad\qquad\quad O$$

Step 3:

$:\!\overset{\cdot\cdot}{\underset{\cdot\cdot}{O}}\!-\!N\!-\!O$	, then	$:\!\overset{\cdot\cdot}{\underset{\cdot\cdot}{O}}\!-\!N\!-\!O$	, then	$:\!\overset{\cdot\cdot}{\underset{\cdot\cdot}{O}}\!-\!N\!-\!\overset{\cdot\cdot}{\underset{\cdot\cdot}{O}}\!:$
$\qquad\quad\mid$		$\qquad\quad\mid$		$\qquad\quad\mid$
$\qquad\quad O$		$\qquad\quad :\!\overset{}{\underset{\cdot\cdot}{O}}\!:$		$\qquad\quad :\!\overset{}{\underset{\cdot\cdot}{O}}\!:$
One octet done, 12 electrons assigned		Two octets done, 18 electrons assigned		Three octets done, all 24 electrons assigned

Step 4: The N needs one more bond to complete its octet. Because any one of the O atoms could supply the needed lone pair, there are three resonance structures:

$$
\left[:\!\overset{\cdot\cdot}{O}\!=\!N\!-\!\overset{\cdot\cdot}{\underset{\cdot\cdot}{O}}\!: \atop {\mid \atop :\!\overset{}{\underset{\cdot\cdot}{O}}\!:}\right]^{-}
\qquad
\left[:\!\overset{\cdot\cdot}{\underset{\cdot\cdot}{O}}\!-\!N\!=\!\overset{\cdot\cdot}{O}\!: \atop {\mid \atop :\!\overset{}{\underset{\cdot\cdot}{O}}\!:}\right]^{-}
\qquad
\left[:\!\overset{\cdot\cdot}{\underset{\cdot\cdot}{O}}\!-\!N\!-\!\overset{\cdot\cdot}{\underset{\cdot\cdot}{O}}\!: \atop {\| \atop :\!\overset{}{O}\!:}\right]^{-}
$$

5.83 Step 1: The hypothetical O_2^{2+} has 10 valence electrons: $2 \times 6 = 12$ from $\cdot\overset{\displaystyle\cdot}{\underset{\displaystyle\cdot}{O}}:$ and subtract 2 to account for the 2+ charge on the ion.

Step 2: O—O   2 electrons assigned

Step 3: $:\!\overset{\cdot\cdot}{\underset{\cdot\cdot}{O}}\!-\!O$, then $:\!\overset{\cdot\cdot}{\underset{\cdot\cdot}{O}}\!-\!\overset{\cdot\cdot}{O}$

One octet done, 8 electrons assigned   Still only one octet done, all 10 electrons assigned

Step 4: Form a triple bond to give both atoms an octet:

$$[:O\equiv O:]^{2+}$$

5.84 Step 1: C_2H_4O has 18 valence electrons: $2 \times 4 = 8$ from $\cdot\overset{\displaystyle\cdot}{C}\cdot$, $4 \times 1 = 4$ from $\cdot H$, and 6 from $\cdot\overset{\displaystyle\cdot}{\underset{\displaystyle\cdot}{O}}:$.

Step 2: Already done!

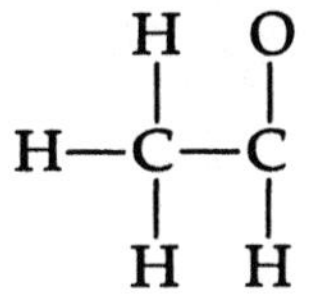

12 electrons assigned

Step 3:

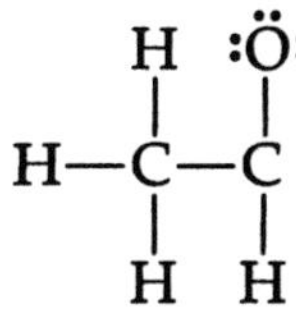

One octet done,
all 18 electrons assigned

Step 4: The C attached to O needs one more bond, meaning you must move one lone pair off the O:

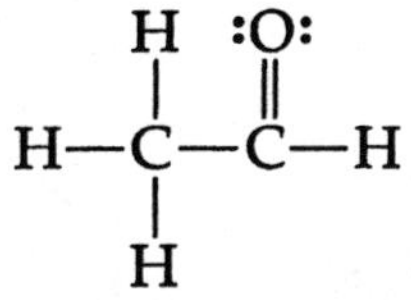

5.85 Step 1: 24 valence electrons: $2 \times 4 = 8$ from $\cdot\overset{\displaystyle\cdot}{C}\cdot$, $4 \times 1 = 4$ from $\cdot H$, and $2 \times 6 = 12$ from $\cdot\overset{\displaystyle\cdot}{\underset{\displaystyle\cdot}{O}}:$.

Step 2:

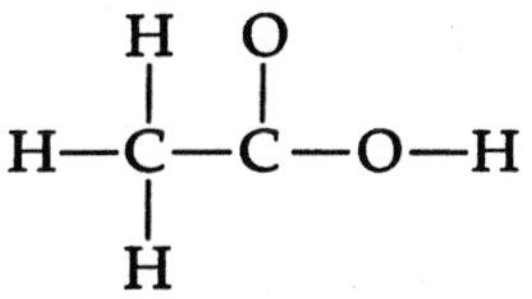

14 electrons assigned

Step 3:

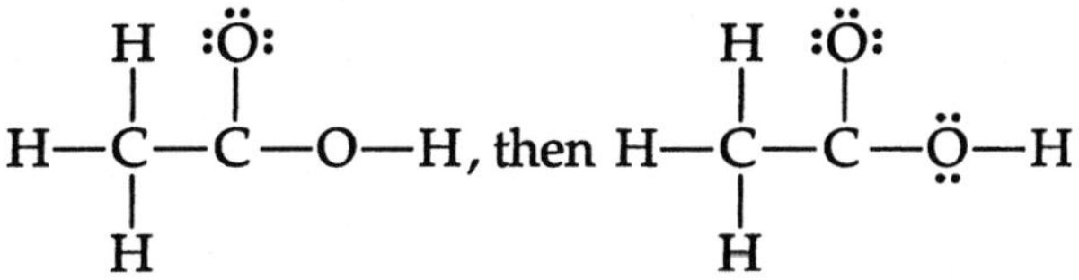

, then

One octet done,   Two octets done,
20 electrons assigned   all 24 electrons assigned

Step 4: The C attached to the two O needs one more bond, which you take from the O having the higher number of lone pairs:

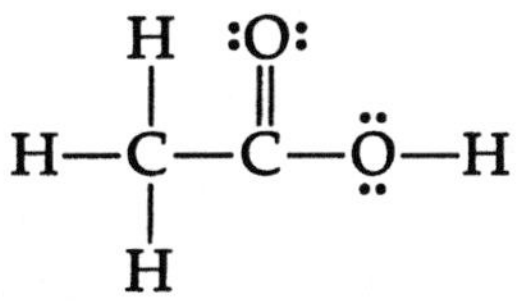

(You may have taken a lone pair from the other O, to get

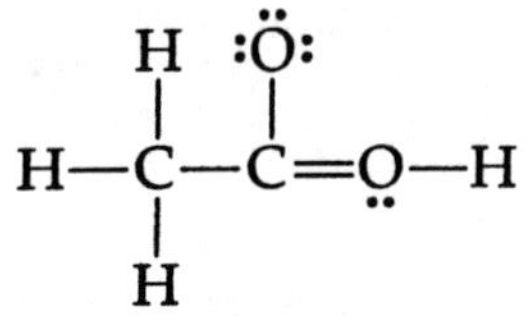

$$
\begin{array}{cc}
\text{H} & :\ddot{\text{O}}: \\
| & | \\
\text{H}-\text{C}-\text{C}=\underset{\cdot\cdot}{\text{O}}-\text{H} \\
| \\
\text{H}
\end{array}
$$

Although this resonance form obeys the octet rule, oxygen atoms generally bond to other atoms such that the O takes part in two covalent bonds and has two lone pairs on it. Therefore this latter resonance form is very unlikely to occur.)

5.86 Step 1: 24 valence electrons: $2 \times 4 = 8$ from $\cdot\dot{\text{C}}\cdot$, $3 \times 1 = 3$ from $\cdot\text{H}$, and $2 \times 6 = 12$ from $\cdot\ddot{\text{O}}:$, and one more to account for the $1-$ charge.

Step 2: 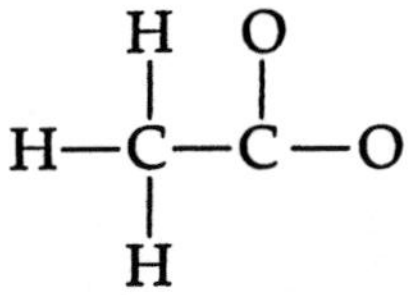
$$
\begin{array}{cc}
\text{H} & \text{O} \\
| & | \\
\text{H}-\text{C}-\text{C}-\text{O} \quad \text{12 electrons assigned}\\
| \\
\text{H}
\end{array}
$$

Step 3:
$$
\begin{array}{cc}
\text{H} & :\ddot{\text{O}}: \\
| & | \\
\text{H}-\text{C}-\text{C}-\text{O}, \text{ then} \\
| \\
\text{H}
\end{array}
\qquad
\begin{array}{cc}
\text{H} & :\ddot{\text{O}}: \\
| & | \\
\text{H}-\text{C}-\text{C}-\ddot{\text{O}}: \\
| \\
\text{H}
\end{array}
$$

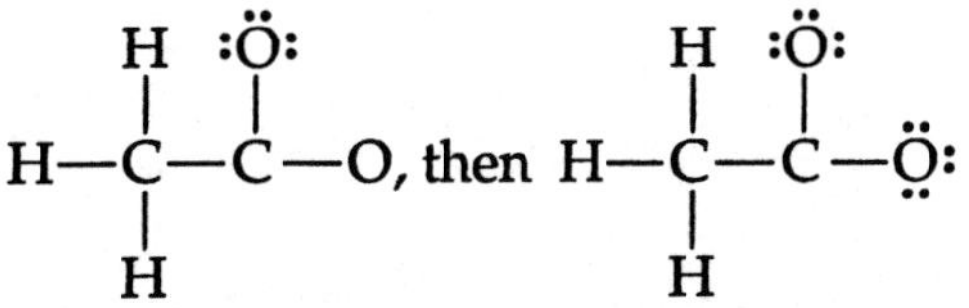

One octet done, Two octets done,
18 electrons   all 24 electrons
assigned   assigned

Step 4: Use an O lone pair to give C the one more bond it needs. Because the two O have the same number of lone pairs, either one can contribute and you get resonance forms:

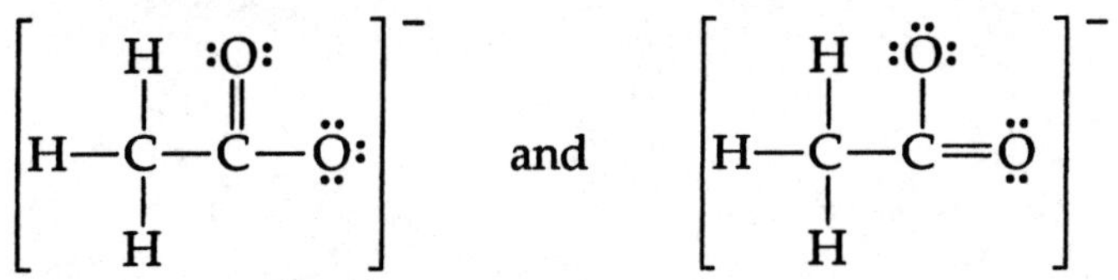

$$
\left[
\begin{array}{cc}
\text{H} & :\text{O}: \\
| & \| \\
\text{H}-\text{C}-\text{C}-\ddot{\text{O}}: \\
| \\
\text{H}
\end{array}
\right]^{-}
\quad \text{and} \quad
\left[
\begin{array}{cc}
\text{H} & :\ddot{\text{O}}: \\
| & | \\
\text{H}-\text{C}-\text{C}=\ddot{\text{O}} \\
| \\
\text{H}
\end{array}
\right]^{-}
$$

5.87 Step 1: 32 valence electrons: 1 from $\cdot\text{H}$, 7 from $:\dot{\ddot{\text{Cl}}}:$, and $4 \times 6 = 24$ from $\cdot\ddot{\text{O}}:$.

Step 2: 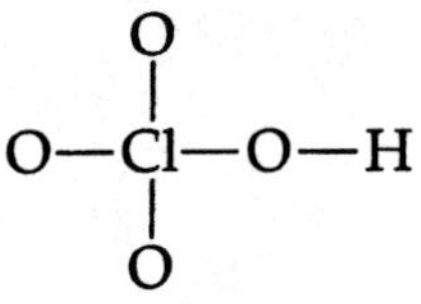
$$
\begin{array}{c}
\text{O} \\
| \\
\text{O}-\text{Cl}-\text{O}-\text{H} \quad \text{10 electrons assigned}\\
| \\
\text{O}
\end{array}
$$

Step 3:
$$
\begin{array}{c}
:\ddot{\text{O}}: \\
| \\
:\ddot{\text{O}}-\text{Cl}-\ddot{\text{O}}-\text{H} \\
| \\
:\underset{\cdot\cdot}{\text{O}}:
\end{array}
$$

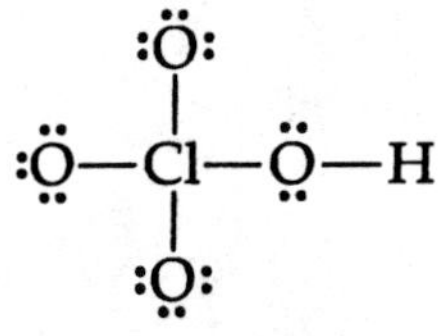

All octets done,
all 32 electrons assigned

5.88 Step 1: 16 valence electrons: 5 from $\cdot\ddot{\text{N}}\cdot$, $2 \times 6 = 12$ from $\cdot\ddot{\text{O}}:$ and subtract one to account for the $1+$ charge.

Step 2: O—N—O   4 electrons assigned

Step 3: $:\ddot{O}-N-\ddot{O}:$

Two octets done,
all 16 electrons assigned

Step 4: N needs two more bonds. Take one lone pair from each O:

$$\left[:\ddot{O}=N=\ddot{O}:\right]^+$$

5.89 The structure as drawn in the problem has 24 electrons assigned, but there are 30 valence electrons: $6 \times 4 = 24$ from $\cdot\dot{C}\cdot$ plus $6 \times 1 = 6$ from $\cdot H$. Because each C needs one more bond, use the 6 electrons to form three C=C bonds. Because all six C are equivalent, you end up with two resonance forms:

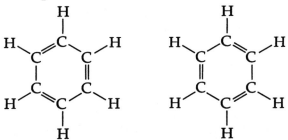

5.90 Eight valence electrons on each carbon atom and two valence electrons on each hydrogen atom, as there must be to satisfy the octet rule.

5.91 (a) The 1− charge means this ion has one more valence electron than the seven found on a neutral I atom: $\left[:\ddot{\underset{..}{I}}:\right]^-$

(b) The 2− charge means two more electrons than the six on a neutral O atom: $\left[:\ddot{\underset{..}{O}}:\right]^{2-}$

(c) The 1− charge means one more electron than the seven on a neutral Cl atom: $\left[:\ddot{\underset{..}{Cl}}:\right]^-$

(d) The 1+ charge means one electron fewer than the one on a neutral H atom—in other words, no electrons: H^+

5.92 An ionic bond is the attractive force between oppositely charged ions that were formed by a transfer of electrons. It is similar to a covalent bond in that both types of bonds have approximately the same strength and both are the result of the attraction between positive and negative charges (attractions of electrons for nuclei in covalent bonds; attractions of ions for oppositely charged ions in ionic bonds). An ionic bond differs from a covalent bond in that an ionic bond is the result of a transfer of electrons, whereas a covalent bond is the result of a sharing of electrons.

5.93 Electrons must be transferred from one atom to another.

5.94 Between a metal and a nonmetal.

5.95 Cl_2 is a covalent compound, which means the electrons are shared. $MgCl_2$ is an ionic compound, which means electrons are transferred. The metal magnesium loses electrons (two because it is a group IIA metal), and the nonmetal chlorine gains them. The dot structures are:

$$:\ddot{\underset{..}{Cl}}-\ddot{\underset{..}{Cl}}: \quad \rightarrow \quad \left[:\ddot{\underset{..}{Cl}}:\right]^- Mg^{2+} \left[:\ddot{\underset{..}{Cl}}:\right]^-$$

5.96 (a) Magnesium is a group IIA metal and tends to lose two electrons to form Mg^{2+}. Bromine is a group VIIA nonmetal and tends to gain one electron to form Br^-. Therefore two Br^- must react with one Mg^{2+}: $MgBr_2$.

(b) Beryllium is a group IIA metal and tends to lose two electrons to form Be^{2+}. Oxygen is a group VIA nonmetal and tends to gain two electrons to form O^{2-}. Therefore these two substances react in a one-to-one ratio: BeO.

(c) Sodium is a group IA metal and loses one electron to form Na^+. Iodine is a group VIIA nonmetal and gains one electron to form I^-. These two substances therefore react in a one-to-one ratio: NaI.

5.97 (a) Calcium, group IIA, loses two electrons to form Ca^{2+}. Iodine, group VIIA, gains one electron to form I^-. These two elements form CaI_2.

(b) Calcium, group IIA, loses two electrons to form Ca^{2+}. Oxygen, group VIA, gains two electrons to form O^{2-}. These two elements form CaO.

(c) Aluminum, group IIIA, loses three electrons to form Al^{3+}. Sulfur, group VIA, gains two electrons to form S^{2-}. These two elements form Al_2S_3.

(d) Calcium, group IIA, forms Ca^{2+}. Bromine, group VIIA, forms Br^-. These two elements form $CaBr_2$.

5.98 Because NaCl is an ionic compound, it exists as a large network of ions called an ionic lattice. There are no molecules of NaCl, only a sea of ions. Water, on the other hand, exists as a collection of H_2O molecules whose atoms are held together by covalent bonds.

5.99 The important missing word is *shared*. Electronegativity is an indication of an atom's ability to attract *shared* electrons to itself.

5.100 Because N, O, Cl, and F are the most electronegative elements, they strongly attract electrons and can be thought of as "hogging" the electrons they share with other elements.

5.101 Fluorine is the most electronegative element; francium is the least electronegative. If these two elements were brought together, the one valence electron of Fr would be transferred to F to form the ionic compound FrF.

5.102 Metals tend to have low electronegativities; nonmetals tend to have high electronegativities.

5.103 (a) Electronegativity decreases going down a group.

(b) Electronegativity increases going across a period from left to right.

(c) Electronegativity increases going from the bottom left corner to the upper right corner.

5.104 Two nonmetal atoms, $\Delta EN = 0$ covalent bond

Two nonmetal atoms, $\Delta EN > 0$ polar covalent bond*

One metal atom, one nonmetal atom, $\Delta EN < 1.7$ polar covalent bond

One metal atom, one nonmetal atom, $\Delta EN \geq 1.7$ ionic bond

*Some species made up of all nonmetal atoms are classified as ionic. NH_4Cl is one example.

5.105 In a covalent bond, the electrons are shared roughly equally by the two atoms. In a polar covalent bond, the electrons spend more time near the atom with the higher electronegativity than near the other atom. Diatomic covalent molecules are F_2, O_2, N_2, or any other diatomic molecule made up of atoms of the same element, for in all these cases $\Delta EN = 0$. Diatomic polar covalent molecules are CO, NO, LiAt, or any other diatomic molecule made up either of two nonidentical nonmetal atoms or of a metal/nonmetal combination with $\Delta EN < 1.7$.

5.106 The electronegativities are C = 2.5 and H = 2.1. Because $\Delta EN > 0$ but < 1.7, the C–H bonds are polar covalent.

5.107 The bonding would be covalent because $\Delta EN = 0$.

5.108 The ΔEN values are H–H 0, C–O 0.5, H–S 0.4, H–O 1.4 telling you that H_2O has the bonds that are most polar covalent.

5.109 Anytime electrons are shared between atoms, the bond can be considered covalent. However, if the shared electrons spend more time nearer one atom than the other, it is as though the electrons have been partially transferred to one atom from the other—in other words, that an ionic bond has formed. Current thinking about covalent and ionic bonds is that they are not completely different from each other but rather exist along a continuum where one type blends into the other.

5.110 Y is more electronegative because the larger sphere indicates the electrons spend more time near it.

5.111 A is more electronegative because it carries the partial negative charge ($\delta-$), indicating that the electrons spend more time closer to A.

5.112 To make the bond ionic, increase the electronegativity of the more electronegative atom and decrease the electronegativity of the less electronegative atom. To make the bond covalent, increase the electronegativity of the less electronegative atom and decrease the electronegativity of the more electronegative atom.

5.113 Numerous answers possible.

5.114 If the two atoms are of the same element (such as in O_2), the bond is purely covalent.

5.115 (a) Br_2 covalent because $\Delta EN = 0$.
  (b) PCl_3 polar covalent because $\Delta EN > 0$ ($3.0 - 2.1 = 0.9$) and all atoms are nonmetals.
  (c) LiCl ionic because $\Delta EN > 1.7$ ($3.0 - 1.0 = 2.0$) and one atom (Li) is a metal.
  (d) ClF polar covalent because $\Delta EN > 0$ ($4.0 - 3.0 = 1.0$) and both atoms are nonmetals.
  (e) $MgCl_2$ ionic because $\Delta EN > 1.7$ ($3.0 - 1.2 = 1.8$) and one atom (Mg) is a metal.

5.116 A binary compound is a compound made up of only two elements. Atmospheric oxygen, O_2, is not a binary compound because it contains only one element.

5.117 The suffix -*ide* indicates the negative part in a binary ionic compound; the negative ion gets this suffix.

5.118 The more electronegative element gets the suffix -*ide* in a binary covalent compound because it is the more negative of the two elements.

5.119 Because the overall charge on the compound must be zero, the number of positive ions and negative ions must result in a total charge of zero. Examples are MgO (2+ and 2−) and $CaCl_2$ (2+ and two 1−).

5.120 (a) Al_2O_3 is the binary ionic compound because $\Delta EN > 1.7$ ($3.5 - 1.5 = 2.0$) and Al is a metal. N_2O_3 is the binary covalent compound because $\Delta EN > 0$ ($3.5 - 3.0 = 0.5$) and all atoms are nonmetals.
  (b) The formulas of binary ionic compounds are fixed by the charges on the ions, and therefore the names do not need to include Greek prefixes. Because the charge on a given nonmetal atom can vary from one binary covalent compound to another, mentioning only the element in the name is not sufficient to indicate the molecular formula of the compound. For this reason, Greek prefixes are used in binary covalent compounds to indicate the number of each type of atom.

5.121 (a) Calcium nitride   (b) Aluminum fluoride   (c) Sodium oxide   (d) Calcium sulfide

5.122 (a) $CaBr_2$ (b) Na_2S (c) K_3N (d) Li_2O

5.123 The transition metals can form more than one kind of cation. A roman numeral in parentheses is used to indicate the magnitude of the positive charge.

5.124 (a) CuCl   copper(I) chloride, cuprous chloride.
    $CuCl_2$ copper(II) chloride, cupric chloride.
  (b) $Fe(OH)_2$ iron (II) hydroxide, ferrous hydroxide.
    $Fe(OH)_3$ iron (III) hydroxide, ferric hydroxide

5.125 (a) Sodium sulfate   (b) Ammonium phosphate   (c) Potassium hypochlorite
  (d) Calcium carbonate   (e) Aluminum nitrate

5.126 (a) $NH_4C_2H_3O_2$. (Note that $CH_3CO_2^-$ is the same as $C_2H_3O_2^-$. They are two ways of indicating the acetate polyatomic ion.)
  (b) $(NH_4)_2CO_3$ (c) $Fe(NO_3)_2$ (d) $Fe(OH)_3$ (e) $Ca(ClO)_2$

5.127 (a) Phosphorus trichloride   (b) Sulfur dioxide   (c) Dinitrogen tetroxide
  (d) Pentaphosphorus decoxide

5.128 The *-ate* and *-ite* suffixes tell you about the relative number of oxygen atoms in the oxyan-ion. In any -ate/-ite pair, the -ate species has more oxygen atoms.

5.129 The oxide ion is a monoatomic anion of oxygen, whereas the peroxide ion is a diatomic anion of oxygen (both have an overall 2− charge).

$$:\ddot{O}:^{2-} \qquad \left[:\ddot{O}-\ddot{O}:\right]^{2-}$$

Oxide ion   Peroxide ion

5.130 Iodine is a halogen just as chlorine is. Therefore they form many of the same types of poly-atomic ions, and you can replace the Cl in the perchlorate ion, ClO_4^-, to make the perio-date ion: IO_4^-. Because this ion carries a 1− charge, the formula for magnesium periodate is $Mg(IO_4)_2$.

5.131 Ammonia is the electrically neutral molecule NH_3. Ammonium is the cation NH^+_4.

$$H-\ddot{N}-H \qquad \left[\begin{matrix} & H & \\ & | & \\ H- & N & -H \\ & | & \\ & H & \end{matrix}\right]^+$$

     H

Ammonia   Ammonia ion

5.132 Magnesium hydroxide consists of Mg^{2+} and OH^- ions. To form an electrically neutral com-pound, there must be two hydroxide anions per magnesium cation. The formula $MgOH_2$ indicates not two OH^- but rather two H and only one O. The correct formula requires a set of parentheses to indicate that the subscript 2 applies to both O and H: $Mg(OH)_2$.

5.133 In the formula for a binary covalent compound, the less electronegative atom (N in this case) appears first, making N_2O correct and ON_2 incorrect. In the name, the more elec-tronegative atom (O in this case) is given the *-ide* suffix because it is this atom that has the partial negative charge, and *-ide* means "negative."

5.134 Sodium oxide is a binary *ionic* compound ($\Delta EN > 1.7$), and Greek prefixes, such as *di-*, are used only in naming binary *covalent* compounds. There is no ambiguity in *sodium oxide* because sodium always has a charge of 1+ in a compound. Because the oxide ion has a charge of 2−, there must be two sodium ions per oxide to achieve electrical neutrality. Saying *disodium oxide* is redundant.

5.135 You know the anion names from the *-ide* rule for single-atom ions and from having memo-rized the polyatomic ions in Table 5.5. (If you haven't memorized them yet, go do it now!) Two rules govern acid names: (1) with acids containing no O, add the prefix *hydro-* and the suffix *-ic acid* to the anion name; (2) with oxyacids, change the ending *-ate* in the name of a polyatomic ion to *-ic* and add the word *acid*, and change the ending *-ite* in the name of a polyatoic ion to *-ous* and add *acid*. If you have followed these rules, your table should look like this:

Anion	Anion name	Acid formula	Acid name
F^-	Fluoride	HF	Hydrofluoric acid
NO_3^-	Nitrate	HNO_3	Nitric acid
Cl^-	Chloride	HCl	Hydrochloric acid
$C_2H_3O_2^-$	Acetate	$HC_2H_3O_2$	Acetic acid
NO_2^-	Nitrite	HNO_2	Nitrous acid

5.136 You use these suffixes when the acid is an oxyacid. When the name of the anion in the acid ends in *-ate*, change the ending to *-ic*. When the name of the anion ends in *-ite*, change the ending to *-ous*.

5.137 Table 5.5 in the textbook tells you NO_3^- is the nitrate ion. Because the oxyacid HNO_3 contains this ion, change the *-ate* in *nitrate* to *-ic acid*; this is nitric acid. The anion NO_2^- has fewer O than the nitrate ion and must therefore be the nit*rite* ion, which means HNO_2 is nitrous acid.

5.138 The *-ic* in acetic acid tells you this acid name came from an anion ending in *-ate*. The ace*tate* ion carries a 1− charge, $C_2H_3O_2^-$, meaning the acid is formed by attaching one H^+: $HC_2H_3O_2$. The *-ous* in sulfurous acid tells you the anion in the acid is sulfite, SO_3^{2-}, and therefore the acid has two H^+: H_2SO_3. The *-ic* in phosporic acid means the anion in the acid is phosph*ate*, PO_4^{3-}, meaning the acid contains three H^+: H_3PO_4.

5.139 Hypochlor*ous* acid is formed from the hypochlorite anion, ClO^-; the molecular formula for the acid is $HClO$. Perchlor*ic* acid is formed from the perchlor*ate* anion, ClO_4^-; the acid formula is $HClO_4$.

5.140 The four oxyanions of chlorine are ClO^- hypochlorite, ClO_2^- chlorite, ClO_3^- chlorate, and ClO_4^- perchlorate. Each becomes an acid by combining with one H^+ ion. The acid is named by changing *-ite* to *-ous* and *-ate* to *-ic*. Thus it is impossible to have hypochlor*ic* acid. You can have only hypochlor*ous* acid.

5.141 Subtract the roman-numeral group number of element from 8.

5.142 It is not electron–*electron* forces but rather electron–*proton* forces that hold molecules together. Forces between electrons are repulsive because like charges repel each other. In a molecule, the attractive force between the electrons of one atom and the protons in the nucleus of another atom hold the molecule together.

5.143 Because they already have a valence octet of electrons.

5.144 One. The electron configuration on this group VA atom is $\cdot\ddot{P}\cdot$, and each unpaired electron bonds with one Cl atom to form

$$Cl-\ddot{P}-Cl$$
$$|$$
$$Cl$$

5.145 You must look at the dot diagrams to answer this question:

$$\cdot\ddot{\underset{\cdot\cdot}{F}}: + \cdot\ddot{\underset{\cdot\cdot}{F}}: \longrightarrow :\ddot{\underset{\cdot\cdot}{F}}-\ddot{\underset{\cdot\cdot}{F}}:$$

$$\cdot\ddot{O}: + \cdot\ddot{O}: + \cdot\ddot{O}: \longrightarrow :\ddot{O}-O-\ddot{O}: \longrightarrow :\underset{\cdot\cdot}{O}=O=\underset{\cdot\cdot}{O}:$$

$$H\cdot + \cdot\dot{C}\cdot + \cdot\ddot{N}\cdot \longrightarrow H-C-\ddot{N}: \longrightarrow H-C\equiv\ddot{N}$$

$$H\cdot + H\cdot + \cdot\dot{C}\cdot + \cdot\ddot{O}: \longrightarrow H-\underset{\underset{H}{|}}{C}-\ddot{O}: \longrightarrow H-\underset{\underset{H}{|}}{C}=\underset{\cdot\cdot}{O}:$$

5.146 (b) is correct. (a) does not have an octet on C, and (c) does not have an octet on O. In addition, (c) violates the rule of thumb that, excluding H, the least electronegative atom is usually the central one: for C, EN = 2.5; for O, EN = 3.5.

5.147 (b) is correct. (a) and (c) have all octets satisfied but incorrect numbers of electrons. There are 12 electrons to be assigned in this molecule—$2 \times 1 = 2$ from H and $2 \times 5 = 10$ from N. (a) has 14 electrons, and (c) has 10.

5.148 Step 1: 16 electrons to be assigned: 5 from N, 4 from C, 6 from O, and 1 for the 1− charge.
Step 2: Least electronegative atom central:

N—C—O   4 electrons assigned

Step 3: $\ddot{\text{N}}$—C—O, then $\ddot{\text{N}}$—C—$\ddot{\text{O}}$:

One octet done,   Two octets done,
10 electrons   all 16 electrons
assigned   assigned

Step 4: $\left[\ddot{\text{N}}\!=\!\text{C}\!=\!\ddot{\text{O}}\right]^{-}$ $\longleftrightarrow$ $\left[:\text{N}\!\equiv\!\text{C}\!-\!\ddot{\text{O}}:\right]^{-}$ $\longleftrightarrow$ $\left[:\ddot{\text{N}}\!-\!\text{C}\!\equiv\!\text{O}:\right]^{-}$

5.149 Steps 1 and 2: 28 electrons: $2 \times 1 = 2$ H, $3 \times 6 = 18$ O, $2 \times 4 = 8$ C; 12 already assigned.

Step 3:

$$\text{H}-\ddot{\text{O}}-\overset{\overset{\displaystyle :\ddot{\text{O}}:}{|}}{\text{C}}-\overset{\overset{\displaystyle :\ddot{\text{O}}:}{|}}{\text{C}}-\text{H}$$

Step 4:

$$\text{H}-\ddot{\text{O}}-\overset{\overset{\displaystyle :\text{O}:}{\|}}{\text{C}}-\overset{\overset{\displaystyle :\text{O}:}{\|}}{\text{C}}-\text{H}$$

(a) Two double bonds.   (b) Six lone pairs.

5.150 Only (d) has resonance forms:

$$\left[\overset{\displaystyle \ddot{\text{N}}}{\ddot{\text{O}}\!=\!\!\diagdown\ddot{\text{O}}:}\right]^{-} \text{ and } \left[\overset{\displaystyle \ddot{\text{N}}}{:\ddot{\text{O}}\diagdown\!=\!\ddot{\text{O}}:}\right]^{-}$$

With only two atoms, (c) cannot have resonance forms. Both (a) and (b) have bonds to H, which can be only single bonds.

5.151 Two: $\left[:\ddot{\text{F}}-\ddot{\text{B}}\text{r}-\ddot{\text{F}}:\right]^{+}$

5.152 (a) is correct. The right diagram of (b) has S with less than an octet of electrons. The right diagram of (c) gives one oxygen less than an octet and the other oxygen more than an octet.

5.153 Calcium. You can determine relative electronegativities from the guideline that the lowest values are at the lower left of the periodic table and highest values are at the upper right.

5.154 (c). Another way of stating this question is, what type of bond—pure covalent, polar covalent, or ionic—forms between H and Be? Because Be is a metal, you can rule out pure covalent, but that still leaves the four choices presented in the problem statement. The guideline is that a metal/nonmental compound is called ionic if the ionic character of the bond is 50% or greater. The graph on page 185 of the textbook tells you this percentage corresponds to ΔEN = 1.7. The EN values here are Be 1.5 and H 2.1, meaning ΔEN = 0.6. Thus the bond is polar covalent rather than ionic. That H is more electronegative than Be tells you the electrons spend more time around H, giving it the partial negative charge.

5.155 ionic

5.156 (a) This is not an ionic compound because it contains only nonmetals. Thus the P cannot have a full ionic charge, which rules out (c) and (d). The eletronegativities are P 2.1 and Cl 3.0, menaing the electrons spend more time around Cl, leaving P with a partial positive charge.

5.157 (d) because the two I atoms have the same electronegativity.

5.158 PBr_3 < $MgBr_2$ < KBr < CsBr. Percent ionic character depends on ΔEN. The values here are PBr_3 0.7, $MgBr_2$ 1.6, KBr 2.0, CsBr 2.1. Remember, though, that you don't need the numerical values to do relative ranking. Just look at the relative periodic-table positions of the four atoms bonding to Br.

5.159

Name	Formula
Silver nitrate	$AgNO_3$
Aluminum selenide	Al_2Se_3
Lithium oxide	Li_2O
Ammonium iodide	NH_4I
Copper(II) sulfate or cupric sulfate	$CuSO_4$
Potassium permanganate	$KMnO_4$
Calcium chlorate	$Ca(ClO_3)_2$

5.160

Name	Formula
Sodium hydrogen carbonate or sodium bicarbonate	$NaHCO_3$
Magnesium acetate	$Mg(CH_3CO_2)_2$
Barium hypochlorite	$Ba(ClO)_2$
Iron(III) nitrate or ferric nitrate	$Fe(NO_3)_3$
Ammonium sulfate	$(NH_4)_2SO_4$
Calcium phosphate	$Ca_3(PO_4)_2$
Cobalt(III) chromate or cobaltic chromate	$Co_2(CrO_4)_3$

5.161

Name	Formula
Cadmium telluride	$CdTe$
Nitrogen triiodide	NI_3
Silicon tetriodide	SiI_4
Bromine trifluoride	BrF_3
Hydroiodic acid	HI (dissolved in water)
Hydrogen iodide	HI (as a pure gas)
Tetrasulfur tetranitride	S_4N_4

5.162

Name	Formula
Xenon tetrafluoride	XeF_4
Xenon difluoride	XeF_2
Iodine monochloride	ICl
Bromine trichloride	$BrCl_3$
Diboron hexahydride	B_2H_6
Dinitrogen oxide	N_2O
Tetrasulfur dioxide	S_4O_2

5.163 You need a metal/nonmetal combination to have an ionic compound, meaning you know (a), (b), and (e) are molecular compounds. For the other four, you should recognize Cl^- plus the anions from Table 5.5 of the textbook and therefore classify them as ionic compounds.

(a) Molecular; chlorine; 14 electrons: :C̈l—C̈l:

(b) Molecular (because this is *gaseous* HCl); hydrogen chloride gas; 8 electrons: H—C̈l:

(c) Ionic; sodium chloride; anion, 8 electrons: $\left[:\ddot{C}l:\right]^-$

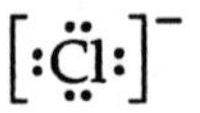

(d) Ionic; magnesium chlorite; anion, 20 electrons: $\left[:\ddot{O}-\ddot{C}l-\ddot{O}:\right]^-$

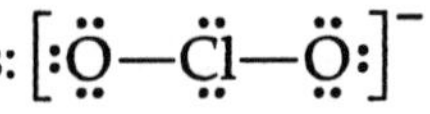

(e) Molecular; methanol; 14 electrons:

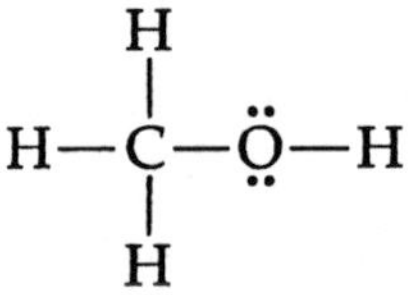

$$H-\overset{\displaystyle H}{\underset{\displaystyle H}{\vert \atop C \atop \vert}}-\ddot{O}-H$$

(f) Ionic; iron(III); nitrate or ferric nitrate; anion, 24 electrons:
$$\left[\ddot{O}=\overset{}{N}-\ddot{O}: \atop :\ddot{O}:\right]^-$$

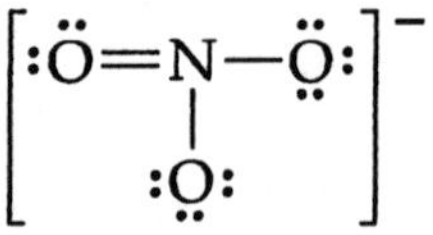

(g) Ionic; lead acetate; anion, 24 electrons:
$$\left[H-\overset{\displaystyle H}{\underset{\displaystyle H}{\vert \atop C \atop \vert}}-\overset{\displaystyle :O: \atop \parallel}{C}-\ddot{O}: \right]^-$$

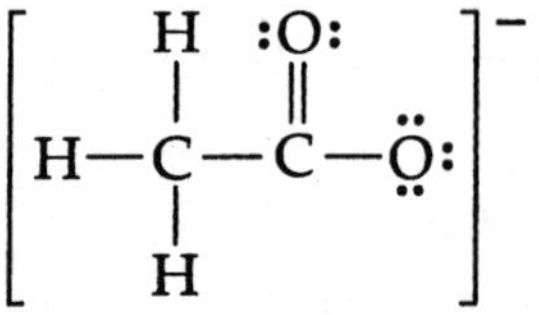

5.164 The roman numeral tells you the Ni atom loses two electrons in both cases.

5.165 Because in binary covalent compounds, the less electronegative element is listed first.

5.166 Step 1: CF_2Cl_2, 32 electrons; CH_2FCH_3, 20 electrons

Step 2:

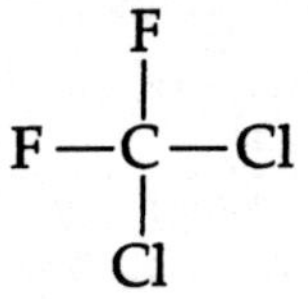

$$F-\overset{\displaystyle F}{\underset{\displaystyle Cl}{\vert \atop C \atop \vert}}-Cl \qquad\qquad H-\overset{\displaystyle F}{\underset{\displaystyle H}{\vert \atop C \atop \vert}}-\overset{\displaystyle H}{\underset{\displaystyle H}{\vert \atop C \atop \vert}}-H$$

  8 electrons assigned 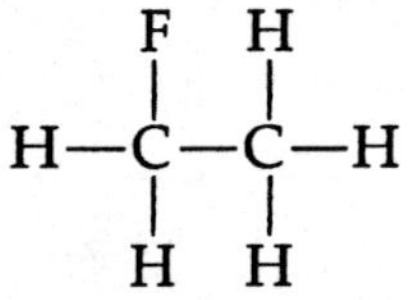   14 electrons assigned

Step 3:

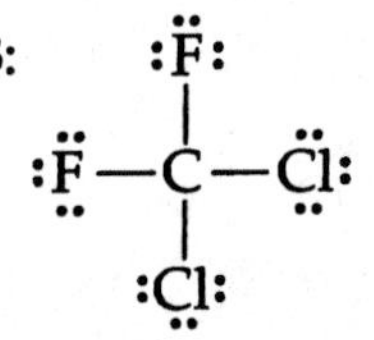

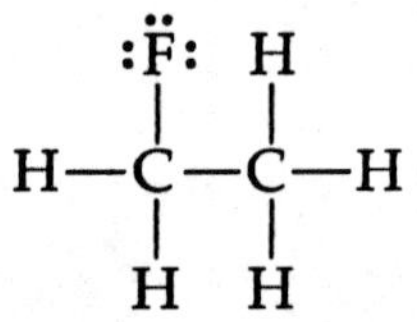

$$:\ddot{F}-\overset{\displaystyle :\ddot{F}:}{\underset{\displaystyle :\ddot{Cl}:}{\vert \atop C \atop \vert}}-\ddot{C}l: \qquad\qquad H-\overset{\displaystyle :\ddot{F}:}{\underset{\displaystyle H}{\vert \atop C \atop \vert}}-\overset{\displaystyle H}{\underset{\displaystyle H}{\vert \atop C \atop \vert}}-H$$

5.167 Because the term *ionic compound* is generally reserved for a metal bonded to a nonmetal. H and F are both nonmetals.

5.168 (a) $Ca_3(PO_4)_2$ (b) K_2HPO_4 (c) $Mg(CN)_2$ (d) $Ba(ClO_3)_2$

5.169 (a) Iron(III) sulfite or ferric sulfite   (b) Gold(III) nitrate
(c) Sodium dihydrogen phosphate   (d) Lead acetate or lead(II) acetate

5.170 Draw the N–O single bond and see how many H atoms are needed to complete octets:

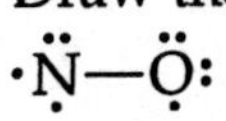

$\cdot\ddot{N}-\ddot{O}:$

The N atom needs two electrons, and O needs one:

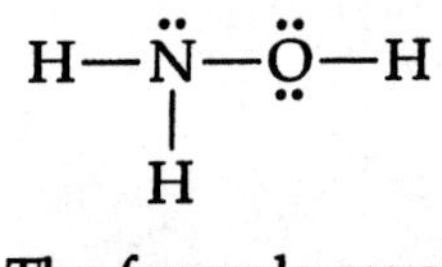

$$H-\overset{\displaystyle \ddot{N}}{\underset{\displaystyle H}{\vert}}-\ddot{O}-H$$

The formula must be NH_2OH.

5.171 (a) K < Li < Be   (b) Si < S < O   (c) Te < I < Br

5.172 (a) Ammonium iodide, ionic (ammonium compounds are ionic)
(b) Dichlorine heptoxide, polar covalent (two nonmetals)
(c) Strontium chloride, ionic (metal/nonmetal, $\Delta EN > 1.7$)
(d) Lithium dichromate, ionic (polyatomic anion)

5.173 (a) Cu_2S, polar covalent (metal/nonmetal, $\Delta EN < 1.7$)

(b) Al_4C_3, polar covalent (metal/nonmetal, $\Delta EN < 1.7$)

(c) I_2O_5, polar covalent (two nonmetals)

(d) ClF_3, polar covalent (two nonmetals)

5.174

$$\overset{\delta-\quad\delta+}{N-Cl} < \overset{\delta+\quad\delta-}{O-Cl} < \overset{\delta-\quad\delta+}{S-O} < \overset{\delta-\quad\delta+}{O-H} < \overset{\delta+\quad\delta-}{C-F}$$

$\Delta EN \qquad 0 \qquad\quad 0.5 \qquad\quad 1.0 \qquad\quad 1.4 \qquad\quad 1.5$

5.175 Hydrogen sulfide refers to the covalent compound in the gas phase, and hydrosulfuric acid refers to the aqueous solution (hydrogen sulfide gas dissolved in water), which acts as an acid by dissociating to give H^+ ions in solution.

5.176 (a) H–F because F is more electronegative than Cl, making ΔEN for H–F greater than ΔEN for H–Cl.

(b) C–F because ΔEN for it is greater than ΔEN for O–F.

5.177 Manganate ion. The *per-* in *permanganate* tells you there are more than two oxyanions in this family, meaning a simple change from *-ate* to *-ite* is not correct. Following the pattern of the Cl oxyanions—perchlorate, chlorate, chlorite, hypochlorite—a loss of one O in the ion, from MnO_4^- to MnO_3^-, changes the name from *permanganate* to *manganate*.

6

The Shape of Molecules

6.1 See solution in textbook.

6.2 Dot diagram:

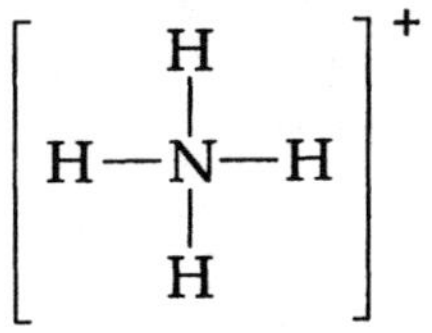

$$\left[\begin{array}{c} H \\ | \\ H-N-H \\ | \\ H \end{array} \right]^{+}$$

Four electron groups around the central N means the electrons are arranged in a tetrahedral shape; the molecular shape is tetrahedral:

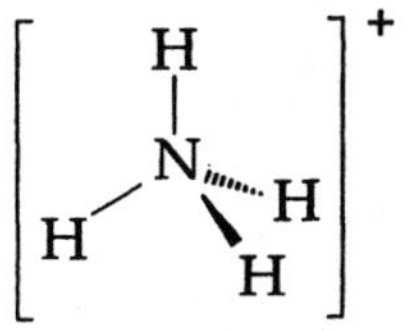

$$\left[\begin{array}{c} H \\ | \\ N_{\text{\tiny{\|\|\|}}}H \\ H \quad H \end{array} \right]^{+}$$ All angles 109.5°

6.3 Dot diagram: :C̈l—C≡C—C̈l:

Two groups of electrons around each carbon atom (remember that we count multiple bonds as single bonds when determining how the electrons are arranged) means the electrons are 180° apart; the molecular shape is therefore linear, and all bond angles are 180°:

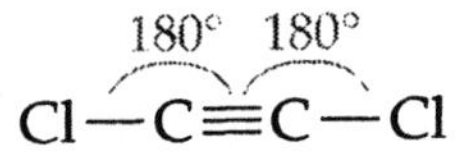

180° 180°
Cl—C≡C—Cl

6.4 Dot diagram:

:O:
‖
C
:C̈l   C̈l:

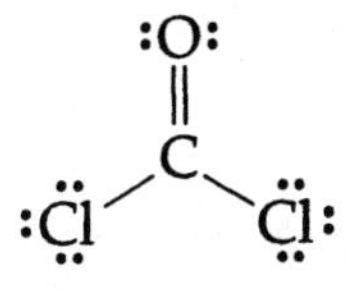

Three electron groups around the central atom are arranged in one plane at the corners of a triangle; the molecular shape is trigonal planar:

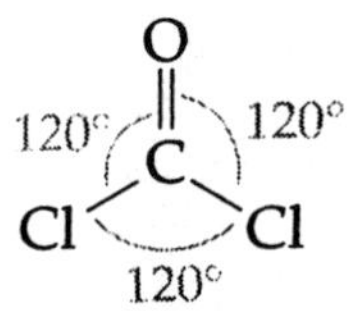

6.5 See solution in textbook.

6.6 Dot diagram:

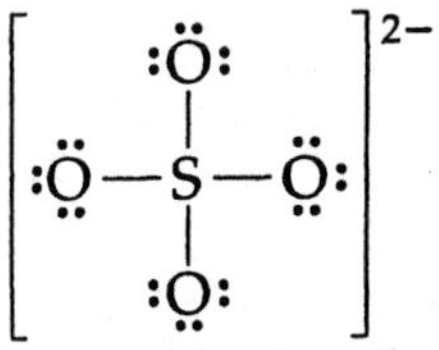

There are four bonding groups around the central atom. The electron-group geometry is therefore tetrahedral. Because there are no lone pairs, the molecular shape is also tetrahedral, with bond angles of 109.5°.

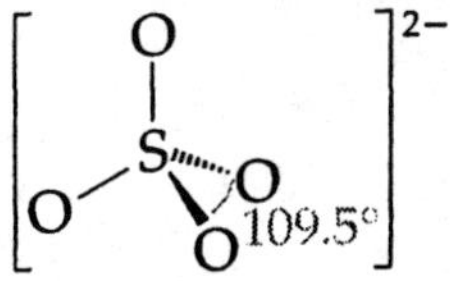

6.7 Dot diagram:

$$H-C\equiv N:$$

There are two bonding groups around the central C and no lone pairs (remember that lone pairs on peripheral atoms do not influence shape). Therefore the electron-group geometry and molecular shape are both linear:

6.8 Dot diagram:

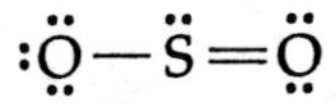

$$:\ddot{O}-\ddot{S}=\ddot{O}$$

There are three groups of electrons around the sulfur—two bonding groups and one lone pair. Table 6.2 of the textbook tells you this combination creates an electron-group geometry that is trigonal planar and a molecular shape that is bent, with bond angles of approximately 118°:

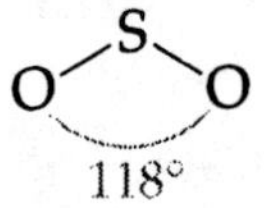

6.9 Dot diagram:

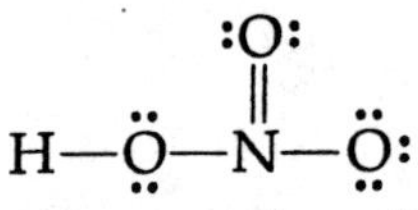

There are three bonding groups of electrons around the nitrogen and no lone pairs. Therefore the electron-group geometry is trigonal planar, and the molecular shape is also trigonal planar, with bond angles of 120° around the N:

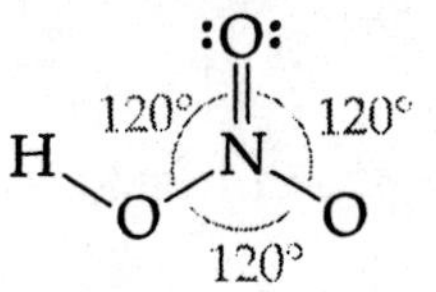

6.10 See solution in textbook.

6.11 $CHCl_3$ is polar. The dot diagram

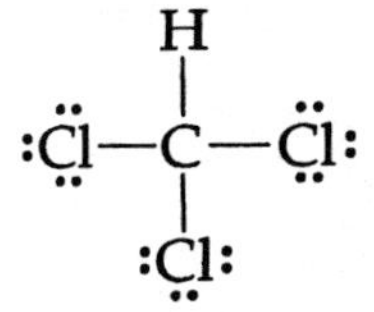

$$
\begin{array}{c}
\ddot{H} \\
| \\
:\ddot{C}l-C-\ddot{C}l: \\
| \\
:\ddot{C}l:
\end{array}
$$

with its four electron groups around the central C tells you the molecule is tetrahedral. The C–H bond is treated as nonpolar, and the electronegativity difference between C and Cl tells you all three C–Cl bonds are polar. In a tetrahedral shape, there is no way three polar bonds can cancel one another, meaning the molecular is polar:

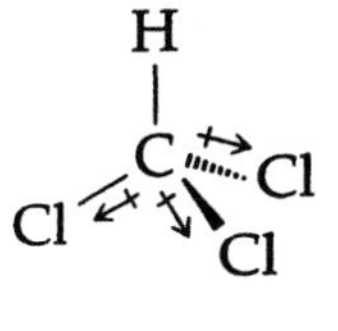

Individual bond   Overall molecule
dipole moments   dipole moments

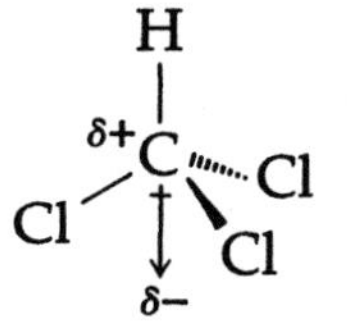

6.12 PCl_3: $CHCl_3$:

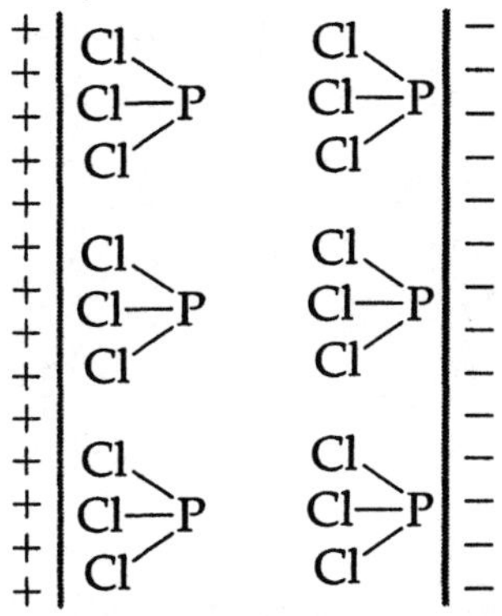

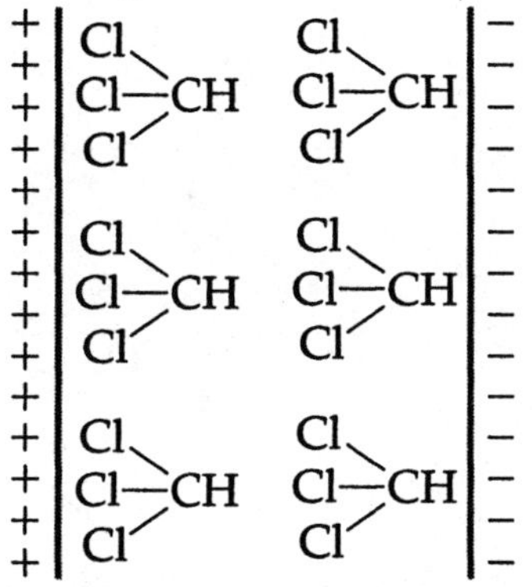

In all cases, the $\delta-$ end of each molecule lines up close to the positive plate and the $\delta+$ end lines up close to the negative plate.

6.13 Because the bonding electrons can be farther apart from one another with 109.5° angles. Because electrons repel one another, they want to be as far apart as possible.

6.14 Answers will vary. One possible evolution scheme would be to produce an enzyme whose pocket is too small for the –SOOH grouping in sulfanilimide but large enough for the –COOH group in PABA.

6.15 Because it is only the *valence shell electrons* that are involved in bonding, and that determine the shape of molecules.

6.16

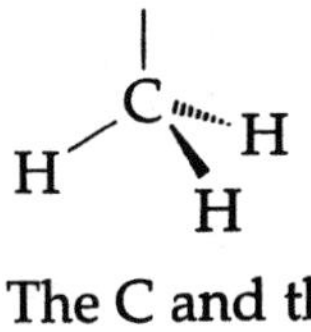

The C and the two H's bonded to it by lines are in the plane of the page. The solid-wedge H sticks out above the plane of the page, and the dashed-wedge H sticks down below the plane of the page.

6.17

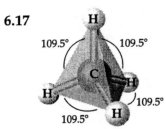

6.18 (a) (1)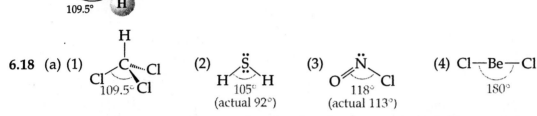

(b) Electron-group geometry and molecular shape come from Table 6.2 of the textbook. (1) Four bonding groups and no lone pairs around C means tetrahedral electron-group arrangement and tetrahedral molecular shape. (2) Two bonding groups and two lone pairs around S means tetrahedral electron arrangement and bent shape. (3) Two bonding groups and one lone pair around N means trigonal planar electron arrangement and bent shape. (4) Two bonding groups and no lone pairs around Be means linear electron arrangement and linear shape. (Note that the Be bonding in this dot diagram violates the octet rule. Chemists do not actually know whether the bonding is as shown or instead is $\ddot{C}l\!=\!Be\!=\!\ddot{C}l$. Either structure would result in a linear molecular shape because both have two bonding groups and no lone pairs around Be.

6.19 (a)

| (1) | (2) | (3) | (4) |

$\left[\begin{array}{c}\text{O}\\[2pt]\overset{\displaystyle\text{O}}{\underset{\displaystyle\text{O}}{\text{P}}}\text{O}\end{array}\right]^{3-}$ 109.5° $\left[\begin{array}{c}\text{O}\\[2pt]\overset{\displaystyle\text{O}}{\underset{\displaystyle\text{O}}{\text{N}}}\end{array}\right]^{-}$ 120°   Cl—As—Cl 107° Cl (predicted)   :Br—Se—Br: 105° (predicted)

(b) (1) Tetrahedral electron geometry, tetrahedral shape. (2) Trigonal planar electron geometry, trigonal planar shape. (3) Tetrahedral electron geometry, pyramidal shape. (4) Tetrahedral electron geometry, bent shape.

6.20 The fact that all the electrons in a multiple bond occupy roughly the same region of space.

6.21 It is possible because the extent of bending depends on how many lone pairs surround the central atom. In a 118° bent molecule, a central atom is surrounded by two bonding groups and one lone pair. Think of this as a modification of a central atom having three bonding groups spaced 120° apart. Because a lone pair takes up more space than a bonding pair, however, the lone pair repels the two bonding groups slightly, and the bond angle is compressed by about 2°, from 120° to 118°. In a 105° bent molecule, a central atom is surrounded by two bonding groups and two lone pairs. Think of this as a modification of a central atom having four bonding groups spaced 109.5° apart. The two lone pairs repel the bonding groups even more than a single long pair does, and so the bond angle is compressed by about 4°, from 109.5° to 105°.

6.22 Because of the lone pair on the nitrogen. The extra repulsion of the lone pair forces the bonding pairs closer together.

6.23 The shape of a molecule is determined by the arrangement of the atoms in the molecule, ignoring any lone pairs around the central atom. We do not call ammonia a tetrahedral molecule because the one N and three H atoms form a pyramid, as Table 6.2 of the textbook shows. The NH_3 molecule thus has a pyramidal shape.

6.24 (a)

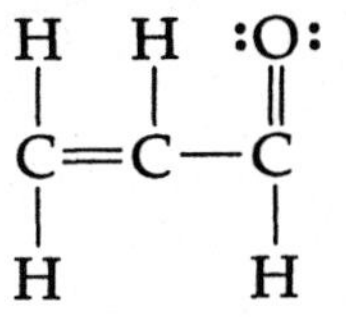

$$H \quad H \quad :O:$$

C=C—C with H below each left carbons and H below the right C, double bond C=C and double bond to O.

(b) and (c) Because each C has three bonding groups and no lone pairs, the electron-group geometry is trigonal planar about each C, and the shape about each C is also trigonal planar. Therefore all the atoms lie in the same plane, and the bond angles are 120°:

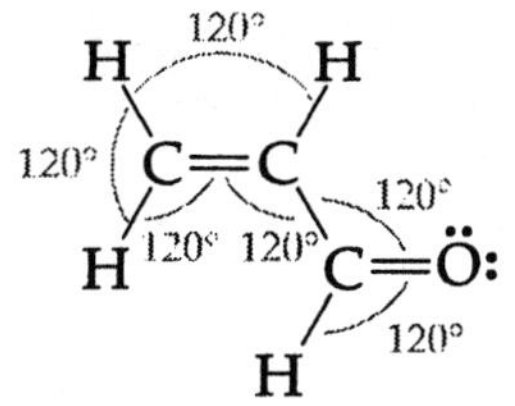

6.25 (a)

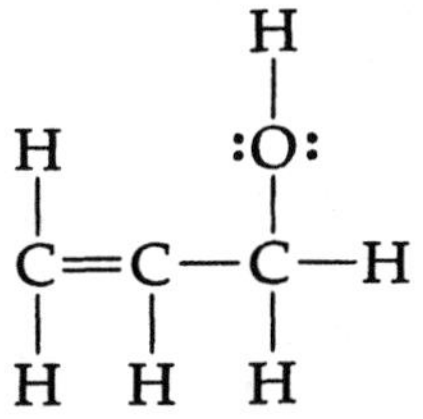

C=C—C—H structure with H, O, and H substituents

(b) and (c) Call the carbons C1, C2, C3 from left to right. C1 and C2 have three bonding groups each, no lone pairs, meaning the shape in this part of the molecule is trigonal planar with 120° angles. C3 has four bonding groups, no lone pairs, and therefore the shape around this C is tetrahedral with 109.5° angles. The O has two bonding groups, two lone pairs, meaning the shape in this part of the molecule is bent with a 105° angle:

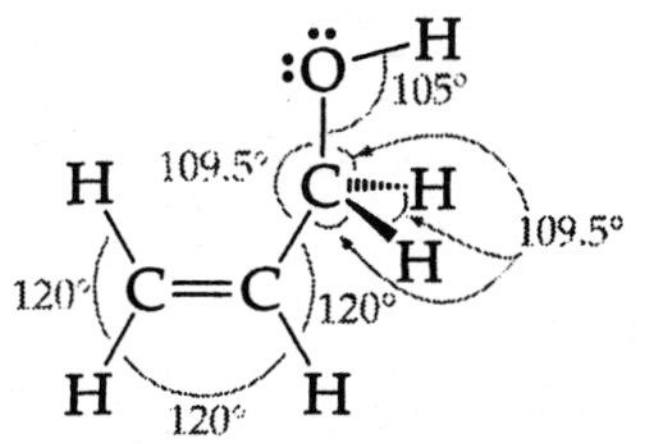

6.26 The shape of a molecule depends on the number of electron groups around each interior atom. That number can be determined only by using a correct Lewis dot diagram.

6.27 (1) is the flat molecule because the bond angles around each carbon are 120° (each carbon has three bonding groups around it). In (2), each carbon has four bonding groups around it, resulting in bond angles of 109.5°. Therefore (2) is not a flat molecule.

6.28

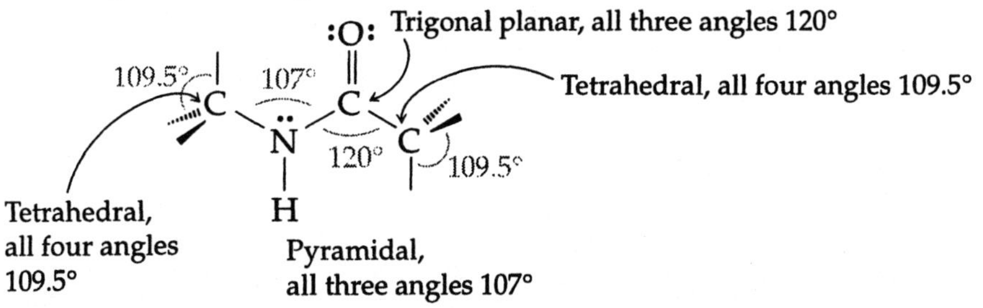

6.29 When it lines up in a specific orientation when placed between two metal plates of opposite electrical charge.

6.30 Yes; you must know (1) which, if any, bonds in the molecule are polar (based on the relative electronegativities of the connected atoms) and (2) the shape of the molecule.

6.31 False. A molecule containing polar bonds is nonpolar if the individual dipole moments cancel each other, as in CO_2.

6.32 (a) HCl, because the electronegativity difference is greater in HCl than in HBr.
(b) HCl, because the molecular dipole moment is greater.

6.33 The degree of the unequal sharing of the electrons in the bond. The longer the arrow, the larger the magnitude of the dipole moment and the more polar the bond.

6.34 Using just a number would not tell us which atom of the dipole pair has the smaller portion of the shared electrons ($\delta+$) and which atom of the pair has the larger portion of the shared electrons ($\delta-$).

6.35 The difference in the electronegativity value of the two bonded atoms determines the bond dipole moment; the greater the electronegativity difference, the more negative one atom is relative to the other and the greater the bond dipole moment.

6.36 With an arrow pointing from the positive end of the bond to the negative end. The head of the arrow is at the negative end of the dipole, and the tail of the arrow carries a small perpendicular line so that this end looks like a plus sign: $\longmapsto$.

6.37 Because the molecule is linear, the two bond dipole moments cancel each other:

$$\overset{\longleftarrow\;\;\longrightarrow}{O=C=O}$$

Net dipole = 0

6.38 Because the molecule is bent (two bonding groups, one lone pair) the two bond dipole moments do not cancel each other:

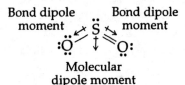

Instead, the two bond moments add vectorially to give a nonzero molecular moment.

6.39 (a) HF, because the electronegativity difference is greatest: $4.0 - 2.1 = 1.9$.
(b) HAt, because the electronegativity difference is least: $2.1 - 2.1 = 0$.

(c) $\overset{\longmapsto}{H-F} \quad \overset{\longmapsto}{H-Cl} \quad \overset{\longmapsto}{H-Br} \quad \overset{\mapsto}{H-I} \quad H-At$

6.40 There is only one bond dipole moment in CO, with the negative end in the direction of the oxygen, making the molecule polar. In CO_2, there are two opposite but equal bond dipole moments that cancel each other, resulting in a nonpolar molecule:

$$\underset{\longmapsto}{:C\equiv O:} \qquad \overset{\longleftrightarrow}{:\overset{..}{O}=C=\overset{..}{O}:}$$

6.41 (a) Individual bond dipole moments

lead to molecular dipole moment

(b) Because there is only one polar bond in the molecule, the bond dipole moment and molecular dipole moment are identical:

$$\underset{H}{\overset{Br\ \delta-}{\underset{|}{\underset{C}{\overset{|}{}}}}}\ \delta+$$

H⋯⋯C δ+
  / \
 H   H
 |
 H

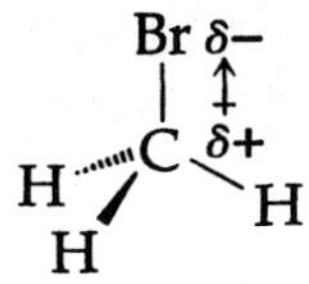

(c) Individual bond dipole moments

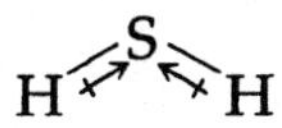

$$H\overset{S}{\underset{}{\rightleftarrows}}H$$

lead to molecular dipole moment

$$\underset{\delta+}{\overset{\delta-}{\underset{S}{}}}$$

H — S — H
   δ+

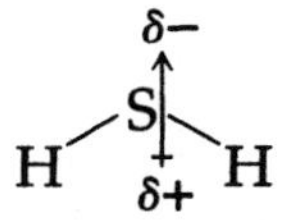

(d) Because N and Cl have the same electronegativity value (3.0), the N–Cl bond is nonpolar. With only one polar bond in the molecule, the bond dipole moment and molecular dipole moment are identical:

$$\delta-O\overset{\delta+}{=}N-Cl$$

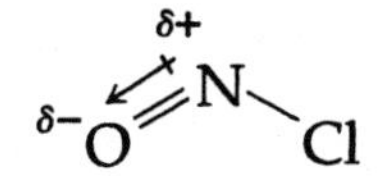

(e) This is a nonpolar molecule. The two bond dipole moments cancel so that there is no molecular dipole moment:

$$Cl\overset{\leftarrow}{—}C\equiv C\overset{\rightarrow}{—}Cl$$

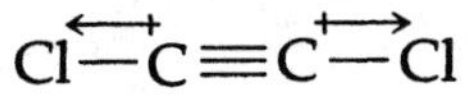

6.42 The attractive force between the partially negative portion of one polar molecule and the partially positive portion of another polar molecule. Some examples are the attraction between two water molecules and the attraction between two NH_3 molecules:

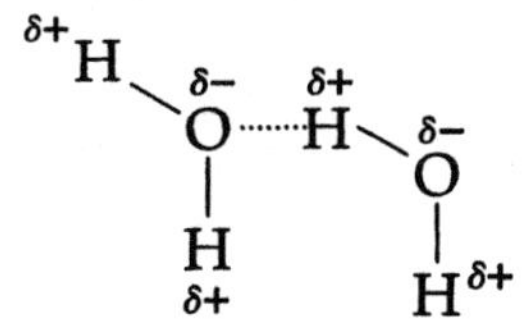

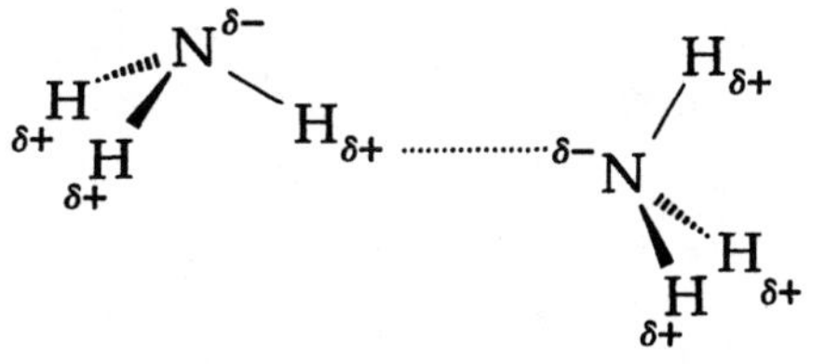

6.43 No. Dipole–dipole forces have only a fraction of the strength of the forces between ions because ions carry full electrical charges but dipole charges are partial.

6.44 Intermolecular forces are forces *between* molecules. The evidence that these forces exist is that molecules "stick" to one another to form solids and liquids.

6.45
$$\underset{Cl}{\overset{\delta+}{H}}\cdots\underset{}{\overset{\delta-}{Cl}}$$

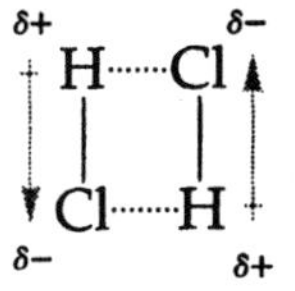

6.46

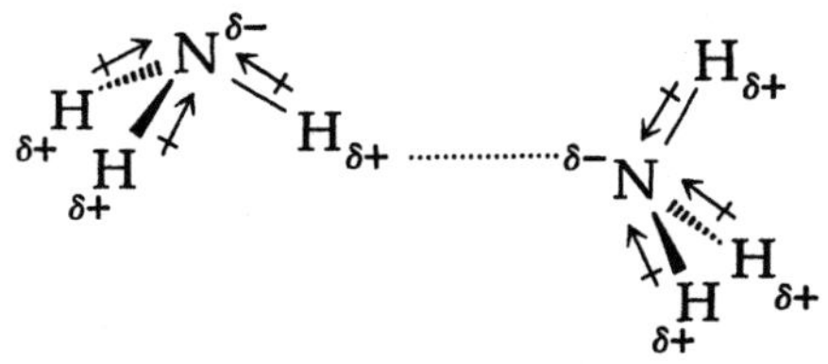

6.47 The lone pairs are important in determining the electron-groups geometry around an atom and thus in determining the shape of the molecule.

6.48 (a) The diagram is incorrect (even though each atom has an octet) because the number of electrons is wrong. The diagram needs 18 electrons, six from each atom. This gives the correct diagram:

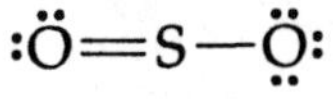

$$:\ddot{O}=S-\ddot{O}:$$

(b) Correct diagram: two bonding groups and one lone pair around S, bent shape and polar molecule:

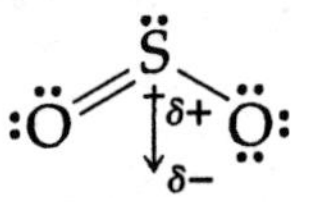

Incorrect diagram: two bonding groups and no lone pairs around S, linear shape and nonpolar molecule:

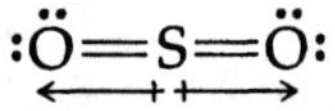

$$:\ddot{O}=S=\ddot{O}:$$

The two bond dipole moments cancel each other.

6.49 (a)

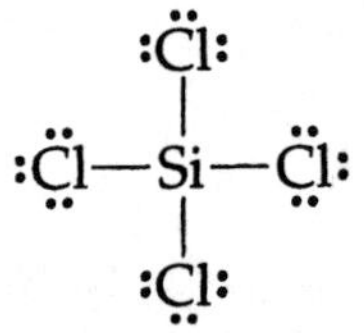

(b) and (c) Four bonding groups, no lone pairs around Si makes this a tetrahedral molecule:

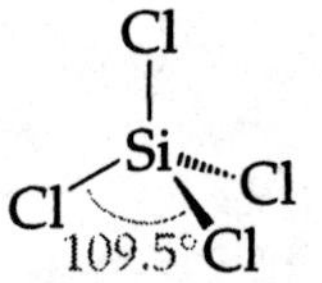

All bond angles 109.5°

(d) Because Cl is more electronegative than Si, the Cl atoms take the lion's share of the electrons:

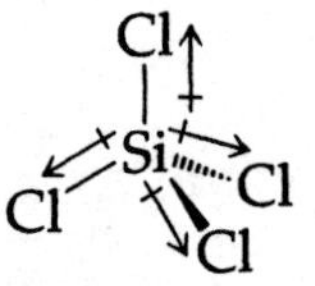

(e) The molecule is nonpolar because the four bond dipole moments cancel one another.

6.50 (a)

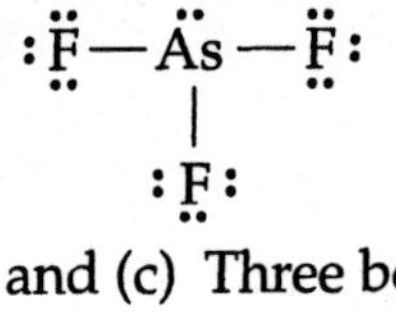

(b) and (c) Three bonding groups, one lone pair around As makes this a pyramidal molecule:

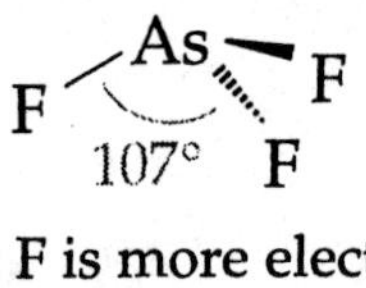

(d) Because F is more electronegative than As, the F atoms take the lion's share of the electrons:

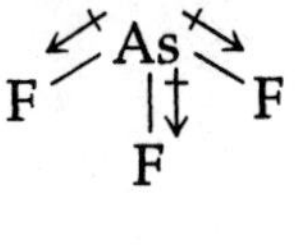

(e) The molecule is polar:

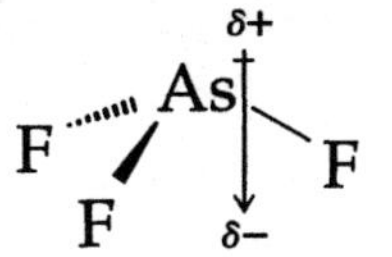

6.51 (a)

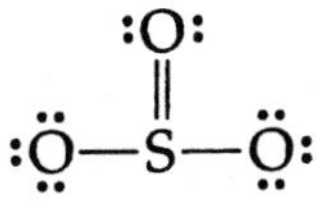

(b) and (c) Three bonding groups, no lone pairs, trigonal planar molecule:

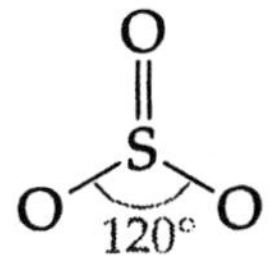

(d) O is more electronegative than S:

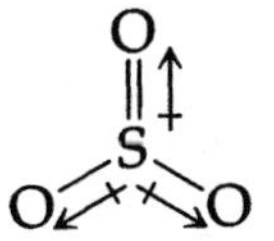

(e) The molecule is nonpolar because the three bond dipole moments, being 120° apart, all cancel.

6.52 (a) $H-\ddot{S}-C\equiv N\!:$

(b) Treat each interior atom separately, as described in the hints in Problems 6.24 and 6.25. S: two bonding groups, two lone pairs, bent shape with 105° angle; C: two bonding groups, no lone pairs, linear shape:

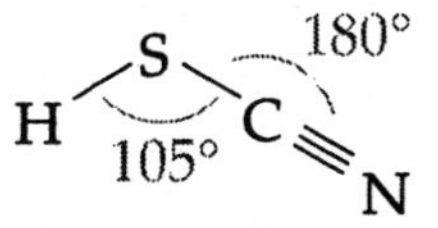

(c) Treat each bond separately:

S is more electronegative than H, H—S

S and C equal electronegativity values, S—C

N more electronegative than C, C≡N

The bond dipole moments therefore are

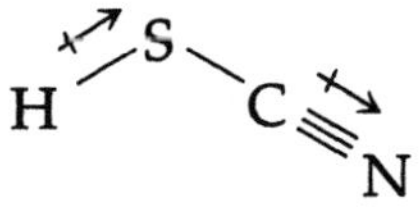

(d) The molecule is polar, with a molecular dipole moment

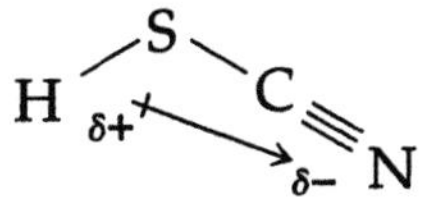

6.53 (a)

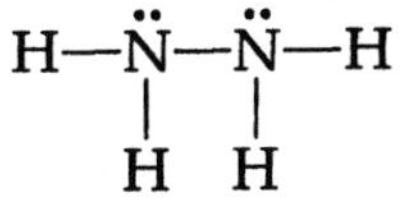

(b) and (c) There are three bonding groups and one lone pair around each N, meaning the shape is pyramidal around each N. The electron-group geometry is tetrahedral, which means the bond angles should be 109.5°. However, the lone pair on each N compresses the angles to about 107°:

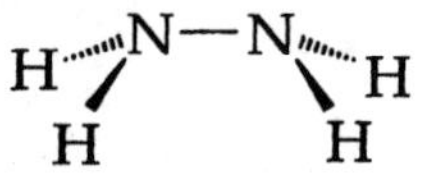

All angles 107°
(2° compression rule for period 2 atoms)

(d) N is more electronegative than H:

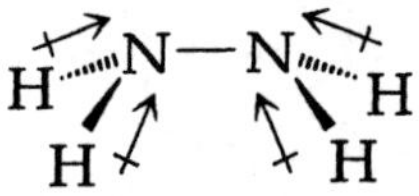

(e) The molecule is polar because the individual bond dipole moments do not cancel:

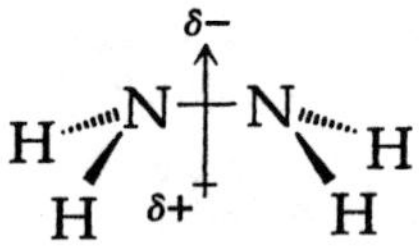

6.54 (a) 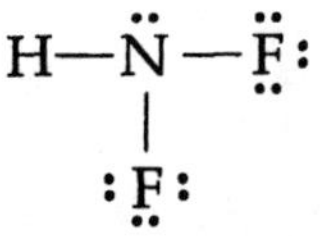 $H-\overset{\cdot\cdot}{N}-\overset{\cdot\cdot}{\underset{\cdot\cdot}{F}}:$
        |
        $:\overset{\cdot\cdot}{\underset{\cdot\cdot}{F}}:$

(b) and (c) Three bonding groups, one lone pair around N, pyramidal shape. The one lone pair compresses the bond angles from 109.5° to 107°:

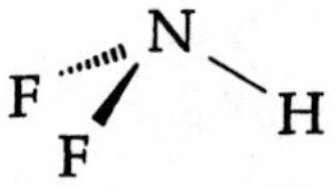

All angles 107° (2° compression rule)

(d) F is more electronegative than N, N is more electronegative than H:

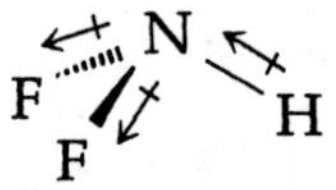

(e) The molecule is polar. Because the N–F electronegativity difference (1.0) is slightly greater than the N–H electronegativity difference (0.9), the $\delta-$ end of the molecular dipole moment is near the F atoms:

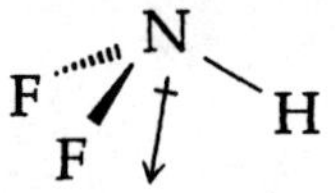

6.55 (a) 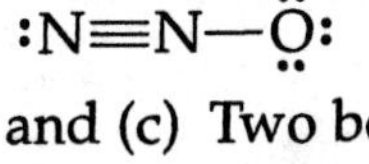 $:N\equiv N-\overset{\cdot\cdot}{\underset{\cdot\cdot}{O}}:$

(b) and (c) Two bonding groups, no lone pairs around the central N makes this a linear molecule with 180° bond angles:

N≡N—O
   180°

(d) O is more electronegative than N:

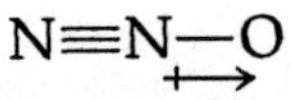

N≡N—O

(e) The molecule is polar because there is only one bond dipole moment. The bond dipole moment and molecular dipole moment are identical.

6.56 (a) NO_2 has an odd number of valence electrons: $5 + 6(2) = 17$. This makes it impossible to show only electron pairs in the dot diagram.

(b) $:\ddot{O}—\dot{N}=\ddot{O}:$

(c) The electron-group geometry around N most closely corresponds to two bonding groups, one lone pair, and Table 6.2 of the textbook tells you that geometry gives a bent molecular shape. (That there is only a single lone electron rather than a pair lets you guess that the bond angle is a bit larger than the 118° shown in Table 6.2.) Because the molecule is bent, the two bond dipole moments do not cancel each other, and therefore the molecule is polar:

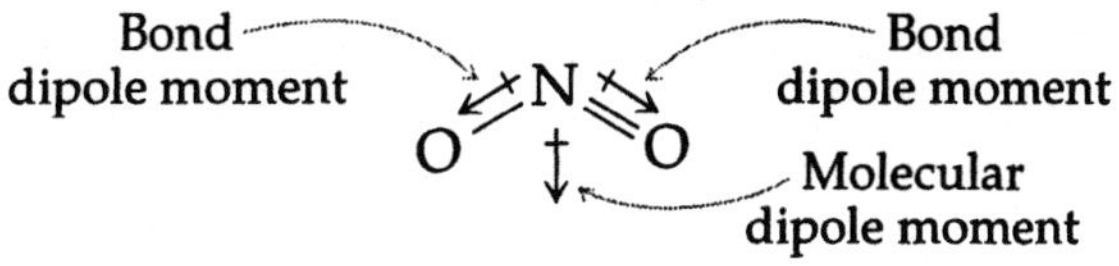

6.57 (a)

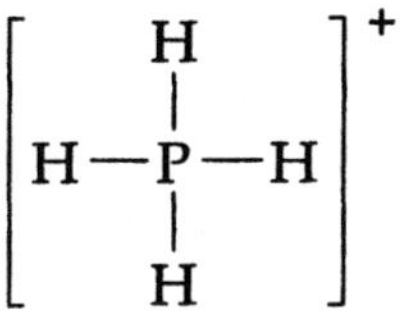

(b) and (c) Four bonding groups, no lone pairs, tetrahedral shape:

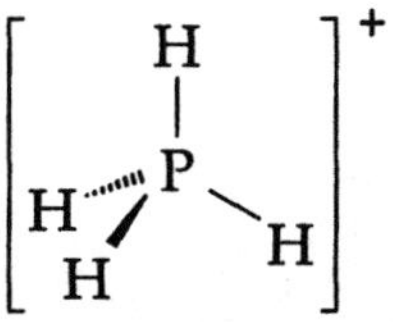

All bond angles 109.5°

(d) Because P and H have the same electronegativity value, there are no bond dipole moments in this molecule.

6.58 The boiling point should increase because the increased molecular dipole moments would mean stronger intermolecular forces. As the molecules "stick" to one another more tightly, it takes more heat energy to cause them to leave the liquid phase and enter the gas phase.

6.59 Because the P–H bonds are nonpolar. (The electronegativity difference is 0 for these two atoms: P 2.1, H 2.1.)

6.60 109.5° is the maximum bond angle that can be achieved for four bonds about a central atom. This angle gets the bonding electron pairs as far apart from one another as possible, minimizing the repulsion between them.

6.61 Consider each C atom separately. Each has four bonding groups and no lone electrons, meaning the molecular shape is tetrahedral about each C:

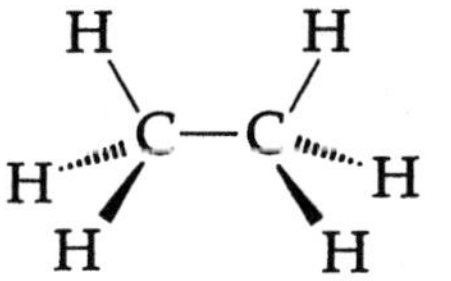

All bond angles 109.5°

6.62 Consider each C atom separately. Left C: three bonding groups, no lone pairs, trigonal planar shape with 120° bond angles; right C: four bonding groups, no lone pairs, tetrahedral shape with 109.5° bond angles:

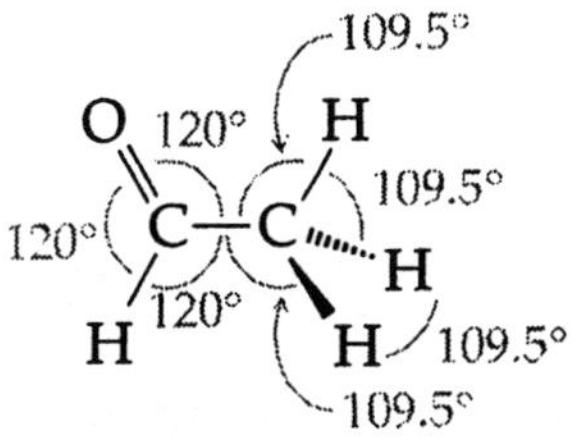

6.63 Consider each interior atom separately. Left C: four bonding groups, no lone pairs, tetrahedral shape with 109.5° bond angles. O: two bonding groups, two lone pairs, bent shape with 105° bond angles. Right C: same as left C.

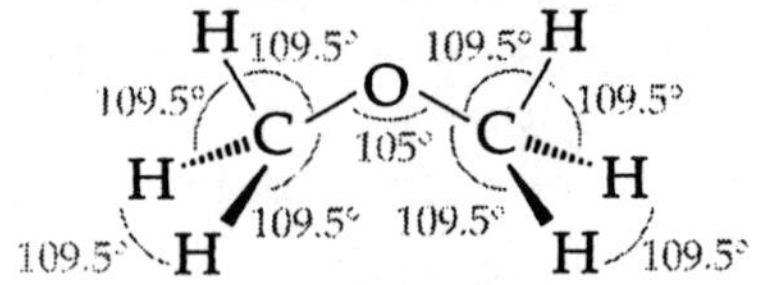

6.64 Three bonding groups, one lone pair around central O, pyramidal shape with 107° bond angles.

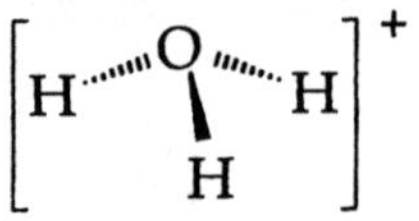

6.65 CH$_4$

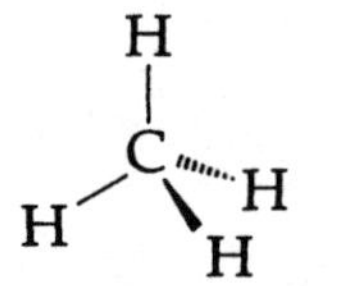

Because the C–H bond is taken to be nonpolar in this course, there are no dipole moments, and the molecule is nonpolar.

CH$_3$Cl

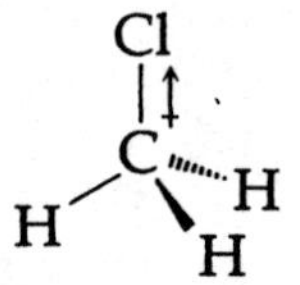

The C–Cl bond is the only polar bond here, making the molecule polar.

CH$_2$Cl$_2$

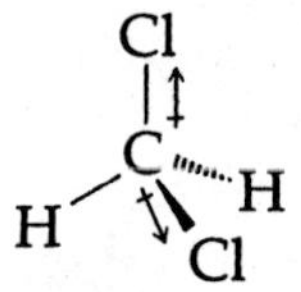

The two C–Cl bonds are polar, and the geometry of the molecule is such that the bond dipole moments do not cancel each other. Therefore the molecule is polar. Do not be misled by the *seeming* symmetry in the drawing. Remember, the molecule in three dimensions is a tetrahedron with the C buried in the interior. No matter which two corners hold the Cl atoms, the two dipole moments do not cancel each other.

CHCl$_3$

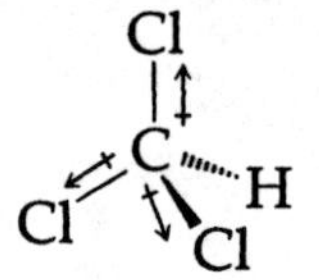

The three C–Cl dipole moments pull electrons to one side of the molecule, making it a polar molecule.

CCl$_4$

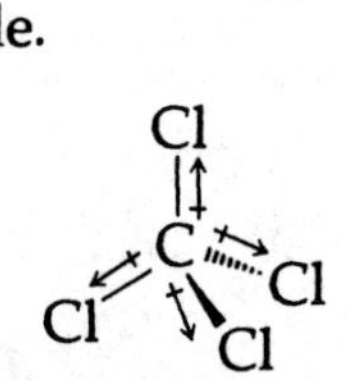

The symmetry in this molecule means all the bond dipole moments cancel, with the result that the molecule is nonpolar.

6.66 Consider each C separately. Left C: four bonding groups, no lone pairs, tetrahedral shape with 109.5° bond angles. Middle C: two bonding groups, no lone electrons, linear shape with 180° bond angles. Right C: same as middle C.

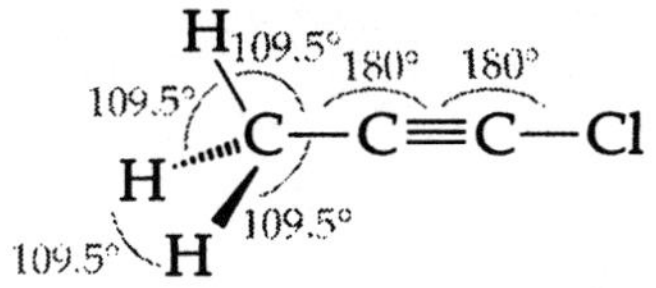

$$
\begin{array}{c}
\text{H}_{109.5°}\;180°\;180° \\
109.5°\;\diagdown\;\text{C}\!-\!\text{C}\!\equiv\!\text{C}\!-\!\text{Cl} \\
\text{H}\quad\diagup\!109.5° \\
109.5°\;\backslash\text{H}
\end{array}
$$

6.67 (a)

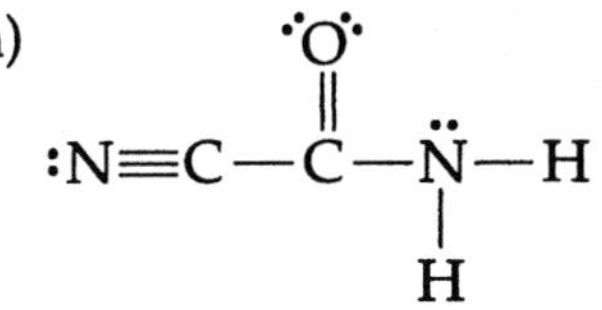

$$
\begin{array}{c}
\cdot\ddot{\text{O}}\cdot \\
\parallel \\
:\text{N}\!\equiv\!\text{C}\!-\!\text{C}\!-\!\ddot{\text{N}}\!-\!\text{H} \\
\mid \\
\text{H}
\end{array}
$$

(b) Consider each interior atom separately. Left C: two bonding groups, no lone pairs, linear shape with 180° bond angles. Middle C: three bonding groups, no lone pairs, trigonal planar shape with 120° bond angles. N: three bonding groups, one lone pair, pyramidal shape with 107° bond angles.

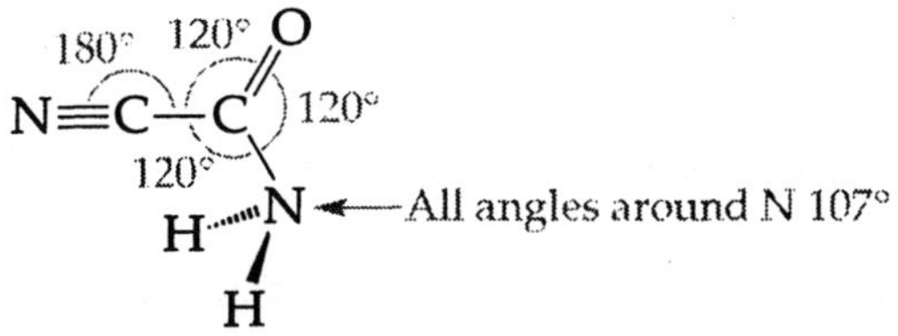

$$
\begin{array}{c}
180°\;\;120°\;\;\text{O} \\
\text{N}\!\equiv\!\text{C}\!-\!\text{C}\;)\,120° \\
120°\quad\diagdown \\
\text{H}^{\cdots\cdots}\text{N}\longleftarrow\text{All angles around N 107°} \\
\diagup \\
\text{H}
\end{array}
$$

6.68 (a)

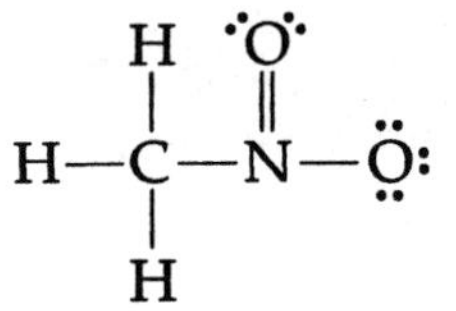

$$
\begin{array}{c}
\text{H}\quad\cdot\ddot{\text{O}}\cdot \\
\mid\qquad\parallel \\
\text{H}\!-\!\text{C}\!-\!\text{N}\!-\!\ddot{\text{O}}: \\
\mid \\
\text{H}
\end{array}
$$

(b) Consider each interior atom separately. C: four bonding groups, no lone pairs, tetrahedral shape with 109.5° bond angles. N: three bonding groups, no lone pairs, trigonal planar shape with 120° bond angles.

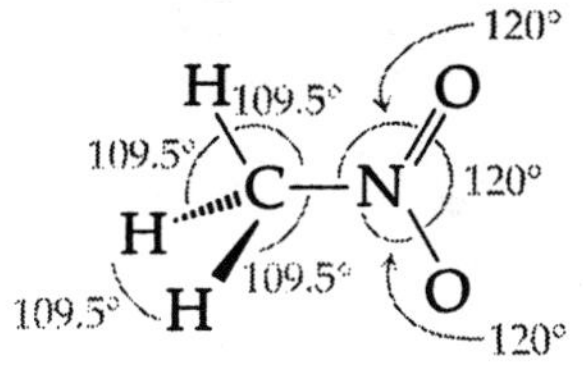

$$
\begin{array}{c}
\qquad\qquad-120° \\
\text{H}_{109.5°}\;)\,\text{O} \\
109.5°\;\diagdown\;\text{C}\!-\!\text{N}\;)\,120° \\
\text{H}\;\diagup\!109.5° \\
109.5°\;\backslash\text{H}\qquad\text{O} \\
\qquad\qquad-120°
\end{array}
$$

6.69

$$[:\text{C}\!\equiv\!\text{N}:]^-$$

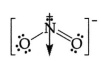

Linear

(a)

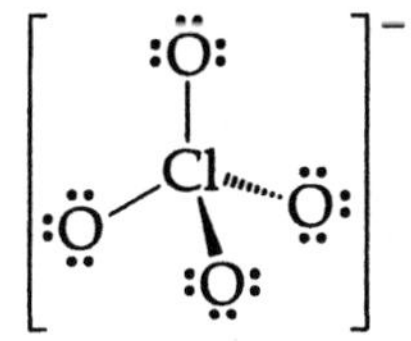

Tetrahedral,
no dipole moment

(b)

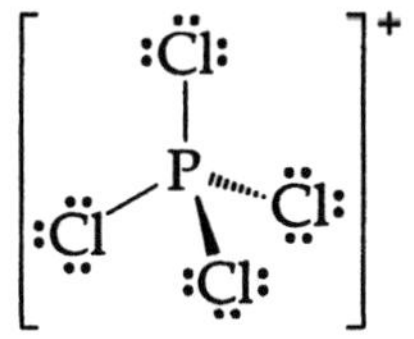

Tetrahedral,
no dipole moment

(c)

Bent, 118° angle

(d)

6.70

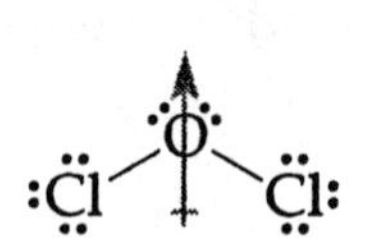

Bent, 105° angle
(a)

Bent, 118° angle
(b)

Pyramidal
(c)

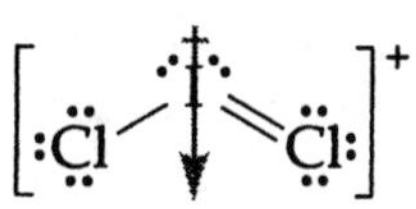

$$\left[\text{:}\ddot{\text{C}}\text{l} \diagup\overset{\cdot\cdot}{\text{I}}\diagdown \text{C}\ddot{\text{l}}\text{:} \right]^{+}$$

Bent, 105° angle
(d)

6.71

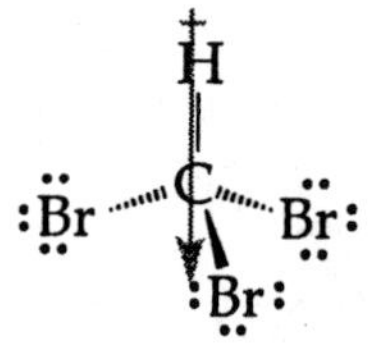

Tetrahedral
(a)

Pyramidal
(b)

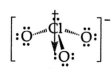

Pyramidal
(c)

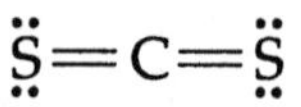

$$\ddot{\text{S}}\text{=}\text{C}\text{=}\ddot{\text{S}}$$

Linear, no dipole moment
(d)

6.72 Dot diagrams:

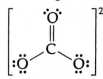

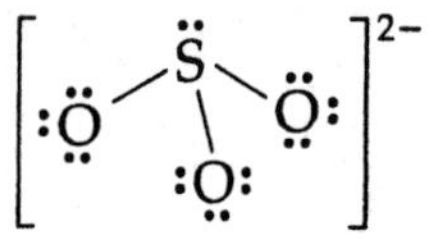

Electron-group geometry: CO_3^{2-} trigonal planar, SO_3^{2-} tetrahedral.
Anion shape: CO_3^{2-} trigonal planar, SO_3^{2-} pyramidal.
Polarity: only SO_3^{2-} is polar, with the $\delta-$ toward the O atoms and the $\delta+$ toward S (because O is more electronegative than S). The CO_3^{2-} is nonpolar because the three C–O bond dipole moments pull toward the three corners of an equilateral triangle and therefore cancel.

6.73 All three are linear molecules, but only CO_2 and CSO have bond dipole moments:

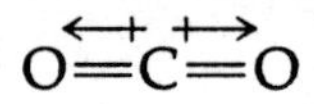

$$O\text{=}C\text{=}O \qquad\qquad S\text{=}C\text{=}S \qquad\qquad S\text{=}C\text{=}O$$

C–O ΔEN = 1.0 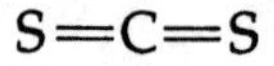   C–S ΔEN = 0
                                no bond dipole moments

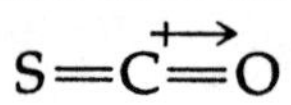

CO_2 is a nonpolar molecule because the two bond dipole moments cancel each other. CS_2 is a nonpolar molecule because there are no bond dipole moments anywhere in the molecule. Only CSO is a polar molecule, because of its one bond dipole moment. The molecular dipole moment is identical to the bond dipole moment.

6.74 The individual bond dipole moments cancel for the nonpolar form. For the polar forms, the individual moments add vectorially to give a molecular dipole moment.

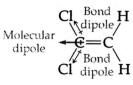

Polar 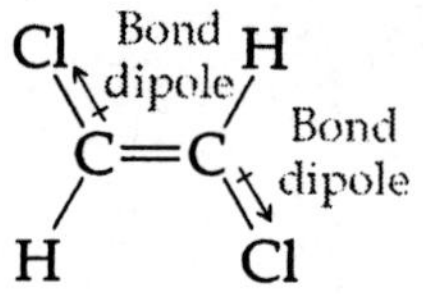   Nonpolar, no   Polar
                       molecular dipole

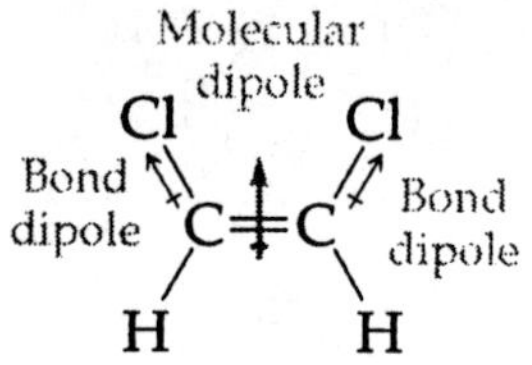

6.75 All three molecules are polar.

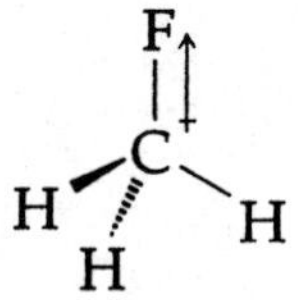

Tetrahdedral, all angles 109.5° 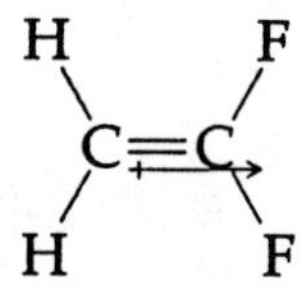   Trigonal planar, all angles 120° 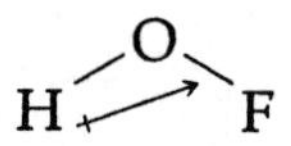   Bent, 105° angle

6.76 (a) Calculate the electronegativity difference for the two bonded atoms. If ΔEN is not zero, the covalent bond is polar.

(b) First determine the shape of the molecule by applying VSEPR theory to a dot diagram. Then use the procedure in part (a) to determine any individual bond dipole moments. If there are any, add the bond dipole moment vectors (do the tug-of-war test). If all the vectors cancel, the molecule is nonpolar. If they do not cancel, the molecule is polar.

6.77 H_2 is nonpolar because $\Delta EN = 0$. CO_2 is nonpolar because the molecule is linear and as a result the individual C–O dipole moments cancel each other. Both CH_3F and CH_3I are polar, but a C–F bond is more polar than a C–I bond. Therefore CH_3F has the largest molecular dipole moment.

6.78 In NCl_3, the N has three bonding groups and one lone pair. This means the electron-group geometry is tetrahedral and the molecular shape is pyramidal. The molecule is nonpolar because nitrogen and chlorine both have an electronegativity of 3.0.

6.79 The student did not consider the three-dimensional shape of the molecule. The four electron groups have a tetrahedral arrangement, not the two-dimensional orientation shown in the dot diagram. Because there are two bonding groups and two lone pairs, the molecule has a tetrahedral electron-group geometry and a bent shape, no matter how it is drawn on paper.

6.80 *Intermolecular* forces are attractions *between* molecules, such as dipole–dipole forces. *Intra*molecular forces are ionic or covalent bonds *within* a molecule and are much stronger than intermolecular forces.

6.81 In S_2F_2, two bonding groups and two lone pairs around each S means a bent shape with 105° bond angles. In N_2F_2, two bonding groups and one lone pair around each N means a bent shape with 118° bond angles.

6.82 The three-dimensional shape of the molecule.

6.83 The bonding is

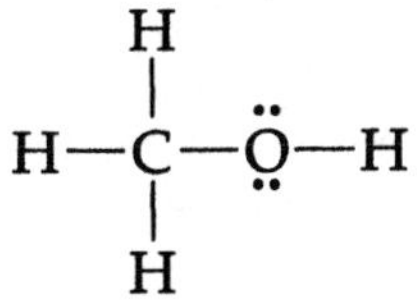

Four bonding groups around C means tetrahedral shape with 109.5° angles. Two bonding groups and two lone pairs around O means bent shape with a 105° angle:

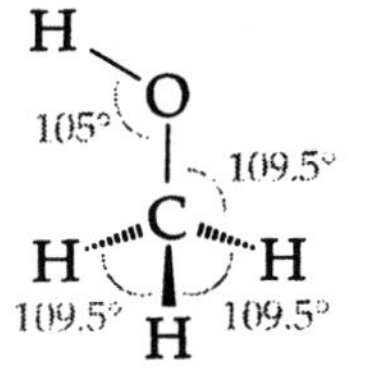

The molecule is polar because O is more electronegative than either H or C:

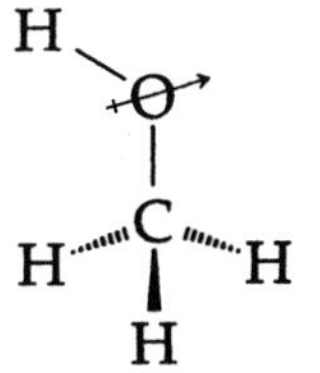

6.84 (a) $\ddot{\text{O}}{=}\dot{\text{N}}{-}\ddot{\text{O}}{-}\ddot{\text{O}}{-}\text{H}$

(b) Consider each interior atom separately. N: two bonding groups, one lone pair, bent shape with 118° angle. First O: two bonding groups, two lone pairs, bent shape with 105° angle. Second O, same as first O.

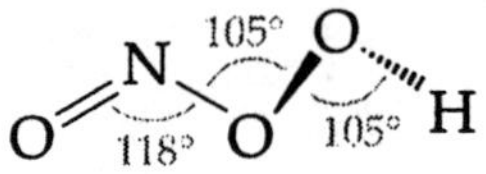

(c) Table 6.2 of the textbook tells you that the electron-group geometry around N is trigonal planar and the shape is bent. Around each O, the electron-group geometry is tetrahedral and the shape is bent.

6.85 The electron-group geometry around an atom A in a molecule tells you the spatial arrangement of all the atoms bonded to A and any lone pairs associated with A. The molecular shape around A tells you the spatial arrangement of only the atoms bonded to A. When determining molecular shape, you use all the bonding groups shown in the electron-group geometry but none of the lone pairs.

6.86 (a)

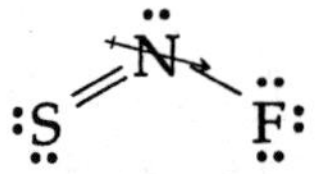

Two bonding groups, one lone pair around N means trigonal planar geometry and bent shape with 118° angle. The electronegativity differences, 1.0 for N–F and 0.5 for S–N, give a molecular dipole moment with $\delta-$ toward F.

(b) $\left[:\text{N}{\equiv}\text{C}{-}\ddot{\text{O}}:\right]^{-}$

Two bonding groups and no lone pairs around C means both electron-group geometry and molecular shape are linear. The electronegativity differences, 0.5 for N–C and 1.0 for C–O, give a molecular dipole moment with $\delta-$ toward O.

(c)

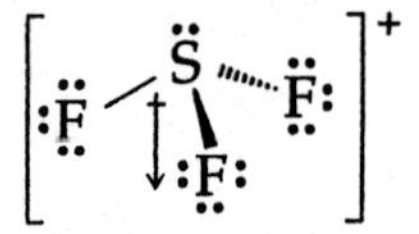

Three bonding groups and one lone pair around S means tetrahedral electron-group geometry and pyramidal molecular shape. The 1.5 S–F electronegativity difference gives a molecular dipole moment with $\delta-$ toward the F atoms.

(d) $\ddot{\text{O}}{=}\text{Si}{=}\ddot{\text{O}}$

Two bonding groups and no lone pairs around Si means both electron-group geometry and molecular shape are linear. There is an electronegativity difference between Si and O, but the symmetry of the molecule means the two bond dipole moments cancel, giving a molecular dipole moment of zero.

6.87 If it had a trigonal planar shape, the NH_3 molecule would have no molecular dipole moment, and as a result there would be no dipole–dipole forces between molecules. With the correct pyramidal shape, NH_3 does have a molecular dipole moment, and consequently there are strong dipole–dipole forces between molecules.

6.88 Whenever there are no lone pairs on the central atom.

6.89 The dot diagram,

$$\left[\ddot{\text{N}}{=}\text{N}{=}\ddot{\text{N}}\right]^{-}$$

shows two bonding groups and no lone pairs around the central atom, meaning the molecular shape is linear and the bond angle is 180°.

6.90 H_2O. All three molecules are bent:

| Two bonding groups, one lone pair | Two bonding groups, two lone pairs | Two bonding groups, two lone pairs |

and therefore any bond dipole moments can lead to a molecular dipole moment. There are no bond dipole moments in O_3 because $\Delta EN = 0$ for both bonds. Because ΔEN for O–H is greater than ΔEN for O–F, H_2O has the larger molecular dipole moment.

6.91 Oxygen, nitrogen, and fluorine are electron "hogs," meaning they have a high electronegativity. This makes the O–H, N–H, and F–H bonds very polar, with the result that molecules containing these bonds have large molecular dipole moments and relatively strong intermolecular forces.

6.92 Dot diagram: $H—\ddot{O}—\ddot{O}—\ddot{O}—H$

Each O has two bonding groups and two lone pairs, meaning the shape is bent around each O with 105° bond angles:

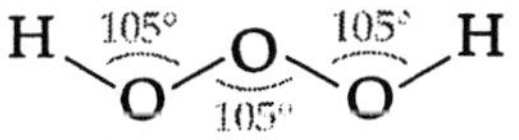

6.93 (a) $:N≡C—C≡N:$

Linear electron-group geometry and linear molecular shape around each C. The two N–C bond dipole moments cancel so that there is no molecular dipole moment.

(b)

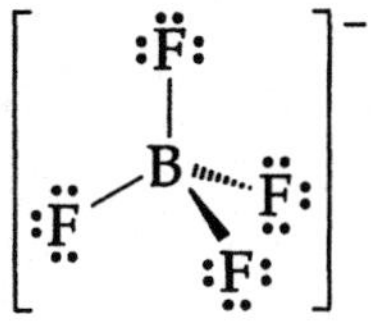

Tetrahedral electron-group geometry and tetrahedral molecular shape around B. The four B–F bond dipole moments cancel so that there is no molecular dipole moment.

(c)

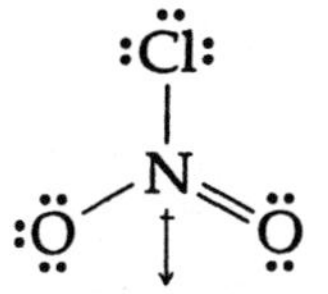

Trigonal planar electron-group geometry and trigonal planar molecular shape around N. Because Cl and N have the same electronegativity value, there is no Cl–N bond dipole moment. Because O is more electronegative than N, each N–O bond has a dipole moment, and these two moments add vectorially to give the molecular dipole moment shown.

(d)

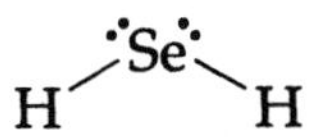

Tetrahedral electron-group geometry and bent molecular shape around Se. The Se–H electrognegativity difference is 0.3, a bit smaller than the C–H difference of 0.4. Therefore because we consider the C–H bond to be nonpolar, we can assume the same about the Se–H bond. Therefore there are no bond dipole moments and no molecular dipole moment.

6.94 For clarity, label the atoms P1, P2, P3, P4. Following the hint, you should have, after assigning the 20 electrons,

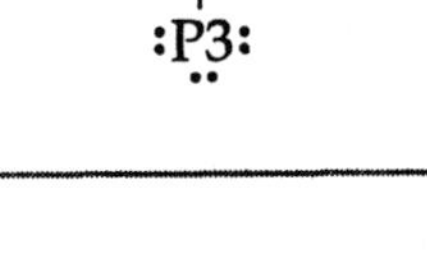

$:\ddot{P}2—P1—P4:$
     $|$
   $:P3:$

Now use one pair of P2 electrons to form the P2–P3 bond and one pair of P3 electrons to form the P3–P4 bond:

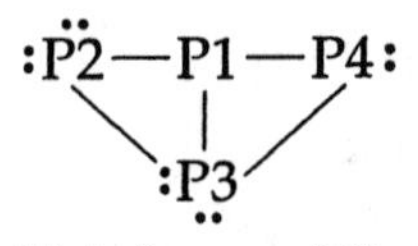

$:\overset{\cdot\cdot}{P}2\!-\!P1\!-\!P4:$
$\diagdown\;\;\vert\;\;\diagup$
$:P3$
$\overset{\cdot\cdot}{}$

This leaves P3 with two electrons too many, a problem you can fix by moving two P3 electrons to P1 (remember, in a dot diagram you can assign the electron pairs anywhere to satisfy the octet rule):

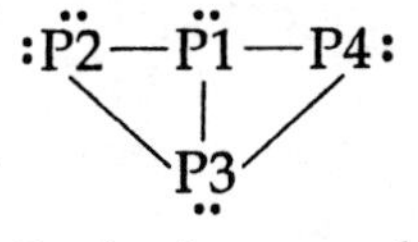

$:\overset{\cdot\cdot}{P}2\!-\!\overset{\cdot\cdot}{P}1\!-\!P4:$
$\diagdown\;\;\vert\;\;\diagup$
$P3$
$\overset{\cdot\cdot}{}$

So far in your drawing, P1 is connected to all three other atoms, and P3 is, too. To make the same true for P2 and P4, and to complete the P4 octet, use either P2 pair to form the P2–P4 bond:

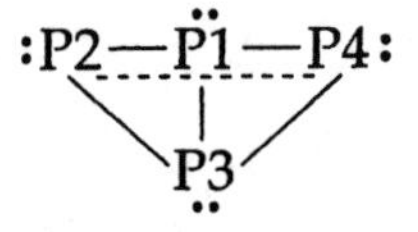

$:P2\text{---}\overset{\cdot\cdot}{P}1\text{---}P4:$
$\diagdown\;\;\vert\;\;\diagup$
$P3$
$\overset{\cdot\cdot}{}$

Each P has three bonding groups and one lone pair, making the shape pyramidal around each P:

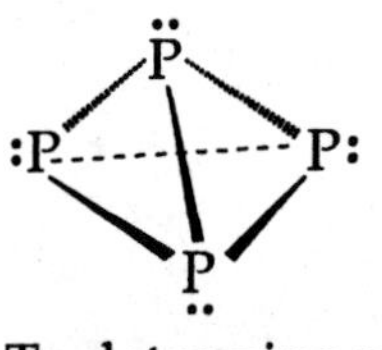

To determine angles, you need to remember from high school that in any equilateral triangle, all three angles are 60°. Your final drawing shows that, even though the shape is pyramidal about each P, the overall shape is a tetrahedron. Because a tetrahedron is defined as comprising four equilateral triangles, all the bond angles in P_4 are 60°. (Such tight angles make P_4 extremely unstable.)

6.95 The dot diagrams,

$$H\!-\!B\!-\!H \qquad H\!-\!\overset{\cdot\cdot}{P}\!-\!H$$
$$\vert \qquad\qquad\quad \vert$$
$$H \qquad\qquad\quad H$$

tell you the electron-group geometry is trigonal planar in BH_3 but tetrahedral in PH_3. The molecular shapes are different, too: trigonal planar in BH_3 and pyramidal in PH_3. BH_3 is nonpolar because the B–H bond ($\Delta EN = 0.1$) is essentially nonpolar.

CHAPTER
7

Chemical Reactions

7.1 See solution in textbook.

7.2 (1) Only O is unbalanced; balance O by putting a 2 in front of H_2O:
$CaH_2 + 2\,H_2O \longrightarrow Ca(OH)_2 + H_2$.
(2) What you did just unbalanced H; rebalance by putting a 2 in front of H_2:
$CaH_2 + 2\,H_2O \longrightarrow Ca(OH)_2 + 2\,H_2$.
(3) The equation is balanced. Verify by counting atoms: one Ca on each side, six H on each side, two O on each side.

7.3 (1) Balance C by putting a 6 in front of CO_2: $C_6H_{12}O_6 + O_2 \longrightarrow 6\,CO_2 + H_2O$.
(2) Balance H by putting a 6 in front of H_2O: $C_6H_{12}O_6 + O_2 \longrightarrow 6\,CO_2 + 6\,H_2O$.
(3) Balance O by putting a 6 in front of O_2: $C_6H_{12}O_6 + 6\,O_2 \longrightarrow 6\,CO_2 + 6\,H_2O$.
(4) The equation is balanced. Verify by counting atoms: six C on each side, 12 H on each side, 18 O on each side.

7.4 (1) Balance H by putting a 2 in front of HCl: $2\,HCl + Na_2CO_3 \longrightarrow NaCl + CO_2 + H_2O$
(2) Balance Cl by putting a 2 in front of NaCl: $2\,HCl + Na_2CO_3 \longrightarrow 2\,NaCl + CO_2 + H_2O$
(3) The equation is balanced. Verify by counting atoms: two H on each side, two Cl on each side, two Na on each side, one C on each side, three O on each side.

7.5 See solution in textbook.

7.6 (1) Only O is unbalanced, with two O left and five O right. Because O on the left appears with no other atoms, you can easily balance O without unbalancing any other atoms. Do so by writing 2.5 O_2, so that the left side has $2.5 \times 2 = 5$ O: $C_6H_{12}(l) + 2.5\,O_2(g) \longrightarrow H_2C_6H_8O_4(l) + H_2O(l)$.
(2) The equation is balanced, but you should multiply through by 2 to get all whole-number coefficients: $2\,C_6H_{12}(l) + 5\,O_2(g) \longrightarrow 2\,H_2C_6H_8O_4(l) + 2\,H_2O(l)$.
(3) Verify by counting atoms: 12 C on each side, 24 H on each side, 10 O on each side.

7.7 (1) You have five H left and two H right, which you can balance by putting a 2 in front of CH_3NH_2 and a 5 in front of H_2O. This step also balances N: $2\,CH_3NH_2 + O_2 \longrightarrow CO_2 + 5\,H_2O + N_2$.
(2) What you just did unbalanced C, which you can fix by putting a 2 in front of CO_2:
$2\,CH_3NH_2 + O_2 \longrightarrow 2\,CO_2 + 5\,H_2O + N_2$.

(3) You now have everything balanced except O—two left, nine right. Balance by putting a 4.5 in front of O_2 to get $4.5 \times 2 = 9$ O left: $2\,CH_3NH_2 + 4.5\,O_2 \longrightarrow 2\,CO_2 + 5\,H_2O + N_2$.

(4) The equation is balanced, but you should multiply through by 2 to get all whole-number coefficients: $4\,CH_3NH_2 + 9\,O_2 \longrightarrow 4\,CO_2 + 10\,H_2O + 2\,N_2$.

(5) Verify by counting atoms: four C on each side, 20 H on each side, four N on each side, 18 O on each side.

7.8 See solution in textbook.

7.9 $2\,Pb(NO_3)_2(s) \xrightarrow{\text{Heat}} 2\,PbO(s) + 4\,NO(g) + 3\,O_2(g)$; decomposition.

7.10 $C_2H_4 + C_2Cl_4 \xrightarrow{\text{Catalyst}} 2\,C_2H_2Cl_2$; combination.

7.11 See solution in textbook.

7.12 (a) In order to know what the spectator ions are, you must write the complete ionic equation.

Step 1: Identify the ions present initially: Pb^{2+}, NO_3^-, Na^+, SO_4^{2-}.

Step 2: Identify all possible new combinations: Pb^{2+} with SO_4^{2-}, Na^+ with NO_3^-.

Step 3: Determine whether any insoluble salts form. $PbSO_4$ is insoluble in water; all sodium salts are water-soluble. Therefore Na^+ and NO_3^- remain in solution. The complete ionic equation is

$$Pb^{2+}(aq) + 2\,NO_3^-(aq) + 2\,Na^+(aq) + SO_4^{2-}(aq) \longrightarrow$$
$$PbSO_4(s) + 2\,NO_3^-(aq) + 2\,Na^+(aq)$$

The spectator ions are Na^+ and NO_3^-.

(b) $Pb^{2+}(aq) + SO_4^{2-}(aq) \longrightarrow PbSO_4(s)$

7.13 (a) In order to know what the spectator ions are, you must write the complete ionic equation.

Step 1: Identify the ions present initially: Ni^{2+}, NO_3^-, NH_4^+, PO_4^{3-}.

Step 2: Identify all possible new combinations: Ni^{2+} with PO_4^{3-}, NH_4^+ with NO_3^-.

Step 3: Determine whether any insoluble salts form. Table 7.1 of the textbook shows that $Ni_3(PO_4)_2$ is not soluble in water; all ammonium salts are soluble. Therefore NH_4^+ and NO_3^- remain in solution. The complete ionic equation is

$$3\,Ni^{2+}(aq) + 6\,NO_3^-(aq) + 6\,NH_4^+(aq) + 2\,PO_4^{3-}(aq) \longrightarrow$$
$$Ni_3(PO_4)_2(s) + 6\,NO_3^-(aq) + 6\,NH_4^+(aq)$$

The spectator ions are NO_3^- and NH_4^+.

(b) $3\,Ni^{2+}(aq) + 2\,PO_4^{3-}(aq) \longrightarrow Ni_3(PO_4)_2(s)$

7.14 See solution in textbook.

7.15 It is true because neutralization requires one OH^- for every one H^+. Because 1 mole of HCl yields 1 mole of H^+, 1 mole of NaOH is sufficient for neutralization. Because 1 mole of H_2SO_4 yields 2 moles of H^+, 2 moles of NaOH are needed for neutralization.

7.16 Intact-molecule equation:

$$2\,HF(aq) + Ca(OH)_2(aq) \longrightarrow CaF_2(s) + 2\,H_2O(l)$$

To get the net ionic equation, you need to see the complete ionic equation:

$$2\,H^+(aq) + 2\,F^-(aq) + Ca^{2+}(aq) + 2\,OH^-(aq) \longrightarrow CaF_2(s) + 2\,H_2O(l)$$

Because there are no spectator ions, the net ionic equation is identical to the complete ionic equation. The salt formed is calcium fluoride.

7.17 Equation (a) represents a chemical reaction because new substances are produced. Equation (b) does not represent a chemical reaction because no new substances are produced; the products are the same substances as the reactants, but in different form.

7.18 You would have to demonstrate that at least one new substance was produced by the reaction.

7.19 The properties of a heterogeneous mixture of the reactants could be compared with those of the product. If electricity did not pass through the reactant mixture with zero resistance and/or if a magnet did not hover above the reactant mixture cooled to 90K, that would be evidence that reactant and product are different substances.

7.20 Under no circumstances; it *always* takes energy to break a chemical bond.

7.21 Two Cl–Cl bonds and two C–H bonds (one from each carbon) must be broken. Two H–Cl bonds and two C–Cl bonds (one to each carbon) are formed.

7.22 From collisions between the fast-moving gas molecules.

7.23 Cooling the reaction mixture slows down the molecules. When they are slowed down enough, the collisions will not have enough energy to break bonds in the reactants.

7.24 When a chemical reaction occurs, some of the bonds in the reactant molecules are broken, and new bonds are formed. Therefore the structures of the reactant molecules have been changed, resulting in the new compounds that are the products.

7.25 Increasing the number of reactant molecules means more chances for collisions between molecules in a given time period. More collisions mean more chances for reactant bonds to break, which means more reactant molecules can be converted to product molecules in the given time period. In other words, the reaction goes faster.

7.26 Because matter is neither created nor destroyed during a chemical reaction. The numbers of each kind of atom must be equal on the two sides of the equation to indicate that the amount of matter present after the reaction is the same as the amount present before the reaction.

7.27 Changing subscripts changes the chemical identity of a substance, which means the (altered) reactants shown in the equation do not represent the reaction.

7.28 Balancing first C by writing $2 CO_2$, then H by writing $2 H_2O$, then O by writing $3 O_2$ gives you the balanced equation $C_2H_4 + 3 O_2 \longrightarrow 2 CO_2 + 2 H_2O$.

7.29 Either "1 mole of methane and 2 moles of oxygen react to give 1 mole of carbon dioxide and 2 moles of water" or "1 molecule of methane and 2 molecules of oxygen react to give 1 molecule of carbon dioxide and 2 molecules of water."

7.30 (1) Because Fe and C appear as single atoms, leave them for last and begin with O. To balance the three O left, you can get $1.5 \times 2 = 3$ O right by writing $1.5 CO_2$:
$Fe_2O_3 + C \longrightarrow Fe + 1.5 CO_2$.
(2) Balance Fe by writing 2 Fe: $Fe_2O_3 + C \longrightarrow 2 Fe + 1.5 CO_2$.
(3) Balance C by writing 1.5 C: $Fe_2O_3 + 1.5 C \longrightarrow 2 Fe + 1.5 CO_2$.
(4) Multiply through by 2 to get the balanced equation $2 Fe_2O_3 + 3 C \longrightarrow 4 Fe + 3 CO_2$.

7.31 If you balance in the order Al, Cl, H, the O is automatically balanced to give $Al_2Cl_6 + 6 H_2O \longrightarrow 2 Al(OH)_3 + 6 HCl$.

7.32 The only atom that needs balancing is O. A coefficient of 1.5 in front of O_2 gives you three O left and $1.5 \times 2 = 3$ O right: $KClO_3 \longrightarrow KCl + 1.5 O_2$ or, multiplying by 2 to obtain whole-number coefficients, $2 KClO_3 \longrightarrow 2 KCl + 3 O_2$.

7.33 H is balanced. Balancing C by putting a 2 in front of CO_2 gives you two O left and five O right, which you balance by giving O_2 a coefficient of 2.5: $C_2H_2 + 2.5 O_2 \longrightarrow H_2O + 2 CO_2$. Multiplying through by 2 to obtain whole-number coefficients gives $2 C_2H_2 + 5 O_2 \longrightarrow 2 H_2O + 4 CO_2$.

7.34 Either "2 moles of acetylene and 5 moles of oxygen react to give 2 moles of water and 4 moles of carbon dioxide" or "2 molecules of acetylene and 5 molecules of oxygen react to give 2 molecules of water and 4 molecules of carbon dioxide."

7.35 Two approaches possible. (1) Writing $2 NO_2$ to balance N gives five O left, six O right. Balance O by writing $0.5 O_2$ to remove one O from right, then multiply through by 2 to get whole-number coefficients. (2) Writing $2 NO_2$ to balance N gives five O left, six O right. To balance, you need more O left, and the only way to get more is to write $2 N_2O_5$. Then rebalance N by writing $4 NO_2$, a step that also balances O. Either way, the balanced equation is $2 N_2O_5(g) \longrightarrow 4 NO_2(g) + O_2(g)$; decomposition.

7.36 C and O are balanced. Balance N by writing $0.5 N_2$ to get $0.5 \times 2 = 1$ N right, then multiply through by 2 to get $2 CO(g) + 2 NO(g) \longrightarrow 2 CO_2(g) + N_2(g)$; single replacement (O in NO replaced by N to form N_2).

7.37 If you balance first Fe by writing 2 $Fe(NO_3)_3$, then N by writing 6 $NaNO_3$, then Na by writing 3 Na_2S, S and O are automatically balanced: 2 $Fe(NO_3)_3(aq)$ + 3 $Na_2S(aq)$ ⟶ $Fe_2S_3(s)$ + 6 $NaNO_3(aq)$. This is both a double-replacement reaction and a precipitation reaction.

7.38 S is inititally balanced. To balance O, remove one O from left by writing 0.5 O_2. Then multiply through by 2: 2 $SO_2(g)$ + $O_2(g)$ ⟶ 2 $SO_3(g)$; combination.

7.39 Two approaches possible. (1) First balance Li by writing 3 Li, then balance N by writing 0.5 N_2, then multiply through by 2. (2) First balance N by writing 2 Li_3N, then balance Li by writing 6 Li. Either way, you get the balanced equation: 6 $Li(s)$ + $N_2(g)$ ⟶ 2 $Li_3N(s)$; combination.

7.40 Balance C by writing 5 CO_2, then balance H by writing 5 H_2O. Doing so gives four O left, 15 O right. You need to do something that either changes the left side to have an odd number of O or changes the right side to have an even number of O. Because changing O number on the right also changes either C or H, keep things simple by working with O_2. You need 15 O left, meaning 13 O in addition to the two O in $C_5H_{10}O_2$. Get 13 O by writing $^{13}\!/_2$ O_2 = 6.5 O_2, and the equation is balanced: $C_5H_{10}O_2(l)$ + 6.5 $O_2(g)$ ⟶ 5 $CO_2(g)$ + 5 $H_2O(g)$. As usual, multiply through by 2 to get whole-number coefficients.

7.41 2 $H_2O_2(l)$ ⟶ 2 $H_2O(l)$ + $O_2(g)$; decomposition.

7.42 A combination reaction brings two or more substances together to form a new substance: A + B ⟶ AB. A decomosition reaction breaks one substance up into two or more new substances: AB ⟶ A + B. For example, 2 $H_2O_2(l)$ ⟶ 2 $H_2O(l)$ + $O_2(g)$ is a decomposition reaction, and 2 $H_2O(l)$ + $O_2(g)$ ⟶ 2 $H_2O_2(l)$ is a combination reaction.

7.43

Name	Formula	Soluble or insoluble in water?
Sodium phosphate	Na_3PO_4	Soluble
Barium acetate	$Ba(CH_3CO_2)_2$	Soluble
Ammonium sulfide	$(NH_4)_2S$	Soluble
Iron(II) carbonate	$FeCO_3$	Insoluble
Mercury(II) chloride	$HgCl_2$	Soluble
Cobalt(II) hydroxide	$Co(OH)_2$	Insoluble
Mercury(I) chloride	$HgCl$	Insoluble

7.44 $CH_3OH(l)$  $Na_3PO_4(s)$

Methanol, a molecular compound, dissolves but does not dissociate into ions. Sodium phosphate, an ionic compound, dissolves and completely dissociates into ions.

7.45 $Ca^{2+}(aq)$ + $B_4O_7^{2-}(aq)$ ⟶ $CaB_4O_7(s)$
$Mg^{2+}(aq)$ + $B_4O_7^{2-}(aq)$ ⟶ $MgB_4O_7(s)$
$Na^+(aq)$ ions replace the $Ca^{2+}(aq)$ and $Mg^{2+}(aq)$ ions in the hard water.

7.46 $Pb^{2+}(aq)$ + 2 $Cl^-(aq)$ ⟶ $PbCl_2(s)$ (lead(II) chloride not water-soluble)
$Ba^{2+}(aq)$ + $SO_4^{2-}(aq)$ ⟶ $BaSO_4(s)$ (barium sulfate not water-soluble)
Nothing precipitates because all Na^+ salts and all K^+ salts are water-soluble.

7.47 $Bi^{3+}(aq)$ + 3 $OH^-(aq)$ ⟶ $Bi(OH)_3(s)$
$Sr^{2+}(aq)$ + $SO_4^{2-}(aq)$ ⟶ $SrSO_4(s)$
3 $Cu^{2+}(aq)$ + 2 $PO_4^{3-}(aq)$ ⟶ $Cu_3(PO_4)_2(s)$

7.48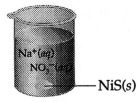
$$Ni^{2+}(aq) + S^{2-}(aq) \longrightarrow NiS(s)$$

$Na^+(aq)$
$NO_3^-(aq)$

—— $NiS(s)$

7.49 Iron(III) hydroxide and barium sulfate precipitate:
Balanced equation: $Fe_2(SO_4)_3(aq) + 3\,Ba(OH)_2(aq) \longrightarrow 2\,Fe(OH)_3(s) + 3\,BaSO_4(s)$
Complete ionic equation: $2\,Fe^{3+}(aq) + 3\,SO_4^{2-}(aq) + 3\,Ba^{2+}(aq) + 6\,OH^-(aq) \longrightarrow$
$$2\,Fe(OH)_3(s) + 3\,BaSO_4(s)$$
Because there are no spectator ions, the net ionic equation is identical to the complete ionic equation.

7.50 Calcium carbonate precipitates:
Balanced equation: $CaCl_2(aq) + K_2CO_3(aq) \longrightarrow CaCO_3(s) + 2\,KCl(aq)$
Complete ionic equation: $Ca^{2+}(aq) + 2\,Cl^-(aq) + 2\,K^+(aq) + CO_3^{2-}(aq) \longrightarrow$
$$CaCO_3(s) + 2\,K^+(aq) + 2\,Cl^-(aq)$$
Net ionic equation: $Ca^{2+}(aq) + CO_3^{2-}(aq) \longrightarrow CaCO_3(s)$

7.51 Numerous answers possible. You could mix an aqueous solution of calcium nitrate, $Ca(NO_3)_2$, with an aqueous solution of sodium sulfate, Na_2SO_4, and $CaSO_4(s)$ would precipitate. You could then filter the solution to isolate the $CaSO_4(s)$.

7.52 Table 7.1 of the textbook tells you all hydroxide salts except NaOH, KOH, $Ca(OH)_2$, and $Ba(OH)_2$ are insoluble in water. Mix an aqueous solution of any one of these with an aqueous solution of any water-soluble Ni^{2+} salt, such as $NiCl_2$ or $Ni(NO_3)_2$, and then filter off the $Ni(OH)_2(s)$ that forms.

7.53 The cloudiness means a precipitation reaction has taken place. According to Table 7.1 of the textbook, all nitrate salts are water-soluble, meaning the precipitate must be a silver salt. From Table 7.1 you see that the possibilities are AgCl, AgBr, AgI, Ag_3PO_4, Ag_2CO_3, Ag_2S, or AgOH.

7.54 (a) $Ca^{2+}(aq) + SO_4^{2-}(aq) \longrightarrow CaSO_4(s)$
(b) $Ca(NO_3)_2(aq) + (NH_4)_2SO_4(aq) \longrightarrow CaSO_4(s) + 2\,NH_4NO_3(aq)$

7.55 (a) $H_2S(aq) + 2\,Na^+(aq) + 2\,OH^-(aq) \longrightarrow 2\,Na^+(aq) + S^{2-}(aq) + 2\,H_2O(l)$
(b) Sodium sulfide, $Na_2S(s)$.

7.56 (a) $H_2S(aq) \longrightarrow 2\,H^+(aq) + S^{2-}(aq)$
(b) Any compound that dissociates in water to produce $H^+(aq)$ ions is an acid, meaning that $H_2S(aq)$ is an acid.
(c) $Cu^{2+}(aq) + S^{2-}(aq) \longrightarrow CuS(s)$

7.57 Combine an aqueous solution of the oxalic acid with an aqueous solution of sodium hydroxide,
$$H_2C_2O_4(aq) + 2\,NaOH(aq) \longrightarrow Na_2C_2O_4(aq) + 2\,H_2O(l)$$
and then evaporate off the $H_2O(l)$ to leave behind $Na_2C_2O_4(s)$.

7.58 $H_2SO_4(aq) + Ca(OH)_2(aq) \longrightarrow CaSO_4(s) + 2\,H_2O(l)$; the salt is calcium sulfate.

7.59 (a) Lead(II) sulfate.
(b) $Pb^{2+}(aq) + SO_4^{2-}(aq) \longrightarrow PbSO_4(s)$.
(c) No, because $Pb(NO_3)_2$ is not a base. After the precipitation reaction, there is still $H^+(aq)$ in solution, making the solution acidic.

7.60 $NH_4^+(aq) \longrightarrow NH_3(aq) + H^+(aq)$

7.61 (a) $Ca(OH)_2(aq) + 2\,HNO_3(aq) \longrightarrow Ca(NO_3)_2(aq) + 2\,H_2O(l)$.
(b) $H^+(aq) + OH^-(aq) \longrightarrow H_2O(l)$

7.62 (a) $H^+(aq) + Br^-(aq) + Na^+(aq) + OH^-(aq) \longrightarrow Br^-(aq) + Na^+(aq) + H_2O(l)$;
$H^+(aq) + OH^-(aq) \longrightarrow H_2O(l)$; sodium bromide, NaBr.

(b) $Ca^{2+}(aq) + 2\,OH^-(aq) + 2\,H^+(aq) + 2\,NO_3^-(aq) \longrightarrow Ca^{2+}(aq) + 2\,NO_3^-(aq) + 2\,H_2O(l)$;
$OH^-(aq) + H^+(aq) \longrightarrow H_2O(l)$; calcium nitrate, $Ca(NO_3)_2$.

(c) $Ca^{2+}(aq) + 2\,OH^-(aq) + 2\,H^+(aq) + 2\,Br^-(aq) \longrightarrow Ca^{2+}(aq) + 2\,Br^-(aq) + 2\,H_2O(l)$;
$OH^-(aq) + H^+(aq) \longrightarrow H_2O(l)$; calcium bromide, $CaBr_2$.

(d) $Mg(OH)_2(s) + 2\,H^+(aq) + 2\,Cl^-(aq) \longrightarrow Mg^{2+}(aq) + 2\,Cl^-(aq) + 2\,H_2O(l)$;
$Mg(OH)_2(s) + 2\,H^+(aq) \longrightarrow Mg^{2+}(aq) + 2\,H_2O(l)$; magnesium chloride, $MgCl_2$.

7.63 (a) The hydrogen atom written at the right end of the formula, CH_3COOH.

(b) In methyl acetate, all the hydrogen atoms are covalently bonded to carbon. In acetic acid, the acidic hydrogen is bonded to oxygen. Whether or not a hydrogen atom is acidic must have something to do with which element it bonds to in a compound.

7.64 Energy, usually in the form of heat, is always released when bonds form. Formation of ionic bonds in the precipitate is the source of the heat energy.

7.65 In any covalent bond A:B, the electron from A is attracted both to its own nucleus and to nucleus B, and the electron from B is attracted both to its own nucleus and to nucleus A. Thus using H1 and H2 to differentiate the two atoms in H_2, you can say that the added energy is used to pull the H1 electron in the bond away from the H2 nucleus and to pull the H2 electron away from the H1 nucleus.

7.66 The energy is used to pull the oppositely charged ions away from each other—in other words, to overcome the attractive force between oppositely charged ions.

7.67 (a) $SiO_2(s) + 2\,C(s) \longrightarrow Si(s) + 2\,CO(g)$; single replacement (the compound containing O replaces Si with C).

(b) Equation balanced as written; double replacement.

(c) $4\,Al(s) + 3\,O_2(g) \longrightarrow 2\,Al_2O_3(s)$; combination.

(d) $(NH_4)_2Cr_2O_7(s) \longrightarrow N_2(g) + Cr_2O_3(s) + 4\,H_2O(g)$; decomposition.

7.68 (a) Yes, because iron(III) sulfide is not soluble in water.

(b) $2\,Fe^{3+}(aq) + 3\,S^{2-}(aq) \longrightarrow Fe_2S_3(s)$.

7.69 (a) $CaCl_2$ and K_2CO_3.

(b) Yes, because calcium carbonate is insoluble in water.

(c) $Ca^{2+}(aq) + CO_3^{2-}(aq) \longrightarrow CaCO_3(s)$.

7.70 Both solids dissolve in the water. The new combination possibilities when both dissolve are Ca^{2+} with NO_3^- and Na^+ with Cl^-. However, because all sodium salts and all nitrate salts are water-soluble, there is no precipitation.

7.71 Any sodium salt whose anion forms a water-insoluble precipitate with Cu^{2+}: Na_2CO_3, Na_3PO_4, NaOH, or Na_2S.

7.72 (a) Add any water-soluble chloride, bromide, or iodide to precipitate $PbX_2(s)$, where X stands for the halide anion, or add an OH^- compound to precipitate $Pb(OH)_2$. Both BaX_2 and $Ba(OH)_2$ are soluble in water, so that Ba^{2+} stays in solution.

(b) Add any water-soluble sulfate, phosphate, carbonate, or sulfide to precipitate the insoluble Ba^{2+} and Pb^{2+} salts since these two cations form precipitates with any of these four anions.

7.73 (a)

$$\left[\begin{array}{c} :\overset{..}{O} \\ | \\ :\overset{..}{O}\!-\!N\!-\!\overset{..}{O}: \end{array} \right]^-$$

(b)

$$\begin{array}{c} :O: \\ \| \\ H\!-\!\overset{..}{O}\!-\!N\!-\!\overset{..}{O}: \end{array}$$

(c) Nitrate ion, because HNO_3 dissociates in water to form $H^+(aq)$ and $NO_3^-(aq)$.

7.74 $HClO_4(aq) + NaOH(aq) \longrightarrow NaClO_4(aq) + H_2O(l)$; $H^+(aq) + OH^-(aq) \longrightarrow H_2O(l)$; sodium perchlorate, $NaClO_4$.

7.75 First add NaCl(aq), NaBr(aq), or NaI(aq) to precipitate the water-insoluble lead(II) halide, which can be isolated via filtration. Then to the filtered solution, add any sodium salt whose anion forms a water-insoluble compound with $Ba^{2+}(aq)$—Na_2SO_4, Na_3PO_4, Na_2CO_3, or Na_2S.

This will precipitate the insoluble Ba^{2+} salt, which can be isolated by filtration. The solution now contains just $Na^+(aq)$ cations.

7.76 First add an aqueous solution of some ionic compound whose anion forms an insoluble salt with only one of these three cations. Once you work through the possibilities in Table 7.1 of the textbook, you will see that a hydroxide is your only choice. (Any sulfate precipitates Ca^{2+} and Ba^{2+}; any sulfide precipitates Fe^{3+} and Ba^{2+}; any phosphate or carbonate precipitates all three cations.) Therefore add $NaOH(aq)$ or $KOH(aq)$ and filter off the solid $Fe(OH)_3$.

Next add to the filtered solution an aqueous solution of some ionic compound whose anion forms an insoluble salt with either $Ca^+(aq)$ or $Ba^+(aq)$. When you again work through the possibilities in Table 7.1, you'll see that a sulfide, which precipitates $BaS(s)$, is your only choice, and so add either $Na_2S(aq)$ or $K_2S(aq)$.

After you filter off $BaS(s)$, the solution contains $Ca^+(aq)$ and either $Na^+(aq)$ or $K^+(aq)$, depending on which hydroxide and which sulfide you used earlier. Add any sulfate salt to precipitate $CaSO_4(s)$. Your separated species are $Fe(OH)_3(s)$, $BaS(s)$, and $CaSO_4(s)$.

An alternative approach. If you want to avoid adding $Na^+(aq)$ or $K^+(aq)$ to your solution, use either $Ca(OH)_2(aq)$ or $Ba(OH)_2(aq)$ in the first step. Filter off $Fe(OH)_3(s)$, add $CaS(aq)$, and filter off $BaS(s)$. Your separated species are now $Fe(OH)(s)$, $BaS(s)$, and $Ca^{2+}(aq)$.

7.77 Balance first C by writing 7 CO_2, then H by writing 8 H_2O, and last O by writing 11 O_2:
$C_7H_{16}(l) + 11\ O_2(g) \longrightarrow 7\ CO_2(g) + 8\ H_2O(g)$.

7.78 Balance first C by writing 2 CO_2, then H by writing 3 H_2O, and last O by writing 3 O_2:
$C_2H_5OH(l) + 3\ O_2(g) \longrightarrow 2\ CO_2(g) + 3\ H_2O(g)$.

7.79 $2\ NaCl + Br_2 \longrightarrow 2\ NaBr + Cl_2$

7.80 (a) Broken: one $N\equiv N$, three Br–Br.
Formed: six N–Br.
(b) Broken: four P–P, six H–H.
Formed: twelve P–H.
(c) Broken: one K–F, one Na–I.
Formed: one K–I, one Na–F.
(d) Broken: one C–H, one Cl–Cl.
Formed: one C–Cl, one H–Cl.

7.81 Initially, Fe and Cd are balanced, but you have two Cl on the left and three Cl on the right. Being that the subscript on the left Cl is 2, writing 1.5 in front of $CdCl_2$ gives you $2 \times 1.5 = 3$ Cl left (Cl is now balanced), but you've unbalanced Cd. Rebalance by writing 1.5 in front of Cd: $Fe + 1.5\ CdCl_2 \longrightarrow FeCl_3 + 1.5\ Cd$. Then multiply through by 2 to get $2\ Fe + 3\ CdCl_2 \longrightarrow 2\ FeCl_3 + 3\ Cd$; single replacement.

7.82 K_2S, $Mg(NO_3)_2$, and $(NH_4)_3PO_4$ are soluble; $BaCO_3$ and $CaSO_4$ are insoluble.

7.83 The reaction should go faster because the reactants are moving faster at the higher temperature, resulting in more collisions having enough energy to cause the reactant bonds to break.

7.84 (a)

Broken: one C–H, one I–I. Formed: one C–I, one H–I.

(b)

Broken: one of the bonds in C=C, one F–F. Formed: two C–F.

7.85 (b) and (c) represent chemical reactions because new substances are formed. In (a) and (d), no new substances are formed.

7.86 $Sn + 2\,HF \longrightarrow H_2 + SnF_2$

7.87 An acid is an H^+ donor; a base is an OH^- donor. Thus if a compound contains neither H nor OH, you know the compound is a salt.

(a) KCl salt, no H or OH.

(b) CH_3COOH acid, but note that only H bonded to O is acidic. The three H bonded to C are not acidic.

(c) $Al(OH)_3$ base because of OH.

(d) H_3BO_3 acid because of the three H.

(e) $LiC_2H_3O_2$ salt, because all three H are attached to one of the C and are therefore not acidic. The structure is

$$
\begin{array}{c}
\quad\;\; H \\
\quad\;\; | \\
H - C - C - OLi \\
\quad\;\; | \quad\; \| \\
\quad\;\; H \quad\; O
\end{array}
$$

7.88 Balance first C by writing 5 CO_2, then H by writing 6 H_2O, and last O by writing 8 O_2:
$C_5H_{12} + 8\,O_2 \longrightarrow 5\,CO_2 + 6\,H_2O$

7.89 Calcium is balanced. Balance first N by writing 2 HNO_3, then H by writing 2 H_2O. Doing so also balances O: $2\,HNO_3 + Ca(OH)_2 \longrightarrow Ca(NO_3)_2 + 2\,H_2O$

Complete ionic: $2\,H^+ + 2\,NO_3^- + Ca^{2+} + 2\,OH^- \longrightarrow Ca^{2+} + 2\,NO_3^- + 2\,H_2O$

Net ionic: $H^+ + OH^- \longrightarrow H_2O$

7.90 Translating the words into chemical symbols gives $P + O_2 \longrightarrow P_2O_5$. Balance P by writing 2 P, balance O by writing 2.5 O_2, then multiply through by 2 to get whole-number coefficients: $4\,P + 5\,O_2 \longrightarrow 2\,P_2O_5$

7.91 (a) $Al(OH)_3$ (b) $Ca_3(PO_4)_2$ (c) $MgCO_3$

7.92 Translating the words into chemical symbols gives $Fe + O_2 \longrightarrow Fe_2O_3$. Balance Fe by writing 2 Fe, balance O by writing 1.5 O_2, then multiply through by 2 to get whole-number coefficients: $4\,Fe + 3\,O_2 \longrightarrow 2\,Fe_2O_3$; combination.

7.93 Balance Ca by writing 3 $Ca(OH)_2$, P by writing 2 H_3PO_4, H by writing 6 H_2O. Doing all this balances O automatically: $2\,H_3PO_4 + 3\,Ca(OH)_2 \longrightarrow Ca_3(PO_4)_2 + 6\,H_2O$; double replacement, which you can see more clearly by writing HOH for water: $2\,H_3PO_4 + 3\,Ca(OH)_2 \longrightarrow Ca_3(PO_4)_2 + 6\,HOH$.

7.94 Translating the words gives $NH_3 + Cl_2 \longrightarrow NH_4Cl + NCl_3$. Ordinarily, you'd begin with N, but note there are no species containing only H atoms. This means balancing H is going to change the count of other atoms. To try to avoid having to rebalance either N or Cl later on, begin with H, which you balance by writing 4 NH_3 and 3 NH_4Cl. This step also balanaces N. Now balance Cl by writing 3 Cl_2, and the equation is balanced: $4\,NH_3 + 3\,Cl_2 \longrightarrow 3\,NH_4Cl + NCl_3$

7.95 (a) Decomposition.   (b) Decomposition.   (c) Single-replacement.   (d) Double-replacement.

7.96 (a) 2 moles of NaOH because 1 mole of H_2SO_4 can provide 2 moles of H^+ ions.

(b) 1 mole of NaOH because 1 mole of HI dissociates to yield 1 mole of H^+ ions.

(c) 3 moles of NaOH because 1 mole of H_3PO_4 can provide 3 moles of H^+ ions.

(d) 1 mole of NaOH because 1 mole of HNO_3 dissociates to yield 1 mole of H^+ ions.

(e) 1 mole of NaOH because 1 mole of CH_3COOH dissociates to yield 1 mole of H^+ ions.
(Remember, only the H bonded to O is acidic; the three H bonded to C are not acidic.)

7.97 Translating the words gives $KClO_3 \longrightarrow KCl + O_2$. With K and Cl already balanced, balance O by writing 1.5 O_2 to get $1.5 \times 2 = 3$ O right. Then multiply through by 2 to get whole-number coefficients: $2\,KClO_3 \longrightarrow 2\,KCl + 3\,O_2$

7.98 (a) $Zn + 2\,HCl \longrightarrow ZnCl_2 + H_2$
(b) $Na_2O + H_2O \longrightarrow 2\,NaOH$
(c) $CH_4 + 2\,H_2S \longrightarrow CS_2 + 4\,H_2$
(d) $CO + 2\,H_2 \longrightarrow CH_3OH$

7.99 $Ca(OH)_2 + 2\,HCl \longrightarrow CaCl_2 + 2\,H_2O$

7.100 Translating the words gives $CaCO_3 \xrightarrow{\text{Heat}} CO_2 + CaO$, which is the balanced equation.

7.101 K and O are balanced. With nine S left and two S right, writing $4.5\,K_2S_2O_3$ balances S but unbalances K and O, telling you that is not the way to go. Because the K subscript is the same left and right and the O subscript is the same left and right, the only way to balance these atoms is to have the K_2SO_3 coefficient be the same as the $K_2S_2O_3$ coefficient. If you use brute force and try each numeric coefficient in turn, you will discover that the lowest number that balances S is $8\,K_2SO_3 + S_8 \longrightarrow 8\,K_2S_2O_3$; combination.

7.102 (a) Nitric acid, HNO_3, and potassium hydroxide, KOH
(b) Phosphoric acid, H_3PO_4, and calcium hydroxide, $Ca(OH)_2$
(c) Sulfuric acid, H_2SO_4, and lithium hydroxide, $LiOH$
(d) Hydroiodic acid, HI, and sodium hydroxide, $NaOH$

7.103 Translating the words gives $ZnS + O_2 \longrightarrow ZnO + SO_2$, with only O unbalanced. Write $1.5\,O_2$, and then multiply through by 2 to get $2\,ZnS + 2\,O_2 \longrightarrow 2\,ZnO + 2\,SO_2$.

7.104 Broken; formed

7.105 Translating to chemical symbols gives $C_3H_8 + O_2 \longrightarrow CO_2 + H_2O$. Balance first C by writing $3\,CO_2$, then H by writing $4\,H_2O$, then O by writing $5\,O_2$: $C_3H_8 + 5\,O_2 \longrightarrow 3\,CO_2 + 4\,H_2O$.

7.106 Balance K by writing $2\,KNO_3$, then Cr by writing $3\,K_2CrO_4$. Doing this unbalances K, forcing you to restore K balance by changing $2\,KNO_3$ to $6\,KNO_3$. Now balance Al by writing $2\,Al(NO_3)_3$, a step that also balances N. A count shows O balanced at 30 left, 30 right. The balanced equation is therefore $3\,K_2CrO_4 + 2\,Al(NO_3)_3 \longrightarrow Al_2(CrO_4)_3 + 6\,KNO_3$; double-displacement.

7.107 Translating to chemical symbols gives $CO + H_2O \longrightarrow CO_2 + H_2$, which is balanced.

7.108 Salt; water

7.109 $Mn + 2\,S \longrightarrow MnS_2$; combination.

7.110 NO_3^-, Br^-, and SO_4^{2-}.

7.111 The words translate to $H_2S + O_2 \longrightarrow SO_2 + H_2O$, which is balanced by writing $1.5\,O_2$ and then multiplying through by 2: $2\,H_2S + 3\,O_2 \longrightarrow 2\,SO_2 + 2\,H_2O$

7.112 $2\,MgO \longrightarrow 2\,Mg + O_2$

7.113 (a) Cl^-, Br^-, I^-, PO_4^{3-}, CO_3^{2-}, S^{2-}, or OH because the sodium salt of any of these anions is soluble in water but the silver(I) salt of any of them is insoluble.
(b) SO_4^{2-}, PO_4^{3-}, or CO_3^{2-} because the sodium salt of any of these anions is soluble in water but the calcium salt is insoluble.

7.114 With H already balanced, balance O by writing $0.5\,O_2$ and then multiplying through by 2: $2\,H_2O_2 \longrightarrow 2\,H_2O + O_2$; decomposition.

7.115 In each case you must first write the balanced equation, then convert to a complete ionic equation and identify the spectator ions. Then you have the information needed to write the net ionic equation.
(a) $Al(NO_3)_3(aq) + 3\,NaOH(aq) \longrightarrow Al(OH)_3(s) + 3\,NaNO_3(aq)$
$Al^{3+}(aq) + 3\,NO_3^-(aq) + 3\,Na^+(aq) + 3\,OH^-(aq) \longrightarrow Al(OH)_3(s) + 3\,Na^+(aq) + 3\,NO_3(aq)$
$Al^{3+}(aq) + 3\,OH^-(aq) \longrightarrow Al(OH)_3(s)$
(b) $2\,K_3PO_4(aq) + 3\,CaCl_2(aq) \longrightarrow Ca_3(PO_4)_2(s) + 6\,KCl(aq)$
$6\,K^+(aq) + 2\,PO_4^{3-}(aq) + 3\,Ca^{2+}(aq) + 6\,Cl^-(aq) \longrightarrow Ca_3(PO_4)_2(s) + 6\,K^+(aq) + 6\,Cl^-(aq)$
$2\,PO_4^{3-}(aq) + 3\,Ca^{2+}(aq) \longrightarrow Ca_3(PO_4)_2(s)$
(c) $MgSO_4(aq) + Na_2CO_3(aq) \longrightarrow MgCO_3(s) + Na_2SO_4(aq)$
$Mg^{2+}(aq) + SO_4^{2-}(aq) + 2\,Na^+(aq) + CO_3^{2-}(aq) \longrightarrow MgCO_3(s) + 2\,Na^+(aq) + SO_4^{2-}(aq)$
$Mg^{2+}(aq) + CO_3^{2-}(aq) \longrightarrow MgCO_3(s)$

7.116 $MgCO_3 \xrightarrow{\text{Heat}} MgO + CO_2$; decomposition.

7.117 Double-replacement, which you can see more easily by writing the water molecule in the form HOH.

7.118 (a) A precipitate of water-insoluble AgI forms.

(b) No precipitate because the only two possible products—$LiC_2H_3O_2$ and Ag_2SO_4—are both water-soluble.

(c) No precipitate because the only two possible products—Na_2SO_4 and NH_4Cl—are both water-soluble.

7.119 That the compound exists in solution as ions; there are no intact units in the solution.

7.120 Net; complete

7.121 Balanced: $2\,KCl(aq) + Pb(NO_3)_2(aq) \longrightarrow PbCl_2(s) + 2\,KNO_3(aq)$

Complete ionic: $2\,K^+(aq) + 2\,Cl^-(aq) + Pb^{2+}(aq) + 2\,NO_3^-(aq) \longrightarrow$
$$PbCl_2(s) + 2\,K^+(aq) + 2\,NO_3^-(aq)$$

Net ionic: $2\,Cl^-(aq) + Pb^{2+}(aq) \longrightarrow PbCl_2(s)$

7.122 H^+; OH^-

7.123 Neutralization

7.124 $H_2CO_3(aq) + 2\,LiOH(aq) \longrightarrow Li_2CO_3(s) + 2\,H_2O(l)$

7.125 Neutralization because an acid (H_2SO_4) and a base [$Ca(OH)_2$] react to form a salt ($CaSO_4$) plus water; double replacement because SO_4^{2-} replaces OH^- in the calcium compound and OH^- replaces SO_4^{2-} in the "hydrogen compound"; precipitation because the water-insoluble $CaSO_4$ forms.

7.126 (a) False. A combination reaction involves forming one product from two or more reactants, whereas a single-displacement reaction involves two reactants and two products.

(b) True.

7.127 Slower because there will be fewer collisions in the increased volume in which the molecules are moving.

7.128 $NH_4NO_3 \xrightarrow[\text{heat}]{\text{Gentle}} N_2O + 2\,H_2O$

7.129 You need the balanced equation before you can write the ionic equations, and so write that first.

(a) Balanced: $AgNO_3(aq) + KI(aq) \longrightarrow AgI(s) + KNO_3(aq)$
Complete ionic: $Ag^+(aq) + NO_3^-(aq) + K^+(aq) + I^-(aq) \longrightarrow AgI(s) + K^+(aq) + NO_3^-(aq)$
Net ionic: $Ag^+(aq) + I^-(aq) \longrightarrow AgI(s)$

(b) Balanced: $Li_2SO_4(aq) + 2\,AgC_2H_3O_2(aq) \longrightarrow 2\,LiC_2H_3O_2(aq) + Ag_2SO_4(aq)$
Complete ionic: $2\,Li^+(aq) + SO_4^{2-}(aq) + 2\,Ag^+(aq) + 2\,C_2H_3O_2^-(aq) \longrightarrow$
$$2\,Li^+(aq) + 2\,C_2H_3O_2^-(aq) + 2\,Ag^+(aq) + SO_4^{2-}(aq)$$

There is no net ionic equation because all the ions in the complete ionic equation are spectator ions. No reaction is occurring, and the balanced equation is more properly written $Li_2SO_4(aq) + 2\,AgC_2H_3O_2(aq) \longrightarrow$ No reaction.

7.130 (a) The phosphide ion is P^{3-} because P, group VA element, has five valence electrons and needs three more to complete its octet. The words describing the reaction translate to $Ca(s) + P_4(s) \longrightarrow Ca_3P_2(s)$. Balance Ca by writing 3 Ca, balance P by writing 0.5 P_4, then multiply through by 2 to get $6\,Ca(s) + P_4(s) \longrightarrow 2\,Ca_3P_2(s)$.

(b) The words translate to $Na(s) + H_2O(l) \longrightarrow NaOH(aq) + H_2(g)$. With Na and O already balanced, balance H by writing 0.5 H_2 and then multiply through by 2 to get $2\,Na(s) + 2\,H_2O(l) \longrightarrow 2\,NaOH(aq) + H_2(g)$.

(c) The words translate to $NH_4NO_3(s) \longrightarrow N_2(g) + O_2(g) + H_2O(g)$. With N balanced, balance H by writing 2 H_2O, balance O by writing 0.5 O_2, and multiply through by 2 to get $2\,NH_4NO_3(s) \longrightarrow 2\,N_2(g) + O_2(g) + 4\,H_2O(g)$.

7.131 (a) The unbalanced equation is $NH_3(g) + F_2(g) \longrightarrow NH_4F(s) + N_2(g)$. Your first thought might be to balance N, but you'll just unbalance N when you balance H because you cannot change H numbers without simultaneously changing N numbers. So begin with H, which you balance by writing $4\ NH_3$ and $3\ NH_4F$:

$4\ NH_3 + F_2 \longrightarrow 3\ NH_4F + N_2$

Now balance F by writing $1.5\ F_2$ to get $1.5 \times 2 = 3$ F left:

$4\ NH_3 + 1.5\ F_2 \longrightarrow 3\ NH_4F + N_2$

All that's left is N, which stands at four left, five right. To lose one N right, write $0.5\ N_2$:

$4\ NH_3 + 1.5\ F_2 \longrightarrow 3\ NH_4F + 0.5\ N_2$

Multiply through by 2 and you are finished:

$8\ NH_3(g) + 3\ F_2(g) \longrightarrow 6\ NH_4F(s) + N_2(g)$

(b)

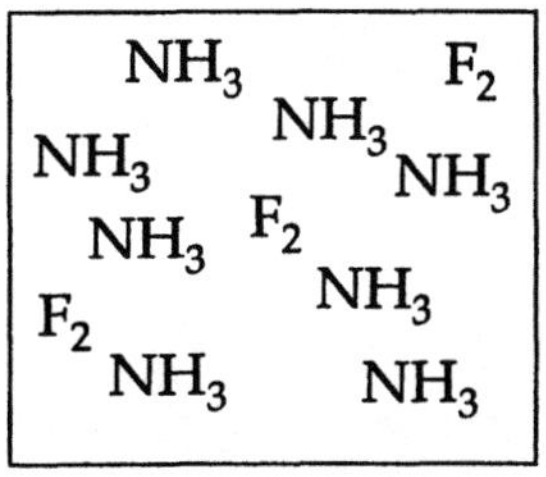

NH_3 F_2
NH_3 NH_3
NH_3 NH_3
NH_3 F_2
F_2 NH_3
NH_3 NH_3

(c)

N_2
NH_4F NH_4F NH_4F
NH_4F NH_4F NH_4F

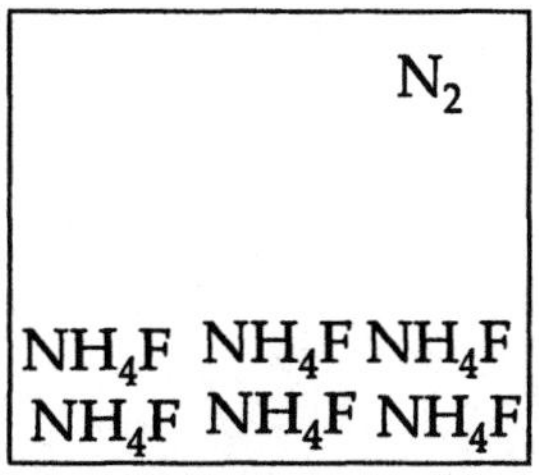

7.132 Balanced: $2\ HBr(aq) + Ba(OH)_2(aq) \longrightarrow BaBr_2(aq) + 2\ H_2O(l)$
Complete ionic: $2\ H^+(aq) + 2\ Br^-(aq) + Ba^{2+}(aq) + 2\ OH^-(aq) \longrightarrow$
$Ba^{2+}(aq) + 2\ Br^-(aq) + 2\ H_2O(l)$
Net ionic: $H^+(aq) + OH^-(aq) \longrightarrow H_2O(l)$

8

Stoichiometry and the Mole

8.1 See solution in textbook.

8.2 One cup of sugar requires 5 eggs, and therefore 3 cups of sugar requires 15 eggs.

8.3 To go from the 3 blocks of cream cheese in the recipe to the 21 blocks of the question, we multiplied the 3 blocks by 7, and the same is done to the number of eggs in the recipe: 7×5 eggs $= 35$ eggs.

8.1 Second time See solution in textbook.

8.2 Second time The two possible conversion factors are

$$\frac{1 \text{ cup sugar}}{5 \text{ eggs}} \quad \text{and} \quad \frac{5 \text{ eggs}}{1 \text{ cup sugar}}$$

Because you want your answer in eggs, use the one with eggs in the numerator:

$$3 \text{ cups sugar} \times \frac{5 \text{ eggs}}{1 \text{ cup sugar}} = 15 \text{ eggs}$$

8.3 Second time The two possible conversion factors are

$$\frac{3 \text{ blocks cream cheese}}{5 \text{ eggs}} \quad \text{and} \quad \frac{5 \text{ eggs}}{3 \text{ blocks cream cheese}}$$

Use the second one because you want your answer in eggs:

$$21 \text{ blocks cream cheese} \times \frac{5 \text{ eggs}}{3 \text{ blocks cream cheese}} = \frac{21 \times 5}{3} \text{ eggs} = 35 \text{ eggs}$$

8.4 See solution in textbook.

8.5 (a) $0.10 \text{ mol U} \times \dfrac{6.022 \times 10^{23} \text{ atoms U}}{1 \text{ mol U}} = 6.0 \times 10^{22} \text{ atoms U}$

(b) $0.10 \text{ mol U} \times \dfrac{238.029 \text{ g U}}{1 \text{ mol U}} = 23.803 \text{ g U}$, which you must report as 24 g because 0.10 has only two significant digits.

8.6 (a) $120.11 \text{ g C} \times \dfrac{1 \text{ mol C}}{12.011 \text{ g C}} = 10.000 \text{ mol C}$

(b) $10.000 \text{ mol C} \times \dfrac{6.022 \times 10^{23} \text{ atoms C}}{1 \text{ mol C}} = 6.022 \times 10^{24} \text{ atoms C}$

8.7 See solution in textbook.

8.8 From Practice Problem 8.7, you know 1 mole of propane has a mass of 44.096 g; therefore 2 moles of propane has a mass of

$2 \text{ mol propane} \times \dfrac{44.096 \text{ g propane}}{1 \text{ mol propane}} = 88.192 \text{ g propane}$

8.9 The molecular formula for propane is C_3H_8—3 moles of C atoms for every 1 mole of propane. Therefore

$2 \text{ mol propane} \times \dfrac{3 \text{ mol carbon atoms}}{1 \text{ mol propane}} = 6 \text{ mol carbon atoms}$

8.10 1 mole of propane and 5 moles of oxygen react to give 3 moles of carbon dioxide and 4 moles of water.

8.11 See solution in textbook.

8.12 (a) $0.565 \text{ mol HI} \times \dfrac{127.9 \text{ g HI}}{1 \text{ mol HI}} = 72.3 \text{ g HI}$

(b) $0.565 \text{ mol HI} \times \dfrac{6.022 \times 10^{23} \text{ molecules HI}}{1 \text{ mol HI}} = 3.40 \times 10^{23} \text{ molecules HI}$

8.13 (a) $5.000 \times 10^{24} \text{ molecules CH}_4 \times \dfrac{1 \text{ mol CH}_4}{6.022 \times 10^{23} \text{ molecules CH}_4} = 8.303 \text{ mol CH}_4$

(b) The molar mass of CH_4 is $(1 \times 12.011 \text{ g C}) + (4 \times 1.0079 \text{ g H}) = 16.043 \text{ g/mol}$. Thus

$8.303 \text{ mol CH}_4 \times \dfrac{16.043 \text{ g CH}_4}{1 \text{ mol CH}_4} = 133.2 \text{ g CH}_4$

8.14 See solution in textbook.

8.15 (a) $C_6H_6 + 3 H_2 \longrightarrow C_6H_{12}$

(b) 1 mole of benzene and 3 moles of hydrogen react to give 1 mole of cyclohexane.

(c) The molar mass of benzene is $(6 \times 12.011 \text{ g C}) + (6 \times 1.0079 \text{ g H}) = 78.113 \text{ g/mol}$. The balanced equation tells you you need 1 mole of C_6H_6 to form 1 mole of C_6H_{12}:

$1 \text{ mol C}_6\text{H}_{12} \times \dfrac{1 \text{ mol C}_6\text{H}_6}{1 \text{ mol C}_6\text{H}_{12}} \times \dfrac{78.113 \text{ g C}_6\text{H}_6}{1 \text{ mol C}_6\text{H}_6} = 78.113 \text{ g C}_6\text{H}_6$

The molar mass of hydrogen is $(2 \times 1.0079 \text{ g H}) = 2.0158 \text{ g/mol}$. Because the equation says that 1 mole of C_6H_{12} requires 3 moles of hydrogen,

$1 \text{ mol C}_6\text{H}_{12} \times \dfrac{3 \text{ mol H}_2}{1 \text{ mol C}_6\text{H}_{12}} \times \dfrac{2.0158 \text{ g H}_2}{1 \text{ mol H}_2} = 6.0474 \text{ g H}_2$

(d) The most you can form is 1 mole of cyclohexane. The molar mass of cyclohexane is $(6 \times 12.011 \text{ g C}) + (12 \times 1.0079 \text{ g H}) = 84.161 \text{ g/mol}$. This 84.161 g is the theoretical yield of C_6H_{12}.

(e) $\text{Percent yield} = \dfrac{\text{Actual yield}}{\text{Theoretical yield}} \times 100 = \dfrac{24.0 \text{ g}}{84.161 \text{ g}} \times 100 = 28.5\%$

8.16 (a) $C_6H_{12}O_6 + 6\,O_2 \longrightarrow 6\,CO_2 + 6\,H_2O$

(b) 1 mole of glucose and 6 moles of oxygen react to give 6 moles of carbon dioxide and 6 moles of water.

(c) The molar mass of glucose is $(6 \times 12.011 \text{ g C}) + (12 \times 1.0079 \text{ g H}) + (6 \times 15.999 \text{ g O}) = 180.155 \text{ g/mol}$.

$$6 \text{ mol H}_2\text{O} \times \frac{1 \text{ mol glucose}}{6 \text{ mol H}_2\text{O}} \times \frac{180.155 \text{ g glucose}}{1 \text{ mol glucose}} = 180.155 \text{ g glucose}$$

The molar mass of O_2 is $(2 \times 15.999 \text{ g O}) = 31.998 \text{ g/mol}$.

$$6 \text{ mol H}_2\text{O} \times \frac{6 \text{ mol O}_2}{6 \text{ mol H}_2\text{O}} \times \frac{31.998 \text{ g O}_2}{1 \text{ mol O}_2} = 191.99 \text{ g O}_2$$

(d) The theoretical yield is 6 moles of CO_2. The molar mass of CO_2 is 44.009 g. The theoretical yield in grams is therefore

$$6 \text{ mol CO}_2 \times \frac{44.009 \text{ mol CO}_2}{6 \text{ mol CO}_2} = 264.05 \text{ g CO}_2$$

(e) $\text{Percent yield} = \dfrac{\text{Actual yield}}{\text{Theoretical yield}} \times 100 = \dfrac{196.0 \text{ g}}{264.05 \text{ g}} \times 100 = 74.23\%$

8.17 See solution in textbook.

8.18 $10.0 \text{ g glucose} \times \dfrac{1 \text{ mol glucose}}{180.155 \text{ g glucose}} \times \dfrac{6 \text{ mol H}_2\text{O}}{1 \text{ mol glucose}} \times \dfrac{18.015 \text{ g H}_2\text{O}}{1 \text{ mol H}_2\text{O}} = 6.00 \text{ g H}_2\text{O}$

8.19 $10.0 \text{ g glucose} \times \dfrac{1 \text{ mol glucose}}{180.155 \text{ g glucose}} \times \dfrac{6 \text{ mol CO}_2}{1 \text{ mol glucose}} \times \dfrac{44.009 \text{ g CO}_2}{1 \text{ mol CO}_2} = 14.7 \text{ g CO}_2$

8.20 $10.0 \text{ g CO}_2 \times \dfrac{1 \text{ mol CO}_2}{44.009 \text{ g CO}_2} \times \dfrac{1 \text{ mol glucose}}{6 \text{ mol CO}_2} \times \dfrac{180.155 \text{ g glucose}}{1 \text{ mol glucose}} = 6.82 \text{ g glucose}$

8.21 See solution in textbook.

8.22 $10.0 \text{ g Al}_2\text{O}_3 \times \dfrac{1 \text{ mol Al}_2\text{O}_3}{101.96 \text{ g Al}_2\text{O}_3} \times \dfrac{2 \text{ mol Al}}{1 \text{ mol Al}_2\text{O}_3} \times \dfrac{6.022 \times 10^{23} \text{ Al atoms}}{1 \text{ mol Al}} = 1.18 \times 10^{23} \text{ Al atoms}$

8.23 $10.0 \text{ g H}_2\text{O} \times \dfrac{1 \text{ mol H}_2\text{O}}{18.015 \text{ g H}_2\text{O}} \times \dfrac{6.022 \times 10^{23} \text{ H}_2\text{O molecules}}{1 \text{ mol H}_2\text{O}} = 3.34 \times 10^{23} \text{ H}_2\text{O molecules}$

8.24 See solution in textbook.

8.25 (a) Step 1: $C_3H_8 + 5\,O_2 \longrightarrow 3\,CO_2 + 4\,H_2O$

Step 2: $100.0 \text{ g C}_3\text{H}_8 \times \dfrac{1 \text{ mol C}_3\text{H}_8}{44.096 \text{ g C}_3\text{H}_8} = 2.268 \text{ mol C}_3\text{H}_8$

No step 2a necessary because reaction run in balanced fashion.

Step 3: $2.268 \text{ mol C}_3\text{H}_8 \times \dfrac{5 \text{ mol O}_2}{1 \text{ mol C}_3\text{H}_8} = 11.34 \text{ mol O}_2$

Step 4: $11.34 \text{ mol O}_2 \times \dfrac{31.998 \text{ g O}_2}{1 \text{ mol O}_2} = 362.9 \text{ g O}_2$

(b) Because the reaction is run in a balanced fashion, you may use either reactant to calculate theoretical yield:

$$2.268 \text{ mol } C_3H_8 \times \frac{4 \text{ mol } H_2O}{1 \text{ mol } C_3H_8} \times \frac{18.015 \text{ g } H_2O}{1 \text{ mol } H_2O} = 163.4 \text{ g } H_2O \text{ theoretical yield}$$

or

$$11.34 \text{ mol } O_2 \times \frac{4 \text{ mol } H_2O}{5 \text{ mol } O_2} \times \frac{18.015 \text{ g } H_2O}{1 \text{ mol } H_2O} = 163.4 \text{ g } H_2O \text{ theoretical yield}$$

8.26 (a) $2 \text{ ZnS} + 3 \text{ O}_2 \longrightarrow 2 \text{ ZnO} + 2 \text{ SO}_2$

(b) Calculate molar masses:

ZnS   65.39 g/mol Zn + 32.06 g/mol S = 97.45 g/mol
O_2 15.999 × 2 = 31.998 g/mol
ZnO   65.39 g/mol Zn + 15.999 g/mol O = 81.39 g/mol
SO_2 32.06 g/mol S + 2 × 15.999 g/mol O = 64.06 g/mol

Step 1: Done

Step 2: $10.0 \text{ g ZnS} \times \dfrac{1 \text{ mol ZnS}}{97.45 \text{ g ZnS}} = 0.103 \text{ mol ZnS}$

$$10.0 \text{ g } O_2 \times \frac{1 \text{ mol } O_2}{31.998 \text{ g } O_2} = 0.313 \text{ mol } O_2$$

Step 2a: ZnS $\dfrac{0.103}{2} = 0.0515$

O_2 $\dfrac{0.313}{3} = 0.104$

ZnS is limiting reactant because of smaller ratio.

Step 3: $0.103 \text{ mol ZnS} \times \dfrac{2 \text{ mol ZnO}}{2 \text{ mol ZnS}} = 0.103 \text{ mol ZnO}$

$$0.103 \text{ mol ZnS} \times \frac{2 \text{ mol } SO_2}{2 \text{ mol ZnS}} = 0.103 \text{ mol } SO_2$$

Step 4: $0.103 \text{ mol ZnO} \times \dfrac{81.39 \text{ g ZnO}}{1 \text{ mol ZnO}} = 8.39 \text{ g ZnO}$

$$0.103 \text{ mol } SO_2 \times \frac{64.06 \text{ g } SO_2}{1 \text{ mol } SO_2} = 6.60 \text{ g } SO_2$$

(c) The excess reactant is the O_2. From step 2 above, you know that the 10.0 g of O_2 is 0.313 mole. Figure out how much of that combined with the 0.103 mole of ZnS:

$$0.103 \text{ mol ZnS} \times \frac{3 \text{ mol } O_2}{2 \text{ mol ZnS}} = 0.155 \text{ mol } O_2$$

This is the amount of O_2 consumed, which means 0.313 mole − 0.155 mole = 0.158 mole of O_2 is left over, which is

$$0.158 \text{ mol } O_2 \times \frac{31.998 \text{ g } O_2}{1 \text{ mol } O_2} = 5.06 \text{ g } O_2 \text{ left over}$$

(d) Percent yield $= \dfrac{7.50 \text{ g}}{8.39 \text{ g}} \times 100 = 89.4\%$

8.27 (a) Step 1: Convert grams of CO_2 to moles of C and grams of H_2O to moles of H:

$$0.686 \text{ g } CO_2 \times \frac{1 \text{ mol } CO_2}{44.009 \text{ g } CO_2} \times \frac{1 \text{ mol C}}{1 \text{ mol } CO_2} = 0.0156 \text{ mol C}$$

$$0.561 \text{ g } H_2O \times \frac{1 \text{ mol } H_2O}{18.015 \text{ g } H_2O} \times \frac{2 \text{ mol H}}{1 \text{ mol } H_2O} = 0.0623 \text{ mol H}$$

Step 2: Convert to grams of C and H:

$$0.0156 \text{ mol C} \times \frac{12.011 \text{ g C}}{1 \text{ mol C}} = 0.187 \text{ g C}$$

$$0.0623 \text{ mol H} \times \frac{1.0079 \text{ g H}}{1 \text{ mol H}} = 0.0628 \text{ g H}$$

Step 3: Determine whether there is any O in the compound and, if so, convert to moles:

$$0.250 \text{ g sample} - (0.0628 \text{ g H} + 0.187 \text{ g C}) = 0 \text{ g O}$$

Step 4: Divide subscripts through by the smallest subscript:

$$C_{\frac{0.0156}{0.0156}} H_{\frac{0.0623}{0.0156}} \rightarrow C_{1.00} H_{3.99} \rightarrow CH_4 \text{ molecular formula}$$

(b)
$$\frac{0.187 \text{ g C}}{0.250 \text{ g compound}} \times 100 = 74.8\% \text{ C}$$

$$\frac{0.0628 \text{ g H}}{0.250 \text{ g compound}} \times 100 = 25.1\% \text{ H}$$

(c) $CH_4 + 2 O_2 \longrightarrow 2 H_2O + CO_2$

8.28 (a) Step 1: Convert grams of CO_2 to moles of C and grams of H_2O to moles of H:

$$0.478 \text{ g } CO_2 \times \frac{1 \text{ mol } CO_2}{44.009 \text{ g } CO_2} \times \frac{1 \text{ mol C}}{1 \text{ mol } CO_2} = 0.0109 \text{ mol C}$$

$$0.293 \text{ g } H_2O \times \frac{1 \text{ mol } H_2O}{18.015 \text{ g } H_2O} \times \frac{2 \text{ mol H}}{1 \text{ mol } H_2O} = 0.0325 \text{ mol H}$$

Step 2: Convert to grams of C and H:

$$0.0109 \text{ mol C} \times \frac{12.011 \text{ g C}}{1 \text{ mol C}} = 0.131 \text{ g C}$$

$$0.0325 \text{ mol H} \times \frac{1.0079 \text{ g H}}{1 \text{ mol H}} = 0.0328 \text{ g H}$$

Step 3: Determine whether there is any O in the compound and, if so, convert to moles:

$$0.250 \text{ g sample} - (0.131 \text{ g C} + 0.0328 \text{ g H}) = 0.0862 \text{ g O}$$

$$0.0862 \text{ g O} \times \frac{1 \text{ mol O}}{15.999 \text{ g O}} = 0.00539 \text{ mol O}$$

Step 4: Divide subscripts through by the smallest subscript:

$$C_{\frac{0.0109}{0.00539}} H_{\frac{0.0328}{0.00539}} O_{\frac{0.00539}{0.00539}} \rightarrow C_{2.02} H_{6.09} O_{1.00} \rightarrow C_2H_6O$$

(b) $\dfrac{0.131 \text{ g C}}{0.250 \text{ g compound}} \times 100 = 52.4\% \text{ C}$

$\dfrac{0.0328 \text{ g H}}{0.250 \text{ g compound}} \times 100 = 13.1\% \text{ H}$

$\dfrac{0.0862 \text{ g O}}{0.250 \text{ g compound}} \times 100 = 34.5\% \text{ O}$

(c) $C_2H_6O + 3\ O_2 \longrightarrow 2\ CO_2 + 3\ H_2O$

8.29 (a) Step 1: Convert grams of CO_2 to moles of C and grams of H_2O to moles of H:

$$0.999 \text{ g } CO_2 \times \frac{1 \text{ mol } CO_2}{44.009 \text{ g } CO_2} \times \frac{1 \text{ mol C}}{1 \text{ mol } CO_2} = 0.0227 \text{ mol C}$$

$$0.409 \text{ g } H_2O \times \frac{1 \text{ mol } H_2O}{18.015 \text{ g } H_2O} \times \frac{2 \text{ mol H}}{1 \text{ mol } H_2O} = 0.0454 \text{ mol H}$$

Step 2: Convert to grams of C and H:

$$0.0227 \text{ mol C} \times \frac{12.011 \text{ g C}}{1 \text{ mol C}} = 0.273 \text{ g C}$$

$$0.0454 \text{ mol H} \times \frac{1.0079 \text{ g H}}{1 \text{ mol H}} = 0.0458 \text{ g H}$$

Step 3: Determine whether there is any O in the compound and, if so, convert to moles:

$$0.500 \text{ g sample} - (0.273 \text{ g C} + 0.0458 \text{ g H}) = 0.181 \text{ g O}$$

$$0.181 \text{ g O} \times \frac{1 \text{ mol O}}{15.999 \text{ g O}} = 0.0113 \text{ mol O}$$

Step 4: $C_{\frac{0.0227}{0.0113}} H_{\frac{0.0454}{0.0113}} O_{\frac{0.0113}{0.0113}} \rightarrow C_{2.01}H_{4.02}O_{1.00} \rightarrow C_2H_4O$ empirical formula

(b) $\dfrac{0.273 \text{ g C}}{0.500 \text{ g compound}} \times 100 = 54.6\% \text{ C}$

$\dfrac{0.0458 \text{ g H}}{0.500 \text{ g compound}} \times 100 = 9.16\% \text{ H}$

$\dfrac{0.181 \text{ g O}}{0.500 \text{ g compound}} \times 100 = 36.2\% \text{ O}$

(c) Divide the given molar mass of the compound by the molar mass of the empirical formula:

$$\frac{\text{Molar mass of compound}}{\text{Molar mass of } C_2H_4O} = \frac{132.159 \text{ g/mol}}{44.053 \text{ g/mol}} = 3$$

The molecular formula is therefore $C_{3\times2}H_{3\times4}O_{3\times1} \longrightarrow C_6H_{12}O_3$.

(d) See solution in textbook.

8.30 (a) Step 1: Convert grams of CO_2 to moles of C and grams of H_2O to moles of H:

$$3.137 \text{ g } CO_2 \times \frac{1 \text{ mol } CO_2}{44.009 \text{ g } CO_2} \times \frac{1 \text{ mol C}}{1 \text{ mol } CO_2} = 0.07128 \text{ mol C}$$

$$1.284 \text{ g } H_2O \times \frac{1 \text{ mol } H_2O}{18.015 \text{ g } H_2O} \times \frac{2 \text{ mol H}}{1 \text{ mol } H_2O} = 0.1425 \text{ mol H}$$

Step 2: Convert to grams of C and H:

$$0.07128 \text{ mol C} \times \frac{12.011 \text{ g C}}{1 \text{ mol C}} = 0.8561 \text{ g C}$$

$$0.1425 \text{ mol H} \times \frac{1.0079 \text{ g H}}{1 \text{ mol H}} = 0.1436 \text{ g H}$$

Step 3: Determine whether there is any O in the compound and, if so, convert to moles:

$$1.000 \text{ g sample} - (0.1436 \text{ g H} + 0.8561 \text{ g C}) = 0 \text{ g O}$$

Step 4: $C_{\frac{0.07128}{0.07128}} H_{\frac{0.1436}{0.07128}} \rightarrow C_{1.00}H_{2.01} \rightarrow CH_2$ empirical formula

(b) $\dfrac{\text{Molar mass of compound}}{\text{Molar mass of } CH_2} = \dfrac{28.054 \text{ g/mol}}{14.027 \text{ g/mol}} = 2$

The molecular formula is therefore $C_{2\times1}H_{2\times2} \longrightarrow C_2H_4$.

(c) $C_2H_4 + 3 O_2 \longrightarrow 2 CO_2 + 2 H_2O$

8.31 Step 1: Begin by assuming you have 1 mole of H_2O_2, and calculate the mass in grams of each element in that 1 mole of H_2O_2:

$$1 \text{ mol } H_2O_2 \times \frac{2 \text{ mol H}}{1 \text{ mol } H_2O_2} \times \frac{1.0079 \text{ g H}}{1 \text{ mol H}} = 2.0158 \text{ g H}$$

$$1 \text{ mol } H_2O_2 \times \frac{2 \text{ mol O}}{1 \text{ mol } H_2O_2} \times \frac{15.999 \text{ g O}}{1 \text{ mol O}} = 31.998 \text{ g O}$$

Step 2: Divide each calculated mass by the mass of the 1 mole of H_2O_2 you are assumed to be working with and multiply by 100: The mass of 1 mol H_2O_2 is its molar mass—34.014 g.

$$\frac{2.0158 \text{ g H}}{34.014 \text{ g } H_2O_2} \times 100 = 5.926\% \text{ H}$$

$$\frac{31.998 \text{ g O}}{34.014 \text{ g } H_2O_2} \times 100 = 94.07\% \text{ O}$$

8.32 Step 1: Assume you have 1 mole of TNT, and calculate the mass in grams of each element in that 1 mole:

$$1 \text{ mol TNT} \times \frac{7 \text{ mol C}}{1 \text{ mol TNT}} \times \frac{12.011 \text{ g C}}{1 \text{ mol C}} = 84.08 \text{ g C}$$

$$1 \text{ mol TNT} \times \frac{5 \text{ mol H}}{1 \text{ mol TNT}} \times \frac{1.0079 \text{ g H}}{1 \text{ mol H}} = 5.040 \text{ g H}$$

$$1 \text{ mol TNT} \times \frac{3 \text{ mol N}}{1 \text{ mol TNT}} \times \frac{14.007 \text{ g N}}{1 \text{ mol N}} = 42.02 \text{ g N}$$

$$1 \text{ mol TNT} \times \frac{6 \text{ mol O}}{1 \text{ mol TNT}} \times \frac{15.999 \text{ g O}}{1 \text{ mol O}} = 95.99 \text{ g O}$$

Step 2: The molar mass of TNT is 227.1 g/mol. Therefore

$$\frac{84.08 \text{ g C}}{227.1 \text{ g TNT}} \times 100 = 37.02\% \text{ C}$$

$$\frac{5.040 \text{ g H}}{227.1 \text{ g TNT}} \times 100 = 2.219\% \text{ H}$$

$$\frac{42.02 \text{ g N}}{227.1 \text{ g TNT}} \times 100 = 18.50\% \text{ N}$$

$$\frac{95.99 \text{ g O}}{227.1 \text{ g TNT}} \times 100 = 42.27\% \text{ O}$$

8.33 Step 1: To get the empirical formula from percent composition, assume 100 g of compound (that way, percent values become grams):

$$89.09\% \text{ Cl} \longrightarrow 89.09 \text{ g Cl} \times \frac{1 \text{ mol Cl}}{35.453 \text{ g Cl}} = 2.513 \text{ mol Cl}$$

$$10.06\% \text{ C} \longrightarrow 10.06 \text{ g C} \times \frac{1 \text{ mol C}}{12.011 \text{ g C}} = 0.8376 \text{ mol C}$$

$$0.84\% \text{ H} \longrightarrow 0.84 \text{ g H} \times \frac{1 \text{ mol H}}{1.0079 \text{ g H}} = 0.8334 \text{ mol H}$$

Step 2: Use the calculated number of moles as subscripts and divide through by the smallest:

$$\text{Cl}_{\frac{2.513}{0.8334}} \text{C}_{\frac{0.8376}{0.8334}} \text{H}_{\frac{0.8334}{0.8334}} \rightarrow \text{Cl}_{3.02}\text{C}_{1.01}\text{H}_{1.00} \rightarrow \text{Cl}_3\text{CH} \text{ empirical formula}$$

The molecular mass of this empirical formula is 119.4 g/mol. That the molar mass of the compound is given as 119.378 g/mol tells you the molecular formula is the same as the empirical formula.

8.34 Because the percentages of C and H do not add up to 100%, you know the compound contains O:

$$100\% - (54.53\% \text{ C} + 9.15\% \text{ H}) = 36.32\% \text{ O}$$

Step 1: To get the empirical formula from percent composition, assume 100 g of compound (that way, percent values become grams):

$$53.53\% \text{ C} \longrightarrow 54.53 \text{ g C} \times \frac{1 \text{ mol C}}{12.011 \text{ g C}} = 4.540 \text{ mol C}$$

$$9.15\% \text{ H} \longrightarrow 9.15 \text{ g H} \times \frac{1 \text{ mol H}}{1.0079 \text{ g H}} = 9.08 \text{ mol H}$$

$$36.32\% \text{ O} \longrightarrow 36.32 \text{ g O} \times \frac{1 \text{ mol O}}{15.999 \text{ g O}} = 2.27 \text{ mol O}$$

Step 2: Use the calculated number of moles as subscripts and divide through by the smallest:

$$\text{C}_{\frac{4.540}{2.27}} \text{H}_{\frac{9.08}{2.27}} \text{O}_{\frac{2.27}{2.27}} \rightarrow \text{C}_{2.00}\text{H}_{4.00}\text{O}_{1.00} \rightarrow \text{C}_2\text{H}_4\text{O} \text{ empirical formula}$$

$$\frac{\text{Molar mass of compound}}{\text{Molar mass of C}_2\text{H}_4\text{O}} = \frac{88.106 \text{ g/mol}}{44.053 \text{ g/mol}} = 2$$

The molecular formula is therefore $\text{C}_{2\times2}\text{H}_{2\times4}\text{O}_{2\times1} \longrightarrow \text{C}_4\text{H}_8\text{O}_2$.

8.35 A balanced equation is like a recipe because the equation specifies how much of each reactant must be used to give a certain amount of product.

8.36 (a) $\dfrac{1 \text{ egg}}{2 \text{ cups flour}}$, $\dfrac{1 \text{ egg}}{3 \text{ cups sugar}}$, $\dfrac{2 \text{ cups flour}}{3 \text{ cups sugar}}$, $\dfrac{\frac{1}{4} \text{ pound butter}}{3 \text{ cups sugar}}$, $\dfrac{1 \text{ cup milk}}{1 \text{ dozen sugar cookies}}$,

$\dfrac{1 \text{ dozen sugar cookies}}{\frac{1}{4} \text{ pound butter}}$

Many other conversion factors possible.

(b) $30 \text{ cookies} \times \dfrac{1 \text{ dozen cookies}}{12 \text{ cookies}} \times \dfrac{2 \text{ cups flour}}{1 \text{ dozen cookies}} = 5 \text{ cups flour}$

(c) You don't have the conversion factor for how many cups of milk are in a container of milk.

(d) $1 \text{ container of milk} \times \dfrac{4 \text{ cups milk}}{1 \text{ container of milk}} \times \dfrac{1 \text{ egg}}{1 \text{ cup milk}} = 4 \text{ eggs}$

(e) 1 egg + 2 cups flour + 3 cups sugar + $\frac{1}{4}$ pound butter + 1 cup milk $\longrightarrow$ 1 dozen cookies

8.37 (a) $3 \text{ cakes} \times \dfrac{5 \text{ eggs}}{1 \text{ cake}} = 15 \text{ eggs}$

(b) $63 \text{ blocks of cream cheese} \times \dfrac{5 \text{ eggs}}{3 \text{ blocks of cream cheese}} = 105 \text{ eggs}$

8.38 One mole represents the quantity 6.022×10^{23}, just as one dozen represents the quantity 12.

8.39 Always.

8.40 6 billion = 6×10^9.

$\% = \dfrac{6 \times 10^9}{6.022 \times 10^{23}} \times 100 = 9.96 \times 10^{-13}\%$

8.41 There are 6.022×10^{23} bicycles in 1 mole of bicycles. Because there are 2 tires on every bicycle, the number of tires in 1 mole of bicycles is 2 times 6.022×10^{23}, or 1.204×10^{24}.

8.42 There are 6.022×10^{23} O_2 molecules in 1 mole of O_2 molecules. Because there are two O atoms in every O_2 molecule, the number of O atoms in one mole of O_2 molecules is 2 times 6.022×10^{23}, or 1.204×10^{24}.

8.43 $2.5 \text{ moles of pennies} \times \dfrac{6.022 \times 10^{23} \text{ pennies}}{1 \text{ mole of pennies}} = 1.5 \times 10^{24} \text{ pennies}$

$1.5 \times 10^{24} \text{ pennies} \times \dfrac{1 \text{ dollar}}{100 \text{ pennies}} = 1.5 \times 10^{22} \text{ dollars}$

8.44 1 mole of seconds = 6.022×10^{23} s; thus

$6.022 \times 10^{23} \text{ s} \times \dfrac{1 \text{ min}}{60 \text{ s}} \times \dfrac{1 \text{ h}}{60 \text{ min}} \times \dfrac{1 \text{ day}}{24 \text{ h}} \times \dfrac{1 \text{ year}}{365 \text{ days}} = 1.91 \times 10^{16} \text{ years}$

8.45 2 molecules of sulfur dioxide react with 1 molecule of oxygen to give 2 molecules of sulfur trioxide. 2 moles of sulfur dioxide react with 1 mole of oxygen to give 2 moles of sulfur trioxide.

8.46 There is no such thing as a fractional molecule, such as (5/2) molecules of oxygen. The word *moles* solves the difficulty because a fraction of a mole can be measured out.

8.47 The mass of 1 mole of atoms of an element is equal to the element's atomic mass expressed in grams.

8.48 The mass of 1 mole of any molecule is the molecule's mass expressed in grams.

8.49 A compound's molar mass is calculated by summing the molar masses of all the atoms in the compound.

8.50 Chemical equations "speak" in moles, but you need to measure substances in grams. Molar mass allows you to translate from moles to grams or from grams to moles.

8.51 The atomic mass of this isotope is exactly 12 amu, by definition. Therefore the molar mass is exactly 12 g, meaning that 12 g of $^{12}_{6}C$ is 1 mole and must contain 6.022×10^{23} atoms.

8.52 The periodic table tells you that 12.011 amu is the atomic mass of carbon. Thus from the definition of molar mass, you know that 12.011 g of carbon is 1 mole of carbon, containing 6.022×10^{23} atoms.

8.53 The subscript on each atom in the chemical formula tells you the number of moles of the atom in 1 mole of the compound:

(a) $1 \text{ mol } C_6H_{12}O_6 \times \dfrac{6 \text{ mol C}}{1 \text{ mol } C_6H_{12}O_6} = 6 \text{ mol C}$

(b) $1 \text{ mol } C_6H_{12}O_6 \times \dfrac{12 \text{ mol H}}{1 \text{ mol } C_6H_{12}O_6} = 12 \text{ mol H}$

(c) $1 \text{ mol } C_6H_{12}O_6 \times \dfrac{6 \text{ mol O}}{1 \text{ mol } C_6H_{12}O_6} \times \dfrac{6.022 \times 10^{23} \text{ atoms O}}{1 \text{ mol O}} = 3.613 \times 10^{24} \text{ atoms O}$

8.54 The subscripts in the formula give the number of moles of each atom in each mole of the compound:

(a) $1 \text{ mol } NH_3 \times \dfrac{3 \text{ mol H}}{1 \text{ mol } NH_3} = 3 \text{ mol H}$

(b) $2 \text{ mol } NH_3 \times \dfrac{3 \text{ mol H}}{1 \text{ mol } NH_3} = 6 \text{ mol H}$

(c) $2 \text{ mol } NH_3 \times \dfrac{1 \text{ mol N}}{1 \text{ mol } NH_3} \times \dfrac{6.022 \times 10^{23} \text{ atoms N}}{1 \text{ mol N}} = 1.204 \times 10^{24} \text{ atoms N}$

8.55 The theoretical yield of a reaction is the maximum amount of product that can be made from a given amount of reactants.

8.56 The actual yield is the amount of product that is actually recovered after a chemical reaction.

8.57 Some reactions have competing side reactions that use up reactants to produce unwanted side products. Sometimes difficulties in collecting the desired product make it impossible to recover all of it.

8.58 The percent yield of any reaction is the actual yield expressed as a percent of the theoretical yield.

$$\text{Percent yield} = \dfrac{\text{Actual yield}}{\text{Theoretical yield}} \times 100$$

8.59 $\text{Percent yield} = \dfrac{15.5 \text{ g}}{40.0 \text{ g}} \times 100 = 38.8\%$

8.60 (a) $2 NO + O_2 \longrightarrow 2 NO_2$
(b) 2 moles of nitrogen monoxide and 1 mole of oxygen react to give 2 moles of nitrogen dioxide.

(c) You need 2 moles of NO and 1 mole of O_2. The molar masses are $14.007 + 15.999 = 30.006$ g/mol for NO and $2 \times 15.999 = 31.9988$ g/mol for O_2.

$$2 \text{ mol NO} \times \frac{30.006 \text{ g NO}}{1 \text{ mol NO}} = 60.012 \text{ g NO}$$

$$1 \text{ mol } O_2 \times \frac{31.998 \text{ g } O_2}{1 \text{ mol } O_2} = 31.998 \text{ } O_2$$

(d) The theoretical yield is 2 moles of NO_2, and the molar mass of NO_2 is 46.006 g/mol:

$$2 \text{ mol } NO_2 \times \frac{46.006 \text{ g } NO_2}{1 \text{ mol } NO_2} = 92.012 \text{ g } NO_2$$

(e) Percent yield $= \dfrac{\text{Actual yield}}{\text{Theoretical yield}} \times 100 = \dfrac{22.5 \text{ g}}{92.012 \text{ g}} \times 100 = 24.5\%$

8.61 (a) $2 \text{ HCl} + \text{Zn} \longrightarrow H_2 + \text{ZnCl}_2$

(b) 2 moles of hydrogen chloride and 1 mole of zinc react to give 1 mole of hydrogen and 1 mole of zinc chloride.

(c) You need 2 moles of HCl and 1 mole of Zn. The molar masses are $1.0079 + 35.453 = 36.461$ g/mol for HCl and 65.39 g/mol for Zn:

$$2 \text{ mol HCl} \times \frac{36.461 \text{ g}}{1 \text{ mol HCl}} = 72.922 \text{ g HCl}$$

$$1 \text{ mol Zn} \times \frac{65.39 \text{ g}}{1 \text{ mol Zn}} = 65.39 \text{ Zn}$$

(d) The theoretical yield is 1 mole of H_2, and the molar mass of H_2 is 2.0158 g/mol:

$$1 \text{ mol } H_2 \times \frac{2.0158 \text{ g } H_2}{1 \text{ mol } H_2} = 2.0158 \text{ g } H_2$$

(e) Percent yield $= \dfrac{\text{Actual yield}}{\text{Theoretical yield}} \times 100 = \dfrac{2.00 \text{ g}}{2.0158 \text{ g}} \times 100 = 99.2\%$

8.62 (a) $2 \text{ Na} + \text{Cl}_2 \longrightarrow 2 \text{ NaCl}$

(b) 2 moles of sodium and 1 mole of chlorine react to give 2 moles of sodium chloride.

(c) Because the equation is written for 2 moles of NaCl but you want to produce only 1 mole, you need to divide the reactant amounts by 2, which means you need 1 mole of Na and 0.5 mole of Cl_2. The molar masses are 22.9898 g/mol for Na and $2 \times 35.453 = 70.906$ g/mol for Cl_2:

$$1 \text{ mol Na} \times \frac{22.9898 \text{ g Na}}{1 \text{ mol Na}} = 22.9898 \text{ g Na}$$

$$0.5 \text{ mol } Cl_2 \times \frac{70.906 \text{ g } Cl_2}{1 \text{ mol } Cl_2} = 35.453 \text{ g } Cl_2$$

(d) The theoretical yield is 1 mole of NaCl, which is

$$1 \text{ mol NaCl} \times \frac{58.443 \text{ g NaCl}}{1 \text{ mol NaCl}} = 58.443 \text{ g NaCl}$$

(e) Percent yield $= \dfrac{\text{Actual yield}}{\text{Theoretical yield}} \times 100 = \dfrac{45.50 \text{ g}}{58.443 \text{ g}} \times 100 = 77.85\%$

8.63 $\dfrac{6\text{ mol C atoms}}{1\text{ mol }C_6H_{12}O_6}$, $\dfrac{12\text{ mol H atoms}}{1\text{ mol }C_6H_{12}O_6}$, $\dfrac{1\text{ mol }C_6H_{12}O_6}{6\text{ mol O atoms}}$, $\dfrac{6\text{ mol C atoms}}{12\text{ mol H atoms}}$,

$\dfrac{12\text{ mol H atoms}}{6\text{ mol O atoms}}$, $\dfrac{12\text{ mol H atoms}}{6\text{ mol C atoms}}$; others possible.

8.64 From the equation:

$\dfrac{2\text{ mol AgBr}}{2\text{ mol Ag}}$, $\dfrac{2\text{ mol AgBr}}{1\text{ mol }Br_2}$, $\dfrac{2\text{ mol Ag}}{1\text{ mol }Br_2}$, $\dfrac{2\text{ mol Ag}}{2\text{ mol AgBr}}$, $\dfrac{1\text{ mol }Br_2}{2\text{ mol AgBr}}$, $\dfrac{1\text{ mol }Br_2}{2\text{ mol Ag}}$

From the formulas:

$\dfrac{1\text{ mol Ag atoms}}{1\text{ mol AgBr molecules}}$, $\dfrac{1\text{ mol AgBr molecules}}{1\text{ mol Ag atoms}}$, $\dfrac{1\text{ mol Br atoms}}{1\text{ mol AgBr molecules}}$,

$\dfrac{1\text{ mol AgBr molecules}}{1\text{ mol Br atoms}}$, $\dfrac{2\text{ mol Br atoms}}{1\text{ mol }Br_2\text{ molecules}}$, $\dfrac{1\text{ mol }Br_2\text{ molecules}}{2\text{ mol Br atoms}}$

8.65 (a) $I_2 + 3\,Cl_2 \longrightarrow 2\,ICl_3$

(b) $\dfrac{1\text{ mol }I_2}{3\text{ mol }Cl_2}$, $\dfrac{1\text{ mol }I_2}{2\text{ mol }ICl_3}$, $\dfrac{3\text{ mol }Cl_2}{2\text{ mol }ICl_3}$, $\dfrac{3\text{ mol }Cl_2}{1\text{ mol }I_2}$, $\dfrac{2\text{ mol }ICl_3}{1\text{ mol }I_2}$, $\dfrac{2\text{ mol }ICl_3}{3\text{ mol }Cl_2}$

(c) $\dfrac{2\text{ mol I atoms}}{1\text{ mol }I_2\text{ molecules}}$, $\dfrac{1\text{ mol }I_2\text{ molecules}}{2\text{ mol I atoms}}$, $\dfrac{2\text{ mol Cl atoms}}{1\text{ mol }Cl_2\text{ molecules}}$, $\dfrac{1\text{ mol }Cl_2\text{ molecules}}{2\text{ mol Cl atoms}}$,

$\dfrac{1\text{ mol I atoms}}{1\text{ mol }ICl_3\text{ molecules}}$, $\dfrac{1\text{ mol }ICl_3\text{ molecules}}{1\text{ mol I atoms}}$, $\dfrac{3\text{ mol Cl atoms}}{1\text{ mol }ICl_3\text{ molecules}}$,

$\dfrac{1\text{ mol }ICl_3\text{ molecules}}{3\text{ mol Cl atoms}}$

8.66 $2.0158\text{ g H atoms} \times \dfrac{1\text{ mol H atoms}}{1.0079\text{ g H atoms}} \times \dfrac{6.022\times10^{23}\text{ H atoms}}{1\text{ mol H atoms}} = 1.204\times10^{24}\text{ H atoms}$

8.67 $24.0\text{ g }O_2 \times \dfrac{1\text{ mol }O_2}{31.998\text{ g }O_2} = 0.750\text{ mol }O_2$

8.68 $24.0\text{ g }O_2 \times \dfrac{1\text{ mol }O_2}{31.998\text{ g }O_2} \times \dfrac{2\text{ mol O atoms}}{1\text{ mol }O_2} = 1.50\text{ mol O atoms}$

8.69 (a) The molar mass is

H $2 \times 1.0079\text{ g/mol} = 2.0158\text{ g/mol}$
S $1 \times 32.064\text{ g/mol} = 32.064\text{ g/mol}$
O $4 \times 15.999\text{ g/mol} = \underline{63.996\text{ g/mol}}$
H_2SO_4 $\qquad\qquad\qquad 98.076\text{ g/mol}$

(b) 98.076 g

(c) $2.50\text{ mol }H_2SO_4 \times \dfrac{98.076\text{ g }H_2SO_4}{1\text{ mol }H_2SO_4} = 245\text{ g}$

(d) $1000\text{ molecules }H_2SO_4 \times \dfrac{1\text{ mol }H_2SO_4}{6.022\times10^{23}\text{ molecules }H_2SO_4} \times \dfrac{98.076\text{ g }H_2SO_4}{1\text{ mol }H_2SO_4}$

$= 1.629\times10^{-19}\text{ g }H_2SO_4$

8.70 $1.00 \text{ g O}_2 \times \dfrac{1 \text{ mol O}_2}{31.998 \text{ g O}_2} \times \dfrac{6.022 \times 10^{23} \text{ molecules O}_2}{1 \text{ mol O}_2} = 1.88 \times 10^{22} \text{ molecules O}_2$

8.71 $1.00 \times 10^9 \text{ molecules H}_2\text{O} \times \dfrac{1 \text{ mol H}_2\text{O}}{6.022 \times 10^{23} \text{ molecules H}_2\text{O}} \times \dfrac{18.015 \text{ g H}_2\text{O}}{1 \text{ mol H}_2\text{O}} = 2.99 \times 10^{-14} \text{ g H}_2\text{O}$

8.72 $5.00 \times 10^{30} \text{ atoms C} \times \dfrac{1 \text{ mol C}}{6.022 \times 10^{23} \text{ atoms C}} \times \dfrac{1 \text{ mol C}_6\text{H}_{12}\text{O}_6}{6 \text{ mol C}}$

$\times \dfrac{180.15 \text{ g C}_6\text{H}_{12}\text{O}_6}{1 \text{ mol C}_6\text{H}_{12}\text{O}_6} = 2.49 \times 10^8 \text{ g C}_6\text{H}_{12}\text{O}_6$

8.73 (a) $20.0 \text{ g H}_2\text{O}_2 \times \dfrac{1 \text{ mol H}_2\text{O}_2}{34.014 \text{ g H}_2\text{O}_2} \times \dfrac{2 \text{ mol H}_2\text{O}}{2 \text{ mol H}_2\text{O}_2} \times \dfrac{18.015 \text{ g H}_2\text{O}}{1 \text{ mol H}_2\text{O}} = 10.6 \text{ g H}_2\text{O}$

(b) $20.0 \text{ g H}_2\text{O} \times \dfrac{1 \text{ mol H}_2\text{O}}{18.015 \text{ g H}_2\text{O}} \times \dfrac{2 \text{ mol H}_2\text{O}_2}{2 \text{ mol H}_2\text{O}} \times \dfrac{34.014 \text{ g H}_2\text{O}_2}{1 \text{ mol H}_2\text{O}_2} = 37.8 \text{ g H}_2\text{O}_2$

(c) $20.0 \text{ g O}_2 \times \dfrac{1 \text{ mol O}_2}{31.998 \text{ g O}_2} \times \dfrac{2 \text{ mol H}_2\text{O}_2}{1 \text{ mol O}_2} \times \dfrac{34.014 \text{ g H}_2\text{O}_2}{1 \text{ mol H}_2\text{O}_2} = 42.5 \text{ g H}_2\text{O}_2$

8.74 (a) $5.000 \text{ g SCl}_4 \times \dfrac{1 \text{ mol SCl}_4}{173.88 \text{ g SCl}_4} \times \dfrac{2 \text{ mol H}_2\text{O}}{1 \text{ mol SCl}_4} \times \dfrac{18.015 \text{ g H}_2\text{O}}{1 \text{ mol H}_2\text{O}} = 1.036 \text{ g H}_2\text{O}$

(b) $10.00 \text{ g H}_2\text{O} \times \dfrac{1 \text{ mol H}_2\text{O}}{18.015 \text{ g H}_2\text{O}} \times \dfrac{1 \text{ mol SO}_2}{2 \text{ mol H}_2\text{O}} \times \dfrac{64.064 \text{ g SO}_2}{1 \text{ mol SO}_2} = 17.78 \text{ g SO}_2$

(c) Because the mass of H_2O you calculated in part (a) is exactly the mass of H_2O that reacts with 5.000 g of SCl_4, you may use either reactant to calculate the amount of HCl formed:

$5.000 \text{ g SCl}_4 \times \dfrac{1 \text{ mol SCl}_4}{173.88 \text{ g SCl}_4} \times \dfrac{4 \text{ mol HCl}}{1 \text{ mol SCl}_4} \times \dfrac{36.460 \text{ g HCl}}{1 \text{ mol HCl}} = 4.194 \text{ g HCl}$

or

$1.036 \text{ g H}_2\text{O} \times \dfrac{1 \text{ mol H}_2\text{O}}{18.015 \text{ g H}_2\text{O}} \times \dfrac{4 \text{ mol HCl}}{2 \text{ mol H}_2\text{O}} \times \dfrac{36.460 \text{ g HCl}}{1 \text{ mol HCl}} = 4.193 \text{ g HCl}$

8.75 The reaction was run with B as the limiting reactant.

8.76 To determine which is the limiting ingredient, multiply each given amount by the appropriate conversion factor:

$3 \text{ cups flour} \times \dfrac{1 \text{ dozen cookies}}{2 \text{ cups flour}} = 1.5 \text{ dozen cookies}$

$3 \text{ cups sugar} \times \dfrac{1 \text{ dozen cookies}}{3 \text{ cups sugar}} = 1 \text{ dozen cookies}$

Because it gives the smaller number, the sugar is the limiting ingredient. You can make only 1 dozen cookies.

8.77 To determine which is the limiting ingredient, multiply each given amount by the appropriate conversion factor:

$$25 \text{ eggs} \times \frac{1 \text{ cheesecake}}{5 \text{ eggs}} = 5 \text{ cheesecakes}$$

$$9 \text{ blocks cream cheese} \times \frac{1 \text{ cheesecake}}{3 \text{ blocks cream cheese}} = 3 \text{ cheesecakes}$$

$$4 \text{ cups sugar} \times \frac{1 \text{ cheesecake}}{1 \text{ cup sugar}} = 4 \text{ cheesecakes}$$

Because it gives the smallest number, the cream cheese is the limiting ingredient. You can make 3 cheesecakes.

8.78 (a) $5.00 \text{ g } H_2 \times \dfrac{1 \text{ mol } H_2}{2.0158 \text{ g } H_2} \times \dfrac{2 \text{ mol } H_2O}{2 \text{ mol } H_2} \times \dfrac{18.015 \text{ g } H_2O}{1 \text{ mol } H_2O} = 44.7 \text{ g } H_2O$

(b) $5.00 \text{ g } H_2O \times \dfrac{1 \text{ mol } H_2O}{18.015 \text{ g } H_2O} \times \dfrac{1 \text{ mol } O_2}{2 \text{ mol } H_2O} \times \dfrac{31.998 \text{ g } O_2}{1 \text{ mol } O_2} = 4.44 \text{ g } O_2$

(c) The number of moles of H_2 in 100.0 g is

$$100.0 \text{ g } H_2 \times \frac{1 \text{ mol } H_2}{2.0158 \text{ g } H_2} = 49.61 \text{ mol } H_2$$

The number of moles of O_2 required to react in a stoichiometric fashion with 49.61 moles of H_2 is

$$49.61 \text{ mol } H_2 \times \frac{1 \text{ mol } O_2}{2 \text{ mol } H_2} = 24.81 \text{ mol } O_2$$

This many moles of O_2 expressed in grams is

$$24.81 \text{ mol } O_2 \times \frac{31.998 \text{ g } O_2}{1 \text{ mol } O_2} = 793.9 \text{ g } O_2$$

(d) $50.0 \text{ g } O_2 \times \dfrac{1 \text{ mol } O_2}{31.998 \text{ g } O_2} \times \dfrac{2 \text{ mol } H_2O}{1 \text{ mol } O_2} \times \dfrac{18.015 \text{ g } H_2O}{1 \text{ mol } H_2O} = 56.3 \text{ g } H_2O$

(e) $56.3 \text{ g } H_2O \times \dfrac{1 \text{ mol } H_2O}{18.015 \text{ g } H_2O} \times \dfrac{6.022 \times 10^{23} \text{ molecules } H_2O}{1 \text{ mol } H_2O} = 1.88 \times 10^{24} \text{ molecules } H_2O$

8.79 The first thing you must do is balance the equation: $4 P + 5 O_2 \longrightarrow 2 P_2O_5$.

(a) $20.0 \text{ g } O_2 \times \dfrac{1 \text{ mol } O_2}{31.998 \text{ g } O_2} \times \dfrac{4 \text{ mol } P}{5 \text{ mol } O_2} \times \dfrac{30.973 \text{ g } P}{1 \text{ mol } P} = 15.5 \text{ g } P$

(b) Because part (a) was calculated for running the reaction in a balanced fashion, you may use either mass to calculate the theoretical yield:

$$20.0 \text{ g } O_2 \times \frac{1 \text{ mol } O_2}{31.998 \text{ g } O_2} \times \frac{2 \text{ mol } P_2O_5}{5 \text{ mol } O_2} \times \frac{141.941 \text{ g } P_2O_5}{1 \text{ mol } P_2O_5} = 35.5 \text{ g } P_2O_5$$

or

$$15.5 \text{ g } P \times \frac{1 \text{ mol } P}{30.973 \text{ g } P} \times \frac{2 \text{ mol } P_2O_5}{4 \text{ mol } P} \times \frac{141.941 \text{ g } P_2O_5}{1 \text{ mol } P_2O_5} = 35.5 \text{ g } P_2O_5$$

8.80 The balanced equation is $3\,H_2 + N_2 \longrightarrow 2\,NH_3$.

(a) $10.0\ \text{g}\,H_2 \times \dfrac{1\ \text{mol}\,H_2}{2.0158\ \text{g}\,H_2} \times \dfrac{1\ \text{mol}\,N_2}{3\ \text{mol}\,H_2} \times \dfrac{28.014\ \text{g}\,N_2}{1\ \text{mol}\,N_2} = 46.3\ \text{g}\,N_2$

(b) Because the masses of part (a) are for the reaction run in a balanced fashion, you may use either mass to determine the mass of product:

$10.0\ \text{g}\,H_2 \times \dfrac{1\ \text{mol}\,H_2}{2.0158\ \text{g}\,H_2} \times \dfrac{2\ \text{mol}\,NH_3}{3\ \text{mol}\,H_2} \times \dfrac{17.031\ \text{g}\,NH_3}{1\ \text{mol}\,NH_3} = 56.3\ \text{g}\,NH_3$

or

$46.3\ \text{g}\,N_2 \times \dfrac{1\ \text{mol}\,N_2}{28.014\ \text{g}\,N_2} \times \dfrac{2\ \text{mol}\,NH_3}{3\ \text{mol}\,N_2} \times \dfrac{17.031\ \text{g}\,NH_3}{1\ \text{mol}\,NH_3} = 56.3\ \text{g}\,NH_3$

(c) $56.3\ \text{g}\,NH_3 \times \dfrac{1\ \text{mol}\,NH_3}{17.031\ \text{g}\,NH_3} \times \dfrac{6.022 \times 10^{23}\ \text{molecules}\,NH_3}{1\ \text{mol}\,NH_3} = 1.99 \times 10^{24}\ \text{molecules}\,NH_3$

8.81 (a) $H_2 + Br_2 \longrightarrow 2\,HBr$

(b) The balanced equation tells you the H_2 and Br_2 combine in a one-to-one ratio. Because you have 7.00 moles of Br_2 but only 5.00 moles of H_2, the H_2 is the limiting reactant.

(c) Because H_2 is the limiting reactant, you must use it to calculate the theoretical yield:

$5.00\ \text{mol}\,H_2 \times \dfrac{2\ \text{mol}\,HBr}{1\ \text{mol}\,H_2} = 10.0\ \text{mol}\,HBr$

(d) $10.0\ \text{mol}\,HBr \times \dfrac{80.912\ \text{g}\,HBr}{1\ \text{mol}\,HBr} = 809\ \text{g}\,HBr$

(e) You begin with 5.00 moles of H_2 and 7.00 moles of Br_2. You know from the one-to-one reactant ratio in the balanced equation that 5.00 moles of Br_2 react with 5.00 moles of H_2. Therefore the excess amount of Br_2 is 7.00 mol − 5.00 mol = 2.00 mol.

(f) $2.00\ \text{mol}\,Br_2 \times \dfrac{159.81\ \text{g}\,Br_2}{1\ \text{mol}\,Br_2} = 320\ \text{g}\,Br_2$

8.82 Because the amounts given are not easy-to-work-with whole numbers as they were in the preceding problem, use the four-step procedure given in the textbook.

(a) Step 1: $Cl_2 + 3\,F_2 \longrightarrow 2\,ClF_3$

(b) Step 2 is unnecesssary because amounts are given in moles. Step 2a:

$Cl_2 \quad \dfrac{2.50}{1} = 2.50$

$F_2 \quad \dfrac{6.15}{3} = 2.05$

Its smaller mole-to-coefficient ratio tells you F_2 is the limiting reactant.

(c) Step 3: $6.15\ \text{mol}\,F_2 \times \dfrac{2\ \text{mol}\,ClF_3}{3\ \text{mol}\,F_2} = 4.10\ \text{mol}\,ClF_3$

(d) Step 4: $4.10\ \text{mol}\,ClF_3 \times \dfrac{92.447\ \text{g}\,ClF_3}{1\ \text{mol}\,ClF_3} = 379\ \text{g}\,ClF_3$

(e) The excess reactant is Cl_2, and you began with 2.50 moles of it. Because this problem deals with theoretical yields, you can assume the entire 6.15 moles of limiting reactant F_2 was used up. The amount of Cl_2 consumed was

$$6.15 \text{ mol } F_2 \times \frac{1 \text{ mol } Cl_2}{3 \text{ mol } F_2} = 2.05 \text{ mol } Cl_2$$

The leftover Cl_2 is therefore 2.50 mol − 2.05 mol = 0.45 mol.

(f) $0.45 \text{ mol } Cl_2 \times \dfrac{70.906 \text{ g } Cl_2}{1 \text{ mol } Cl_2} = 32 \text{ g } Cl_2$

8.83 (a) Step 1: $2 \text{ Na}(s) + Br_2(l) \longrightarrow 2 \text{ NaBr}(s)$

(b) Step 2: $5.00 \text{ g Na} \times \dfrac{1 \text{ mol Na}}{22.9898 \text{ g Na}} = 0.217 \text{ mol Na}$

$$30.0 \text{ g } Br_2 \times \frac{1 \text{ mol } Br_2}{159.8 \text{ g } Br_2} = 0.188 \text{ mol } Br_2$$

Step 2a: Na $\quad \dfrac{0.217}{2} = 0.109$

$Br_2 \quad \dfrac{0.188}{1} = 0.188$

Because 0.109 is the smaller number, Na is the limiting reactant.

(c) Steps 3 and 4:

$$0.217 \text{ mol Na} \times \frac{2 \text{ mol NaBr}}{2 \text{ mol Na}} \times \frac{102.89 \text{ g NaBr}}{1 \text{ mol NaBr}} = 22.3 \text{ g NaBr}$$

(d) Because the problem deals with theoretical yields, all the 5.00 g = 0.217 moles of limiting reactant Na is used up. The amount of Br_2 it combined with is

$$0.217 \text{ mol Na} \times \frac{1 \text{ mol } Br_2}{2 \text{ mol Na}} \times \frac{159.82 \text{ g } Br_2}{1 \text{ mol } Br_2} = 17.3 \text{ g } Br_2$$

The leftover Br_2 is therefore 30.0 g − 17.3 g = 12.7 g.

(e) $\dfrac{14.7 \text{ g NaBr}}{22.3 \text{ g NaBr}} \times 100 = 65.9\%$

8.84 (a) Step 1: $Cl_2 + 3 F_2 \longrightarrow 2 \text{ ClF}_3$

(b) Step 2: $10.00 \text{ g } Cl_2 \times \dfrac{1 \text{ mol } Cl_2}{70.906 \text{ g } Cl_2} = 0.1410 \text{ mol } Cl_2$

$$10.00 \text{ g } F_2 \times \frac{1 \text{ mol } F_2}{37.996 \text{ g } F_2} = 0.2632 \text{ mol } F_2$$

Step 2a: $Cl_2 \quad \dfrac{0.1410}{1} = 0.1410$

$F_2 \quad \dfrac{0.2632}{3} = 0.08773 \text{ limiting}$

(c) Steps 3 and 4:

$$0.2632 \text{ mol } F_2 \times \frac{2 \text{ mol } ClF_3}{3 \text{ mol } F_2} \times \frac{92.447 \text{ g } ClF_3}{1 \text{ mol } ClF_3} = 16.22 \text{ g } ClF_3$$

(d) All of the F_2 is used up, consuming

$$0.2632 \text{ mol } F_2 \times \frac{1 \text{ mol } Cl_2}{3 \text{ mol } F_2} \times \frac{70.906 \text{ g } Cl_2}{1 \text{ mol } Cl_2} = 6.221 \text{ g } Cl_2$$

The leftover Cl_2 is $10.00 \text{ g} - 6.221 \text{ g} = 3.78 \text{ g}$.

(e) $\dfrac{12.50 \text{ g } ClF_3}{16.22 \text{ g } ClF_3} \times 100 = 77.07\%$

8.85 (a) Step 1: $2 \text{ Na} + H_2 \longrightarrow 2 \text{ NaH}$

(b) Step 2: $10.00 \text{ g Na} \times \dfrac{1 \text{ mol Na}}{22.9898 \text{ g Na}} = 0.4350 \text{ mol Na}$

$0.0235 \text{ g } H_2 \times \dfrac{1 \text{ mol } H_2}{2.0158 \text{ g } H_2} = 0.0117 \text{ mol } H_2$

Step 2a: Na $\dfrac{0.4350}{2} = 0.2175$

H_2 $\dfrac{0.0117}{1} = 0.0117$ limiting reactant

(c) Steps 3 and 4:

$0.0117 \text{ mol } H_2 \times \dfrac{2 \text{ mol NaH}}{1 \text{ mol } H_2} \times \dfrac{23.998 \text{ g NaH}}{1 \text{ mol NaH}} = 0.562 \text{ g NaH}$

(d) All of the H_2 is used up, consuming

$0.0117 \text{ mol } H_2 \times \dfrac{2 \text{ mol Na}}{1 \text{ mol } H_2} \times \dfrac{22.9898 \text{ g Na}}{1 \text{ mol Na}} = 0.538 \text{ g Na}$

The leftover Na is therefore $10.00 \text{ g} - 0.538 \text{ g} = 9.46 \text{ g}$.

(e) $\dfrac{0.428 \text{ g NaH}}{0.562 \text{ g NaH}} \times 100 = 76.2\%$

8.86 (a) Step 1: $2 \text{ C}_4\text{H}_{10} + 13 \text{ O}_2 \longrightarrow 8 \text{ CO}_2 + 10 \text{ H}_2\text{O}$

(b) Step 2: $10.00 \text{ g } C_4H_{10} \times \dfrac{1 \text{ mol } C_4H_{10}}{58.123 \text{ g } C_4H_{10}} = 0.1720 \text{ mol } C_4H_{10}$

$10.00 \text{ g } O_2 \times \dfrac{1 \text{ mol } O_2}{31.998 \text{ g } O_2} = 0.3125 \text{ mol } O_2$

Step 2a: C_4H_{10} $\dfrac{0.1720}{2} = 0.0860$

O_2 $\dfrac{0.3125}{13} = 0.0240$ limiting reactant

(c) $0.3125 \text{ mol } O_2 \times \dfrac{8 \text{ mol } CO_2}{13 \text{ mol } O_2} \times \dfrac{44.009 \text{ g } CO_2}{1 \text{ mol } CO_2} = 8.463 \text{ g } CO_2$

$0.3125 \text{ mol } O_2 \times \dfrac{10 \text{ mol } H_2O}{13 \text{ mol } O_2} \times \dfrac{18.015 \text{ g } H_2O}{1 \text{ mol } H_2O} = 4.331 \text{ g } H_2O$

(d) $0.3125 \text{ mol } O_2 \times \dfrac{2 \text{ mol } C_4H_{10}}{13 \text{ mol } O_2} \times \dfrac{58.123 \text{ g } C_4H_{10}}{1 \text{ mol } C_4H_{10}} = 2.794 \text{ g } C_4H_{10} \text{ consumed}$

$10.00 \text{ g} - 2.794 \text{ g} = 7.21 \text{ g } C_4H_{10} \text{ left over}$

(e) Find the total number of grams of O_2 needed to run the reaction in balanced fashion with 10.00 g of C_4H_{10}:

$$10.00 \text{ g } C_4H_{10} \times \dfrac{1 \text{ mol } C_4H_{10}}{58.123 \text{ g } C_4H_{10}} \times \dfrac{13 \text{ mol } O_2}{2 \text{ mol } C_4H_{10}} \times \dfrac{31.998 \text{ g } O_2}{1 \text{ mol } O_2} = 35.78 \text{ g } O_2$$

$35.78 \text{ g } O_2 \text{ needed} - 10.00 \text{ g } O_2 \text{ present} = 25.78 \text{ g additional } O_2$

8.87 Step 1: $\dfrac{\text{Molar mass of compound}}{\text{Molar mass of empirical formula}} = \dfrac{90 \text{ g/mol}}{44.053 \text{ g/mol}} = 2 \text{ approximately}$

Step 2: $C_{2\times2}H_{2\times4}O_{2\times1} \longrightarrow C_4H_8O_2$

8.88 (a) Step 1: $\dfrac{26 \text{ g/mol}}{13.02 \text{ g/mol}} = 2 \text{ approximately}$

Step 2: $C_{2\times1}H_{2\times1} \longrightarrow C_2H_2$

(b) Step 1: $\dfrac{52 \text{ g/mol}}{13.02 \text{ g/mol}} = 4 \text{ approximately}$

Step 2: $C_{4\times1}H_{4\times1} \longrightarrow C_4H_4$

(c) Step 1: $\dfrac{78 \text{ g/mol}}{13.02 \text{ g/mol}} = 6 \text{ approximately}$

Step 2: $C_{6\times1}H_{6\times1} \longrightarrow C_6H_6$

8.89 (a) To find mass percents, begin with the first three steps of the procedure given in the textbook for Determining a Molecular Formula from Combustion Analysis Data:

Step 1: Convert grams of CO_2 to moles of C and grams of H_2O to moles of H:

$$2.257 \text{ g } CO_2 \times \dfrac{1 \text{ mol } CO_2}{44.009 \text{ g } CO_2} \times \dfrac{1 \text{ mol } C}{1 \text{ mol } CO_2} = 0.05128 \text{ mol } C$$

$$0.9241 \text{ g } H_2O \times \dfrac{1 \text{ mol } H_2O}{18.015 \text{ g } H_2O} \times \dfrac{2 \text{ mol } H}{1 \text{ mol } H_2O} = 0.1026 \text{ mol } H$$

Step 2: Convert to grams of C and H:

$$0.05128 \text{ mol } C \times \dfrac{12.011 \text{ g } C}{1 \text{ mol } C} = 0.6159 \text{ g } C$$

$$0.1026 \text{ mol } H \times \dfrac{1.0079 \text{ g } H}{1 \text{ mol } H} = 0.1034 \text{ g } H$$

Step 3: Determine whether there is any O in the compound and, if so, convert to moles [you do not need moles of O for this calculation, but you will in part (b)]:

$$1.540 \text{ g sample} - \left(0.1034 \text{ g } H + 0.6159 \text{ g } C\right) = 0.8207 \text{ g } O$$

$$0.8207 \text{ g } O \times \dfrac{1 \text{ mol } O}{15.999 \text{ g } O} = 0.05130 \text{ mol } O$$

Now you have enough information to calculate mass percents:

$$\frac{0.6159 \text{ g C}}{1.540 \text{ g compound}} \times 100 = 39.99\% \text{ C}$$

$$\frac{0.1034 \text{ g H}}{1.540 \text{ g compound}} \times 100 = 6.714\% \text{ H}$$

$$\frac{0.8207 \text{ g O}}{1.540 \text{ g compound}} \times 100 = 53.29\% \text{ O}$$

(b) From part (a), you know the subscripts x, y, z are $C_{0.05128}H_{0.1026}O_{0.05130}$. Dividing through by the smallest subscript gives an empirical formula of:

$$C_{\frac{0.05128}{0.05128}} H_{\frac{0.1026}{0.05128}} O_{\frac{0.05130}{0.05128}} \rightarrow C_{1.00}H_{2.00}O_{1.00} \rightarrow CH_2O$$

(c) The molar mass of the empirical formula is 30.03 g/mol.

Step 1: $\dfrac{30 \text{ g/mol}}{30.03 \text{ g/mol}} = 1$ approximately

Step 2: Because the ratio from step 1 is 1, the molecular formula is the same as the empirical formula.

8.90 (a) Calculate the element masses by using the first three steps of the procedure for Determining a Molecular Formula from Combustion Analysis Data:

Step 1: $6.258 \text{ g CO}_2 \times \dfrac{1 \text{ mol CO}_2}{44.009 \text{ g CO}_2} \times \dfrac{1 \text{ mol C}}{1 \text{ mol CO}_2} = 0.1422 \text{ mol C}$

$1.274 \text{ g H}_2O \times \dfrac{1 \text{ mol H}_2O}{18.015 \text{ g H}_2O} \times \dfrac{2 \text{ mol H}}{1 \text{ mol H}_2O} = 0.1414 \text{ mol H}$

Step 2: $0.1422 \text{ mol C} \times \dfrac{12.011 \text{ g C}}{1 \text{ mol C}} = 1.708 \text{ g C}$

$0.1414 \text{ mol H} \times \dfrac{1.0079 \text{ g H}}{1 \text{ mol H}} = 0.1425 \text{ g H}$

Step 3: $2.230 \text{ g sample} - (1.708 \text{ g C} + 0.1425 \text{ g H}) = 0.3795 \text{ g O}$

$$\left(0.3795 \text{ g O} \times \dfrac{1 \text{ mol O}}{15.999 \text{ g O}} = 0.02373 \text{ mol O}\right)$$

The mass percents are

$$\frac{1.708 \text{ g C}}{2.230 \text{ g compound}} \times 100 = 76.59\% \text{ C}$$

$$\frac{0.1425 \text{ g H}}{2.230 \text{ g compound}} \times 100 = 6.390\% \text{ H}$$

$$\frac{0.3795 \text{ g O}}{2.230 \text{ g compound}} \times 100 = 17.02\% \text{ O}$$

(b) From part (a), you know the subscripts x, y, z are $C_{0.1422}H_{0.1414}O_{0.02373}$. Dividing through by the smallest gives $C_{5.99}H_{5.96}O_1 \rightarrow C_6H_6O$ for the empirical formula.

(c) Step 1: $\dfrac{94 \text{ g/mol}}{94.11 \text{ g/mol}} = 1$ approximately

Step 2: Because the ratio is 1, the molecular formula is the same as the empirical formula.

8.91 (a) Step 1: $3.383 \text{ g } CO_2 \times \dfrac{1 \text{ mol } CO_2}{44.009 \text{ g } CO_2} \times \dfrac{1 \text{ mol C}}{1 \text{ mol } CO_2} = 0.07687 \text{ mol C}$

$0.692 \text{ g } H_2O \times \dfrac{1 \text{ mol } H_2O}{18.015 \text{ g } H_2O} \times \dfrac{2 \text{ mol H}}{1 \text{ mol } H_2O} = 0.0768 \text{ mol H}$

Step 2: $0.07687 \text{ mol C} \times \dfrac{12.011 \text{ g C}}{1 \text{ mol C}} = 0.9233 \text{ g C}$

$0.0768 \text{ mol H} \times \dfrac{1.0079 \text{ g H}}{1 \text{ mol H}} = 0.0774 \text{ g H}$

Step 3: $1.000 \text{ g sample} - (0.9233 \text{ g C} + 0.07741 \text{ g H}) = 0 \text{ g O}$
Mass percents:

$\dfrac{0.9233 \text{ g C}}{1.000 \text{ g compound}} \times 100 = 92.33\% \text{ C}$

$\dfrac{0.0774 \text{ g H}}{1.000 \text{ g compound}} \times 100 = 7.74\% \text{ H}$

(b) $C_{\frac{0.07687}{0.0768}} H_{\frac{0.0768}{0.0768}} \rightarrow C_{1.00} H_{1.00} \rightarrow CH$

(c) Step 1: $\dfrac{78 \text{ g/mol}}{13.02 \text{ g/mol}} = 6$ approximately

Step 2: $C_{6\times1} H_{6\times1} \longrightarrow C_6H_6$

8.92 Knowing that the sample contains only C and H, you can work the problem knowing only the H_2O mass. Once you use this mass to calculate grams of H, get grams of C by difference.

(a) Step 1: $1.284 \text{ g } H_2O \times \dfrac{1 \text{ mol } H_2O}{18.015 \text{ g } H_2O} \times \dfrac{2 \text{ mol H}}{1 \text{ mol } H_2O} = 0.1425 \text{ mol H}$

Step 2: $0.1425 \text{ mol H} \times \dfrac{1.0079 \text{ g H}}{1 \text{ mol H}} = 0.1436 \text{ g H}$

The C mass must be $1.000 \text{ g sample} - 0.1436 \text{ g H} = 0.8564 \text{ g C}$, and the mass percents are

$\dfrac{0.8564 \text{ g C}}{1.000 \text{ g compound}} \times 100 = 85.64\% \text{ C}$

$\dfrac{0.1436 \text{ g H}}{1.000 \text{ g compound}} \times 100 = 14.36\% \text{ H}$

(b) You need to convert the mass of C to moles to get the empirical formula:

$0.8564 \text{ g C} \times \dfrac{1 \text{ mol C}}{12.011 \text{ g C}} = 0.07130 \text{ mol C}$

$C_{\frac{0.07130}{0.07130}} H_{\frac{0.1425}{0.07130}} \rightarrow C_{1.00} H_{2.00} \rightarrow CH_2$

(c) Step 1: $\dfrac{71 \text{ g/mol}}{14.03 \text{ g/mol}} = 5$ approximately

Step 2: $C_{5\times 1}H_{5\times 2} \longrightarrow C_5H_{10}$

8.93 (a) Step 1: $6.162 \text{ g CO}_2 \times \dfrac{1 \text{ mol CO}_2}{44.009 \text{ g CO}_2} \times \dfrac{1 \text{ mol C}}{1 \text{ mol CO}_2} = 0.1400 \text{ mol C}$

$9.008 \text{ g H}_2O \times \dfrac{1 \text{ mol H}_2O}{18.015 \text{ g H}_2O} \times \dfrac{2 \text{ mol H}}{1 \text{ mol H}_2O} = 0.1000 \text{ mol H}$

Step 2: $0.1400 \text{ mol C} \times \dfrac{12.011 \text{ g C}}{1 \text{ mol C}} = 1.682 \text{ g C}$

$0.1000 \text{ mol H} \times \dfrac{1.0079 \text{ g H}}{1 \text{ mol H}} = 0.1008 \text{ g H}$

Knowing the compound contains only C, H, and Cl, you calculate the mass of Cl by difference:

3.200 g sample $-$ (1.682 g C + 0.1008 g H) = 1.417 g Cl

Mass percents:

$\dfrac{1.682 \text{ g C}}{3.200 \text{ g compound}} \times 100 = 52.56\% \text{ C}$

$\dfrac{0.1008 \text{ g H}}{3.200 \text{ g compound}} \times 100 = 3.150\% \text{ H}$

$\dfrac{1.417 \text{ g Cl}}{3.200 \text{ g compound}} \times 100 = 44.28\% \text{ Cl}$

8.94 (a) Step 1: $2.724 \text{ g CO}_2 \times \dfrac{1 \text{ mol CO}_2}{44.009 \text{ g CO}_2} \times \dfrac{1 \text{ mol C}}{1 \text{ mol CO}_2} = 0.06190 \text{ mol C}$

$0.5575 \text{ g H}_2O \times \dfrac{1 \text{ mol H}_2O}{18.015 \text{ g H}_2O} \times \dfrac{2 \text{ mol H}}{1 \text{ mol H}_2O} = 0.06189 \text{ mol H}$

Step 2: $0.06190 \text{ mol C} \times \dfrac{12.011 \text{ g C}}{1 \text{ mol C}} = 0.7435 \text{ g C}$

$0.06189 \text{ mol H} \times \dfrac{1.0079 \text{ g H}}{1 \text{ mol H}} = 0.06238 \text{ g H}$

Determine the mass of Cl by difference:

3.000 g sample $-$ (0.7435 g C + 0.06238 g H) = 2.194 g Cl

Mass percents:

$\dfrac{0.7435 \text{ g C}}{3.000 \text{ g compound}} \times 100 = 24.78\% \text{ C}$

$\dfrac{0.06238 \text{ g H}}{3.000 \text{ g compound}} \times 100 = 2.079\% \text{ H}$

$\dfrac{2.194 \text{ g Cl}}{3.000 \text{ g compound}} \times 100 = 73.13\% \text{ Cl}$

(b) To determine subscripts for the empirical formula, you need numbers of moles. You already have that information for C and H. The calculation for Cl is

$$2.194 \text{ g Cl} \times \frac{1 \text{ mol Cl}}{35.453 \text{ g Cl}} = 0.06188 \text{ mol Cl}$$

The empirical formula is

$$C_{\frac{0.06190}{0.06188}}H_{\frac{0.06189}{0.06188}}Cl_{\frac{0.06188}{0.06188}} \rightarrow C_{1.00}H_{1.00}Cl_{1.00} \rightarrow CHCl$$

8.95 Step 1: To get the empirical formula from percent composition, assume 100 g of compound (that way, percent values become grams):

$$66.63\% \text{ C} \rightarrow 66.63 \text{ g C} \times \frac{1 \text{ mol C}}{12.011 \text{ g C}} = 5.547 \text{ mol C}$$

$$11.18\% \text{ H} \rightarrow 11.18 \text{ g H} \times \frac{1 \text{ mol H}}{1.0079 \text{ g H}} = 11.09 \text{ mol H}$$

$$22.19\% \text{ O} \rightarrow 22.19 \text{ g O} \times \frac{1 \text{ mol O}}{15.999 \text{ g O}} = 1.387 \text{ mol O}$$

Step 2: Use the calculated numbers of moles as subscripts and divide through by the smallest:

$$C_{\frac{5.547}{1.387}}H_{\frac{11.09}{1.387}}O_{\frac{1.387}{1.387}} \rightarrow C_{4.00}H_{8.00}O_{1.00} \rightarrow C_4H_8O$$

8.96 Step 1: Assume 100 g of compound and convert element masses to moles:

$$58.5\% \text{ C} \rightarrow 58.5 \text{ g C} \times \frac{1 \text{ mol C}}{12.011 \text{ g C}} = 4.87 \text{ mol C}$$

$$4.91\% \text{ H} \rightarrow 4.91 \text{ g H} \times \frac{1 \text{ mol H}}{1.0079 \text{ g H}} = 4.87 \text{ mol H}$$

$$19.5\% \text{ O} \rightarrow 19.5 \text{ g O} \times \frac{1 \text{ mol O}}{15.999 \text{ g O}} = 1.22 \text{ mol O}$$

$$17.1\% \text{ N} \rightarrow 17.1 \text{ g N} \times \frac{1 \text{ mol N}}{14.007 \text{ g N}} = 1.22 \text{ mol N}$$

Step 2: $C_{\frac{4.87}{1.22}}H_{\frac{4.87}{1.22}}O_{\frac{1.22}{1.22}}N_{\frac{1.22}{1.22}} \rightarrow C_{3.99}H_{3.99}O_{1.00}N_{1.00} \rightarrow C_4H_4ON$

8.97 First determine the percent by mass oxygen:

100% − (26.4% Na + 36.8% S) = 36.8% O

Step 1: Assume 100 g of compound and convert masses to moles:

$$26.4\% \text{ Na} \rightarrow 26.4 \text{ g Na} \times \frac{1 \text{ mol Na}}{22.9898 \text{ g Na}} = 1.15 \text{ mol Na}$$

$$36.8\% \text{ S} \rightarrow 36.8 \text{ g S} \times \frac{1 \text{ mol S}}{32.066 \text{ g S}} = 1.15 \text{ mol S}$$

$$36.8\% \text{ O} \rightarrow 36.8 \text{ g O} \times \frac{1 \text{ mol O}}{15.999 \text{ g O}} = 2.30 \text{ mol O}$$

Step 2: $Na_{\frac{1.15}{1.15}}S_{\frac{1.15}{1.15}}O_{\frac{2.30}{1.15}} \rightarrow Na_{1.00}S_{1.00}O_{2.00} \rightarrow NaSO_2$

8.98 First determine the mass percent of oxygen:

100% − (43.2% K + 39.1% Cl) = 17.7% O

Step 1: Assume 100 g of compound and convert masses to moles:

$$43.2\% \text{ K} \rightarrow 43.2 \text{ g K} \times \frac{1 \text{ mol K}}{39.098 \text{ g K}} = 1.10 \text{ mol K}$$

$$39.1\% \text{ Cl} \rightarrow 39.1 \text{ g Cl} \times \frac{1 \text{ mol Cl}}{35.453 \text{ g Cl}} = 1.10 \text{ mol Cl}$$

$$17.7\% \text{ O} \rightarrow 17.7 \text{ g O} \times \frac{1 \text{ mol O}}{15.999 \text{ g O}} = 1.11 \text{ mol O}$$

Step 2: $K_{\frac{1.10}{1.10}}Cl_{\frac{1.10}{1.10}}O_{\frac{1.11}{1.10}} \rightarrow K_{1.00}Cl_{1.00}O_{1.01} \rightarrow KClO$

8.99 Step 1: Assume you have 1 mole of C_2H_6O. That way, the subscripts tell you how many moles you have of each element in the compound. Use this information to convert element moles to element masses:

$$2 \text{ mol C} \times \frac{12.011 \text{ g C}}{1 \text{ mol C}} = 24.022 \text{ g C}$$

$$6 \text{ mol H} \times \frac{1.0079 \text{ g H}}{1 \text{ mol H}} = 6.0474 \text{ g H}$$

$$1 \text{ mol O} \times \frac{15.999 \text{ g O}}{1 \text{ mol O}} = 15.999 \text{ g O}$$

Step 2: Divide each mass calculated in step 1 by the mass of the 1 mole of C_2H_6O you are assumed to have. The mass in grams of that 1 mole is numerically equal to the molar mass. The molar mass of C_2H_6O is 46.068 g/mol, which means you are working with 46.068 g of C_2H_6O. Multiply each quotient by 100 to get the mass percent of each element:

$$\frac{24.022 \text{ g C}}{46.068 \text{ g C}_2\text{H}_6\text{O}} \times 100 = 52.14\% \text{ C}$$

$$\frac{6.0474 \text{ g C}}{46.068 \text{ g C}_2\text{H}_6\text{O}} \times 100 = 13.13\% \text{ H}$$

$$\frac{15.999 \text{ g C}}{46.068 \text{ g C}_2\text{H}_6\text{O}} \times 100 = 34.73\% \text{ O}$$

8.100 Step 1: Assume you have 1 mole of $C_2H_6O_2$, so that the subscripts tell you how many moles of each element you have. Convert moles to masses:

$$2 \text{ mol C} \times \frac{12.011 \text{ g C}}{1 \text{ mol C}} = 24.022 \text{ g C}$$

$$6 \text{ mol H} \times \frac{1.0079 \text{ g H}}{1 \text{ mol H}} = 6.0474 \text{ g H}$$

$$2 \text{ mol O} \times \frac{15.999 \text{ g O}}{1 \text{ mol O}} = 31.998 \text{ g O}$$

Step 2: The molar mass of $C_2H_6O_2$ is 62.067 g/mol, meaning the assumed 1 mole you are working with has a mass of 62.067 g. Divide each element mass by this mass and multiply by 100 to get mass percents:

$$\frac{24.022 \text{ g C}}{62.067 \text{ g C}_2\text{H}_6\text{O}_2} \times 100 = 38.70\% \text{ C}$$

$$\frac{6.0474 \text{ g H}}{62.067 \text{ g C}_2\text{H}_6\text{O}_2} \times 100 = 9.743\% \text{ H}$$

$$\frac{31.998 \text{ g P}}{62.067 \text{ g C}_2\text{H}_6\text{O}_2} \times 100 = 51.55\% \text{ O}$$

8.101 Step 1: Assume you have 1 mole of $C_{16}H_{18}N_2O_4S$, so that the subscripts tell you moles of each element. Convert moles to masses:

$$16 \text{ mol C} \times \frac{12.011 \text{ g C}}{1 \text{ mol C}} = 192.18 \text{ g C}$$

$$18 \text{ mol H} \times \frac{1.0079 \text{ g H}}{1 \text{ mol H}} = 18.142 \text{ g H}$$

$$2 \text{ mol N} \times \frac{14.007 \text{ g N}}{1 \text{ mol N}} = 28.014 \text{ g N}$$

$$4 \text{ mol O} \times \frac{15.999 \text{ g O}}{1 \text{ mol O}} = 63.996 \text{ g O}$$

$$1 \text{ mol S} \times \frac{32.066 \text{ g S}}{1 \text{ mol S}} = 32.066 \text{ g S}$$

Step 2: The molar mass of $C_{16}H_{18}N_2O_4S$ is 334.40 g/mol, meaning the assumed 1 mole you have has a mass of 334.40 g. Divide each element mass by this mass and multiply by 100 to get mass percents:

$$\frac{192.18 \text{ g C}}{334.40 \text{ g C}_{16}\text{H}_{18}\text{N}_2\text{O}_4\text{S}} \times 100 = 57.470\% \text{ C}$$

$$\frac{18.142 \text{ g H}}{334.40 \text{ g C}_{16}\text{H}_{18}\text{N}_2\text{O}_4\text{S}} \times 100 = 5.4252\% \text{ H}$$

$$\frac{28.014 \text{ g N}}{334.40 \text{ g C}_{16}\text{H}_{18}\text{N}_2\text{O}_4\text{S}} \times 100 = 8.3774\% \text{ N}$$

$$\frac{63.996 \text{ g O}}{334.40 \text{ g C}_{16}\text{H}_{18}\text{N}_2\text{O}_4\text{S}} \times 100 = 19.138\% \text{ O}$$

$$\frac{32.066 \text{ g S}}{334.40 \text{ g C}_{16}\text{H}_{18}\text{N}_2\text{O}_4\text{S}} \times 100 = 9.589\% \text{ S}$$

8.102 Step 1: Assume 1 mole of $C_{15}H_{11}NO_4I_4$, so that the subscripts tell you moles of each element. Convert moles to masses:

$$15 \text{ mol C} \times \frac{12.011 \text{ g C}}{1 \text{ mol C}} = 180.17 \text{ g C}$$

$$11 \text{ mol H} \times \frac{1.0079 \text{ g H}}{1 \text{ mol H}} = 11.087 \text{ g H}$$

$$1 \text{ mol N} \times \frac{14.007 \text{ g N}}{1 \text{ mol N}} = 14.007 \text{ g N}$$

$$4 \text{ mol O} \times \frac{15.999 \text{ g O}}{1 \text{ mol O}} = 63.996 \text{ g O}$$

$$4 \text{ mol I} \times \frac{126.90 \text{ g I}}{1 \text{ mol I}} = 507.60 \text{ g I}$$

Step 2: The molar mass of $C_{15}H_{11}NO_4I_4$ is 776.86 g/mol, meaning your 1 mole has a mass of 776.86 g. Divide each element mass by this mass and multiply by 100 to get mass percents:

$$\frac{180.17 \text{ g C}}{776.86 \text{ g C}_{15}\text{H}_{11}\text{NO}_4\text{I}_4} \times 100 = 23.192\% \text{ C}$$

$$\frac{11.087 \text{ g H}}{776.86 \text{ g C}_{15}\text{H}_{11}\text{NO}_4\text{I}_4} \times 100 = 1.4272\% \text{ H}$$

$$\frac{14.007 \text{ g N}}{776.86 \text{ g C}_{15}\text{H}_{11}\text{NO}_4\text{I}_4} \times 100 = 1.8030\% \text{ N}$$

$$\frac{63.996 \text{ g O}}{776.86 \text{ g C}_{15}\text{H}_{11}\text{NO}_4\text{I}_4} \times 100 = 8.2378\% \text{ O}$$

$$\frac{507.60 \text{ g I}}{776.86 \text{ g C}_{15}\text{H}_{11}\text{NO}_4\text{I}_4} \times 100 = 65.340\% \text{ I}$$

8.103 (a)   5 mol C = 5 × 12.011 g/mol = 60.055 g/mol
            10 mol H = 10 × 1.0079 g/mol = 10.079 g/mol
            $\underline{\text{5 mol O} = \text{5} \times 15.999 \text{ g/mol} = 79.995 \text{ g/mol}}$
            1 mol $C_5H_{10}O_5$ ⟶   150.129 g/mol

(b) $3.87 \text{ mol} \times \frac{150.129 \text{ g}}{1 \text{ mol}} = 581 \text{ g}$

(c) $3.87 \text{ mol} \times \frac{6.022 \times 10^{23} \text{ molecules}}{1 \text{ mol}} = 2.33 \times 10^{24} \text{ molecules}$

(d) $3.87 \text{ mol ribose} \times \frac{5 \text{ mol O}}{1 \text{ mol ribose}} \times \frac{6.022 \times 10^{23} \text{ atoms O}}{1 \text{ mol O}} = 1.16 \times 10^{25} \text{ atoms O}$

(e) $1.16 \times 10^{25} \text{ atoms O} \times \frac{15.999 \text{ g}}{6.022 \times 10^{23} \text{ atoms O}} = 309 \text{ g}$

8.104 (a) Mass of one S atom: 32.064 amu; mass of one O_2 molecule: 2 × 15.999 amu = 31.998 amu. The S atom has more mass.

(b) The molar mass of S_8 is 8 × 32.064 g/mol = 256.5 g/mol. Therefore

$$0.125 \text{ mol S}_8 \times \frac{256.5 \text{ g S}_8}{1 \text{ mol S}_8} = 32.06 \text{ g S}_8$$

The molar mass of O_3 is 3 × 15.999 g/mol = 47.997 g/mol. Therefore

$$0.670 \text{ mol O}_3 \times \frac{47.997 \text{ g O}_3}{1 \text{ mol O}_3} = 32.16 \text{ g O}_3$$

The O_3 sample has more mass.

8.105 No, because the theoretical yield is 100% of what you can possibly get.

8.106 (a) $2 Na(s) + 2 H_2O(l) \longrightarrow 2 NaOH(aq) + H_2(g)$

(b) $100.0 \text{ g Na} \times \dfrac{1 \text{ mol Na}}{22.9898 \text{ g Na}} = 4.350 \text{ mol Na}$

Mole-to-coefficient ratios:

Na $\quad \dfrac{4.350}{2} = 2.175$

$H_2O \quad \dfrac{4.00}{2} = 2.00$

H_2O is the limiting reactant because it has the lower ratio.

8.107 C_2H_4 molar mass

$$\begin{array}{l} 2 \times 12.011 \text{ g/mol} = 24.022 \text{ g/mol} \\ 4 \times 1.0079 \text{ g/mol} = \underline{4.032 \text{ g/mol}} \\ 28.054 \text{ g/mol} \end{array}$$

CO molar mass

$$\begin{array}{l} 1 \times 12.011 \text{ g/mol} = 12.011 \text{ g/mol} \\ 1 \times 15.999 \text{ g/mol} = \underline{15.999 \text{ g/mol}} \\ 28.010 \text{ g/mol} \end{array}$$

N_2 molar mass $\quad 2 \times 14.007 \text{ g/mol} = 28.014 \text{ g/mol}$

The 1 mole of C_2H_4 has the greatest mass.

8.108 100%

8.109 (a)
$$\begin{array}{l} 12 \times 12.011 \text{ g/mol C} = 144.13 \text{ g/mol} \\ 22 \times 1.0079 \text{ g/mol H} = 22.17 \text{ g/mol} \\ 11 \times 15.999 \text{ g/mol O} = \underline{175.99 \text{ g/mol}} \\ 342.29 \text{ g/mol } C_{12}H_{22}O_{11} \end{array}$$

(b) $1.25 \text{ mol} \times \dfrac{342.29 \text{ g}}{1 \text{ mol}} = 428 \text{ g}$

(c) $1.25 \text{ mol} \times \dfrac{6.022 \times 10^{23} \text{ molecules}}{1 \text{ mol}} = 7.53 \times 10^{23} \text{ molecules}$

(d) $1.25 \text{ mol sucrose} \times \dfrac{22 \text{ mol H}}{1 \text{ mol sucrose}} \times \dfrac{6.022 \times 10^{23} \text{ H atoms}}{1 \text{ mol H}} = 1.66 \times 10^{25} \text{ H atoms}$

(e) $1.66 \times 10^{25} \text{ H atoms} \times \dfrac{1.0079 \text{ amu}}{1 \text{ H atom}} \times \dfrac{1.661 \times 10^{-24} \text{ g}}{1 \text{ amu}} = 27.8 \text{ g}$

8.110 (a) $2 Al(s) + 3 Cl_2(g) \longrightarrow 2 AlCl_3(s)$

(b) $100.0 \text{ g Al} \times \dfrac{1 \text{ mol Al}}{26.98 \text{ g Al}} = 3.706 \text{ mol Al}$

Al $\quad \dfrac{3.760}{2} = 1.853$

$Cl_2 \quad \dfrac{5.00}{3} = 1.667$ smaller ratio, limiting reactant

8.111 (a) $2 Cu_2O(s) + C(s) \longrightarrow 4 Cu(s) + CO_2(g)$

(b) Begin by converting the Cu_2O mass from tons to grams:

$$1.000 \text{ ton} \times \dfrac{2000 \text{ lb}}{1 \text{ ton}} \times \dfrac{1 \text{ kg}}{2.205 \text{ lb}} \times \dfrac{1000 \text{ g}}{1 \text{ kg}} = 9.070 \times 10^5 \text{ g}$$

Convert to moles:

$$9.070 \times 10^5 \text{ g Cu}_2\text{O} \times \frac{1 \text{ mol Cu}_2\text{O}}{143.08 \text{ g Cu}_2\text{O}} = 6339 \text{ mol Cu}_2\text{O}$$

Use the equation coefficients to determine the number of moles of C that react with this much Cu_2O, then convert to mass:

$$6339 \text{ mol Cu}_2\text{O} \times \frac{1 \text{ mol C}}{2 \text{ mol Cu}_2\text{O}} = 3170 \text{ mol C}$$

$$3170 \text{ mol C} \times \frac{12.011 \text{ g C}}{1 \text{ mol C}} = 3.807 \times 10^4 \text{ g C}$$

This is the amount of C you need but you must account for the fact that the coke is only 95% by mass C:

$$3.807 \times 10^4 \text{ g C} \times \frac{100 \text{ g coke}}{95 \text{ g C}} \times \frac{1 \text{ kg}}{1000 \text{ g}} = 40.07 \text{ kg coke}$$

8.112 For 100 g of sample,

$$17.552\% \text{ Na} \rightarrow 17.552 \text{ g Na} \times \frac{1 \text{ mol Na}}{22.9898 \text{ g Na}} = 0.7635 \text{ mol Na}$$

$$39.696\% \text{ Cr} \rightarrow 39.696 \text{ g Cr} \times \frac{1 \text{ mol Cr}}{51.996 \text{ g Cr}} = 0.7634 \text{ mol Cr}$$

$$42.752\% \text{ O} \rightarrow 42.752 \text{ g O} \times \frac{1 \text{ mol O}}{15.999 \text{ g O}} = 2.672 \text{ mol O}$$

$$Na_{\frac{0.7635}{0.7635}} Cr_{\frac{0.7634}{0.7634}} O_{\frac{2.672}{0.7634}} \rightarrow Na_{1.00} Cr_{1.00} O_{3.50}$$

To remove the decimal subscript on O, multiply through by 2, to get an empirical formula of $Na_2Cr_2O_7$.

8.113 (a) $10.0 \text{ g PF}_3 \times \dfrac{1 \text{ mol PF}_3}{87.968 \text{ g PF}_3} \times \dfrac{3 \text{ mol CO}}{2 \text{ mol PF}_3} \times \dfrac{28.010 \text{ g CO}}{1 \text{ mol CO}} = 4.78 \text{ g CO}$

(b) Determine the limiting reactant:

$$Fe(CO)_5 \quad \frac{5.0}{1} = 5.0$$

$$PF_3 \quad \frac{8.0}{2} = 4.0 \text{ smallest ratio, limiting reactant}$$

$$H_2 \quad \frac{6.0}{1} = 6.0$$

$$8.0 \text{ mol PF}_3 \times \frac{3 \text{ mol CO}}{2 \text{ mol PF}_3} \times \frac{28.010 \text{ g CO}}{1 \text{ mol CO}} = 3.4 \times 10^2 \text{ g CO}$$

(c) $25.0 \text{ g Fe(CO)}_5 \times \dfrac{1 \text{ mol Fe(CO)}_5}{195.9 \text{ g Fe(CO)}_5} = 0.128 \text{ mol Fe(CO)}_5$

$$10.0 \text{ g PF}_3 \times \frac{1 \text{ mol PF}_3}{87.968 \text{ g PF}_3} = 0.114 \text{ mol PF}_3$$

$$Fe(CO)_5 \quad \frac{0.128}{1} = 0.128$$

$$PF_3 \quad \frac{0.114}{2} = 0.057 \text{ limiting reactant}$$

$$0.114 \text{ mol PF}_3 \times \frac{3 \text{ mol CO}}{2 \text{ mol PF}_3} = 0.171 \text{ mol CO}$$

(d) $5.00 \text{ L H}_2 \times \dfrac{0.0820 \text{ g H}_2}{1 \text{ L H}_2} \times \dfrac{1 \text{ mol H}_2}{2.0158 \text{ g H}_2} = 0.203 \text{ mol H}_2$

$$0.203 \text{ mol H}_2 \times \frac{3 \text{ mol CO}}{1 \text{ mol H}_2} \times \frac{28.010 \text{ g CO}}{1 \text{ mol CO}} = 17.1 \text{ g CO theoretical yield}$$

$$\text{Percent yield} = \frac{13.5 \text{ g}}{17.1 \text{ g}} \times 100 = 78.9\%$$

8.114 (a) $CH_4(g) + 2 O(g) \longrightarrow CO_2(g) + 2 H_2O(g)$

(b)

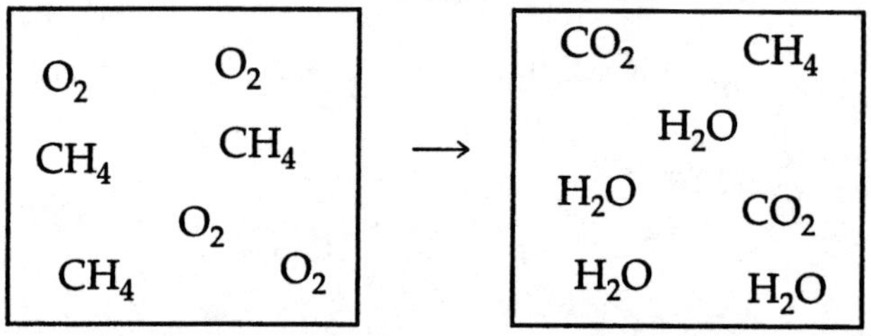

Mixture before reaction   Mixture after reaction

(c) The balanced equation tells you one CH_4 molecule needs two O_2 molecules, meaning that three CH_4 molecules need six O_2 molecules. With only four O_2 molecules available, O_2 is the limiting reactant. You should have one unreacted CH_4 molecule in your "after" drawing.

8.115 (a) $5.00 \text{ g AgNO}_3 \times \dfrac{1 \text{ mol AgNO}_3}{169.9 \text{ g AgNO}_3} = 0.0294 \text{ mol AgNO}_3$

(b) $0.0294 \text{ mol AgNO}_3 \times \dfrac{3 \text{ mol O}}{1 \text{ mol AgNO}_3} = 0.0882 \text{ mol O}$

(c) $0.0294 \text{ mol AgNO}_3 \times \dfrac{1 \text{ mol N}}{1 \text{ mol AgNO}_3} \times \dfrac{14.007 \text{ g N}}{1 \text{ mol N}} = 0.412 \text{ g N}$

(d) $0.0294 \text{ mol AgNO}_3 \times \dfrac{1 \text{ mol Ag}}{1 \text{ mol AgNO}_3} \times \dfrac{6.022 \times 10^{23} \text{ Ag atoms}}{1 \text{ mol Ag}} = 1.77 \times 10^{22} \text{ Ag atoms}$

8.116 (a) $N_2 \quad \dfrac{0.50}{1} = 0.50$ (b) $N_2 \quad \dfrac{12.0}{1} = 12.0$

$ F_2 \quad \dfrac{0.50}{3} = 0.17 \text{ limiting}$ $ F_2 \quad \dfrac{20.0}{3} = 6.67 \text{ limiting}$

(c) $N_2 \quad \dfrac{2.5}{1} = 2.5$ $\left.\begin{array}{l}\end{array}\right\}$ no limiting reactant   (d) $N_2 \quad \dfrac{100}{1} = 100 \text{ limiting}$

$ F_2 \quad \dfrac{7.5}{3} = 2.5$ $ F_2 \quad \dfrac{500}{3} = 167$

(e) $5.00 \text{ g N}_2 \times \dfrac{1 \text{ mol N}_2}{28.014 \text{ g N}_2} = 0.178 \text{ mol N}_2$

$15.0 \text{ g F}_2 \times \dfrac{1 \text{ mol F}_2}{37.997 \text{ g F}_2} = 0.395 \text{ mol F}_2$

$\text{N}_2 \quad \dfrac{0.178}{1} = 0.178$

$\text{F}_2 \quad \dfrac{0.395}{3} = 0.132 \text{ limiting}$

(f) $20.0 \text{ mg N}_2 \times \dfrac{1 \text{ mol N}_2}{28.014 \text{ g N}_2} \times \dfrac{1 \text{ g}}{1000 \text{ mg}} = 7.14 \times 10^{-4} \text{ mol N}_2$

$70.0 \text{ mg F}_2 \times \dfrac{1 \text{ mol F}_2}{37.997 \text{ g F}_2} \times \dfrac{1 \text{ g}}{1000 \text{ mg}} = 1.84 \times 10^{-3} \text{ mol F}_2$

$\text{N}_2 \quad \dfrac{7.14 \times 10^{-4}}{1} = 7.14 \times 10^{-4}$

$\text{F}_2 \quad \dfrac{1.84 \times 10^{-3}}{3} = 6.13 \times 10^{-4} \text{ limiting reactant}$

8.117 (a) $0.50 \text{ mol F}_2 \times \dfrac{1 \text{ mol N}_2}{3 \text{ mol F}_2} = 0.17 \text{ mol N}_2$

$0.50 \text{ mol N}_2 - 0.17 \text{ mol N}_2 = 0.33 \text{ mol N}_2 \text{ left over}$

(b) $20.0 \text{ mol F}_2 \times \dfrac{1 \text{ mol N}_2}{3 \text{ mol F}_2} = 6.67 \text{ mol N}_2 \text{ used up}$

$12.0 \text{ mol N}_2 - 6.67 \text{ mol N}_2 = 5.3 \text{ mol N}_2 \text{ left over}$

(c) The two reactants are present in the needed 3:1 ratio, meaning both are used up completely.

(d) $100 \text{ molecules N}_2 \times \dfrac{3 \text{ molecules F}_2}{1 \text{ molecule N}_2} = 300 \text{ molecules F}_2 \text{ used up}$

$500 \text{ molecules F}_2 - 300 \text{ molecules F}_2 = 200 \text{ molecules F}_2 \text{ left over}$

(e) From the preceding problem, $15.0 \text{ g F}_2 = 0.395 \text{ mol F}_2$

$0.395 \text{ mol F}_2 \times \dfrac{1 \text{ mol N}_2}{3 \text{ mol F}_2} = 0.132 \text{ mol N}_2 \text{ used up}$

$0.132 \text{ mol N}_2 \times \dfrac{28.014 \text{ g N}_2}{1 \text{ mol N}_2} = 3.69 \text{ g N}_2 \text{ used up}$

$5.00 \text{ g N}_2 - 3.69 \text{ g N}_2 = 1.31 \text{ g N}_2 \text{ left over}$

(f) From the preceding problem, $70.0 \text{ mg F}_2 = 1.84 \times 10^{-3} \text{ mol F}_2$

$1.84 \times 10^{-3} \text{ mol F}_2 \times \dfrac{1 \text{ mol N}_2}{3 \text{ mol F}_2} = 6.13 \times 10^{-4} \text{ mol N}_2 \text{ used up}$

$6.13 \times 10^{-4} \text{ mol N}_2 \times \dfrac{28.018 \text{ g N}_2}{1 \text{ mol N}_2} = 0.0172 \text{ g N}_2 = 17.2 \text{ mg N}_2 \text{ used up}$

$20.0 \text{ g N}_2 - 17.2 \text{ mg N}_2 = 2.8 \text{ mg N}_2 \text{ left over}$

8.118 $5789.25 \, \cancel{g} \times \dfrac{1 \, \cancel{penny}}{2.49 \, \cancel{g}} \times \dfrac{1 \, dollar}{100 \, \cancel{pennies}} = \$23.25$

8.119 (a) $Ca_3P_2 + 6 \, H_2O \longrightarrow 3 \, Ca(OH)_2 + 2 \, PH_3$

(b) $60.0 \, \cancel{g \, Ca_3P_2} \times \dfrac{1 \, mol \, Ca_3P_2}{182.2 \, \cancel{g \, Ca_3P_2}} = 0.329 \, mol \, Ca_3P_2$

$0.329 \, \cancel{mol \, Ca_3P_2} \times \dfrac{6 \, \cancel{mol \, H_2O}}{1 \, \cancel{mol \, Ca_3P_2}} \times \dfrac{18.015 \, g \, H_2O}{1 \, \cancel{mol \, H_2O}} = 35.6 \, g \, H_2O$

(c) Because you calculated the exact amount of H_2O needed to react completely with 60.0 g of Ca_3P_2, you may use either reactant to calculate theoretical yield:

$60.0 \, g \, Ca_3P_2 = 0.329 \, \cancel{mol \, Ca_3P_2} \times \dfrac{2 \, \cancel{mol \, PH_3}}{1 \, \cancel{mol \, Ca_3P_2}} \times \dfrac{33.998 \, g \, PH_3}{1 \, \cancel{mol \, PH_3}} = 22.4 \, g \, PH_3$

$35.6 \, \cancel{g \, H_2O} \times \dfrac{1 \, \cancel{mol \, H_2O}}{18.015 \, \cancel{g \, H_2O}} \times \dfrac{2 \, \cancel{mol \, PH_3}}{6 \, \cancel{mol \, H_2O}} \times \dfrac{33.998 \, g \, PH_3}{1 \, \cancel{mol \, PH_3}} = 22.4 \, g \, PH_3$

8.120 Iron(III) carries a 3+ charge, and the sulfate ion carries a 2− charge. The chemical formula is therefore $Fe_2(SO_4)_3$.

$0.262 \, \cancel{mol \, Fe_2(SO_4)_3} \times \dfrac{12 \, \cancel{mol \, O}}{1 \, \cancel{mol \, Fe_2(SO_4)_3}} \times \dfrac{6.022 \times 10^{23} \, O \, atoms}{1 \, \cancel{mol \, O}} = 1.89 \times 10^{24} \, O \, atoms$

8.121 Assume you have 1 mole of $C_8H_9NO_2$.

$8 \, \cancel{mol \, C} \times \dfrac{12.011 \, g \, C}{1 \, \cancel{mol \, C}} = 96.088 \, g \, C$

$9 \, \cancel{mol \, H} \times \dfrac{1.0079 \, g \, H}{1 \, \cancel{mol \, H}} = 9.0711 \, g \, H$

$1 \, \cancel{mol \, N} \times \dfrac{14.007 \, g \, N}{1 \, \cancel{mol \, N}} = 14.007 \, g \, N$

$2 \, \cancel{mol \, O} \times \dfrac{15.999 \, g \, O}{1 \, \cancel{mol \, O}} = 31.998 \, g \, O$

The molar mass of $C_8H_9NO_2$ is 151.16 g/mol, meaning your 1 mole has a mass of 151.16 g.

$\dfrac{96.088 \, g \, C}{151.16 \, mol \, C_8H_9NO_2} \times 100 = 63.57\% \, C$

$\dfrac{9.0711 \, g \, H}{151.16 \, mol \, C_8H_9NO_2} \times 100 = 6.001\% \, H$

$\dfrac{14.007 \, g \, N}{151.16 \, mol \, C_8H_9NO_2} \times 100 = 9.266\% \, N$

$\dfrac{31.998 \, g \, O}{151.16 \, mol \, C_8H_9NO_2} \times 100 = 21.17\% \, g \, O$

8.122 The balanced equation is $2 \, KCl + 3 \, O_2 \longrightarrow 2 \, KClO_3$. The limiting reactant is

$42.6 \, \cancel{g \, KCl} \times \dfrac{1 \, mol \, KCl}{74.56 \, \cancel{g \, KCl}} = 0.571 \, mol \, KCl$

$$36.5 \text{ g } O_2 \times \frac{1 \text{ mol } O_2}{31.998 \text{ g } O_2} = 1.14 \text{ mol } O_2$$

$$\text{KCl} \quad \frac{0.571}{2} = 0.286 \text{ limiting}$$

$$O_2 \quad \frac{1.14}{3} = 0.380$$

$$0.571 \text{ mol KCl} \times \frac{2 \text{ mol } KClO_3}{2 \text{ mol KCl}} \times \frac{122.6 \text{ g } KClO_3}{1 \text{ mol } KClO_3} = 70.0 \text{ g } KClO_3$$

This is the theoretical yield. The amount you actually get is $0.560 \times 70.0 \text{ g} = 39.2 \text{ g}$.

8.123 The balanced equation is $C_{12}H_{22}O_{11} + 12 \, O_2 \longrightarrow 12 \, CO_2 + 11 \, H_2O$.

$$2.00 \text{ g sucrose} \times \frac{1 \text{ mol sucrose}}{342.3 \text{ g sucrose}} = 5.84 \times 10^{-3} \text{ mol sucrose}$$

$$5.84 \times 10^{-3} \text{ mol sucrose} \times \frac{12 \text{ mol } CO_2}{1 \text{ mol sucrose}} \times \frac{44.009 \text{ g } CO_2}{1 \text{ mol } CO_2} = 3.08 \text{ g } CO_2$$

$$5.84 \times 10^{-3} \text{ mol sucrose} \times \frac{11 \text{ mol } H_2O}{1 \text{ mol sucrose}} \times \frac{18.015 \text{ g } H_2O}{1 \text{ mol } H_2O} = 1.16 \text{ g } H_2O$$

8.124 The name tells you the molecular formula is CCl_4.

$$44.6 \text{ g } CCl_4 \times \frac{1 \text{ mol } CCl_4}{153.82 \text{ g } CCl_4} \times \frac{4 \text{ mol } Cl}{1 \text{ mol } CCl_4} \times \frac{6.022 \times 10^{23} \text{ Cl atoms}}{1 \text{ mol } Cl} = 6.98 \times 10^{23} \text{ Cl atoms}$$

8.125 (a) $4 \, BF_3 + 3 \, H_2O \longrightarrow H_3BO_3 + 3 \, HBF_4$
(b) Theoretical yield is

$$24.2 \text{ g } BF_3 \times \frac{1 \text{ mol } BF_3}{67.81 \text{ g } BF_3} \times \frac{3 \text{ mol } HBF_4}{4 \text{ mol } BF_3} \times \frac{87.81 \text{ g } HBF_4}{1 \text{ mol } HBF_4} = 23.5 \text{ g } HBF_4$$

$$\% \text{ yield} = \frac{14.8 \text{ g}}{23.5 \text{ g}} \times 100 = 63.0\%$$

8.126 (a) $5 \text{ eggs} \times \dfrac{1 \text{ dozen cupcakes}}{2 \text{ eggs}} \times \dfrac{12 \text{ cupcakes}}{1 \text{ dozen cupcakes}} = 30 \text{ cupcakes}$

(b) $5 \text{ eggs} \times \dfrac{1 \text{ cup sugar}}{2 \text{ eggs}} = 2.5 \text{ cups sugar}$
or

$$30 \text{ cupcakes} \times \frac{1 \text{ cup sugar}}{12 \text{ cupcakes}} = 2.5 \text{ cups sugar}$$

8.127 Assume 100 g of chrome yellow.

$$64.11\% \text{ Pb} \rightarrow 64.11 \text{ g Pb} \times \frac{1 \text{ mol Pb}}{207.19 \text{ g Pb}} = 0.3094 \text{ mol Pb}$$

$$16.09\% \text{ Cr} \rightarrow 16.09 \text{ g Cr} \times \frac{1 \text{ mol Cr}}{51.996 \text{ g Cr}} = 0.3094 \text{ mol Cr}$$

$$19.80\% \text{ O} \rightarrow 19.80 \text{ g O} \times \frac{1 \text{ mol O}}{15.999 \text{ g O}} = 1.238 \text{ mol O}$$

$$Pb_{\frac{0.3094}{0.3094}} Cr_{\frac{0.3094}{0.3094}} O_{\frac{1.238}{0.3094}} \rightarrow Pb_{1.00} Cr_{1.00} O_{4.00} \rightarrow PbCrO_4$$

8.128 1.62×10^{25} molecules $H_2S \times \dfrac{1 \text{ mol } H_2S}{6.022 \times 10^{23} \text{ molecules } H_2S} \times \dfrac{34.08 \text{ g } H_2S}{1 \text{ mol } H_2S} = 917 \text{ g } H_2S$

8.129 The balanced equation is $3 \text{ SiCl}_4 + 4 \text{ NH}_3 \longrightarrow \text{Si}_3\text{N}_4 + 12 \text{ HCl}$. Find out which reactant is the limiting one:

$64.2 \text{ g SiCl}_4 \times \dfrac{1 \text{ mol SiCl}_4}{169.9 \text{ g SiCl}_4} = 0.378 \text{ mol SiCl}_4$

$20.0 \text{ g NH}_3 \times \dfrac{1 \text{ mol NH}_3}{17.03 \text{ g NH}_3} = 1.17 \text{ mol NH}_3$

$\text{SiCl}_4 \quad \dfrac{0.378}{3} = 0.126$ limiting reactant

$\text{NH}_3 \quad \dfrac{1.17}{4} = 0.293$

The theoretical yield is

$0.378 \text{ mol SiCl}_4 \times \dfrac{1 \text{ mol Si}_3\text{N}_4}{3 \text{ mol SiCl}_4} \times \dfrac{140.3 \text{ g Si}_3\text{N}_4}{1 \text{ mol Si}_3\text{N}_4} = 17.7 \text{ g Si}_3\text{N}_4$

Actual yield $= 0.960 \times 17.7 \text{ g} = 17.0 \text{ g Si}_3\text{N}_4$

8.130 Step 1: $0.240 \text{ g CO}_2 \times \dfrac{1 \text{ mol CO}_2}{44.009 \text{ g CO}_2} \times \dfrac{1 \text{ mol C}}{1 \text{ mol CO}_2} = 5.45 \times 10^{-3} \text{ mol C}$

$0.0655 \text{ g H}_2\text{O} \times \dfrac{1 \text{ mol H}_2\text{O}}{18.015 \text{ g H}_2\text{O}} \times \dfrac{2 \text{ mol H}}{1 \text{ mol H}_2\text{O}} = 7.27 \times 10^{-3} \text{ mol H}$

Step 2: $5.45 \times 10^{-3} \text{ mol C} \times \dfrac{12.011 \text{ g C}}{1 \text{ mol C}} = 6.55 \times 10^{-2} \text{ g C}$

$7.27 \times 10^{-3} \text{ mol H} \times \dfrac{1.0079 \text{ g H}}{1 \text{ mol H}} = 7.33 \times 10^{-3} \text{ g H}$

Step 3: $0.160 \text{ g sample} - (6.55 \times 10^{-2} \text{ g C} + 7.33 \times 10^{-3} \text{ g H})$

$= 8.71 \times 10^{-2} \text{ g O} \times \dfrac{1 \text{ mol O}}{15.999 \text{ g O}} = 5.45 \times 10^{-3} \text{ mol O}$

Step 4: $C_{\frac{5.45 \times 10^{-3}}{5.45 \times 10^{-3}}} H_{\frac{7.27 \times 10^{-3}}{5.45 \times 10^{-3}}} O_{\frac{5.45 \times 10^{-3}}{5.45 \times 10^{-3}}} \rightarrow C_{1.00} H_{1.33} O_{1.00}$

Find a multiplier that gives H a whole-number subscript:

$1.33 \times 2 = 2.66$
$1.33 \times 3 = 3.99 \quad$ close enough!

The empirical formula is $C_{3 \times 1.00} H_{3 \times 1.33} O_{3 \times 1.00} \longrightarrow C_3H_4O_3$. The molecular formula is

$\dfrac{176 \text{ g / mol vitamin C}}{88.06 \text{ g / mol } C_3H_4O_3} = 2.00$

$C_{2 \times 3} H_{2 \times 4} O_{2 \times 3} = C_6H_8O_6$

8.131 The balanced equation is $Cr_2O_3 + 3\,H_2S \longrightarrow Cr_2S_3 + 3\,H_2O$.

(a) $13.6\ \text{g}\ Cr_2O_3 \times \dfrac{1\ \text{mol}\ Cr_2O_3}{151.99\ \text{g}\ Cr_2O_3} \times \dfrac{3\ \text{mol}\ H_2S}{1\ \text{mol}\ Cr_2O_3} \times \dfrac{34.080\ \text{g}\ H_2S}{1\ \text{mol}\ H_2S} = 9.15\ \text{g}\ H_2S$

(b) $13.6\ \text{g}\ Cr_2O_3 \times \dfrac{1\ \text{mol}\ Cr_2O_3}{151.99\ \text{g}\ Cr_2O_3} \times \dfrac{1\ \text{mol}\ Cr_2S_3}{1\ \text{mol}\ Cr_2O_3} \times \dfrac{200.2\ \text{g}\ Cr_2S_3}{1\ \text{mol}\ Cr_2S_3} = 17.9\ \text{g}\ Cr_2S_3$

or

$9.15\ \text{g}\ H_2S \times \dfrac{1\ \text{mol}\ H_2S}{34.080\ \text{g}\ H_2S} \times \dfrac{1\ \text{mol}\ Cr_2S_3}{3\ \text{mol}\ H_2S} \times \dfrac{200.2\ \text{g}\ Cr_2S_3}{1\ \text{mol}\ Cr_2S_3} = 17.9\ \text{g}\ Cr_2S_3$

8.132 Magnesium is a group IIA metal and therefore forms 2+ cations. The phosphate anion is PO_4^{3-}, making the formula for this compound $Mg_3(PO_4)_2$. Assume 1 mole of the compound, which contains 3 moles of Mg, 2 moles of P, and 8 moles of O.

$3\ \text{mol}\ Mg \times \dfrac{24.312\ \text{g}\ Mg}{1\ \text{mol}\ Mg} = 72.936\ \text{g}\ Mg$

$2\ \text{mol}\ P \times \dfrac{30.974\ \text{g}\ P}{1\ \text{mol}\ P} = 61.948\ \text{g}\ P$

$8\ \text{mol}\ O \times \dfrac{15.999\ \text{g}\ O}{1\ \text{mol}\ O} = 127.99\ \text{g}\ O$

The molar mass of $Mg_3(PO_4)_2$ is 262.9 g/mol.

$\dfrac{72.936\ \text{g}\ Mg}{262.9\ \text{g compound}} \times 100 = 27.74\%\ Mg$

$\dfrac{61.948\ \text{g}\ P}{262.9\ \text{g compound}} \times 100 = 23.56\%\ P$

$\dfrac{127.99\ \text{g}\ O}{262.9\ \text{g compound}} \times 100 = 48.68\%\ O$

8.133 (a) $SiCl_4 + 2\,H_2O \longrightarrow SiO_2 + 4\,HCl$

(b) $120.0\ \text{g}\ HCl \times \dfrac{1\ \text{mol}\ HCl}{36.46\ \text{g}\ HCl} = 3.291\ \text{mol}\ HCl$

$3.291\ \text{mol}\ HCl \times \dfrac{1\ \text{mol}\ SiCl_4}{4\ \text{mol}\ HCl} \times \dfrac{169.9\ \text{g}\ SiCl_4}{1\ \text{mol}\ SiCl_4} = 139.8\ \text{g}\ SiCl_4$

$3.291\ \text{mol}\ HCl \times \dfrac{2\ \text{mol}\ H_2O}{4\ \text{mol}\ HCl} \times \dfrac{18.015\ \text{g}\ H_2O}{1\ \text{mol}\ H_2O} = 29.64\ \text{g}\ H_2O$

(c) $3.291\ \text{mol}\ HCl \times \dfrac{1\ \text{mol}\ SiO_2}{4\ \text{mol}\ HCl} \times \dfrac{60.08\ \text{g}\ SiO_2}{1\ \text{mol}\ SiO_2} = 49.44\ \text{g}\ SiO_2$

or

$139.8\ \text{g}\ SiCl_4 \times \dfrac{1\ \text{mol}\ SiCl_4}{169.9\ \text{g}\ SiCl_4} \times \dfrac{1\ \text{mol}\ SiO_2}{1\ \text{mol}\ SiCl_4} \times \dfrac{60.08\ \text{g}\ SiO_2}{1\ \text{mol}\ SiO_2} = 49.43\ \text{g}\ SiO_2$

or

$29.64\ \text{g}\ H_2O \times \dfrac{1\ \text{mol}\ H_2O}{18.015\ \text{g}\ H_2O} \times \dfrac{1\ \text{mol}\ SiO_2}{2\ \text{mol}\ H_2O} \times \dfrac{60.08\ \text{g}\ SiO_2}{1\ \text{mol}\ SiO_2} = 49.42\ \text{g}\ SiO_2$

8.134 Assume 100 g of compound.

$$91.77\% \text{ Si} \rightarrow 91.77 \text{ g Si} \times \frac{1 \text{ mol Si}}{28.086 \text{ g Si}} = 3.267 \text{ mol Si}$$

$$8.23\% \text{ H} \rightarrow 8.23 \text{ g H} \times \frac{1 \text{ mol H}}{1.0079 \text{ g H}} = 8.165 \text{ mol H}$$

$$\text{Si}_{\frac{3.267}{3.267}}\text{H}_{\frac{8.165}{3.267}} \rightarrow \text{Si}_{1.00}\text{H}_{2.50} \rightarrow \text{Si}_{2\times1.00}\text{H}_{2\times2.50} \rightarrow \text{Si}_{2.00}\text{H}_{5.00} \rightarrow \text{Si}_2\text{H}_5 \text{ empirical formula}$$

$$\frac{122 \text{ g / mol compound}}{61.21 \text{ g / mol empirical formula}} = 2 \text{ approximately}$$

The molecular formula is $\text{Si}_{2\times2}\text{H}_{2\times5} \longrightarrow \text{Si}_4\text{H}_{10}$.

8.135 The balanced equation is $\text{Fe}_2\text{O}_3 + 3 \text{ CO} \longrightarrow 2 \text{ Fe} + 3 \text{ CO}_2$.

$$24.0 \text{ g Fe}_2\text{O}_3 \times \frac{1 \text{ mol Fe}_2\text{O}_3}{159.687 \text{ g Fe}_2\text{O}_3} = 0.150 \text{ mol Fe}_2\text{O}_3$$

$$34.0 \text{ g CO} \times \frac{1 \text{ mol CO}}{28.01 \text{ g CO}} = 1.21 \text{ mol CO}$$

$$\text{Fe}_2\text{O}_3 \quad \frac{0.150}{1} = 0.150 \text{ limiting reactant}$$

$$\text{CO} \quad \frac{1.21}{3} = 0.403$$

Theoretical yield:

$$0.150 \text{ mol Fe}_2\text{O}_3 \times \frac{3 \text{ mol CO}_2}{1 \text{ mol Fe}_2\text{O}_3} \times \frac{44.009 \text{ g CO}_2}{1 \text{ mol CO}_2} = 19.8 \text{ g CO}_2$$

8.136 The balanced equation is $2 \text{ C}_{13}\text{H}_{18}\text{O}_2 + 33 \text{ O}_2 \longrightarrow 26 \text{ CO}_2 + 18 \text{ H}_2\text{O}$.

$$0.250 \text{ g ibuprofen} \times \frac{1 \text{ mol ibuprofen}}{206.3 \text{ g ibuprofen}} \times \frac{26 \text{ mol CO}_2}{2 \text{ mol ibuprofen}} \times \frac{44.009 \text{ g CO}_2}{1 \text{ mol CO}_2} = 0.693 \text{ g CO}_2$$

$$0.250 \text{ g ibuprofen} \times \frac{1 \text{ mol ibuprofen}}{206.3 \text{ g ibuprofen}} \times \frac{18 \text{ mol H}_2\text{O}}{2 \text{ mol ibuprofen}} \times \frac{18.015 \text{ g H}_2\text{O}}{1 \text{ mol H}_2\text{O}} = 0.196 \text{ g H}_2\text{O}$$

8.137 $200.0 \text{ g N}_2\text{O}_5 \times \dfrac{1 \text{ mol N}_2\text{O}_5}{108.0 \text{ g N}_2\text{O}_5} \times \dfrac{2 \text{ mol N}}{1 \text{ mol N}_2\text{O}_5} \times \dfrac{6.022 \times 10^{23} \text{ N atoms}}{1 \text{ mol N}} = 2.230 \times 10^{24} \text{ N atoms}$

$$200.0 \text{ g N}_2\text{O}_5 \times \frac{1 \text{ mol N}_2\text{O}_5}{108.0 \text{ g N}_2\text{O}_5} \times \frac{5 \text{ mol O}}{1 \text{ mol N}_2\text{O}_5} \times \frac{6.022 \times 10^{23} \text{ O atoms}}{1 \text{ mol O}} = 5.576 \times 10^{24} \text{ O atoms}$$

8.138 The balanced equation is $4 \text{ KNO}_3 \longrightarrow 2 \text{ K}_2\text{O} + 2 \text{ N}_2 + 5 \text{ O}_2$.

$$18.6 \text{ g KNO}_3 \times \frac{1 \text{ mol KNO}_3}{101.1 \text{ g KNO}_3} \times \frac{5 \text{ mol O}_2}{4 \text{ mol KNO}_3}$$

$$\times \frac{6.022 \times 10^{23} \text{ molecules O}_2}{1 \text{ mol O}_2} = 1.38 \times 10^{23} \text{ molecules O}_2$$

8.139 The balanced equation is $P_4O_{10} + 6\,H_2O \longrightarrow 4\,H_3PO_4$.

$$52.5\ \text{g}\ P_4O_{10} \times \frac{1\ \text{mol}\ P_4O_{10}}{283.9\ \text{g}\ P_4O_{10}} = 0.185\ \text{mol}\ P_4O_{10}$$

$$25.0\ \text{g}\ H_2O \times \frac{1\ \text{mol}\ H_2O}{18.015\ \text{g}\ H_2O} = 1.39\ \text{mol}\ H_2O$$

$$P_4O_{10} \quad \frac{0.185}{1} = 0.185\ \text{limiting reactant}$$

$$H_2O \quad \frac{1.39}{6} = 0.232$$

$$0.185\ \text{mol}\ P_4O_{10} \times \frac{4\ \text{mol}\ H_3PO_4}{1\ \text{mol}\ P_4O_{10}} \times \frac{97.9\ \text{g}\ H_3PO_4}{1\ \text{mol}\ H_3PO_4} = 72.4\ \text{g}\ H_3PO_4$$

8.140 The formula is $Al_2(SO_4)_3$. Assume 1 mole of the compound, which contains 2 moles of Al, 3 moles of S, and 12 moles of O.

$$2\ \text{mol}\ Al \times \frac{26.98\ \text{g}\ Al}{1\ \text{mol}\ Al} = 53.96\ \text{g}\ Al$$

$$3\ \text{mol}\ S \times \frac{32.064\ \text{g}\ S}{1\ \text{mol}\ S} = 96.19\ \text{g}\ S$$

$$12\ \text{mol}\ O \times \frac{15.999\ \text{g}\ O}{1\ \text{mol}\ O} = 192.0\ \text{g}\ O$$

The molar mass of the compound is 342.2 g/mol.

$$\frac{53.96\ \text{g}\ Al}{342.2\ \text{g}\ Al_2(SO_4)_3} \times 100 = 15.77\%\ Al$$

$$\frac{96.19\ \text{g}\ S}{342.2\ \text{g}\ Al_2(SO_4)_3} \times 100 = 28.11\%\ S$$

$$\frac{192.0\ \text{g}\ O}{342.2\ \text{g}\ Al_2(SO_4)_3} \times 100 = 56.11\%\ O$$

8.141 The balanced equation is $Cl_2O_7 + H_2O \longrightarrow 2\,HClO_4$.

(a) Rearrange the percent yield equation by solving for theoretical yield:

$$\text{Percent yield} = \frac{\text{Actual yield}}{\text{Theoretical yield}} \times 100$$

$$\text{Theoretical yield} = \frac{\text{Actual yield}}{\text{Percent yield}} \times 100 = \frac{52.8\ \text{g}\ HClO_4}{82.0\%} \times 100 = 64.4\ \text{g}\ HClO_4$$

(b) You must use the theoretical yield in calculating how much of each reactant was used up.

$$64.4\ \text{g}\ HClO_4 \times \frac{1\ \text{mol}\ HClO_4}{100.5\ \text{g}\ HClO_4} \times \frac{1\ \text{mol}\ Cl_2O_7}{2\ \text{mol}\ HClO_4} \times \frac{182.9\ \text{g}\ Cl_2O_7}{1\ \text{mol}\ Cl_2O_7} = 58.6\ \text{g}\ Cl_2O_7$$

$$64.4\ \text{g}\ HClO_4 \times \frac{1\ \text{mol}\ HClO_4}{100.5\ \text{g}\ HClO_4} \times \frac{1\ \text{mol}\ H_2O}{2\ \text{mol}\ HClO_4} \times \frac{18.015\ \text{g}\ H_2O}{1\ \text{mol}\ H_2O} = 5.77\ \text{g}\ H_2O$$

8.142 Step 1: $0.755 \text{ g CO}_2 \times \dfrac{1 \text{ mol CO}_2}{44.009 \text{ g CO}_2} \times \dfrac{1 \text{ mol C}}{1 \text{ mol CO}_2} = 0.0172 \text{ mol C}$

$0.124 \text{ g H}_2\text{O} \times \dfrac{1 \text{ mol H}_2\text{O}}{18.015 \text{ g H}_2\text{O}} \times \dfrac{2 \text{ mol H}}{1 \text{ mol H}_2\text{O}} = 0.0138 \text{ mol H}$

Step 2: $0.0172 \text{ mol C} \times \dfrac{12.011 \text{ g C}}{1 \text{ mol C}} = 0.207 \text{ g C}$

$0.0138 \text{ mol H} \times \dfrac{1.0079 \text{ g H}}{1 \text{ mol H}} = 0.0139 \text{ g H}$

Step 3: $0.220 \text{ g} - (0.207 \text{ g} + 0.0139 \text{ g}) = 0$
There is no O in naphthalene.

Step 4: $C_{\frac{0.0172}{0.0138}} H_{\frac{0.0138}{0.0138}} \rightarrow C_{1.24} H_{1.00} \rightarrow C_{4 \times 1.24} H_{4 \times 1.00} \rightarrow C_{4.96} H_{4.00} \rightarrow C_5 H_4$

The molecular formula is

$\dfrac{128 \text{ g / mol naphthalene}}{64.0 \text{ g / mol } C_5H_4} = 2$

$C_{2 \times 5} H_{2 \times 4} \rightarrow C_{10} H_8$

8.143 The balanced equation is $C_2H_4(g) + 6 F_2(g) \longrightarrow 2 CF_4(g) + 4 HF(g)$.

$2.78 \text{ g C}_2\text{H}_4 \times \dfrac{1 \text{ mol C}_2\text{H}_4}{28.054 \text{ g C}_2\text{H}_4} = 0.0991 \text{ mol C}_2\text{H}_4$

$0.0991 \text{ mol C}_2\text{H}_4 \times \dfrac{2 \text{ mol CF}_4}{1 \text{ mol C}_2\text{H}_4} \times \dfrac{88.003 \text{ g CF}_4}{1 \text{ mol CF}_4} = 17.4 \text{ g CF}_4$

$0.0991 \text{ mol C}_2\text{H}_4 \times \dfrac{4 \text{ mol HF}}{1 \text{ mol C}_2\text{H}_4} \times \dfrac{20.006 \text{ g HF}}{1 \text{ mol HF}} = 7.93 \text{ g HF}$

8.144 The name tells you the molecular formula is SF_6. Thus

$5.25 \times 10^{24} \text{ F atoms} \times \dfrac{1 \text{ mol F}}{6.022 \times 10^{23} \text{ F atoms}} \times \dfrac{1 \text{ mol SF}_6}{6 \text{ mol F}} \times \dfrac{146.05 \text{ g SF}_6}{1 \text{ mol SF}_6} = 212 \text{ g SF}_6$

8.145 The balanced equation is $2 \text{ HSbCl}_4 + 3 \text{ H}_2\text{S} \longrightarrow \text{Sb}_2\text{S}_3 + 8 \text{ HCl}$.

$118.2 \text{ g HSbCl}_4 \times \dfrac{1 \text{ mol HSbCl}_4}{264.6 \text{ g HSbCl}_4} = 0.4467 \text{ mol HSbCl}_4$

$47.9 \text{ g H}_2\text{S} \times \dfrac{1 \text{ mol H}_2\text{S}}{34.080 \text{ g H}_2\text{S}} = 1.41 \text{ mol H}_2\text{S}$

$\text{HSbCl}_4 \quad \dfrac{0.4467}{2} = 0.2234 \text{ limiting reactant}$

$\text{H}_2\text{S} \quad \dfrac{1.41}{3} = 0.470$

Theoretical yield:

$0.4467 \text{ mol HSbCl}_4 \times \dfrac{8 \text{ mol HCl}}{2 \text{ mol HSbCl}_4} \times \dfrac{36.46 \text{ g HCl}}{1 \text{ mol HCl}} = 65.15 \text{ g HCl}$

$\text{Percent yield} = \dfrac{41.6 \text{ g}}{65.15 \text{ g}} \times 100 = 63.9\%$

8.146 Assume 100 g of caffeine.

$$49.48\% \; C \;\rightarrow\; 49.48 \; g\,C \times \frac{1 \; mol \; C}{12.011 \; g\,C} = 4.120 \; mol \; C$$

$$5.19\% \; H \;\rightarrow\; 5.19 \; g\,H \times \frac{1 \; mol \; H}{1.0079 \; g\,H} = 5.15 \; mol \; H$$

$$28.85\% \; N \;\rightarrow\; 28.85 \; g\,N \times \frac{1 \; mol \; N}{14.007 \; g\,N} = 2.060 \; mol \; N$$

$$16.48\% \; O \;\rightarrow\; 17.1 \; g\,O \times \frac{1 \; mol \; O}{15.999 \; g\,O} = 1.030 \; mol \; O$$

$$C_{\frac{4.120}{1.030}} H_{\frac{5.15}{1.030}} N_{\frac{2.060}{1.030}} O_{\frac{1.030}{1.030}} \rightarrow C_{4.00}H_{5.00}N_{2.00}O_{1.00} \rightarrow C_4H_5N_2O \; \text{empirical formula}$$

$$\frac{194 \; g \,/\, mol \; caffeine}{97.1 \; g \,/\, mol \; C_4H_5N_2O} = 2 \; \text{approximately}$$

$$C_{2\times4}H_{2\times5}N_{2\times2}O_{2\times1} \longrightarrow C_8H_{10}N_4O_2 \; \text{molecular formula}$$

8.147 (a) $4 \, NH_3 + 6 \, NO \longrightarrow 5 \, N_2 + 6 \, H_2O$

(b) $15 \; g\,NH_3 \times \dfrac{1 \; mol \; NH_3}{17.03 \; g\,NH_3} = 0.881 \; mol \; NH_3$

$$22.0 \; g\,NO \times \frac{1 \; mol \; NO}{30.01 \; g\,NO} = 0.733 \; mol \; NO$$

$$NH_3 \quad \frac{0.881}{4} = 0.220$$

$$NO \quad \frac{0.733}{3} = 0.122 \; \text{limiting reactant}$$

$$0.733 \; mol\,NO \times \frac{5 \; mol\,N_2}{6 \; mol\,NO} \times \frac{28.014 \; g \; N_2}{1 \; mol\,N_2} = 17.1 \; g \; N_2 \; \text{theoretical yield}$$

$$\frac{13.3 \; g}{17.1 \; g} \times 100 = 77.8\% \; \text{yield}$$

8.148 Assume 1 mole of nicotine, which contains 10 moles of C, 13 moles of H, and 2 moles of N.

$$10 \; mol\,C \times \frac{12.011 \; g \; C}{1 \; mol\,C} = 120.11 \; g \; C$$

$$13 \; mol\,H \times \frac{1.0079 \; g \; H}{1 \; mol\,H} = 13.103 \; g \; H$$

$$2 \; mol\,N \times \frac{14.007 \; g \; N}{1 \; mol\,N} = 28.014 \; g \; N$$

The molar mass of nicotine is 161.23 g/mol.

$$\frac{120.11 \; g \; C}{161.23 \; g \; nicotine} \times 100 = 74.50\% \; C$$

$$\frac{13.103 \; g \; H}{161.23 \; g \; nicotine} \times 100 = 8.127\% \; H$$

$$\frac{28.014 \; g \; N}{161.23 \; g \; nicotine} \times 100 = 17.38\% \; N$$

8.149 The balanced equation is $CaC_2 + 3\,CO \longrightarrow 4\,C + CaCO_3$. That some CaC_2 is left over tells you CO is the limiting reactant and therefore the one to use to calculate theoretical yield. Determine what mass of CO was used to get the $CaCO_3$:

$$135.4 \text{ g } CaCO_3 \times \frac{1 \text{ mol } CaCO_3}{100.1 \text{ g } CaCO_3} \times \frac{3 \text{ mol } CO}{1 \text{ mol } CaCO_3} \times$$

$$\frac{28.01 \text{ g } CO}{1 \text{ mol } CO} = 113.7 \text{ g } CO \text{ present at beginning of reaction}$$

Now determine what mass of CaC_2 combined with the 113.7 g of CO:

$$113.7 \text{ g } CO \times \frac{1 \text{ mol } CO}{28.01 \text{ g } CO} \times \frac{1 \text{ mol } CaC_2}{3 \text{ mol } CO} \times \frac{64.10 \text{ g } CaC_2}{1 \text{ mol } CaC_2} = 86.73 \text{ g } CaC_2 \text{ used up}$$

$$\begin{array}{l} 86.73 \text{ g } CaC_2 \text{ used} \\ \underline{38.5 \text{ g } CaC_2 \text{ left over}} \\ 125.2 \text{ g } CaC_2 \text{ present at beginning of reaction} \end{array}$$

8.150 Assume 100 g of beryl.

$$5.03\% \text{ Be} \;\rightarrow\; 5.03 \text{ g } Be \times \frac{1 \text{ mol Be}}{9.012 \text{ g } Be} = 0.558 \text{ mol Be}$$

$$10.04\% \text{ Al} \;\rightarrow\; 10.04 \text{ g } Al \times \frac{1 \text{ mol Al}}{26.98 \text{ g } Al} = 0.3721 \text{ mol Al}$$

$$31.35\% \text{ Si} \;\rightarrow\; 31.35 \text{ g } Si \times \frac{1 \text{ mol Si}}{28.09 \text{ g } Si} = 1.116 \text{ mol Si}$$

$$53.58\% \text{ O} \;\rightarrow\; 53.58 \text{ g } O \times \frac{1 \text{ mol O}}{15.999 \text{ g } O} = 3.349 \text{ mol O}$$

$$Be_{\frac{0.558}{0.3721}} Al_{\frac{0.3721}{0.3721}} Si_{\frac{1.116}{0.3721}} O_{\frac{3.349}{0.3721}} \rightarrow Be_{1.50}Al_{1.00}Si_{3.00}O_{9.00}$$

Multiplying through by 2 to get a whole number for the Be subscript gives $Be_3Al_2Si_6O_{18}$ for the empirical formula, the molar mass of which iss 537.5 g/mol. Because the molar mass of the mineral is given as 538 g/mol, the molecular formula is the same as the empirical formula.

8.151 (a) $S + 2\,H_2SO_4 \longrightarrow 3\,SO_2 + 2\,H_2O$

(b) $4.80 \text{ g } S \times \dfrac{1 \text{ mol S}}{32.06 \text{ g } S} = 0.150 \text{ mol S}$

$$16.20 \text{ g } H_2SO_4 \times \frac{1 \text{ mol } H_2SO_4}{98.07 \text{ g } H_2SO_4} = 0.1652 \text{ mol } H_2SO_4$$

$$S \qquad \frac{0.150}{1} = 0.150$$

$$H_2SO_4 \qquad \frac{0.1652}{2} = 0.0826 \text{ limiting reactant}$$

$$0.1652 \text{ mol } H_2SO_4 \times \frac{3 \text{ mol } SO_2}{2 \text{ mol } H_2SO_4} \times \frac{64.06 \text{ g } SO_2}{1 \text{ mol } SO_2} = 15.87 \text{ g } SO_2$$

8.152 Assume 1 mole of AZT, which contains 10 moles of C, 13 moles of H, 5 moles of N, and 5 moles of O.

$$10 \text{ mol C} \times \frac{12.011 \text{ g C}}{1 \text{ mol C}} = 120.11 \text{ g C}$$

$$13 \text{ mol H} \times \frac{1.0079 \text{ g H}}{1 \text{ mol H}} = 13.103 \text{ g H}$$

$$5 \text{ mol N} \times \frac{14.007 \text{ g N}}{1 \text{ mol N}} = 70.035 \text{ g N}$$

$$5 \text{ mol O} \times \frac{15.999 \text{ g O}}{1 \text{ mol O}} = 79.995 \text{ g O}$$

The molar mass of AZT is 283.2 g/mol.

$$\frac{120.11 \text{ g C}}{283.2 \text{ g AZT}} \times 100 = 42.41\% \text{ C}$$

$$\frac{13.103 \text{ g H}}{283.2 \text{ g AZT}} \times 100 = 4.627\% \text{ H}$$

$$\frac{70.035 \text{ g N}}{283.2 \text{ g AZT}} \times 100 = 24.73\% \text{ N}$$

$$\frac{79.995 \text{ g O}}{283.2 \text{ g AZT}} \times 100 = 28.24\% \text{ O}$$

8.153 No. The number of moles is proportional to the number of product and reactant particles, which can change during a reaction. For example, in the reaction $2 H_2 + O_2 \longrightarrow 2 H_2O$, you begin with 3 moles of reactants and end up with 2 moles of product.

8.154 (a) $N_2O_4 + 2 N_2H_4 \longrightarrow 3 N_2 + 4 H_2O$

(b) Work back from actual yield to theoretical yield and then use theoretical yield to find out how many grams of reactants were needed to form the theoretical amount of product. (Even though this amount of product was not recovered because of the low yield, it was created.)

$$\text{Theoretical yield} = \frac{\text{Actual yield}}{\% \text{ yield}} \times 100 = \frac{42.32 \text{ g}}{67.5\%} \times 100 = 62.70 \text{ g N}_2 \text{ theoretically possible}$$

$$62.70 \text{ g N}_2 \times \frac{1 \text{ mol N}_2}{28.014 \text{ g N}_2} \times \frac{1 \text{ mol N}_2O_4}{3 \text{ mol N}_2} \times \frac{92.01 \text{ g N}_2O_4}{1 \text{ mol N}_2O_4} = 68.64 \text{ g N}_2O_4$$

$$62.70 \text{ g N}_2 \times \frac{1 \text{ mol N}_2}{28.014 \text{ g N}_2} \times \frac{2 \text{ mol N}_2H_4}{3 \text{ mol N}_2} \times \frac{32.046 \text{ g N}_2H_4}{1 \text{ mol N}_2H_4} = 47.82 \text{ g N}_2H_4$$

8.155 The balanced equation is $2 NH_4F + Ca(NO_3)_2 \longrightarrow CaF_2 + 2 N_2O + 4 H_2O$.

$$22.8 \text{ g NH}_4F \times \frac{1 \text{ mol NH}_4F}{37.04 \text{ g NH}_4F} = 0.616 \text{ mol NH}_4F$$

$$38.2 \text{ g Ca(NO}_3)_2 \times \frac{1 \text{ mol Ca(NO}_3)_2}{164.1 \text{ g Ca(NO}_3)_2} = 0.233 \text{ mol Ca(NO}_3)_2$$

$NH_4F \quad \dfrac{0.616}{2} = 0.308$

$Ca(NO_3)_2 \quad \dfrac{0.233}{1} = 0.233$ limiting reactant

$0.233 \text{ mol } Ca(NO_3)_2 \times \dfrac{1 \text{ mol } CaF_2}{1 \text{ mol } Ca(NO_3)_2} \times \dfrac{78.08 \text{ g } CaF_2}{1 \text{ mol } CaF_2} = 18.2 \text{ g } CaF_2$

$0.233 \text{ mol } Ca(NO_3)_2 \times \dfrac{2 \text{ mol } N_2O}{1 \text{ mol } Ca(NO_3)_2} \times \dfrac{44.01 \text{ g } N_2O}{1 \text{ mol } N_2O} = 20.5 \text{ g } N_2O$

$0.233 \text{ mol } Ca(NO_3)_2 \times \dfrac{4 \text{ mol } H_2O}{1 \text{ mol } Ca(NO_3)_2} \times \dfrac{18.015 \text{ g } H_2O}{1 \text{ mol } H_2O} = 16.8 \text{ g } H_2O$

8.156 As usual, assume 1 mole of compound.
Calcium citrate, molar mass 498.3 g/mol:

$3 \text{ mol } Ca \times \dfrac{40.08 \text{ g } Ca}{1 \text{ mol } Ca} = 120 \text{ g } Ca$ in 1 mol $Ca_3(C_6H_5O_7)_2$

$\dfrac{120 \text{ g } Ca}{498.3 \text{ g calcium citrate}} \times 100 = 24.1\% \text{ Ca}$

Calcium carbonate, molar mass 100.0 g/mol:

$1 \text{ mol } Ca \times \dfrac{40.08 \text{ g } Ca}{1 \text{ mol } Ca} = 40.08 \text{ g } Ca$ in 1 mol $CaCO_3$

$\dfrac{40.08 \text{ g } Ca}{100.0 \text{ g calcium carbonate}} \times 100 = 40.1\% \text{ Ca}$

The carbonate form contains a higher percentage of Ca.

8.157 The balanced equation is $PbS + 4 H_2O_2 \longrightarrow PbSO_4 + 4 H_2O$.

(a) $63.2 \text{ g } PbS \times \dfrac{1 \text{ mol } PbS}{239.3 \text{ g } PbS} = 0.264 \text{ mol } PbS$

$48.0 \text{ g } H_2O_2 \times \dfrac{1 \text{ mol } H_2O_2}{34.01 \text{ g } H_2O_2} = 1.41 \text{ mol } H_2O_2$

$PbS \quad \dfrac{0.264}{1} = 0.264$ limiting reactant

$H_2O_2 \quad \dfrac{1.41}{4} = 0.352$

(b) $0.264 \text{ mol } PbS \times \dfrac{4 \text{ mol } H_2O_2}{1 \text{ mol } PbS} \times \dfrac{34.01 \text{ g } H_2O_2}{1 \text{ mol } H_2O_2} = 35.9 \text{ g } H_2O_2$ used up

Because the reaction began with 48.0 g of H_2O_2, the amount remaining is 48.0 g − 35.9 g = 12.1 g.

8.158 $3.34 \text{ g } CO_2 \times \dfrac{1 \text{ mol } CO_2}{44.009 \text{ g } CO_2} \times \dfrac{1 \text{ mol } C}{1 \text{ mol } CO_2} = 0.0759 \text{ mol } C$

$0.913 \text{ g } H_2O \times \dfrac{1 \text{ mol } H_2O}{18.015 \text{ g } H_2O} \times \dfrac{2 \text{ mol } H}{1 \text{ mol } H_2O} = 0.101 \text{ mol } H$

$$0.0759 \text{ mol C} \times \frac{12.011 \text{ g C}}{1 \text{ mol C}} = 0.912 \text{ g C}$$

$$0.101 \text{ mol H} \times \frac{1.0079 \text{ g H}}{1 \text{ mol H}} = 0.102 \text{ g H}$$

$$1.15 \text{ g} - (0.912 \text{ g} + 0.102 \text{ g}) = 0.136 \text{ g O} \times \frac{1 \text{ mol O}}{15.999 \text{ g O}} = 0.00850 \text{ mol O}$$

$$C_{\frac{0.0759}{0.00850}} H_{\frac{0.101}{0.00850}} O_{\frac{0.00850}{0.00850}} \rightarrow C_{8.93}H_{11.85}O_{1.00} \rightarrow C_9H_{12}O \text{ empirical formula}$$

$$\frac{272 \text{ g / mol estradiol}}{136 \text{ g / mol } C_9H_{12}O} = 2$$

$$C_{2\times9}H_{2\times12}O_{2\times1} \longrightarrow C_{18}H_{24}O_2 \text{ molecular formula}$$

8.159 The balanced equation is $CaCN_2 + 3\ H_2O \longrightarrow CaCO_3 + 2\ NH_3$.

$$5.65 \text{ g CaCN}_2 \times \frac{1 \text{ mol CaCN}_2}{80.11 \text{ g CaCN}_2} = 0.0705 \text{ mol CaCN}_2$$

$$12.2 \text{ g H}_2O \times \frac{1 \text{ mol H}_2O}{18.015 \text{ g H}_2O} = 0.677 \text{ mol H}_2O$$

$$CaCN_2 \quad \frac{0.0705}{1} = 0.0705 \text{ limiting reactant}$$

$$H_2O \quad \frac{0.667}{3} = 0.226$$

$$0.0705 \text{ mol CaCN}_2 \times \frac{2 \text{ mol NH}_3}{1 \text{ mol CaCN}_2} \times \frac{17.03 \text{ g NH}_3}{1 \text{ mol NH}_3} = 2.40 \text{ g NH}_3 \text{ theoretical yield}$$

Actual yield = $0.860 \times 2.40 \text{ g} = 2.06 \text{ g NH}_3$

8.160 Assume 100 g of saccharin.

$$45.90\% \text{ C} \rightarrow 45.90 \text{ g C} \times \frac{1 \text{ mol C}}{12.011 \text{ g C}} = 3.821 \text{ mol C}$$

$$2.75\% \text{ H} \rightarrow 2.75 \text{ g H} \times \frac{1 \text{ mol H}}{1.0079 \text{ g H}} = 2.728 \text{ mol H}$$

$$26.20\% \text{ O} \rightarrow 26.20 \text{ g O} \times \frac{1 \text{ mol O}}{15.999 \text{ g O}} = 1.638 \text{ mol O}$$

$$7.65\% \text{ N} \rightarrow 7.65 \text{ g N} \times \frac{1 \text{ mol N}}{14.007 \text{ g N}} = 0.546 \text{ mol N}$$

$$17.50\% \text{ S} \rightarrow 17.50 \text{ g S} \times \frac{1 \text{ mol S}}{32.064 \text{ g S}} = 0.546 \text{ mol S}$$

$$C_{\frac{3.821}{0.546}} H_{\frac{2.728}{0.546}} O_{\frac{1.638}{0.546}} N_{\frac{0.546}{0.546}} S_{\frac{0.546}{0.546}} \rightarrow C_{7.00}H_{5.00}O_{3.00}N_{1.00}S_{1.00} \rightarrow C_7H_5O_3NS \text{ empirical formula}$$

$$\frac{183.19 \text{ g / mol saccharin}}{183.2 \text{ g / mol } C_7H_5O_3NS} = 1$$

The molecular formula is the same as the empirical formula.

8.161 5.00×10^{11} Ti atoms $\times \dfrac{47.90 \text{ amu}}{1 \text{ Ti atom}} \times \dfrac{1.66 \times 10^{-24} \text{ g}}{1 \text{ amu}} = 3.98 \times 10^{-11} \text{ g}$

8.162 The theoretical yield of NO is

$$25.0 \text{ g Cu} \times \frac{1 \text{ mol Cu}}{63.54 \text{ g Cu}} \times \frac{2 \text{ mol NO}}{3 \text{ mol Cu}} \times \frac{30.01 \text{ g NO}}{1 \text{ mol NO}} = 7.87 \text{ g NO}$$

Percent yield $= \dfrac{7.24 \text{ g}}{7.87 \text{ g}} \times 100 = 92.0\%$

8.163 Assume 100 g of arginine.

$41.37\% \text{ C} \rightarrow 41.37 \text{ g C} \times \dfrac{1 \text{ mol C}}{12.011 \text{ g C}} = 3.444 \text{ mol C}$

$8.10\% \text{ H} \rightarrow 8.10 \text{ g H} \times \dfrac{1 \text{ mol H}}{1.0079 \text{ g H}} = 8.037 \text{ mol H}$

$32.16\% \text{ N} \rightarrow 32.16 \text{ g N} \times \dfrac{1 \text{ mol N}}{14.007 \text{ g N}} = 2.296 \text{ mol N}$

$18.37\% \text{ O} \rightarrow 18.37 \text{ g O} \times \dfrac{1 \text{ mol O}}{15.999 \text{ g O}} = 1.148 \text{ mol O}$

$C_{\frac{3.444}{1.148}} H_{\frac{8.037}{1.148}} N_{\frac{2.296}{1.148}} O_{\frac{1.148}{1.148}} \rightarrow C_{3.00}H_{7.00}N_{2.00}O_{1.00} \rightarrow C_3H_7O_2N$ empirical formula

$\dfrac{174 \text{ g / mol arginine}}{87.1 \text{ g / mol } C_3H_7N_2O} = 2$ approximately

$C_{2\times3}H_{2\times7}N_{2\times2}O_{2\times1} \longrightarrow C_6H_{14}N_4O_2$ molecular formula

8.164 The balanced equation is $As_4S_6 + 9 O_2 \longrightarrow As_4O_6 + 6 SO_2$.

(a) $58.9 \text{ g As}_4\text{S}_6 \times \dfrac{1 \text{ mol As}_4\text{S}_6}{492.1 \text{ g As}_4\text{S}_6} \times \dfrac{9 \text{ mol O}_2}{1 \text{ mol As}_4\text{S}_6} \times \dfrac{31.998 \text{ g O}_2}{1 \text{ mol O}_2} = 34.5 \text{ g O}_2$

(b) $58.9 \text{ g As}_4\text{S}_6 \times \dfrac{1 \text{ mol As}_4\text{S}_6}{492.1 \text{ g As}_4\text{S}_6} \times \dfrac{6 \text{ mol SO}_2}{1 \text{ mol As}_4\text{S}_6} \times \dfrac{64.06 \text{ g SO}_2}{1 \text{ mol SO}_2} = 46.0 \text{ g SO}_2$ theoretical yield

Percent yield $= \dfrac{41.2 \text{ g}}{46.0 \text{ g}} \times 100 = 89.6\%$

8.165 $11.0 \text{ g Cu}_2\text{O} \times \dfrac{1 \text{ mol Cu}_2\text{O}}{143.09 \text{ g Cu}_2\text{O}} \times \dfrac{2 \text{ mol Cu}}{1 \text{ mol Cu}_2\text{O}} \times \dfrac{63.546 \text{ g Cu}}{1 \text{ mol Cu}} = 9.77 \text{ g Cu}$

$12.6 \text{ g Cu}_2\text{S} \times \dfrac{1 \text{ mol Cu}_2\text{S}}{159.16 \text{ g Cu}_2\text{S}} \times \dfrac{2 \text{ mol Cu}}{1 \text{ mol Cu}_2\text{S}} \times \dfrac{63.546 \text{ g Cu}}{1 \text{ mol Cu}} = 10.06 \text{ g Cu}$

The Cu_2S sample contains more Cu.

8.166 (a) In the reaction, the number of moles of A equals the number of moles of C, meaning every 1 mole of A used up forms 1 mole of C. This relationship holds for any number of moles—0.3 mol A $\longrightarrow$ 0.3 mol C, 0.278 mol A $\longrightarrow$ 0.278 mol C, and so on. So even though you don't know what the mole number is for these particular reactant and product masses, you do know it is the same for A and C. Thus 8.0 g of A and 10.0 g of C represent the same number of moles. Say that number is 1, for simplicity: 8.0 g/mol A, 10.0 g/mol C, giving C the greater molar mass.

(b) The number of moles of B consumed is half the number of moles of A consumed. Because the 6.0 g of B consumed is more than half the 8.0 g of A consumed, the molar mass of B must be greater than that of A.

(c) The number of moles of A consumed is twice the number of moles of D produced. The 8.0 g of A consumed is twice the mass of the 4.0 g of D produced, telling you A and D must have the same molar mass (even though they are different substances).

(d) For simplicity, begin by saying that the masses given in the problem statement correspond to the mole numbers indicated by the equation coefficients, so that 8 g is 2 moles of A, 6 g is 1 mole of B, 10 g is 2 moles of C, and 4 grams is 1 mole of D. Dividing by the coefficients tells you that

$8/2 = 4$ g/mol is the molar mass of A
$6/1 = 6$ g/mol is the molar mass of B
$10/2 = 5$ g/mol is the molar mass of C
$4/1 = 4$ g/mol is the molar mass of D

Because the stated molar mass of A, 24 g/mol, tells you your hypothetical value of 4 g/mol was multiplied by 6, multiply the other hypothetical values to get true values:

B $\quad 6 \times 6 = 36$ g/mol
C $\quad 6 \times 5 = 30$ g/mol
D $\quad 6 \times 4 = 24$ g/mol

8.167 $\quad 4.25 \times 10^{22}$ atoms S $\times \dfrac{1 \text{ mol S}}{6.022 \times 10^{23} \text{ atoms S}} = 0.0706$ mol S

0.0706 mol S $\times \dfrac{1 \text{ mol Al}_2\text{S}_3}{3 \text{ mol S}} = 0.0235$ mol Al_2S_3

0.0235 mol $\text{Al}_2\text{S}_3 \times \dfrac{150.2 \text{ mol Al}_2\text{S}_3}{1 \text{ mol Al}_2\text{S}_3} = 3.53$ g Al_2S_3

8.168 The balanced equation is $2 \text{ Al}_2\text{O}_3 + 3 \text{ C} \longrightarrow 3 \text{ CO}_2 + 4 \text{ Al}$. First get the theoretical yield of Al:

Theoretical yield $= \dfrac{284 \text{ kg Al}}{94.7\%} \times 100 = 300.$ kg Al

Now figure out how much of each reactant was needed to form this mass of Al. Because masses are in kilograms, you can save yourself a conversion step by working in kilomoles.

$300.$ kg Al $\times \dfrac{1 \text{ kmol Al}}{26.98 \text{ kg Al}} \times \dfrac{2 \text{ kmol Al}_2\text{O}_3}{4 \text{ kmol Al}} \times \dfrac{102.0 \text{ kg Al}_2\text{O}_3}{1 \text{ kmol Al}_2\text{O}_3} = 567$ kg Al_2O_3

$300.$ kg Al $\times \dfrac{1 \text{ kmol Al}}{26.98 \text{ kg Al}} \times \dfrac{3 \text{ kmol C}}{4 \text{ kmol Al}} \times \dfrac{12.011 \text{ kg C}}{1 \text{ kmol C}} = 100.$ kg C

8.169 $\quad 250$ mg $\times \dfrac{1 \text{ g}}{1000 \text{ mg}} \times \dfrac{1 \text{ mol C}_9\text{H}_8\text{O}_4}{180.2 \text{ g C}_9\text{H}_8\text{O}_4} \times \dfrac{6.022 \times 10^{23} \text{ molecules C}_9\text{H}_8\text{O}_4}{1 \text{ mol C}_9\text{H}_8\text{O}_4}$

$= 8.35 \times 10^{20}$ molecules $\text{C}_9\text{H}_8\text{O}_4$

There are nine C atoms in each molecule:

8.35×10^{20} molecules $\text{C}_9\text{H}_8\text{O}_4 \times \dfrac{9 \text{ atoms C}}{1 \text{ molecule C}_9\text{H}_8\text{O}_4} = 7.52 \times 10^{21}$ atoms C

8.170 The balanced equation is $3\ Ca + N_2 \longrightarrow Ca_3N_2$.

(a) $33.8\ \text{g Ca} \times \dfrac{1\ \text{mol Ca}}{40.08\ \text{g Ca}} = 0.834\ \text{mol Ca}$

$20.4\ \text{g N}_2 \times \dfrac{1\ \text{mol N}_2}{28.014\ \text{g N}_2} = 0.728\ \text{mol N}_2$

$\text{Ca} \quad \dfrac{0.843}{3} = 0.281\ \text{limiting reactant}$

$\text{N}_2 \quad \dfrac{0.728}{1} = 0.728$

(b) $0.843\ \text{mol Ca} \times \dfrac{1\ \text{mol Ca}_3\text{N}_2}{3\ \text{mol Ca}} \times \dfrac{148.3\ \text{g Ca}_3\text{N}_2}{1\ \text{mol Ca}_3\text{N}_2} = 41.7\ \text{g Ca}_3\text{N}_2\ \text{theoretical yield}$

Actual yield $= 0.724 \times 41.7\ \text{g Ca}_3\text{N}_2 = 30.2\ \text{g Ca}_3\text{N}_2$

8.171 $1.04\ \text{g CO}_2 \times \dfrac{1\ \text{mol CO}_2}{44.009\ \text{g CO}_2} \times \dfrac{1\ \text{mol C}}{1\ \text{mol CO}_2} = 0.0236\ \text{mol C}$

$0.213\ \text{g H}_2\text{O} \times \dfrac{1\ \text{mol H}_2\text{O}}{18.015\ \text{g H}_2\text{O}} \times \dfrac{2\ \text{mol H}}{1\ \text{mol H}_2\text{O}} = 0.0236\ \text{mol H}$

$0.0236\ \text{mol C} \times \dfrac{12.011\ \text{g C}}{1\ \text{mol C}} = 0.283\ \text{g C}$

$0.0236\ \text{mol H} \times \dfrac{1.0079\ \text{g H}}{1\ \text{mol H}} = 0.0238\ \text{g H}$

$0.450\ \text{g} - (0.283\ \text{g} + 0.0238\ \text{g}) = 0.143\ \text{g O}$

$0.143\ \text{g O} \times \dfrac{1\ \text{mol O}}{15.999\ \text{g O}} = 0.00895\ \text{mol O}$

$C_{\frac{0.0236}{0.00895}} H_{\frac{0.0236}{0.00895}} O_{\frac{0.00895}{0.00895}} \rightarrow C_{2.64}H_{2.64}O_{1.00}$

Find a multiplier that makes the C and H subscripts whole numbers:

$2 \times 2.64 = 5.28$
$3 \times 2.64 = 7.92$ close enough to 8
$C_{3\times2.64}H_{3\times2.64}O_{3\times1.00} \longrightarrow C_8H_8O_3$ empirical formula

$\dfrac{152\ \text{g / mol vanillin}}{152\ \text{g / mol C}_8\text{H}_8\text{O}_3} = 1$

The molecular formula is the same as the empirical formula.

8.172 The balanced equation is $3\ Ca(OH)_2 + 2\ H_3PO_4 \longrightarrow Ca_3(PO_4)_2 + 6\ H_2O$.

(a) $34.6\ \text{g Ca(OH)}_2 \times \dfrac{1\ \text{mol Ca(OH)}_2}{74.09\ \text{g Ca(OH)}_2} \times \dfrac{2\ \text{mol H}_3\text{PO}_4}{3\ \text{mol Ca(OH)}_2} \times \dfrac{97.99\text{g H}_3\text{PO}_4}{1\ \text{mol H}_3\text{PO}_4} = 30.5\ \text{g H}_3\text{PO}_4$

(b) $34.6\ \text{g Ca(OH)}_2 \times \dfrac{1\ \text{mol Ca(OH)}_2}{74.09\ \text{g Ca(OH)}_2} \times \dfrac{1\ \text{mol Ca}_3(\text{PO}_4)_2}{3\ \text{mol Ca(OH)}_2} \times \dfrac{310.2\ \text{g Ca}_3(\text{PO}_4)_2}{1\ \text{mol Ca}_3(\text{PO}_4)_2}$

$= 48.3\ \text{g Ca}_3(\text{PO}_4)_2$

or

$$30.5 \text{ g H}_3\text{PO}_4 \times \frac{1 \text{ mol H}_3\text{PO}_4}{97.99 \text{ g H}_3\text{PO}_4} \times \frac{1 \text{ mol Ca}_3(\text{PO}_4)_2}{2 \text{ mol H}_3\text{PO}_4} \times \frac{310.2 \text{ g Ca}_3(\text{PO}_4)_2}{1 \text{ mol Ca}_3(\text{PO}_4)_2}$$

$$= 48.3 \text{ g Ca}_3(\text{PO}_4)_2$$

8.173 The balanced equation is $16 \text{ Cr} + 3 \text{ S}_8 \longrightarrow 8 \text{ Cr}_2\text{S}_3$. First determine the theoretical yield:

$$\text{Theoretical yield} = \frac{\text{Actual yield}}{\text{Percent yield}} \times 100 = \frac{235.0 \text{ g Cr}_2\text{S}_3}{63.80\%} \times 100 = 368.3 \text{ g Cr}_2\text{S}_3$$

$$368.3 \text{ g Cr}_2\text{S}_3 \times \frac{1 \text{ mol Cr}_2\text{S}_3}{200.2 \text{ g Cr}_2\text{S}_3} \times \frac{16 \text{ mol Cr}}{8 \text{ mol Cr}_2\text{S}_3} \times \frac{52.00 \text{ g Cr}}{1 \text{ mol Cr}} = 191.3 \text{ g Cr}$$

$$368.3 \text{ g Cr}_2\text{S}_3 \times \frac{1 \text{ mol Cr}_2\text{S}_3}{200.2 \text{ g Cr}_2\text{S}_3} \times \frac{3 \text{ mol S}_8}{8 \text{ mol Cr}_2\text{S}_3} \times \frac{256.5 \text{ g S}_8}{1 \text{ mol S}_8} = 177.0 \text{ g S}_8$$

8.174 The balanced equation is $\text{Al}_2\text{S}_3 + 6 \text{ H}_2\text{O} \longrightarrow \text{Al(OH)}_3 + 3 \text{ H}_2\text{S}$.

(a) $56.0 \text{ g Al}_2\text{S}_3 \times \dfrac{1 \text{ mol Al}_2\text{S}_3}{150.2 \text{ g Al}_2\text{S}_3} = 0.373 \text{ mol Al}_2\text{S}_3$

$48.2 \text{ g H}_2\text{O} \times \dfrac{1 \text{ mol H}_2\text{O}}{18.015 \text{ g H}_2\text{O}} = 2.68 \text{ mol H}_2\text{O}$

$\text{Al}_2\text{S}_3 \quad \dfrac{0.373}{1} = 0.373 \text{ limiting reactant}$

$\text{H}_2\text{O} \quad \dfrac{2.68}{6} = 0.447$

Because Al_2S_3 is the limiting reactant, the H_2O is the excess reactant.

(b) $0.373 \text{ mol Al}_2\text{S}_3 \times \dfrac{6 \text{ mol H}_2\text{O}}{1 \text{ mol Al}_2\text{S}_3} \times \dfrac{18.015 \text{ g H}_2\text{O}}{1 \text{ mol H}_2\text{O}} = 40.3 \text{ g H}_2\text{O used up}$

$48.2 \text{ g} - 40.3 \text{ g} = 7.9 \text{ g H}_2\text{O left over}$

CHAPTER
9

The Transfer of Electrons from One Atom to Another in a Chemical Reaction

9.1 See solution in textbook.

9.2 (a) Dot diagram: $\ddot{O}{=}C{=}\ddot{O}$.

We determine oxidation number by subtracting the number of valence electrons assigned by oxidation-state bookkeeping from the number of valence electrons each free atom normally owns. Because O is more electronegative than C, all the electrons in the dot diagram are assigned to one or the other O and none is assigned to C:

$:\ddot{O}:_A \quad C \quad :\ddot{O}:_B$

Atom	Valence electrons in free atom		Electrons assigned by oxidation-state bookkeeping		Oxidation state
C	4	−	0	=	+4
Left O_A	6	−	8	=	−2
Right O_B	6	−	8	=	−2

(b) None, because it is the less electronegative element in the C−O bonds.

(c) Four fewer, because a free C atom has four valence electrons.

(d) Correct, because assigning C no electrons in part (a) is only a technique for determining oxidation number and does not reflect the number of electrons actually around C in CO_2. (That actual number, from the dot structure, is eight, to satisfy the octet rule.)

9.3 (a) Dot diagram:
$$H:\overset{\displaystyle H}{\underset{\displaystyle H}{\ddot{C}}}:H$$

We determine oxidation number by subtracting the number of valence electrons assigned by oxidation-state bookkeeping from the number of valence electrons each free atom normally

---

149

owns. Because C is more electronegative than H, all the electrons in the dot diagram are assigned to C and none is assigned to H:

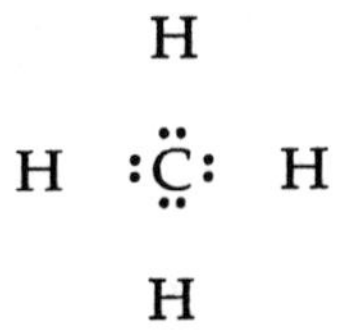

$$
\begin{array}{c}
\text{H} \\
\text{H} \;\; :\!\overset{\cdot\cdot}{\underset{\cdot\cdot}{\text{C}}}\!: \;\; \text{H} \\
\text{H}
\end{array}
$$

Atom	Valence electrons in free atom		Electrons assigned by oxidation-state bookkeeping		Oxidation state
C	4	−	8	=	−4
Each H	1	−	0	=	+1

(b) Eight

(c) Four more because a free C atom has four valence electrons.

9.4 (a) Dot diagram:
$$
\begin{array}{c}
\text{H} \\
:\!\overset{\cdot\cdot}{\underset{\cdot\cdot}{\text{Cl}}}\!:\overset{\cdot\cdot}{\text{C}}:\!\overset{\cdot\cdot}{\underset{\cdot\cdot}{\text{Cl}}}\!: \\
:\!\overset{\cdot\cdot}{\underset{\cdot\cdot}{\text{Cl}}}\!:
\end{array}
$$

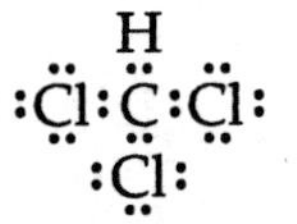

We determine oxidation number by subtracting the number of valence electrons assigned by oxidation-state bookkeeping from the number of valence electrons each free atom normally owns. C being more electronegative than H means C gets both electrons of the C–H bond; Cl being more electronegative than C means each Cl gets both the electrons in its respective C–Cl bond:

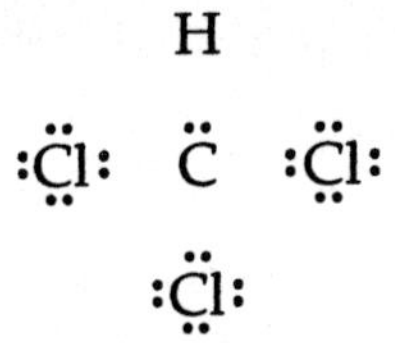

$$
\begin{array}{c}
\text{H} \\
:\!\overset{\cdot\cdot}{\underset{\cdot\cdot}{\text{Cl}}}\!: \;\; \overset{\cdot\cdot}{\text{C}} \;\; :\!\overset{\cdot\cdot}{\underset{\cdot\cdot}{\text{Cl}}}\!: \\
:\!\overset{\cdot\cdot}{\underset{\cdot\cdot}{\text{Cl}}}\!:
\end{array}
$$

Atom	Valence electrons in free atom		Electrons assigned by oxidation-state bookkeeping		Oxidation state
C	4	−	2	=	+2
H	1	−	0	=	+1
Each Cl	7	−	8	=	−1

(b) Two

(c) Two fewer because a free C atom has four valence electrons.

(d) Correct, because assigning C only two electrons in part (a) is merely a technique for determining oxidation number and does not reflect the number of electrons actually around C in $CHCl_3$. (That actual number is eight, to satisfy the octet rule.)

9.5 See solution in textbook.

9.6 Mg +2 (rule 5); each Br −1 (halide rule applies because Br more electronegative than Mg).

9.7 Each O −2 (rule 2; O assigned first because no rule for Fe); each Fe +3 (rule 7: three O of oxidation state −2 is $3 \times (-2) = -6$, which means combined oxidation state of the two Fe must be +6: $+6/2 = +3$ for each Fe).

9.8 H +1 (rule 3); O −2 (rule 2); Cl +1 (rule 7: $[1 \times (+1)] + [1 \times (-2)] = -1$, $-1 + ? = 0$, $? = +1$; halide rule does not apply because Cl less electronegative than O.)

9.9 Each O −2 (rule 2); C +4 (rule 7: three O of oxidation state −2 is 3 × (−2) = −6; charge on ion is 2−, meaning charge on C must be such that C + 3 O sum is −2: −6 + 4 = −2).

9.10 Cu +2 (rule 6).

9.11 See solution in textbook.

9.12 This is a redox reaction. The oxidation number of Fe changes from 0 to +3 (each Fe *loses* three electrons), and the oxidation number of O changes from 0 to −2 (each O atom *gains* two electrons). The Fe is oxidized, and the O is reduced.

9.13 This is a redox reaction. The oxidation number of Ca changes from 0 to +2 (Ca loses two electrons), and the oxidation number of H changes from +1 to 0 (each H atom gains one electron). The Ca is oxidized, and the H is reduced.

9.14 This is not a redox reaction because none of the oxidation numbers change during the reaction. Na remains +1, Br remains −1, Mg remains +2, and O remains −2.

9.15 See solution in textbook.

9.16 Fe is oxidized, and O is reduced (see Practice Problem 9.12). Therefore Fe is the reducing agent, and O_2 is the oxidizing agent.

9.17 Ca is oxidized, and H is reduced (see Practice Problem 9.13). Therefore Ca is the reducing agent, and H^+ is the oxidizing agent.

9.18 See solution in textbook.

9.19 (a) Pb^{2+} (reduced from +2 to 0)
(b) Ni (oxidized from 0 to +2)
(c) The Pb cathode because Pb metal plates out on the electrode.
(d) The Ni anode because Ni metal atoms from the electrode dissolve and become Ni^{2+} ions in solution.

9.20 (a) Fe (oxidation state changes from 0 to +3).
(b) Ag^+ (oxidation state changes from +1 to 0).
(c)

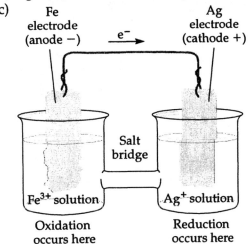

9.21 See solution in textbook.

9.22 Only (a) occurs spontaneously because Al is more active than Zn. (Al is higher on the EMF list.) Al gives electrons to Zn^{2+} (reaction a), but Zn does not give electrons to Al^{3+} (reaction b).

9.23 Draw two beakers, one containing a solid Al electrode in a solution of Al^{3+} ions and the other containing a solid Zn electrode in a solution of Zn^{2+} ions. Connect the electrodes by a wire and the beakers by a salt bridge. Because Al is higher than Zn on the EMF list, electrons flow from the Al electrode to the Zn electrode, making Al the anode (−) and Zn the cathode (+).

Al atoms lose electrons, which means they are oxidized. Zn^{2+} ions gain electrons, which means they are reduced.

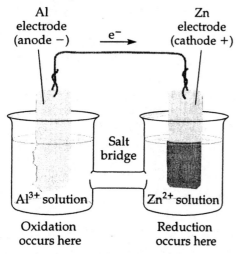

9.24 Because lead is higher than copper in the EMF series, Pb gives electrons to Cu^{2+} to produce Pb^{2+} ions and Cu: $Pb + Cu^{2+} \longrightarrow Pb^{2+} + Cu$. Pb loses electrons, which means it is oxidized and therefore is the reducing agent. Cu^{2+} gains electrons, which means it is reduced and therefore is the oxidizing agent.

9.25 The electrical voltage is analogous to water pressure, and the electron flow is analogous to water flow.

9.26 By moving copper wire through a magnetic field. Coils of copper wire are wound around a rotor and spun in a magnetic field by a turbine powered by either steam or moving water.

9.27 One in which atoms of one of the reactants lose electrons while atoms of some other reactant gain electrons.

9.28 To keep track of how many electrons each atom owns before and after a chemical reaction takes place. This process of "electron bookkeeping" makes it possible to determine whether electron transfer occurs during the reaction.

9.29 Electron bookkeeping is a method of keeping track of all of the electrons owned by every atom on both sides of an equation representing a redox reaction.

9.30 Both methods are correct. The double-counting method of the octet rule is used when determining the correctness of electron dot structures, and the oxidation-state method is used when determining oxidation states.

9.31 Because the oxidation state of the atom is the difference between the number of valence electrons in the free atom and the number of valence electrons assigned to the atom by oxidation-state bookkeeping. The number of valence electrons in the free atom must be known in order to determine this difference.

9.32 The more electronegative of the two bonded atoms.

9.33 Dot diagram: $:\ddot{F}—\ddot{N}—\ddot{F}:$
$\qquad\qquad\qquad\quad |$
$\qquad\qquad\qquad\quad H$

Because F is more electronegative than N, each F owns eight electrons, all three of its lone pairs plus both electrons from the F–N bond. Because N is more electronegative than H, N owns four electrons, its one lone pair plus both electrons from the N–H bond. Having given its one electron to the more electronegative N, H owns no electrons: $:\ddot{F}: \quad \ddot{N} \quad :\ddot{F}:$.

$\qquad\qquad\qquad\qquad\qquad\qquad\qquad\qquad\qquad\qquad H$

9.34 Dot diagram: $H\!-\!\overset{\displaystyle ..}{\underset{\displaystyle ..}{O}}\!-\!\overset{\displaystyle ..}{\underset{\displaystyle ..}{O}}\!-\!H$

Each O owns both electrons from its O–H bond (because O is more electronegative than H) and one of the electrons from its O–O bond (because the two atoms of the bond have the same electronegativity), for a total of three electrons. Each O also owns both its lone pairs, for a grand total of $3 + 4 = 7$ electrons. Each H, having given its electron from its O–H bond to the more electronegative O, owns no electrons: H $\;:\!\overset{\displaystyle ..}{\underset{\displaystyle ..}{O}}\!\cdot\;\;\cdot\!\overset{\displaystyle ..}{\underset{\displaystyle ..}{O}}\!:\;$ H.

9.35 Dot diagram: $\left[\;:\!\overset{\displaystyle ..}{\underset{\displaystyle ..}{O}}\!-\!N\!=\!\overset{\displaystyle ..}{\underset{\displaystyle ..}{O}}\;\right]^{-}$ with $\underset{\displaystyle :\overset{..}{\underset{..}{O}}:}{\vert}$ below N

Because O is more electronegative than N, each O owns eight electrons, all of its lone pairs plus all electrons from the N–O bonds. The N owns no electrons because it gave all its electrons from its N–O bonds to the more electronegative O: $\left[\;:\!\overset{\displaystyle ..}{\underset{\displaystyle ..}{O}}\!:\quad N\quad:\!\overset{\displaystyle ..}{\underset{\displaystyle ..}{O}}\!:\;\right]^{-}$ with $:\!\overset{\displaystyle ..}{\underset{\displaystyle ..}{O}}\!:$ below.

9.36 NF_2H Electron-bookkeeping method:

    Each F: 7 free-atom valence e^- $-$ 8 assigned e^- = -1 oxidation state

    N: 5 free-atom valence e^- $-$ 4 assigned e^- = $+1$ oxidation state

    H: 1 free-atom valence e^- $-$ 0 assigned e^- = $+1$ oxidation state

    Shortcut rules:

    Each F: -1 (halide rule holds because F more electronegative than N)

    H: $+1$ (rule 3)

    N: $+1$ (rule 7: $2 \times (-1) + (+1) = -1$; therefore N must be $+1$ to sum to zero: $-1 + (+1) = 0$

H_2O_2 Electron-bookkeeping method:

    Each H: 1 free-atom valence e^- $-$ 0 assigned e^- = $+1$ oxidation state

    Each O: 6 free-atom valence e^- $-$ 7 assigned e^- = -1 oxidation state

    Shortcut rules:

    Each H: $+1$ (rule 3)

    Each O: rule 2 says O is almost always -2, but that oxidation state would mean the sum of all oxidation states in the H_2O_2 molecule is not zero: $2 \times (+1) + 2 \times (-2) = -2$. Therefore rule 2 does not work and you must turn to rule 7: $2 \times (+1) = +2$ for H, meaning the sum of the O oxidation states must be -2, or -1 for each O.

NO_3^- Electron-bookkeeping method:

    N: 5 free-atom valence e^- $-$ 0 assigned e^- = $+5$ oxidation state

    Each O: 6 free-atom valence e^- $-$ 8 assigned e^- = -2 oxidation state

    Shortcut rules:

    Each O: -2 (rule 2)

    N: $+5$ (rule 7: $3 \times (-2) = -6$ for O, and the oxidation states of all the atoms must sum to the charge on the ion, -1: $-6 + ? = -1$, $? = +5$)

9.37 (a) Dot diagram: $H\!:\!H$. Each H owns one electron because the two atoms have the same electronegativity. Oxidation state = 1 free-atom valence e^- $-$ 1 assigned e^- = 0 oxidation state.

(b) Dot diagram: $:\!\overset{\displaystyle ..}{\underset{\displaystyle ..}{O}}\!::\!\overset{\displaystyle ..}{\underset{\displaystyle ..}{O}}\!:$. Each O owns six electrons, four from its two lone pairs plus two from the double bond because the two atoms have the same electronegativity. Oxidation number = 6 free-atom valence e^- $-$ 6 assigned e^- = 0 oxidation state.

(c) Dot diagram: $:\ddot{C}l:\ddot{C}l:$. Each Cl owns seven electrons, six from its three lone pairs plus one of the bond electrons. Oxidation state = 7 free-atom valence e^- − 7 assigned e^- = 0 oxidation state.

9.38 That the oxidation number of each atom in a diatomic element is always 0.

9.39 The sum must always equal the overall charge on the molecule.

9.40 (a) The equation for calculating oxidation state is "number of free-atom valence electrons − number of assigned electrons." In order for this quantity to be a positive number, as is the +3 oxidation state of this problem, the term "number of free-atom valence electrons" must be greater than the term "number of assigned electrons." Thus any atom having a positive oxidation state has been assigned fewer electrons than the number of free-atom valence electrons.

(b) The +3 tells you the number of electrons assigned has to be three fewer than the number of valence electrons in the free atom.

9.41 (a) The equation for calculating oxidation state is "number of free-atom valence electrons − number of assigned electrons." In order for this quantity to be a negative number, as is the −2 oxidation state of this problem, the term "number of assigned electrons" must be greater than the term "number of free-atom valence electrons." Thus any atom having a negative oxidation state has been assigned more electrons than the number of free-atom valence electrons.

(b) The −2 tells you the number of electrons assigned must be two more than the number of valence electrons in the free atom.

9.42 Add up the oxidation numbers of all the other atoms in the compound. Subtract this sum from the total charge on the species. The difference is the oxidation number of the remaining atom.

9.43 (a) Each Cl −1 by the halide rule (applies because Cl more electronegative than P); P +3 by rule 7: $3 \times (-1) = -3$, $-3 + ? = 0$, $? = +3$.

(b) Each H +1 by rule 3; S −2 by rule 7: $2 \times (+1) = +2$, $+2 + ? = 0$, $? = -2$.

(c) Each O −2 by rule 2; Mn +7 by rule 7: $4 \times (-2) = -8$, $-8 + ? = -1$, $? = +7$.

(d) H +1 by rule 3; each O −2 by rule 2; N +5 by rule 7: $[1 \times (+1)] + [3 \times (-2)] = -5$, $-5 + ? = 0$, $? = +5$.

(e) Each H +1 by rule 3; each O −2 by rule 2; C +2 by rule 7: $[2 \times (+1)] + [2 \times (-2)] = -2$, $-2 + ? = 0$, $? = +2$.

(f) Each O −2 by rule 2; each S +2 by rule 7: $3 \times (-2) = -6$, $-6 + ? = -2$, $? = +4$. This +4 oxidation state must be spread over the two S, giving each S a +2 state.

9.44 (a) O −2 by rule 2; C +2 by rule 7: $-2 + ? = 0$, $? = +2$.

(b) Each H +1 by rule 3; each Cl −1 by the halide rule (applies because Cl more electronegative than C); C 0 by rule 7: $[2 \times (+1)] + [2 \times (-1)] = 0$, $0 + ? = 0$, $? = 0$.

(c) H +1 by rule 3; each O −2 by rule 2; C +2 by rule 7: $+1 + [2 \times (-2)] = -3$, $-3 + ? = -1$, $? = +2$.

(d) Each Cl −1 by halide rule (applies because Cl more electronegative than Pt); Pt +4 by rule 7: $6 \times -1 = -6$, $-6 + ? = -2$; $? = +4$.

9.45 (a) O −2 by rule 6.

(b) Each Li +1 by rule 4; N −3 by rule 7: $3 \times (+1) = +3$, $+3 + ? = 0$, $? = -3$.

(c) Mg +2 by rule 5; each O −2 by rule 2; S +6 by rule 7: $+2 + [4 \times (-2)] = -6$, $-6 + ? = 0$, $? = +6$.

(d) Each O −2 by rule 2; Mn +4 by rule 7: $2 \times (-2) = -4$; $-4 + ? = 0$, $? = +4$.

9.46 (a) The halide rule works for $AlCl_3$ because Cl is more electronegative than Al.

(b) The halide rule does not work for ClO^- because Cl is less electronegative than O.

(c) ClO^-: O −2 by rule 2; Cl +1 by rule 7: $-2 + ? = -1$, $? = +1$.

$AlCl_3$: each Cl −1 by halide rule; Al +3 by rule 7: $3 \times (-1) = -3$, $-3 + ? = 0$, $? = +3$.

9.47 Dot diagram: $:\ddot{\underset{..}{I}}-\ddot{\underset{..}{F}}:$. Because F is the more electronegative element, it owns both of the

shared electrons: $:\ddot{\underset{.}{I}}\quad:\ddot{\underset{..}{F}}:$.

F: 7 free-atom valence e^- − 8 assigned e^- = −1
I: 7 free-atom valence e^- − 6 assigned e^- = +1

9.48 (a) Two oxygens, each with a −2 oxidation state, and six hydrogens, each with a +1 oxidation state, sum to +2. This means the sum of the oxidation numbers of the three carbons must be −2 to achieve charge neutrality for the molecule. This is not enough information to assign the carbons a unique set of oxidation numbers.

(b) Redraw the dot diagram given in the problem statement so that it shows each valence electron on the atom that owns it, assigning electrons according to the electronegativity ranking O > C > H:

$$\begin{matrix} H & :\ddot{\underset{..}{O}}: & & H \\ H & :\ddot{\underset{..}{C}}\cdot & \cdot C & :\ddot{\underset{..}{O}}: & \ddot{\underset{..}{C}}: & H \\ H & & & H \end{matrix}$$

Each H: 1 free-atom valence e^- − 0 assigned e^- = +1
Left C: 4 free-atom valence e^- − 7 assigned e^- = −3
Middle C: 4 free-atom valence e^- − 1 assigned e^- = +3
Right C: 4 free-atom valence e^- − 6 assigned e^- = −2
Each O: 6 free-atom valence e^- − 8 assigned e^- = −2

9.49 Reduction is the gain of electrons by an atom or ion in an oxidation–reduction reaction.

9.50 Oxidation is the loss of electrons by an atom or ion in an oxidation–reduction reaction.

9.51 If the oxidation number of any atom changes during a reaction, the reaction is a redox reaction.

9.52 Oxidation state decreases when an atom is reduced.

9.53 Oxidation state increases when an atom is oxidized.

9.54 That one or more electrons move from one atom to another.

9.55 Because the oxidation and reduction that occur in the redox reaction involve a transfer of electrons, by definition. Electrons are transferred from the species being oxidized to the species being reduced.

9.56 (a) and (c), because they are the only reactions in which oxidation numbers change. In (a), sodium, the oxidation number changes from 0 in Na to +1 in Na^{+1}, and the hydrogen oxidation number changes from +1 in H_2O to 0 in H_2.

In (c), the carbon oxidation number changes from +2 in CO to +4 in CO_2, and the oxygen oxidation number changes from 0 in O_2 to −2 in CO_2.

In (b), the charge remains unchanged on each ion—Mg^{2+}, Br^-, Na^+, F^-—meaning the oxidation numbers have not changed.

In (d), the sulfur oxidation number is +4 in both SO_2 and H_2SO_3, the hydrogen oxidation number is +1 in both H_2O and H_2SO_3, and the oxygen oxidation number is −2 in all three compounds.

9.57 (a) In reaction (a), the oxidation-state change 0 → +1 for Na means Na lost an electron and so was oxidized; the change +1 → 0 for H means H gained an electron and so was reduced.
In reaction (c), the change +2 → +4 for C means C lost two electrons and so was oxidized; the change 0 → −2 for O means O gained two electrons and so was reduced.

(b) The oxidizing agent is the reactant that contains the atom that is reduced: H_2O in reaction (a) and O_2 in reaction (c).

(c) The reducing agent is the reactant that contains the atom that is oxidized: Na in reaction (a) and CO in reaction (c).

9.58 (b), (c), and (d). In (a), the Cr oxidation number is +6 in both $CrO_4{}^{2-}$ and $Cr_2O_7{}^{2-}$; the O oxidation number is -2 in $CrO_4{}^{2-}$, $Cr_2O_7{}^{2-}$, and H_2O; and the H oxidation number is +1 in both H^+ and H_2O.

In (b), Fe changes from 0 in Fe to +3 in Fe^{3+} and N changes from +5 in $NO_3{}^-$ to +2 in NO.

In (c), C changes from -3 in C_2H_6 to +4 in CO_2 and O changes from 0 in O_2 to -2 in CO_2 and H_2O.

In (d), Ag changes from +1 in AgBr to 0 in Ag and Br changes from -1 in AgBr to 0 in Br_2.

9.59 (a) In reaction (b), the oxidation-state change $0 \rightarrow +3$ for Fe means Fe lost electrons and so was oxidized; the change $+5 \rightarrow +2$ for N means N gained electrons and so was reduced.

In (c), the change $-3 \rightarrow +4$ for C means C lost electrons and so was oxidized; the change $0 \rightarrow -2$ for O means O gained electrons and so was reduced.

In (d), the change $+1 \rightarrow 0$ for Ag^+ means Ag^+ gained an electron and so was reduced; the change $-1 \rightarrow 0$ for Br^- means Br^- lost an electron and so was oxidized.

(b) The oxidizing agent is the reactant containing the atom that is reduced: $NO_3{}^-$ in (b), O_2 in (c), and AgBr in (d).

(c) The reducing agent is the reactant containing the atom that is oxidized: Fe in (b), C_2H_6 in (c), and AgBr in (d). (AgBr acts as both reducing agent and oxidizing agent because it is the only reactant present. The Ag^+ is reduced and can therefore be thought of as the "true" oxidizing agent; the Br^- is oxidized and can be thought of as the "true" reducing agent.)

9.60 (a) Pb: 0 by rule 1. PbO_2: each O -2 by rule 2; Pb +4 by rule 7: $2 \times (-2) = -4$, $-4 + ? = 0$, $? = +4$.

H_2SO_4: each H +1 by rule 3; each O -2 by rule 2;
  S +6 by rule 7: $[2 \times (+1)] + [4 \times (-2)] = -6$, $-6 + ? = 0$, $? = +6$.

$PbSO_4$: Pb +2 by rule 6: in order for $PbSO_4$ to be electrically neutral with the $2-$
  charge on $SO_4{}^{2-}$, the cation charge must be 2+, Pb^{2+}; each O -2 by rule 2;
  S +6 by rule 7: $2 + [4 \times (-2)] = -6$, $-6 + ? = 0$, $? = +6$.

H_2O: each H +1 by rule 3; O -2 by rule 2.

(b) Elemental Pb is oxidized (from 0 to +2); Pb as Pb^{4+} in PbO_2 is reduced (from +4 to +2).

(c) PbO_2 is the oxidizing agent (the substance that is reduced is the oxidizing agent); Pb is the reducing agent (the substance that is oxidized is the reducing agent).

9.61 Yes, because the reaction is an electron-transfer (redox) reaction.

9.62 Yes, because oxidation numbers change. From the dot diagrams $\ddot{O}{=}\ddot{O}$ and $\ddot{:}\ddot{O}{-}\ddot{O}{=}\ddot{O}$, you can assign electrons as $:\ddot{O}\quad :\ddot{O}:$ for O_2 and $:\ddot{O}\cdot\quad\cdot\ddot{O}:\quad :\ddot{O}:$ for O_3. Therefore the oxidation states are

O_2: each O 6 free-atom valence e^- $-$ 6 assigned e^- = 0
O_3: left O 6 free-atom valence e^- $-$ 7 assigned e^- = -1
  middle O 6 free-atom valence e^- $-$ 5 assigned e^- = $+1$
  right O 6 free-atom valence e^- $-$ 6 assigned e^- = 0
O: 0 by rule 1

Two of the four O reactant atoms ($2\,O_2$) have changed oxidation state:

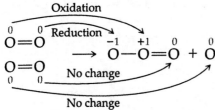

9.63 (a) In hydroquinone, the two C bonded to O are oxidized from +1 to +2. This can be seen when you assign oxidation numbers to the hydroquinone atoms and the quinone atoms:

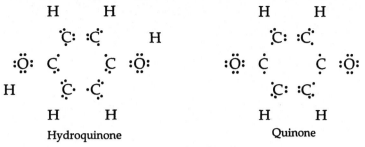

Hydroquinone   Quinone

In hydroquinone, the oxidation state of these two C is:

4 free-atom valence e⁻ − 3 assigned e⁻ = +1.

In quinone, their oxidation state is:

4 free-atom valence e⁻ − 2 assigned e⁻ = +2.

Each C has lost an electron and so has been oxidized.

(b) Ag is reduced, changing from Ag^+ as a reactant to Ag as a product. Each Ag^+ gained an electron.

(c) The oxidizing agent is the reactant containing the atom that is reduced, AgBr.

(d) The reducing agent is the reactant containing the atom that is oxidized, hydroquinone.

9.64 (a) Fe is oxidized. It loses electrons in changing from Fe, oxidation state 0 (rule 1), to Fe^{2+}, oxidation state +2 (rule 6).

(b) Cu^{2+} is reduced. It gains electrons in changing from Cu^{2+}, oxidation state +2 (rule 6), to Cu, oxidation state 0 (rule 1).

(c) Cu^{2+}, the species being reduced, is the oxidizing agent.

(d) Fe, the species being oxidized, is the reducing agent.

(e) The iron will dissolve over time as Fe metal is oxidized to Fe^{2+} ions in solution.

(f) They move from Fe to Cu^{2+}, which means from reducing agent to oxidizing agent.

(g) The nail and the penny are your two electrodes. Connect them with a metal wire, through which electrons will flow, and then place the nail in one of two beakers connected by a salt bridge and the penny in the second beaker. Add an Fe^{2+} solution to the nail beaker and a Cu^{2+} solution to the penny beaker. The nail is the anode (−), and the penny is the cathode (+). Because iron is above copper in the EMF series, the iron is oxidized at the anode and copper ions are reduced at the cathode.

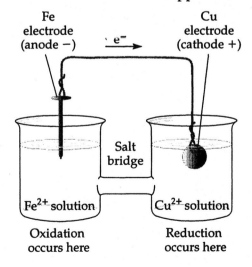

Fe electrode (anode −)   e⁻   Cu electrode (cathode +)

Salt bridge

Fe²⁺ solution   Cu²⁺ solution

Oxidation occurs here   Reduction occurs here

9.65

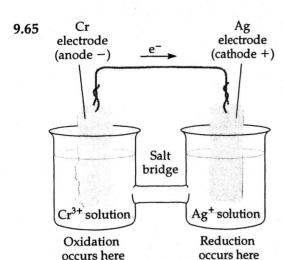

Cr
electrode
(anode −)

e^-

Ag
electrode
(cathode +)

Salt
bridge

Cr^{3+} solution

Ag$^+$ solution

Oxidation
occurs here

Reduction
occurs here

Cr is oxidized from 0 to +3. Ag$^+$ is reduced from +1 to 0.

9.66 (a) Ag$^+$, the species being reduced, is the oxidizing agent.

(b) Cr, the species being oxidized, is the reducing agent.

(c) The Ag electrode, as Ag$^+$ ions converted to Ag metal atoms plate out on the electrode.

(d) The Cr electrode, as Cr atoms leave the electrode to become Cr^{3+} ions in solution.

9.67

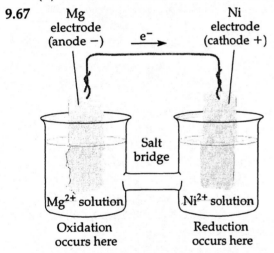

Mg
electrode
(anode −)

e^-

Ni
electrode
(cathode +)

Salt
bridge

Mg^{2+} solution

Ni^{2+} solution

Oxidation
occurs here

Reduction
occurs here

Mg is oxidized from 0 to +2. Ni^{2+} is reduced from +2 to 0.

9.68 (a) Ni^{2+}, the species being reduced, is the oxidizing agent.

(b) Mg, the species being oxidized, is the reducing agent.

(c) The Ni electrode, as Ni^{2+} ions converted to Ni metal atoms plate out on the electrode.

(d) The Mg electrode, as Mg atoms leave the electrode to become Mg^{2+} ions in solution.

9.69 (a) The increase in Sn^{2+} concentration tells you that the reaction Sn $\longrightarrow$ Sn^{2+} + 2 e$^-$ is taking place, meaning the tin is being oxidized (from 0 to +2).

(b) The decrease in Cu^{2+} concentration tells you that the reaction Cu^{2+} + 2 e$^-$ $\longrightarrow$ Cu is taking place, meaning Cu^{2+} is being reduced (from +2 to 0).

(c)

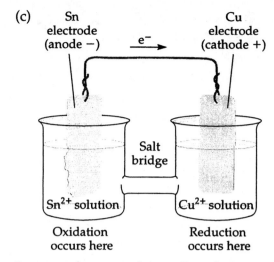

9.70 Because electrons always flow from anode (−) to cathode (+).

9.71 Electrons are negative and flow from the negative electrode (like charges repel) to the positive electrode (unlike charges attract). Because electrons always flow from the anode to the cathode, the anode must be negative and the cathode positive. Or, you can remember that a *ca*tion is positive (so is a *ca*thode) and an *an*ion is negative (so is an *an*ode).

9.72 (a) $B + A^+ \longrightarrow B^+ + A$; because B is more active, it gives up electrons more readily than A does.

(b) A^+ because it is the species being reduced.

(c) B because it is the species being oxidized.

(d) From B to A^+. The species being oxidized (B) loses electrons, which flow to the species being reduced (A^+).

9.73 (a), (b), (d), (e), (f): See diagram below.

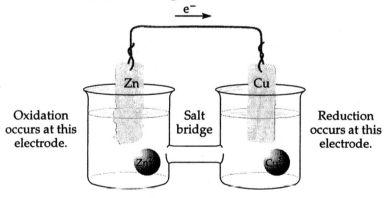

(c) $Zn + Cu^{2+} \longrightarrow Zn^{2+} + Cu$.

(g) The Zn^{2+} concentration increases with time as Zn atoms are oxidized to Zn^{2+} ions.

(h) The Cu^{2+} concentration decreases with time as Cu^{2+} ions are reduced to Cu atoms.

(i) The Zn electrode is eaten away as Zn atoms leave the electrode and enter the solution as Zn^{2+} ions.

(j) The Cu electrode gains mass as Cu^{2+} plates out as Cu.

9.74 You would have to do competitive redox experiments, two metals at a time. You could first test metals X and Y, and see which electrode is eaten away (and which one gains mass). The metal that is eaten away is the more active metal. Next, you could repeat the experiment for Y and Z, then again for X and Z. By comparing the results, you could properly order X, Y, and Z according to their relative activities.

9.75 It allows us to predict which reactions occur spontaneously when we place metals in solutions of ions. We can use this information to construct batteries to generate electricity.

9.76 The active metal gives up electrons to the ions of the less active metal. In the process, the active metal dissolves (as its atoms are oxidized to ions) and the ions of the less active metal are reduced to metal atoms.

9.77 No reaction occurs.

9.78 (a) is spontaneous because K is more active than Al; (b) is not spontaneous for the same reason.

9.79 (a) is spontaneous because Ag is more active than Au; (b) is not spontaneous for the same reason.

9.80 (a)

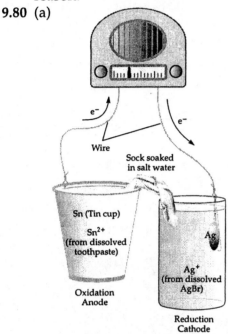

Being higher on the EMF list, Sn transfers electrons to Ag^+ ions. Therefore a battery made with Sn and Ag as the electrodes could be used to generate electricity. The electron flow is from the Sn cup anode to the Ag pendant cathode.

(b) The Sn is eaten away as it is oxidized to Sn^{2+} ions.

(c) Ag^+ is reduced, which means it is the oxidizing agent.

(d) Sn is oxidized, which means it is the reducing agent.

9.81

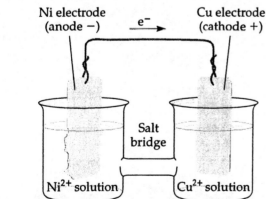

The reaction is $Cu^{2+} + Ni \longrightarrow Cu + Ni^{2+}$ because Ni is higher than Cu on the EMF list. The Ni is oxidized from 0 to +2 and the Cu^{2+} is reduced from +2 to 0.

9.82 (a) $Pb + Cu^{2+} \longrightarrow Pb^{2+} + Cu$, because Pb is higher than Cu on the EMF list.
(b) $Pb^{2+} + Cu \longrightarrow Pb + Cu^{2+}$

9.83 Li and Au should combine to give the highest-voltage battery because Li has the greatest tendency to lose electrons and Au^{3+} has the least resistance to accepting electrons.

9.84 (a) Oxidation is the loss of electrons; oxidation is a combining of some other element with oxygen.
(b) The two definitions are compatible whenever the element combining with oxygen is less electronegative than oxygen.
(c) The reaction in which the metals combine with oxygen, as in $4\,Fe + 3\,O_2 \longrightarrow 2\,Fe_2O_3$.

9.85 Magnesium is higher than iron on the EMF list and therefore is oxidized more easily than iron. When magnesium is in contact with iron in its oxidized state (Fe^{2+}), the magnesium oxidizes and loses electrons to the iron, reducing it back to elemental iron.

9.86 The next best metal would be Pt (platinum) because, after gold, it is the least active metal in the series.

9.87 The statue is made of sheets of copper metal placed over a steel (iron) skeleton. Iron is more active than copper. When the copper sheets began to oxidize ($Cu \longrightarrow Cu^{2+}$), the iron skeleton gave up its electrons to reduce the copper ions ($Cu^{2+} \longrightarrow Cu$), meaning that the iron skeleton was being eaten away as Fe atoms oxidized to Fe^{2+} ions. The solution to the problem was to replace the dissolving steel skeleton with a reinforced, corrosion-resistant, stainless steel skeleton incorporating high-tech plastics to isolate the steel from the copper.

9.88 The conversion of Zn to Zn^{2+} could result in weak spots along the surface of the battery.

9.89 +7 by rule 7: each H +1; each O -2; therefore because $[2 \times (+1)] + [6 \times (-2)] = -10$, I is $-10 + ? = -3, ? = +7$.

9.90 Being the only reactant, $(NH_4)_2Cr_2O_7$ has to be both the oxidizing agent and the reducing agent. To show that you understand the chemistry, you should show which part of it is oxidized and which part is reduced. You could use a dot diagram to assign oxidation numbers in $(NH_4)_2Cr_2O_7$, but it is simpler to apply the shortcut rules to the two ions of this compound (recalling from Table 5.5 of the textbook that the ionic charges are $NH_4{}^+$ and $Cr_2O_7{}^{2-}$).
$NH_4{}^+$: each H +1 by rule 3; N -3 by rule 7: $4 \times (+1) = +4, +4 + ? = +1, ? = -3$.
$Cr_2O_7{}^{2-}$: each O -2 by rule 2; each Cr +6 by rule 7: Cr_2 is $7 \times (-2) = -14, -14 + ? = -2$,
    $? = +12$, meaning each Cr is $+12/2 = +6$.
N_2: each N 0 by rule 1.
Cr_2O_3: each O -2 by rule 2; each Cr +3 by rule 7: Cr_2 is $3 \times (-2) = -6, -6 + ? = 0, ? = +6$,
    meaning each Cr is $+6/2 = +3$.
H_2O: each H +1 by rule 3; O -2 by rule 2.
The oxidation-state changes are Cr $+6 \rightarrow +3$ and N $-3 \rightarrow 0$. Thus Cr gains electrons, is reduced, and is the "true" oxidizing agent. N loses electrons, is oxidized, and is the "true" reducing agent.

9.91 C in C_8H_{18} is oxidized; O in O_2 is reduced.
C_8H_{18}: The shortcut method, with +1 for each H, yields a fractional oxidation state for each C, making the electron-bookkeeping method a better choice. Assigning all electrons to the more electronegative C, the electron-assignment diagram is

H   H   H   H   H   H   H   H

H :C̈· ·C̈· ·C̈· ·C̈· ·C̈· ·C̈· ·C̈· ·C̈: H

H   H   H   H   H   H   H   H

Two terminal C: 4 free-atom valence e^- $-$ 7 assigned $e^- = -3$.
Six interior C: 4 free-atom valence e^- $-$ 6 assigned $e^- = -2$.
Each H: 1 free-atom valence e^- $-$ 0 assigned $e^- = +1$.

CO_2: each O -2 by rule 2; C $+4$ by rule 7: $2 \times (-2) = -4$, $-4 + ? = 0$, $? = +4$.
The C atoms in C_8H_{18} are oxidized either from -3 to $+4$ or from -2 to $+4$.

O_2: each O 0 by rule 1.
H_2O: each H $+1$ by rule 3; O -2 by rule 2.
CO_2: each O -2 by rule 2.
The O in O_2 are reduced from 0 to -2.

9.92 Mg, the metal highest up on the EMF list in the textbook.

9.93 Spontaneous reactions occur in (c) because Zn is more active than Ag and in (e) because Cu is more active than Hg. In (a), (b), and (d), the metal of which the strip is made is less active than the metal whose ions are in solution.

9.94 No. Corrosion in iron usually means Fe atoms oxidized to Fe^{2+} and Fe^{3+} ions; protecting an iron structure means preventing this oxidation. Because nickel is less active than iron (Ni lower on EMF list), the reaction $Fe \longrightarrow Fe^{2+} + 2\,e^-$ is more likely than the reaction $Ni \longrightarrow Ni^{2+} + 2\,e^-$. Any element above Fe on the EMF list would make a better sacrificial metal than nickel.

9.95 Li^+. To reduce an ion means to add electrons to it. The fact that Li metal is easier to oxidize than Mn, Hg, Fe, or Mg (Li highest in textbook EMF series), means the reduction $Li^+ + e^- \longrightarrow Li$ is most difficult to accomplish.

9.96 $Cr_2O_7^{2-}$: each O -2 by rule 2; each Cr $+6$ by rule 7: Cr_2 $7 \times (-2) = -14$, $-14 + ? = -2$, $? = +12$, which means each Cr $+12/2 = +6$.
C_2H_5OH: each H $+1$ by rule 3; O -2 by rule 2; each C -2 by rule 7: C_2 $[6 \times (+1)] + -2 = +4$, $+4 + ? = 0$, $? = -4$, which means each C $-4/2 = -2$.
H^+: $+1$ by rule 3.
Cr^{3+}: $+3$ by rule 6.
CO_2: each O -2 by rule 2; C $+4$ by rule 7: $2 \times (-2) = -4$, $-4 + ? = 0$, $? = +4$.
H_2O: each H $+1$ by rule 3; O -2 by rule 2.

The oxidizing agent, which is the reactant containing the atom that is reduced, is $Cr_2O_7^{2-}$ because the Cr is reduced from $+6$ to $+3$.

The reducing agent, which is the reactant containing the atom that is oxidized, is C_2H_5OH because the C is oxidized from -2 to $+4$.

9.97 Because copper is the anode, it is being oxidized to Cu^{2+} and losing electrons. At the cathode, Rh^{3+} ions gain electrons to form Rh metal. Because copper metal can give electrons to Rh^{3+} ions, rhodium must be lower in the EMF series than copper. (The series shown in the textbook is not exhaustive, which is why Rh is not shown.)

9.98 Dot diagram: $\left[\ddot{\ddot{N}} \!=\! N \!=\! \ddot{\ddot{N}} \right]^-$

Electron assignment: $\left[\ddot{\ddot{N}}\!: \; :\!N\!: \; :\!\ddot{\ddot{N}} \right]^-$

Each terminal N: 5 free-atom valence e^- $-$ 6 assigned e^- $= -1$.
Center N: 5 free-atom valence e^- $-$ 4 assigned e^- $= +1$.

9.99 (a) and (c).
(a) SeO_3^{2-}: each O -2 by rule 2; Se $+4$ by rule 7: $3 \times (-2) = -6$, $-6 + ? = -2$, $? = +4$.
Se: 0 by rule 1.
Se reduced from $+4$ to 0, making SeO_3^{2-} the oxidizing agent (which is the reactant containing the atom that is reduced).

I^-: -1 by rule 6.
I_2: each I 0 by rule 1.
I^- oxidized from -1 to 0, making I^- the reducing agent (which is the reactant containing the atom that is oxidized).

(c) HCl: H +1 by rule 3; Cl −1 by either rule 6 or halide rule.
Cl_2: each Cl 0 by rule 1.
Cl oxidized from −1 to 0, making HCl the reducing agent (which is the reactant containing the atom that is oxidized).

O_2: each O 0 by rule 1.
H_2O: each H +1 by rule 3; O −2 by rule 2.
O reduced from 0 to −2, making O_2 the oxidizing agent (the reactant containing the atom that is reduced).

9.100 Tin (Sn) is lower in the EMF series than iron, meaning tin is the less active metal and therefore less likely to corrode than iron.

9.101 Electron assignment:

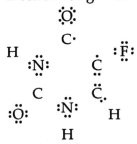

Each O: 6 free-atom valence e^- − 8 assigned e^- = −2
Each H: 1 free-atom valence e^- − 0 assigned e^- = +1
F: 7 free-atom valence e^- − 8 assigned e^- = −1
Each N: 5 free-atom valence e^- − 8 assigned e^- = −3
12 o'clock C: 4 free-atom valence e^- − 1 assigned e^- = +3
2 o'clock C: 4 free-atom valence e^- − 3 assigned e^- = +1
4 o'clock C: 4 free-atom valence e^- − 4 assigned e^- = 0
8 o'clock C: 4 free-atom valence e^- − 0 assigned e^- = +4

9.102 A reducing agent is a substance that gets oxidized. Thus to ask which is the better reducing agent is another way of asking which is more easily oxidized. Being higher than Pb on the EMF list, Zn is more easily oxidized and is therefore the better reducing agent.

9.103 (a) Each H +1 by rule 3; each C −3 by rule 7: CC 6 × (+1) = +6, +6 + ? = 0, ? = −6, making each C −6/2 = −3.
    (b) Each H +1 by rule 3; each C −2 by rule 7: CC 4 × (+1) = +4, +4 + ? = 0, ? = −4, making each C −4/2 = −2.
    (c) Each H +1 by rule 3; each C −1 by rule 7: CC 2 × (+1) = +2, +2 + ? = 0, ? = −2, making each C −2/2 = −1.

9.104 (a) Cd^{2+} gains electrons, meaning it is reduced and is therefore the oxidizing agent.
    (b) Mn loses electrons, meaning it is oxidized and is therefore the reducing agent.
    (c) Cd is the electrode at which reduction takes place, making it the cathode.
    (d) Mn is the electrode at which oxidation takes place, making it the anode.

9.105 Na_2SO_3: each Na +1 by rule 4; each O −2 by rule 2; S +4 by rule 7: [2 × (+1)] + [3 × (−2)]
        = −4, −4 + ? = 0, ? = +4.
    $KMnO_4$: K +1 by rule 4; each O −2 by rule 2; Mn +7 by rule 7: [1 × (+1)] + [4 × (−2)]
        = −7, −7 + ? = 0, ? = +7.
    H_2O: each H +1 by rule 3; O −2 by rule 2.
    Na_2SO_4: each Na +1 by rule 4; each O −2 by rule 2; S +6 by rule 7: [2 × (+1)] + [4 × (−2)]
        = −6, −6 + ? = 0, ? = +6.
    MnO_2: each O −2 by rule 2; Mn +4 by rule 7: 2 × (−2) = −4, −4 + ? = 0, ? = +4.
    KOH: K +1 by rule 4; O −2 by rule 2; H +1 by rule 3.

Mn is reduced from +7 to +4, making $KMnO_4$ the oxidizing agent (which is the reactant containing the atom that is reduced).

S is oxidized from +4 to +6, making Na_2SO_3 the reducing agent (which is the reactant containing the atom that is oxidized).

9.106 Either Al or Mn. The illustration on page 347 of the textbook shows that combining a metal with ions of a metal lower in the EMF series (Cu in Ag^+ in the illustration) leads to a redox reaction. Combining a metal with ions of a metal higher in the series (Ag in Cu^{2+} in the illustration) leads to no reaction. That the unknown metal reacted with Zn^{2+} means the metal is higher than Zn in the series. That the unknown metal did not react with Mg^{2+} means the metal is lower than Mg in the series. The only metals meeting both these conditions are Al and Mn.

9.107 (a) Each F −1 by the halide rule, which applies because P is less electronegative than F; P +5 by rule 7: $6 \times (-1) = -6$, $-6 + ? = -1$, $? = +5$.

(b) Each O −2 by rule 2; each Mo +6 by rule 7: Mo_2 $7 \times (-2) = -14$, $-14 + ? = -2$, $? = +12$, making each Mo $+12/2 = +6$.

(c) H +1 by rule 3; each O −2 by rule 2; Pb +2 by rule 7: $[1 \times (+1)] + [2 \times (-2)] = -3$, $-3 + ? = -1$, $? = +2$.

(d) H +1 by rule 3; each O −2 by rule 2; each C +3 by rule 7: C_2 $[1 \times (+1)] + [4 \times (-2)]$ $= -7$, $-7 + ? = -1$, $? = +6$, making each C $+6/2 = +3$.

9.108 No; electricity is an electron flow that can be used to do work, just as flowing water can be used to do work. The electrons are not used up; all they do is move from one position to another.

9.109 (a) Because it is the cathode, the nickel electrode gains electrons converting Ni^{2+} to Ni(s). This conversion lowers the amount of positive charge on the cathode side, and to compensate K^+ ions flow toward the cathode to neutralize the buildup of negative charge.

(b) Because it is the anode, the zinc electrode gives up electrons as Zn atoms are converted to Zn^{2+} ions in solution. This conversion raises the amount of positive charge on the anode side, and to compensate Cl^- ions flow toward the anode to neutralize the buildup of positive charge.

9.110 With the electronegativity values O 3.5, N 3.0, C 2.5, H 2.1, the electron-assignment

diagram is

Each H: 1 free-atom valence e^- − 0 assigned e^- = +1
N: 5 free-atom valence e^- − 8 assigned e^- = −3
Left C: 4 free-atom valence e^- − 5 assigned e^- = −1
Right C: 4 free-atom valence e^- − 1 assigned e^- = +3
Each O: 6 free-atom valence e^- − 8 assigned e^- = −2

9.111 IO_4^-: each O −2 by rule 2; I +7 by rule 7: $4 \times (-2) = -8$, $-8 + ? = -1$, $? = +7$
I^-: −1 by rule 6
H^+: +1 by rule 3
I_2: each I 0 by rule 1
H_2O: each H +1 by rule 3, O −2 by rule 2

The only changes in oxidation number are for I^- and for the I in IO_4^-. The I in IO_4^- is reduced from +7 to 0, meaning IO_4^- is the oxidizing agent (which is the reactant containing the atom that is reduced). The I^- is oxidized from −1 to 0, meaning it is the reducing agent (which is the reactant containing the atom that is oxidized).

9.112 Aluminum is higher than silver in the EMF series. Therefore aluminum atoms in the foil give up electrons to the Ag^+ ions in Ag_2S, reducing Ag^+ to Ag metal and thereby causing the Ag_2S tarnish to disappear.

9.113 Only when the fluorine is in F_2, where, by rule 1, each F has an oxidation state of 0. Otherwise, fluorine will always get complete ownership of all bonding electrons because it is the most electronegative atom. Owning all bonding electrons (eight) always gives fluorine an oxidation state of -1 because the free atom has seven valence electrons.

9.114 (a) S changes from $+4$ in H_2SO_3 to $+6$ in H_2SO_4; S loses electrons, which means H_2SO_3 is oxidized and is therefore the reducing agent. N changes from $+5$ in HNO_3 to $+2$ in NO; N gains electrons, which means HNO_3 is reduced and is therefore the oxidizing agent.

(b) Mg changes from 0 in Mg to $+2$ in $Mg(OH)_2$; Mg loses electrons, which means it is oxidized and is the reducing agent. H changes from $+1$ in H_2O to 0 in H_2; H gains an electron, meaning H_2O is reduced and is the oxidizing agent.

(c) This is not an electron-transfer reaction because S stays $+4$, O stays -2, and H stays $+1$.

(d) Pb changes from $+2$ in PbO to 0 in Pb; Pb gains electrons, which means PbO is reduced and is the oxidizing agent. C changes from $+2$ in CO to $+4$ in CO_2; C loses electrons, meaning CO is oxidized and is the reducing agent.

9.115 Dot diagram: $H—C\equiv\ddot{N}$ Electron assignment: $H \quad :C \quad :\ddot{\underset{..}{N}}:$

H: 1 free-atom valence e^- $- 0$ assigned $e^- = +1$
C: 4 free-atom valence e^- $- 2$ assigned $e^- = +2$
N: 5 free-atom valence e^- $- 8$ assigned $e^- = -3$

9.116 (a) That the lead electrode loses mass tells you Pb metal atoms are changing to Pb^{2+} ions; this is a loss of electrons, which is oxidation. Oxidation occurs at the anode, making Pb the anode.

(b) That the palladium electrode gains mass tells you Pd^{2+} ions are plating out as Pd metal atoms; this is a gain of electrons, which is reduction. Reduction occurs at the cathode, making Pd the cathode.

(c) $Pb + Pd^{2+} \longrightarrow Pb^{2+} + Pd$

9.117 $+4$ to -4. In a compound such as CF_4, carbon has no bonding electrons assigned to it because fluorine is more electronegative: 4 free-atom valence e^- $- 0$ assigned $e^- = +4$. In a compound such as CH_4, carbon is assigned all eight bonding electrons because hydrogen is less electronegative than carbon: 4 free-atom valence e^- $- 8$ assigned $e^- = -4$.

9.118 The only two species that change oxidation number are N and Zn. NO_3^- is reduced as N changes from $+5$ in NO_3^- to -3 in NH_3; thus NO_3^- is the oxidizing agent. Zn is oxidized from 0 in Zn to $+2$ in $Zn(OH)_4^{2-}$; thus Zn is the reducing agent.

9.119 Because zinc is a more active metal than iron. If any iron is oxidized to Fe^{2+}, the zinc metal transfers electrons to the Fe^{2+} and reduces it back to iron metal. In this way zinc acts as a sacrificial electrode. The zinc ions formed from the zinc metal form a protective coating of $Zn_2(OH)_2CO_3$.

9.120 (a) Because Zn is higher than Hg on the EMF list, Zn loses electrons more easily and therefore is the anode. The electrons flow to the Hg electrode, which is the cathode.

(b) Because Zn metal atoms lose electrons and are converted to Zn^{2+} ions, the Zn electrode loses mass over time.

9.121 (a) Not an electron-transfer reaction; P stays $+3$, F stays -1, H stays $+1$, O stays -2.

(b) H_2: each H 0 by rule 1.
Cl_2: each Cl 0 by rule 1.
HCl: H $+1$ by rule 1, Cl -1 by rule 7 or halide rule.
H_2 is oxidized as H changes from 0 in H_2 to $+1$ in HCl; thus H_2 is the reducing agent.
Cl_2 is reduced as Cl changes from 0 in Cl_2 to -1 in HCl; thus Cl_2 is the oxidizing agent.

(c) Cr_2O_3: each O −2 by rule 2; each Cr +3 by rule 7: Cr_2 $3 \times (-2) = -6$, $-6 + ? = 0$, ? = +6, making each Cr +6/2 = +3.

Si: 0 by rule 1.

Cr: 0 by rule 1.

SiO_2: each O −2 by rule 2; Si +4 by rule 7: $2 \times (-2) = -4$, $-4 + ? = 0$, ? = +4.

Cr_2O_3 is reduced as Cr changes from +3 in Cr_2O_3 to 0 in Cr; thus Cr_2O_3 is the oxidizing agent. Si is oxidized from 0 in Si to +4 in SiO_2; thus Si is the reducing agent.

(d) Not an electron-transfer reaction; H stays +1, Cl stays −1, Na stays +1, O stays −2.

9.122 The fact that Cu metal atoms plate out tells you something is providing electrons for the reaction $Cu^{2+} + 2\,e^- \longrightarrow Cu$. That "something" cannot be gold because gold is lower in the EMF series than copper and therefore does not give up electrons to Cu^{2+} ions. Silver is also lower in the EMF series, meaning the ring cannot be made of silver either. It must be made of a metal higher than Cu in the EMF series.

9.123 (a) Na +1 by rule 4; O −2 by rule 2; P +5 by rule 7: $[1 \times (+1)] + [3 \times (-2)] = -5$, $-5 + ? = 0$, ? = +5.

(b) Each O −2 by rule 2; each H +1 by rule 3; B +3 by rule 7: $[3 \times -2)] + [3 \times (+1)] = -3$, $-3 + ? = 0$, ? = +3. (Alternatively, you can say that B, which must carry a 3+ ionic charge to balance the 3 OH^-, is +3 by rule 6.)

(c) Each O −2 by rule 2; each V +5 by rule 7: V_2 $5 \times (-2) = -10$, $-10 + ? = 0$, ? = +10, making each V +10/2 = +5.

(d) Each K +1 by rule 4; each F −1 by the halide rule; Ti +4 by rule 7: $[2 \times (+1)] + [6 \times (-1)] = -4$, $-4 + ? = 0$, ? = +4.

9.124 Cu^{2+}: +2 by rule 6.

I_2: each I 0 by rule 1.

Cu^+: +1 by rule 6.

I^-: −1 by rule 6.

Both Cu^{2+} and I_2 are reduced, Cu^{2+} from +2 to +1 and I_2 from 0 to −1. In order for one species to gain electrons, another must lose electrons. Because both Cu^{2+} and I_2 would gain electrons in this reaction, it is not possible.

9.125 That the Zn^{2+} concentration decreases tells you Zn^{2+} is being reduced to Zn metal atoms. That the Ti^{2+} concentration increases tells you Ti metal atoms are being oxidized to Ti^{2+} ions.

(a) The titanium electrode is the anode because the anode is where oxidation occurs.

(b) The zinc electrode is the cathode because the cathode is where reduction occurs.

(c) Because titanium gives up electrons to Zn^{2+}, titanium must be higher on the EMF scale than zinc.

(d) $Ti + Zn^{2+} \longrightarrow Ti^{2+} + Zn$

CHAPTER
10

Intermolecular Forces and the Phases of Matter

10.1 See solution in textbook.

10.2 HF. Because F is more electronegative than Br, the dipole moment of the H–F bond is greater than the dipole moment of the H–Br bond. Consequently, the partial charges in HF are stronger than those in HBr, resulting in a greater attraction between HF molecules than between HBr molecules and a higher boiling point for HF.

10.3

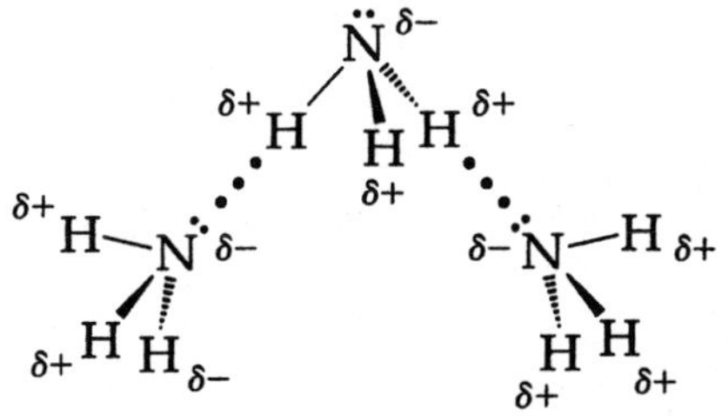

10.4 H_2O. Because O is more electronegative than S, the dipole moment of the O–H bonds is greater than the dipole moment of the S–H bonds. Consequently, the partial charges in H_2O are stronger than those in H_2S, resulting in a greater attraction between H_2O molecules than between H_2S molecules and a higher boiling point for H_2O.

10.5 See solution in textbook.

10.6 Both ethylene and polyethylene are nonpolar molecules. Therefore the only intermolecular forces involved are London forces. Polyethylene is a very large molecule containing many electrons, which means many London forces between molecules and consequently a high melting point, making this substance a solid at room temperature. The much smaller ethylene molecule contains a relatively small number of electrons. This means relatively few London forces between molecules and low melting and boiling points, making this substance a gas at room temperature.

10.7 (a) One electron from each H, five from N: H:N̈:H
    Ḧ

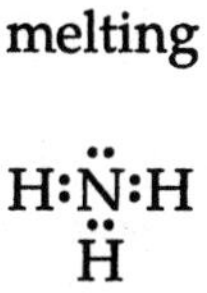

One electron from each H, five from P: H:P̈:H
    Ḧ

167

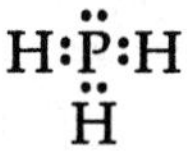

(b) NH_3 is polar because the H–N electronegativity difference causes the bonding electrons to be closer to the N. PH_3 is nonpolar because there is no H–P electronegativity difference.

(c) In PH_3 because this molecule has more electrons (18) than NH_3 (10 electrons).

(d) PH_3 because of stronger London forces. This is in fact not the case, however. See Practice Problem 10.8 for additional information.

10.8 See solution in textbook.

10.9

10.10 (a) Because HF is the only one of the four compounds where the molecules can hydrogen-bond. (Hydrogen bonds are possible only with H–N, H–O, or H–F bonds.)

(b) Because HI has more electrons than HBr or HCl and therefore stronger intermolecular London forces and a higher boiling point.

10.11 See solution in textbook.

10.12 Both iron and sodium chloride are nonmolecular solids. The forces holding iron and sodium chloride together are true bonds—metallic bonds in iron and ionic bonds in NaCl. Because both bonds are very strong, high temperatures are required to break them in order to melt either solid.

10.13 The intermolecular London forces holding the lattice together.

10.14 Ionic, network, and metallic solids have high melting points because true chemical bonds must be broken in order to melt these substances. Molecular solids have low melting points because here melting involves breaking only intermolecular attractive forces, which are weaker than true bonds.

(a) Metallic; the element Zr is classified as a metal.

(b) Metallic; the element Pb is classified as a metal.

(c) Ionic; Ca is a group 2 element that ionizes to Ca^{2+}, and it is combined with the non-metal N in the form of N^{3-} ions.

(d) Network; the very high sublimation point tells you this is a nonmolecular solid. The absence of ions tells you it is not an ionic nonmolecular solid. That C is classified as a nonmetal tells you graphite is not a metallic nonmolecular solid. Therefore it must be a network nonmolecular solid.

(e) Molecular, indicated by the low melting point.

10.15 They move constantly in straight-line paths at very high speeds, changing direction only when they collide with one another or with the walls of their container.

10.16 Cooling a gas slows the molecules down to a speed at which they are not moving fast enough to overcome the attractive forces that cause them to condense to the liquid phase.

10.17 The gas could never be liquefied.

10.18 Yes. Molecules in the liquid phase are still very much in motion. They are jostling past one another constantly but remain in close proximity to one another.

10.19 Heating causes the molecules of the liquid to move faster and faster until they have enough energy to overcome the attractive forces holding them in the liquid phase. When they overcome the attractive forces, they escape into the gas phase.

10.20 That the temperature at which $H_2O(g)$ becomes $H_2O(l)$ is much higher than the temperature at which $N_2(g)$ becomes $N_2(l)$ tells you that water has the stronger intermolecular attractive forces. The stronger these attractive forces, the higher the temperature at which the gas condenses.

10.21 Because in both solids and liquids the molecules are very close to one another. They are *condensed* into a volume much smaller than what the gas phase occupies.

10.22 Because gas molecules are not bound to one another the way molecules in solids and liquids are. Gas molecules are essentially independent of one another and can travel around in the entire volume of their container.

10.23 Gases have the least order, with the molecules moving everywhere in the volume of the container. Solids have the most order, with the molecules essentially fixed in position and unable to migrate. The order in liquids is between that in solids and that in gases; the molecules are confined to the liquid but free to migrate throughout the liquid.

10.24 (a) C–D. The greater dipole moment of C–D means stronger intermolecular attractive forces, which means less energy needs to be removed from the liquid in order to form a solid. Therefore C–D freezes at a higher temperature than the less polar A–B.

(b) C–D. The stronger intermolecular attractive forces mean more energy must be added to the liquid in order for the molecules to overcome the attractive forces and escape into the gas phase.

10.25
$$\overset{\delta+}{H}-\overset{\delta-}{Br}$$
$$\overset{\delta+}{H}-\overset{\delta-}{Br}\cdots\overset{\delta+}{H}-Br$$

The intermolecular forces holding the molecules together are dipole–dipole interactions.

10.26 London forces are the result of the partial charge separation that develops and disappears instantaneously. The charge separation is due to momentary electron imbalances and occurs constantly in all molecules, both polar and nonpolar.

10.27 CBr_4. Both molecules are nonpolar and therefore their liquid phase involves only London forces. Because CBr_4 is the larger molecule, it has more electrons and therefore stronger London forces. The stronger the London forces, the higher the boiling point.

10.28 (1) Chloromethane is a polar molecule, and therefore the molecules in the liquid are subject to dipole–dipole interactions, which are absent in the nonpolar CH_4. (2) Chloromethane is the larger molecule and therefore the molecules in the liquid experience stronger London forces.

10.29 Because propane molecules are much smaller than octane molecules, there are weaker London forces between propane molecules. Weaker London forces to overcome allows the propane molecules to separate more easily and enter the gas phase.

10.30 The strength of London forces depends on the size of the molecules involved. For this reason, the sum of the London forces holding a group of large molecules together can be greater than the dipole–dipole forces holding a group of small molecules together.

10.31 (a) HF is more polar because the H–F electronegativity difference is greater than the H–Cl electronegativity difference.

(b) For HF because the partial charges in the HF molecules are greater than those in the HCl molecules, leading to a larger dipole moment in HF.

(c) HF. Because they have the larger dipole moment, HF molecules experience stronger intermolecular forces, and stronger intermolecular forces mean less energy needs to be removed to change $HF(g)$ to $HF(l)$. That HF liquifies first is another way of saying HF has the higher condensation temperature. Because condensation temperature (gas → liquid) and boiling temperature (liquid → gas) are numerically equal, HF also has the higher boiling point.

(d) Yes; HCl experiences greater London forces because it is the larger molecule and so contains more electrons.

10.32 Because the hydrogen bonds formed by the $-\overset{\cdot\cdot}{\text{O}}\text{H}$ groups are much stronger than the London forces between molecules.

10.33 All three substances are nonpolar and therefore involve only London forces. The electron counts are Cl_2 34, Br_2 70, I_2 106. Cl_2 molecules have the fewest electrons and therefore the weakest London forces. I_2 molecules have the most electrons and therefore the strongest London forces. Br_2 molecules fall between these two extremes. Thus it is reasonable that at room temperature Cl_2 is a gas, Br_2 is a liquid, and I_2 is a solid.

10.34 Because waxes are very large molecules, they contain many electrons, and therefore the London forces between wax molecules are quite strong, strong enough to make waxes solid at room temperature.

10.35 Whenever the molecules contain O–H, N–H, and/or F–H bonds.

10.36 The hydrogen atom has only one electron. For this reason, the atom resembles a naked proton when bonded to a very electronegative atom, and its partial positive charge is very high because a proton carries a full positive charge. The interaction between the highly $\delta+$ H on one molecule and the highly $\delta-$ atom on another molecule is very strong.

10.37 The compound with the higher boiling point must have hydrogen-bonding.

10.38 (a) Because molecular size increases as you go from H_2S to H_2Se to H_2Te. Larger molecules mean more electrons, and therefore the intermolecular London forces to be overcome are greatest in H_2Te, giving this compound the highest boiling point.

(b) H_2O is the only compound of the four in which hydrogen-bonding is possible.

10.39 We mean the momentary dipole caused (induced) in one molecule by instantaneous electron imbalance in a neighboring molecule.

10.40 Because hydrogen bonds are not covalent bonds within a molecule (which we represent by solid lines).

10.41 Because there are numerous N–H groups in the molecule. The H atom in an N–H can hydrogen-bond either to some other N in the molecule or to an O.

10.42 DNA molecules must be very stable but still able to break into two strands when involved in protein-building. Covalent bonds would be too strong to allow the strands to break apart, and London forces would be too weak to provide the connection needed between the two strands.

10.43 If the nonpolar molecules are much larger than the polar molecules, the London forces in the nonpolar liquid will be quite substantial and can be stronger than the dipole–dipole interactions in the polar liquid. The greater London forces make the boiling point of the nonpolar liquid higher than that of the polar liquid.

10.44 A molecular substance is made up of individual molecules. The substance is held together by intermolecular attractive forces between the molecules. A nonmolecular substance is an array of ions or atoms bonded together by covalent, ionic, or metallic bonds. There are no discrete molecules in a nonmolecular substance.

10.45 Sometimes. Compounds containing a group IA (1) or IIA (2) metal plus a nonmetal are usually ionic and therefore nonmolecular. Metals are nonmolecular compounds. It is generally not possible, however, to look at the formula of a covalent compound and tell whether its solid phase is molecular or nonmolecular.

10.46 A repeating pattern of positive and negative ions held together by ionic bonds.

10.47 Because nonmolecular solids are held together by much stronger forces—namely, covalent, ionic, or metallic bonds. Molecular solids are held together only by the much weaker intermolecular attractive forces—London forces, dipole–dipole interactions, and hydrogen-bonding.

10.48 A network covalent substance is a nonmolecular solid that consists of a large network of atoms held together by covalent bonds. Examples include diamond and quartz.

10.49 The high melting points of some metals, such as gold and iron, are evidence that metallic bonds can be as strong as ionic or covalent bonds.

10.50 Because chlorine atoms are larger than fluorine atoms, carbon tetrachloride is larger than carbon tetrafluoride and contains more electrons. In general, if the intermolecular attractive forces are the same type, larger molecules have stronger forces and therefore condense to the liquid phase at higher temperatures.

10.51 (a) Metallic; potassium is classified as a metal.

(b) Ionic; made of K^+ and Cl^- ions.

(c) Network; the high melting point tells you this is a nonmolecular solid. The absence of ions tells you it is not ionic, that P is a nonmetal tells you it is not metallic, and so it must be a network nonmolecular solid.

(d) Molecular solid, indicated by the relatively low melting point.

10.52 The smaller the distance between two molecules, the greater the attraction between them.

10.53 Because the attraction is the result of opposite partial charges attracting each other to form a hydrogen bond. If the molecules are oriented $\delta+$ to $\delta+$ or $\delta-$ to $\delta-$, there can be no hydrogen bond formed:

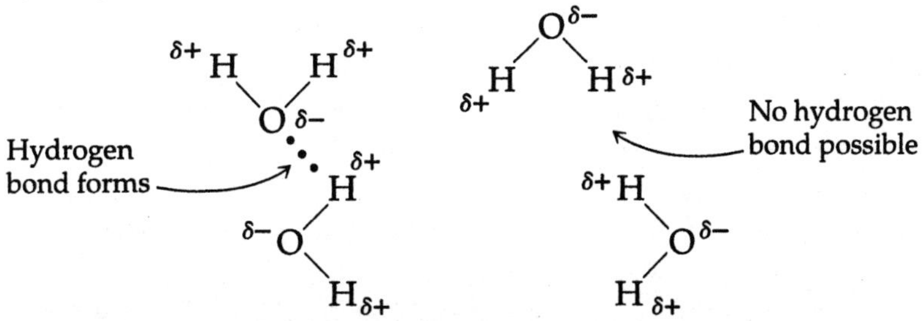

10.54 The molecules move faster and faster because the added heat energy increases their kinetic energy (energy of motion).

10.55 Because density defines the number of molecules per unit volume, there must be more water molecules per unit volume in the (denser) liquid phases than in the solid phase. (The molecules are packed more tightly in the liquid phase).

10.56 (d). (a) and (b) describe the solid phase; (c) describes the gas phase.

10.57 The intermolecular forces between Br_2 molecules are greater than those between F_2 molecules or Cl_2 molecules.

10.58 (a) and (b) because they are nonpolar molecules. The As–H bond is considered nonpolar because the electronegativity difference for these two atoms is so slight $(2.1 - 2.0)$; the molecular dipole moment is therefore zero in AsH_3, making the molecule nonpolar. CO_2 is a linear molecule because there are two bonding groups and no lone pairs around C, causing the two opposed C–O dipole moments to cancel and make the molecule nonpolar: $O{=}C{=}O$.

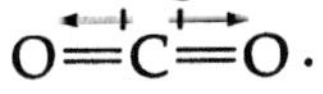

H_2O and $SeCl_2$ are bent molecules because in each case there are two bonding groups and two lone pairs around the central atom. Because of this nonlinear shape, the two bond dipole moments in each molecule do not cancel. The molecular dipole moment is therefore nonzero, leading to dipole–dipole intermolecular forces:

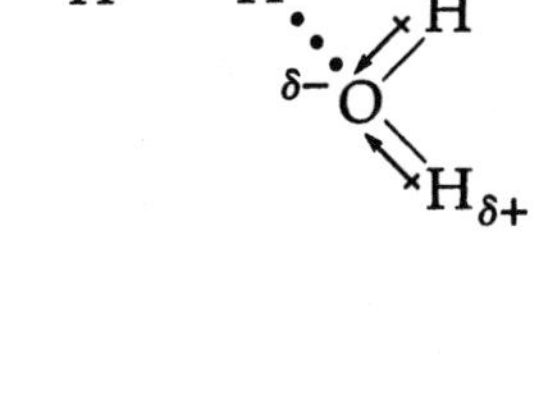

10.59 CH_4 because it is both smaller and nonpolar. That CH_4 contains fewer electrons than CH_2Cl_2 means weaker London forces in CH_4 than in CH_2Cl_2; weaker London forces to overcome allows CH_4 to enter the gas phase at a lower temperature. That CH_4 is nonpolar means there are no intermolecular dipole–dipole attractions to be overcome. Because CH_2Cl_2 is slightly polar, there is also the possibility of intermolecular dipole–dipole attractions, which require more heat energy to overcome and therefore give CH_2Cl_2 a higher boiling point, making it more likely than CH_4 to be liquid at room temperature.

10.60 (d), because an H–N bond, H–O bond, or H–F bond must be present in order for hydrogen bonds to form.

10.61 To determine relative boiling points, you must first determine the types of intermolecular forces in each substance. The weaker these forces, the easier it is to separate the molecules and consequently the lower the boiling point. (a) and (b) are nonpolar molecules, meaning only London forces. (c) has an –OH group, which means hydrogen bonds. (d) is polar, which means dipole–dipole attractions. Because hydrogen bonds are the strongest of the three, (c) should have the highest boiling point.

10.62 (b); because C_2H_2 is small and nonpolar, the only intermolecular forces are London forces. Weak intermolecular forces mean it takes very little heat energy to get C_2H_2 molecules moving fast enough to overcome the London forces and enter the gas phase. Both (a), an ionic compound, and (c), a metal, typically have very high melting and boiling points. (d) is polar, and therefore the dipole–dipole intermolecular forces are stronger than the London forces of (b).

10.63 (a) CH_3OH hydrogen bonding; CH_3Cl dipole–dipole forces; CH_3CH_3 London forces; $CH_3CH_2CH_3$ London forces.

(b) $CH_3CH_3 < CH_3CH_2CH_3 < CH_3Cl < CH_3OH$. The reason nonpolar CH_3CH_3 has a lower boiling point than nonpolar $CH_3CH_2CH_3$ is that CH_3CH_3 is smaller and therefore fewer London forces are at work in a sample of CH_3CH_3.

10.64

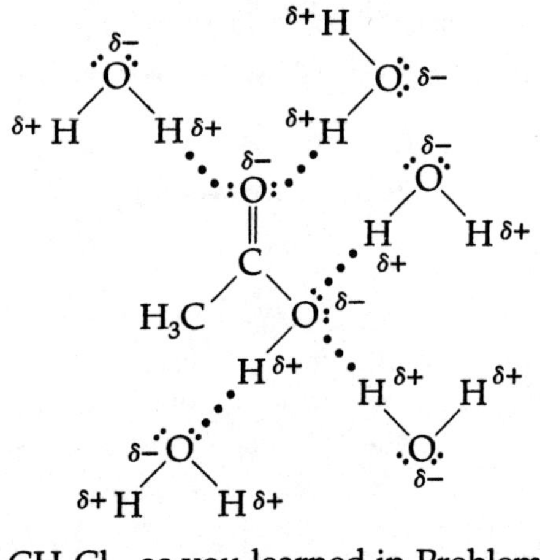

10.65 CH_2Cl_2, as you learned in Problem 6.74, can be polar or nonpolar. In the nonpolar form, there is no specific molecule-to-molecule orientation. In the polar form, the $\delta+$ portion of one molecule attracts the $\delta-$ portion of another:

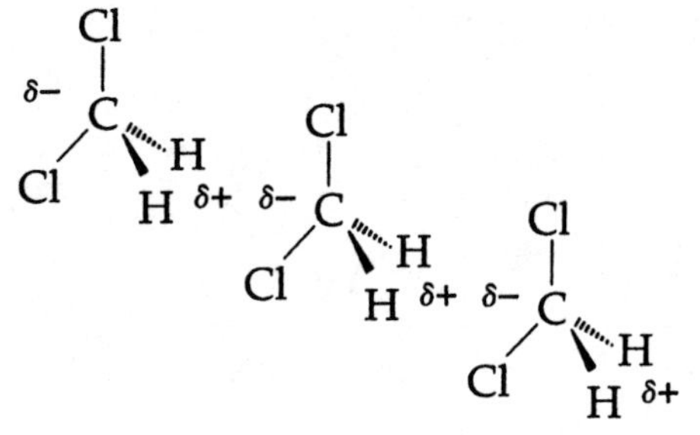

10.66 (a) $CH_4 < Cl_2 < Br_2 < CBr_4$

(b) All four molecules are nonpolar, meaning that in each liquid the only intermolecular forces are London forces, which increase as the molecules become larger and therefore contain more electrons. CH_4 is the smallest of the four, with 10 electrons, followed by Cl_2 (34 electrons), Br_2 (70 electrons), and CBr_4 (146 electrons).

10.67 (a) $H_2 < CH_4 < HCl < CH_3OH$

(b) H_2 and CH_4 are both nonpolar, meaning only the weakest intermolecular forces—London forces—are operating. Because H_2 has fewer electrons than CH_4, H_2 has weaker London forces and therefore the lower boiling point. In polar HCl, dipole–dipole attractions are present, and in polar CH_3OH, the –OH means hydrogen-bonding is present. Because hydrogen bonds are stronger than dipole–dipole interactions, HCl has a lower boiling point than CH_3OH.

10.68 (a) and (d) because they are nonpolar. The two polar compounds, (b) and (c), experience dipole–dipole intermolecular forces in addition to London forces. CBr_4 is tetrahedral (four bonding groups, no lone pairs around C), with the four Br arranged so that the individual bond dipole moments cancel; the molecular dipole moment is therefore zero, and the molecule is nonpolar:

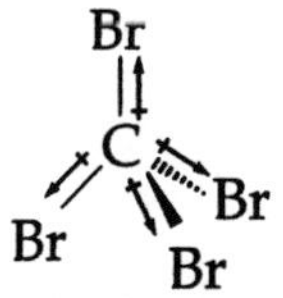

CH_3Br is also a tetrahedron (four bonding groups, no lone pairs around C), but now there is only one bond dipole moment because the three C–H bonds are considered nonpolar. The molecular dipole moment is therefore nonzero, and the molecule is polar:

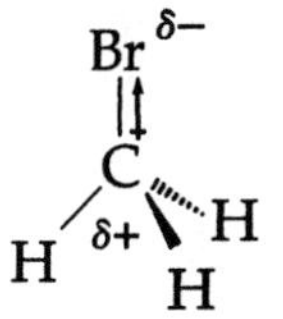

PBr_3 is pyramidal (three bonding groups, one lone pair around P) and has a nonzero molecular dipole moment, making it a polar molecule:

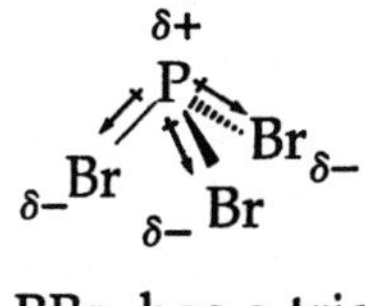

BBr_3 has a trigonal planar shape (three bonding groups, no lone pairs around B). The three B–Br dipole moments, because they are all in the same plane, cancel to give a zero molecular dipole moment and a nonpolar molecule:

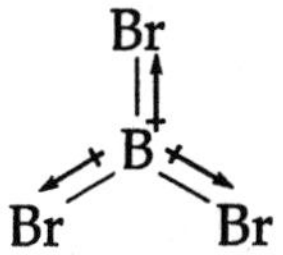

10.69 (a) London forces. Each B–F bond is polar, but the symmetry of the trigonal planar molecule causes the three B–F dipole moments to cancel one another. The molecule is therefore nonpolar, and so only London forces are possible.

(b) Hydrogen-bonding, because of the –OH group.

(c) London forces. That Xe is a noble gas tells you there are no ionic or covalent bonds. It's not a molecule and therefore you can rule out dipole–dipole interactions. Hydrogen-bonding is impossible because there are no –OH, –NH, or –FH groups.

(d) Hydrogen-bonding, because of the HF "groups."

(e) Both dipole–dipole and London forces present; dipole–dipole is the stronger force.

10.70 (a) because it is an ionic compound and (c) because it is a metal.

10.71 SiO_2 is a network solid held together by covalent bonds. At room temperature, the atoms do not have anywhere near the energy required to break these bonds, which means the substance is a solid.

In a sample of CO_2, only London forces act between molecules. These forces are so weak that even at room temperature the CO_2 molecules have enough energy to overcome them, making CO_2 a gas at room temperature.

10.72 $C_2H_6 < CH_3OH < NaCl < SiO_2$. Molecular substances generally have lower melting points than nonmolecular substances, and the molecular substance with the weakest intermolecular forces is the one with the lowest melting point. Because C_2H_6 is a molecular substance and has only nonpolar C–H and C–C bonds, only London forces, the weakest intermolecular forces, are present. In CH_3OH, there is hydrogen-bonding because of the –OH group, and therefore this molecular substance has a melting point higher than that of C_2H_6. NaCl is an ionic nonmolecular solid, and, as noted in the textbook, SiO_2 is a network nonmolecular solid. Thus you expect these two substances to have melting points much higher than those of C_2H_6 and CH_3OH. To get the proper ranking $NaCl < SiO_2$, recall that the textbook mentions the melting point of NaCl as being 800°C and that of SiO_2 as being above 1700°C.

10.73 The substance having the stronger intermolecular forces has the higher boiling point, and hydrogen bonds are stronger than London forces. Thus ethylene glycol boils at the higher temperature because of the two –OH groups and the hydrogen-bonding they make possible. Pentane is essentially nonpolar because it contains only nonpolar C–C and C–H bonds. For this reason, the only intermolecular forces in pentane are London forces.

10.74

10.75 (a) Because C–C bonds are nonpolar, each graphite sheet must be nonpolar. This means the only attractive forces between sheets are London forces.

(b) Because the London forces between sheets in graphite are relatively weak, the sheets can slip past one another, making graphite slippery. The carbon atoms in diamond are all locked in position by extremely strong covalent bonds, preventing the atoms from moving and making diamond a very hard substance.

10.76 Because in diamond and NaCl, melting involves breaking covalent and ionic bonds, respectively. Melting ice, a molecular solid, requires breaking only hydrogen bonds. Because no covalent bonds are broken when ice melts, this substance cannot be used for a covalent/ionic comparison.

10.77 The valence electrons in a piece of metal are free to move about the entire lattice of metal atoms.

10.78 Boiling point increases because the strength of the London forces between atoms increases down the group as the number of electrons per atom increases.

10.79 Because eicosane is so large—a string of 20 carbon atoms bonded to 42 hydrogen atoms—it contains a large number of electrons. The resulting London forces between molecules combine to produce an overall intermolecular attraction that is stronger than the hydrogen-bonding between water molecules. The substance with the greater intermolecular attraction has the higher melting and boiling points.

10.80 Absolutely nothing because melting involves breaking bonds between molecules (*inter*molecular bonds); it does not involve any covalent bonds inside the molecules (*intra*molecular bonds).

10.81 $CO_2 < SO_2 < CH_3CH_2OH < Al$. CO_2 is nonpolar (linear shape), meaning only London forces are possible. SO_2 is polar (bent shape) and experiences stronger dipolar attractive forces between molecules, giving it a higher boiling point than CO_2. Hydrogen-bonding is the strongest intermolecular force in CH_3CH_2OH, giving this substance a higher boiling point than either CO_2 or SO_2. Al is a metal, and the metallic bond is stronger than either London forces or hydrogen bonds, giving this substance the highest boiling point of the four.

CHAPTER
11

What If There Were No Intermolecular Forces? The Ideal Gas

11.1 See solution in textbook.

11.2 $10.50 \text{ g H}_2 \times \dfrac{1 \text{ mol H}_2}{2.0158 \text{ g H}_2} = 5.209 \text{ mol H}_2$

11.3 (a) $5 \times 760 \text{ mm Hg} = 3800 \text{ mm Hg} = 3.80 \times 10^3 \text{ mm Hg}$

(b) $3.80 \times 10^3 \text{ mm Hg} \times \dfrac{1 \text{ cm}}{10 \text{ mm}} \times \dfrac{1 \text{ in.}}{2.54 \text{ cm}} = 150 \text{ in. Hg}$

11.4 Too low because the air in the tube will push down on the mercury column, causing the column to be shorter than it would be if there were a vacuum above the column.

11.5 See solution in textbook.

11.6 $P = \dfrac{nRT}{V}$

$T = \dfrac{PV}{nR}$

n is number of moles, P must be in atmospheres, T must be in kelvins, and V must be in liters.

$\text{Mol N}_2 = 3.00 \text{ g N}_2 \times \dfrac{1 \text{ mol N}_2}{28.014 \text{ g N}_2} = 0.107 \text{ mol N}_2$

$\text{Pressure in atm} = 450.5 \text{ mm Hg} \times \dfrac{1 \text{ atm}}{760 \text{ mm Hg}} = 0.5928 \text{ atm}$

Substitute these values into the ideal gas equation solved for T:

$T = \dfrac{PV}{nR} = \dfrac{0.5928 \text{ atm} \times 2.00 \text{ L}}{0.107 \text{ mol N}_2 \times \dfrac{0.0821 \text{ L} \cdot \text{atm}}{\text{K} \cdot \text{mol}}} = 135 \text{ K}$

$135 \text{ K} - 273.15 = -138°\text{C}$

11.7 $P = \dfrac{nRT}{V}$

$n = \dfrac{PV}{RT}$

Pressure in atm = $40.0 \text{ lb/in.}^2 \times \dfrac{760 \text{ mm Hg}}{14.696 \text{ lb/in.}^2} \times \dfrac{1 \text{ atm}}{760 \text{ mm Hg}} = 2.72 \text{ atm}$

Because 760 mm Hg = 1 atm, you could also use the conversion factor
1 atm = 14.696 lb/in.^{2}:

$40.0 \text{ lb/in.}^2 \times \dfrac{1 \text{ atm}}{14.696 \text{ lb/in.}^2} = 2.72 \text{ atm}$

Volume in L = $10.5 \text{ gal} \times \dfrac{3.785 \text{ L}}{1 \text{ gal}} = 39.7 \text{ L}$

$22.5°C + 273.15 = 295.7 \text{ K}$

$n = \dfrac{PV}{RT} = \dfrac{2.72 \text{ atm} \times 39.7 \text{ L}}{\dfrac{0.0821 \text{ L} \cdot \text{atm}}{\text{K} \cdot \text{mol}} \times 295.7 \text{ K}} = 4.45 \text{ mol O}_2$

$4.45 \text{ mol O}_2 \times \dfrac{31.998 \text{ g O}_2}{1 \text{ mol O}_2} = 142 \text{ g O}_2$

11.8 See solution in textbook.

11.9 See solution in textbook.

11.10 You are asked for an answer in pounds, and from Chapter 2 of the textbook you know the relationship between pounds and the mass units grams and kilograms. You also know the molar mass of H_2, 2.0158 g/mol. All this indicates you should use the ideal gas equation expressed in terms of molar mass and sample mass. First convert the given data to units used in the ideal gas equation, then calculate grams of H_2, then convert grams of H_2 to pounds of H_2.

$1000.0 \text{ gal} \times \dfrac{3.785 \text{ L}}{1 \text{ gal}} = 3785 \text{ L}$

$K = °C + 273.15 = -4.50°C + 273.15 = 268.65 \text{ K}$

$m = \dfrac{PV(MM)}{RT} = \dfrac{32.6 \text{ atm} \times 3785 \text{ L} \times 2.0158 \text{ g / mol}}{0.0821 \dfrac{\text{L} \cdot \text{atm}}{\text{K} \cdot \text{mol}} \times 268.65 \text{ K}}$

$= 1.13 \times 10^4 \text{ g H}_2 \times \dfrac{1 \text{ lb H}_2}{453.6 \text{ g H}_2} = 24.9 \text{ lb H}_2$

11.11 Mass divided by molar mass gives number of moles:

$\dfrac{m}{MM} = \dfrac{g}{g / \text{mol}} = g \div \dfrac{g}{\text{mol}} = g \times \dfrac{\text{mol}}{g} = \text{mol}$

11.12 See solution in textbook.

11.13 See solution in textbook.

11.14 Step 1: $P_i = 2.00 \text{ atm}$ $P_f = ?$
$T_i = 200.0 \text{ K}$ $T_f = 220.0 \text{ K}$
$V_i = 50.0 \text{ mL}$ $V_f = 25.0 \text{ mL}$
$n_i = ?$ $n_f = ? = n_i$

Step 2: $\dfrac{P_iV_i}{n_iT_i} = \dfrac{P_fV_f}{n_fT_f} \longrightarrow \dfrac{P_iV_i}{\cancel{n_i}T_i} = \dfrac{P_fV_f}{\cancel{n_i}T_f} \longrightarrow \dfrac{P_iV_i}{T_i} = \dfrac{P_fV_f}{T_f}$

Step 3:

(a) $P_f = \dfrac{T_fP_iV_i}{V_fT_i} = \dfrac{220.0\ \cancel{K} \times 2.00\ \text{atm} \times 50.0\ \cancel{mL}}{25.0\ \cancel{mL} \times 200.0\ \cancel{K}} = 4.40\ \text{atm}$

(b) $50.0\ \cancel{mL} \times \dfrac{1\ L}{1000\ \cancel{mL}} = 0.0500\ L$

$25.0\ \cancel{mL} \times \dfrac{1\ L}{1000\ \cancel{mL}} = 0.0250\ L$

$P_f = \dfrac{220.0\ \cancel{K} \times 2.00\ \text{atm} \times 0.0500\ \cancel{L}}{0.0250\ \cancel{L} \times 200\ \cancel{K}} = 4.40\ \text{atm}$

(c) No. Because R does not appear in the initial-condition, final-condition equation, there are no restrictions on units used for V, P, or n. (T still must be in kelvins, though.)

(d) Because one of the units in R is liters.

11.15 Because the molecules in the gas phase are moving rapidly throughout the container. There is no order to their movement; it is completely random. In the liquid phase, the molecules are confined to a smaller space and are moving throughout the liquid only rather than throughout the container. In the solid phase, the molecules remain in relatively fixed positions.

11.16 The molecules of an ideal gas are assumed to be moving independently of one another and exerting no attractive forces on one another. We are justified in making this assumption because the molecules are moving very fast in straight-line paths and are relatively far apart. (If they attracted one another, they would not move in straight-line paths.)

11.17 Yes, the gas will leak out even though the pressure inside the container is the same as the pressure outside. Because all the gas molecules in the container are moving along random straight-line paths, some will find themselves on paths that carry them through the tiny hole.

11.18 By colliding with the walls of its container. Pressure is defined as force per unit area, and any gas molecule hitting the container wall exerts a force on the wall.

11.19 Because the air pressure above the liquid inside the straw has been decreased. (You have created a near-vacuum inside the straw.) The unchanged air pressure outside the straw pushes down on the liquid outside the straw, forcing some of it up into the straw.

11.20 A mercury barometer measures atmospheric pressure by showing the height of a mercury column that rises in a glass tube sealed at one end. The open end of the tube is submerged in a dish of liquid mercury. Air pressure pushes down on the mercury in the dish, causing a column of mercury to rise in the tube. Numbers printed on the tube indicate the atmospheric pressure.

11.21 760 mm Hg; 1 atm.

11.22 True: $1\ \cancel{\text{atm}} \times \dfrac{760\ \cancel{\text{mm Hg}}}{1\ \cancel{\text{atm}}} \times \dfrac{1\ \text{cm Hg}}{10\ \cancel{\text{mm Hg}}} = 76\ \text{cm Hg}$

11.23 (a) $29.7\ \cancel{\text{in. Hg}} \times \dfrac{2.54\ \cancel{\text{cm}}}{1\ \cancel{\text{in.}}} \times \dfrac{10\ \text{mm}}{1\ \cancel{\text{cm}}} = 754\ \text{mm Hg}$

(b) $754\ \cancel{\text{mm Hg}} \times \dfrac{1\ \text{atm}}{760\ \cancel{\text{mm Hg}}} = 0.992\ \text{atm}$

11.24 (a) $2000.5 \text{ lb/in.}^2 \times \dfrac{760.00 \text{ mm Hg}}{14.696 \text{ lb/in.}^2} = 1.0346 \times 10^5 \text{ mm Hg}$

(b) $1.0346 \times 10^5 \text{ mm Hg} \times \dfrac{1 \text{ atm}}{760.00 \text{ mm Hg}} = 136.13 \text{ atm}$

11.25 By adding 273.15 to the Celsius temperature: $22.0°C + 273.15 = 295.2 \text{ K}$.

11.26 $K = °C + 273.15 = -100.5°C + 273.15 = 172.7 \text{ K}$

11.27 $K = °C + 273.15 = -2.0°C + 273.15 = 271.2 \text{ K}$

$2.35 \text{ g CH}_4 \times \dfrac{1 \text{ mol CH}_4}{16.04 \text{ g CH}_4} = 0.147 \text{ mol CH}_4$

11.28 $600.2 \text{ lb/in.}^2 \times \dfrac{760.0 \text{ mm Hg}}{14.696 \text{ lb/in.}^2} \times \dfrac{1 \text{ atm}}{760.0 \text{ mm Hg}} = 40.84 \text{ atm}$

Because 760.0 mm Hg = 1 atm, you could also use the conversion factor 1 atm = 14.696 lb/in.^{2}:

$600.2 \text{ lb/in.}^2 \times \dfrac{1 \text{ atm}}{14.696 \text{ lb/in.}^2} = 40.84 \text{ atm}$

$48.5 \text{ lb C}_2\text{H}_2 \times \dfrac{453.6 \text{ g}}{1 \text{ lb}} \times \dfrac{1 \text{ mol C}_2\text{H}_2}{26.038 \text{ g}} = 845 \text{ mol C}_2\text{H}_2$

11.29 The pressure decreases. The pressure is due to collisions between the gas molecules and the walls of the container. If the container is bigger, the molecules have farther to go before they hit the walls and therefore hit the walls less frequently. Less-frequent collisions result in lower pressure.

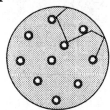

Large volume,
less frequent collisions with walls,
low pressure

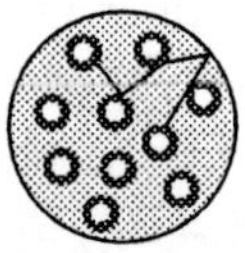

Small volume,
frequent collisions with walls,
high pressure

11.30 The pressure decreases. Pressure depends on the frequency and force with which gas molecules collide with the container walls. If the temperature is decreased, the molecules will move more slowly and will consequently hit the walls less frequently and with less force. Fewer, less forceful collisions result in lower pressure.

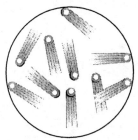

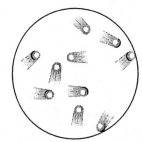

High temperature,
fast-moving molecules,
high pressure

Low temperature,
slow-moving molecules,
low pressure

11.31 The pressure increases. The pressure is due to collisions between the gas molecules and the walls of the container. If there are more molecules inside the container, there are more collisions per unit time and the pressure increases.

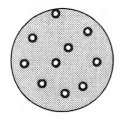
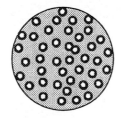

Few gas molecules, few collisions with walls, low pressure

Many gas molecules, many collisions with walls, high pressure

11.32 (a) Sample 1. Because this sample has the fewest molecules in the largest available space, the molecules collide least frequently with the container walls.

(b) Sample 3. Because this sample has the greatest number of molecules in the smallest available space, the molecules collide most frequently with the container walls.

11.33 Sample 2. In fact, the temperature of this sample has been lowered to the point where the gas has condensed to the liquid phase, which is why the molecules are clumped together at the bottom of the container. Because sample 2 is really a liquid and not a gas, we used quotation marks for "gas."

11.34 The pressure of a gas is inversely proportional to volume: P is proportional to $1/V$.

11.35 The pressure of a gas is directly proportional to temperature: P is proportional to T.

11.36 The pressure of a gas is directly proportional to the amount of gas (number of moles) present: P is proportional to n.

11.37 Inverse proportionality means that as one value *increases*, the other one *decreases*; or that as one value *decreases*, the other one *increases*. Direct proportionality means that as one value *increases*, the other one *also increases*; or that as one value *decreases*, the other one *also decreases*. An example of inverse proportionality is the way gas pressure varies with volume. If a certain gas sample exerts a pressure of 4 atm when it occupies a volume of 10 L at a temperature T, it will exert a pressure of 2 atm when it occupies a volume of 20 L at the same temperature T. An example of direct proportionality is the relationship between gas volume and temperature. If a gas occupies a volume of 3 L at 200 K and a pressure P, it will occupy a volume of 6 L at 400 K and the same pressure P.

11.38 It tells you that as the value of y increases, the value of x decreases, and as the value of y decreases, the value of x increases. Example: $x = 1/y$; for $y = 6$, $x = 0.167$; for $y = 12$, $x = 0.0833$; for $y = 3$, $x = 0.333$.

11.39 Inverse proportion. As his age increases, his hair decreases.

11.40 Inverse proportion. As the distance between molecules increases, the strength of the intermolecular force decreases; as the distance between molecules decreases, the strength of the intermolecular force increases.

11.41 Liters-atmospheres ÷ kelvins-moles: L · atm/K · mol. The units are important because they indicate the units in which the volume, pressure, temperature, and quantity of gas must be expressed when using the ideal gas law. The volume must be in *liters*, the pressure in *atmospheres*, the temperature in *kelvins*, and the quantity of gas in *moles*.

11.42 $P = \dfrac{nRT}{V}$

$VP = \dfrac{\cancel{V}nRT}{\cancel{V}} = nRT$

$\dfrac{V\cancel{P}}{\cancel{P}} = \dfrac{nRT}{P}$

$V = \dfrac{nRT}{P}$

11.43 $P = \dfrac{nRT}{V}$

$PV = \dfrac{nRT\cancel{V}}{\cancel{V}}$

$PV = nRT$

$\dfrac{PV}{nR} = \dfrac{\cancel{n}\cancel{R}T}{\cancel{n}\cancel{R}}$

$\dfrac{PV}{nR} = T,$ or, more conventionally, $T = \dfrac{PV}{nR}$

11.44 $P = \dfrac{nRT}{V}$

$VP = \dfrac{\cancel{V}nRT}{\cancel{V}} = nRT$

$\dfrac{VP}{RT} = \dfrac{n\cancel{R}\cancel{T}}{\cancel{R}\cancel{T}} = n$

11.45 You should get the value of R, as you can see by solving the ideal gas equation for R:

$P = \dfrac{nRT}{V}$

$PV = \dfrac{nRT\cancel{V}}{\cancel{V}}$

$PV = nRT$

$\dfrac{PV}{nT} = \dfrac{\cancel{n}R\cancel{T}}{\cancel{n}\cancel{T}}$

$\dfrac{PV}{nT} = R$

For an ideal gas, the ratio PV/nT *always* gives the numeric value 0.0821 (and the units, of course, are L · atm/K · mol).

11.46 The pressure would increase fourfold. According to the ideal gas law, $P = nRT/V$, doubling n doubles the pressure and halving V also doubles the pressure. Making both changes at once results in a fourfold increase in pressure:

$P = \dfrac{nRT}{V}$

$\dfrac{(2n)RT}{0.5V} = \dfrac{4nRT}{V} = 4P$

11.47 The pressure would increase sixfold. According to the ideal gas law, $P = nRT/V$, doubling n doubles the pressure and tripling T triples the pressure. Making both changes at once results in a sixfold increase in pressure:

$$P = \frac{nRT}{V}$$

$$\frac{(2n)R(3T)}{V} = \frac{6nRT}{V} = 6P$$

11.48 The student is wrong because temperatures must be expressed in kelvins in the ideal gas equation. He should learn that there are restrictions on units when gas-law calculations are being done. Pressures *must* be in atmospheres, volumes *must* be in liters, quantities *must* be in moles, temperatures *must* be in kelvins. To get the correct answer, convert 25.0°C to kelvins, double that Kelvin temperature, then convert to °C.

25.0°C + 273.15 = 298.2 K

2 × 298.2 K = 596.4 K

°C = 596.4 K − 273.15 = 323.3°C

(The temperature increase is 323.3°C − 25.0°C = 298.3 C°.)

11.49 You use the ideal gas law solved for n. First, though, you must change the pressure to atmospheres, the volume to liters, and the temperature to kelvins.

$$745.5 \text{ mm Hg} \times \frac{1 \text{ atm}}{760.0 \text{ mm Hg}} = 0.9809 \text{ atm}$$

$$250.0 \text{ mL} \times \frac{1 \text{ L}}{1000 \text{ mL}} = 0.2500 \text{ L}$$

25.5°C + 273.15 = 298.7 K

$$n = \frac{PV}{RT} = \frac{0.9809 \text{ atm} \times 0.2500 \text{ L}}{\dfrac{0.0821 \text{ L} \cdot \text{atm}}{\text{K} \cdot \text{mol}} \times 298.7 \text{ K}} = 0.0100 \text{ mol}$$

11.50 Use the ideal gas equation solved for V: $V = nRT/P$. All quantities are in the correct units except temperature.

0.00°C + 273.15 = 273.15 K

$$V = \frac{nRT}{P} = \frac{2.0 \text{ mol} \times \dfrac{0.0821 \text{ L} \cdot \text{atm}}{\text{K} \cdot \text{mol}} \times 273.15 \text{ K}}{2.5 \text{ atm}} = 18 \text{ L}$$

The volume of the gas would need to be adjusted to 18 liters.

11.51 $T = \dfrac{PV}{nR} = \dfrac{100 \text{ atm} \times 4.0 \text{ L}}{2.0 \text{ mol} \times \dfrac{0.0821 \text{ L} \cdot \text{atm}}{\text{K} \cdot \text{mol}}} = 2.4 \times 10^3 \text{ K}$

°C = K − 273.15 = 2.4 × 10³ − 273.15 = 2.4 × 10³ − 0.27315 × 10³ = 2.1 × 10³ °C

11.52 Because $V = nRT/P$, V = 0 L when T = 0 K, and volume of 0 L does not make sense. What really happens is that the gas becomes a liquid as it approaches absolute zero, and the ideal gas law no longer governs its behavior.

11.53 (a) Before using the ideal gas law solved for moles, you must change the pressure to atmospheres and the temperature to kelvins.

$$30 \ \text{psi} \times \frac{1 \ \text{atm}}{14.696 \ \text{psi}} = 2.0 \ \text{atm}$$

$$22°C + 273.15 = 295 \ K$$

$$n = \frac{PV}{RT} = \frac{2.0 \ \text{atm} \times 20.0 \ L}{\dfrac{0.0821 \ L \cdot \text{atm}}{K \cdot \text{mol}} \times 295 \ K} = 1.7 \ \text{mol}$$

(b) $\quad 1.7 \ \text{mol } N_2 \times \dfrac{28.01 \ \text{g } N_2}{1 \ \text{mol } N_2} = 48 \ \text{g } N_2$

$$48 \ \text{g } N_2 \times \frac{1 \ \text{lb } N_2}{453.6 \ \text{g } N_2} = 0.11 \ \text{lb } N_2$$

11.54 Because the ideal gas law assumes the molecules feel absolutely no intermolecular attractive forces. This is not strictly true. In any real gas, the molecules feel enough intermolecular attractions to make the gas behavior deviate from that predicted by the ideal gas law.

11.55 (a) Use the ideal gas equation solved for V: $V = nRT/P$. All quantities are in the correct units except temperature.

$$22.5°C + 273.15 = 295.7 \ K$$

$$V = \frac{nRT}{P} = \frac{1 \ \text{mol} \times \dfrac{0.0821 \ L \cdot \text{atm}}{K \cdot \text{mol}} \times 295.7 \ K}{1.00 \ \text{atm}} = 24.3 \ L \ H_2$$

(b) $1 \ \text{mol } H_2 \times \dfrac{2 \ \text{mol HCl}}{1 \ \text{mol } H_2} = 2 \ \text{mol HCl} \quad$ or $\quad 1 \ \text{mol } Cl_2 \times \dfrac{2 \ \text{mol HCl}}{1 \ \text{mol } Cl_2} = 2 \ \text{mol HCl}$

$$V = \frac{nRT}{P} = \frac{2 \ \text{mol} \times \dfrac{0.0821 \ L \cdot \text{atm}}{K \cdot \text{mol}} \ 295.7 \ K}{1.00 \ \text{atm}} = 48.6 \ L \ HCl$$

11.56 Divide the mass by the molar mass: $n = m/MM$. Unit check:

$$g \div \frac{g}{\text{mol}} = g \times \frac{\text{mol}}{g} = \text{mol}$$

11.57 Use the ideal gas law expressed in terms of sample mass and molar mass. The given temperature and pressure must be converted to the proper units.

$$25.0°C + 273.15 = 298.2 \ K$$

$$765.0 \ \text{mm Hg} \times \frac{1 \ \text{atm}}{760.0 \ \text{mm Hg}} = 1.007 \ \text{atm}$$

$$\frac{m}{MM} = \frac{PV}{RT}$$

$$mRT = (MM)PV$$

$$MM = \frac{mRT}{PV} = \frac{7.24 \ \text{g} \times 0.0821 \dfrac{L \cdot \text{atm}}{K \cdot \text{mol}} \times 298.2 \ K}{1.007 \ \text{atm} \times 4.00 \ L} = 44.0 \ \text{g / mol}$$

11.58 (a) $250.0 \text{ mL} \times \dfrac{1 \text{ L}}{1000 \text{ mL}} = 0.2500 \text{ L}$

$1255.6 \text{ mm Hg} \times \dfrac{1 \text{ atm}}{760.0 \text{ mm Hg}} = 1.6521 \text{ atm}$

$22.7°C + 273.15 = 295.9 \text{ K}$

$MM = \dfrac{m_{sample}RT}{PV}$

$= \dfrac{1.56 \text{ g} \times 0.0821 \dfrac{\text{L} \cdot \text{atm}}{\text{K} \cdot \text{mol}} \times 295.9 \text{ K}}{1.6521 \text{ atm} \times 0.2500 \text{ L}} = 91.8 \text{ g/mol}$

(b) You know how to work with empirical and molecular formulas from Section 8.5 of the textbook. Because the molar mass of NO_2, 46.005 g/mol, is not the same as the molar mass calculated in (a), you must divide to get a multiplying factor for the subscripts of the empirical formula:

$\dfrac{91.8 \text{ g / mol}}{46.005 \text{ g / mol}} = 2.00$

$N_{2 \times 1}O_{2 \times 2} = N_2O_4$

11.59 Use the ideal gas law expressed in terms of molar mass and sample mass. The given volume, pressure, and temperature must be converted to the proper units, and the molar mass of H_2 is 2.0158 g/mol.

$1610.2 \text{ mL} \times \dfrac{1 \text{ L}}{1000 \text{ mL}} = 1.6102 \text{ L}$

$745.4 \text{ mm Hg} \times \dfrac{1 \text{ atm}}{760.0 \text{ mm Hg}} = 0.9808 \text{ atm}$

$22.7°C + 273.15 = 295.9 \text{ K}$

$\dfrac{m}{MM} = \dfrac{PV}{RT}$

$m = \dfrac{(MM)PV}{RT} = \dfrac{2.0158 \text{ g / mol} \times 0.9808 \text{ atm} \times 1.6102 \text{ L}}{0.0821 \dfrac{\text{L} \cdot \text{atm}}{\text{K} \cdot \text{mol}} \times 295.9 \text{ K}} = 0.131 \text{ g}$

11.60 $24.5°C + 273.15 = 297.7 \text{ K}$

$768.0 \text{ mm Hg} \times \dfrac{1 \text{ atm}}{760.0 \text{ mm Hg}} = 1.011 \text{ atm}$

The molar mass of He is 4.003 g/mol.

$\text{Density} = \dfrac{m_{sample}}{V} = \dfrac{(MM)P}{RT}$

$= \dfrac{4.003 \text{ g / mol} \times 1.011 \text{ atm}}{0.0821 \dfrac{\text{L} \cdot \text{atm}}{\text{K} \cdot \text{mol}} \times 297.7 \text{ K}} = 0.166 \text{ g / L}$

$\dfrac{0.166 \text{ g}}{\text{L}} \times \dfrac{1 \text{ L}}{1000 \text{ mL}} = 0.000166 \text{ g / mL} = 1.66 \times 10^{-4} \text{ g / mL}$

11.61 (a) The definition of density is mass divided by volume. You know a form of the ideal gas law that contains m and V, and if you solve this equation for m/V, you'll have an expression that tells you something about the density of these two gases.

$$\frac{m}{MM} = \frac{PV}{RT}$$

$$\frac{m}{V} = \frac{(MM)P}{RT} = \text{Density}$$

P and T are the same in the two balloons, and R is a constant. Therefore you can ignore them and focus on the relationship between MM and density. MM being in the numerator means density is directly proportional to MM. Because the molar masses are 2.0158 g/mol for H_2 and 4.003 g/mol for He, the density must be greater in the He balloon.

(b) H_2 density $= 2.0158 \text{ g} / \text{mol} \times \dfrac{P}{RT}$

He density $= 4.003 \text{ g} / \text{mol} \times \dfrac{P}{RT}$

$$\frac{4.003}{2.0158} = 1.986$$

The He density is 1.986 times greater than the H_2 density.

11.62 $25.0°C + 273.15 = 298.2$ K

$$V = \frac{nRT}{P}$$

$$V_{CO} = \frac{1.00 \text{ mol} \times 0.0821 \dfrac{\text{L} \cdot \text{atm}}{\text{K} \cdot \text{mol}} \times 298.2 \text{ K}}{1.00 \text{ atm}} = 24.5 \text{ L}$$

$$V_{CO_2} = \frac{1.00 \text{ mol} \times 0.0821 \dfrac{\text{L} \cdot \text{atm}}{\text{K} \cdot \text{mol}} \times 298.2 \text{ K}}{1.00 \text{ atm}} = 24.5 \text{ L}$$

(b) Equal molar amounts of different gases at the same temperature and pressure occupy the same volume.

11.63 $10.0°C + 273.15 = 283.2$ K

$20.0°C + 273.15 = 293.2$ K

$$50.5 \text{ lb} / \text{in.}^2 \times \frac{1 \text{ atm}}{14.70 \text{ lb} / \text{in.}^2} = 3.44 \text{ atm}$$

Step 1: $P_i = 3.44$ atm $P_f = ?$

$\qquad\quad V_i = ?$ $V_f = ? = V_i$

$\qquad\quad n_i = ?$ $n_f = ? = n_i$

$\qquad\quad T_i = 283.2$ K $T_f = 293.2$ K

Step 2: $\dfrac{P_i V_i}{n_i T_i} = \dfrac{P_f V_f}{n_f T_f}$

$\qquad\quad \dfrac{P_i V_i}{n_i T_i} = \dfrac{P_f V_i}{n_i T_f}$

$\qquad\quad \dfrac{P_i}{T_i} = \dfrac{P_f}{T_f}$

Step 3: $P_f = \dfrac{T_f P_i}{T_i} = \dfrac{293.2 \text{ K} \times 3.44 \text{ atm}}{283.2 \text{ K}} = 3.56 \text{ atm}$

$$3.56 \text{ atm} \times \dfrac{14.70 \text{ lb / in.}^2}{1 \text{ atm}} = 52.3 \text{ lb / in.}^2$$

11.64 The pressure of a gas doubles only when its temperature *in kelvins* doubles. *Never use °C in a gas law calculation.*

11.65 Step 1: $P_i = 3.44 \text{ atm}$ $P_f = ? = 2P_i$
             $V_i = ?$ $V_f = ? = V_i$
             $n_i = ?$ $n_f = ? = n_i$
             $T_i = 283.2 \text{ K}$ $T_f = ?$

Step 2: $\dfrac{P_i V_i}{n_i T_i} = \dfrac{P_f V_f}{n_f T_f}$

$$\dfrac{P_i V_i}{n_i T_i} = \dfrac{2 P_i V_i}{n_i T_f}$$

$$\dfrac{1}{T_i} = \dfrac{2}{T_f}$$

Step 3: $T_f = 2T_i = 2 \times 283.2 \text{ K} = 566.4 \text{ K}$
        $566.4 \text{ K} - 273.15 = 293.3°\text{C}$

11.66 Step 1: $P_i = 6.70 \text{ atm}$ $P_f = ?$
             $V_i = ?$ $V_f = V_i$
             $n_i = 20.0 \text{ mol}$ $n_f = 30.0 \text{ mol}$
             $T_i = 298.2 \text{ K}$ $T_f = 318.2 \text{ K}$

Step 2: $\dfrac{P_i V_i}{n_i T_i} = \dfrac{P_f V_f}{n_f T_f}$

$$\dfrac{P_i V_i}{n_i T_i} = \dfrac{P_f V_i}{n_f T_f}$$

$$\dfrac{P_i}{n_i T_i} = \dfrac{P_f}{n_f T_f}$$

Step 3: $P_f = \dfrac{n_f T_f P_i}{n_i T_i} = \dfrac{30.0 \text{ mol} \times 318.2 \text{ K} \times 6.70 \text{ atm}}{20.0 \text{ mol} \times 298.2 \text{ K}} = 10.7 \text{ atm}$

11.67 Step 1: $P_i = ?$ $P_f = ?$
             $V_i = ?$ $V_f = ? = 0.5V_i$
             $n_i = ?$ $n_f = ? = n_i$
             $T_i = ?$ $T_f = ? = 2T_i$

Step 2: $\dfrac{P_i V_i}{n_i T_i} = \dfrac{P_f V_f}{n_f T_f}$

$$\frac{P_i V_i}{n_i T_i} = \frac{P_f \times 0.5\, V_i}{n_i \times 2\, T_i}$$

$$P_i = \frac{0.5\, P_f}{2}$$

$$\frac{2\, P_i}{0.5} = P_f = 4\, P_i$$

The final pressure is four times greater than the initial pressure.

11.68 Because the reaction is run at STP, the 22.4 L of O_2 gas is 1 mole of O_2 gas. (At STP, 1 mole of any gas occupies a volume of 22.4 L.) The balanced equation tells you that 2 moles of H_2 gas reacts with 1 mole of O_2 gas, meaning you need

$$2\ \text{mol}\ H_2(g) \times \frac{22.4\ \text{L}\ H_2(g)}{1\ \text{mol}\ H_2(g)} = 44.8\ \text{L}\ H_2(g)$$

The 2 moles of H_2O gas formed occupies a volume of

$$2\ \text{mol}\ H_2O(g) \times \frac{22.4\ \text{L}\ H_2O(g)}{1\ \text{mol}\ H_2O(g)} = 44.8\ \text{L}\ H_2O(g)$$

11.69 (a) The reaction stoichiometry tells you that it takes 1 mole of $O_2(g)$ to produce 2 moles of $SO_3(g)$. At STP, 1 mole of O_2 gas has a volume of 22.4 L.

(b) The required amount is still 1 mole of $O_2(g)$, but now conditions are not STP, which means you must use the ideal gas equation to calculate the required volume.

$25.0°C + 273.15 = 298.2\ K$

$$V = \frac{nRT}{P} = \frac{1\ \text{mol} \times 0.0821\ \dfrac{L \cdot atm}{K \cdot mol} \times 298.2\ K}{1\ \text{atm}} = 24.5\ L$$

11.70 Method 1—using the ideal gas equation:

$$500.0\ \text{g}\ H_2O \times \frac{1\ \text{mol}\ H_2O}{18.015\ \text{g}\ H_2O} \times \frac{2\ \text{mol}\ H_2}{2\ \text{mol}\ H_2O} = 27.75\ \text{mol}\ H_2$$

$$V = \frac{nRT}{P} = \frac{27.75\ \text{mol}\ H_2 \times 0.08210\ \dfrac{L \cdot atm}{K \cdot mol} \times 273.15\ K}{1\ \text{atm}} = 622.3\ L\ H_2$$

$$500.0\ \text{g}\ H_2O \times \frac{1\ \text{mol}\ H_2O}{18.015\ \text{g}\ H_2O} \times \frac{1\ \text{mol}\ O_2}{2\ \text{mol}\ H_2O} = 13.88\ \text{mol}\ O_2$$

$$V = \frac{nRT}{P} = \frac{13.88\ \text{mol}\ O_2 \times 0.08210\ \dfrac{L \cdot atm}{K \cdot mol} \times 273.15\ K}{1\ \text{atm}} = 311.3\ L\ O_2$$

Method 2—because the reaction is run at STP, you can use the fact that under these conditions 1 mole of any gas occupies a volume of 22.4 L. You want to produce

$$500.0 \text{ g H}_2\text{O} \times \frac{1 \text{ mol H}_2\text{O}}{18.015 \text{ g H}_2\text{O}} = 27.75 \text{ mol H}_2\text{O}$$

The balanced equation tells you that you need

$$27.75 \text{ mol H}_2\text{O} \times \frac{2 \text{ mol H}_2}{2 \text{ mol H}_2\text{O}} = 27.75 \text{ mol H}_2$$

$$27.75 \text{ mol H}_2\text{O} \times \frac{1 \text{ mol O}_2}{2 \text{ mol H}_2\text{O}} = 13.88 \text{ mol O}_2$$

Both these reactants are gases, meaning the volumes at STP are

$$27.75 \text{ mol H}_2 \times \frac{22.4 \text{ L H}_2}{1 \text{ mol H}_2} = 622 \text{ L H}_2$$

$$13.88 \text{ mol O}_2 \times \frac{22.4 \text{ L O}_2}{1 \text{ mol O}_2} = 311 \text{ L O}_2$$

11.71 First find out how much H_2 gas must be present to create the given pressure in the cylinder at the given temperature. Then use stoichiometry to find out the mass of Zn needed to produce that amount of H_2 gas.

$$25.0°C + 273.15 = 298.2 \text{ K}$$

$$n = \frac{PV}{RT} = \frac{10.0 \text{ atm} \times 50.0 \text{ L}}{0.0821 \dfrac{\text{L} \cdot \text{atm}}{\text{K} \cdot \text{mol}} \times 298.2 \text{ K}} = 20.4 \text{ mol H}_2$$

$$20.4 \text{ mol H}_2 \times \frac{1 \text{ mol Zn}}{1 \text{ mol H}_2} \times \frac{65.39 \text{ g Zn}}{1 \text{ mol Zn}} = 1.33 \times 10^3 \text{ g Zn}$$

11.72 The sample at 200°C. At 101°C, the water is only 1 Celsius degree above its boiling point and thus very close to making a phase transition to the liquid state, where attractive interactions between molecules cannot be ignored as they are in the ideal gas model.

11.73 Because the model assumes that all gases consist of identical particles that have no attraction for one another and do not interact with one another in any way. Because there is no interaction, the chemical identity of the particles does not matter.

11.74

$$0.8004 \text{ g He} \times \frac{1 \text{ mol He}}{4.003 \text{ g He}} = 0.2000 \text{ mol He}$$

$$107.0°C + 273.15 = 380.2 \text{ K}$$

$$P = \frac{nRT}{V} = \frac{0.2000 \text{ mol} \times 0.0821 \dfrac{\text{L} \cdot \text{atm}}{\text{K} \cdot \text{mol}} \times 297.2 \text{ K}}{5.00 \text{ L}} = 1.25 \text{ atm}$$

$$1.25 \text{ atm} \times \frac{760 \text{ mm Hg}}{1 \text{ atm}} = 950 \text{ mm Hg}$$

11.75 Convert the given data to match the units in R, use the ideal gas law to find the number of moles of H_2 produced, then convert moles to grams.

$$100.0 \text{ mL} \times \frac{1 \text{ L}}{1000 \text{ mL}} = 0.1000 \text{ L}$$

$$745.5 \text{ mm Hg} \times \frac{1 \text{ atm}}{760.0 \text{ mm Hg}} = 0.9809 \text{ atm}$$

$$24.0°C + 273.15 = 297.2 \text{ K}$$

$$n = \frac{PV}{RT} = \frac{0.9809 \text{ atm} \times 0.1000 \text{ L}}{0.0821 \frac{\text{L} \cdot \text{atm}}{\text{K} \cdot \text{mol}} \times 297.2 \text{ K}} = 4.02 \times 10^{-3} \text{ mol } H_2$$

$$4.02 \times 10^{-3} \text{ mol } H_2 \times \frac{2.0158 \text{ g } H_2}{1 \text{ mol } H_2} = 8.10 \times 10^{-3} \text{ g } H_2$$

11.76 STP means 0°C (273.15 K) and 1 atm.

$$\text{Density} = \frac{m}{V} = \frac{(MM)P}{RT} = \frac{28.014 \text{ g / mol} \times 1 \text{ atm}}{0.0821 \frac{\text{L} \cdot \text{atm}}{\text{K} \cdot \text{mol}} \times 273.15 \text{ K}} = 1.249 \text{ g / L}$$

11.77 (a) $$MM = \frac{mRT}{PV} = \frac{2.678 \text{ g} \times 0.0821 \frac{\text{L} \cdot \text{atm}}{\text{K} \cdot \text{mol}} \times 273.15 \text{ K}}{1 \text{ atm} \times 2.00 \text{ L}} = 30.0 \text{ g / mol}$$

(b) To determine the empirical formula, assume you have 100.0 g of the sample rather than the 2.678 g mentioned in the problem statement. The percentages then equal the grams.

$$80.0\% \text{ C} \rightarrow 80.0 \text{ g C} \times \frac{1 \text{ mol C}}{12.011 \text{ g C}} = 6.66 \text{ mol C}$$

$$20.0\% \text{ H} \rightarrow 20.0 \text{ g H} \times \frac{1 \text{ mol H}}{1.0079 \text{ g H}} = 19.8 \text{ mol H}$$

$$C_{\frac{6.66}{6.66}} H_{\frac{19.8}{6.66}} \rightarrow C_1 H_{2.97} \rightarrow CH_3$$

(c) The molar mass of the empirical formula CH_3 determined in (b) is 15.035 g/mol. The molar mass of the compound is, from (a), 30.0 g/mol.

$$\frac{30.0 \text{ g / mol}}{15.035 \text{ g / mol}} = 2.00$$

$$C_{2 \times 1} H_{2 \times 3} \rightarrow C_2 H_6$$

11.78 $$150.0 \text{ mL} \times \frac{1 \text{ L}}{1000 \text{ mL}} = 0.1500 \text{ L}$$

$$22.0°C + 273.15 = 295.2 \text{ K}$$

$$780.5 \text{ mm Hg} \times \frac{1 \text{ atm}}{760.0 \text{ mm Hg}} = 1.027 \text{ atm}$$

$$n = \frac{PV}{RT} = \frac{1.027 \text{ atm} \times 0.1500 \text{ L}}{0.0821 \frac{\text{L} \cdot \text{atm}}{\text{K} \cdot \text{mol}} \times 295.2 \text{ K}} = 6.356 \times 10^{-3} \text{ mol } O_2$$

$$6.356 \times 10^{-3} \, \text{mol } O_2 \times \frac{2 \, \text{mol } KClO_3}{3 \, \text{mol } O_2} = 4.237 \times 10^{-3} \, \text{mol } KClO_3$$

$$4.237 \times 10^{-3} \, \text{mol } KClO_3 \times \frac{122.5 \, \text{g } KClO_4}{1 \, \text{mol } KClO_4} = 0.5190 \, \text{g } KClO_4$$

11.79 Step 1: $P_i = ?$ $\qquad$ $P_f = 3P_i$
$\quad\quad\quad\quad\quad$ $V_i = ?$ $\qquad\quad$ $V_f = 2V_i$
$\quad\quad\quad\quad\quad$ $n_i = ?$ $\qquad\quad$ $n_f = n_i$
$\quad\quad\quad\quad\quad$ $T_i = 293.2 \, \text{K}$ $\quad$ $T_f = ?$

Step 2: $\dfrac{P_i V_i}{n_i T_i} = \dfrac{P_f V_f}{n_f T_f}$

$\quad\quad\quad$ $\dfrac{P_i V_i}{n_i T_i} = \dfrac{3P_i 2V_i}{n_i T_f}$

$\quad\quad\quad$ $\dfrac{1}{T_i} = \dfrac{6}{T_f}$

Step 3: $T_f = 6T_i = 6 \times 293.2 \, \text{K} = 1759 \, \text{K}$
$\quad\quad\quad$ $1759 \, \text{K} - 273.15 = 1486°\text{C}$

11.80 Step 1: $P_i = 700.0 \, \text{mm Hg}$ $\quad$ $P_f = 760.0 \, \text{mm Hg}$
$\quad\quad\quad\quad\quad$ $V_i = 15.0 \, \text{mL}$ $\qquad\quad$ $V_f = ?$
$\quad\quad\quad\quad\quad$ $n_i = ?$ $\qquad\qquad\quad$ $n_f = n_i$
$\quad\quad\quad\quad\quad$ $T_i = 0.0°\text{C}$ $\qquad\quad$ $T_f = T_i$

Note that it is not necessary to convert any of these variables to the units found in R, $L \cdot \text{atm}/\text{K} \cdot \text{mol}$, because R is not used in initial-condition, final-condition problems and the temperature does not appear in the final equation to be used.

Step 2: $\dfrac{P_i V_i}{n_i T_i} = \dfrac{P_f V_f}{n_f T_f}$

$\quad\quad\quad$ $\dfrac{P_i V_i}{n_i T_i} = \dfrac{P_f V_f}{n_i T_i}$

$\quad\quad\quad$ $P_i V_i = P_f V_f$

Step 3: $V_f = \dfrac{P_i V_i}{P_f} = \dfrac{700.0 \, \text{mm Hg} \times 15.0 \, \text{mL}}{760.0 \, \text{mm Hg}} = 13.8 \, \text{mL}$

11.81 Use the ideal gas law expressed in terms of molar mass and sample mass. Because the equation requires volume to be in liters, convert the density to grams per liter:

$$\frac{2.26 \times 10^{-3} \, \text{g}}{\text{mL}} \times \frac{1000 \, \text{mL}}{1 \, \text{L}} = 2.26 \, \text{g} / \text{L}$$

$$655 \, \text{mm Hg} \times \frac{1 \, \text{atm}}{760 \, \text{mm Hg}} = 0.862 \, \text{atm}$$

You know density is mass/volume, meaning you can replace m/V by the density value.
$25.0°\text{C} + 273.15 = 298.2 \, \text{K}$

$$MM = \frac{mRT}{PV} = \frac{m}{V} \times \frac{RT}{P} = \text{Density} \times \frac{RT}{P} = 2.26 \frac{\text{g}}{\text{L}} \times \frac{0.0821 \frac{\text{L} \cdot \text{atm}}{\text{K} \cdot \text{mol}} \times 298.2 \, \text{K}}{0.862 \, \text{atm}} = 64.2 \, \text{g} / \text{mol}$$

11.82 (a) You know that equal volumes of gases at the same temperature and pressure contain equal numbers of moles. Because both gases are at STP, 6.0 L of $H_2(g)$ contains three times as many moles as 2.0 L of $N_2(g)$. This is the stoichiometry shown in the balanced equation, which tells you the reaction is being run in a balanced fashion.

(b) $200.0 \text{ lb/in.}^2 \times \dfrac{760.0 \text{ mm Hg}}{14.70 \text{ lb/in.}^2} \times \dfrac{1 \text{ atm}}{760.0 \text{ mm Hg}} = 13.61 \text{ atm } N_2 \text{ pressure}$

$22.0°C + 273.15 = 295.2 \text{ K}$

$240.0 \text{ lb/in.}^2 \times \dfrac{760.0 \text{ mm Hg}}{14.70 \text{ lb/in.}^2} \times \dfrac{1 \text{ atm}}{760.0 \text{ mm Hg}} = 16.33 \text{ atm } H_2 \text{ pressure}$

Convert both reactant amounts of moles:

$$n = \frac{PV}{RT}$$

$$n_{N_2} = \frac{13.61 \text{ atm} \times 50.0 \text{ L}}{0.0821 \dfrac{\text{L} \cdot \text{atm}}{\text{K} \cdot \text{mol}} \times 295.2 \text{ K}} = 28.1 \text{ mol } N_2$$

$$n_{H_2} = \frac{16.33 \text{ atm} \times 100.0 \text{ L}}{0.0821 \dfrac{\text{L} \cdot \text{atm}}{\text{K} \cdot \text{mol}} \times 295.2 \text{ K}} = 67.4 \text{ mol } H_2$$

The balanced equation tells you that 1 mole of N_2 reacts with 3 moles of H_2, which means 28.1 moles of N_2 reacts with $3 \times 28.1 = 84.3$ moles of H_2. Because you do not have this much H_2, this is a limiting-reactant problem as described in Section 8.4 of the textbook. You have moles for both reactants, and therefore your next step is to determine mole-to-coefficient ratios:

$N_2: \dfrac{28.1}{1} = 28.1 \qquad H_2: \dfrac{67.4}{3} = 22.5 \leftarrow$ Smaller number, limiting reactant

Now use the limiting reactant to determine the amount of NH_3 formed:

$67.4 \text{ mol } H_2 \times \dfrac{2 \text{ mol } NH_3}{3 \text{ mol } H_2} \times \dfrac{17.031 \text{ g } NH_3}{1 \text{ mol } NH_3} = 765 \text{ g } NH_3$

11.83 $230.0 \text{ mL} \times \dfrac{1 \text{ L}}{1000 \text{ mL}} = 0.2300 \text{ L}$

$745.0 \text{ mm Hg} \times \dfrac{1 \text{ atm}}{760.0 \text{ mm Hg}} = 0.9803 \text{ atm}$

$34.0°C + 273.15 = 307.2 \text{ K}$

$n = \dfrac{PV}{RT} = \dfrac{0.9803 \text{ atm} \times 0.2300 \text{ L}}{0.0821 \dfrac{\text{L} \cdot \text{atm}}{\text{K} \cdot \text{mol}} \times 307.2 \text{ K}} = 8.940 \times 10^{-3} \text{ mol } N_2O_4$

$8.940 \times 10^{-3} \text{ mol } N_2O_4 \times \dfrac{2 \text{ mol N atoms}}{1 \text{ mol } N_2O_4} \times \dfrac{6.022 \times 10^{23} \text{ N atoms}}{1 \text{ mol N atoms}} = 1.077 \times 10^{22} \text{ N atoms}$

11.84 Increase because V is directly proportional to T when P and n are held constant.

11.85 The same in both containers because the identity of the gas does not matter. $P = nRT/V$, $n = 1$ mol in both containers, R is the same in both containers, $T = 300$ K in both containers, $V = 1$ L in both containers. Therefore P must be the same in the two containers.

11.86 Higher in the hydrogen container because the number of moles of H_2 gas is greater than the number of moles of He gas:

$$1.0 \text{ g He} \times \frac{1 \text{ mol He}}{4.003 \text{ g He}} = 0.25 \text{ mol He}$$

$$1.0 \text{ g H}_2 \times \frac{1 \text{ mol H}_2}{2.0158 \text{ g H}_2} = 0.50 \text{ mol H}_2$$

The ideal gas equation, $P = nRT/V$, tells you that pressure is directly proportional to number of moles.

11.87 $25.0°C + 273.15 = 298.2$ K

$$0.200 \text{ g O}_2 \times \frac{1 \text{ mol O}_2}{31.998 \text{ g O}_2} \times \frac{1 \text{ mol N}_2O_4}{2 \text{ mol O}_2} = 3.13 \times 10^{-3} \text{ mol N}_2O_4$$

$$V = \frac{nRT}{P} = \frac{3.13 \times 10^{-3} \text{ mol} \times 0.0821 \frac{\text{L} \cdot \text{atm}}{\text{K} \cdot \text{mol}} \times 298.2 \text{ K}}{0.996 \text{ atm}} = 0.0769 \text{ L} = 76.9 \text{ mL N}_2O_4$$

11.88 Step 1:

$P_i = 25.0$ atm	$P_f = ?$
$V_i = ?$	$V_f = ? = V_i$
$n_i = ?$	$n_f = ? = n_i$
$T_i = 25°C = 298$ K	$T_f = 40°C = 313$ K

Step 2:
$$\frac{P_iV_i}{n_iT_i} = \frac{P_fV_f}{n_fT_f}$$

$$\frac{P_iV_i}{n_iT_i} = \frac{P_fV_i}{n_iT_f}$$

$$\frac{P_i}{T_i} = \frac{P_f}{T_f}$$

$$P_f = \frac{P_iT_f}{T_i} = \frac{25.0 \text{ atm} \times 313 \text{ K}}{298 \text{ K}} = 26.3 \text{ atm}$$

11.89 The ideal gas equation solved for V, $V = nRT/P$, tells you that the volume of a gas is *directly* proportional to the temperature. Thus if the temperature decreases (as it would in a freezer), the volume must also decrease.

11.90 $25.0°C + 273.15 = 298.2$ K

$$n = \frac{PV}{RT} = \frac{7.35 \text{ atm} \times 10.0 \text{ L}}{0.0821 \frac{\text{L} \cdot \text{atm}}{\text{K} \cdot \text{mol}} \times 298.2 \text{ K}} = 3.00 \text{ mol Ne}$$

$$3.00 \text{ mol Ne} \times \frac{20.180 \text{ g Ne}}{1 \text{ mol Ne}} = 60.5 \text{ g Ne}$$

11.91 (a) n and V constant. That the bulb is sealed tells you n is constant. That the bulb is made of glass, a rigid material, tells you V is constant. That T changes is stated in the problem. P changes because T changes and, according to the ideal gas law, P is directly proportional to T. (Here P increases because T increases.)

(b) n and P constant. The balloon can be assumed to be tied tightly, making n constant because no He can escape. That T changes is stated in the problem. P is constant because the pressure inside the balloon must equal the exterior (atmospheric) pressure at all times. V changes because T changes and the ideal gas equation shows that V is directly proportional to T: $P = nRT/V$, $V = nRT/P$. (Here V decreases because T decreases.)

(c) T and V constant. That n changes is stated in the problem. Because the cylinder is made of steel and is sealed, V cannot change. T is constant because the CO_2 is assumed to behave ideally. P changes because it is directly proportional to n. (Here P increases because n increases.) [Note: For any real gas, T would increase slightly as n was increased at constant V.]

11.92 When they are cooled to near the temperature at which the gas liquifies and when they are under such high pressure that they are very close to one another.

11.93 $\text{Density} = \dfrac{m}{V} = \dfrac{(MM)P}{RT}$

Because all the gases are at 0.0°C and 1.0 atm, P, T, and R can be ignored so that this expression reduces to

$\text{Density} = \dfrac{m}{V}$ is proportional to MM

Thus, the greater the molar mass, the greater the density. The molar masses are CO_2, 44 g/mol; H_2, 2 g/mol; O_2, 32 g/mol; CH_4, 16 g/mol; He, 4 g/mol. Therefore the order of increasing density is $H_2 < He < CH_4 < O_2 < CO_2$.

11.94 $792 \text{ mm Hg} \times \dfrac{1 \text{ atm}}{760 \text{ mm Hg}} = 1.04 \text{ atm}$

$250°C + 273.15 = 523 \text{ K}$

$n = \dfrac{PV}{RT} = \dfrac{1.04 \text{ atm} \times 1.80 \text{ L}}{0.0821 \dfrac{\text{L} \cdot \text{atm}}{\text{K} \cdot \text{mol}} \times 523 \text{ K}} = 0.0437 \text{ mol}$

11.95 Molar mass; all the others are needed in the ideal gas equation.

11.96 At STP, any gas has a temperature of 0°C = 273.15 K and a pressure of 1 atm.

(a) $V = \dfrac{nRT}{P} = \dfrac{5.38 \text{ mol} \times 0.0821 \dfrac{\text{L} \cdot \text{atm}}{\text{K} \cdot \text{mol}} \times 273.15 \text{ K}}{1 \text{ atm}} = 121 \text{ L}$

(b) $859 \text{ mL} \times \dfrac{1 \text{ L}}{1000 \text{ mL}} = 0.859 \text{ L}$

$n = \dfrac{PV}{RT} = \dfrac{1 \text{ atm} \times 0.859 \text{ L}}{0.0821 \dfrac{\text{L} \cdot \text{atm}}{\text{K} \cdot \text{mol}} \times 273.15 \text{ K}} = 0.0383 \text{ mol}$

(c) $n = \dfrac{PV}{RT} = \dfrac{1\ \text{atm} \times 0.518\ \text{L}}{0.0821\ \dfrac{\text{L} \cdot \text{atm}}{\text{K} \cdot \text{mol}} \times 273.15\ \text{K}} = 0.0231\ \text{mol}$

11.97 In each case, solve the ideal gas equation for the unknown quantity.

<u>Gas A</u>

$757\ \text{mm Hg} \times \dfrac{1\ \text{atm}}{760\ \text{mm Hg}} = 0.996\ \text{atm}$

$952\ \text{mL} \times \dfrac{1\ \text{L}}{1000\ \text{mL}} = 0.952\ \text{L}$

$T = \dfrac{PV}{nR} = \dfrac{0.996\ \text{atm} \times 0.952\ \text{L}}{0.300\ \text{mol} \times 0.0821\ \dfrac{\text{L} \cdot \text{atm}}{\text{K} \cdot \text{mol}}} = 38.5\ \text{K}$

$38.5\ \text{K} - 273.15 = -234.7°\text{C}$

<u>Gas B</u>

$27.0°\text{C} + 273.15 = 300.2\ \text{K}$

$V = \dfrac{nRT}{P} = \dfrac{5.00\ \text{mol} \times 0.0821\ \dfrac{\text{L} \cdot \text{atm}}{\text{K} \cdot \text{mol}} \times 300.2\ \text{K}}{1.20\ \text{atm}} = 103\ \text{L}$

<u>Gas C</u>

$800.0\ \text{mm Hg} \times \dfrac{1\ \text{atm}}{760.0\ \text{mm Hg}} = 1.053\ \text{atm}$

$n = \dfrac{PV}{RT} = \dfrac{1.053\ \text{atm} \times 1.20\ \text{L}}{0.0821\ \dfrac{\text{L} \cdot \text{atm}}{\text{K} \cdot \text{mol}} \times 298\ \text{K}} = 0.0516\ \text{mol}$

<u>Gas D</u>

$750\ \text{mL} \times \dfrac{1\ \text{L}}{1000\ \text{mL}} = 0.750\ \text{L}$

$0.0°\text{C} + 273.15 = 273.2\ \text{K}$

$P = \dfrac{nRT}{V} = \dfrac{0.0875\ \text{mol} \times 0.0821\ \dfrac{\text{L} \cdot \text{atm}}{\text{K} \cdot \text{mol}} \times 273.2\ \text{K}}{0.750\ \text{L}} = 2.62\ \text{atm}$

11.98 Less dense, because the molecules in gases are farther apart than the molecules in liquids and solids, resulting in less mass in a given volume and therefore lower density.

11.99 Step 1: $P_i = 1\ \text{atm}$ $P_f = 1\ \text{atm} = P_i$

   $V_i = 2.40\ \text{L}$ $V_f = 7.20\ \text{L}$

   $n_i = ?$ $n_f = ? = n_i$

   $T_i = 22°\text{C} = 295\ \text{K}$ $T_f = ?$

Step 2: $\dfrac{P_iV_i}{n_iT_i} = \dfrac{P_fV_f}{n_fT_f}$

$\dfrac{\cancel{P_i}V_i}{\cancel{n_i}T_i} = \dfrac{\cancel{P_i}V_f}{\cancel{n_i}T_f}$

$\dfrac{V_i}{T_i} = \dfrac{V_f}{T_f}$

Step 3: $T_f = \dfrac{T_iV_f}{V_i} = \dfrac{295 \text{ K} \times 7.20 \cancel{L}}{2.40 \cancel{L}} = 885 \text{ K}$

$885 \text{ K} - 273.15 = 612°\text{C}$

11.100 Use the ideal gas law solved for R, after converting the mass to moles and the temperature to kelvins.

$$4.505 \text{ g } \cancel{CO_2} \times \dfrac{1 \text{ mol}}{44.009 \text{ g } \cancel{CO_2}} = 0.1024 \text{ mol}$$

$$23°\text{C} + 273.15 = 296 \text{ K}$$

$$R = \dfrac{PV}{nT} = \dfrac{0.9960 \text{ atm} \times 2.50 \text{ L}}{0.1024 \text{ mol} \times 296 \text{ K}} = 0.0821 \dfrac{\text{L} \cdot \text{atm}}{\text{K} \cdot \text{mol}}$$

11.101 (a) $25.0°\text{C} + 273.15 = 298.2 \text{ K}$

(b) $5.00 \text{ gallons} \times \dfrac{3.785 \text{ L}}{1 \text{ gallon}} = 18.9 \text{ L}$

(c) $755 \text{ mm Hg} \times \dfrac{1 \text{ atm}}{760 \text{ mm Hg}} = 0.993 \text{ atm}$

11.102 In the ideal gas law, pressure must be expressed in units of <u>atmospheres</u>, volume must be expressed in units of <u>liters</u>, temperature must be expressed in <u>kelvins</u>, and n represents the number of <u>moles</u>.

11.103 $\dfrac{5}{9} \times (32°\text{F} - 32) = 0°\text{C} + 273.15 = 273 \text{ K}$

$\dfrac{5}{9} \times (80°\text{F} - 32) = 27°\text{C} + 273.15 = 300 \text{ K}$

Step 1: $P_i = 2.20 \text{ atm}$ $P_f = ?$
$V_i = ?$ $V_f = ? = V_i$
$n_i = ?$ $n_f = ? = n_i$
$T_i = 273 \text{ K}$ $T_f = 300 \text{ K}$

Step 2: $\dfrac{P_iV_i}{n_iT_i} = \dfrac{P_fV_f}{n_fT_f}$

$\dfrac{P_i\cancel{V_i}}{\cancel{n_i}T_i} = \dfrac{P_f\cancel{V_i}}{\cancel{n_i}T_f}$

$\dfrac{P_i}{T_i} = \dfrac{P_f}{T_f}$

Step 3: $P_f = \dfrac{T_f P_i}{T_i} = \dfrac{300\ K \times 2.20\ atm}{273\ K} = 2.42\ atm$

11.104 $23°C + 273.15 = 296\ K$

$$n = \frac{PV}{RT} = \frac{1.2\ atm \times 60.8\ L}{0.0821\dfrac{L \cdot atm}{K \cdot mol} \times 296\ K} = 3.0\ mol$$

$$\frac{84.0\ g}{3.0\ mol} = 28\ g/mol$$

11.105 False. Because the relationship between P, V, T, and n in an ideal gas is independent of the identity of the gas.

11.106 Because density is mass/volume, use the ideal gas law expressed in terms of molar mass and sample mass, and manipulate the equation so that m/V is alone on one side of the equals sign.

$22°C + 273.15 = 295\ K$

$$\frac{m}{MM} = \frac{PV}{RT}$$

$$\frac{m}{V} = \frac{(MM)P}{RT} = \frac{4.003\ g/mol \times 1.52\ atm}{0.0821\dfrac{L \cdot atm}{K \cdot mol} \times 295\ K} = 2.51\ g/L$$

11.107 (a) For this stoichiometry problem, you need the molar mass of $KClO_3$, which is 122.5 g/mole.

$$500.0\ g\ KClO_3 \times \frac{1\ mol\ KClO_3}{122.5\ g\ KClO_3} \times \frac{3\ mol\ O_2}{2\ mol\ KClO_3} = 6.123\ mol\ O_2$$

(b) $24.0°C + 273.15 = 297.2\ K$

$$750.0\ mm\ Hg \times \frac{1\ atm}{760.0\ mm\ Hg} = 0.9868\ atm$$

$$V = \frac{nRT}{P} = \frac{6.123\ mol \times .0821\dfrac{L \cdot atm}{K \cdot mol} \times 297.2\ K}{0.9868\ atm} = 151.4\ L$$

(c) STP means $0°C = 273.15\ K$ and 1 atm.

$$V = \frac{6.123\ mol \times .0821\dfrac{L \cdot atm}{K \cdot mol} \times 273.15\ K}{1\ atm} = 137.3\ L$$

11.108 In an ideal gas, the molecules are considered to have no <u>intermolecular</u> forces.

11.109 (a) If the temperature of a gas is doubled while the pressure is kept constant, the volume of the gas <u>doubles</u>. (Volume is directly proportional to temperature.)

(b) If the pressure of a gas is halved while the temperature is kept constant, the volume of the gas <u>doubles</u>. (Volume is inversely proportional to pressure.)

11.110 $T = \dfrac{PV}{nR} = \dfrac{8.500\ atm \times 12.00\ L}{3.200\ mol \times 0.0821\dfrac{L \cdot atm}{K \cdot mol}} = 388.2\ K$

$388.2\ K - 273.15 = 115.1°C$

11.111 (a) $MM = \dfrac{m_{sample}RT}{PV} = \dfrac{1.25 \text{ g} \times 0.0821 \dfrac{\text{L} \cdot \text{atm}}{\text{K} \cdot \text{mol}} \times 273 \text{ K}}{0.400 \text{ atm} \times 2.50 \text{ L}} = 28.0 \text{ g} / \text{mol}$

(b) The molar mass of CH_2 is 14.027 g/mol.

$$\dfrac{28.0 \text{ g} / \text{mol}}{14.027 \text{ g} / \text{mol}} = 2.00$$

$$C_{2 \times 1}H_{2 \times 2} = C_2H_4$$

11.112 $850 \text{ mL} \times \dfrac{1 \text{ L}}{1000 \text{ mL}} = 0.850 \text{ L}$

$750 \text{ mm Hg} \times \dfrac{1 \text{ atm}}{760 \text{ mm Hg}} = 0.987 \text{ atm}$

$1200 \text{ mm Hg} \times \dfrac{1 \text{ atm}}{760 \text{ mm Hg}} = 1.58 \text{ atm}$

Step 1: $\quad P_i = 0.987 \text{ atm} \qquad P_f = 1.58 \text{ atm}$
$\qquad\quad V_i = 0.850 \text{ L} \qquad\quad V_f = ?$
$\qquad\quad n_i = ? \qquad\qquad\quad n_f = ? = n_i$
$\qquad\quad T_i = 300 \text{ K} \qquad\quad\; T_f = 200 \text{ K}$

Step 2: $\dfrac{P_iV_i}{n_iT_i} = \dfrac{P_fV_f}{n_fT_f}$

$\qquad\quad \dfrac{P_iV_i}{\cancel{n_i}T_i} = \dfrac{P_fV_f}{\cancel{n_i}T_f}$

$\qquad\quad \dfrac{P_iV_i}{T_i} = \dfrac{P_fV_f}{T_f}$

Step 3: $V_f = \dfrac{T_fP_iV_i}{T_iP_f} = \dfrac{200 \text{ K} \times 0.987 \text{ atm} \times 0.850 \text{ L}}{300 \text{ K} \times 1.58 \text{ atm}} = 0.354 \text{ L} = 354 \text{ mL}$

11.113 (a) $30.2 \text{ in. Hg} \times \dfrac{760 \text{ mm Hg}}{29.9 \text{ in. Hg}} = 768 \text{ mm Hg}$

(b) $890.0 \text{ mm Hg} \times \dfrac{1 \text{ atm}}{760 \text{ mm Hg}} = 1.17 \text{ atm}$

(c) $300.0 \text{ lb / in.}^2 \text{ Hg} \times \dfrac{1 \text{ atm}}{14.696 \text{ lb / in.}^2} = 20.41 \text{ atm}$

11.114 $28°C + 273.15 = 301 \text{ K}$

$P = \dfrac{nRT}{V} = \dfrac{8.50 \text{ mol} \times 0.0821 \dfrac{\text{L} \cdot \text{atm}}{\text{K} \cdot \text{mol}} \times 301 \text{ K}}{25.0 \text{ L}} = 8.40 \text{ atm}$

11.115 $40°C + 273.15 = 313 \text{ K}$

$MM = \dfrac{m_{sample}RT}{PV} = \dfrac{48.3 \text{ g} \times 0.0821 \dfrac{\text{L} \cdot \text{atm}}{\text{K} \cdot \text{mol}} \times 313 \text{ K}}{3.10 \text{ atm} \times 10.0 \text{ L}} = 40.0 \text{ g} / \text{mol}$

11.116 (a) Step 1: $P_i = 6.80$ atm $P_f = ?$
                $V_i = ?$ $V_f = 2\,V_i$
                $n_i = ?$ $n_f = n_i$
                $T_i = ?$ $T_f = T_i$

Step 2: $\dfrac{P_i V_i}{n_i T_i} = \dfrac{P_f V_f}{n_f T_f}$

$\dfrac{P_i V_i}{n_i T_i} = \dfrac{P_f 2V_i}{n_i T_i}$

$P_i = 2\,P_f$

Step 3: $P_f = \dfrac{P_i}{2} = \dfrac{6.80\text{ atm}}{2} = 3.40$ atm

Doubling the volume halves the pressure. Pressure is inversely proportional to volume.

(b) Step 1: $P_i = 6.80$ atm $P_f = ?$
                $V_i = ?$ $V_f = V_i/4 = 0.250\,V_i$
                $n_i = ?$ $n_f = n_i$
                $T_i = ?$ $T_f = T_i$

Step 2: $\dfrac{P_i V_i}{n_i T_i} = \dfrac{P_f V_f}{n_f T_f}$

$\dfrac{P_i V_i}{n_i T_i} = \dfrac{P_f(0.250\,V_i)}{n_i T_i}$

$P_i = 0.250\,P_f$

Step 3: $P_f = \dfrac{P_i}{0.250} = \dfrac{6.80\text{ atm}}{0.250} = 27.2$ atm

Decreasing the volume by a factor of 4 increases the pressure by a factor of 4. Pressure is inversely proportional to volume.

11.117 Because you are given density, which is mass/volume, use the ideal gas law expressed in terms of molar mass and sample mass. That way you can use the density value for m/V in the equation.

$0°C + 273.15 = 273$ K

$$\frac{m}{MM} = \frac{PV}{RT}$$

$$MM = \frac{mRT}{PV} = \frac{m}{V} \times \frac{RT}{P} = 1.52\,\frac{\text{g}}{\text{L}} \times \frac{0.0821\dfrac{\text{L} \cdot \text{atm}}{\text{K} \cdot \text{mol}} \times 273\,\text{K}}{1\text{ atm}} = 34.1 \text{ g / mol}$$

11.118 Because gas molecules don't attract one another, they move about freely until they fill the container. In liquids and solids, the molecules are held relatively close to one another by intermolecular attractive forces and therefore cannot expand to fill the container.

11.119 (a) The volume is halved because volume is inversely proportional to pressure.

(b) The volume is doubled because volume is directly proportional to temperature.

(c) The volume remains unchanged because the two changes cancel each other. Doubling P changes the volume to $0.5\ V_i$, and doubling T changes the volume to $2\ V_i$: $(0.5 \times 2)V_i = V_i$.

CHAPTER

12

Solutions

12.1 See solution in textbook.

12.2 In each case, the solvent is the component present in the greater (or greatest) amount.
    (a) Water solvent (70%); acetone solute (30%).
    (b) Nitrogen solvent (78%); oxygen, water vapor, other gases solutes (none can be greater than 100% − 78% = 22%).
    (c) Iron solvent; chromium, nickel, carbon solutes.
    (d) Water solvent; aspirin solute.

12.3 Because 135-proof vodka is $135/2 = 67.5\%$ alcohol and $100.0\% − 67.5\% = 32.5\%$ water, alcohol is the major component and therefore the solvent.

12.4 See solution in textbook.

12.5 Less than in water. Because carbon tetrachloride is a nonpolar molecule, it does not attract ions. With little or no attraction between the Na^+ and Cl^- ions and the carbon tetrachloride molecules, there is little or no energy released in the solvation step.

12.6 Greater for $MgCl_2$ because the attraction between the 2+ magnesium ions and the negative chloride ions is stronger than the attraction between the 1+ sodium ions and the chloride ions. The attractive force between oppositely charged particles increases as the magnitude of the charge increases.

12.7 See solution in textbook.

12.8 Larger for the solid ionic solute. Because gaseous molecules have very little attraction for one another and are already separated, $\Delta E_{\text{solute separation}}$ is negligible for a gaseous solute.

12.9 Because $\Delta E_{\text{solvation}}$ is the only negative energy value when a solute dissolves, a more negative ΔE_{total} usually means a more negative $\Delta E_{\text{solvation}}$, which measures how strongly solute and solvent particles attract one another. The stronger this attraction, the more likely the solute is to dissolve in the solvent.

12.10 (a) Because Mg is in group IIA (2) of the periodic table and therefore has two valence electrons that it easily gives up to acquire a completely filled valence shell. Losing two electrons changes the electrically neutral Mg atom to the 2+ ion.
    (b) $\Delta E_{\text{solute separation}}$ is a measure of the energy needed to break up the solute lattice. Because the attraction between Mg^{2+} ions and Cl^- ions is stronger than the attraction between Na^+ ions and Cl^- ions (because of Coulomb's law), more energy is needed to break the $MgCl_2$ lattice, making $\Delta E_{\text{solute separation}}$ greater for $MgCl_2$.

(c) Even though $\Delta E_{\text{solute separation}}$ is greater for $MgCl_2$ than for NaCl, $\Delta E_{\text{solvation}}$ is much larger for Mg^{2+} than for Na^+ because the strength of the ion–dipole attractions with water increases as the magnitude of the ionic charge increases.

12.11 See solution in textbook.

12.12 The mass of 500 mL of water is

$$500.0 \text{ mL water} \times \frac{1.000 \text{ g water}}{1 \text{ mL water}} = 500.0 \text{ g water}$$

The KCl solubility is

$$500.0 \text{ g water} \times \frac{56.7 \text{ g KCl}}{100.0 \text{ g water}} = 284 \text{ g KCl}$$

12.13 The biggest difference is in the solute-separation step. Gases do not exist in a lattice, which means the solute particles are already separated. Hence, $\Delta E_{\text{solute separation}}$ is essentially zero for gases. For both solvent separation and solvation, the energy needed in dissolution of a gas is roughly the same as the energy needed in dissolution of a solid.

12.14 See solution in textbook.

12.15 $25.0 \text{ g glucose} \times \dfrac{1 \text{ mol glucose}}{180.155 \text{ g glucose}} \times \dfrac{1 \text{ L solution}}{2.55 \text{ mol glucose}} \times \dfrac{1000 \text{ mL solution}}{1 \text{ L solution}}$

$$= 54.4 \text{ mL solution}$$

12.16 $200.0 \text{ mL solution} \times \dfrac{1 \text{ L solution}}{1000 \text{ mL solution}} \times \dfrac{2.00 \text{ mol ethanol}}{1 \text{ L solution}} \times \dfrac{46.068 \text{ g ethanol}}{1 \text{ mol ethanol}}$

$$= 18.4 \text{ g ethanol}$$

12.17 $400.0 \text{ mL solution} \times \dfrac{1 \text{ L solution}}{1000 \text{ mL solution}} \times \dfrac{2.00 \text{ mol NaCl}}{1 \text{ L solution}} \times \dfrac{58.443 \text{ g NaCl}}{1 \text{ mol NaCl}}$

$$= 46.8 \text{ g NaCl required}$$

After placing this amount of solid NaCl in a 400-mL volumetric flask, add some water, swirl to dissolve the solid, and then add enough water to raise the level to the 400.0-mL mark. Because the NaCl takes up some volume (even after it has dissolved), the amount of water added is slightly less than 400.0 mL.

12.18 First determine the number of moles of NaCl in 400.0 mL of a 2.00 M NaCl solution:

$$400.0 \text{ mL solution} \times \frac{1 \text{ L solution}}{1000 \text{ mL solution}} \times \frac{2.00 \text{ mol NaCl}}{1 \text{ L solution}} = 0.800 \text{ mol NaCl}$$

Now determine what volume of the stock solution contains this number of moles of NaCl:

$$0.800 \text{ mol NaCl} \times \frac{1 \text{ L solution}}{3.00 \text{ mol}} \times \frac{1000 \text{ mL solution}}{1 \text{ L solution}} = 267 \text{ mL stock solution}$$

Thus to make the solution you need, you must transfer 267 mL of the stock solution to a 400-mL volumetric flask and dilute to the 400-mL mark with water.

Alternatively, you could use the dilution equation to determine what volume of stock solution you need:

$$V_{\text{stock solution}} = \frac{M_{\text{diluted solution}} \times V_{\text{diluted solution}}}{M_{\text{stock solution}}} = \frac{2.00 \text{ M} \times 400.0 \text{ mL}}{3.00 \text{ M}} = 267 \text{ mL}$$

12.19 See solution in textbook.

12.20 The appropriate percent composition is percent by volume because both component amounts are given in volume units.

$$\text{Percent by volume} = \frac{\text{mL solute}}{\text{mL solution}} \times 100 = \frac{90.0 \text{ mL ethanol}}{1000 \text{ mL solution}} \times 100 = 9.00 \text{ vol \%}$$

12.21 $65.0 \text{ g solution} \times \dfrac{12.5 \text{ g sucrose}}{100 \text{ g solution}} = 8.12 \text{ g sucrose}$

12.22 See solution in textbook.

12.23 See solution in textbook.

12.24 $255.0 \text{ mL} \times \dfrac{1 \text{ L}}{1000 \text{ mL}} = 0.2550 \text{ L of solution}$

Moles of glucose = Volume of glucose solution in liters $\times$ Molarity of glucose solution

$$= 0.2550 \text{ L} \times \frac{0.998 \text{ mol}}{1 \text{ L}} = 0.254 \text{ mol}$$

12.25 Number of moles = Volume of solution in liters $\times$ Molarity of solution

$$\text{Volume} = \frac{\text{Number of moles}}{\text{Molarity}} = \frac{0.500 \text{ mol}}{0.350 \text{ mol}/\text{L}} = 1.43 \text{ L}$$

You can also solve this problem by using molarity as a conversion factor:

$$0.500 \text{ mol BaCl}_2 \times \frac{1 \text{ L solution}}{0.350 \text{ mol BaCl}_2} = 1.43 \text{ L solution}$$

12.26 You know from the solubility rules of Table 7.1 of the textbook that $BaCl_2$ completely dissociates in solution, which means each mole of $BaCl_2$ yields 2 moles of Cl^- ions.

$$0.500 \text{ mol Cl}^- \times \frac{1 \text{ mol BaCl}_2}{2 \text{ mol Cl}^-} \times \frac{1 \text{ L solution}}{0.350 \text{ mol BaCl}_2} = 0.714 \text{ L solution}$$

12.27 See solution in textbook.

12.28 $\text{Percent yield} = \dfrac{\text{Actual yield}}{\text{Theoretical yield}} \times 100 = \dfrac{8.24 \text{ g}}{9.70 \text{ g}} \times 100 = 84.9\%$

12.29 Step 1: $Fe^{3+}(aq) + 3 \text{ OH}^-(aq) \longrightarrow Fe(OH)_3(s)$

Step 2: $20.0 \text{ g Fe(OH)}_3 \times \dfrac{1 \text{ mol Fe(OH)}_3}{106.9 \text{ g Fe(OH)}_3} = 0.187 \text{ mol Fe(OH)}_3$

Step 3: $0.187 \text{ mol Fe(OH)}_3 \times \dfrac{1 \text{ mol Fe}^{3+}}{1 \text{ mol Fe(OH)}_3} = 0.187 \text{ mol Fe}^{3+}$

$$0.187 \text{ mol Fe(OH)}_3 \times \frac{3 \text{ mol OH}^-}{1 \text{ mol Fe(OH)}_3} = 0.561 \text{ mol OH}^-$$

Step 4: $0.187 \text{ mol Fe}^{3+} \times \dfrac{1 \text{ mol Fe(NO}_3)_3}{1 \text{ mol Fe}^{3+}} \times \dfrac{1 \text{ L Fe(NO}_3)_3 \text{ solution}}{0.250 \text{ mol Fe(NO}_3)_3}$

$$= 0.748 \text{ L Fe(NO}_3)_3 \text{ solution}$$

$$0.561 \text{ mol OH}^- \times \frac{1 \text{ mol Ba(OH)}_2}{2 \text{ mol OH}^-} \times \frac{1 \text{ L Ba(OH)}_2 \text{ solution}}{0.150 \text{ mol Ba(OH)}_2} = 1.87 \text{ L Ba(OH)}_2 \text{ solution}$$

Combine 0.748 L of the iron(III) nitrate solution with 1.87 L of the barium hydroxide solution, and then filter off the precipitated $Fe(OH)_3$. The amount to be collected for a 67.5% yield is

$$\text{Actual yield} = \frac{\%\text{ yield} \times \text{Theoretical yield}}{100} = \frac{67.5\% \times 20.0\text{ g}}{100} = 13.5\text{ g }Fe(OH)_3$$

12.30 See solution in textbook.

12.31 Step 1: $H^+(aq) + OH^-(aq) \longrightarrow H_2O(l)$

Step 2: $0.03860\text{ L NaOH solution} \times \dfrac{0.100\text{ mol }OH^-}{1\text{ L NaOH solution}} = 0.00386\text{ mol }OH^-$

Step 3: $0.00386\text{ mol }OH^- \times \dfrac{1\text{ mol }H^+}{1\text{ mol }OH^-} \times \dfrac{1\text{ mol }H_3PO_4}{3\text{ mol }H^+} = 1.29 \times 10^{-3}\text{ mol }H_3PO_4$

Step 4: $\dfrac{1.29 \times 10^{-3}\text{ mol }H_3PO_4}{0.05000\text{ L}} = 0.0258\text{ M }H_3PO_4$

12.32 (a) Step 1: $H^+(aq) + OH^-(aq) \longrightarrow H_2O(l)$

Step 2: $0.02748\text{ L NaOH solution} \times \dfrac{1.000\text{ mol }OH^-}{1\text{ L NaOH solution}} = 0.02748\text{ mol }OH^-$

Step 3: $0.02748\text{ mol }OH^- \times \dfrac{1\text{ mol }H^+}{1\text{ mol }OH^-} \times \dfrac{1\text{ mol acid}}{1\text{ mol }H^+} = 0.02748\text{ mol acid}$

Step 4: $\dfrac{0.02748\text{ mol acid}}{0.02500\text{ L}} = 1.099\text{ M acid}$

(b) $\dfrac{1.65\text{ g acid}}{0.02748\text{ mol acid}} = 60.0\text{ g/mol}$

(c) The molar mass of the empirical formula CH_2O is $12.001 + (2 \times 1.0079) + 15.999 = 30.016$ g/mol. That the molar mass calculated in (b) is just about twice this molar mass for the empirical formula tells you the molecular formula must be twice the empirical formula, or $C_2H_4O_2$ (Section 8.5). Writing the one acidic H separately gives the formula $HC_2H_3O_2$. Because $C_2H_3O_2^-$ is the acetate ion, the acid is acetic acid.

12.33 See solution in textbook.

12.34 See solution in textbook.

12.35 When the vapor pressure of an aqueous solution at sea level is 760 mm Hg (1 atm), the solution boils. Therefore one way to determine the temperature at which the solution has a vapor pressure of 760 mm Hg is to determine the boiling point.

That $Ca(NO_3)_2$ is dissolved tells you the boiling point is higher than 100.0°C. Therefore calculate how much the dissolved salt elevates the boiling point and you have the temperature at which the vapor pressure is 760 mm Hg.

Each mole of calcium nitrate dissociates in water to produce 3 moles of solute particles: $Ca(NO_3)_2 \longrightarrow Ca^{2+} + 2\,NO_3^-$. The number of moles of solute particles in solution is therefore

$$100.0\text{ g }Ca(NO_3)_2 \times \frac{1\text{ mol }Ca(NO_3)_2}{164.1\text{ g }Ca(NO_3)_2} \times \frac{3\text{ mol solute particles}}{1\text{ mol }Ca(NO_3)_2} = 1.828\text{ mol solute particles}$$

This amount of solute particles causes a boiling-point elevation of

$$\Delta T_b = \frac{0.52\ \dfrac{C° \cdot \text{kg solvent}}{\text{mol solute particles}} \times 1.828\text{ mol solute particles}}{0.4500\text{ kg solvent}} = 2.1\ C°$$

The elevated boiling point is therefore 100.0°C + 2.1°C = 102.1°C, and it is at this temperature that the vapor pressure is 760 mm Hg.

12.36 That the phase change liquid → solid is happening tells you the solution is freezing. You know from Table 12.2 of the textbook that the normal freezing point for cyclohexane is 6.47°C and thus can calculate how much the freezing point has been depressed. Then use that information in the ΔT_f expression to determine the molar amount of solute particles:

$6.47°C - 2.70°C = 3.77\ C° = \Delta T_f$

$$\text{Mol solute particles} = \frac{\Delta T_f \times \text{kg solvent}}{K_f} = \frac{3.77\ \cancel{C°} \times 0.225\ \cancel{\text{kg solvent}}}{20.0\dfrac{\cancel{C°} \cdot \cancel{\text{kg solvent}}}{\text{mol solute particles}}} = 0.0424\ \text{mol solute}$$

The molar mass is

$$\frac{45.0\ \text{g}}{0.0424\ \text{mol}} = 1.06 \times 10^3\ \text{g/mol}$$

12.37 A solute is any substance in a solution other than the solvent.
A solvent is the substance in a solution present in the greatest amount.
A solution is a homogeneous mixture of two or more substances.

12.38 The mixture is not a solution because it is not homogeneous at the molecular level. It consists of flour particles and sugar particles in a nonuniform mixture.

12.39 Only if there are no visible bubbles of CO_2 gas. If such bubbles are visible, the CO_2 is in the gas phase and you have a heterogeneous mixture. If there are no bubbles visible, then the soft drink is indeed a solution of CO_2 gas, sugar, coloring agents, and so forth dissolved in water.

12.40 It is appropriate to call the atmosphere a solution because it is a homogeneous mixture of $N_2(g)$, $O_2(g)$, $H_2O(g)$, and other gases.

12.41 As noted in Section 12.1 of the textbook, vinegar is mostly water. Therefore the solvent is water because it is the component present in the greater amount. The solute is the acetic acid dissolved in the water.

12.42 A homogeneous mixture of two or more solids. Metal alloys, such as brass and steel, are examples.

12.43 (a) Solution; the two molten metals mix completely and uniformly, with the result that the cooled solid is uniform in composition and therefore a solution.
(b) Solution; the filtering removes anything not in solution.
(c) Heterogeneous mixture; visual inspection shows you the non-uniformity.
(d) Solution; what you exhale is a solution of various gases, just as the atmosphere you inhale is.
(e) Heterogeneous mixture; no matter how much you shake, sooner or later the two components separate, telling you a true solution never formed.

12.44 Because the gases are present in equal amounts, you may call either one the solute and the other the solvent.

12.45 Heterogeneous mixture because each solid exists only in its own lattice and cannot mix into the other lattice.

12.46 The + end of the dipole moment vector is incorrectly shown at the more electronegative oxygen atom. The + indicates the $\delta+$ portion of the molecule, and the head of the arrow indicates the $\delta-$ portion. Because O is more electronegative than H, the vector should be reversed:

12.47 Intermolecular attractive forces are responsible for gas molecules' coming together and condensing to the liquid and sold phases. Therefore any everyday instance of liquid H_2O—raindrops, the ocean—or solid H_2O—ice, snow—is evidence of these attractive forces.

12.48 Only the gas phase because intermolecular attractive forces are what allow the liquid and solid phases to form.

12.49 When a piece of NaCl is melted, the lattice is broken and the Na^+ and Cl^- ions become mobile. The same thing happens when NaCl dissolves in water. The difference is that in melting, the energy provided by the heat breaks the bonds, and in dissolving, the solute–solvent interactions break the bonds.

12.50 Because in melting there are no solute–solvent interactions to provide any of the energy required to break apart the ion lattice. When NaCl is dissolving, there are solute–solvent interactions that aid in the dissolution.

12.51 Absorbs energy because attractive forces must be overcome. Overcoming an attractive force *always* requires an input of energy.

12.52 Absorbs energy because the attractive forces between solvent molecules must be overcome. Overcoming an attractive force *always* requires an input of energy.

12.53 The surrounding of solute particles by molecules of water.

12.54 Releases energy because attractive forces are formed between the solute particles and the water molecules. Forming an attractive force *always* releases energy.

12.55 (1) Solute separation—solute–solute attractive forces overcome (solute lattice broken apart):

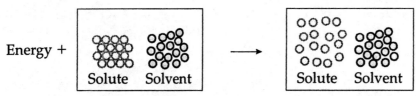

(2) Solvent separation—solvent–solvent attractive forces overcome:

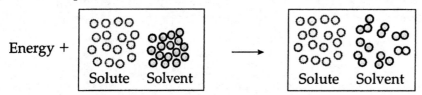

(3) Solvation—solute–solvent attractive forces formed:

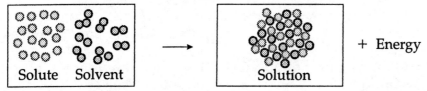

12.56 Breaking up the NaCl lattice because ionic bonds are always stronger than hydrogen bonds. The stronger a bond is the greater the amount of energy required to break it.

12.57 The attraction between the ions and water molecules. The Na^+ ions are attracted to the $\delta-$ end of the water molecules; the Cl^- ions are attracted to the $\delta+$ ends of the water molecules. Once the ions are surrounded by H_2O molecules, there is very little tendency to re-form the NaCl lattice.

12.58 An ion–dipole force. The force acts between the positively charged Na$^+$ and the negatively charged end of a water molecule:

With the chloride ion, the ion–dipole force acts between the ion and the positively charged end of a water molecule:

12.59 The water molecule forms a hydrogen bond with the alcohol. The bond is either between the O of the alcohol –OH group and one water H or between the H of the alcohol –OH group and the water O:

This interaction is rightly called hydration because it is a solvation process with water as the solvent.

12.60 Because solvation is the only energy-releasing step in the process. If the amount of energy released during this step is greater than the amount of energy absorbed during solute separation and solvent separation, the solute will probably dissolve. If the amount of energy released during this step is less than the amount absorbed during solute separation and solvent separation, the solute will probably not dissolve.

12.61 Probably not soluble at all. The step in which solute–solvent interactions take place is the solvation step. Because the energy released during this step is a lot less than the energy absorbed for solute separation and solvent separation, ΔE_{total} is positive, indicating the solid is insoluble in this solvent.

12.62 It is possible because the amount of energy released during the solvation step is greater than the amount absorbed during the solute-separation and solvent-separation steps. The excess energy is in the form of thermal energy, and so the water heats up.

12.63 When the energy released in the solvation step is less than the energy required in the solute-separation and solvent-separation steps, the solution components remove heat from the water, and therefore the water gets colder.

12.64 Insoluble, because ΔE_{total} is positive. Hydration, which is the solvation step with water as the solvent, is the only energy-releasing step, making $\Delta E_{solvation}$ negative. (Both

$\Delta E_{\text{solute separation}}$ and $\Delta E_{\text{solvent separation}}$ are positive numbers.) Because $\Delta E_{\text{solute separation}}$ is so much greater than $\Delta E_{\text{solvation}}$, ΔE_{total} is positive.

12.65 Because water molecules are polar and hexane molecules are nonpolar. The Na^+ and Cl^- ions are strongly attracted to the $\delta+$ and $\delta-$ parts of the water molecules, and consequently the solvation step releases more energy than what is absorbed during solute separation and solvent separation. ΔE_{total} is negative, and the solid NaCl dissolves in water. The ions are not attracted to the nonpolar hexane molecules, and consequently the solvation step releases very little energy, less than what is absorbed during solute separation and solvent separation. ΔE_{total} is positive, and the solid NaCl does not dissolve in hexane.

12.66 The solvent-separation step because it takes far less energy to break the weak London forces between hexane molecules than to break the much stronger hydrogen bonds between water molecules.

12.67 $AlCl_3$ because hydration energy is a function of how strongly solute particles and solvent particles attract each other. Both $AlCl_3$ and NaCl are ionic compounds, and so the interaction with water molecules is an ion–dipole interaction. Because the attraction gets stronger with increasing charge on the ion, the Al^{3+}–H_2O attraction is stronger than the Na^+–H_2O attraction.

12.68 $\Delta E_{\text{solute separation}}$ for the less soluble compound would have to be much higher than $\Delta E_{\text{solute separation}}$ for the more soluble compound.

12.69 Polar solutes dissolve in polar solvents; nonpolar solutes dissolve in nonpolar solvents.

12.70 ΔE_{total} is the sum of the energies required for the solute-separation, solvent-separation, and solvation steps. It is important to know the value of ΔE_{total} because it is this value that predicts whether a compound is soluble or not. If ΔE_{total} is positive, the solute probably will not dissolve. If ΔE_{total} is negative, the solute probably will dissolve.

12.71 (a) Because attractive forces between solute particles are being broken.
   (b) Because attractive forces between solvent particles are being broken.
   (c) Because attractive forces between solute particles and solvent particles are being formed.
   (d) Soluble because ΔE_{total} is negative.
   (e) Warmer because the energy released in the solvation step is more than the energy absorbed in the solute-separation and solvent-separation steps. The excess energy released is heat energy that warms the solution.

12.72 That the ion is surrounded by and attracted to water molecules.

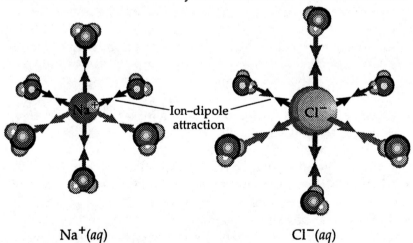

Na$^+$(aq)   Cl$^-$(aq)

12.73 B. The described difference means that $\Delta E_{\text{solute separation, A}}$ is larger than $\Delta E_{\text{solute separation, B}}$. That this is the only significant difference tells you that $\Delta E_{\text{solvent separation, A}} = \Delta E_{\text{solvent separation, B}}$ and $\Delta E_{\text{solvation, A}} = \Delta E_{\text{solvation, B}}$. Mathematically, this means that $\Delta E_{\text{total, B}}$ is more negative than

$\Delta E_{\text{total, A}}$. The more negative ΔE_{total}, the more soluble a compound. (Note that a number does not have to be negative in order to be "more negative." For instance, 3 is more negative than 4.)

12.74 The solute-separation step because there is no lattice to be broken in a gas solute. The gas molecules are already separated from one another.

12.75 The intermolecular attractive forces holding the liquid solute molecules are overcome. The step absorbs energy because attractive forces are being overcome.

12.76 CCl_4 is least soluble because it is a nonpolar molecule and therefore the only interactions possible between CCl_4 molecules and water molecules are relatively weak London forces. CH_3OH is most soluble because the presence of the –OH group means CH_3OH molecules can form relatively strong hydrogen bonds with water molecules.

12.77 Because the interactions between the nonpolar oil molecules and the solvent water molecules are not strong. Thus very little energy is released in the solvation step, and as a result, ΔE_{total} for the dissolution is likely to be positive, making the oil insoluble.

12.78 A measure of the amount of disorder in a system. The more ordered a system is, the lower its entropy. The more disordered a system is, the higher its entropy.

12.79 In order for anything to happen spontaneously, the entropy of the universe must increase.

12.80 The justification is that the probability of achieving a less-ordered state during any event is greater than the probability of achieving a more-ordered state. That the less-ordered state is the result means the entropy of the universe increases.

12.81 Because the state of higher entropy is the one in which the dye molecules are dispersed. There are many more ways to have the dye molecules randomly dispersed than to have them grouped together in the original blue drop.

12.82 Entropy is important only when ΔE_{total} is slightly positive. It is not important when ΔE_{total} is either negative (solute dissolves because there is enough energy) or very positive (entropy increase not enough to cancel unfavorable energy conditions).

12.83 True. The second law of thermodynamics tells you that anytime a process occurs spontaneously, the entropy of the universe increases.

12.84 Because NaCl is an ionic compound and hexane is a nonpolar compound, there are no significant solute–solvent interactions. Therefore ΔE_{total} is too positive for the entropy change to be the deciding factor.

12.85 Total chaos, in which everything has gone back to a totally random state.

12.86 (a) Solubility increases; (b) solubility decreases.

12.87 Increasing pressure increases the solubility of gaseous solutes because the increased pressure above the solution forces more solute molecules into solution.

12.88 The bends occur when nitrogen gas dissolved in the blood comes out of solution too rapidly as a diver ascends too quickly. The reason the gas comes out of solution is that the decrease in water pressure as the diver rises causes a decrease in the solubility of nitrogen.

12.89 The trend is an increase in solubility as temperature increases.

12.90 NaCl solubility increases very little as the temperature increases; this is indicated by the nearly horizontal graph for NaCl. Cerium(III) sulfate, $Ce_2(SO_4)_3$, violates the general trend by becoming less soluble as the temperature increases.

12.91 Aquatic life can survive only if the water it lives in contains dissolved O_2 gas. Discharging hot water heats all the water in the river or lake, and at the higher temperatures less O_2 gas can dissolve in the water.

12.92 Because all the dissolved CO_2 gas escapes from the liquid.

12.93 The sucrose solubility graph in the textbook tells you the solubility at 90°C is 420.0 g/100.0 g of water.

$$100.0 \text{ lb water} \times \frac{453.6 \text{ g water}}{1 \text{ lb water}} \times \frac{420.0 \text{ g sucrose}}{100.0 \text{ g water}} = 1.905 \times 10^5 \text{ g sucrose}$$

12.94 (a)

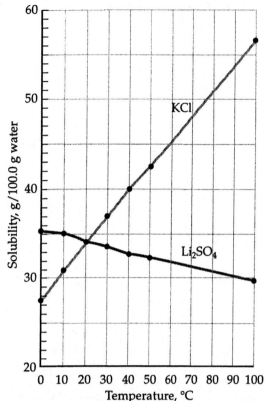

(b) Go to the 70°C line on the horizontal scale, and then move upward along that line until your finger intersects your Li_2SO_4 plot. Move your finger to the left edge of the graph and read solubility off the vertical scale—about 31.5 g/100 g water. The point where the vertical 70°C line intersects your KCl plot gives you the solubility of KCl at 70°C—about 48.2 g/100 g water.

(c) $75 \text{ g water} \times \dfrac{48.2 \text{ g KCl}}{100 \text{ g water}} = 36 \text{ g KCl}$

$75 \text{ g water} \times \dfrac{31.5 \text{ g } Li_2SO_4}{100 \text{ g water}} = 24 \text{ g } Li_2SO_4$

12.95 At 10°C:

$250.0 \text{ g water} \times \dfrac{35.0 \text{ g } Li_2SO_4}{100 \text{ g water}} = 87.5 \text{ g } Li_2SO_4$

At 50° C:

$250.0 \text{ g water} \times \dfrac{32.5 \text{ g } Li_2SO_4}{100 \text{ g water}} = 81.3 \text{ g } Li_2SO_4$

87.5 g − 81.3 g = 6.2 g more at 10°C.

12.96 The data in Problem 12.94 tell you the solubility of KCl at 40°C is 40.0 g/100 g water. This amount of KCl in 40°C water produces a saturated solution. First convert pounds of water to grams and then use solubility as a conversion factor:

$5.00 \text{ lb water} \times \dfrac{453.6 \text{ g water}}{1 \text{ lb water}} \times \dfrac{40.0 \text{ g KCl}}{100 \text{ g water}} = 907 \text{ g KCl}$

12.97 Problem 12.94 tells you that at 50°C the solubility of KCl is 42.6 g/100 g water.

$$2.00 \text{ L water} \times \frac{1000 \text{ mL water}}{1 \text{ L water}} \times \frac{1.00 \text{ g water}}{1 \text{ mL water}} \times \frac{42.6 \text{ g KCl}}{100 \text{ g water}} = 852 \text{ g KCl}$$

12.98 $CH_3-CH_2-CH_2-CH_2-CH_2-CH_2-CH_2-CH_2-CH_2-CH_2-CH_2-C \overset{\displaystyle O}{\underset{\displaystyle O^- Na^+}{\big\|}}$

Nonpolar hydrocarbon tail   **Polar head**

The nonpolar tail has an affinity for nonpolar molecules, such as grease and oil.

The polar head has an affinity for polar molecules, such as water.

12.99 Hydrophobic means "water-fearing"; hydrophilic means "water-loving."

12.100 The nonpolar hydrophobic tail of each soap molecule needs to be isolated from the water. With the soap molecules grouped together to form a sphere, the tails can be in the interior of the sphere, away from the water, and the polar heads making up the sphere surface keep water molecules away from the tails. If the micelle were flat and two-dimensional, the water would be in direct contact with the hydrophobic chains because there would be no protective surface formed by the polar heads.

12.101 By forming a micelle that keeps the hydrophobic portion of each soap molecule away from the water.

12.102 The oily, nonpolar dirt dissolves in the interior, hydrophobic region of the micelle and is washed away with the water-soluble micelle.

12.103 The hydrophobic portion is the hydrocarbon chain. The hydrophilic portion is

$$O-\overset{\displaystyle O}{\underset{\displaystyle O}{\overset{\displaystyle \|}{\underset{\displaystyle \|}{S}}}}-O^- \; Na^+.$$

12.104 Number of moles of solute in 1 L of solution: molarity = moles of solute/liter of solution.

12.105 You know from the definition of molarity that 1.00 L of a 1.00 M $CaCl_2$ solution contains 1.00 mole of $CaCl_2$. Because your assistant needs to know what mass of $CaCl_2$ to use, your first step is to determine the number of grams in 1.00 mole:

$$1.00 \text{ L solution} \times \frac{1.00 \text{ mol CaCl}_2}{1 \text{ L solution}} \times \frac{110 \text{ g CaCl}_2}{1 \text{ mol CaCl}_2} = 111.0 \text{ g CaCl}_2$$

Your instructions should therefore be, "Place 111.0 g of $CaCl_2$ in a 1-L volumetric flask, dissolve in about 500 mL of water, and then add enough water to bring the volume to the 1-L mark."

12.106 $1.00 \text{ L solution} \times \dfrac{1.00 \text{ mol C}_{12}\text{H}_{22}\text{O}_{11}}{1 \text{ L solution}} \times \dfrac{342.295 \text{ g C}_{12}\text{H}_{22}\text{O}_{11}}{1 \text{ mol C}_{12}\text{H}_{22}\text{O}_{11}} = 342 \text{ g C}_{12}\text{H}_{22}\text{O}_{11}$

Place 342 g of $C_{12}H_{22}O_{11}$ in the 1-L volumetric flask, add enough water to dissolve the $C_{12}H_{22}O_{11}$, and then add additional water to bring the volume to 1.00 L.

12.107 You know from the definition of molarity that 1.00 L of a 0.250 M sucrose solution contains 0.250 mole of sucrose. Because your assistant needs to know what mass of sucrose to use, your first step is to determine the number of grams in 0.250 mole:

$$1.00 \text{ L solution} \times \frac{0.250 \text{ mol C}_{12}\text{H}_{22}\text{O}_{11}}{1 \text{ L solution}} \times \frac{342.3 \text{ g C}_{12}\text{H}_{22}\text{O}_{11}}{1 \text{ mol C}_{12}\text{H}_{22}\text{O}_{11}} = 85.6 \text{ g C}_{12}\text{H}_{22}\text{O}_{11}$$

Your instructions should therefore be, "Place 85.6 g of sucrose in a 1-L volumetric flask, dissolve in about 500 mL of water, and then add enough water to bring the volume to the 1-L mark."

12.108 $0.500 \text{ L solution} \times \dfrac{1.50 \text{ mol } C_{12}H_{22}O_{11}}{1 \text{ L solution}} \times \dfrac{342.295 \text{ g } C_{12}H_{22}O_{11}}{1 \text{ mol } C_{12}H_{22}O_{11}} = 257 \text{ g } C_{12}H_{22}O_{11}$

Place 257 g of $C_{12}H_{22}O_{11}$ in the 0.50-L volumetric flask, dissolve in about 300 mL of water, and then add enough water to bring the volume to 0.50 L.

12.109 (a) $2.50 \text{ mol NaCl} \times \dfrac{58.443 \text{ g NaCl}}{1 \text{ mol NaCl}} = 146 \text{ g NaCl}$

(b) Yes. Proof:

$$\dfrac{2.50 \text{ mol NaCl}}{500.0 \text{ mL}} \times \dfrac{1000 \text{ mL}}{1 \text{ L}} = \dfrac{5.00 \text{ mol NaCl}}{\text{L}} = 5.00 \text{ M}$$

12.110 You fire him. To prepare a 2.00 M solution of NaCl, he should add just enough water to the 116.886 g of NaCl to bring *the total volume of solution* to 1.00 L. Adding exactly 1.00 L of water to the solid NaCl gives a total volume greater than 1.00 L because the NaCl, even when dissolved and therefore no longer visible, occupies some volume. As a result, the concentration is not 2.00 M but rather some value slightly less than 2.00 M.

12.111 $2500.0 \text{ mL} \times \dfrac{1 \text{ L}}{1000 \text{ mL}} \times \dfrac{0.250 \text{ mol NaCl}}{1 \text{ L}} \times \dfrac{58.443 \text{ g NaCl}}{1 \text{ mol NaCl}} = 36.5 \text{ g NaCl}$

12.112 $45.0 \text{ mL} \times \dfrac{1 \text{ L}}{1000 \text{ mL}} \times \dfrac{0.250 \text{ mol sucrose}}{1 \text{ L}} \times \dfrac{342.295 \text{ g sucrose}}{1 \text{ mol sucrose}} = 3.85 \text{ g sucrose}$

12.113 $5.00 \text{ g NaCl} \times \dfrac{1 \text{ mol NaCl}}{58.443 \text{ g NaCl}} \times \dfrac{1 \text{ L}}{1 \text{ mol NaCl}} \times \dfrac{1000 \text{ mL}}{1 \text{ L}} = 85.6 \text{ mL}$

12.114 $100.0 \text{ g glucose} \times \dfrac{1 \text{ mol glucose}}{180.1548 \text{ g glucose}} \times \dfrac{1 \text{ L}}{0.250 \text{ mol glucose}} \times \dfrac{1000 \text{ mL}}{1 \text{ L}} = 2.22 \times 10^3 \text{ mL}$

12.115 You need to know what volume of stock solution goes into a 250-mL volumetric flask. You can determine this volume either by calculating numbers of moles or by using the dilution equation. Working with moles, you find

$250.0 \text{ mL} \times \dfrac{1 \text{ L}}{1000 \text{ mL}} \times \dfrac{0.348 \text{ mol glucose}}{1 \text{ L}} = 0.0870 \text{ mol sucrose needed in 250-mL flask}$

$0.0870 \text{ mol sucrose} \times \dfrac{1 \text{ L stock solution}}{0.500 \text{ mol sucrose}} = 0.174 \text{ L stock solution} = 174 \text{ L stock solution}$

With the dilution equation, you get

$V_{\text{stock solution}} = \dfrac{0.348 \text{ M} \times 250.0 \text{ mL}}{0.500 \text{ M}} = 174 \text{ mL}$

Therefore your instructions should be, "Place 174 mL of the stock solution in a 250-mL volumetric flask and add enough water to bring the total volume to 250.0 mL."

12.116 You need to know what volume of stock solution goes into a 100-mL volumetric flask. You can determine this volume either by calculating numbers of moles or by using the dilution equation. Working with moles, you find

$100.0 \text{ mL} \times \dfrac{1 \text{ L}}{1000 \text{ mL}} \times \dfrac{4.00 \text{ mol NaCl}}{1 \text{ L}} = 0.400 \text{ mol NaCl needed in 100-mL flask}$

$$0.400 \text{ mol NaCl} \times \frac{1 \text{ L stock solution}}{4.50 \text{ mol NaCl}} = 0.0889 \text{ L stock solution} = 88.9 \text{ mL stock solution}$$

With the dilution equation, you get

$$V_{\text{stock solution}} = \frac{4.00 \text{ M} \times 100.0 \text{ mL}}{4.50 \text{ M}} = 88.9 \text{ mL stock solution}$$

Put 88.9 mL of the stock solution in a 100-mL volumetric flask and add enough water to bring the volume to 100.0 mL.

12.117 Moles, because molarity is moles per liter:

$$\frac{\text{Moles}}{\text{Liter}} \times \text{Liters} = \text{Moles}$$

12.118 $\text{Percent by mass} = \dfrac{\text{Grams of solute}}{\text{Grams of solution}} \times 100$

$\text{Percent by volume} = \dfrac{\text{Volume of solute}}{\text{Volume of solution}} \times 100$

$\text{Percent by mass/volume} = \dfrac{\text{Grams of solute}}{\text{Milliliters of solution}} \times 100$

12.119 A concentration of 90 proof means 90/2 = 45% alcohol. If this is volume percent, a 90-proof drink contains 45 mL of alcohol in every 100 mL of the drink.

12.120 $\text{Percent by mass} = \dfrac{\text{Grams of alcohol}}{\text{Grams of solution}} \times 100 = \dfrac{22.5 \text{ g}}{22.5 \text{ g} + 49.6 \text{ g}} \times 100 = 31.2 \text{ mass \% alcohol}$

12.121 (a) $100.0 \text{ g solution} \times \dfrac{25.0 \text{ g solute}}{100 \text{ g solution}} = 25.0 \text{ g solute}$

(b) $48.0 \text{ g solution} \times \dfrac{25.0 \text{ g solute}}{100 \text{ g solution}} = 12.0 \text{ g solute}$

(c) $56.5 \text{ g solute} \times \dfrac{100 \text{ g solution}}{25.0 \text{ g solute}} = 226 \text{ g solution}$

12.122 $2.00 \text{ kg solution} \times \dfrac{1000 \text{ g solution}}{1 \text{ kg solution}} \times \dfrac{30.0 \text{ g NaCl}}{100 \text{ g solution}} = 600 \text{ g NaCl}$

Place 600 g of NaCl in a 2-L flask or beaker and add 1.40 kg of water.

12.123 $1.00 \text{ L solution} \times \dfrac{1000 \text{ mL solution}}{1 \text{ L solution}} \times \dfrac{5.00 \text{ mL alcohol}}{100.0 \text{ mL solution}} = 50.0 \text{ mL alcohol}$

You would place 50.0 mL of alcohol in a 1-L volumetric flask, add about 900 mL of water, mix thoroughly, and then add water to the 1-L mark.

12.124 $200.0 \text{ mL alcohol} \times \dfrac{100.0 \text{ mL solution}}{35.00 \text{ mL alcohol}} = 571.4 \text{ mL solution}$

12.125 A concentration of 25.0 mass % means 25.0 g of NaCl per 100.0 g of solution. First use this information to get the number of moles of NaCl in 100.0 g of solution, then use density to get the volume of the 100.0 g of solution. You then have enough information to calculate molarity:

$$25.0 \text{ g NaCl} \times \frac{1 \text{ mol NaCl}}{58.443 \text{ g NaCl}} = 0.428 \text{ mol NaCl in 100.0 g of solution}$$

$$100.0 \text{ g solution} \times \frac{1 \text{ mL solution}}{1.05 \text{ g solution}} = \frac{1 \text{ L solution}}{1000 \text{ mL solution}} = 0.0952 \text{ L solution}$$

$$\frac{0.428 \text{ mol NaCl}}{100.0 \text{ g solution}} \times \frac{100.0 \text{ g solution}}{0.0952 \text{ L solution}} = 4.50 \frac{\text{mol NaCl}}{\text{L solution}} = 4.50 \text{ M NaCl}$$

12.126 A sphere of water molecules surrounding a dissolved solute particle. A molecule or ion dissolved in water is attracted to the water molecules that surround it and form a "cage." The cage of water molecules gets dragged along with the dissolved particle as it moves through the solution.

12.127 We mean the particles move in random, zigzag paths through the solution. They move this way because they are constantly buffeted by moving solvent molecules.

12.128 (a) $Pb^{2+}(aq) + S^{2-}(aq) \longrightarrow PbS(s)$

(b) $10.00 \text{ g PbS} \times \frac{1 \text{ mol PbS}}{239.3 \text{ g PbS}} = 0.04179 \text{ mol PbS}$

$$0.04179 \text{ mol PbS} \times \frac{1 \text{ mol Pb}^{2+}}{1 \text{ mol PbS}} \times \frac{1 \text{ mol Pb(NO}_3)_2}{1 \text{ mol Pb}^{2+}} \times \frac{1000 \text{ mL Pb(NO}_3)_2 \text{ solution}}{1.00 \text{ mol Pb(NO}_3)_2}$$

$$= 41.8 \text{ mL Pb(NO}_3)_2 \text{ solution}$$

$$0.04179 \text{ mol PbS} \times \frac{1 \text{ mol S}^{2-}}{1 \text{ mol PbS}} \times \frac{1 \text{ mol Na}_2\text{S}}{1 \text{ mol S}^{2-}} \times \frac{1000 \text{ mL Na}_2\text{S solution}}{1.50 \text{ mol Na}_2\text{S}}$$

$$= 27.9 \text{ mL Na}_2\text{S solution}$$

(c) From Section 8.3 of the textbook,

$$\% \text{ yield} \times \frac{\text{Actual yield}}{\text{Theoretical yield}} \times 100$$

Because you know % yield (50.0%) and actual yield (10.00 g), your unknown is theoretical yield:

$$\text{Theoretical yield} = \frac{\text{Actual yield}}{\% \text{ yield}} \times 100 = \frac{10.00 \text{ g}}{50.0\%} \times 100 = 20.0 \text{ g}$$

Because 20.0 g is twice 10.00 g, you know without further calculation that you must double the volumes calculated in part (b), to 83.6 mL Pb(NO$_3$)$_2$ solution and 55.8 mL Na$_2$S solution. If the theoretical yield were some value other than the easy-to-work-with 50.0%, you would have to use the percent-yield equation solved for theoretical yield to calculate the theoretical mass of PbS formed and then repeat the calculations of part (b) with this theoretical mass.

You could also use the short-cut method of dividing each volume calculated in (b) by the percent yield in decimal form:

$$\frac{41.8 \text{ mL Pb(NO}_3)_2 \text{ solution}}{0.500} = 83.6 \text{ mL Pb(NO}_3)_2 \text{ solution}$$

$$\frac{27.9 \text{ mL Na}_2\text{S solution}}{0.500} = 55.8 \text{ mL Na}_2\text{S solution}$$

12.129 (a) $Ba^{2+}(aq) + 2\,OH^-(aq) \longrightarrow Ba(OH)_2(s)$

(b) $5.00 \text{ g Ba(OH)}_2 \times \dfrac{1 \text{ mol Ba(OH)}_2}{171.3 \text{ g Ba(OH)}_2} = 0.0292 \text{ mol Ba(OH)}_2$

$$0.0292 \text{ mol Ba(OH)}_2 \times \frac{1 \text{ mol Ba}^{2+}}{1 \text{ mol Ba(OH)}_2} \times \frac{1 \text{ mol Ba(NO}_3)_2}{1 \text{ mol Ba}^{2+}} \times \frac{1000 \text{ mL Ba(NO}_3)_2 \text{ solution}}{0.755 \text{ mol Ba(NO}_3)_2}$$

$$= 38.7 \text{ mL Ba(NO}_3)_2 \text{ solution}$$

$$0.0292 \text{ mol Ba(OH)}_2 \times \frac{2 \text{ mol OH}^-}{1 \text{ mol Ba(OH)}_2} \times \frac{1 \text{ mol Ca(OH)}_2}{2 \text{ mol OH}^-} \times \frac{1000 \text{ mL Ca(OH)}_2 \text{ solution}}{1.250 \text{ mol Ca(OH)}_2}$$

$$= 23.4 \text{ mL Ca(OH)}_2 \text{ solution}$$

(c) From Section 8.3 of the textbook,

$$\% \text{ yield} \times \frac{\text{Actual yield}}{\text{Theoretical yield}} \times 100$$

$$\text{Theoretical yield} = \frac{\text{Actual yield}}{\% \text{ yield}} \times 100 = \frac{5.00 \text{ g}}{85.0\%} \times 100 = 5.88 \text{ g}$$

$$5.88 \text{ g Ba(OH)}_2 \times \frac{1 \text{ mol Ba(OH)}_2}{171.3 \text{ g Ba(OH)}_2} = 0.0343 \text{ mol Ba(OH)}_2$$

$$0.0343 \text{ mol Ba(OH)}_2 \times \frac{1 \text{ mol Ba}^{2+}}{1 \text{ mol Ba(OH)}_2} \times \frac{1 \text{ mol Ba(NO}_3)_2}{1 \text{ mol Ba}^{2+}} \times \frac{1000 \text{ mL Ba(NO}_3)_2 \text{ solution}}{0.755 \text{ mol Ba(NO}_3)_2}$$

$$= 45.4 \text{ mL Ba(NO}_3)_2 \text{ solution}$$

$$0.0343 \text{ mol Ba(OH)}_2 \times \frac{2 \text{ mol OH}^-}{1 \text{ mol Ba(OH)}_2} \times \frac{1 \text{ mol Ca(OH)}_2}{2 \text{ mol OH}^-} \times \frac{1000 \text{ mL Ca(OH)}_2 \text{ solution}}{1.250 \text{ mol Ca(OH)}_2}$$

$$= 27.4 \text{ mL Ca(OH)}_2 \text{ solution}$$

You could also use the short-cut method of dividing each volume calculated in (b) by the percent yield in decimal form:

$$\frac{38.7 \text{ mL Ba(NO}_3)_2 \text{ solution}}{0.850} = 45.5 \text{ mL Ba(NO}_3)_2 \text{ solution}$$

$$\frac{23.4 \text{ mL Ca(OH)}_2 \text{ solution}}{0.850} = 27.5 \text{ mL Ca(OH)}_2 \text{ solution}$$

12.130 (a) $2 Fe^{3+}(aq) + 3 CO_3^{2-}(aq) \longrightarrow Fe_2(CO_3)_3(s)$

(b) The procedure for determining theoretical yield is described in Section 8.4 of the textbook.

Step 1: See part (a).

Step 2: $200.0 \text{ mL Fe(NO}_3)_3 \text{ solution} \times \dfrac{0.650 \text{ mol Fe(NO}_3)_3}{1000 \text{ mL Fe(NO}_3)_3 \text{ solution}}$

$\times \dfrac{1 \text{ mol Fe}^{3+}}{1 \text{ mol Fe(NO}_3)_3} = 0.130 \text{ mol Fe}^{3+}$

$200.0 \text{ mL (NH}_4)_2CO_3 \text{ solution} \times \dfrac{1.500 \text{ mol (NH}_4)_2CO_3}{1000 \text{ mL (NH}_4)_2CO_3 \text{ solution}} \times$

$\dfrac{1 \text{ mol CO}_3^{2-}}{1 \text{ mol (NH}_4)_2CO_3} = 0.3000 \text{ mol CO}_3^{2-}$

Step 2a: $\dfrac{0.130 \text{ mol Fe}^{3+}}{2} = 0.065 \leftarrow$ Smaller number, limiting reactant

$\dfrac{0.3000 \text{ mol CO}_3^{2-}}{3} = 0.1000$

Steps 3 and 4: $0.130 \text{ mol Fe}^{3+} \times \dfrac{1 \text{ mol Fe}_2(CO_3)_3}{2 \text{ mol Fe}^{3+}} \times$

$\dfrac{291.71 \text{ g Fe}_2(CO_3)_3}{1 \text{ mol Fe}_2(CO_3)_3} = 19.0 \text{ g Fe}_2(CO_3)_3$

(c) You must first determine the number of moles of CO_3^{2-} not used in the reaction. Use the equation coefficients to determine how much CO_3^{2-} reacted with the Fe^{3+}:

$0.130 \text{ mol Fe}^{3+} \times \dfrac{3 \text{ mol CO}_3^{2-}}{2 \text{ mol Fe}^{3+}} = 0.195 \text{ mol CO}_3^{2-}$ consumed

$0.3000 \text{ mol CO}_3^{2-} - 0.195 \text{ mol CO}_3^{2-} = 0.105 \text{ mol CO}_3^{2-}$ remaining
This amount of CO_3^{2-} is present in $200.0 \text{ mL} + 200.0 \text{ mL} = 400.0 \text{ mL}$ of solution, making the molar CO_3^{2-} concentration
$\dfrac{0.105 \text{ mol}}{0.400 \text{ L}} = 0.263 \text{ M}$

12.131 (a) $3 Pb^{2+}(aq) + 2 PO_4^{3-}(aq) \longrightarrow Pb_3(PO_4)_2(s)$

(b) The procedure for determining theoretical yield when one reactant is limiting is described in Section 8.4 of the textbook.
Step 1: See part (a).

Step 2: $50.0 \text{ mL Pb(C}_2H_3O_2)_2 \text{ solution} \times \dfrac{0.800 \text{ mol Pb(C}_2H_3O_2)_2}{1000 \text{ mL Pb(C}_2H_3O_2)_2 \text{ solution}} \times$

$\dfrac{1 \text{ mol Pb}^{2+}}{1 \text{ mol Pb(C}_2H_3O_2)_2} = 0.0400 \text{ mol Pb}^{2+}$

$100.0 \text{ mL Na}_3PO_4 \text{ solution} \times \dfrac{0.800 \text{ mol Na}_3PO_4}{1000 \text{ mL Na}_3PO_4 \text{ solution}} \times \dfrac{1 \text{ mol PO}_4^{3-}}{1 \text{ mol Na}_3PO_4}$

$= 0.0800 \text{ mol PO}_4^{3-}$

Step 2a: $\dfrac{0.0400 \text{ mol Pb}^{2+}}{3} = 0.0133 \leftarrow$ Smaller number, limiting reactant

$\dfrac{0.0800 \text{ mol PO}_4^{3-}}{2} = 0.0400$

Steps 3 and 4: $0.0400 \text{ mol Pb}^{2+} \times \dfrac{1 \text{ mol Pb}_3(\text{PO}_4)_2}{3 \text{ mol Pb}^{2+}} \times$

$\dfrac{811.5 \text{ g Pb}_3(\text{PO}_4)_2}{1 \text{ mol Pb}_3(\text{PO}_4)_2} = 10.8 \text{ g Pb}_3(\text{PO}_4)_2$

(c) You must first determine the number of moles of PO_4^{3-} not used:

$0.400 \text{ mol Pb}^{2+} \times \dfrac{2 \text{ mol PO}_4^{3-}}{3 \text{ mol Pb}^{2+}} = 0.0267 \text{ mol PO}_4^{3-}$ consumed

$0.0800 \text{ mol PO}_4^{3-} - 0.0267 \text{ mol PO}_4^{3-} = 0.0533 \text{ mol PO}_4^{3-}$ remaining

This amount of PO_4^{3-} is present in 100.0 mL + 50.0 mL = 150.0 mL of solution, making the molar PO_4^{3-} concentration

$\dfrac{0.0533 \text{ mol}}{0.1500 \text{ L}} = 0.355 \text{ M}$

12.132 (a) $H^+(aq) + OH^-(aq) \longrightarrow H_2O(l)$

(b) First determine the number of moles of acid neutralized by the NaOH:

$0.04328 \text{ L NaOH} \times \dfrac{0.1001 \text{ mol NaOH}}{1 \text{ L NaOH}} \times \dfrac{1 \text{ mol OH}^-}{1 \text{ mol NaOH}} \times$

$\dfrac{1 \text{ mol H}^+}{1 \text{ mol OH}^-} \times \dfrac{1 \text{ mol HBr}}{1 \text{ mol H}^+} = 0.004332 \text{ mol HBr}$

This number of moles in the 25.00-mL acid sample means the molar concentration of HBr is

$\dfrac{0.004332 \text{ mol}}{0.02500 \text{ L}} = 0.1733 \text{ M}$

12.133 (a) $H^+(aq) + OH^-(aq) \longrightarrow H_2O(l)$

(b) First determine the number of moles of acid neutralized:

$0.02755 \text{ L NaOH} \times \dfrac{1.0002 \text{ mol NaOH}}{1 \text{ L NaOH}} \times \dfrac{1 \text{ mol OH}^-}{1 \text{ mol NaOH}} \times$

$\dfrac{1 \text{ mol H}^+}{1 \text{ mol OH}^-} \times \dfrac{1 \text{ mol H}_2\text{SO}_4}{2 \text{ mol H}^+} = 0.01378 \text{ mol H}_2\text{SO}_4$

This number of moles of H_2SO_4 in the 25.00 mL of solution makes the molar concentration of H_2SO_4

$\dfrac{0.01378 \text{ mol}}{0.02500 \text{ L}} = 0.5512 \text{ M}$

12.134 (a) First determine the number of moles of acid neutralized by the base:

$0.03682 \text{ L NaOH} \times \dfrac{0.1001 \text{ mol NaOH}}{1 \text{ L NaOH}} \times \dfrac{1 \text{ mol OH}^-}{1 \text{ mol NaOH}} \times$

$\dfrac{1 \text{ mol H}^+}{1 \text{ mol OH}^-} \times \dfrac{1 \text{ mol proprionic acid}}{1 \text{ mol H}^+} = 0.003686 \text{ mol proprionic acid}$

This number of moles in 100.0 mL of solution makes the proprionic acid molar concentration

$$\frac{0.003686\ \text{mol}}{0.1000\ \text{L}} = 0.03686\ \text{M}$$

(b) $\dfrac{0.273\ \text{g}}{0.003686\ \text{mol}} = 74.1\ \text{g}/\text{mol}$

12.135 (a) A heating curve tells you (1) when a substance is changing phase (horizontal portions) and (2) when the temperature of the substance is changing (sloping portions). Melting is the phase change from solid to liquid, and therefore the lower horizontal portion tells you that the melting point for this substance is −115.0°C.

(b) Freezing is the phase change from liquid to solid, which means the same horizontal portion used in part (a) also tells you the freezing point, −115.0°C.

(c) Boiling is the phase change from liquid to gas, and therefore the upper horizontal portion of the heating curve tells you that the boiling point for this substance is 78.4°C.

(d) Condensation is the phase change from gas to liquid, which means the upper horizontal line tells you the condensation point as well as the boiling point. Both are 78.4°C.

(e) Because the temperature of a substance does not change whenever the substance is changing phase at its freezing/melting point or its boiling/condensing point.

(f) Ethanol.

12.136 Obtain a piece of the plastic that you know for certain is in the ordered phase and imbed a thermometer in it. Then heat the plastic continuously and graph its temperature as time passes. You will get a graph that looks like this:

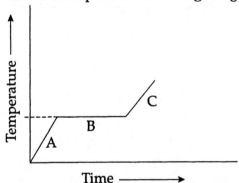

Stop heating once you have reached the C portion of the graph because at that point, the phase change is complete. Extrapolate the horizontal portion leftward to the temperature axis, and this is the temperature at which the phase change occurs.

12.137 To break the hydrogen bonds holding the water molecules together in the liquid phase.

12.138 Dynamic equilibrium between liquid water and water vapor occurs when the evaporation rate equals the condensation rate.

12.139 The pressure exerted by the gas phase of a substance when the gas phase is in dynamic equilibrium with the liquid phase of the substance.

12.140 (a) That at any given temperature, hexane evaporates faster than water.

(b) Hexane, because vapor pressure and volatility are both measures of a liquid's "urge" to evaporate. The more volatile the liquid, the greater its urge to evaporate and therefore the greater its vapor pressure.

(c) Water, because the more volatile a liquid is, the lower its boiling point.

(d) Because the London forces between hexane molecules are weaker than the hydrogen bonds between water molecules. This means it is easier for hexane molecules in the liquid phase to separate and enter the gas phase.

12.141 Water boils when its vapor pressure is equal to the downward pressure exerted by the air on the water surface. Because the vapor pressure of water at 20°C is 17.54 mm Hg, you get water to boil at this temperature by using a vacuum pump to reduce the air pressure above the water surface to 17.54 mm Hg or less.

12.142 In this model, one arrow representing vapor pressure and one arrow representing atmospheric pressure are placed head-to-head at the surface of a liquid. When the liquid is much cooler than its boiling point, the upward-pointing vapor-pressure arrow is much smaller than the downward-pointing atmospheric-pressure arrow. As more and more heat energy is added to the liquid, the vapor-pressure arrow gets larger while the atmospheric-pressure arrow does not change. When enough heat energy has been added to make the vapor-pressure arrow the same size as the atmospheric-pressure arrow, the liquid boils.

The lengthening vapor-pressure arrow represents the fact that the added heat energy is increasing the liquid's vapor pressure, and the two arrows of equal length as boiling begins represents the fact that a liquid boils when its vapor pressure equals atmospheric pressure.

12.143 Any liquid boils when its vapor pressure is equal to atmospheric pressure, which is normally 760 mm Hg. Because 80.1°C is the normal boiling point of benzene, the vapor pressure at that temperature must be atmospheric pressure, 760 mm Hg.

12.144 A colligative property of a solution is one that depends only on the number of dissolved solute particles present in the solution, not on their nature. Examples are boiling point elevation, freezing point depression, and vapor pressure depression.

12.145 The two solutions have the same freezing point when they contain the same number of moles of solute particles. NaCl dissociates to 2 moles of solute particles for every 1 mole of NaCl, which means the number of moles of solute particles in the 28.7 g is

$$28.7 \text{ g NaCl} \times \frac{1 \text{ mol NaCl}}{58.443 \text{ g NaCl}} \times \frac{2 \text{ mol solute particles}}{1 \text{ mol NaCl}} = 0.982 \text{ mol solute particles}$$

Because sucrose does not dissociate when it dissolves, each mole of sucrose yields 1 mole of solute particles. You therefore need 0.982 mole of sucrose, which means a mass of

$$0.982 \text{ mol sucrose} \times \frac{342 \text{ g sucrose}}{1 \text{ mol sucrose}} = 336 \text{ g sucrose}$$

12.146 Because boiling point elevation depends on the number of moles of dissolved solute particles, you must know whether either solute ionizes. $Ca(NO_3)_2$ does, yielding 3 moles of solute particles for each 1 mole of $Ca(NO_3)_2$. Glucose does not, which means each 1 mole of glucose yields 1 mole of dissolved solute particles. The two aqueous solutions have the same boiling point when they contain the same number of moles of dissolved particles.

$$36.9 \text{ g Ca(NO}_3)_2 \times \frac{1 \text{ mol Ca(NO}_3)_2}{164.086 \text{ g Ca(NO}_3)_2} \times \frac{3 \text{ mol solute particles}}{1 \text{ mol Ca(NO}_3)_2}$$

$$= 0.675 \text{ mol solute particles in Ca(NO}_3)_2 \text{ solution}$$

So he needs 0.675 mole of solute particles in the glucose solution.

$$0.675 \text{ mol solute particles} \times \frac{1 \text{ mol glucose}}{1 \text{ mol solute particles}} \times \frac{180.155 \text{ g glucose}}{1 \text{ mol glucose}} = 122 \text{ g glucose}$$

12.147 The two solutions have the same vapor pressure when they contain the same number of moles of solute particles. Because each mole of Na_2SO_4 dissociates to 3 moles of solute particles, the Na_2SO_4 solution contains

$$45.6 \text{ g } Na_2SO_4 \times \frac{1 \text{ mol } Na_2SO_4}{142 \text{ g } Na_2SO_4} \times \frac{3 \text{ mol solute particles}}{1 \text{ mol } Na_2SO_4} = 0.963 \text{ mol solute particles}$$

She therefore needs 0.963 mol of solute particles from NaCl, where 1 mole of the salt yields 2 moles of particles:

$$0.963 \text{ mol solute particles} \times \frac{1 \text{ mol NaCl}}{2 \text{ mol solute particles}} \times \frac{58.4 \text{ g NaCl}}{1 \text{ mol NaCl}} = 28.1 \text{ g NaCl}$$

12.148 (a) $38.6 \text{ g } Na_3PO_4 \times \dfrac{1 \text{ mol } Na_3PO_4}{163.9 \text{ g } Na_3PO_4} \times \dfrac{4 \text{ mol solute particles}}{1 \text{ mol } Na_3PO_4} = 0.942 \text{ mol solute particles}$

In the expression for boiling-point elevation, solvent mass is used rather than volume, meaning you must convert:

$$200.0 \text{ mL water} \times \frac{1.00 \text{ g water}}{1 \text{ mL water}} \times \frac{1 \text{ kg water}}{1000 \text{ g water}} = 0.200 \text{ kg water}$$

The change in boiling point is

$$\Delta T_b = \frac{0.52 \dfrac{C° \cdot \text{kg solvent}}{\text{mol solute}} \times 0.942 \text{ mol solute}}{0.200 \text{ kg solvent}} = 2.45 \text{ C}°$$

Because the presence of solute raises the boiling point, you must add this change to water's normal boiling point:

$$100.0°C + 2.45°C = 102.5°C$$

(b) The change in freezing point is

$$\Delta T_f = \frac{1.86 \dfrac{C° \cdot \text{kg solvent}}{\text{mol solute}} \times 0.942 \text{ mol solute}}{0.200 \text{ kg solvent}} = 8.76 \text{ C}°$$

Because the presence of solute lowers the freezing point, you must subtract this change from water's normal freezing point:

$$0.00°C - 8.76°C = -8.76°C$$

12.149 The ΔT_b and ΔT_f equations require the solvent mass in kilograms:

$$100.0 \text{ mL benzene} \times \frac{0.874 \text{ g benzene}}{1 \text{ mL benzene}} \times \frac{1 \text{ kg benzene}}{1000 \text{ g benzene}} = 0.0874 \text{ kg benzene}$$

The equations require the solute particles in moles. The solute cetyl alcohol does not dissociate when it dissolves:

$$5.75 \text{ g } C_{16}H_{34}O \times \frac{1 \text{ mol } C_{16}H_{34}O}{242.4 \text{ g } C_{16}H_{34}O} \times \frac{1 \text{ mol solute particles}}{1 \text{ mol } C_{16}H_{34}O} = 0.0237 \text{ mol solute particles}$$

(a) $\Delta T_b = \dfrac{2.53 \dfrac{C° \cdot \text{kg benzene}}{\text{mol solute particles}} \times 0.0237 \text{ mol solute particles}}{0.0874 \text{ kg benzene}} = 0.686 \text{ C}°$

Elevated boiling point = Normal boiling point + ΔT_b = 80.1°C + 0.686 C° = 80.8°C

(b) $\Delta T_f = \dfrac{5.12\,\dfrac{\text{C°}\cdot\text{kg benzene}}{\text{mol solute particles}}\times 0.0237\ \text{mol solute particles}}{0.0874\ \text{kg benzene}} = 1.39\ \text{C°}$

Depressed freezing point = Normal freezing point − ΔT_f = 5.53°C − 1.39 C° = 4.14°C

12.150 (a) Because you begin with a liquid solution, the graph must show the phase change from liquid to solid, and where the horizontal portion of the graph intersects the temperature axis tells you the freezing point of the solution is −31.15°C. Table 12.2 of the textbook gives −22.96°C as the normal freezing point of CCl_4. Therefore, ΔT_f = −31.15°C − (−22.96°C) = −8.19 C°. (You are concerned only with the absolute value of ΔT_f and so can ignore the minus sign.)

Now rearrange the ΔT_f equation to determine how much solute caused the 8.19 C° depression:

$$\text{Mol solute} = \frac{\Delta T_f \times \text{kg solvent}}{K_f} = \frac{8.19\ \text{C°} \times 1000\ \text{kg solvent}}{31.8\,\dfrac{\text{C°}\cdot\text{kg solvent}}{\text{mol solute}}} = 0.0258\ \text{mol solute}$$

This is the number of moles of caffeine in the solution, making the molar mass

$$\frac{5.00\ \text{g}}{0.0258\ \text{mol}} = 194\ \text{g/mol}$$

(b) The empirical formula $C_4H_5N_2O$ has a molar mass of 97.10 g/mol, and 194/97.1 = 2.00, making the molecular formula of caffeine twice the empirical formula, or $C_8H_{10}N_4O_2$.

12.151 The ΔT_f equation solved for moles of solute particles tells you how many moles of cholesterol is represented by the 1.56 g. To use the equation, you'll need the solvent mass in kilograms and a value for ΔT_f:

$$50.0\ \text{mL cyclohexane} \times \frac{0.779\ \text{g cyclohexane}}{1\ \text{mL cyclohexane}} \times \frac{1\ \text{kg cyclohexane}}{1000\ \text{g cyclohexane}} = 0.0390\ \text{kg cyclohexane}$$

ΔT_f = Normal freezing point − Depressed freezing point = 6.47°C − 4.40°C = 2.07°C

$$\Delta T_f = \frac{K_f \times \text{Mol solute particles}}{\text{Kilograms solvent}}$$

$$\text{Mol solute particles} = \frac{\text{Kilograms solvent} \times \Delta T_f}{K_f} = \frac{0.0390\ \text{kg cyclohexane} \times 2.07\ \text{C°}}{20.0\,\dfrac{\text{C°}\cdot\text{kg cyclohexane}}{\text{mol solute particles}}}$$

$$= 0.00404\ \text{mol solute particles}$$

Assuming cholesterol does not dissociate when it dissolves, you can say

$$0.00404\ \text{mol solute particles} \times \frac{1\ \text{mol cholesterol}}{1\ \text{mol solute particles}} = 0.00404\ \text{mol cholesterol}$$

This is the number of moles of cholesterol in the 1.56 g, making the molar mass

$$\frac{1.56\ \text{g}}{0.00404\ \text{mol}} = 386\ \text{g/mol}$$

12.152 $Mg(OH)_2(s)$ releases the most hydration energy because it produces 2+ ions in solution and the strength of ion–dipole forces increases with the charge of the ion. Therefore the $Mg^{2+}\cdots H_2O$ attractions are stronger than the $K^+\cdots H_2O$ attractions.

$CO_2(g)$ releases the least energy because it is a covalent substance rather than an ionic one. As a result, the $CO_2 \cdots H_2O$ attractions are only weak London forces.

12.153 The amount of hydration energy released is proportional to the strength of the intermolecular forces between solute molecule and water molecule. The stronger these forces, the greater the amount of energy released. Therefore $CH_3CH_2OH(l)$ releases the most energy because these molecules contain an $-OH$ group and can therefore form hydrogen bonds with water molecules. $C_8H_{18}(l)$ releases the least energy because the only forces posible between these nonpolar molecules and water molecules are London forces. Because hydrogen bonds are stronger than London forces, $CH_3CH_2OH(l)$ releases more energy.

An intermediate amount of energy is released by $CH_3Cl(l)$, which interact with water molecules via dipole–dipole interactions. (Recall from Section 10.3 of the textbook that hydrogen bonds are considerably stronger than dipole–dipole interactions.)

12.154 The lattice in $Mg(OH)_2$ because ionic bonds in a lattice get stronger as the charge on the ions increases. Of these three ionic compounds, only $Mg(OH)_2$ has 2+ ions; the other two compounds have 1+ ions.

12.155 Step (b) because a negative ΔE value means, by convention, that energy is released, and energy is released whenever two particles attract each other. Steps (a) and (c) both have a positive energy change (these steps absorb energy).

12.156 (c). Henry's law says gas solubility is directly proportional to pressure. Statements (a), (b), and (d) contradict Henry's law.

12.157 $0.02886 \text{ L solution} \times \dfrac{5.20 \times 10^{-3} \text{ mol KMnO}_4}{1 \text{ L solution}} = 1.50 \times 10^{-4} \text{ mol KMnO}_4$

12.158 (a) $0.5000 \text{ L solution} \times \dfrac{0.300 \text{ mol NaOH}}{1 \text{ L solution}} \times \dfrac{39.997 \text{ g NaOH}}{1 \text{ mol NaOH}} = 6.00 \text{ g NaOH}$

(b) Measure out 6.00 g of NaOH on a balance, transfer it to a 500-mL volumetric flask, add about 400 mL of water, shake to dissolve the solid, and then add water up to the 500-mL mark. (You may need to let the solution cool to room temperature before doing the final step.)

12.159 The dilution equation tells you how much stock solution you need to dilute:

$$V_{\text{stock solution}} = \frac{0.350 \text{ M} \times 250.0 \text{ mL}}{6.00 \text{ M}} = 14.6 \text{ mL}$$

Transfer 14.6 mL of the stock solution to a 250-mL volumetric flask and dilute to the mark with water.

12.160 The graph tells you that at 40°C the solubility of $NaNO_3$ is 104 g per 100.0 g of water.

$$50.0 \text{ g NaNO}_3 \times \frac{100.0 \text{ g water}}{104 \text{ g NaNO}_3} = 48.1 \text{ g water}$$

12.161 Because molarity is moles per liter, the first step is to convert the given volume to liters:

$$200 \text{ cm}^3 \times \frac{1 \text{ mL}}{1 \text{ cm}^3} \times \frac{1 \text{ L}}{1000 \text{ mL}} = 0.200 \text{ L}$$

(a) $0.200 \text{ L} \times \dfrac{0.200 \text{ mol NaCl}}{\text{L}} \times \dfrac{1 \text{ mol Na}^+}{1 \text{ mol NaCl}} = 0.0400 \text{ mol Na}^+$

$0.200 \text{ L} \times \dfrac{0.200 \text{ mol NaCl}}{\text{L}} \times \dfrac{1 \text{ mol Cl}^-}{1 \text{ mol NaCl}} = 0.0400 \text{ mol Cl}^-$

(b) $0.200 \text{ L} \times \dfrac{0.350 \text{ mol K}_3\text{PO}_4}{\text{L}} \times \dfrac{3 \text{ mol K}^+}{1 \text{ mol K}_3\text{PO}_4} = 0.210 \text{ mol K}^+$

$0.200 \text{ L} \times \dfrac{0.350 \text{ mol K}_3\text{PO}_4}{\text{L}} \times \dfrac{1 \text{ mol PO}_4{}^{3-}}{1 \text{ mol K}_3\text{PO}_4} = 0.0700 \text{ mol PO}_4{}^{3-}$

(c) $0.200 \text{ L} \times \dfrac{1.44 \text{ mol Al(NO}_3)_3}{\text{L}} \times \dfrac{1 \text{ mol Al}^{3+}}{1 \text{ mol Al(NO}_3)_3} = 0.288 \text{ mol Al}^{3+}$

$0.200 \text{ L} \times \dfrac{1.44 \text{ mol Al(NO}_3)_3}{\text{L}} \times \dfrac{3 \text{ mol NO}_3{}^-}{1 \text{ mol Al(NO}_3)_3} = 0.864 \text{ mol NO}_3{}^-$

12.162 NaBr $\qquad \dfrac{3.96 \text{ g NaBr} \times \dfrac{1 \text{ mol NaBr}}{102.894 \text{ g NaBr}}}{0.150 \text{ L}} = 0.257 \text{ M}$

Ba(OH)$_2$ $\qquad 2.58 \text{ g Ba(OH)}_2 \times \dfrac{1 \text{ mol Ba(OH)}_2}{171.341 \text{ g Ba(OH)}_2} \times \dfrac{1 \text{ L solution}}{0.0800 \text{ mol Ba(OH)}_2} = 0.188 \text{ L}$

(NH$_4$)$_2$SO$_4$ $\qquad \dfrac{8.65 \text{ g (NH}_4)_2\text{SO}_4 \times \dfrac{1 \text{ mol (NH}_4)_2\text{SO}_4}{132.139 \text{ g (NH}_4)_2\text{SO}_4}}{2.40 \text{ L}} = 0.0273 \text{ M}$

NH$_4$Cl $\qquad 4.20 \text{ L solution} \times \dfrac{0.420 \text{ mol NH}_4\text{Cl}}{1 \text{ L solution}} \times \dfrac{53.492 \text{ g NH}_4\text{Cl}}{1 \text{ mol NH}_4\text{Cl}} = 94.4 \text{ g NH}_4\text{Cl}$

12.163 (a) $4.70 \text{ g CuSO}_4 \times \dfrac{1 \text{ mol CuSO}_4}{160 \text{ g CuSO}_4} = 0.0294 \text{ mol CuSO}_4$

$\dfrac{0.0294 \text{ mol}}{150.0 \text{ cm}^3} \times \dfrac{1 \text{ cm}^3}{1 \text{ mL}} \times \dfrac{1000 \text{ mL}}{1 \text{ L}} = 0.196 \text{ mol / L} = 0.196 \text{ M}$

(b) $1.00 \text{ mL} \times \dfrac{1 \text{ L}}{1000 \text{ mL}} \times \dfrac{0.196 \text{ mol}}{\text{L}} = 1.96 \times 10^{-4} \text{ mol}$

(c) To calculate percent by mass, both solute amount and solution amount must be in mass units. You already have solute mass and therefore need to calculate only solution mass:

$150.0 \text{ cm}^3 \times \dfrac{1 \text{ mL}}{1 \text{ cm}^3} \times \dfrac{1.01 \text{ g}}{\text{mL}} = 1.52 \text{ g}$

$\dfrac{4.70 \text{ g solute}}{152 \text{ g solution}} \times 100 = 3.09 \text{ mass \%}$

12.164 Your first step in each case should be to convert grams of solute to moles of solute. Neither glucose nor urea dissociates when it dissolves in water.

(a) $18.4 \text{ g glucose} \times \dfrac{1 \text{ mol glucose}}{180.2 \text{ g glucose}} = 0.102 \text{ mol glucose}$

$\Delta T_f = \dfrac{\dfrac{1.86 \text{ C}° \cdot \text{kg solvent}}{\text{mol solute particles}} \times 0.102 \text{ mol solute particles}}{0.0955 \text{ kg solvent}} = 1.99 \text{ C}°$

Depressed freezing point = Normal freezing point $- \Delta T_f = 0.00°C - 1.99$ C° $= -1.99°C$

$$\Delta T_b = \frac{\dfrac{0.52 \text{ C°} \cdot \text{kg solvent}}{\text{mol solute particles}} \times 0.102 \text{ mol solute particles}}{0.0955 \text{ kg solvent}} = 0.56 \text{ C°}$$

Elevated boiling point = 100.00°C + 0.56 C° = 100.56°C

(b) $15.00 \text{ g urea} \times \dfrac{1 \text{ mol urea}}{60.056 \text{ g urea}} = 0.2498 \text{ mol urea}$

$$\Delta T_f = \frac{\dfrac{1.86 \text{ C°} \cdot \text{kg solvent}}{\text{mol solute particles}} \times 0.2498 \text{ mol solute particles}}{0.0750 \text{ kg solvent}} = 6.20 \text{ C°}$$

Depressed freezing point = 0.00°C − 6.20 C° = −6.20°C

$$\Delta T_b = \frac{\dfrac{0.52 \text{ C°} \cdot \text{kg solvent}}{\text{mol solute particles}} \times 0.2498 \text{ mol solute particles}}{0.0750 \text{ kg solvent}} = 1.7 \text{ C°}$$

Elevated boiling point = 100.00°C + 1.7 C° = 101.7°C

12.165 Get the empirical formula from the combustion data, assuming a 100.0-g sample so that percents can be directly converted to grams. The amount of O is determined by difference: 100.0% − 40.9% C − 4.58% H = 54.5% O.

$$40.9 \text{ g C} \times \frac{1 \text{ mol C}}{12.011 \text{ g C}} = 3.41 \text{ mol C}$$

$$4.58 \text{ g H} \times \frac{1 \text{ mol H}}{1.0079 \text{ g H}} = 4.54 \text{ mol H}$$

$$54.5 \text{ g O} \times \frac{1 \text{ mol O}}{15.999 \text{ g O}} = 3.41 \text{ mol O}$$

$$C_{\frac{3.41}{3.41}}H_{\frac{4.54}{3.41}}O_{\frac{3.41}{3.41}} \rightarrow C_{1.00}H_{1.33}O_{1.00} \rightarrow C_{1.00\times3}H_{1.33\times3}O_{1.00\times3} = C_3H_4O_3$$

A compound having this empirical formula has a molar mass of 88.1 g/mol. To determine whether or not this empirical formula is the molecular formula, you need to know the vitamin C molar mass, which you get from the freezing point of the vitamin C solution:

$$\text{Mol solute} = \frac{\Delta T_f \times \text{kg solvent}}{K_f} = \frac{2.05 \text{ C°} \times 0.100 \text{ kg solvent}}{1.86 \dfrac{\text{C°} \cdot \text{kg solvent}}{\text{mol solute}}} = 0.110 \text{ mol solute}$$

The molar mass of the vitamin C is therefore

$$\frac{19.40 \text{ g}}{0.110 \text{ mol}} = 176 \text{ g/mol}$$

because (176 g/mol)/(88.1 g/mol) = 2, the molecular formula is $C_{2\times3}H_{2\times4}O_{2\times3} = C_6H_8O_6$.

12.166 If HF remains primarily undissociated, each mole of it yields 1 mole of solute particles. Therefore the temperature change for the undissociated form is

$$\Delta T_f = \frac{\dfrac{1.86\ C° \cdot kg\ solvent}{mol\ solute\ particles} \times 0.200\ mol\ solute\ particles}{2.00\ kg\ solvent} = 0.186\ C°$$

This value means the depressed freezing point is $-0.186°C$ if no HF dissociates. It is twice this, $-0.372°C$ if the HF dissociates completely. Therefore, HF remains mostly undissociated and must be a weak acid because it is so poor at producing H^+ ions.

12.167 Wine that is 24 proof is $24/2 = 12\%$ alcohol, by definition, which means each gallon of wine contains 0.12 gallon of alcohol, as you can see by rearranging the expression for percent composition by volume:

$$\text{Volume of solute} = \frac{12\% \times 1\ gallon\ wine}{100} = 0.12\ gallon\ alcohol$$

$$0.100\ gallon\ alcohol \times \frac{1\ gallon\ wine}{0.12\ gallon\ alcohol} = 0.83\ gallon\ wine$$

12.168

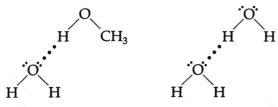

Both solvent and solute are capable of hydrogen bonding, making this a case of like dissolving like.

12.169 (a) Use the dilution equation with $V_{\text{diluted solution}} = 125.0\ mL + 50.0\ mL = 175.0\ mL$:

$$M_{\text{diluted solution}} = \frac{0.250\ M \times 50.0\ mL}{175.0\ mL} = 0.0714\ M$$

(b) $0.0714\ M\ (NH_4)_3PO_4 \times \dfrac{3\ mol\ NH_4^+}{1\ mol\ (NH_4)_3PO_4} = 0.214\ M\ NH_4^+$

(c) $0.0714\ M\ (NH_4)_3PO_4 \times \dfrac{1\ mol\ PO_4^{3-}}{1\ mol\ (NH_4)_3PO_4} = 0.0714\ M\ PO_4^{3-}$

12.170 (a) $\dfrac{0.250\ mol\ Ca(NO_3)_2}{L} \times 0.0500\ L = 0.0125\ mol\ Ca(NO_3)_2$

$$+$$

$$\dfrac{0.835\ mol\ Ca(NO_3)_2}{L} \times 0.1000\ L = \underline{0.0835\ mol\ Ca(NO_3)_2}$$

$$0.0960\ mol\ Ca(NO_3)_2$$

Molarity in combined solution $= \dfrac{0.0960\ mol\ Ca(NO_3)_2}{0.1500\ L} = 0.640\ M$

(b) $\dfrac{0.640\ mol\ Ca(NO_3)_2}{L} \times \dfrac{1\ mol\ Ca^{2+}}{1\ mol\ Ca(NO_3)_2} = \dfrac{0.640\ mol\ Ca^{2+}}{L} = 0.640\ M$

(c) $\dfrac{0.640 \text{ mol Ca(NO}_3)_2}{\text{L}} \times \dfrac{2 \text{ mol NO}_3^-}{1 \text{ mol Ca(NO}_3)_2} = \dfrac{1.28 \text{ mol NO}_3^-}{\text{L}} = 1.28 \text{ M}$

12.171 The net ionic equation is $Ba^{2+}(aq) + SO_4^{2-}(aq) \longrightarrow BaSO_4(s)$. In order to determine how much sulfate ion you need, you must know how much barium ion you have:

$$0.2500 \text{ L} \times \dfrac{0.600 \text{ mol Ba(NO}_3)_2}{\text{L}} \times \dfrac{1 \text{ mol Ba}^{2+}}{1 \text{ mol Ba(NO}_3)_2} = 0.150 \text{ mol Ba}^{2+}$$

You therefore need 0.150 mole of SO_4^{2-}, and the volume of sodium sulfate solution containing that amount of SO_4^{2-} is

$$0.150 \text{ mol SO}_4^{2-} \times \dfrac{1 \text{ mol Na}_2SO_4}{1 \text{ mol SO}_4^{2-}} \times \dfrac{1 \text{ L}}{0.500 \text{ mol Na}_2SO_4} = 0.300 \text{ L}$$

12.172 $M_{\text{stock solution}} = \dfrac{M_{\text{diluted solution}} \times V_{\text{diluted solution}}}{V_{\text{stock solution}}} = \dfrac{0.0478 \text{ M} \times 100.0 \text{ mL}}{5.00 \text{ mL}} = 0.956 \text{ M}$

12.173 The complete ionic equation is

$$2 \text{ Na}^+(aq) + 2 \text{ I}^-(aq) + Pb^{2+}(aq) + 2 \text{ C}_2H_3O_2^-(aq) \longrightarrow PbI_2(s) + 2 \text{ Na}^+(aq) + 2 \text{ C}_2H_3O_2^-(aq)$$

telling you the spectator ions are $Na^+(aq)$ and $C_2H_3O_2^-(aq)$. The amount of lead ion in the 100.0 mL of $Pb(C_2H_3O_2)_2$ solution is

$$0.1000 \text{ L} \times \dfrac{0.300 \text{ mol Pb(C}_2H_3O_2)_2}{\text{L}} \times \dfrac{1 \text{ mol Pb}^{2+}}{1 \text{ mol Pb(C}_2H_3O_2)_2} = 0.0300 \text{ mol Pb}^{2+}$$

Because 1 mole of Pb^{2+} reacts with 2 moles of I^-, the volume of NaI solution needed is

$$0.0300 \text{ mol Pb}^{2+} \times \dfrac{2 \text{ mol I}^-}{1 \text{ mol Pb}^{2+}} \times \dfrac{1 \text{ mol NaI}}{1 \text{ mol I}^-} \times \dfrac{1 \text{ L}}{0.245 \text{ mol NaI}} = 0.245 \text{ L}$$

12.174 (a) This is an acid–base neutralization: $H^+(aq) + OH^-(aq) \longrightarrow H_2O(l)$. The number of moles of citric acid in the 100.0 mL of solution is

$$0.02755 \text{ L NaOH solution} \times \dfrac{0.1001 \text{ mol OH}^-}{1 \text{ L NaOH solution}} \times \dfrac{1 \text{ mol H}^+}{1 \text{ mol OH}^-} \times \dfrac{1 \text{ mol citric acid}}{3 \text{ mol H}^+}$$

$$= 9.192 \times 10^{-4} \text{ mol citric acid}$$

The molar concentration is therefore

$$\dfrac{9.192 \times 10^{-4} \text{ mol}}{0.1000 \text{ L}} = 9.192 \times 10^{-3} \text{ M}$$

(b) $\dfrac{0.177 \text{ g}}{9.192 \times 10^{-4} \text{ mol}} = 193 \text{ g / mol}$

12.175 Adding the 27.65 mL of water to the flask does not change the number of moles of acid in the flask. All the acid that reacts with the NaOH comes from the 25.00-mL sample. The number of moles of HCl in this sample is

$$0.02870 \text{ L NaOH} \times \dfrac{0.1004 \text{ mol OH}^-}{1 \text{ L NaOH}} \times \dfrac{1 \text{ mol H}^+}{1 \text{ mol OH}^-} \times \dfrac{1 \text{ mol HCl}}{1 \text{ mol H}^+} = 0.002881 \text{ mol HCl}$$

Because this number of moles is in 25.00 mL, the concentration of the sample solution is

$$\dfrac{0.002881 \text{ mol}}{0.02500 \text{ L}} = 0.1152 \text{ mol / L} = 0.1152 \text{ M}$$

Remember, in a titration, it's the number of moles in the flask that is important, not the volume of solution in the flask.

12.176 The solvent is always the substance present in the greater or greatest amount. (a) Cu solvent; Zn solute. (b) Water solvent; ammonia solute. (c) Sucrose solvent; water solute.

12.177 No. A compound is a single pure substance, but a solution must contain at least two substances, mixed homogeneously.

12.178 Solute separation: The lattice of iodine molecules in the solid iodine comes apart into individual I_2 molecules as the intermolecular London forces that hold the lattice together are overcome.

Solvent separation: The CCl_4 molecules are pulled away from one another as the intermolecular London forces between CCl_4 molecules are overcome. Solvation: The I_2 molecules occupy the open spaces in the solvent and are distributed homogeneously throughout the solution as London forces develop between I_2 molecules and CCl_4 molecules.

12.179 More soluble. I_2 and CCl_4 are both nonpolar molecules, and H_2O is a polar molecule. Because "like dissolves like," you expect I_2 to be more soluble in CCl_4 than in H_2O. In terms of energy, the attractive forces that develop between I_2 and CCl_4 are greater than the forces that develop between I_2 and H_2O. The I_2–CCl_4 attractions release more energy to drive the energy-absorbing solute-separation and solvent-separation steps.

12.180 *Solvation* is the general term for the development of intermolecular attractions between solute molecules and solvent molecules; this term applies to all solvents. *Hydration* is solvation with water as the solvent. You cannot say that solvation always releases more energy than hydration or vice versa. How much energy is released in any given dissolution depends on the nature of the solute and the solvent.

12.181 Aluminum phosphate contains Al^{3+} ions, which carry three times the positive charge of the Na^+ ions in sodium phosphate. Because of this higher charge, the ionic bonds in the $AlPO_4$ lattice are stronger than those in the Na_3PO_4 lattice. The strongly held together $AlPO_4$ lattice makes $AlPO_4$ insoluble, and the much weaker ionic bonds in the Na_3PO_4 lattice make Na_3PO_4 very soluble.

12.182 Because ethanol forms more hydrogen bonds with water,

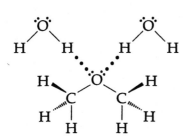

Diethyl ether, two possibilities
for hydrogen bonding

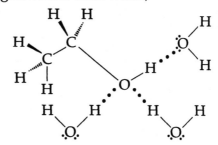

Ethanol, three possibilities
for hydrogen bonding

the amount of energy released in the ethanol solvation step is much greater than that released in the diethyl ether solvation step. The difference in $\Delta E_{solvation}$ is more than enough to compensate for the fact that $\Delta E_{solute\ separation}$ is greater for ethanol.

12.183 Whether or not a solute dissolves in a solvent is decided not only by changes in energy but also by changes in <u>entropy</u>.

12.184 A solute can dissolve even when the energy *released* by the solute–solvent interactions is less than the energy absorbed by the solute–solute and solvent–solvent interactions because the entropy of the system *increases*.

First error: Solute–solvent interactions mean some form of bonding is taking place, and the formation of bonds *always releases* energy.

Second error: Usually, having $\Delta E_{\text{solvation}}$ less than $\Delta E_{\text{solute separation}} + \Delta E_{\text{solvent separation}}$ means a solute does not dissolve. When $\Delta E_{\text{solvation}}$ is only slightly less, however, the *increase* in entropy that occurs as solute particles dissolve and become more disordered can tip the balance in favor of dissolution.

12.185 (a) An endothermic reaction is one that absorbs energy from its surroundings. According to the convention taught in the textbook, a reaction that absorbs energy has a positive ΔE_{total} value.

(b) The entropy for the universe increases when the solute dissolves because there is less order in the arrangement of the dissolved solute particles than in their arrangement in the undissolved solid.

12.186 (a) is correct because it expresses a direct proportionality between s and P—as pressure increases, so does gas solubility. (b) expresses an inverse proportionality and predicts that gas solubility decreases as pressure increases, counter to Henry's law. (c) predicts no dependence of gas solubility on pressure, also counter to Henry's law.

12.187 The graph tells you that, at 20.0°C, the solubility of NaCl in water is 38 g per 100.0 g of water. In 75 g of 20.0°C water, therefore, you can dissolve

$$75 \text{ g water} \times \frac{38 \text{ g NaCl}}{100.0 \text{ g water}} = 29 \text{ g NaCl}$$

Only 29 g of NaCl dissolves, which means the answer is no.

12.188 Yes. The solubility plot on page 439 of the textbook indicates that the solubility of $NaNO_3$ in water at 60.0°C is about 124 g per 100 g of water. The maximum amount of $NaNO_3$ soluble in 90.0 g of water at 60.0°C is therefore

$$90.0 \text{ g water} \times \frac{124 \text{ g NaNO}_3}{100 \text{ g water}} = 112 \text{ g NaNO}_3$$

12.189 The graph tells you that, at 20.0°C, the solubility of glucose in water is 86 g per 100.0 g of water. In 60.0 g of 20.0°C water, therefore, a saturated solution contains

$$60.0 \text{ g water} \times \frac{86 \text{ g glucose}}{100.0 \text{ g water}} = 52 \text{ g glucose}$$

12.190 As temperature increases, water molecules move faster and consequently collide more forcefully with the solid lattice, helping to release more molecules or ions from the solute lattice.

12.191

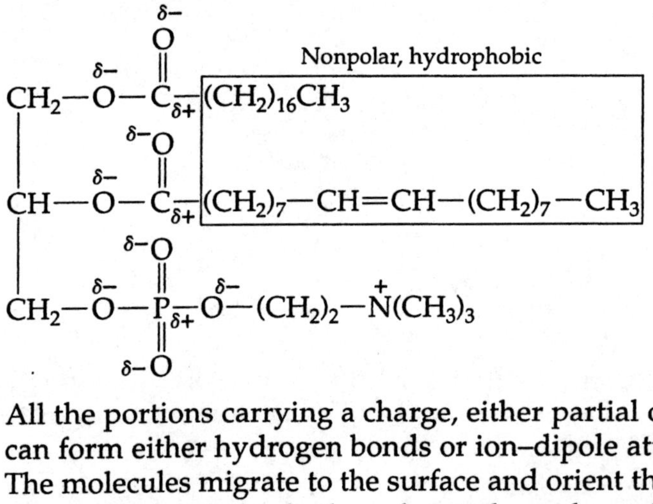

All the portions carrying a charge, either partial or full are hydrophilic because they can form either hydrogen bonds or ion–dipole attractions with water molecules.

12.192 The molecules migrate to the surface and orient themselves as shown in the drawing so that the hydrophobic hydrocarbon tails can be as far away from the water as possible.

12.193 Fat molecule:

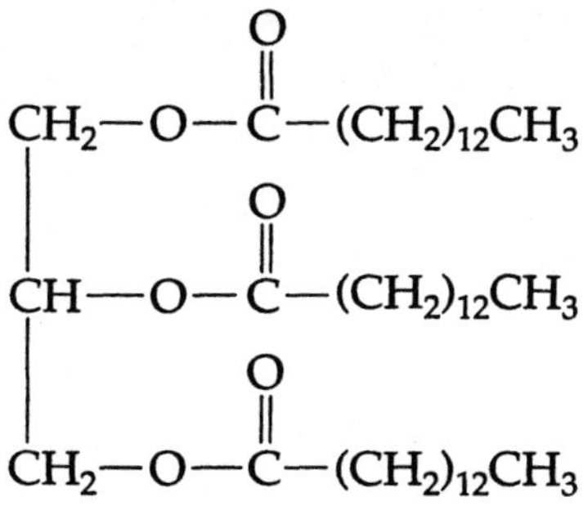

$$\begin{array}{l} \text{CH}_2\text{—O—}\overset{\displaystyle\overset{\text{O}}{\|}}{\text{C}}\text{—}(\text{CH}_2)_{12}\text{CH}_3 \\[1.5em] \text{CH—O—}\overset{\displaystyle\overset{\text{O}}{\|}}{\text{C}}\text{—}(\text{CH}_2)_{12}\text{CH}_3 \\[1.5em] \text{CH}_2\text{—O—}\overset{\displaystyle\overset{\text{O}}{\|}}{\text{C}}\text{—}(\text{CH}_2)_{12}\text{CH}_3 \end{array}$$

Each soap molecule is

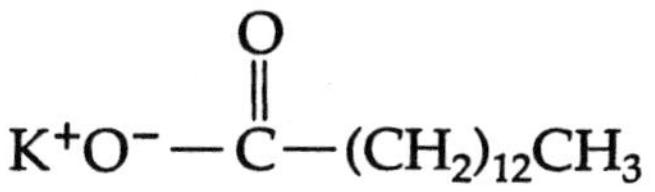

$$\text{K}^+\text{O}^-\text{—}\overset{\displaystyle\overset{\text{O}}{\|}}{\text{C}}\text{—}(\text{CH}_2)_{12}\text{CH}_3$$

12.194 (a)

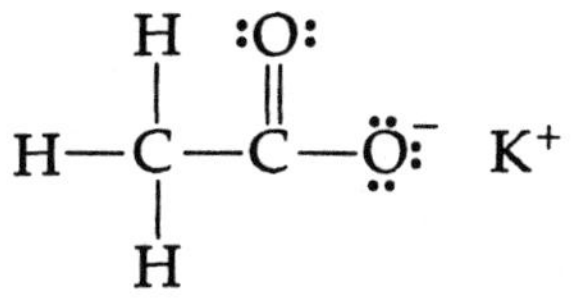

$$\text{H—}\overset{\displaystyle\overset{\text{H}}{|}}{\underset{\displaystyle\underset{\text{H}}{|}}{\text{C}}}\text{—}\overset{\displaystyle\overset{:\text{O}:}{\|}}{\text{C}}\text{—}\ddot{\text{O}}:^- \quad \text{K}^+$$

Potassium acetate

(b) 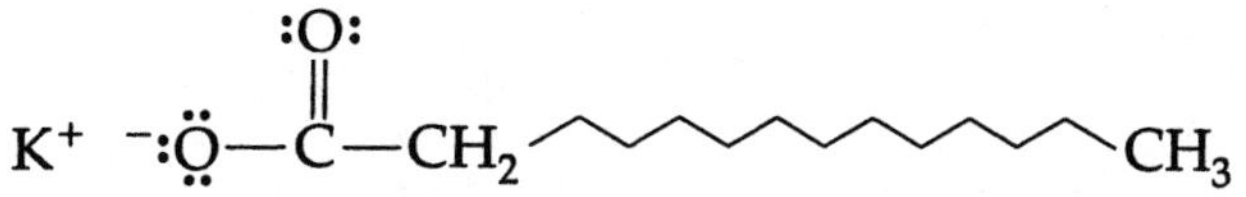 $\text{K}^+ \quad {}^-:\ddot{\text{O}}\text{—}\overset{\displaystyle\overset{:\text{O}:}{\|}}{\text{C}}\text{—CH}_2\text{\textasciitilde\textasciitilde\textasciitilde CH}_3$

Both have a cation plus an amino containing the $-\overset{\displaystyle\overset{}{\underset{\displaystyle\underset{\text{O}}{\|}}{\text{C}}}-\text{O}^-$ unit,

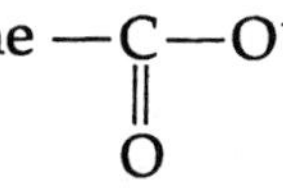

but potassium acetate does not have a nonpolar hydrocarbon tail. (Thus it cannot act as a soap.)

(c) Because Ca^{2+} carries a 2+ charge, it bonds with two soap molecules. The Ca^{2+}—soap bond forms at the negative site on the soap molecule, so that the scum molecule looks like this:

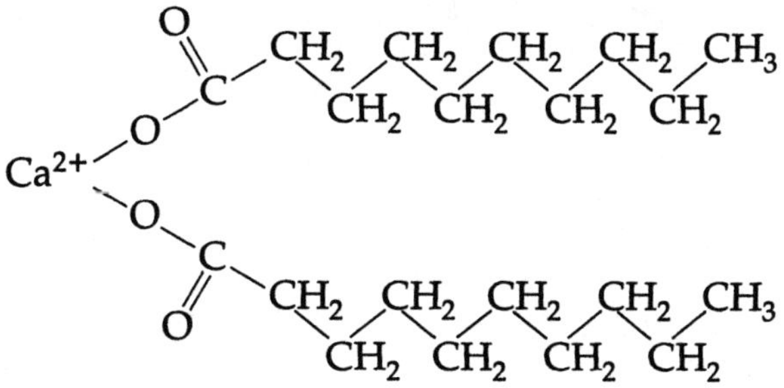

12.195 The soap molecules in a vesicle align themselves such that there are polar heads (gray circles in the textbook drawing) lining both the outside and the hollowed-out center of the structure. (The tails from the two layers intermingle and "dissolve" into one another.) Because there are polar heads at the center, polar water molecules migrate there to interact with the polar heads.

12.196 (a) $M_{\text{diluted solution}} = \dfrac{2.00\text{ M} \times 75.0\text{ mL}}{2.00\text{ L}} \times \dfrac{1\text{ L}}{1000\text{ mL}} = 0.0750\text{ M}$

(b) $\dfrac{0.075 \text{ mol Fe(NO}_3)_3}{\text{L}} \times \dfrac{1 \text{ mol Fe}^{3+}}{1 \text{ mol Fe(NO}_3)_3} = \dfrac{0.075 \text{ mol Fe}^{3+}}{\text{L}} = 0.075 \text{ M}$

(c) $\dfrac{0.075 \text{ mol Fe(NO}_3)_3}{\text{L}} \times \dfrac{3 \text{ mol NO}_3^{-}}{1 \text{ mol Fe(NO}_3)_3} = \dfrac{0.225 \text{ mol NO}_3^{-}}{\text{L}} = 0.225 \text{ M}$

12.197 (a) $M_{\text{diluted solution}} = \dfrac{0.500 \text{ M} \times 0.0450 \text{ L}}{1.50 \text{ L}} = 0.0150 \text{ M}$

(b) The formula for aluminum sulfate is $Al_2(SO_4)_3$.

$\dfrac{0.0150 \text{ mol Al}_2(SO_4)_3}{1 \text{ L}} \times \dfrac{2 \text{ mol Al}^{3+}}{1 \text{ mol Al}_2(SO_4)_3} = 0.0300 \dfrac{\text{mol Al}^{3+}}{\text{L}} = 0.0300 \text{ M}$

(c) $\dfrac{0.0150 \text{ mol Al}_2(SO_4)_3}{1 \text{ L}} \times \dfrac{3 \text{ mol SO}_4^{2-}}{1 \text{ mol Al}_2(SO_4)_3} = 0.0450 \dfrac{\text{mol SO}_4^{2-}}{\text{L}} = 0.0450 \text{ M}$

12.198 You must determine the number of moles of NaOH in the 60.0 mL + 60.0 mL = 120.0 mL of solution. Because the product MV is always equal to number of moles, you can say

$0.250 \text{ M} \times 0.0600 \text{ L} = \dfrac{0.250 \text{ mol}}{\text{L}} \times 0.0600 \text{ L} = 0.0150 \text{ mol NaOH}$ from the 0.250 M solution

$0.125 \text{ M} \times 0.0600 \text{ L} = \dfrac{0.125 \text{ mol}}{\text{L}} \times 0.0600 \text{ L} = 0.00750 \text{ mol NaOH}$ from the 0.125 M solution

You therefore have 0.0150 mol + 0.00750 mol = 0.0225 mol NaOH in 120.0 mL, for a molarity of

$\dfrac{0.0225 \text{ mol}}{120.0 \text{ mL}} \times \dfrac{1000 \text{ mL}}{1 \text{ L}} = 0.188 \text{ M}$

12.199 Your first step is to determine the number of moles of each base in the 60.0 mL + 60.0 mL = 120.0 mL of solution. Because the product MV equals number of moles, you can say (remembering that V must be in liters)

$0.250 \text{ M} \times 0.0600 \text{ L} = 0.0150 \text{ mol NaOH}$

$0.125 \text{ M} \times 0.0600 \text{ L} = 0.00750 \text{ mol Ba(OH)}_2$

Now determine how much OH^{-} these quantities yield:

$0.0150 \text{ mol NaOH} \times \dfrac{1 \text{ mol OH}^{-}}{1 \text{ mol NaOH}} = 0.0150 \text{ mol OH}^{-}$

$0.00750 \text{ mol Ba(OH)}_2 \times \dfrac{2 \text{ mol OH}^{-}}{1 \text{ mol Ba(OH)}_2} = 0.0150 \text{ mol OH}^{-}$

You therefore have 0.0150 mol + 0.0150 mol = 0.0300 mol OH^{-} in the 120.0 mL, meaning the molarity is

$\dfrac{0.0300 \text{ mol}}{0.1200 \text{ L}} = 0.250 \dfrac{\text{mol}}{\text{L}} = 0.250 \text{ M}$

12.200 $0.1000 \text{ L} \times \dfrac{1.00 \text{ mol Ca(NO}_3)_2}{\text{L}} \times \dfrac{2 \text{ mol N}}{1 \text{ mol Ca(NO}_3)_2} \times \dfrac{14.007 \text{ g N}}{1 \text{ mol N}} = 2.80 \text{ g N}$

12.201 $0.5000 \text{ L solution} \times \dfrac{0.300 \text{ mol NaOH}}{1 \text{ L solution}} \times \dfrac{39.997 \text{ g NaOH}}{1 \text{ mol NaOH}} = 6.00 \text{ g NaOH}$

12.202 $\dfrac{0.0025 \text{ mol}}{0.00369 \text{ L}} = 0.68 \text{ M}$

12.203 The product MV gives number of moles (V must be in liters).

$5.20 \times 10^{-3} \text{ M} \times 0.02868 \text{ L} = 149 \times 10^{-4} \text{ mol}$

12.204 One mole of NaOH neutralizes 1 mole of HNO_3. First determine the number of moles of H^+ to be neutralized:

$$0.0500 \text{ L } HNO_3 \text{ solution} \times \frac{0.0100 \text{ mol } HNO_3}{1 \text{ L } HNO_3 \text{ solution}} \times \frac{1 \text{ mol } H^+}{1 \text{ mol } HNO_3} = 5.00 \times 10^{-4} \text{ mol } H^+$$

Then determine what volume of the NaOH solution contains this number of moles of OH^-:

$$5.00 \times 10^{-4} \text{ mol } OH^- \times \frac{1 \text{ mol } NaOH}{1 \text{ mol } OH^-} \times \frac{1 \text{ L } NaOH \text{ solution}}{0.0150 \text{ mol } NaOH} = 0.0333 \text{ L } NaOH \text{ soln} = 33.3 \text{ mL}$$

12.205 The number of moles of H^+ to be neutralized is

$$0.0500 \text{ L} \times \frac{0.0100 \text{ mol } H_2SO_4}{1 \text{ L}} \times \frac{2 \text{ mol } H^+}{1 \text{ mol } H_2SO_4} = 0.00100 \text{ mol } H^+$$

The volume of base solution containing this many moles of OH^- is

$$0.00100 \text{ mol } OH^- \times \frac{1 \text{ mol } NaOH}{1 \text{ mol } OH^-} \times \frac{1 \text{ L } NaOH \text{ solution}}{0.0150 \text{ mol } NaOH} = 0.0667 \text{ L} = 66.7 \text{ mL}$$

12.206 The number of moles of OH^- consumed in the neutralization is

$$0.04735 \text{ L } NaOH \text{ solution} \times \frac{0.01020 \text{ mol } NaOH}{1 \text{ L } NaOH \text{ solution}} \times \frac{1 \text{ mol } OH^-}{1 \text{ mol } NaOH} = 4.830 \times 10^{-4} \text{ mol } OH^-$$

Thus there must be this number of moles of H^+ in the titrated sample. The number of moles of HCl is therefore

$$4.830 \times 10^{-4} \text{ mol } H^+ \times \frac{1 \text{ mol HCl}}{1 \text{ mol } H^+} = 4.830 \times 10^{-4} \text{ mol HCl}$$

and the concentration of the HCl solution is

$$\frac{4.830 \times 10^{-4} \text{ mol HCl}}{0.05000 \text{ L}} = 0.009660 \frac{\text{mol}}{\text{L}} = 9.660 \times 10^{-3} \text{ M HCl}$$

12.207 Percent composition by mass is calculated with solute and solution masses. Therefore your first step is to use the density to convert the given solvent volume to mass:

$$1.00 \text{ L} \times \frac{1000 \text{ mL}}{1 \text{ L}} \times \frac{1.00 \text{ g}}{\text{mL}} = 1.00 \times 10^3 \text{ g water}$$

$$\frac{5.00 \text{ g sucrose}}{5.00 \text{ g sucrose} + (1.00 \times 10^3 \text{ g water})} \times 100$$

$$= \frac{5.00 \text{ g sucrose}}{(0.00500 \times 10^3 \text{ g sucrose}) + (1.00 \times 10^3 \text{ g water})} \times 100$$

$$= \frac{5.00 \text{ g sucrose}}{1.01 \times 10^3 \text{ g solution}} \times 100 = 0.495 \text{ mass } \%$$

12.208 $\dfrac{4.00 \text{ mL hexane}}{250.0 \text{ mL solution}} \times 100 = 1.60\% \text{ by volume}$

12.209 Air being 21 vol % O_2 means each 100 mL of air contains 21 mL of O_2, information you use as a conversion factor:

$$200.0 \text{ L air} \times \frac{1000 \text{ mL air}}{1 \text{ L air}} \times \frac{21 \text{ mL } O_2}{100 \text{ mL air}} = 4.2 \times 10^4 \text{ mL } O_2 \text{ in } 200.0 \text{ mL of air}$$

Now use the ideal gas equation solved for n to determine moles of O_2 (remembering that you must convert O_2 volume to liters to match the units of R):

$$n = \frac{1.00 \text{ atm} \times 42 \text{ L}}{0.0821 \dfrac{\text{L} \cdot \text{atm}}{\text{K} \cdot \text{mol}} \times 298 \text{ K}} = 1.7 \text{ mol } O_2$$

$$1.7 \text{ mol } O_2 = \frac{31.998 \text{ g } O_2}{1 \text{ mol } O_2} = 54 \text{ g } O_2$$

12.210 (a) $\dfrac{5.00 \text{ g solute}}{100.0 \text{ mL solution}} \times 100 = 5.00\% \text{ by mass / volume}$

(b) You need to know the mass of solvent used to make the solution (either by measuring the mass or by knowing the solvent density). The calculation is:

$$\frac{5.00 \text{ g solute}}{5.00 \text{ g solute} + \text{grams of solvent}} \times 100 = \% \text{ by mass}$$

12.211 11.5 mass % means each 100.0 g of steel contains 11.5 g of Cr.

$$250.0 \text{ lb steel} \times \frac{453.6 \text{ g steel}}{1 \text{ lb steel}} \times \frac{11.5 \text{ g Cr}}{100.0 \text{ g steel}} = 1.30 \times 10^4 \text{ g Cr}$$

12.212 (a) He did not specify which type of percent composition he means (percent by mass, percent by volume, percent by mass/volume).

(b) $\text{Percent by mass} = \dfrac{\text{Grams solute}}{\text{Grams solution}} \times 100$

$$\text{Grams solute} = \frac{\text{Grams solution} \times \text{Percent by mass}}{100} = \frac{500.0 \text{ g} \times 1.00\%}{100} = 5.00 \text{ g}$$

You would mix 5.00 g of hexane with 500.0 g solution − 5.00 g hexane = 495.0 g of dichloromethane.

12.213 (a) The procedure for determining theoretical yield is described in Section 8.4 of the textbook.

Step 1: $Ca^{2+}(aq) + 2 \text{ F}^-(aq) \longrightarrow CaF_2(s)$

Step 2: $0.0265 \text{ L Ca(NO}_3)_2 \text{ solution} \times \dfrac{0.100 \text{ mol Ca(NO}_3)_2}{1 \text{ L Ca(NO}_3)_2 \text{ solution}} \times \dfrac{1 \text{ mol Ca}^{2+}}{1 \text{ mol Ca(NO}_3)_2}$

$= 0.00265 \text{ mol Ca}^{2+}$

$$0.0498 \text{ L NaF solution} \times \frac{0.100 \text{ mol NaF}}{1 \text{ L NaF solution}} \times \frac{1 \text{ mol F}^-}{1 \text{ mol NaF}} = 0.00498 \text{ mol F}^-$$

Step 2a: $\dfrac{0.00265 \text{ mol Ca}^{2+}}{1} = 0.00265$

$\dfrac{0.00498 \text{ mol F}^-}{2} = 0.00294$ ← Smaller number, limiting reactant

Steps 3 and 4: $0.00498 \text{ mol } F^- \times \dfrac{1 \text{ mol } CaF_2}{2 \text{ mol } F^-} \times \dfrac{78.074 \text{ g } CaF_2}{1 \text{ mol } CaF_2} = 0.194 \text{ g } CaF_2$ consumed

(b) You must first determine the number of moles of Ca^{2+} not used in the reaction. Use the equation coefficients to determine how much Ca^{2+} reacted with the F^-:

$$0.00498 \text{ mol } F^- \times \dfrac{1 \text{ mol } CaF_2}{2 \text{ mol } F^-} \times \dfrac{78.074 \text{ g } CaF_2}{1 \text{ mol } CaF_2} = 0.194 \text{ g } CaF_2$$

$0.00265 \text{ mol } Ca^{2+} - 0.00249 \text{ mol } Ca^{2+} = 0.00016 \text{ mol } Ca^{2+}$ left over

This amount of Ca^{2+} is present in 26.5 mL + 49.8 mL = 76.3 mL of solution, making the molar Ca^{2+} concentration

$$\dfrac{0.00016 \text{ mol}}{0.0763 \text{ L}} = 0.0021 \text{ M}$$

12.214 (a) $Fe^{3+}(aq) + 3 \, OH^-(aq) \longrightarrow Fe(OH)_3(s)$

(b) The procedure for determining theoretical yield is described in Section 8.4 of the textbook.

Step 1: See part (a).

Step 2: $0.2000 \text{ L NaOH solution} \times \dfrac{2.50 \text{ mol NaOH}}{1 \text{ L solution}} \times \dfrac{1 \text{ mol } OH^-}{1 \text{ mol NaOH}} = 0.500 \text{ mol } OH^-$

$0.1000 \text{ L } Fe(NO_3)_3 \text{ solution} \times \dfrac{1.50 \text{ mol } Fe(NO_3)_3}{1 \text{ L } Fe(NO_3)_3 \text{ solution}} \times \dfrac{1 \text{ mol } Fe^{3+}}{1 \text{ mol } Fe(NO_3)_3}$

$= 0.150 \text{ mol } Fe^{3+}$

Step 2a: $\dfrac{0.500 \text{ mol } OH^-}{3} = 0.167$

$\dfrac{0.150 \text{ mol } Fe^{3+}}{1} = 0.150$ ← Smaller number, limiting reactant

Steps 3 and 4: $0.150 \text{ mol } Fe^{3+} \times \dfrac{1 \text{ mol } Fe(OH)_3}{1 \text{ mol } Fe^{3+}} \times \dfrac{106.9 \text{ g } Fe(OH)_3}{1 \text{ mol } Fe(OH)_3} = 16.0 \text{ g } Fe(OH)_3$

(c) $\dfrac{10.95 \text{ g}}{16.0 \text{ g}} \times 100 = 68.4\%$

(d) You must first determine the number of moles of OH^- not used in the reaction. Use the equation coefficients to determine how much OH^- reacted with the Fe^{3+}:

$$0.150 \text{ mol } Fe^{3+} \times \dfrac{3 \text{ mol } OH^-}{1 \text{ mol } Fe^{3+}} = 0.450 \text{ mol } OH^- \text{ consumed}$$

$0.500 \text{ mol } OH^- - 0.450 \text{ mol } OH^- = 0.050 \text{ mol } OH^-$ left over

This amount of OH^- is present in 200.0 mL + 100.0 mL = 300.0 mL of solution, making the molar OH^- concentration

$$\dfrac{0.050 \text{ mol}}{0.3000 \text{ L}} = 0.17 \text{ M}$$

12.215 (a) $Ag^+(aq) + Br^-(aq) \longrightarrow AgBr(s)$

(b) $20.0 \text{ g NaBr} \times \dfrac{1 \text{ mol NaBr}}{102.894 \text{ g NaBr}} \times \dfrac{1 \text{ mol Br}^-}{1 \text{ mol NaBr}} = \dfrac{0.194 \text{ mol Br}^-}{1} = 0.194$

$0.0500 \text{ L AgNO}_3 \text{ solution} \times \dfrac{2.00 \text{ mol AgNO}_3}{1 \text{ L solution}} \times \dfrac{1 \text{ mol Ag}^+}{1 \text{ mol AgNO}_3}$

$= \dfrac{0.100 \text{ mol Ag}^+}{1} = 0.100 \leftarrow$ Smaller number, limiting reactant

Use the limiting reactant to calculate theoretical yield:

$0.100 \text{ mol Ag}^+ \times \dfrac{1 \text{ mol AgBr}}{1 \text{ mol Ag}^+} \times \dfrac{187.772 \text{ g AgBr}}{1 \text{ mol AgBr}} = 18.8 \text{ g AgBr}$

(c) $\dfrac{15.0 \text{ g}}{18.8 \text{ g}} \times 100 = 79.8\%$

(d) $0.100 \text{ mol Ag}^+ \times \dfrac{1 \text{ mol Br}^-}{1 \text{ mol Ag}^+} = 0.100 \text{ mol Br}^-$ consumed

The Br^- remaining in the 50.0 mL of solution is thus

$0.194 \text{ mol} - 0.100 \text{ mol} = 0.094 \text{ mol}$

making the Br^- molar concentration

$\dfrac{0.094 \text{ mol}}{0.0500 \text{ L}} = 1.88 \text{ M}$

13

When Reactants Turn into Products

13.1 See solution in textbook.

13.2 (a) 165 kJ/mol

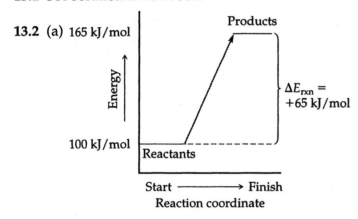

(b) Uphill because the energy of the products is greater than the energy of the reactants.

(c) 165kJ/mol − 100 kJ/mol = +65 kJ/mol

(d) Cold because the reaction is endothermic and therefore absorbs heat from the surroundings.

13.3 (a) Because $\Delta E_{rxn} = E_{products} - E_{reactants}$ is negative, $E_{reactants}$ must be higher than $E_{products}$.

(b) $E_{reactants} = E_{products} - \Delta E_{rxn} = 20 \text{ kJ/mol} - (-450 \text{ kJ/mol}) = +470 \text{ kJ/mol}$.

(c) Exothermic, because ΔE_{rxn} is negative.

(d) Downhill, starting high ($E_{reactants} = 470$ kJ/mol) and ending lower ($E_{products} = 20$ kJ/mol).

(e)

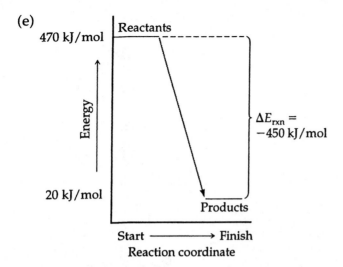

13.4 See solution in textbook.

13.5 (a) That the container gets cold tells you energy (in the form of heat) is absorbed into the reaction mixture. This means the reaction is endothermic, and therefore ΔE_{rxn} must be a positive number: $\Delta E_{forward\ rxn} = +250$ kJ/mol.

    (b) A change of sign gives $\Delta E_{reverse\ rxn} = -250$ kJ/mol.

13.6 (a) That the container gets hot tells you energy (in the form of heat) is released by the reaction mixture. This means the reaction is exothermic, and therefore ΔE_{rxn} must be a negative number: $\Delta E_{forward\ rxn} = -250$ kJ/mol.

    (b) A change of sign gives $\Delta E_{reverse\ rxn} = +250$ kJ/mol.

13.7 See solution in textbook.

13.8 See solution in textbook.

13.9 200 kJ. The negative value of ΔE_{rxn} means an exothermic reaction. Therefore the amount of energy released as product forms is 100 kJ greater than the amount of energy absorbed as reactants break up. The 2 moles of AB formed releases 2 mol × 150 kJ/1 mol = 300 kJ, making the amount absorbed by the reactants 300 kJ − 100 kJ = 200 kJ.

13.10 Practice Problem 13.8:

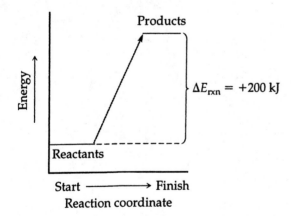

Practice Problem 13.9:

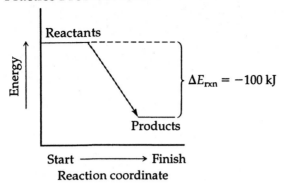

13.11 See solution in textbook.

13.12 Endothermic reaction A must have the energy of the products higher than the energy of the reactants:

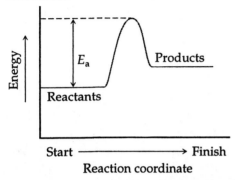

Exothermic reaction B must have the energy of the products lower than the energy of the reactants. You indicate that reaction B proceeds faster than reaction A by making the E_a height less here than in the profile for reaction A:

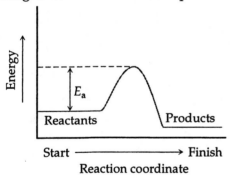

13.13 False. It is the size of the E_a barrier that determines the speed of any exothermic reaction, not how much heat energy is given off as the reaction proceeds.

Reaction A

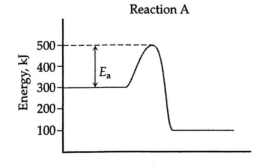

$\Delta E_{rxn} = 100\ kJ - 300\ kJ = -200\ kJ$; more exothermic than reaction B
$E_a = 500\ kJ - 300\ kJ = 200\ kJ$; slower than reaction B

Reaction B

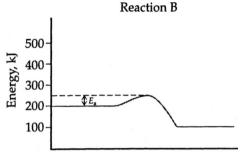

$\Delta E_{rxn} = 100\ kJ - 200\ kJ = -100\ kJ$; less exothermic than reaction A
$E_a = 250\ kJ - 200\ kJ = 50\ kJ$; faster than reaction A

13.14 See solution in textbook.

13.15 (a) The rule of thumb is that reaction rate doubles with every 10 C° increase in temperature. Practice Problem 13.14(b) shows that reaction rate is expressed as number of effective collisions per second. Thus the doubled reaction rate means the number of effective collisions increases from 20 per second to 40 per second.

(b) Because increasing the temperature causes the molecules to have more kinetic energy, and consequently more of them have energy equal to or greater than E_a. In mathematical terms, the energy factor in Equation 13.1 of the textbook increases while the orientation factor remains unchanged. Therefore the number of effective collisions increases.

(c) (200 sufficiently energetic collisions/s) × 0.2 = 40 effective collisions/s, forming 40 CH_3OH molecules/s.

13.16 (a) An orientation factor of 0.1 means colliding molecules have the proper orientation in 10% of the collisions.

(b) (100 sufficiently energetic collisions/s) × 0.1 = 10 effective collisions/s, forming 10 CH_3OH molecules/s.

13.17 See solution in textbook.

13.18 Only reactant concentrations appear in a rate law, along with the rate constant k. Each reactant concentration has an order shown as an exponent:

Rate = $k\ [H_2O_2]^x[I^-]^y[H^+]^z$

13.19 (a) k for the NO reaction is much larger than k for the H_2O_2 reaction. Temperature increases affect reaction rates, as do reactant concentrations. Because both these factors are the same for the two reactions, the vast difference in rates must be due to different k values.

(b) Because faster reactions have smaller E_a values, the NO E_a must be much smaller than the $H_2O_2\ E_a$.

(c) Increase $[H_2O_2]$, $[I^-]$, and/or $[H^+]$; increase the temperature at which the reaction is run; add a catalyst to the reaction mixture.

13.20 Reactant concentrations are proportional to the number of reactant molecules per unit volume. The more reactant molecules there are in a given volume, the greater the number of collisions.

13.21 See solution in textbook.

13.22 (a) and (b) Reaction order with respect to a particular reactant is the exponent on that reactant in the rate law. Thus the order is 1 for Br^- and 2 for H^+.

(c) You get the overall order by adding all the exponents together: $1 + 1 + 2 = 4$.

(d) The rate quadruples. To see this, suppose all concentrations are initially 1 M and that, for simplicity, k is 1 also. The rate initially is $1 \times (1\ M) \times (1\ M) \times (1\ M)^2 = 1\ M/s$.

Double $[H^+]$ and you get $1 \times (1\text{ M}) \times (1\text{ M}) \times (2\text{ M})^2 = 4\text{ M/s}$. You may use any other initial concentrations and the result will be the same: initial $1 \times (3\text{ M}) \times (4\text{ M}) \times (2\text{ M})^2 = 48\text{ M/s}$, double $[H^+]$ and you get $1 \times (3\text{ M}) \times (4\text{ M}) \times (4\text{ M})^2 = 192\text{ M/s}$, $192 \div 48 = 4$; the rate has quadrupled from 48 M/s to 192 M/s.

13.23 Rate $= k[NO]^2[O_2]$. To get the NO exponent, use experiments 1 and 2, which say that when [NO] was doubled while $[O_2]$ was held constant, the rate quadrupled. This means the reaction is second order with respect to NO. (Note that you could have used experiments 3 and 4 to get this same result.)

To get the O_2 exponent, use experiments 1 and 3, which say that when $[O_2]$ was doubled while [NO] was held constant, the rate doubled. This means the reaction is first order with respect to O_2. (Note that you could have used experiments 2 and 4 to get this same result.)

13.24 See solution in textbook.

13.25 (a) and (b) Numerous answers possible, such as

$$
\begin{aligned}
Y_2 + Y_2 &\xrightarrow{\text{Slow}} (Y_3) + (Y) \\
(Y) + X_2 &\xrightarrow{\text{Fast}} XY + (X) \\
(Y_3) + (X) &\xrightarrow{\text{Fast}} XY + Y_2 \\
\hline
X_2 + Y_2 &\longrightarrow XY + XY
\end{aligned}
$$

$$
\begin{aligned}
Y_2 + Y_2 &\xrightarrow{\text{Slow}} (Y_3) + (Y) \\
X_2 + (Y_3) &\xrightarrow{\text{Fast}} XY + (XY_2) \\
(XY_2) &\xrightarrow{\text{Fast}} (X) + Y_2 \\
(X) + (Y) &\xrightarrow{\text{Fast}} XY \\
\hline
X_2 + Y_2 &\longrightarrow XY + XY
\end{aligned}
$$

$$
\begin{aligned}
Y_2 + Y_2 &\xrightarrow{\text{Slow}} (Y_3) + (Y) \\
X_2 + X_2 &\xrightarrow{\text{Fast}} (X_3) + (X) \\
(X) + (Y_3) &\xrightarrow{\text{Fast}} XY + Y_2 \\
(X_3) + (Y) &\xrightarrow{\text{Fast}} XY + Y_2 \\
\hline
X_2 + Y_2 &\longrightarrow XY + XY
\end{aligned}
$$

$$
\begin{aligned}
Y_2 + Y_2 &\xrightarrow{\text{Slow}} (Y_3) + (Y) \\
X_2 + X_2 &\xrightarrow{\text{Fast}} (X_4) \\
(X_4) + (Y) &\xrightarrow{\text{Fast}} XY + (X_3) \\
(Y_3) + (X_3) &\xrightarrow{\text{Fast}} XY + X_2 + Y_2 \\
\hline
X_2 + Y_2 &\longrightarrow XY + XY
\end{aligned}
$$

(c) For any mechanism you postulate, design an experiment that detects one or more of the reaction intermediates.

13.26 $Y_2 \longrightarrow Y + Y$. The rate-determining elementary step that goes with the given rate law has only one reactant, Y_2, and the balancing coefficient for it must be 1. The only thing Y_2 alone can do is split into two Y units.

13.27 There are no C–H bonds in either product, which means all four C–H bonds in $H_2C=CH_2$ were broken. There are no C–C bonds in either product, which means the C=C bond was broken. There are no O–O bonds in either product, which means the three O–O bonds in $3 O_2$ were broken.

There are no C–O bonds in either reactant, meaning four C–O bonds formed to create the $2 CO_2$. There are no O–H bonds in either reactant, meaning four O–H bonds formed to create the $2 H_2O$.

13.28 No, because a single collision breaking all the bonds would require the highly unlikely event of four molecules coming together with the proper orientation and enough energy to tear all the molecules apart at once.

13.29 Yes, because the Cl is substituted for the I.

13.30

13.31 The sequence of steps molecules go through when changing from reactants to products during the chemical reaction.

13.32 Chemical kinetics.

13.33 They study the kinetics of the reaction by determining how the reaction rate changes as temperature and reactant concentrations are varied.

13.34 When a reaction mechanism is understood, the reaction rate can be influenced and new reaction rates can be predicted.

13.35 Because of the way ΔE_{rxn} is defined—$\Delta E_{rxn} = E_{products} - E_{reactants}$—a negative ΔE_{rxn} means the energy of the products is less than the energy of the reactants. Therefore compound B, the product, is at a lower energy level than compound A, the reactant, by 100 kJ/mol.

13.36 Absorb energy from the surroundings because the product, B, has twice the energy of the reactant, A. Therefore $\Delta E_{rxn} = E_{products} - E_{reactants}$ is a positive number, which means the reaction is endothermic and so absorbs energy.

13.37 Compound B, the product, because it has the energy that compound A originally had plus the energy absorbed from the surroundings.

13.38 C is at the higher energy level. D must have less energy than C because some of the energy originally in C was released into the surroundings when C converted to D.

13.39 The reaction in Problem 13.37 is endothermic because it absorbs energy from the surroundings; because it lowers the temperature of the surroundings as it absorbs energy, this reaction can "supply cold." The reaction in Problem 13.38 is exothermic because it releases energy into the surroundings; because it increases the temperature of the surroundings as it releases energy, this reaction can supply heat.

13.40 Endothermic because the reaction had to absorb energy from the surroundings in order to increase the energy from 20 kJ to 60 kJ. $\Delta E_{rxn} = E_{products} - E_{reactants} = 60 \text{ kJ} - 20 \text{ kJ} = +40 \text{ kJ}$.

13.41 Because the definition of ΔE_{rxn} is $E_{products} - E_{reactants}$, a negative ΔE_{rxn} means the energy of the products is less than the energy of the reactants. The energy initially in the reactants but not needed by the products is released into the surroundings, making the reaction exothermic.

13.42 Exothermic because the energy of the product, 1 mole of A, is 20 kJ and the energy of the reactant, 1 mole of B, is 60 kJ. Anytime $E_{products}$ is less than $E_{reactants}$, the reaction is exothermic; $\Delta E_{rxn} = 20 \text{ kJ} - 60 \text{ kJ} = -40 \text{ kJ}$.

13.43 An energy-uphill reaction is one in which the products have more energy than the reactants—in other words, an energy-absorbing, endothermic reaction. An energy-downhill reaction is one in which the products have less energy than the reactants—in other words, an energy-releasing, exothermic reaction.

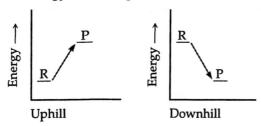

Uphill   Downhill

13.44 Endothermic because $E_{products}$ is greater than $E_{reactants}$; $\Delta E_{rxn} = 240$ kJ/mol $- 190$ kJ/mol $= +50$ kJ/mol.

13.45 The reactants must absorb energy from the surroundings.

13.46 Because the definition of ΔE_{rxn} is $E_{products} - E_{reactants}$ and in an exothermic reaction the products are at a lower energy level than the reactants. Therefore a larger number ($E_{reactants}$) is subtracted from a smaller number ($E_{products}$), making ΔE_{rxn} negative.

13.47 $\Delta E_{rxn} = E_{absorbed} - E_{released} = 800$ kJ $- 400$ kJ $= 400$ kJ. The reaction is endothermic because ΔE_{rxn} is positive, which means the energy absorbed to break reactant bonds is greater than the energy released as product bonds form.

13.48 The ΔE_{rxn} value -800 kJ tells you that, *overall*, the reaction releases 800 kJ. Because 800 kJ was absorbed initially to break reactant bonds, forming the product bonds must release 1600 kJ.

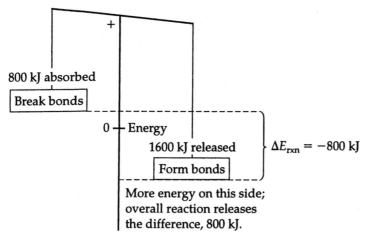

$\Delta E_{rxn} = E_{absorbed} - E_{released}$
$E_{released} = E_{absorbed} - \Delta E_{rxn} = 800$ kJ $- (-800$ kJ$) = 1600$ kJ

13.49 The minimum amount of energy reactant molecules must have in order for a reaction to occur.

13.50 An inverse proportion—the larger the E_a value, the lower the reaction rate (and the slower the reaction); the smaller the E_a value, the higher the reaction rate (and the faster the reaction).

13.51 False. The speed of any chemical reaction depends on the size of E_a, not on whether the reaction is exothermic (energy-downhill) or endothermic (energy-uphill). The smaller the E_a value, the faster the reaction.

13.52

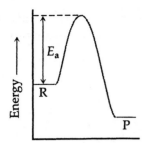

Reaction A. This reaction is downhill because the energy of the products is less than the energy of the reactants, but it is slower than reaction B because E_a here is larger than E_a for reaction B.

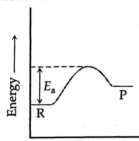

Reaction B. This reaction is uphill because the energy of the products is more than the energy of the reactants, but it is faster than reaction A because E_a here is smaller than E_a for reaction A.

13.53 Exothermic means the products must have less energy than the reactants. You can use any numeric values you like on the energy axis, just so long as there is a 20-kJ difference between $E_{reactants}$ and E_a, and a 40-kJ difference between $E_{reactants}$ and $E_{products}$. Here are just two of the many possibilities for what your graph could look like. Note that no matter what values you use on the energy axis, the shape of the curve never changes.

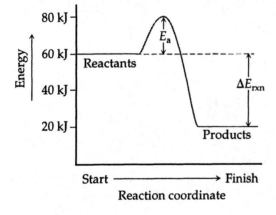

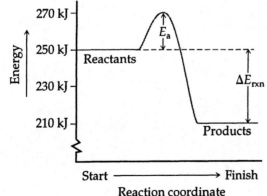

13.54 The point in the reaction when just enough energy has been added to the reaction mixture to cause the reactant bonds to be almost broken and the product bonds to be just beginning to form.

13.55

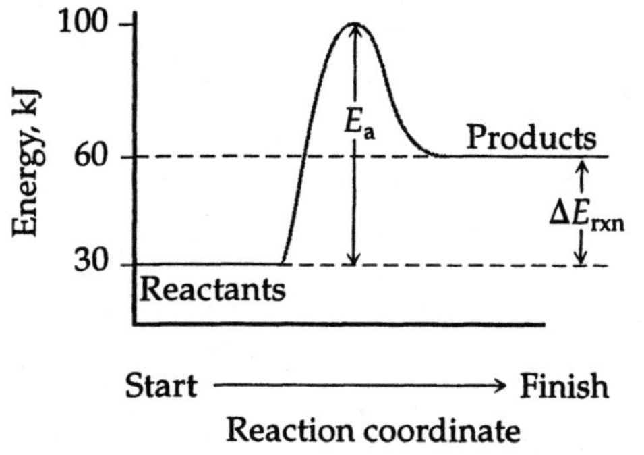

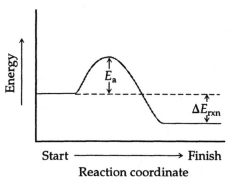

$$\Delta E_{rxn} = E_{products} - E_{reactants} = 60 \text{ kJ} - 30 \text{ kJ} = +30 \text{ kJ}$$
$$E_a = E_{transition\ state} - E_{reactants} = 100 \text{ kJ} - 30 \text{ kJ} = +70 \text{ kJ}$$
The positive ΔE_{rxn} value makes this an endothermic reaction.

13.56 Increase the rate. The lower the activation energy barrier, the faster the reaction proceeds because more molecules have enough energy to climb the energy barrier (E_a).

13.57 Inversely. The larger E_a is, the slower the reaction; the smaller E_a is, the faster the reaction.

13.58 Increase the rate because heating up the reaction mixture increases the energy of the reactants. As a result, more reactant molecules have enough energy to overcome the energy barrier E_a.

13.59 Those that collide with each other with energy greater than or equal to E_a and with the proper orientation.

13.60

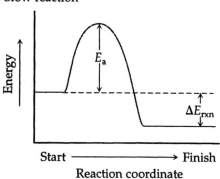

The fast reaction has a lower E_a than the slow reaction. Reaction rate is inversely proportional to E_a.

13.61 Nothing. There is no relationship between E_a and temperature. The only thing changing the temperature does is change the reaction rate. The energy barrier the reactants have to overcome does not change.

13.62 Because the size of E_a depends on the nature of the reactant molecules. Reaction A might have a much larger E_a than reaction B because the reactants in A have very strong bonds. It would therefore take a large amount of energy to break the A reactant bonds, resulting in a large value for E_a.

13.63 The rate generally doubles with every 10 C° increase in temperature.

13.64 In a substitution reaction, an atom or group X is knocked off a molecule and a new atom or group Y takes its place on the molecule. If the molecule initially containing Y does not approach the molecule initially containing X from the side opposite X, no reaction will occur:

$$CH_3Y \text{-----} \overset{\overset{H}{\underset{\diagdown}{}}}{\underset{\underset{H_3C}{\diagup}}{\overset{H\cdots}{}C}} - X = CH_3CH_2Y + CH_3^+ + X^-$$

$$\overset{\overset{H}{\underset{\diagdown}{}}}{\underset{\underset{H_3C}{\diagup}}{\overset{H\cdots}{}C}} - X \text{-----} YCH_3 = \text{No reaction}$$

13.65 Faster, because then all reactants having sufficient energy would be converted to product. Because of the orientation requirement, only a small fraction of energetically favorable molecules are converted to product.

13.66 A substance that increases the rate of a reaction without being used up in the process.

13.67 By providing an alternate pathway that has a lower activation energy E_a.

13.68 The Zn^{2+} bonds with the O of the OH group, and the presence of the Zn^{2+}–O bond weakens the C–OH bond. This weakening makes the C–OH bond easier to break, thus lowering the activation energy for the reaction and speeding it up.

13.69 Enzymes.

13.70 The reactant molecule that fits into an enzyme's active site.

13.71 The lock-and-key mechanism describes how, in a chemical reaction catalyzed by an enzyme, a substrate (the key) fits into the enzyme's active site (the lock). The substrate fits only if it has the correct shape, just as a key fits a lock only if the key has the correct shape.

13.72 Key. Scientists made a sulfanilamide molecule that was a modified version of the PABA key. The sulfanilamide key in the enzyme lock produced faulty vitamin B.

13.73 Because they speed up the processes, thereby decreasing production time and making the processes more financially profitable. Catalysts allow biological processes to proceed at the rate necessary to sustain life at normal temperatures. Without catalysts, the reactions would proceed so slowly that death would occur.

13.74 Because increasing reactant concentration increases the number of collisions between reactant molecules. The more collisions, the faster the rate of reaction.

13.75 Because decreasing the volume of a gas increases the gas concentration. Increasing the reactant concentration this way increases the number of collisions between reactant molecules, thus increasing the rate of the reaction.

13.76 Because both factors in the product depend on inherent (unchanging) properties of the reactants.

13.77 Increase because k depends partially on the fraction of collisions having energy equal to or greater than E_a. As temperature increases, more collisions have sufficient energy and k increases.

13.78 Increase because k partially depends on the fraction of collisions having the proper orientation. A catalyst provides a new mechanism for the reaction that allows a larger fraction of the reactant molecules to have the proper orientation, thus increasing k.

13.79 The fraction of collisions having energy equal to or greater than E_a and the fraction of collisions having the proper orientation.

13.80 k depends on the inherent factors of a reaction, not on whether the reaction is exothermic or endothermic.

13.81 (a) k. The inherent factors (those not influenced by concentration) in the rate law are fraction of collisions having $E \geqslant E_a$ and fraction of collisions having proper orientation, and k is by definition the product of these two factors.
(b) Orders.
(c) By adding up all the individual reactant orders.
(d) $x = 2$, $y = 1$, overall order $= 2 + 1 = 3$.
(e) Its order is 0, and this means the reaction rate does not depend on the concentration of reactant 1.

13.82 False. The orders must be determined experimentally and cannot be assumed to come from the balanced equation except when the reaction occurs in one step.

13.83 By conducting experiments that determine how reaction rate changes when the concentrations of the individual reactants are changed one by one.

13.84 The rate doubles. For a reaction where $k = 1$ and the concentration to be doubled is initially 2 M, for instance,

$$\text{Rate} = 1 \times (2\,\text{M})^1 = 2\,\text{M/s}$$

$$\text{Rate} = 1 \times (4\,\text{M})^1 = 4\,\text{M/s}$$

13.85 The rate quadruples. For a reaction where $k = 1$ and the concentration to be doubled is initially 2 M,

$$\text{Rate} = 1 \times (2\,\text{M})^2 = 4\,\text{M/s}$$

$$\text{Rate} = 1 \times (4\,\text{M})^2 = 16\,\text{M/s}$$

13.86 The rate does not change. For a reaction where $k = 1$ and the concentration to be doubled is initially 2 M, for instance,

$$\text{Rate} = 1 \times (2\,\text{M})^0 = 1 \times 1 = 1$$

$$\text{Rate} = 1 \times (4\,\text{M})^0 = 1 \times 1 = 1$$

13.87 Halving the volume of the balloon doubles the concentration of the reactants. Because rate $= k[\text{A}]$, the reaction is first order with respect to A and zero order with respect to B. Therefore doubling the concentration of A doubles the rate and doubling the concentration of B has no effect. Therefore the rate of the reaction doubles. For $k = 1$ and an initial A concentration of 1 M,

$$\text{Rate} = 1 \times (1\,\text{M}) = 1\,\text{M/s}$$

$$\text{Rate} = 1 \times (2\,\text{M}) = 2\,\text{M/s}$$

13.88 Halving the volume of the balloon doubles the concentration of the reactants. Because rate $= k[\text{A}]^2$, the reaction is second order with respect to A and zero order with respect to B. Therefore doubling the concentration of A quadruples the rate and doubling the concentration of B has no effect, which means the rate quadruples. For $k = 1$ and an initial A concentration of 1 M, for instance,

$$\text{Rate} = 1 \times (1\,\text{M})^2 = 1\,\text{M/s}$$

$$\text{Rate} = 1 \times (2\,\text{M})^2 = 4\,\text{M/s}$$

13.89 Halving the volume of the balloon doubles the concentration of the reactants. Because rate $= k[\text{A}][\text{B}]^2$, the reaction is first order with respect to A and second order with respect to B. Therefore doubling the concentration of A doubles the rate and doubling the concentration of B quadruples the rate. Doubling both concentrations therefore causes the rate to increase eightfold. For $k = 1$, an initial A concentration of 1 M, and an initial B concentration of 1 M,

$$\text{Rate} = 1 \times (1\,\text{M}) \times (1\,\text{M})^2 = 1\,\text{M/s}$$

$$\text{Rate} = 1 \times (2\,\text{M}) \times (2\,\text{M})^2 = 8\,\text{M/s}$$

13.90 Halving the volume of the balloon doubles the concentration of the reactants. Because rate = $k[A][B]$, the reaction is first order with respect to A and first order with respect to B. Therefore doubling the concentration of A doubles the rate and doubling the concentration of B doubles the rate. Doubling both at the same time quadruples the rate. For $k = 1$ and initial concentration of 1 M for A and 3 M for B, for instance,

Rate = $1 \times (1\,M) \times (3\,M) = 3\,M/s$

Rate = $1 \times (2\,M) \times (6\,M) = 12\,M/s$

13.91 A kinetics experiment is one in which the reactant concentrations are changed one at a time and how these changes affect reaction rate is noted. The exponents in an experimental rate law are determined from kinetics experiments.

13.92 You find the order of each reactant by comparing two experiments in which the concentration of that reactant is changed while the concentrations of all other reactants are held constant. Determine the order with respect to H_2O_2 from experiments 1 and 2. Doubling $[H_2O_2]$ causes the reaction rate to double from $1.15 \times 10^{-6}\,M/s$ to $2.30 \times 10^{-6}\,M/s$, making the reaction first order with respect to H_2O_2: rate = $k[H_2O_2]^1[I^-]^?[H^+]^?$.

Determine the order with respect to I^- from experiments 1 and 3. Doubling $[I^-]$ causes the reaction rate to double from $1.15 \times 10^{-6}\,M/s$ to $2.30 \times 10^{-6}\,M/s$, making the reaction first order with respect to I^-: rate = $k[H_2O_2]^1[I^-]^1[H^+]^?$.

Determine the order with respect to H^+ from experiments 1 and 4. Doubling $[H^+]$ has no effect on the rate, making the reaction zero order with respect to H^+: rate = $k[H_2O_2]^1[I^-]^1[H^+]^0$. Because exponent 1 is left unwritten and any zero-order reactant does not appear in the rate law, the law for this reaction is

Rate = $k[H_2O_2][I^-]$

The overall order of the reaction is $1 + 1 = 2$.

13.93 You find the order of each reactant by comparing two experiments in which the concentration of that reactant is changed while the concentrations of all other reactants are held constant. Determine the order with respect to A from experiments 1 and 2. Doubling [A] causes the reaction rate to double from 0.0281 M/s to 0.0562 M/s, making the reaction first order with respect to A: rate = $k[A]^1[B]^?$.

Determine the order with respect to B from experiments 1 and 3. Doubling [B] causes the reaction rate to quadruple from 0.0281 M/s to 0.1124 M/s, making the reaction second order with respect to B: rate = $k[A]^1[B]^2$.

Dropping the exponent 1 by convention, you get the rate law rate = $k[A][B]^2$.

The overall order of the reaction is $1 + 2 = 3$, and this problem confirms that the exponents in the rate law are not necessarily the same as the coefficients in the balanced equation.

13.94 You find the order of each reactant by comparing two experiments in which the concentration of that reactant is changed while the concentrations of all other reactants are held constant. Determine the order with respect to ClO_2 from experiments 1 and 2. Tripling $[ClO_2]$ from 0.020 M in experiment 2 to 0.060 M in experiment 1 causes the reaction rate to increase ninefold from 0.002 76 M/s to 0.024 84 M/s, making the reaction second order with respect to ClO_2: rate = $k[ClO_2]^2[OH]^?$.

Determine the order with respect to OH^- from experiments 2 and 3. Tripling $[OH^-]$ from 0.030 M in experiment 2 to 0.090 M in experiment 3 causes the reaction rate to triple from 0.002 76 M/s to 0.008 28 M/s, making the reaction first order with respect to OH^-: rate = $k[ClO_2]^2[OH]^1$.

Dropping the exponent 1 by convention, you get the rate law rate = $k[ClO_2]^2[OH^-]$.

The overall order of the reaction is $2 + 1 = 3$, and this problem confirms that the exponents in the rate law are not necessarily the same as the coefficients in the balanced equation.

13.95 In order for the reaction to occur in one step, four molecules would have to come together simultaneously, all with the proper orientation. This is very unlikely.

13.96 True, because the slowest elementary step is the rate-determining step, and the balancing coefficients from the rate-determining step are equal to the orders in the rate law.

13.97 One that involves one collision between two reactant molecules.

13.98 If the reaction $A + 2B + C \longrightarrow P$ proceeded in one step (a practically impossible occurrence), the equation must represent a rate-determining elementary step (because it is the *only* step), and therefore the equation coefficients can be used as orders to yield rate = $k[A][B]^2[C]$.

13.99 The slowest step in a reaction mechanism.

13.100 Because in any multistep reaction, the rate law for the overall reaction is the same as the rate law for the rate-determining step.

13.101 No, because it is extremely unlikely that three molecules will come together in the orientation necessary for reaction.

13.102 It cannot be correct because it does not agree with the experimentally determined rate law.

13.103 It cannot be correct.

13.104 All you can say is that the postulated mechanism *may possibly* be the correct mechanism. There may be other mechanisms that also agree with the experimental data. Incorrect mechanisms can be ruled out by experimental evidence, but you cannot prove easily that a given possible mechanism for a reaction is the correct one.

13.105 (a) The first-order dependence on $[(CH_3)_3CBr]$ means the reaction rate doubles when $[(CH_3)_3CBr]$ is doubled, triples when $[(CH_3)_3CBr]$ is tripled, and so forth. The zero-order dependence on $[H_2O]$ means the rate is not affected by any change in $[H_2O]$.

(b) You can rule out mechanism II because it does not agree with the experimental evidence. Its one-step mechanism means the reaction is first order in both $(CH_3)_3CBr$ and H_2O. Mechanism I is plausible because it agrees with the experimental data and the sum of the individual steps yields the balanced equation:

$$(CH_3)_3CBr \xrightarrow{\text{Slow}} (CH_3)_3C^+ + Br^-$$
$$(CH_3)_3C^+ + H_2O \xrightarrow{\text{Fast}} (CH_3)_3COH + H^+$$
$$\underline{H^+ + Br^- \xrightarrow{\text{Fast}} HBr}$$
$$(CH_3)_3CBr + H_2O \longrightarrow (CH_3)_3COH + HBr$$

13.106 The overall balanced equation is determined by adding the steps in the mechanism:

$$Cl_2 \longrightarrow Cl + Cl$$
$$Cl + CHCl_3 \longrightarrow HCl + CCl_3$$
$$\underline{Cl + CCl_3 \longrightarrow CCl_4}$$
$$Cl_2 + CHCl_3 \longrightarrow HCl + CCl_4$$

13.107 Rate = $k[Cl_2]$ because only the reactants in the rate-determining step appear in the rate law. The rate-law exponent indicating order is the same as the reactant coefficient in the rate-determining step—1 in this case.

13.108 Endothermic in the forward direction because the energy of the products is greater than the energy of the reactants; exothermic in the reverse direction because in this direction the energy of the products is lower than the energy of the reactants:

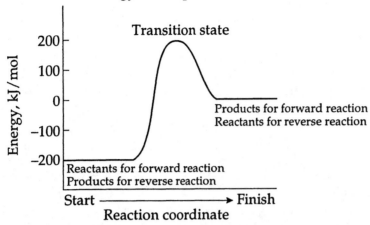

13.109 $\Delta E_{\text{forward rxn}} = E_{\text{products}} - E_{\text{reactants}} = 0 \text{ kJ/mol} - (-200 \text{ kJ/mol}) = +200 \text{ kJ/mol}$;
$\Delta E_{\text{reverse rxn}} = E_{\text{products}} - E_{\text{reactants}} = -200 \text{ kJ/mol} - 0 \text{ kJ/mol} = -200 \text{ kJ/mol}$.

13.110 $E_a = E_{\text{transition state}} - E_{\text{reactants}} = 200 \text{ kJ/mol} - (-200 \text{ kJ/mol}) = 400 \text{ kJ/mol}$.

13.111 $E_a = E_{\text{transition state}} - E_{\text{reactants}} = 200 \text{ kJ/mol} - 0 \text{ kJ/mol} = 200 \text{ kJ/mol}$.

13.112 (c)

13.113 A is endothermic because ΔE_{rxn} is positive: $\Delta E_{\text{rxn}} = E_{\text{products}} - E_{\text{reactants}} = 0 \text{ kJ/mol} - (-200 \text{ kJ/mol}) = +200 \text{ kJ/mol}$. B is exothermic because ΔE_{rxn} is negative: $\Delta E_{\text{rxn}} = E_{\text{products}} - E_{\text{reactants}} = -200 \text{ kJ/mol} - (-100 \text{ kJ/mol}) = -100 \text{ kJ/mol}$.

13.114 Reaction A: $\Delta E_{\text{rxn}} = E_{\text{products}} - E_{\text{reactants}} = 0 \text{ kJ/mol} - (-200 \text{ kJ/mol}) = +200 \text{ kJ/mol}$
Reaction B: $\Delta E_{\text{rxn}} = -200 \text{ kJ/mol} - (-100 \text{ kJ/mol}) = -100 \text{ kJ/mol}$

13.115 A forward: $E_a = E_{\text{transition state}} - E_{\text{reactants}} = 200 \text{ kJ/mol} - (-200 \text{ kJ/mol}) = +400 \text{ kJ/mol}$.
B forward: $E_a = E_{\text{transition state}} - E_{\text{reactants}} = 300 \text{ kJ/mol} - (-100 \text{ kJ/mol}) = +400 \text{ kJ/mol}$.
A reverse: $E_a = E_{\text{transition state}} - E_{\text{reactants}} = 200 \text{ kJ/mol} - 0 \text{ kJ/mol} = 200 \text{ kJ/mol}$.
B reverse: $E_a = E_{\text{transition state}} - E_{\text{reactants}} = 300 \text{ kJ/mol} - (-200 \text{ kJ/mol}) = +500 \text{ kJ/mol}$.

13.116 The forward rates are the same for the two reactions because the activation energies are the same.

13.117 (e). (Choice b is not correct because changing reactant concentrations changes the reaction *rate*, not the reaction *k* value.)

13.118 (a)

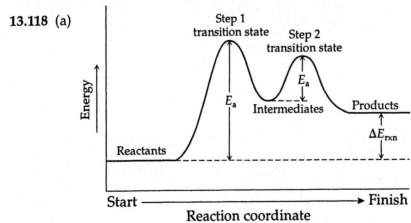

(b) The rate law for the reaction is the rate law for the rate-determining step, which is the slow step. Because this is an elementary step, the exponents in the rate law are the same as the coefficients in the balanced equation:

Rate = $k[A]^1[A]^1 = k[A]^2$

(c) By a factor of 2, which means you double [A]. An order of 2 means that doubling the concentration quadruples the rate. For $k = 1$ and [A] initially 3 M, for instance,

Rate = $1 \times [3\ M]^2 = 9\ M/s$

Rate = $1 \times [6\ M]^2 = 36\ M/s$

13.119

Bonds broken	Bonds formed
(a) One N–N, three H–H	Six N–H
(b) Two P–Cl	One Cl–Cl
(c) One H–H, two I–Cl	One I–I, two H–Cl
(d) Four H–Br, one O–O	Two H–O, two Br–Br

13.120 A reaction is exothermic whenever ΔE_{rxn} is a negative number and whenever heat is a product of the reaction. This means that (b), (c), (d), and (f) are exothermic.

A reaction is endothermic whenever ΔE_{rxn} is a positive number and whenever heat is a reactant. This means (a) and (e) are endothermic.

13.121 When a chemical reaction is in the <u>transition state</u>, the reactant bonds are just ready to break and the product bonds are just ready to form.

13.122 By definition,

k = Fraction of collisions with $E \geq E_a$ × Fraction of collisions between molecules having proper orientation

Therefore (a) $k = 0.42 \times 0.15 = 0.063$ (b) $k = 0.42 \times 0.30 = 0.13$
(c) $k = 0.84 \times 0.15 = 0.13$ (d) $k = 0.84 \times 0.30 = 0.25$

13.123 The order of each reactant (in other words, the rate-law exponent of each reactant) tells you how changing concentration affects rate. In each case below, both k and initial concentrations are arbitrarily given a numeric value of 1.

(a) The order of NO is 2, which means doubling [NO] quadruples the rate: $1 \times (1\ M)^2 \times (1\ M) = 1\ M/s$; $1 \times (2\ M)^2 \times (1\ M) = 4\ M/s$.
(b) The order of Br_2 is 1, which means tripling $[Br_2]$ triples the rate: $1 \times (1\ M)^2 \times (1\ M) = 1\ M/s$; $1 \times (1\ M)^2 \times (3\ M) = 3\ M/s$.
(c) Rate increases ninefold: $1 \times (1\ M)^2 \times (1\ M) = 1\ M/s$; $1 \times (3\ M)^2 \times (1\ M) = 9\ M/s$.
(d) Rate quadruples: $1 \times (1\ M)^2 \times (1\ M) = 1\ M/s$; $1 \times (1\ M)^2 \times (4\ M) = 4\ M/s$.
(e) Rate increases twelvefold: $1 \times (1\ M)^2 \times (1\ M) = 1\ M/s$; $1 \times (2\ M)^2 \times (3\ M) = 12\ M/s$.

13.124 The slowest step in a reaction mechanism is called the <u>rate-determining</u> step.

13.125 (a) First proposed mechanism:

$A + B \longrightarrow AB$
$AB + A \longrightarrow A_2 + B$
$\overline{A + A \longrightarrow A_2}$

Second proposed mechanism:

$A + BC \longrightarrow AB + C$
$A + AB \longrightarrow B + A_2$
$B + C \longrightarrow BC$
$\overline{A + A \longrightarrow A_2}$

(b) The second proposed mechanism is consistent with the rate law because in this mechanism the reactants in the slow step are the species that appear in the rate law. The first proposed mechanism cannot be correct for this reaction because the rate law for its slow step rate = $k[A][B]$, which does not agree with the experimental rate law.

(c) Because it is a catalyst.

13.126 For a reaction mechanism to be valid, the <u>predicted</u> rate law must agree with the <u>experimental</u> rate law.

13.127 (a) Endothermic, because ΔE_{rxn} is a positive number.

(b) The reaction's being endothermic means heat energy is absorbed and is therefore shown as a reactant: $X + \text{Heat} \longrightarrow Y$.

(c) The ΔE_{rxn} values for any forward/reverse pair of reactions always have the same numeric value but opposite signs. Because $\Delta E_{\text{forward rxn}}$ is $+30$ kJ, $\Delta E_{\text{reverse rxn}}$ must be -30 kJ.

(d) Exothermic because ΔE_{rxn} is negative.

(e) Cold because the reaction, being endothermic, absorbs heat from the surroundings.

13.128 E_a is $E_{\text{transition state}} - E_{\text{reactants}}$. The reaction is exothermic if $\Delta E_{rxn} = E_{\text{products}} - E_{\text{reactants}}$ is negative and endothermic if ΔE_{rxn} is positive.

(a) $E_a = 150$ kJ $- 100$ kJ $= +50$ kJ
$\Delta E_{rxn} = 130$ kJ $- 100$ kJ $= +30$ kJ, endothermic

(b) $E_a = 150$ kJ $- 100$ kJ $= +50$ kJ
$\Delta E_{rxn} = 70$ kJ $- 100$ kJ $= -30$ kJ, exothermic

(c) $E_a = 175$ kJ $- 50$ kJ $= +125$ kJ
$\Delta E_{rxn} = 130$ kJ $- 50$ kJ $= +80$ kJ, endothermic

(d) $E_a = 40$ kJ $- 20$ kJ $= +20$ kJ
$\Delta E_{rxn} = 10$ kJ $- 20$ kJ $= -10$ kJ, exothermic

13.129 Because the reaction is exothermic, your profile must show the products having less energy than the reactants:

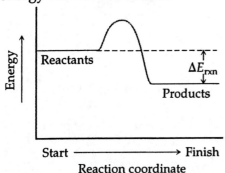

13.130 False. A catalyst decreases the energy gap between the reactants and the transition state—in other words, it decreases the activation energy. The energy gap between reactants and products remains the same with or without a catalyst present.

13.131 A substitution reaction is one in which one atom or group of atoms in a molecule is split off and replaced by another atom or group of atoms. Thus (a) and (d) are substitution reactions. In (a), I is substituted for Br; in (d), OH is substituted for Cl. No such substitution occurs in (b) or in (c).

13.132 (a) Halving the volume doubles [A]. Because the exponent on [A] is 2, the reaction rate quadruples. For $k = 1$ and initial [A] $= 1$ M, $1 \times (1 \text{ M})^2 = 1$ M/s; $1 \times (2 \text{ M})^2 = 4$ M/s.

(b) The reaction occurs nine times as fast: $1 \times (1 \text{ M})^2 = 1$ M/s; $1 \times (3 \text{ M})^2 = 9$ M/s.

13.133 (a) $A_2 + \cancel{Y} \longrightarrow \cancel{AY} + \cancel{A}$
$\cancel{A} + B \longrightarrow \cancel{AB}$
$\cancel{AY} + \cancel{AB} \longrightarrow \cancel{Y} + A_2B$

$\overline{A_2 + B \longrightarrow A_2B}$

(b) Step 1 because it is the slowest step.

(c) Use the balancing coefficients from the step-1 equation as the orders in the rate law:

$$\text{Rate} = k[A_2]^1[Y]^1 = k[A_2][Y]$$

(d) Because the reaction is first order in A_2, the rate doubles when A_2 is doubled.

(e) Y is the catalyst because it is unchanged once the reaction is complete (note that it is a product of step 3). Another way to tell that Y is the catalyst is to note that it appears in elementary steps but not in the overall reaction.

(f) An intermediate is a species produced in one elementary step but consumed in a subsequent step—which means AY, A, and AB in this case. Note that intermediates never appear in the equation for the overall reaciton.

13.134 When weak bonds are broken (absorbing relatively little energy to do so) and strong bonds are formed (releasing relatively large amounts of energy), the reaction absorbs less energy than it releases and is therefore exothermic.

13.135 (a) True, because raising their temperature gives the reactant molecules more kinetic energy.

(b) False. Lowering the temperature of a reaction mixture *slows* the reaction *down.*
OR *Raising* the temperature of a reaction mixture speeds up the reaction.

(c) False. The rate of a reaction depends on the number of collisions per unit time having energy equal to or greater than E_a *and on the fraction of those collisions in which the reactant molecules have the proper orientation with respect to one another.*

(d) True, because orientation factor is a fraction and a fraction can be 1 only when its numerator and denominator are the same. Thus the factor is 1 when, say, there are ten collisions between reactant molecules and all ten result in a reaction: $10/10 = 1$. The molecules can react only when oriented properly, and the fact that all react tells you all must be oriented properly.

13.136 The lower the activation energy, the faster the reaction. Therefore the reaction for which $E_a = 20$ kJ occurs fastest.

13.137 That H_2 and Cl_2 appear in the rate law tells you these two substances must be reactants in your equation. There may also be one or more additional reactants that have an order of zero and therefore do not appear in the rate law, but you do not have to be concerned about them if you can come up with a legitimate reaction between H_2 and Cl_2. You do not need to know the values of x and y because there is no direct relationship between orders in a rate law and coefficients in a balanced equation. The simplest reaction that fits the criterion of having H_2 and Cl_2 as reactants is $H_2 + Cl_2 \longrightarrow$ 2 HCl.

13.138 False. A catalyst is a reactant in the rate-determining step of a reaction. It is not used up because it is regenerated as the product in a subsequent step of the reaction.

13.139 A reaction intermediate appears first in one step as a product and then in a subsequent step as a reactant. A catalyst appears first in one step as a reactant and then in a subsequent step as a product.

13.140 The energy factor is the number of collisions per unit time in which the energy of the colliding particles is equal to or greater than E_a. The orientation factor is the fraction of collisions in which the colliding particles have the proper orientation.

13.141 Only reactants appear in a rate law, and balancing coefficients do not necessarily appear in a rate law.
(a) Rate = $k[NO]^x[O_2]^y$
(b) Rate = $k[H_2O_2]^x$

13.142 Catalysts speed up reactions by lowering E_a values. A company can therefore lower its manufacturing costs by consuming less energy in running the chemical reactions it must run to create its products. (This assumes the savings in energy dollars are greater than the cost of using the catalyst, which is usually true.) Additionally, decreasing the time needed to run a reaction by adding a catalyst decreases the cost of the process (because time is money).

13.143 (a) Exothermic because energy (in the form of heat) is *released*.
(b) Reactants because the reaction releases energy, leaving the products in a lower energy state than the reactants.
(c) Downhill because the products have less energy than the reactants.
(d) You must show reactants higher on the energy axis than products. Because no information is given for E_a, choose any value you like for the peak of your curve, just as long as your peak value (transition-state value) is higher in energy than the reactants. Because you are told the reaction releases 900 kJ, label the energy difference between reactants energy and products energy with this numeric value:

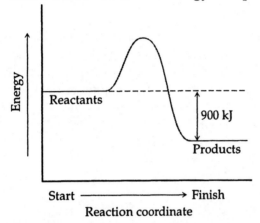

13.144 k is defined by two factors describing the collisions between reactant particles. One factor is the fraction of collisions having energy equal to or greater than E_a. When the reaction temperature is increased, the kinetic energy of all the reactant particles is increased. These particles then collide with greater energy, meaning a larger fraction of the collisions have energy equal to or greater than E_a, and therefore k increases.

13.145 (a) True because in this case the exponent for each reactant in the rate law is identical to the reactant's balancing coefficient in the balanced equation.
(b) False. A rate law can *never* be used to prove that a proposed mechanism is correct. *OR* A rate law can be used to prove *only* that a proposed mechanism is *wrong or that a proposed mechanism is* possibly *correct*.
(c) False. The step A + X + Y ⟶ AX + Y in a reaction mechanism is implausible because it proposes the highly unlikely event of three molecules colliding simultaneously.
(d) False. A *catalyst* appears first as a reactant and then as a product in a reaction mechanism. *OR* A reaction intermediate appears first as a *product* and then as a *reactant* in a reaction mechanism.

CHAPTER

14

Chemical Equilibrium

14.1 See solution in textbook.

14.2 Because you want essentially all the reactants to be converted to products before the reaction reaches equilibrium.

14.3 Because the equilibrium lies so far to the right (products side) that there are essentially no reactants present at equilibrium. Therefore the reverse reaction can be ignored, and the reaction is considered a one-way reaction in the forward direction.

14.4 See solution in textbook.

14.5 $K_{eq} = \dfrac{[HI]^2}{[H_2] \times [I_2]}$

14.6 $K_{eq} = \dfrac{[Fe(SCN)^{2+}]}{[Fe^{3+}] \times [SCN^-]}$

14.7 $K_{eq} = \dfrac{[HI]^2}{[H_2] \times [I_2]} = \dfrac{(0.158\ M)^2}{0.021\ M \times 0.021\ M} = 57$

Because K_{eq} is calculated from equilibrium concentrations, the initial concentrations given in the problem statement are extraneous information. All you need are the equilibrium concentrations.

14.8 To the right. If the reaction went to completion (all the way to the right), the concentrations would be [HI] = 0.200 M, [H$_2$] = 0.000 M, [I$_2$] = 0.000 M. The actual equilibrium concentrations are approximately 75% of these values, meaning the equilibrium is to the right.

14.9 $K_{eq} = \dfrac{[CS_2] \times [H_2]^4}{[CH_4] \times [H_2S]^2} = \dfrac{6.10 \times 10^{-3}\,M \times (1.17 \times 10^{-3}\,M)^4}{2.35 \times 10^{-3}\,M \times (2.93 \times 10^{-3}\,M)^2} = 5.67 \times 10^{-7}$

14.10 See solution in textbook.

14.11 To the left so that the rate of the reverse reaction, $2\ SO_2 + O_2 \longleftarrow 2\ SO_3$, increases so as to consume some of the SO$_3$ you added. Adding product to a reaction at equilibrium shifts the reaction toward reactants.

14.12 No shift because N$_2$ is neither a reactant nor a product.

14.13 See solution in textbook.

14.14 (a) is at the lower temperature. The positive ΔE_{rxn} tells you this is an endothermic reaction, meaning the reactants absorb heat from the surroundings. Thus you can think of the reaction as $N_2O_4(g)$ + Heat $\rightleftharpoons$ 2 $NO_2(g)$, with heat as a reactant. Le Chatelier's principle tells you that adding heat (that is, running the reaction at a higher temperature) shifts the equilibrium to the right, forming more brown NO_2. Removing heat (running the reaction at a lower temperature) shifts the equilibrium to the left, forming more colorless N_2O_4.

14.15 (a) A negative ΔE_{rxn} means the reaction is exothermic. Heat is released to the surroundings and is therefore to be written as a product: 2 $CO(g)$ + $O_2(g)$ $\rightleftharpoons$ 2 $CO_2(g)$ + Heat
(b) To the left because raising the temperature is equivalent to adding something to the right side of the equation. The reaction shifts left to use up the added heat.

14.16 See solution in textbook.

14.17 (a) Show no liquids or solids in the K_{eq} expression: $K_{eq} = [O_2]^6/[CO_2]^6$.
(b) It would shift to the right to use up the added CO_2.
(c) No change in equilibrium because $[H_2O]$ does not appear in the K_{eq} expression. (All liquid concentrations are taken to be constant in equilibrium calculations.)
(d) It would shift to the right because the reaction is endothermic (positive ΔE_{rxn}), making heat a reactant.
(e) Addition of a catalyst has no effect on the position of the equilibrium, only on the time required to reach equilibrium.

14.18 (a) Show no solids in the expression: $K_{eq} = [Pb^{2+}] \times [I^-]^2$.
(b) No change in equilibrium because $[PbI_2]$ does not appear in the K_{eq} expression. (All solid concentrations are taken to be constant in equilibrium calculations.)
(c) Because $Pb(NO_3)_2$ dissolves and dissociates into Pb^{2+} and NO_3^- ions, adding it is equivalent to adding Pb^{2+} ions. Because $[Pb^{2+}]$ appears on the right in the reaction equation, the $Pb(NO_3)_2$ addition shifts the equilibrium to the left.

14.19 See solution in textbook.

14.20 See solution in textbook.

14.21 (a) $Mg(OH)_2(s) \rightleftharpoons Mg^{2+}(aq) + 2\ OH^-(aq)$
(b) Show only the (aq) species, no (s) species: $K_{sp} = [Mg^{2+}] \times [OH^-]^2$.

(c) $(1.44 \times 10^{-4} \text{M } Mg^{2+}) \times \dfrac{2\ OH^-}{1\ Mg^{2+}} = 2.88 \times 10^{-4} \text{M } OH^-$

(d) $K_{sp} = [Mg^{2+}] \times [OH^-]^2 = 1.44 \times 10^{-4} \text{ M} \times (2.88 \times 10^{-4} \text{ M})^2 = 1.19 \times 10^{-11}$

14.22 (a) $Al(OH)_3(s) \rightleftharpoons Al^{3+}(aq) + 3\ OH^-(aq)$
(b) $K_{sp} = [Al^{3+}] \times [OH^-]^3$

(c) $(8.58 \times 10^{-9} \text{M } OH^-) \times \dfrac{1\ Al^{3+}}{3\ OH^-} = 2.86 \times 10^{-9} \text{M } Al^{3+}$

(d) $K_{sp} = [Al^{3+}] \times [OH^-]^3 = 2.86 \times 10^{-9} \text{ M} \times (8.58 \times 10^{-9} \text{ M})^3 = 1.81 \times 10^{-33}$

14.23 See solution in textbook.

14.24 By taking the square root of the 25°C solubility product: $s = \sqrt{K_{sp}}$.

14.25 $Ag_2S(s) \rightleftharpoons 2\ Ag^+(aq) + S^{2-}(aq)$
$K_{sp} = [Ag^+]^2 \times [S^{2-}]$
$[S^{2-}] = s = 1.14 \times 10^{-17} \text{ M}$
$[Ag^+] = 2s = 2 \times (1.14 \times 10^{-17} \text{ M}) = 2.28 \times 10^{-17} \text{ M}$

14.26 The state in a chemical reaction where the rate of the forward reaction equals the rate of the reverse reaction.

14.27 We mean the reaction can run both in the forward direction and in the reverse direction.

14.28 No; the reaction only *appeared* to have stopped. The amount of product present was not increasing because the rate of the reverse reaction was equal to the rate of the forward reaction, with the result that product was disappearing at the same rate as it was being formed. Because both the forward reaction and the reverse reaction are going on even though concentrations are not changing, the state is called dynamic equilibrium (dynamic = moving; equilibrium = not changing).

14.29 The position of a reaction's equilibrium refers to whether there are more products or more reactants present at equilibrium. When there are more reactants, the equilibrium is said to lie toward the left end of the reaction coordinate; when there are more products, the equilibrium is said to lie toward the right end of the reaction coordinate; when there are significant amounts of both products and reactants, the equilibrium is said to lie toward the middle of the reaction coordinate.

14.30 Far to the right because, by convention, the left end of the coordinate is taken as the starting point of the reaction and the right end is taken as the 100% point.

14.31 Far to the left. That the reaction appears not to occur means the reaction vessel contains essentially all reactants—in other words, the reaction is still at the starting point. By convention, the left end of the reaction coordinate is taken as the starting point.

14.32 That the reaction is reversible and runs in both directions, reactants converting to products and products simultaneously converting to reactants.

14.33 The reaction would produce very little product if the equilibrium lay far to the left, meaning the chemist would end up with a vessel containing mostly the reactants she started with, no matter how long she waited.

14.34 As the forward reaction proceeds, there is a decrease in the amount of forward-reaction reactants. As the concentration of these reactants decreases, the forward reaction slows down.

14.35 Initially there are no forward-reaction products in the vessel. Because these products are the reverse-reaction reactants, the reverse reaction rate is initially zero.

14.36 As the forward reaction proceeds, there is an increase in the amount of forward-reaction products. Because these products are the reverse-reaction reactants, as their concentration increases, the reverse reaction speeds up.

14.37 The reverse reaction because those products present are the reverse-reaction reactants. At the moment after loading, there are no forward-reaction reactants in the vessel, which means the forward reaction cannot occur. Therefore the reverse reaction must be going faster because the rate of the forward reaction is zero.

14.38 Yes. Once the reverse reaction produces products, these products become forward-reaction reactants. As time passes, the reverse reaction slows down (because reverse-reaction reactants are consumed) and the forward reaction speeds up (because forward-reaction reactants are being formed). Equilibrium is attained when $\text{rate}_{\text{forward}} = \text{rate}_{\text{reverse}}$.

14.39 Yes. In the sealed container, the liquid water evaporates until the air in the container is saturated with water vapor. After that point, the rate at which liquid water evaporates is equal to the rate at which water vapor condenses, which means the water level remains constant.

14.40 Equilibrium is the state in which the rate of the forward reaction is equal to the rate of the reverse reaction. Because the general form of the rate law is Rate = $k[\text{Reactants}]^{\text{order}}$, the definition for equilibrium is

$\text{Rate}_{\text{forward}} = \text{Rate}_{\text{reverse}}$

$k_{\text{forward}}[\text{Reactants}]^{\text{order}} = k_{\text{reverse}}[\text{Products}]^{\text{order}}$

14.41 No, because it is not possible to reach equilibrium if both rates increase, which is what the rate meters show. As the reverse reaction proceeds, the reverse-reaction reactant concentrations decrease, which means $\text{Rate}_{\text{reverse}} = k_{\text{reverse}}[\text{Reactants}]^{\text{order}}$ must decrease.

14.42 Because the reverse reaction must slow down, the equilibrium position for the two reactions must show the needles both pointing to some value less than the time-zero reverse-rate needle:

At time zero   At equilibrium

Forward rate =   Reverse rate =   Forward rate =   Reverse rate =
  0 units   3 units   2 units   2 units

14.43 For simplicity, assume the order of R is 1 for both the forward and the reverse reaction. Then

$$\text{Rate}_{\text{forward}} = k_f[R]$$

$$\text{Rate}_{\text{reverse}} = k_r[P]$$

At equilibrium, $k_f[R] = k_r[P]$. To solve for k_f/k_r, divide both sides of this expression by k_r:

$$\frac{k_f[R]}{k_r} = \frac{\cancel{k_r}[P]}{\cancel{k_r}}$$

$$\frac{k_f[R]}{k_r} = [P]$$

Then divide both sides by [R]:

$$\frac{k_f\cancel{[R]}}{k_r\cancel{[R]}} = \frac{[P]}{[R]}$$

$$\frac{k_f}{k_r} = \frac{[P]}{[R]}$$

14.44 Because k_f and k_r are defined for a specific temperature, neither changes at a given temperature. Therefore k_f/k_r stays constant, too.

14.45 K_{eq}, the equilibrium constant.

14.46 Greater than 1. K_{eq} is defined as the fraction k_f/k_r, and whenever the numerator of a fraction is larger than the denominator, the fraction is greater than 1.

14.47 No matter how many reactants you have—one, two, or 200—all of them go in the denominator because the definition of K_{eq} is in the form

$$\frac{\text{Concentrations of products}}{\text{Concentrations of reactants}}$$

When there are more than one reactant concentration, you multiply:

$$K_{eq} = \frac{[\text{Product 1}]^a}{[\text{Reactant 1}]^b \times [\text{Reactant 2}]^c \times [\text{Reactant 3}]^d \times \cdots}$$

The same holds true for products:

$$K_{eq} = \frac{[\text{Product 1}]^a \times [\text{Product 2}]^b \times [\text{Product 3}]^c \times \cdots}{[\text{Reactant 1}]^d \times [\text{Reactant 2}]^e \times [\text{Reactant 3}]^f \times \cdots}$$

14.48 Put product concentrations in the numerator, reactant concentrations in the denominator. Raise each concentration to a power equal to the substance's stoichiometric coefficient in the balanced equation. Because this is a gas-state reaction, all four species are gases and therefore all four appear in the K_{eq} expression:

$$K_{eq} = \frac{[C] \times [D]}{[A]^2 \times [B]^3}$$

14.49 Put product concentrations in the numerator, reactant concentrations in the denominator. Raise each concentration to a power equal to the substance's stoichiometric coefficient in the balanced equation. Because this is a gas-state reaction, all four species are gases and therefore all four appear in the K_{eq} expression:

$$K_{eq} = \frac{[A]^2 \times [B]^3}{[C] \times [D]}$$

14.50 The two K_{eq} values are inversely related: what is numerator in Problem 14.48 is denominator in Problem 14.49; what is denominator in 14.48 is numerator in 14.49. From this you can conclude that the K_{eq} for a reverse reaction is equal to the inverse of the K_{eq} for the forward reaction.

14.51 Put product concentrations in the numerator, reactant concentrations in the denominator. Raise each concentration to a power equal to the substance's stoichiometric coefficient in the balanced equation. Because both species in the reaction are gases, show both of them in the K_{eq} expression:

$$K_{eq} = \frac{[NO_2]^2}{[N_2O_4]}$$

14.52 Put product concentrations in the numerator, reactant concentrations in the denominator. Raise each concentration to a power equal to the substance's stoichiometric coefficient in the balanced equation. Because all species in the reaction are gases, show all of them in the K_{eq} expression:

$$K_{eq} = \frac{[NO]^4 \times [H_2O]^6}{[NH_3]^4 \times [O_2]^5}$$

14.53 You would place some N_2O_4 in a container and allow the reaction to proceed to equilibrium. Then you would determine the concentration of N_2O_4 and NO_2 at equilibrium and substitute those concentration values into the K_{eq} expression shown in the solution to Problem 14.51.

14.54 No, because K_{eq} depends only on temperature. If you react 1 M reactant A with 1 M reactant B at 25°C and use equilibrium concentrations to calculate a K_{eq} of, say, 30, then reacting 10 M reactant A with 7 M reactant B at 25°C also gives K_{eq} = 30. Only if you run the reaction at some temperature other than 25°C will your calculated value for K_{eq} change.

14.55 $K_{eq} = \dfrac{[NO]^2}{[N_2] \times [O_2]} = \dfrac{(0.011\ \text{M})^2}{0.25\ \text{M} \times 1.2\ \text{M}} = 4.0 \times 10^{-4}$

14.56 The equilibrium at 25°C lies farther to the left because K_{eq} is smaller at 25°C than at 2000°C. The K_{eq} value comes from the fraction [Products]/[Reactants]. The smaller the K_{eq} value, therefore, the larger the denominator, the higher the reactant concentration, and the farther to the left the equilibrium lies.

14.57 That the concentration of products at equilibrium is much greater than the concentration of reactants. The general expression shows that the numerator (product concentration) must be much larger than the denominator (reactant concentration) if $K_{eq} > 10^3$.

14.58 No; K_{eq} = 2.05 means the equilibrium lies near the middle of the reaction coordinate. Only for reactions whose equilibria lie extremely far to the right ($K_{eq} > 10^5$) may you use a single arrow to the right, indicating that the reaction goes essentially to completion.

14.59 That the concentration of products at equilibrium is much less than the concentration of reactants. The general expression shows that the numerator (product concentration) must be substantially smaller than the denominator (reactant concentration) if $K_{eq} < 10^{-3}$.

14.60 No, because $K_{eq} = 1.5 \times 10^{-6}$ means the equilibrium lies far to the left. There would be very little product present when the reaction reaches equilibrium.

14.61 $K_{eq} = \dfrac{[CH_4] \times [H_2O]}{[CO] \times [H_2]^3}$

The equilibrium molar concentrations are

$$[CO] = \frac{0.613 \text{ mol}}{10.0 \text{ L}} = 0.0613 \text{ M} \qquad [H_2] = \frac{1.839 \text{ mol}}{10.0 \text{ L}} = 0.1839 \text{ M}$$

$$[CH_4] = \frac{0.387 \text{ mol}}{10.0 \text{ L}} = 0.0387 \text{ M} \qquad [H_2O] = \frac{0.387 \text{ mol}}{10.0 \text{ L}} = 0.0387 \text{ M}$$

$$K_{eq} = \frac{0.0387 \text{ M} \times 0.0387 \text{ M}}{0.0613 \text{ M} \times (0.1839 \text{ M})^3} = 3.93$$

The equilibrium lies about in the middle of the reaction coordinate because 3.93 is roughly midway between $K_{eq} = 10^{-3}$, indicating equilibrium essentially all the way to the left (mainly reactant present), and $K_{eq} = 10^3$, indicating equilibrium essentially all the way to the right (mainly product present).

14.62 Still 3.93 because K_{eq} does not depend on the concentrations in the starting mixture. The ratio of products to reactants at equilibrium is the same as in Problem 14.61 because the temperature has not been changed.

14.63 Because its value does not change if the temperature at which a reaction is run does not change.

14.64 $K_{eq} = \dfrac{[CS_2] \times [H_2]^4}{[CH_4] \times [H_2S]^2} = 3.59$

To determine whether or not the reaction is at equilibrium, substitute in the given concentrations to see if the ratio equals 3.59:

$$\frac{1.51 \text{ M} \times (1.08 \text{ M})^4}{1.15 \text{ M} \times (1.20 \text{ M})^2} = 1.24$$

Because 1.24 is not equal to 3.59, the reaction is not at equilibrium.

14.65 The textbook notes that any reaction for which K_{eq} is greater than 10^5 goes to completion and any reaction for which K_{eq} is less than 10^{-3} hardly occurs at all. Thus reaction a ($K_{eq} \approx 10^{81}$) goes essentially to completion, with virtually all of the reactants converted to products at equilibrium, and reaction b ($K_{eq} = 10^{-95}$) does not happen, with almost none of the reactants converted to products at equilibrium.

14.66 The species in the numerator are the products in the balanced equation; the species in the denominator are the reactants. Exponents in the K_{eq} expression become balancing coefficients in the equation:

$$4 \text{ HCl} + O_2 \rightleftharpoons 2 \text{ H}_2O + 2 \text{ Cl}_2$$

14.67 All species are gases, and so all appear in the expression for K_{eq}:

$$K_{eq} = \frac{[HI]^2}{[H_2] \times [I_2]}$$

The equilibrium molar concentrations are

$$[HI] = \frac{3.00 \text{ mol}}{8.00 \text{ L}} = 0.375 \text{ M} \qquad [H_2] = \frac{0.650 \text{ mol}}{8.00 \text{ L}} = 0.0812 \text{ M} \qquad [I_2] = \frac{0.275 \text{ mol}}{8.00 \text{ L}} = 0.0344 \text{ M}$$

$$K_{eq} = \frac{(0.375 \text{ M})^2}{0.0812 \text{ M} \times 0.0344 \text{ M}} = 50.3$$

The equilibrium lies near the middle of the reaction coordinate because 50.3 is roughly halfway between $K_{eq} = 10^{-3}$, indicating equilibrium essentially all the way to the left (mainly reactants present), and $K_{eq} = 10^3$, indicating equilibrium essentially all the way to the right (mainly product present).

14.68 The two values would be the same because $k_f/k_r = K_{eq}$ whenever the reaction is a one-step reaction.

14.69 The value of K_{eq} does not change because you have not changed the temperature. K_{eq} changes only when the temperature at which the reaction is run changes.

14.70 When a chemical reaction at equilibrium is disturbed, the reaction shifts in such a way as to partially undo the disturbance.

14.71 (a) To the right because Cl_2 appears on the left side of the equation. Equilibrium shifts rightward to consume some of the added Cl_2 via the reaction $PCl_3 + Cl_2 \longrightarrow PCl_5$.

(b) To the left so that the reaction $PCl_5 \longrightarrow PCl_3 + Cl_2$ produces more Cl_2 to replace some of the removed Cl_2.

(c) To the left so that the reaction $PCl_5 \longrightarrow PCl_3 + Cl_2$ uses up some of the added PCl_5.

(d) To the left so that the reaction $PCl_5 \longrightarrow PCl_3 + Cl_2$ produces more PCl_3 to replace some of the removed PCl_3.

(e) No shift because H_2 does not take part in the reaction and therefore does not affect the $PCl_3/Cl_2/PCl_5$ equilibrium.

14.72 Because when you remove reactants, the reaction shifts to the left, converting some of the product to reactants to partially replace the reactants you took away.

14.73 (a) To the left because the reverse reaction, Products $\longrightarrow$ Reactants, speeds up to consume some of the added products and restore equilibrium.

(b) Greater than before the disturbance. Some of the added products are converted to reactants as the new equilibrium is established, but the net result is an increase in the amount of products (and an increase in the amount of reactants, produced when the reaction shifted left). In other words, the equilibrium shift never consumes all of the substance (or substances) added to disturb the equilibrium.

(c) Greater than before the disturbance. See explanation in part (b).

14.74 (a) You are free to choose any arbitrary needle position for the initial setting. The only restriction is that the forward rate must be identical to the reverse rate because the mixture is at equilibrium:

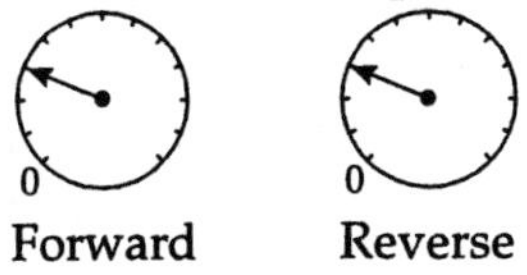

Forward   Reverse

(b) Because PCl_5 appears on the right in the equation, adding it shifts the reaction left. This means the reverse rate increases as the reaction $PCl_5 \longrightarrow PCl_3 + Cl_2$ speeds up to consume some of the added PCl_5; therefore your reverse meter must read higher than in (a). Because the speeded-up reaction $PCl_5 \longrightarrow PCl_3 + Cl_2$ creates more $PCl_3 + Cl_2$, after a few moments the forward rate also increases (only slightly at first):

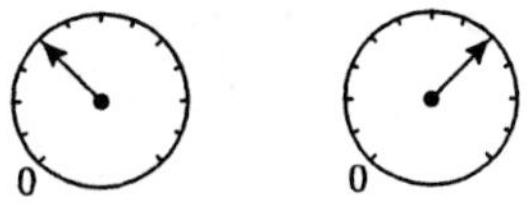

Forward   Reverse

(c) As more and more PCl_3 and Cl_2 are formed, the forward rate continues to increase. At the same time, the reverse rate is decreasing because PCl_5 is being used up. Equilibrium is restored when the increasing forward rate and the decreasing reverse rate meet:

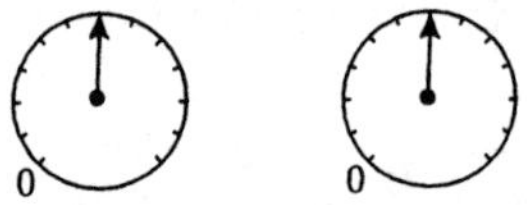

Forward   Reverse

Note that the new equilibrium rate is higher than the initial equilibrium rate of part (a).

(d) Left because the initial disturbance was caused by adding a substance that appears on the right in the balanced equation.

14.75 At a high temperature because this is an endothermic reaction (ΔE_{rxn} positive). Therefore heat is a "reactant": $2 H_2O(g) + \text{Heat} \rightleftharpoons 2 H_2(g) + O_2(g)$. Adding a substance that appears on the left in the equation (heat in this case) shifts the reaction right, forming greater amounts of H_2 and O_2.

14.76 (a) About the middle of the reaction coordinate, with significant amounts of both product and reactants present, because 0.105 is about midway between $K_{eq} = 10^{-3}$ (mainly reactants present) and $K_{eq} = 10^3$ (mainly product present).

(b) No, because with $K_{eq} = 0.105$ there are significant amounts of the reactants present at equilibrium. (You need a reaction having a much larger K_{eq} if you want to isolate pure product.)

(c) You would drive the reaction to completion by causing it to shift continuously to the right.

14.77 (a) To the left, because K_{eq} is smaller at the higher temperature. The smaller the $K_{eq} = [\text{Products}]/[\text{Reactants}]$ value, the smaller the numerator. That the product concentration decreases tells you the reaction has shifted left.

(b) Exothermic, because increasing the temperature (adding heat) causes the reaction to shift to the left. Heat must therefore be a product in the reaction.

(c) $CO(g) + 2 H_2(g) \rightleftharpoons CH_3OH(g) + \text{Heat}$

14.78 (a) Endothermic, because increasing the temperature (adding heat) causes the reaction to shift to the right. Heat must therefore be a "reactant."

(b) Increase because more product is produced, increasing the numerator in $K_{eq} = [\text{Products}]/[\text{Reactants}]$.

(c) $\text{Heat} + N_2O_4(g) \rightleftharpoons 2 NO_2(g)$

14.79 Exothermic, because the reaction shifts left when the reaction mixture is heated. Therefore heat must be a product, $C_{diamond} \rightleftharpoons C_{graphite} + \text{Heat}$.

14.80 An endothermic reaction means heat is a "reactant": $\text{Reactants} + \text{Heat} \rightleftharpoons \text{Products}$. To drive the reaction to the right, therefore, you add heat by increasing the temperature at which the reaction is run.

14.81 An exothermic reaction means heat is a product: $\text{Reactants} \rightleftharpoons \text{Products} + \text{Heat}$.

(a) Heating means adding to the right side of the equation, shifting the reaction left. This causes [Products] to decrease and [Reactants] to increase. Therefore $K_{eq} = [\text{Products}]/[\text{Reactants}]$ decreases.

(b) Cooling means removing from the right side of the equation, shifting the reaction right. This causes [Products] to increase and [Reactants] to decrease. Therefore K_{eq} = [Products]/[Reactants] increases.

14.82 An endothermic reaction means heat is a reactant: Reactants + Heat $\rightleftharpoons$ Products.

(a) Heating means adding to the left side of the equation, shifting the reaction right. This causes [Products] to increase and [Reactants] to decrease. Therefore K_{eq} = [Products]/[Reactants] increases.

(b) Cooling means removing from the left side of the equation, shifting the reaction left. This causes [Products] to decrease and [Reactants] to increase. Therefore K_{eq} = [Products]/[Reactants] decreases.

14.83 Decreased. The negative value for ΔE_{rxn} tells you this is an exothermic reaction. Thus heat is a product, $CO(g) + 2 H_2(g) \rightleftharpoons CH_3OH(g)$ + Heat, and adding it to the reaction mixture by raising the temperature shifts the reaction left. $[H_2]$ and [CO] increase, and $[CH_3OH]$ decreases.

14.84 Cooling slows down the rate of the reaction. It therefore takes longer to form the product.

14.85 Because it speeds up the forward and reverse reactions by the same amount, a catalyst has no effect on either the position of equilibrium or the value of K_{eq}.

14.86 A catalyst decreases the time it takes for a reaction to reach equilibrium by providing an alternative mechanism that has a lower activation energy. A lower activation energy means that more molecules have sufficient energy to react, and the forward and reverse reaction rates both increase.

14.87 (a) That $K_{eq} = [NO]^2/[N_2] \times [O_2]$ is higher at the higher temperature means that at the higher temperature [NO] must be higher and $[N_2] \times [O_2]$ must be lower. Therefore the reaction shifts to the right.

(b) Endothermic. The fact that heating shifts the reaction to the right means heat must be a "reactant."

14.88 One in which not all the reactants and products are in the same phase. A heterogeneous reaction occurs at the interface between the phases present in the reaction mixture.

14.89 Show only (g) and (aq) species in a K_{eq} expression. Put product molar concentrations in the numerator, reactant molar concentrations in the denominator. Raise each concentration to a power equal to the substance's stoichiometric coefficient in the balanced equation.

(a) $K_{eq} = [HCl]^6/[H_2O]^3$
(b) $K_{eq} = [CO_2]^3/[CO]^3$
(c) $K_{eq} = [Pb^{2+}] \times [SO_4^{2-}]$
(d) $K_{eq} = [H_2CO_3]/[CO]$

14.90 Show only (g) and (aq) species in a K_{eq} expression. Put product molar concentrations in the numerator, reactant molar concentrations in the denominator. Raise each concentration to a power equal to the substance's stoichiometric coefficient in the balanced equation.

(a) $K_{eq} = 1/[H_2]^2$
(b) $K_{eq} = [PO_4^{3-}] \times [H_3O^+]^3/[H_3PO_4]$
(c) $K_{eq} = 1/[Pb^{2+}] \times [I^-]^2$
(d) $K_{eq} = [H_3O^+]^2/[Ca^{2+}] \times [CO_2]$

14.91 The fact that the concentrations of solids and liquids do not change during any heterogeneous reaction.

14.92 AgCl(s) precipitates. When the NaCl is added, $[Cl^-]$ increases drastically, causing the product $[Ag^+] \times [Cl^-]$ to exceed K_{sp}.

14.93 (a) Because the sealed vessel keeps the $H_2(g)$ from escaping. In an open container, $H_2(g)$ would escape, continuously shifting the reaction to the left so that no product could form and equilibrium would never be established.

(b) $K_{eq} = \dfrac{1}{[H_2]^2}$

$[H_2]^2 = \dfrac{1}{K_{eq}}$

$\sqrt{[H_2]^2} = \dfrac{\sqrt{1}}{\sqrt{K_{eq}}}$

$[H_2] = \dfrac{1}{\sqrt{K_{eq}}}$

(c) The fact that K_{eq} = [Products]/[Reactants] gets smaller tells you the reaction shifts to the left, with [Products] decreasing and [Reactants] increasing.

(d) That adding heat shifts the reaction left means heat must be a product—$SnO_2(s)$ + $2\,H_2(g) \rightleftharpoons Sn(s) + 2\,H_2O(l)$ + Heat. The reaction therefore is exothermic.

14.94 Any undissolved solid present after equilibrium is established is actually dissolving. It's just that the rate of precipitation equals the rate of dissolution, which makes the undissolved solid seem to just sit there.

14.95 Table 14.2 of the textbook tells you that for any sparingly soluble salt of the form XY_3, the cation equilibrium concentration is equal to the salt solubility s and the anion equilibrium concentration is equal to $3s$. Therefore $[Al^{3+}] = s = 2.86 \times 10^{-9}$ M, $[OH^-] = 3s = 3 \times (2.86 \times 10^{-9}\,\text{M}) = 8.58 \times 10^{-9}$ M.

14.96 Table 14.2 of the textbook tells you that for any sparingly soluble salt of the form X_3Y_2, the cation equilibrium concentration is $3s$, where s is the solubility of the salt, and the equilibrium anion concentration is $2s$. Therefore $[Ca^{2+}] = 3s = 3 \times (2.60 \times 10^{-6}\,\text{M}) = 7.80 \times 10^{-6}$ M, $[PO_4^{3-}] = 2s = 2 \times (2.60 \times 10^{-6}\,\text{M}) = 5.20 \times 10^{-6}$ M.

14.97 (a) $AgC_2H_3O_2(s) \rightleftharpoons Ag^+(aq) + C_2H_3O_2^-(aq)$

(b) $K_{sp} = [Ag^+] \times [C_2H_3O_2^-]$

(c) To calculate K_{sp}, you need the value of $[Ag^+]$ and $[C_2H_3O_2^-]$. Table 14.2 of the textbook tells you that for any sparingly soluble salt of the form XY, the cation equilibrium concentration and the anion equilibrium concentration are both equal to s. You are given solubility but in grams rather than moles. Because concentrations in the K_{sp} expression are molar concentrations, you must convert:

$$s = \frac{10.6\ \text{g}\ AgC_2H_3O_2}{L} \times \frac{1\ \text{mol}\ AgC_2H_3O_2}{166.9\ \text{g}\ AgC_2H_3O_2} = 0.0635\ \text{mol}\ AgC_2H_3O_2\,/\,L = 0.0635\ \text{M}$$

Therefore $[Ag^+] = 0.0635$ M, $[C_2H_3O_2^-] = 0.0635$ M, and

$K_{sp} = [Ag^+] \times [C_2H_3O_2^-] = (0.0635\ \text{M}) \times (0.0635\ \text{M}) = 4.03 \times 10^{-3}$

14.98 (a) Table 14.2 of the textbook tells you that for any sparingly soluble salt of the form XY, the cation equilibrium concentration and the anion equilibrium concentration are both equal to s, the solubility of the salt. Because s is given in milligrams per liter but you are asked for molar concentrations you must convert:

$$s = \frac{6.1\ \text{mg}\ CaC_2O_4}{L} \times \frac{1\ \text{g}\ CaC_2O_4}{1000\ \text{mg}\ CaC_2O_4} \times \frac{1\ \text{mol}\ CaC_2O_4}{128.1\ \text{g}\ CaC_2O_4}$$

$$= 4.8 \times 10^{-5}\ \text{mol}\,/\,L = 4.8 \times 10^{-5}\ \text{M}$$

Therefore $[Ca^{2+}] = [C_2O_4^{2-}] = s = 4.8 \times 10^{-5}$ M.

(b) $K_{sp} = [Ca^{2+}] \times [C_2O_4^{2-}] = 4.8 \times 10^{-5}\ \text{M} \times 4.8 \times 10^{-5}\ \text{M} = 2.3 \times 10^{-9}$

14.99 Lead(II) chloride, because it is the one with the largest K_{sp}.

14.100 (a) $\dfrac{4.49 \times 10^{-10}\,\text{mol Fe(OH)}_3}{\text{L}} \times \dfrac{106.87\,\text{g Fe(OH)}_3}{1\,\text{mol Fe(OH)}_3} = \dfrac{4.80 \times 10^{-8}\,\text{g Fe(OH)}_3}{\text{L}}$

(b) Table 14.2 of the textbook tells you that for any sparingly soluble salt of the form XY_3, the cation equilibrium concentration is equal to s, the salt's solubility, and the anion equilibrium concentration is equal to $3s$. Therefore $[\text{Fe}^{3+}] = s = 4.49 \times 10^{-10}$ M and $[\text{OH}^-] = 3s = 1.35 \times 10^{-9}$ M.

(c) $20{,}000\,\text{gallons} \times \dfrac{3.79\,\text{L}}{1\,\text{gallon}} \times \dfrac{4.80 \times 10^{-8}\,\text{g Fe(OH)}_3}{\text{L}} = 3.64 \times 10^{-3}\,\text{g Fe(OH)}_3$

14.101 (a) Table 14.1 of the textbook gives 3.3×10^{-14} for the 25°C K_{sp} for $PbCO_3$. Because this is a 1:1 salt,

$$s = \sqrt{K_{sp}} = \sqrt{3.3 \times 10^{-14}} = 1.8 \times 10^{-7}\,\text{mol/L}$$

(b) $\dfrac{1.8 \times 10^{-7}\,\text{mol PbCO}_3}{\text{L}} \times \dfrac{267.2\,\text{g PbCO}_3}{1\,\text{mol PbCO}_3} = \dfrac{4.8 \times 10^{-5}\,\text{g PbCO}_3}{\text{L}}$

(c) You know from Table 14.2 of the textbook that for a 1:1 salt the equilibrium concentration of both cation and anion is equal to s. Therefore $[\text{Pb}^{2+}] = [\text{CO}_3^{2-}] = 1.8 \times 10^{-7}$ M.

(d) $1.000 \times 10^6\,\text{gallons} \times \dfrac{3.79\,\text{L}}{1\,\text{gallon}} \times \dfrac{4.8 \times 10^{-5}\,\text{g PbCO}_3}{\text{L}} = 1.8 \times 10^2\,\text{g PbCO}_3$

14.102 From Table 14.1 of the textbook, you know $K_{sp} = 1.0 \times 10^{-26}$. Because the dissolution reaction is $SnS(s) \rightleftharpoons Sn^{2+}(aq) + S^{2-}(aq)$, you know $K_{sp} = [\text{Sn}^{2+}] \times [\text{S}^{2-}]$. Therefore

$$[\text{S}^{2-}] = \frac{K_{sp}}{[\text{Sn}^{2+}]} = \frac{1.0 \times 10^{-26}}{2.00 \times 10^{-1}\,\text{M}} = 5.0 \times 10^{-26}\,\text{M}$$

14.103 $PCl_5(g) \rightleftharpoons PCl_3(g) + Cl_2(g)$; $K_{eq} = [\text{PCl}_3] \times [\text{Cl}_2]/[\text{PCl}_5]$

$$[\text{PCl}_5] = \frac{[\text{PCl}_3] \times [\text{Cl}_2]}{K_{eq}} = \frac{5.50 \times 10^{-3}\,\text{M} \times 0.125\,\text{M}}{7.50 \times 10^{-2}} = 9.17 \times 10^{-3}\,\text{M}$$

14.104 (a) $K_{eq} = \dfrac{[\text{NH}_3]^2}{[\text{H}_2]^3 \times [\text{N}_2]}$

(b)
$$K_{eq} = \frac{[\text{NH}_3]^2}{[\text{H}_2]^3 \times [\text{N}_2]}$$

$$[\text{NH}_3]^2 = K_{eq} \times [\text{H}_2]^3 \times [\text{N}_2]$$

$$[\text{NH}_3] = \sqrt{K_{eq} \times [\text{H}_2]^3 \times [\text{N}_2]}$$

$$= \sqrt{(1.5 \times 10^{-2}) \times (0.20\,\text{M})^3 \times 0.20\,\text{M}} = \sqrt{2.4 \times 10^{-5}} = 4.9 \times 10^{-3}\,\text{M}$$

14.105 (a) To the right. Because the reverse reaction is so much slower than the forward reaction, there must be a large buildup of product (AB) before the reverse reaction is going fast enough to match the rate of the forward reaction. The large amount of AB means the equilibrium lies to the right.

(b) Because the forward rate is so much faster, k_f must be much larger than k_r. Therefore the fraction $k_f/k_r = K_{eq}$ must be a large number, which means the equilibrium lies to the right, just as in part (a).

14.106 Because this is a simple reaction involving a one-step collision between two reactant molecules, the fact that $k_f >> k_r$, established in Problem 14.105, means that E_a for the forward reaction is much smaller than E_a for the reverse reaction. The forward reaction is faster because it has the smaller activation-energy barrier to overcome.

14.107 (a) The reverse reaction is faster because it is the only reaction going on at that moment. The forward reaction is not happening because initially there are no reactants for it in the container.

(b) The balanced equation tells you that if you begin with only NO, the molar amount of O_2 formed must be the same as the molar amount of N_2 formed. Therefore the O_2 concentration must be equal to the N_2 concentration—both are 0.2159 M.

$$K_{eq} = \frac{[NO]^2}{[N_2] \times [O_2]} = \frac{(0.0683 \text{ M})^2}{0.2159 \text{ M} \times 0.2159 \text{ M}} = 0.100$$

14.108 $K_{eq} = \dfrac{[N_2O_4]}{[NO_2]^2}$

$[NO_2]^2 = \dfrac{[N_2O_2]}{K_{eq}}$

$[NO_2] = \sqrt{\dfrac{[N_2O_4]}{K_{eq}}} = \sqrt{\dfrac{0.248 \text{ M}}{0.500}} = \sqrt{0.496} = 7.04 \times 10^{-1}$

14.109 K_{eq} must change because the temperature has changed. In an endothermic reaction—Reactants + Heat $\rightleftharpoons$ Products—heat is a reactant, which means adding heat by increasing the temperature shifts the reaction to the right, creating more product. Therefore [Products] in the fraction [Products]/[Reactants] = K_{eq} increases, [Reactants] decreases, and so K_{eq} increases.

14.110 Show only (g) and (aq) species in a K_{eq} expression. Put product molar concentrations in the numerator, reactant molar concentrations in the denominator. Raise each concentration to a power equal to the substance's stoichiometric coefficient in the balanced equation.

(a) $K_{eq} = [HCl]^4/[H_2O]^2$

(b) $K_{eq} = [CO]/[H_2] \times [CO_2]$

(c) $K_{eq} = [Mn^{2+}] \times [Cl_2]/[H^+]^4 \times [Cl^-]^2$

(d) $K_{eq} = [I_2(g)]$

(e) $K_{eq} = 1/[TiCl_4]$

(f) $K_{eq} = [Ni^{2+}] \times [OH^-]^2$

14.111 (a) $K_{eq} = \dfrac{[NH_3]^2}{[N_2] \times [H_2]^3} = \dfrac{(0.090 \text{ M})^2}{0.25 \text{ M} \times (0.15 \text{ M})^3} = 9.6$

(b) To the right so that, by Le Chatelier's principle, some of the added $H_2(g)$ is used up.

(c) Because there is no mention of changing the temperature, you must assume temperature is held constant as the $H_2(g)$ is added. Therefore K_{eq} does not change because only changes in temperature affect the value of K_{eq}.

(d) The new coefficients mean the expression for K_{eq} changes to

$$K_{eq} = \frac{[NH_3]^4}{[N_2]^2 \times [H_2]^6}$$

To calculate the value of K_{eq}, use the concentrations given at the beginning of the problem, now raised to the new powers:

$$\frac{(0.090 \text{ M})^4}{(0.25 \text{ M})^2 \times (0.15 \text{ M})^6} = 92$$

How can this be? There's been no temperature change, and yet K_{eq} changes from 9.6 in (a) to 92 here just because the equation was multiplied through by 2. The answer is that any numeric value of K_{eq} is constant for a given temperature *but also for a given form of the balanced equation.*

To see why this must be so, think about putting some $N_2(g)$ and $H_2(g)$ together in a reaction vessel held at some constant temperature. (The amounts you use don't matter.) The two gases will react, an equilibrium state will be set up after some time has passed, and at that point the concentrations of N_2, H_2, and NH_3 have attained their (constant) equilibrium values. Plug these values into the two expressions for K_{eq}, and you must get different numbers, as you saw when you calculated your answers to (a) and (d). (Chemists do not usually run into any problem with this interesting phenomenon because published K_{eq} values are by convention taken to be for chemical equations written in their simplest form—in this case $N_2 + 3 H_2 \rightleftharpoons 2 NH_3$ rather than $2 N_2 + 6 H_2 \rightleftharpoons 4 NH_3$.)

(e) A shift to the right means either (1) something was added to the left side of the equation $N_2 + 3 H_2 \rightleftharpoons 2 NH_3$ or (2) something was removed from the right side. Cooling means the removal of heat, and therefore (2) is what happened: heat was removed from the right. Being that the right side is the products side, heat must be a product, which means the reaction is exothermic.

14.112 (a) You know from Table 7.1 of the textbook that halides of silver(I) are insoluble in water. Therefore the precipitate must be silver chloride, AgCl.

(b) $K_{sp} = [\text{Ag}^+] \times [\text{Cl}^-]$

$$[\text{Ag}^+] = \frac{K_{sp}}{[\text{Cl}^-]}$$

Get a value for K_{sp} from Table 14.1 of the textbook:

$$[\text{Ag}^+] = \frac{1.6 \times 10^{-10}}{2.0 \times 10^{-3} \text{M}} = 8.0 \times 10^{-8} \text{M}$$

14.113 Because K_{sp} values are calculated with molar concentrations, a conversion is your first step:

$$\frac{7.51 \text{ g AgC}_2\text{H}_3\text{O}_2}{1 \text{ L}} \times \frac{1 \text{ mol AgC}_2\text{H}_3\text{O}_2}{166.9 \text{ g AgC}_2\text{H}_3\text{O}_2} = \frac{4.50 \times 10^{-2} \text{mol AgC}_2\text{H}_3\text{O}_2}{\text{L}}$$

Because this is a 1:1 salt, this is also the concentration of both Ag^+ and Cl^-. Thus $K_{sp} = [\text{Ag}^+] \times [\text{C}_2\text{H}_3\text{O}_2^-] = (4.50 \times 10^{-2} \text{ M}) \times (4.50 \times 10^{-2} \text{ M}) = 2.03 \times 10^{-3}$

14.114 Because this is a 1:1 salt, the solubility *s* is

$$s = \sqrt{K_{sp}} = \sqrt{1.1 \times 10^{-10}} = 1.0 \times 10^{-5} \text{M}$$

In 200 ml, therefore,

$$\frac{1.0 \times 10^{-5} \text{mol BaSO}_4}{1000 \text{ mL}} \times 200.0 \text{ mL} = 2.0 \times 10^{-6} \text{mol BaSO}_4$$

14.115 The given solubility means that, at 25°C, 1.52×10^{-3} mole of PbI_2 is dissolved in each liter of solution. Therefore

$$2.50 \times 10^{-6}\, \text{gallons} \times \frac{3.79\, L}{1\, \text{gallon}} \times \frac{1.52 \times 10^{-3}\, \text{mol}\, PbI_2}{L} \times \frac{461\, \text{g}\, PbI_2}{1\, \text{mol}\, PbI_2} = 6.64 \times 10^{6}\, \text{g}\, PbI_2$$

14.116 (a) Add solid CuI to water and stir to dissolve. Keep adding more and more CuI and stirring until no more solid dissolves (you'll then see excess solid CuI at the bottom of your container). Filter off the solid, and you are left with a saturated solution.

(b) Because this is a 1:1 salt, the solubility s is

$$s = \sqrt{K_{sp}} = \sqrt{5.1 \times 10^{-12}} = 2.3 \times 10^{-6}\, M$$

In 400.0 mL therefore,

$$0.400\, L \times \frac{2.3 \times 10^{-6}\, \text{mol}\, CuI}{L} \times \frac{190.4\, \text{g}\, CuI}{1\, \text{mol}\, CuI} \times \frac{1000\, \text{mg}\, CuI}{1\, \text{g}\, CuI} = 0.18\, \text{mg}\, CuI$$

(c) The added CuI* solid enters into a dynamic equilibrium with $Cu^+(aq)$ and $I^-(aq)$, $CuI^*(s) \rightleftharpoons Cu^+(aq) + I^{-*}(aq)$, so that soon there are I^{-*} ions in solution.

14.117 $K_{eq} = \dfrac{[N_2O_5]^2}{[NO_2]^4 \times [O_2]}$

$$[NO_2]^4 = \frac{[N_2O_5]^2}{K_{eq} \times [O_2]}$$

$$[NO_2] = \sqrt[4]{\frac{[N_2O_5]^2}{K_{eq} \times [O_2]}} = \sqrt[4]{\frac{(0.300\, M)^2}{0.150 \times 1.20\, M}} = \sqrt[4]{0.500}$$

Use your calculator to get the fourth root. Key in 0.500, then $\sqrt[x]{y}$, then 4 to get the answer 0.841 M.

14.118 (c). The numerator shows products, the denominator shows reactants and each exponent in the K_{eq} expression becomes a coefficient in the balanced equation (*not* a subscript). The other four expressions are

(a) $K_{eq} = \dfrac{[C_3] \times [D_2]}{[A_2] \times [B_3]}$

(b) $K_{eq} = \dfrac{[C]^3 \times [D]^2}{[A]^2 \times [B]^3}$

(d) Cannot be written because A^2, B^3, C^3, and D^2 are not chemical formulas.

(e) $K_{eq} = \dfrac{[A]^3 \times [B]^2}{[C]^2 \times [D]^3}$

14.119 Greater in water because in water the concentration of I^- is initially zero. In NaI solution, the initial concentration of I^- is greater than zero, with the result that the amount of PbI_2 that can dissolve before the numeric value of $[Pb^{2+}] \times [I^-]^2$ exceeds K_{sp} is reduced.

14.120 (a) Right; adding a substance that appears as a reactant in the equation as written shifts the reaction toward product.

(b) Right; reducing the container volume has the effect of increasing the concentration of any gases in the container, and the only gas is the reactant CO_2. Thus you've essentially added to the reactant side, forcing a shift to more product.

(c) Left; adding a substance that appears as a product in the equation as written shifts the reaction toward reactant.

(d) It depends. If *all* the solid $CaCO_3$ is removed, the reaction must shift left because you are taking away from the reactant side, and Le Chatelier's principle says more reactant will be formed. However, if only *some* of the solid $CaCO_3$ is removed, then the constant-density explanation given for graphite on page 565 of the textbook applies and the reaction does not shift.

14.121 (a) K_{sp}, because the reaction is the dissolution in water of a sparingly soluble salt.

(b) $K_{sp} = [Ca^{2+}] \times [F^-]^2$

$$[F^-]^2 = \frac{K_{sp}}{[Ca^{2+}]}$$

$$[F^-] = \sqrt{\frac{K_{sp}}{[Ca^{2+}]}} = \sqrt{\frac{1.4 \times 10^{-10}}{3.3 \times 10^{-4} M}} = \sqrt{4.2 \times 10^{-7}} = 6.5 \times 10^{-4} M$$

(c) The rate constant k_r for the reverse reaction. Because $K < 1$, it must be true that the denominator in the fraction $k_f/k_r = K_{eq}$ is larger than the numerator.

(d) E_a for the forward reaction. The slower the rate of a reaction, the larger the E_a value for the reaction. Because k_f is smaller [see (c)], the forward reaction is slower and therefore has the larger E_a value.

(e) The rate of the reverse reaction because k_r is larger [see (c)].

(f) $Li_2CO_3(s) \rightleftharpoons 2\,Li^+(aq) + CO_3^{2-}(aq)$; $K_{eq} = K_{sp} = [Li^+]^2 \times [CO_3^{2-}]$

(g) Lithium carbonate; because these two salts give the same number of moles of ions when they dissolve (1 mol Ca^{2+} + 2 mol F^- = 3 mol ions; 2 mol Li^+ + 1 mol CO_3^{2-} = 3 mol ions), their solubilities are directly proportional to their K_{sp} values. Li_2CO_3 has the larger K_{sp} value and therefore is more soluble.

CHAPTER

15

Electrolytes, Acids, and Bases

15.1 See solution in textbook.

15.2 (a) Electrolyte.   (b) Nonelectrolyte.   (c) Electrolyte.   (d) Nonelectrolyte.
(e) Electrolyte.   (f) Electrolyte.   (g) Electrolyte.

15.3 (a) 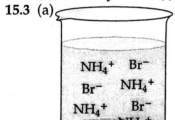   (b) Yes. That NH_4Br dissociates tells you it is an electrolyte.

(c)

15.4 See solution in textbook.

15.5 $H_2CO_3 + 2 H_2O \rightleftarrows 2 H_3O^+ + CO_3^{2-}$

15.6 $H_2CO_3 + H_2O \rightleftarrows H_3O^+ + HCO_3^-$
$HCO_3^- + H_2O \rightleftarrows H_3O^+ + CO_3^{2-}$

15.7 See solution in textbook.

15.8 It would take 1 mole of NaOH to neutralize 1 mole of hydrochloric acid, but 2 moles of NaOH to neutralize 1 mole of sulfuric acid.

The answers to the two questions aren't the same because HCl is monoprotic (contains one dissociable hydrogen) and H_2SO_4 is diprotic (contains two dissociable hydrogens). Thus each mole of H_2SO_4 produces 2 moles of H^+ ions.

15.9 It would take 0.05 mole of $Ba(OH)_2$ to neutralize 0.1 mole of hydrochloric acid because each mole of this base dissociates to 2 moles of OH^- ions.

15.10

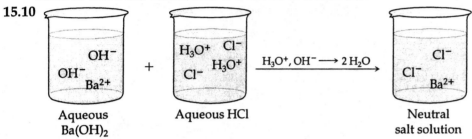

Aqueous $Ba(OH)_2$ Aqueous HCl   Neutral salt solution

15.11 See solution in textbook.

15.12 $H:\overset{..}{\underset{H}{N}}:H + H:\overset{..}{\underset{H}{P}}:H \longrightarrow \left[H:\overset{..}{\underset{H}{N}}:\right]^- + \left[H:\overset{H}{\underset{H}{\overset{..}{P}}}:H\right]^+$

15.13 Water is behaving as an acid because it donates a proton to NH_2^-.

15.14 See solution in textbook.

15.15 As acid: $HCO_3^- + H_2O \rightleftarrows H_3O^+ + CO_3^{2-}$
As base: $HCO_3^- + H_2O \rightleftarrows H_2CO_3 + OH^-$

15.16 (a) HCO_3^- acting as a base lies farther to the right because $K_b > K_a$.
(b) Basic because $K_b > K_a$, which means the solution contains more OH^- than H_3O^+.

15.17 See solution in textbook.

15.18 (a) The solution is basic because the OH^- concentration is 1.55×10^{-4} M, which is greater than 10^{-7} M.

(b) $[H_3O^+] = \dfrac{1 \times 10^{-14}}{1.55 \times 10^{-4}} = 6.45 \times 10^{-11}$ M

15.19 (a) $[H_3O^+] = \dfrac{1.00 \text{ mol } H_3O^+}{0.5000 \text{ L of solution}} = 2.00$ M

(b) $[OH^-] = \dfrac{1 \times 10^{-14}}{2.00} = 5.00 \times 10^{-15}$ M

15.20 (a) Because 0.0100 mole of $Ba(OH)_2$ provides 0.0200 mole of OH^-, the OH^- concentration is

$[OH^-] = \dfrac{0.0200 \text{ mol } OH^-}{0.5000 \text{ L of solution}} = 0.0400$ M

(b) $[H_3O^+] = \dfrac{1 \times 10^{-14}}{0.0400} = 2.50 \times 10^{-13}$ M

15.21 See solution in textbook.

15.22 The logarithm of 10,000 is 4 because 10 must be raised to the fourth power to get 10,000: $10 \times 10 \times 10 \times 10 = 10^4 = 10,000$.

15.23 The logarithm is 1 for both 10 and 10^1 because the number 10 written with no exponent is understood to be raised to the first power: $10 = 10^1$.

15.24 The logarithm of 0.01 is -2. The logarithm of 10^{-2} is also -2 because $0.01 = 10^{-2}$.

15.25 See solution in textbook.

15.26 The logarithm is -11 for both 1.0×10^{-11} and 10^{-11}.

15.27 Because the (positive) logarithm of 10^{-7} is -7, the negative logarithm is $-(-7) = +7$.

15.28 See solution in textbook.

15.29 The pH of solution B is 10. (Recall that the higher the pH, the more basic the solution.) Because pH is a logarithmic scale, each *one*-unit increase in the pH of a basic solution means a *ten*fold increase in OH^- concentration. Thus to be ten times more basic than solution A (pH 9), solution B must have a pH of $9 + 1 = 10$.

15.30 (a) The most acidic solution in the table has a pH of 0. A solution ten times more acidic has a pH of -1. Each *one*-unit decrease in the pH of an acidic solution means a *ten*fold increase in acidity (remember—the lower the pH, the more acidic the solution). Thus to be ten times more acidic than a pH 0 solution, the solution must have a pH of $0 - 1 = -1$.

(b) The concentration of H_3O^+ is 10 raised to the negative of the pH value:

$$[H_3O^+] = 10^{-(-1)}\,M = 10^{+1}\,M = 10\,M.$$

15.31 See solution in textbook.

15.32 A solution 100 times less acidic than one having a pH of 2.56 has a pH of 4.56 (the higher the pH, the *less* acidic the solution). Each one-unit increases in pH means a tenfold decrease in acidity, and so a 100-fold decrease in acidity means a two-unit change in pH: $2.56 + 2 = 4.56$. The H_3O^+ concentration of this less-acidic solution is $10^{-4.56} = 2.75 \times 10^{-5}$.

15.33 $[H_3O^+] = 10^{-5.55} = 2.82 \times 10^{-6}$

$$[OH^-] = \frac{1 \times 10^{-14}}{2.82 \times 10^{-6}} = 3.55 \times 10^{-9}$$

15.34 See solution in textbook.

15.35 CO_3^{2-} is the conjugate base of HCO_3^- because any conjugate base has one fewer H^+ ion than its acid.

15.36 H_2CO_3 is the conjugate acid of HCO_3^- because any conjugate acid has one more H^+ ion than its base.

15.37 See solution in textbook.

15.38 $NH_3 + H_2O \rightleftharpoons NH_4^+ + OH^-$

15.39 This is called a buffer solution because it contains NH_4^+ (from NH_4Cl) and NH_3. Differing by only one proton, NH_4^+ and NH_3 are a weak acid/base conjugate pair.

15.40 $NH_4^+ + OH^- \longrightarrow NH_3 + H_2O$
The added OH^- is converted to the weak base NH_3, resulting in a pH change much smaller than what would occur in an unbuffered solution.

15.41 $NH_3 + H_3O^+ \longrightarrow NH_4^+ + H_2O$
The added H_3O^+ is converted to the weak acid NH_4^+, resulting in a pH change much smaller than what would occur in an unbuffered solution.

15.42 Substances were classified as acids if they had a sour taste, turned litmus red, and reacted with active metals to produce hydrogen gas.

15.43 Substances were classified as bases if they had a bitter taste, turned litmus blue, and formed aqueous solutions that felt slippery to the touch.

15.44 An indicator is a compound that is one color in the presence of an acid and a different color in the presence of a base. Litmus is an example, being red in acids and blue in bases.

15.45 An electrolyte is a substance whose aqueous solution can conduct electricity. A nonelectrolyte is a substance whose aqueous solution cannot conduct electricity. Some examples of electrolytes are $NaCl$, HCl, and $NaOH$. Some examples of nonelectrolytres are CH_3OH, $C_6H_{12}OH$, and CH_4. See Table 15.1 of the textbook for additional examples.

15.46 The setup consists of a beaker containing an aqueous solution of the compound to be tested plus a light bulb attached to a cord terminating in a plug. You cut one wire of the cord and immerse the two cut ends in the solution. Then plug the cord into an electrical outlet. If the bulb lights up, the compound is an electrolyte because it carries electricity from one immersed wire end to the other. If the bulb fails to light up, the solution is not conducting electricity, telling you the compound is not an electrolyte.

15.47 Ethanol does not dissociate into ions when dissolved in water, but magnesium chloride does. In other words, ethanol is a nonelectrolyte, and magnesium chloride is an electrolyte.

15.48 *Dissociation* means "breaking up into ions." An example is that $NaCl$ dissociates in water to produce Na^+ and Cl^- ions.

15.49 Ionic compounds dissociate into ions when they dissolve in water. The compounds are electrolytes because the ions conduct electricity.

15.50 False. Some molecular compounds, such as HX acids, dissociate into ions when placed in water. An example is HBr.

15.51 Ions must be present.

15.52 (a) We mean that HCl is a covalently bonded compound that exists as discrete HCl molecules rather than as H^+ and Cl^- ions.

(b) Yes, it is incorrect to call HCl an ionic compound because it does not consist of a lattice of ions held together by ionic bonds.

(c) It must break up to produce ions.

15.53 (a) Yes, because NaCl does not exist as discrete molecules whose atoms are held together by covalent bonds.

(b) Because it is a water-soluble ionic compound.

15.54 This statement is true because water-soluble compounds that consist of metal and nonmetal atoms are ionic compounds, and all water-soluble ionic compounds are electrolytes.

15.55 (a) Electrolyte.

(b) Nonelectrolyte.

(c) Nonelectrolyte.

(d) Electrolyte.

(e) Electrolyte.

(f) Electrolyte.

(g) Nonelectrolyte.

15.56 $Na_2SO_4(aq) \longrightarrow 2\,Na^+(aq) + SO_4{}^{2-}(aq)$

15.57 $NH_4{}^+$

15.58 $CaBr_2(aq) \longrightarrow Ca^{2+}(aq) + 2\,Br^-(aq)$

15.59 Glucose is a molecular compound that does not dissociate in water.

15.60 We mean that such compounds, even though they consist of molecules rather than ions in the solid phase, do break up into ions when dissolved in water. An example is HI, which exists as HI molecules in the solid phase but forms H_3O^+ and I^- ions when dissolved in water.

15.61 The intense glow indicates a strong electric current and thus a large number of ions in the HCl beaker. HCl is a strong electrolyte that dissociates completely in solution. The dim glow indicates a weak current and thus few ions in the HF beaker. HF is a weak electrolyte that dissociates only partially in solution.

15.62 The halide ion concentration is 0.1 M in the HCl solution and much less than 0.1 M in the HF solution. You know this because you know from the experiment that HCl is a strong electrolyte and HF is a weak electrolyte.

15.63 The dissociation equilibrium lies far to the right for a strong electrolyte (we say the reaction *goes to completion*) and to the left for a weak electrolyte.

15.64 *Partially dissociates* means that only a small fraction of the molecules of a substance break up into ions. Most of the molecules remain undissociated. An example is HF, and in any aqueous solution of HF, you'll always find many HF molecules and only a few H^+ and F^- ions:

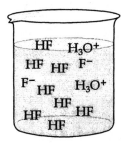

15.65 The hydronium ion, H_3O^+, because all three of these substances are electrolytes and therefore dissociate when dissolved in water.

15.66 It is more correct to write $H_3O^+(aq)$ because any H^+ ions formed in an aqueous solution are always solvated by water molecules.

15.67 It is a weak electrolyte. The low equilibrium constant of 8.2×10^{-6} means that the numerator in the expression [prducts]/[reactants] for the reaction undissociated molecules $\longrightarrow$ ions is much smaller than the denominator. In other words, the product concentration at equilibrium is very low, the equilibrium lies to the left, and most of the molecules are undissociated, which is the definition of a weak electrolyte.

15.68 It is appropriate to ignore equilibrium in this case. That the equilibrium constant is very large means that the reaction goes to completion. Therefore the reverse reaction can be neglected.

15.69 Numerous answers possible. Two strong molecular electrolytes are hydrobromic acid and hydrochloric acid:

$HBr + H_2O \longrightarrow H_3O^+ + Br^-$

$HCl + H_2O \longrightarrow H_3O^+ + Cl^-$

Two weak molecular electrolytes are hydrofluoric acid and ammonia:

$HF + H_2O \rightleftharpoons H_3O^+ + F^-$

$NH_3 + H_2O \rightleftharpoons NH_4^+ + OH^-$

15.70 (a) Hydrochloric acid. (b) Nitric acid. (c) Sulfuric acid.
(d) Hydrofluoric acid. (e) Acetic acid.

15.71 All the compounds are molecular because none contain a metal ion or polyatomic ion.

15.72 All are molecular electrolytes, and they all produce H_3O^+ ions in water.

15.73 They are all acids because they all contain at least one H atom and produce H_3O^+ ions in solution.

15.74 False. Because HF is a weak acid and HCl is a strong acid, a given volume of 1.0 M HCl contains many, many more H^+ ions and is therefore more acidic than the same volume of 1.0 M HF.

15.75 Weak: hydrofluoric, acetic; strong: hydrochloric, nitric, sulfuric. In solutions of equal concentrations, the strong acids produce more H^+ ions than the weak acids do. Therefore the 1.0 M solutions of the strong acids are more acidic than the 1.0 M solutions of the weak acids.

15.76 *Diprotic* means two dissociable hydrogens in the acid. One example is sulfuric acid:

$$H_2SO_4 + H_2O \longrightarrow H_3O^+ + HSO_4^-$$
$$HSO_4^- + H_2O \rightleftarrows H_3O^+ + SO_4^{2-}$$

Another example is carbonic acid:

$$H_2CO_3 + H_2O \longrightarrow H_3O^+ + HCO_3^-$$
$$HCO_3^- + H_2O \rightleftarrows H_3O^+ + CO_3^{2-}$$

15.77 Phosphoric acid is triprotic:

$$H_3PO_4 + H_2O \rightleftarrows H_3O^+ + H_2PO_4^-$$
$$H_2PO_4^- + H_2O \rightleftarrows H_3O^+ + HPO_4^{2-}$$
$$HPO_4^{2-} + H_2O \rightleftarrows H_3O^+ + PO_4^{3-}$$

15.78 After water, CH_3COOH (acetic acid) would be in highest concentration because it is a weak acid and so dissociates only to a very small extent in water ($K_{eq} = 1.8 \times 10^{-5}$).

15.79 After water, H_3O^+ and NO_3^- would be in highest concentration because HNO_3 (nitric acid) is a strong acid and so dissociates completely in water.

15.80 The beaker contains mostly undissociated acid molecules because the acid is weak:

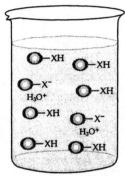

15.81 The beaker contains essentially all dissociated acid ions because the acid is strong:

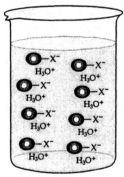

15.82 H:C:C... or H—C—C Dissociating proton

15.83 Section 15.3 of the textbook states that for acetic acid, $K_{eq} = 1.8 \times 10^{-5}$. The small value of K_a tells you that acetic acid dissociates very little in water. In other words, it is a weak acid.

15.84 Section 15.3 of the textbook states that for the first proton in H_2SO_4, $K_{eq} = 1 \times 10^3$. The large value tells you this first proton dissociates essentially completely. In other words, this is a strong acid.

15.85 False. The extent of dissociation is what determines whether an acid is weak or strong, not the number of protons in the chemical formula. A monoprotic acid can be either strong or weak, and a diprotic acid can be either strong or weak. In this case, H_2CO_3 is a weak diprotic acid and HCl is a strong monoprotic acid.

15.86 An Arrhenius base is any electrolyte that contains a metal ion and OH group and produces OH^- ions when dissolved in water.

15.87 Acid–base neutralization is the production of water from the reaction between H_3O^+ supplied by an acid and OH^- supplied by a base:

$$H_3O^+ + OH^- \longrightarrow 2\,H_2O$$

15.88 Strong bases are typically the hydroxides of groups IA (1) and IIA (2) metals (Table 15.3 of the textbook).

15.89 The product of the reaction is the water-soluble salt $CaCl_2$. All water-soluble salts are strong electrolytes, completely dissociating into ions in solution. The ions conduct electricity very well.

15.90 $K^+(aq) + OH^-(aq) + H_3O^+(aq) + Cl^-(aq) \longrightarrow K^+(aq) + Cl^-(aq) + 2\,H_2O(l)$

15.91 $0.50\ \text{mol}\ H_2SO_4 \times \underbrace{\dfrac{2\ \text{mol}\ H_3O^+}{1\ \text{mol}\ H_2SO_4}}_{\substack{\text{Diprotic}}} \times \underbrace{\dfrac{1\ \text{mol}\ OH^-}{1\ \text{mol}\ H_3O^+}}_{\substack{H_3O^+ + OH^- \longrightarrow 2\,H_2O \\ \text{Neutralization}}} \times \underbrace{\dfrac{1\ \text{mol}\ Ba(OH)_2}{2\ \text{mol}\ OH^-}}_{\substack{\text{From formula} \\ Ba(OH)_2}} = 0.50\ \text{mol}\ Ba(OH)_2$

The products of the neutralization are $BaSO_4(s)$ and water. Because the $BaSO_4$ is insoluble in water (see Table 7.1 of the textbook), there are no ions present to conduct electricity. When an excess of $Ba(OH)_2$ is added, Ba^{2+} and OH^- ions are present to conduct electricity.

15.92 $2.5\ \text{mol}\ HNO_3 \times \underbrace{\dfrac{1\ \text{mol}\ H_3O^+}{1\ \text{mol}\ HNO_3}}_{\substack{\text{Monoprotic}}} \times \underbrace{\dfrac{1\ \text{mol}\ OH^-}{1\ \text{mol}\ H_3O^+}}_{\substack{H_3O^+ + OH^- \longrightarrow 2\,H_2O \\ \text{Neutralization}}} \times \underbrace{\dfrac{1\ \text{mol}\ Ba(OH)_2}{2\ \text{mol}\ OH^-}}_{\substack{\text{From formula} \\ Ba(OH)_2}}$

$$= 1.25\ \text{mol}\ Ba(OH)_2$$

15.93 Problem 15.91—$BaSO_4$: $Ba(OH)_2 + H_2SO_4 \longrightarrow BaSO_4 + 2\,H_2O$.
Problem 15.92—$Ba(NO_3)_2$: $Ba(OH)_2 + 2\,HNO_3 \longrightarrow Ba(NO_3)_2 + 2\,H_2O$

15.94

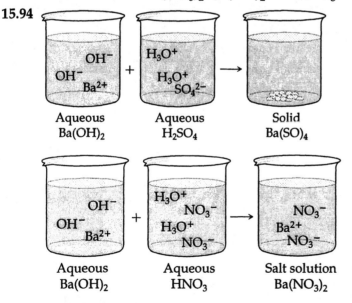

15.95 $NH_3(g) + H_2O \underset{\longrightarrow}{\longleftarrow} NH_4^+(aq) + OH^-(aq)$

15.96 The small value of K_{eq} indicates the equilibrium lies to the left, meaning that NH_3 is the predominant species in solution.

15.97 Because NH_3 contains no OH groups and therefore cannot dissociate to produce OH^- ions in solutions. By definition, an Arrhenius base must produce OH^- ions.

15.98 Brønsted–Lowry bases are proton acceptors. NH_3 has a lone pair of electrons that can accept a proton.

15.99 Water can be thought of as a Brønsted–Lowry acid because it donates a proton to the ammonia:

$$NH_3 + H_2O \rightleftharpoons NH_4^+ + OH^-$$

15.100 (a) $NH_4Cl(s) + NaOH(s) \longrightarrow NH_3(g) + H_2O(l) + Na^+(aq) + Cl^-(aq)$

(b) Once this reaction has begun, enough water is formed to dissolve the initially solid NH_4Cl and NaOH. Then we can think in terms of ions for both reactants and products:

$$NH_4^+(aq) + Cl^-(aq) + Na^+(aq) + OH^-(aq) \longrightarrow$$
$$NH_3(g) + H_2O(l) + Na^+(aq) + Cl^-(aq)$$

Removing the spectator ions, we see that NH_4^+ is the acid and OH^- is the base because NH_4^+ donates a proton to OH^-:

$$NH_4^+ + OH^- \rightleftharpoons NH_3 + H_2O$$

15.101 (a) The very low value of K_{eq} indicates that the equilibrium lies far to the left, which means there are very few $H_3O^+(aq)$ ions present. The solution is therefore only slightly acidic.

(b) Water is acting as a base because it accepts a proton from NH_4^+.

15.102 (a) $CO_3^{2-} + H_2O \rightleftharpoons HCO_3^- + OH^-$

(b) The H_2O is the acid because it donates a proton, and CO_3^{2-} is the base because it accepts a proton.

(c) The low value of K_{eq} indicates that the equilibrium lies to the left, meaning CO_3^{2-} is a weak base.

15.103 (a) $H^- + H_2O \longrightarrow H_2 + OH^-$

(b) The Brønsted–Lowry definition says the base H^- is a proton acceptor, so that H_2 gas forms as H^- combines with the proton it accepted from water: $H^- + H^+ \longrightarrow H_2$.

15.104 $H\!:^- + H\!:\!\ddot{O}\!:\!H \longrightarrow H\!:\!H + {}^-\!\ddot{O}\!:\!H$

15.105 The hydride has a lone pair of electrons.

15.106 NH_3 has a lone pair of electrons available to accept a proton, but CH_4 does not:

$$H\!:\!\ddot{N}\!:\!H \qquad H\!:\!\overset{\overset{\displaystyle H}{}}{\underset{\underset{\displaystyle H}{}}{C}}\!:\!H$$

15.107 The C_2H_5OH donates a proton to the H^-.

15.108 A Brønsted–Lowry weak base is defined as anything that reacts with water to accept a proton and produce OH^- ions. To be a weak base, the reaction equilibrium would have to lie to the left.

15.109 Because it produces relatively few OH^- in aqueous solution.

15.110 These ionic compounds completely dissociate in solution and therefore do not meet the weak-base criterion of producing only low concentrations of OH^- ions in water.

15.111 The LiOH solution is more basic. Because lithium is a group 1 metal, LiOH is a strong base that dissociates completely, meaning a 1 M LiOH solution has an OH^- concentration of 1 M. The weak base NH_3 dissociates very little, meaning a 1 M NH_3 solution has an OH^- concentration of much less than 1 M.

15.112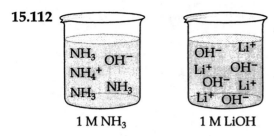

1 M NH_3 1 M LiOH

15.113 (a) $HSO_4^- + H_2O \rightleftharpoons H_3O^+ + SO_4^{2-}$
(b) $HSO_4^- + H_2O \rightleftharpoons H_2SO_4 + OH^-$
(c) You need the K_{eq} values for both reactions. If K_{eq} for reaction (a) is larger, the solution is weakly acidic. If K_{eq} for reaction (b) is larger, the solution is weakly basic.

15.114 (a) 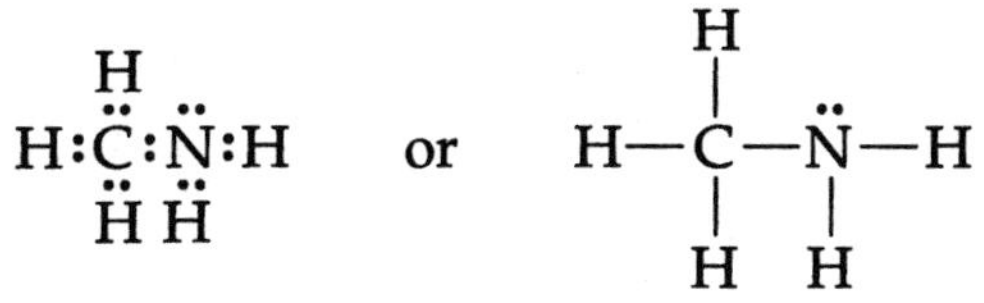 $H:\overset{..}{\underset{..}{C}}:\overset{..}{N}:H$ or $H-\overset{\overset{\textstyle H}{|}}{\underset{\underset{\textstyle H}{|}}{C}}-\overset{..}{\underset{\underset{\textstyle H}{|}}{N}}-H$

(b) 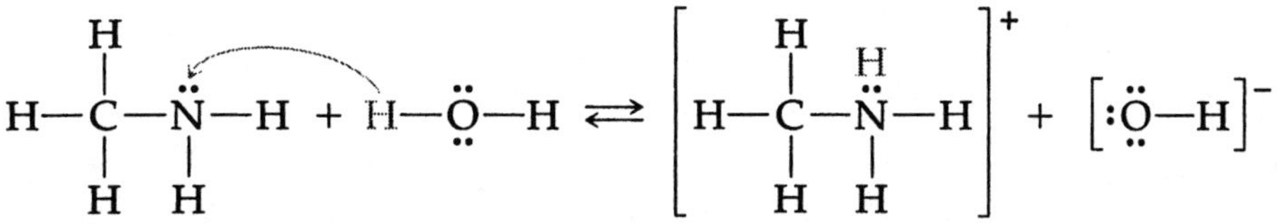 $H-\overset{\overset{\textstyle H}{|}}{\underset{\underset{\textstyle H}{|}}{C}}-\overset{\underset{\textstyle H}{|}}{N}-H + H-\overset{..}{\underset{..}{O}}-H \rightleftharpoons \left[H-\overset{\overset{\textstyle H}{|}}{\underset{\underset{\textstyle H}{|}}{C}}-\overset{\overset{\textstyle ..H}{}}{\underset{\underset{\textstyle H}{|}}{N}}-H \right]^+ + \left[:\overset{..}{\underset{..}{O}}-H \right]^-$

(c) The equilibrium lies to the left, which you know because you were told that amines are all *weak* bases.
(d) Ethane has no lone pairs of electrons:

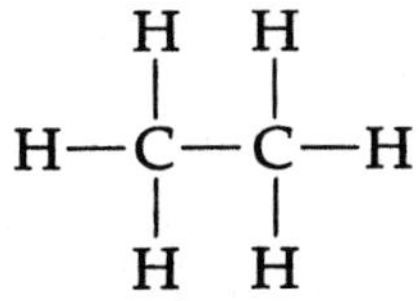

$H-\overset{\overset{\textstyle H}{|}}{\underset{\underset{\textstyle H}{|}}{C}}-\overset{\overset{\textstyle H}{|}}{\underset{\underset{\textstyle H}{|}}{C}}-H$

(e) It is appropriate to call methylamine an electrolyte because, by definition, any weak base is an electrolyte. And for the same reason, it is a weak electrolyte: all weak bases are weak electrolytes. They produce a small amount of ions in solution.

15.115 It must produce OH^- ions in water.
15.116 (a) $H_2PO_4^-$, HPO_4^{2-}, PO_4^{3-}
(b) PO_4^{3-} has no ability to serve as a weak acid because it has no hydrogens.
15.117 The autoionization of water refers to the reaction in which one water molecule donates a proton to another water molecule:

$H_2O + H_2O \rightleftharpoons H_3O^+ + OH^-$

15.118 It is breaking up into its component ions, H^+ (or H_3O^+) and OH^-.
15.119 The autoionization equilibrium lies far to the left. The extremely small K_w value of 1.0×10^{-14} verifies this.
15.120 $K_w = 1.0 \times 10^{-14} = [H_3O^+] \times [OH^-]$
15.121 False. One liter of pure water contains 1.0×10^{-7} mole of H_3O^+ and 1×10^{-7} mole of OH^- because of the equilibrium $2 H_2O \rightleftharpoons H_3O^+ + OH^-$.
15.122 At 25°C, $[H_3O^+]$ and $[OH^-]$ are both 1.0×10^{-7} mol/L.
15.123 Pure water is neutral because $[H_3O^+]$ equals $[OH^-]$.

15.124 (1) An aqueous solution is acidic when $[H_3O^+] > [OH^-]$. (2) An aqueous solution is acidic when $[H_3O^+] > 1.0 \times 10^{-7}$.

15.125 (1) An aqueous solution is basic when $[OH^-] > [H_3O^+]$. (2) An aqueous solution is basic when $[OH^-] > 1.0 \times 10^{-7}$.

15.126 True. There are always some H_3O^+ ions in any aqueous solution because of the autoionization of water.

15.127 True. The product of $[H_3O^+]$ and $[OH^-]$ must always equal 1.0×10^{-14} in an aqueous solution. If one concentration increases, the other must decrease.

15.128 True. The product of $[H_3O^+]$ and $[OH^-]$ must always equal 1.0×10^{-14} in an aqueous solution at 25°C.

15.129 Solve the K_w expression, $[H_3O^+] \times [OH^-] = 1.0 \times 10^{-14}$, for $[OH^-]$:

$$[OH^-] = \frac{1.0 \times 10^{-14}}{[H_3O^+]} = \frac{1.0 \times 10^{-14}}{1.0 \text{ M}} = 1.0 \times 10^{-14} \text{ M}$$

The solution is acidic because $[H_3O^+] > [OH^-]$.

15.130 Solve the K_w expression for $[H_3O^+]$:

$$[H_3O^+] \times [OH^-] = 1.0 \times 10^{-14}$$

$$[H_3O^+] = \frac{1.0 \times 10^{-14}}{[OH^-]} = \frac{1.0 \times 10^{-14}}{1.0 \times 10^{-11} \text{M}} = 1.0 \times 10^{-3} \text{M}$$

The solution is acidic because $[H_3O^+] > [OH^-]$.

15.131 LiOH dissociates to produce 1 mole of OH^- for every 1 mole of LiOH. Therefore

$$[OH^-] = \frac{2.50 \text{ mol OH}^-}{4.00 \text{ L solution}} = 0.625 \text{ M}$$

$$[H_3O^+] = \frac{1.0 \times 10^{-14}}{0.625 \text{ M}} = 1.6 \times 10^{-14} \text{M}$$

15.132 $Ba(OH)_2$ dissociates to produce 2 moles of OH^- for every 1 mole of $Ba(OH)_2$, which means 0.250 mole of $Ba(OH)_2$ produces 0.500 mole OH^-. The molar concentrations are therefore

$$[OH^-] = \frac{0.500 \text{ mol OH}^-}{4.00 \text{ L solution}} = 0.125 \text{ M}$$

$$[H_3O^+] = \frac{1.0 \times 10^{-14}}{0.125 \text{ M}} = 8.0 \times 10^{-14} \text{M}$$

15.133 Molar mass of $Mg(OH)_2$ = 58.319 g/mol.

$$\text{Mol } Mg(OH)_2 = 2.40 \text{ g} \times \frac{1 \text{ mol}}{58.319 \text{ g}} = 0.0412 \text{ mol}$$

$Mg(OH)_2$ dissociates to produce 2 moles of OH^- for every 1 mole of $Mg(OH)_2$, meaning 0.0412 mole of $Mg(OH)_2$ produces 0.0824 mole of OH^-. The concentrations are therefore

$$[OH^-] = \frac{0.0824 \text{ mol}}{4.00 \text{ L solution}} = 0.0206 \text{ M}$$

$$[H_3O^+] = \frac{1.0 \times 10^{-14}}{0.0206 \text{ M}} = 4.85 \times 10^{-13} \text{M}$$

15.134 Because HNO_3 dissociates to produce 1 mole of H_3O^+ for every 1 mole of HNO_3, the concentrations are

$$[H_3O^+] = \frac{2.00 \text{ mol}}{0.800 \text{ L solution}} = 2.50 \text{ M}$$

$$[OH^-] = \frac{1.0 \times 10^{-14}}{2.50 \text{ M}} = 4.0 \times 10^{-15} \text{M}$$

15.135 (a) The solution is acidic because the $[OH^-]$ concentration being below 10^{-7} means the H_3O^+ concentration must be above 10^{-7}.

(b) Because $[OH^-]$ equals 1.0×10^{-11} (same as 10^{-11}), the H_3O^+ concentration must be 1.0×10^{-3} (same as 10^{-3}) because $10^{-11} \times 10^{-3} = 10^{-14}$.

15.136 The base-10 logarithm of any number is the power to which 10 must be raised to get the number.

15.137 -34

15.138 13

15.139 The logarithm of both 10^0 and 1 is 0 ($10^0 = 1$).

15.140 (d)

15.141 The logarithm of 10 is 1 ($10^1 = 10$), and the logarithm of 100 is 2 ($10^2 = 100$). Because 60 is between 10 and 100, the logarithm of 60 must be between 1 and 2.

15.142 (b)

15.143 The logarithm of 0.1 is -1 ($10^{-1} = 0.1$), and the logarithm of 1 is 0 ($10^0 = 1$) by definition. Because 0.73 is between 0.1 and 1, so the logarithm of 0.73 must be between -1 and 0.

15.144 True. As a number increases, its negative logarithm decreases.

15.145 $pH = -\log[H_3O^+]$

15.146 At $pH = 7$, $[H_3O^+] = [OH^-] = 10^{-7}$ M.

15.147 $pH = -\log[H_3O^+] = -\log 0.0010 = -\log 10^{-3} = 3$. The solution is acidic because the pH is below 7.

15.148 $pH = -\log[H_3O^+] = -\log 10^{-6} = 6$. The solution is acidic because the pH is below 7.

15.149 $pH = -\log(6.40 \times 10^{-9}) = 8.19$. The solution is basic because the pH is above 7.

15.150 If $[OH^-] = 10^{-14}$, $[H_3O^+] = 1$ (from the K_w equation). Therefore $pH = -\log 1 = 0$. The solution is acidic because the pH is below 7.

15.151 If $[OH^-] = 2.0 \times 10^{-3}$ M, $[H_3O^+] = 5.0 \times 10^{-12}$ M (from the K_w equation). The pH is therefore $-\log(5.00 \times 10^{-12}) = 11.3$. The solution is basic because the pH is above 7.

15.152 Solution A is more acidic because it has the lower pH. Because each one-unit change in pH corresponds to a tenfold change in H_3O^+ concentration, the three-unit difference in pH means a $10 \times 10 \times 10 = 1000$-fold difference in acidity. Solution A is 1000 times more acidic than solution B.

15.153 $pH = -\log 10.0 = -1.00$. The solution is acidic because the pH is below 7.

15.154 $[H_3O^+] = 10^{-pH} = 10^{-4}$ M. The solution is acidic because the pH is below 7.

15.155 $[H_3O^+] = 10^{-pH} = 10^{-8}$ M. $[OH^-] = 1.0 \times 10^{-14}/10^{-18}$ M $= 10^{-6}$ M. The solution is basic because the pH is above 7.

15.156 $[H_3O^+] = 10^{-pH} = 10^{-(-1)} = 10^1 = 10$ M. $[OH^-] = 1.0 \times 10^{-14}/10$ M $= 10^{-15}$ M. The solution is acidic because the pH is below 7.

15.157 The pH of the HCl solution is lower because acetic acid is a weak acid and HCl is a strong acid. One mole of the weak acid puts only a few H_3O^+ ions into solution, meaning $[H_3O^+] << 1$ M. One mole of the strong acid puts 1 mole of H_3O^+ ions into solution, meaning $[H_3O^+] = 1$ M.

15.158 (a) Aniline must accept a proton to be a base.

(b) Aniline has a lone pair of electrons that can accept a proton.

(c) $C_6H_5NH_3^+$, because the members of any conjugate pair differ by one proton.

15.159 No, the weak acid always has one more proton than its conjugate base. Because protons have a positive charge, the acid always carries one more positive charge than its conjugate base.

15.160 The conjugate acid is a weak acid. The conjugate of any weak base is a weak acid.

15.161 The $NaNO_3$ solution would be neutral. The NO_3^- ion has no tendency to accept protons because doing so forms the strong acid HNO_3, which dissociates immediately and completely. The conjugate of any strong acid is so weak that it is neither acid nor base.

15.162 Because the source of the conjugate base is salt of the weak acid. For example, the source of acetate ion (CH_3COO^-), the conjugate base of acetic acid (CH_3COOH), might be the salt sodium acetate ($NaCH_3COO$) or the salt potassium acetate (KCH_3COO).

15.163 Because Cl^- has no tendency to accept protons to form the strong acid HCl. Strong acids have conjugates that are neither acid nor base; they are neutral. A solution of NaCl is therefore neutral.

15.164 We mean the solution resists any large change in its pH.

15.165 No, because it does not contain significant amounts of either a weak acid and its conjugate base or a weak base and its conjugate acid.

15.166 The recipe is to combine either a weak acid and its conjugate base or a weak base and its conjugate acid. With either combination, the weak acid part of the buffer reacts with added strong base, and the weak base part of the buffer reacts with added strong acid. As a result of either reaction, the change in pH is much less than it would be in an unbuffered solution.

15.167 Blood in living organisms is one biological system that is buffered. The buffer is bicarbonate/carbonate, HCO_3^-/CO_3^{2-}.

15.168 No; if you add enough strong acid or strong base, the buffer will be exhausted.

15.169 Yes, the $NaHCO_3$ dissociates to produce Na^+ and HCO_3^- ions. The solution then contains the weak acid H_2CO_3 and its conjugate base HCO_3^-, components of a buffer solution. The HCO_3^- reacts with added acid according to the reaction: $HCO_3^- + H_3O^+ \longrightarrow H_2CO_3 + H_2O$, and the H_2CO_3 reacts with added base according to the reaction $H_2CO_3 + OH^- \longrightarrow HCO_3^- + H_2O$.

15.170 (a) The pH decreases.

    (b) Because the added strong acid is converted to a weak acid (the conjugate acid in the buffer system). This weak acid dissociates slightly, adding H^+ ions to the solution and thereby decreasing the pH slightly.

15.171 The NaOH reacts with half of the acetic acid to produce sodium acetate, according to the neutralization reaction

$$CH_3COOH + NaOH \longrightarrow Na^+ + CH_3COO^- + H_2O$$

After the neutralization reaction, the solution contains significant amounts of acetic acid and acetate ion, a conjugate pair and therefore components of a buffer solution.

15.172 Dissolve NH_3 and NH_4Cl or any other soluble ammonium salt in water. The salt provides NH_4^+, the conjugate acid of the base NH_3.

15.173 Dissolve HClO and NaClO or any other soluble hypochlorite salt in water, so that the solution contains a weak acid, HClO, and its conjugate base, ClO^-.

15.174 (a) HPO_4^{2-} is the conjugate base of $H_2PO_4^-$.

    (b) $HPO_4^{2-} + H_3O^+ \longrightarrow H_2PO_4^- + H_2O$
       $H_2PO_4^- + OH^- \longrightarrow HPO_4^{2-} + H_2O$

    (c) H_3PO_4 is the conjugate acid of $H_2PO_4^-$.

    (d) $H_3PO_4 + OH^- \longrightarrow H_2PO_4^- + H_2O$
       $H_2PO_4^- + H_3O^+ \longrightarrow H_3PO_4 + H_2O$

15.175 (a) The sodium acetate dissociates completely, forming 2.0 moles of acetate ions and 2.0 moles of sodium ions. One mole of acetate ions reacts with the 1 mole of HCl according to the reaction

$$CH_3COO^- + HCl \longrightarrow CH_3COOH + Cl^-$$

(b) Na^+, Cl^-, CH_3COO^-, and CH_3COOH. The added 1.0 mole of H_3O^+ reacts with half of the sodium acetate, leaving 1.0 mole of CH_3COO^-, 1.0 mole of CH_3COOH, 1.0 mole of Cl^- (from the 1.0 mole of HCl added), and 2.0 moles of Na^+ (from the 2.0 moles of sodium acetate initially dissolved).

(c) Yes, because there is a large amount of both a weak acid, CH_3COOH, and its conjugate base, CH_3COO^-, present in solution.

15.176 The base part of the buffer pair combines with the protons of the added strong acid, locking the protons up in molecules of a weak acid. In an acetic acid/acetate buffer, for instance, the mechanism is

$$CH_3COO^- + H_3O^+ \longrightarrow CH_3COOH + H_2O$$

The strong acid H_3O^+ has been replaced by the weak acid CH_3COOH.

15.177 The acid part of the buffer pair combines with the OH^- ions of the added strong base, locking the OH^- ions up in water molecules. In an acetic acid/acetate buffer, for instance, the mechanism is

$$CH_3COOH + OH^- \longrightarrow CH_3COO^- + H_2O$$

The strong base OH^- has been replaced by the weak base CH_3COO^-.

15.178 The weak acid in the buffer converts the added OH^- ions to water.

15.179 The weak base in the buffer combines with the added protons to form molecules of a weak acid.

15.180 The components of a hypochlorous acid buffer are $HClO$ and ClO^-. The ClO^- defends against added strong acid: $ClO^- + H_3O^+ \longrightarrow HClO + H_2O$. The $HClO$ defends against added strong base: $HClO + OH^- \longrightarrow ClO^- + H_2O$.

15.181 (a) $HClO_4 + H_2O \longrightarrow H_3O^+ + ClO_4^-$.

(b) Because this is a strong acid, it dissociates completely, meaning the solution contains no $HClO_4$, and equal amounts of the two ions from the acid. The relative concentrations are therefore $[H_2O] > [H_3O^+] = [ClO_4^-]$.

(c) Because the acid is monoprotic, each mole of acid yields 1 mole of H^+ and 1 mole of ClO_4^-. The concentrations are therefore $[H_3O^+] = [ClO_4^-] = 0.100$ M.

(d) pH $= -\log 0.100 = -(-1.00) = 1.00$

15.182 (a) $C_6H_5N + H_2O \rightleftharpoons C_6H_5NH^+ + OH^-$

(b) Being a weak base, pyridine dissociates only slightly, and therefore there is much C_6H_5N in the solution and only small amounts of $C_6H_5NH^+$ and OH^-. The relative concentrations are $[H_2O] > [C_6H_5N] > [C_6H_5NH^+] = [OH^-]$.

(c) In 1 L of the solution, there is initially 0.100 mole of C_6H_5N. After 3.2% dissociates, the amount of $C_6H_5NH^+$ and OH^- in the 1 L is

$$0.032 \times 0.100 \text{ mol} = 0.0032 \text{ mol}$$

and the amount of C_6H_5N is

$$0.100 \text{ mol} - 0.0032 \text{ mol} = 0.097 \text{ mol}$$

The concentrations are therefore 0.0032 M for $C_6H_5NH^+$ and OH^- and 0.097 M for C_6H_5N.

(d) $[H_3O^+] = \dfrac{1.0 \times 10^{-14}}{0.0032 \text{ M}} = 3.1 \times 10^{-12} \text{M}$

pH $= -\log 3.1 \times 10^{-12} = -(-11.5) = 11.5$

15.183 (a) $H_2PO_4^-$; the K_{eq} values are given in Equation 15.2 of the textbook. They are 4.2×10^{-13} for HPO_4^{2-} and 6.2×10^{-8} for $H_2PO_4^-$. The species with the larger K_{eq} is the stronger acid.

    (b) H_3O^+

    (c) HCO_2H

    (d) HI; Section 15.1 of the textbook notes that HI is a strong electrolyte, meaning it dissociates completely and has a very high K_{eq} value. Section 15.2 notes that HF is a weak electrolyte and has a very low K_{eq} value.

15.184 You need to neutralize

$$\frac{0.010 \text{ mol HNO}_3}{\cancel{L}} \times 0.0500 \,\cancel{L} = 0.000500 \text{ mol HNO}_3$$

and therefore need 0.000500 mole of the NaOH solution, equivalent to a volume of

$$0.000500 \text{ mol NaOH} \times \frac{1 \text{ L}}{0.015 \text{ mol NaOH}} \times 0.0333 \text{ L} = 3.33 \text{ mL}$$

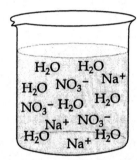

15.185 (a) Basic because the number of moles of OH^- is greater than the number of moles of H_3O^+:

$$\frac{0.015 \text{ mol NaOH}}{\cancel{L}} \times 0.0500 \,\cancel{L} = 0.00075 \text{ mol NaOH yielding } 0.00075 \text{ mol OH}^-$$

$$\frac{0.010 \text{ mol HNO}_3}{\cancel{L}} \times 0.0500 \,\cancel{L} = 0.000500 \text{ mol HNO}_3 \text{ yielding } 0.00050 \text{ mol H}_3\text{O}^+$$

    (b)

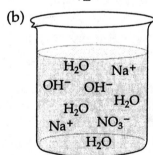

    (c) The 0.00050 mole of H_3O^+ ions reacts with 0.00050 mole of OH^- ions, leaving 0.00025 mole of OH^- in the 100 mL of solution. The pH is therefore

$$[OH^-] = \frac{0.00025 \text{ mol}}{0.100 \text{ L}} = 0.0025 \text{ M}$$

$$[H^+] = \frac{1.0 \times 10^{-14}}{0.0025 \text{ M}} = 4.0 \times 10^{-12} \text{ M}$$

$$pH = -\log 4.0 \times 10^{-12} = -(11.4) = 11.4$$

15.186 0.030 mole of monoprotic HNO_3 yields 0.030 mole of H_3O^+ ions. The H_3O^+ concentration is thus 0.030 mol/0.1 L = 0.30 M, and the pH is $-\log 0.30 = -(-0.52) = 0.52$.

15.187 (a) $HNO_3 + OH^- \rightarrow H_2O + NO_3^-$
(b) $HF + OH^- \rightarrow H_2O + F^-$
(c) $NH_3 + H_2O \rightleftarrows NH_4^+ + OH^-$
(d) $HCO_3^- + H_2O \rightleftarrows H_3O^+ + CO_3^{2-}$

15.188 (a) The H_3O^+ concentration is $10^{-2.14} = 7.24 \times 10^{-3}$ M, much lower than the 0.20 M concentration of HX, telling you HX does not dissociate to any significant extent and is therefore a weak acid.

(b) $K_{eq} = \dfrac{[H_3O^+] \times [X^-]}{[HX]} = \dfrac{(7.24 \times 10^{-3} M) \times (7.24 \times 10^{-3} M)}{0.20 \text{ M}} = 2.6 \times 10^{-4}$

15.189

Substance	Name	Type of electrolyte (strong, weak, or nonelectrolyte)	Type of acid/base (strong or weak)	Reaction(s) in water
NaCl	Sodium chloride	Strong	—	(1) $NaCl \rightarrow Na^+ + Cl^-$
HNO_3	Nitric acid	Strong	Strong acid	(1) $HNO_3 + H_2O \rightarrow H_3O^+ + NO_3^-$
$Mg(NO_3)_2$	Magnesium nitrate	Strong	—	(1) $Mg(NO_3)_2 \rightarrow Mg^{2+} + 2\,NO_3^-$
HF	Hydrofluoric acid	Weak	Weak acid	(1) $HF + H_2O \rightleftarrows H_3O^+ + F^-$
NaF	Sodium fluoride	Strong	Weak base	(1) $NaF \rightarrow Na^+ + F^-$ (2) $F^- + H_2O \rightleftarrows HF + OH^-$
NH_4Cl	Ammonium chloride	Strong	Weak acid	(1) $NH_4Cl \rightarrow NH_4^+ + Cl^-$ (2) $NH_4^+ + H_2O \rightleftarrows NH_3 + H_3O^+$

15.190 Lowest to highest pH means the most acidic solution is first in your list, and therefore begin with a strong acid. There are two, HCl and HNO_3, and the more concentrated one has the higher H_3O^+ concentration and consequently the lower pH. The one weak acid, HCN, comes next, and then look for compounds that are neutral in water—$LiNO_3$. Then do the bases, weak ones followed by strong ones—NaF, then KOH. Your list should be 0.20 M HCl, 0.10 M HNO_3, 0.10 M HCN, 0.10 M $LiNO_3$, 0.10 M NaF, 0.10 M KOH.

15.191 A pH of 2.0 means $[H_3O^+]$ is $10^{-2.0} = 0.010$ M. Nitric acid, HNO_3, is monoprotic and strong, meaning each mole yields 1 mole of H_3O^+ ions. To prepare 200.0 mL of a 0.010 M solution, you need

$\dfrac{0.010 \text{ mol}}{L} \times 0.2000\, L = 0.0020 \text{ mol}$

15.192 OH^- ions because there are 2 moles of OH^- ions for every 1 mole of Ca^{2+} ions.

15.193 (a) $HCO_3^- + OH^- \rightarrow H_2O + CO_3^{2-}$
(b) $HCl + F^- \rightarrow HF + Cl^-$
(c) $H_2CO_3 + OH^- \rightarrow H_2O + HCO_3^-$
(d) $HCN + H_2O \rightleftarrows H_3O^+ + CN^-$

15.194 K^+ and OH^- in equal amounts because this is a strong base and therefore dissociates completely, and the molecular formula is one K^+ for each OH^-.

15.195 (a) $pH = -\log 1.0 = 0$ (b) $pH = -\log 0.1 = 1$
(c) $pH = -\log 0.001 = 3$ (d) $pH = -\log(1.0 \times 10^{-5}) = 5.0$
(e) $pH = -\log(1.10 \times 10^{-7}) = 6.96$

15.196 Because neutralization is described as complete here, assume the acid dissociates completely so that 0.4 mole yields 1.2 moles of H_3O^+ ions. Thus you need 1.2 moles of OH^- ions for complete neutralization. The amount of $Ca(OH)_2$ is

$$1.2 \text{ mol } OH^- \times \frac{1 \text{ mol } Ca(OH)_2}{2 \text{ mol } OH^-} = 0.6 \text{ mol } Ca(OH)_2$$

15.197 First determine the molar concentration of OH^-, then use K_w and OH^- concentration to determine H_3O^+ concentration, then convert to pH:

$$\frac{20.0 \text{ g NaOH}}{2.00 \text{ L}} \times \frac{1 \text{ mol NaOH}}{40.0 \text{ g NaOH}} \times \frac{1 \text{ mol } OH^-}{1 \text{ mol NaOH}} = 0.250 \text{ mol } OH^-/L = 0.250 \text{ M}$$

$$[H_3O^+] = \frac{1.00 \times 10^{-14}}{0.250 \text{ M}} = 4.00 \times 10^{-14}$$

$$pH = -\log(4.00 \times 10^{-14}) = -(-13.4) = 13.4$$

15.198 $H_2SO_4 + H_2O \rightarrow H_3O^+ + HSO_4^-$ $K_{eq} = 1.0 \times 10^3$
$HSO_4^- + H_2O \rightleftharpoons H_3O^+ + SO_4^{2-}$ $K_{eq} = 1.2 \times 10^{-2}$
HSO_4^- is the weak acid.

15.199 In a 0.010 M NaOH solution, $[OH^-] = 0.010$ M. Therefore

$$[H_3O^+] = \frac{1.0 \times 10^{-14}}{0.010 \text{ M}} = 1.0 \times 10^{-12} \text{ M}$$

$$pH = -\log(1.0 \times 10^{-12}) = -(-12) = 12$$

15.200 Calculate $[H_3O^+]$ from the given pH, then use the $[H_3O^+]$ value and K_w to get $[OH^-]$ and $[NaOH]$, then use the molar mass of NaOH to find the number of grams:

$$[H_3O^+] = 10^{-11} = 1.0 \times 10^{-11}$$

$$[OH^-] = \frac{1.0 \times 10^{-14}}{1.0 \times 10^{-11} \text{ M}} = 1.0 \times 10^{-3} \text{ M} = [NaOH]$$

$$\frac{1.0 \times 10^{-3} \text{ mol NaOH}}{L} \times \frac{40.0 \text{ g NaOH}}{1 \text{ mol NaOH}} = 0.040 \text{ g NaOH/L}$$

15.201 KOH and H_2SO_4. The equation is $2 KOH + H_2SO_4 \rightarrow 2 H_2O + K_2SO_4$.

15.202 $pH = -\log 12.1 = -(+1.08) = -1.08$

$$[OH^-] = \frac{1.0 \times 10^{-14}}{12.1 \text{ M}} = 8.26 \times 10^{-16} \text{ M}$$

15.203

Base   Acid

The fluoride ion is the Brønsted–Lowry base because it accepts a proton. The ammonium ion is the Brønsted–Lowry acid because it donates a proton.

15.204 (a) Nonelectrolyte   (b) Electrolyte   (c) Electrolyte   (d) Nonelectrolyte
(e) Electrolyte   (f) Electrolyte   (g) Nonelectrolyte

15.205 A solution that has a pH of 4.20 is acidic, and you cannot add the strong base NaOH to pure water and end up with an acidic solution.

15.206 The K_{eq} values tell you the relative strengths. The smallest value is for the weakest acid. Therefore the weakest-to-strongest ranking is HCN < HClO < HCOOH < HNO$_2$.

15.207

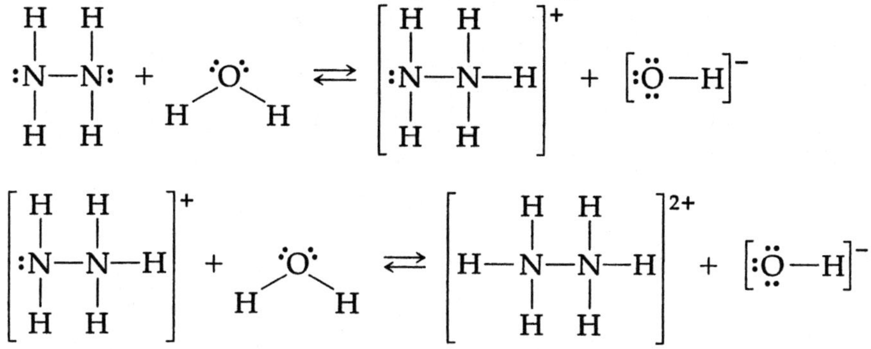

15.208 KOH + C$_2$H$_3$COOH → KC$_2$H$_3$COO + H$_2$O
Because all potassium salts are water-soluble (Table 7.1 of the textbook), the solution contains K$^+$(aq) ions and C$_2$H$_3$COO$^-$(aq) ions. Because an excess of the acid has been added and because it is a weak acid, the solution also contains undissociated C$_2$H$_3$COOH molecules. Because the C$_2$H$_3$COOH and C$_2$H$_3$COO$^-$ are a weak acid–base conjugate pair, the solution is a buffer.

15.209 First figure out what the OH$^-$ ion concentration is, which must also be the LiOH concentration because each LiOH yields one OH$^-$:

$$[OH^-] = \frac{1.0 \times 10^{-14}}{2.30 \times 10^{-13}} = 0.043\ 48\ M$$

Now use the molar mass of LiOH to determine the number of grams in this number of moles of LiOH:

$$\frac{0.04348\ \text{mol LiOH}}{L} \times \frac{23.948\ \text{g LiOH}}{\text{mol LiOH}} \times 0.750\ L = 0.781\ \text{g LiOH}$$

15.210 H$_3$C$_6$H$_5$O$_7$ + H$_2$O $\rightleftarrows$ H$_2$C$_6$H$_5$O$_7^-$ + H$_3$O$^+$
H$_2$C$_6$H$_5$O$_7^-$ + H$_2$O $\rightleftarrows$ HC$_6$H$_5$O$_7^{2-}$ + H$_3$O$^+$
HC$_6$H$_5$O$_7^{2-}$ + H$_2$O $\rightleftarrows$ C$_6$H$_5$O$_7^{3-}$ + H$_3$O$^+$

15.211 One thousand times more acidic means 10 × 10 × 10 times more acidic. Because each one-unit change in pH is a tenfold change in acidity, the more acidic solution must have a pH of 9.20 − 3 = 6.20. Therefore

$$[H_3O^+] = 10^{-6.20} = 6.31 \times 10^{-7}\ M$$

$$[OH^-] = \frac{1.0 \times 10^{-14}}{6.31 \times 10^{-7}\ M} = 1.58^{-8}\ M$$

15.212

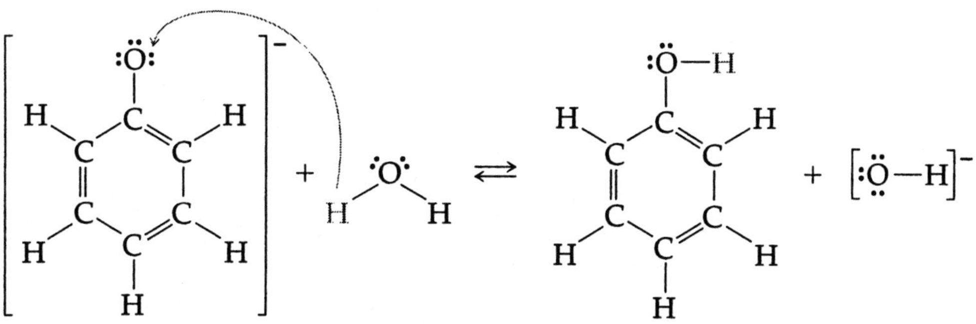

15.213 (a) LiOH + HI → H_2O + LiI

(b) CH_3COOH + NaOH → H_2O + $NaCH_3COO$

(c) 2 HBr + $Ca(OH)_2$ → 2 H_2O + $CaBr_2$

(d) 3 KOH + H_3PO_4 → 3 H_2O + K_3PO_4

15.214 $Mg(OH)_2$ and HNO_3. The equation is $Mg(OH)_2$ + 2 HNO_3 → 2 H_2O + $Mg(NO_3)_2$.

15.215 No. Because HBr is a strong acid, Br^- cannot act as a conjugate base by accepting protons. A buffered solution must contain a weak acid.

15.216 The solution of propionic acid, because its lower K_{eq} value means this acid dissociates less in solution. Therefore it has a lower concentration of H_3O^+ and a higher pH.

15.217 $[H_3O^+] = 10^{-2.40} = 3.98 \times 10^{-3}$ mol/L

Because each HCl gives one H_3O^+, this is also the molar HCl concentration. Use the molar mass of HCl to get grams per liter and then multiply by the desired volume:

$$\frac{3.98 \times 10^{-3} \,\text{mol}}{L} \times \frac{36.46 \text{ g}}{\text{mol}} \times 7.50\,L = 1.09 \text{ g}$$

15.218 (a) Weak electrolyte (b) Strong electrolyte (c) Strong electrolyte

(d) Nonelectrolyte (e) Weak electrolyte (f) Weak electrolyte

(g) Strong electrolyte

15.219 The $NaClO_2$ solution would have the higher pH. Both these sodium salts are soluble in water, which means we must talk about the ions in solution. Because $HClO_4$ is a strong acid, it dissociates completely, with the result that anytime ClO_4^- accepts an H^+ from a water molecule, the $HClO_4$ immediately breaks up. The same is true for Na^+ accepting OH^- from water—the strong base NaOH immediately breaks up. The result is a neutral solution of Na^+ and ClO_4^- ions. The ClO_2^- ions, however, can accept H^+ from water and form the weak acid $HClO_2$. Because the Na^+ in the $NaClO_2$ solution cannot accept OH^- from water, every H_2O that gives an H^+ to ClO_2^- results in a free OH^- and therefore a basic solution. Thus the pH of the $NaClO_4$ solution is 7, and the pH of the $NaClO_2$ solution is above 7.

15.220 Use the $Ba(OH)_2$ molar mass to find out how many moles of $Ba(OH)_2$ you've dissolved in the 3 L:

$$0.250 \text{ g} \times \frac{1 \text{ mol}}{171.34 \text{ g}} = 1.459 \times 10^{-3} \,\text{mol } Ba(OH)_2$$

Each mole of $Ba(OH)_2$ yields 2 moles of OH^-, which means

$$[OH^-] = \frac{2 \times (1.459 \times 10^{-3}) \text{ mol } OH^-}{3 \text{ L}} = 9.727 \times 10^{-4} \,\text{mol } OH^-/L$$

Now use K_w to get $[H_3O^+]$ and then convert to pH:

$$[H_3O^+] = \frac{1 \times 10^{-14}}{9.727 \times 10^{-4} \,M} = 1.03 \times 10^{-11} M$$

$$pH = -\log(1.03 \times 10^{-11}) = -(-11.0) = 11.0$$

15.221 CN^- + H_2O ⇌ HCN + OH^-

15.222 With $[OH^-] = 8.20 \times 10^{-12}$ M,

$$[H_3O^+] = \frac{1 \times 10^{-14}}{8.20 \times 10^{-12} \,M} = 1.22 \times 10^{-3} M$$

The formula HI tells you there is a one-to-one ratio of H^+ to HI, and so 1.22×10^{-3} M must also be the original HI concentration. That is the amount in 1 L, but you want to know how much in 2.75 L:

$$\frac{1.22 \times 10^{-3} \text{ mol HI}}{\cancel{L}} \times 2.75 \cancel{L} = 3.36 \times 10^{-3} \text{ mol HI}$$

15.223 $NaOCl + HNO_3 \longrightarrow NaNO_3 + HOCl$

Because all sodium salts are water-soluble (Table 7.1 of the textbook), the solution contains $Na^+(aq)$ ions and $NO_3^-(aq)$ ions. Because HOCl is a weak acid (Table 15.2B of the textbook), the solution also contains HOCl. And because the NaOCl was added in excess, the solution contains OCl^-. This solution is therefore a buffer of the weak acid HOCl and its conjugate base, OCl^-.

15.224 Use the molar mass of HBr to find out how many moles this mass is and then divide by the volume of the solution:

$$0.378 \text{ g} \times \frac{1 \text{ mol HBr}}{80.91 \text{ g}} = 4.67 \times 10^{-3} \text{ mol HBr}$$

$$\frac{4.67 \times 10^{-3} \text{ mol HBr}}{1.25 \text{ L}} = 3.74 \times 10^{-3} \text{ mol HBr/L}$$

The formula HBr and the fact that HBr is a strong acid (Table 15.2A in the textbook) tell you this is also the H_3O^+ concentration. The OH^- concentration is

$$[OH^-] = \frac{1 \times 10^{-14}}{3.74 \times 10^{-3} \text{ M}} = 2.67 \times 10^{-12} \text{ M}$$

15.225 $\left[H-\ddot{\underset{\cdot\cdot}{S}}{:} \right]^- + H-\ddot{\underset{\cdot\cdot}{O}}-\ddot{\underset{\cdot\cdot}{C}}l{:} \rightleftharpoons H-\underset{\cdot\cdot}{\overset{H}{\underset{|}{S}}}{:} + \left[{:}\ddot{\underset{\cdot\cdot}{O}}-\ddot{\underset{\cdot\cdot}{C}}l{:} \right]^-$

      Base   Acid

15.226 $[H_3O^+] = 10^{-9.66} = 2.19 \times 10^{-10} \text{ M}$

$$[OH^-] = \frac{1 \times 10^{-14}}{2.19 \times 10^{-10} \text{ M}} = 4.57 \times 10^{-5} \text{ M}$$

The solution is basic because the OH^- concentration is greater than 1×10^{-7} M. (Of course, you can also say it's basic because the pH is above 7.)

15.227 Weak acid. X^- is the conjugate base of HX. If HX were a strong acid, X^- would not be able to act as a base by accepting a proton from water and thereby causing the solution to be basic:

$H_2O + X^- \longrightarrow HX + OH^-$

CHAPTER

16

Nuclear Chemistry

16.1 See solution in textbook.

16.2 Radioactive atoms.

16.3 Calculate the mass defect for 1 mole of $^4_2$He:

$$2 \text{ mol protons} \times \frac{1.007\,30 \text{ g}}{1 \text{ mol protons}} = 2.014\,60 \text{ g}$$

$$2 \text{ mol neutrons} \times \frac{1.008\,70 \text{ g}}{1 \text{ mol neutrons}} = 2.017\,40 \text{ g}$$

$$2 \text{ mol electrons} \times \frac{0.000\,55 \text{ g}}{1 \text{ mol electrons}} = 0.001\,1 \text{ g}$$

4.033 1 g	Theoretical $^4_2$He molar mass
−4.003 g	Actual $^4_2$He molar mass from periodic table
0.030 g/mol $^4_2$He	

Because $1 \text{ J} = 1 \text{ kg} \cdot \text{m}^2/\text{s}^2$, you must convert this mass to kilograms for your next calculation:

$$\frac{0.030 \text{ g}}{\text{mol}} \times \frac{1 \text{ kg}}{1000 \text{ g}} = 3.0 \times 10^{-5} \text{kg} / \text{mol}$$

Now use Einstein's energy equation, with the mass defect 3.0×10^{-5} kg/mol as m:

$$E = mc^2 = \frac{3.0 \times 10^{-5} \text{kg}}{\text{mol}} \times (3.00 \times 10^8 \text{ m}/\text{s})^2$$

$$= 2.7 \times 10^{12} \frac{\text{kg} \cdot \text{m}^2/\text{s}^2}{\text{mol}} = 2.7 \times 10^{12} \frac{\text{J}}{\text{mol}} \times \frac{1 \text{ kJ}}{1000 \text{ J}} = 2.7 \times 10^9 \text{ kJ}/\text{mol}$$

16.4 The band curves upward because, in order to be stable, nuclei that contain more than about 60 protons require that the number of neutrons be greater than the number of protons. Therefore $n/p > 1$, which causes the band to curve above the $n/p = 1$ line.

16.5 See solution in textbook.

16.6 Beta emission means a neutron in the nucleus splits into a proton plus an electron (beta particle). The number of protons therefore increases by 1. The number of nucleons does not change because the lost neutron is replaced by the newly formed proton (but the *details* describing the number of nucleons do change, from 14 p + 21 n = 35 nucleons in the parent to 15 p + 20 n = 35 nucleons in the daughter). The periodic table tells you an atom containing 15 protons is phosphorus. The reaction is therefore $^{35}_{14}\text{Si} \longrightarrow {}^{35}_{15}\text{P} + {}^{0}_{-1}\text{e}$.

16.7 Beta emission means a neutron in the nucleus splits into a proton plus an electron (beta particle). $^{40}_{20}\text{Ca}$ has 20 protons, which means the parent must have had 19 protons. The periodic table tells you an atom containing 19 protons is potassium. Because the total number of nucleons does not change in beta emission, the parent nucleus also had 40 nucleons, making the isotope $^{40}_{19}\text{K}$. The reaction was $^{40}_{19}\text{K} \longrightarrow {}^{40}_{20}\text{Ca} + {}^{0}_{-1}\text{e}$.

16.8 See solution in textbook.

16.9 (a) Electron capture means an inner-shell electron and a proton in the nucleus combine to form a neutron. The number of protons therefore decreases by 1. The total number of nucleons does not change because the lost proton is replaced by the newly formed neutron (but the *details* do change, from 18 p + 19 n = 37 nucleons in the parent to 17 p + 20 n = 37 nucleons in the daughter). Any atom containing 17 protons is chlorine, making the reaction $^{37}_{18}\text{Ar} + {}^{0}_{-1}\text{e} \longrightarrow {}^{37}_{17}\text{Cl}$.

(b) Electron capture increases the n/p ratio, from 19/18 = 1.1 to 20/17 = 1.2. This means the n/p ratio for $^{37}_{18}\text{Ar}$ must have been too low, placing this isotope below the dark brown central region of the band of stability.

(c) Chlorine = 37.

16.10 Electron capture means an inner-shell electron and a proton in the nucleus combine to form a neutron. The parent loses a proton, meaning the parent here must have contained 12 + 1 = 13 protons, making it aluminum. The gained neutron means the parent must have contained 13 − 1 = 12 neutrons, for a mass number of 13 p + 12 n = 25. The parent was aluminum-25, $^{25}_{13}\text{Al}$.

16.11 Positron emission means a proton splits into a neutron plus a positron. Therefore the parent must have contained 12 + 1 = 13 protons, making it aluminum. The gained neutron means the parent must have contained 13 − 1 = 12 neutrons, for a mass number of 13 p + 12 n = 25. The parent was aluminum-25, $^{25}_{13}\text{Al}$. If you compare this result with the one given in the solution to Practice Problem 16.10, you'll see that electron capture and positron emission create the same daughter from a given parent.

16.12 Practice Problem 16.10: $^{25}_{13}\text{Al} + {}^{0}_{-1}\text{e} \longrightarrow {}^{25}_{12}\text{Mg}$; Practice Problem 16.11: $^{25}_{13}\text{Al} \longrightarrow {}^{0}_{+1}\text{e} + {}^{25}_{12}\text{Mg}$.

16.13 See solution in textbook.

16.14 Two positron emissions: $^{238}_{92}\text{U} \longrightarrow {}^{0}_{+1}\text{e} + {}^{238}_{91}\text{Pa}$; $^{238}_{91}\text{Pa} \longrightarrow {}^{0}_{+1}\text{e} + {}^{238}_{90}\text{Th}$. One alpha emission: $^{238}_{92}\text{U} \longrightarrow {}^{4}_{2}\text{He} + {}^{234}_{90}\text{Th}$.

16.15 Alpha emission because, of the decay processes covered in the textbook, only alpha emission creates a daughter having an atomic number 2 less than that of the parent.

16.16 One step to the right means the number of protons increased by 1, meaning a neutron turned into a proton, which is the definition of beta emission.

16.17 See solution in textbook.

16.18 All the $^{206}_{82}\text{Pb}$ came from the decay of some of the $^{238}_{92}\text{U}$ initially present in the rock. Hence the sum of $^{238}_{92}\text{U}$ and $^{206}_{82}\text{Pb}$ in the rock today must equal the $^{238}_{92}\text{U}$ initially present.

16.19 The sum of $^{206}_{82}\text{Pb}$ and $^{238}_{92}\text{U}$ atoms present in the rock today is equal to $^{238}_{92}\text{U}$ atoms initially present.

$$1.82\text{ g } {}^{238}_{92}\text{U} \times \frac{1\text{ mol } {}^{238}_{92}\text{U}}{238.029\text{ g } {}^{238}_{92}\text{U}} \times \frac{6.022 \times 10^{23}\text{ atoms U}}{1\text{ mol } {}^{238}_{92}\text{U}} = 4.60 \times 10^{21}\text{ atoms } {}^{238}_{92}\text{U today}$$

$$4.02 \text{ g } ^{206}_{82}\text{Pb} \times \frac{1 \text{ mol } ^{206}_{82}\text{Pb}}{205.974 \text{ g } ^{206}_{82}\text{Pb}} \times \frac{6.022 \times 10^{23} \text{ atoms Pb}}{1 \text{ mol } ^{206}_{82}\text{Pb}} = 1.18 \times 10^{22} \text{ atoms } ^{206}_{82}\text{Pb today}$$

$$(0.460 \times 10^{22}) + (1.18 \times 10^{22}) = 1.64 \times 10^{22} \text{ atoms } ^{238}_{92}\text{U initially present}$$

$$\% \ ^{238}_{92}\text{U remaining in rock} = \frac{4.60 \times 10^{21} \text{ atoms}}{1.64 \times 10^{22} \text{ atoms}} \times 100 = 28.0\%$$

$$\text{Age} = \frac{-2.303 \times \log\left(\dfrac{28.0\%}{100}\right) \times 4.46 \times 10^{9} \text{ years}}{0.693} = 8.19 \times 10^{9} \text{ years}$$

16.20 The missing isotope is $^{147}_{56}\text{Ba}$. The superscripts on the left add up to 240, and those on the right add up to $90 + (3 \times 1) = 93$. The missing element therefore carries a superscript of $240 - 93 = 147$. The subscripts on the left add up to 94, and those on the right add up to 38. The missing element therefore carries a subscript of $94 - 38 = 56$.

16.21 Yes, because the reaction produces more neutrons (three) than it uses up (one).

16.22 The opening of Section 16.5 of the textbook tells you that a nuclear reaction is exothermic (releases energy) whenever mass is lost during the reaction. Thus you could determine whether or not the reaction is exothermic by measuring masses before and after the reaction is run. If the combined mass of the products is less than the combined mass of the reactants, the reaction is exothermic.

A second way would be to compare the relative stabilities of the parent and daughter isotopes. In general, an exothermic reaction occurs whenever a reactant has a chance to convert to some more stable substance. The greater the binding energy per mole of nucleons in a nucleus, the more stable the nucleus. The graph on page 638 of the textbook shows that a nucleus containing 239 nucleons has a binding energy of about 7.3×10^8 kJ/mol nucleons, one containing 90 nucleons has a binding energy of about 8.4×10^8 kJ/mol nucleons, and one containing 147 nucleons has a binding energy of about 8.0×10^8 kJ/mol nucleons. Because both products are more stable than the ^{239}Pu reactant, the reaction is exothermic.

16.23 The mass of the atom is less than the sum of the masses of the particles of which the atom is composed.

16.24 Binding energy is the energy to which the missing mass (mass defect) was converted when the atom formed from its component subatomic particles. You can think of it either as the energy that holds the nucleus together or as the energy required to break the nucleus apart into its subatomic particles.

16.25 True, because a nucleon is either a proton or a neutron and mass number is defined as number of protons plus number of neutrons.

16.26 Statement (1) is true because the more nucleons a nucleus has, the greater the binding energy of the nucleus. Statement (2) can be true because stability is a function not of total binding energy in a nucleus but rather of binding energy *per mole of nucleons* in the nucleus. The example of $^{13}_{6}\text{C}$ and $^{12}_{6}\text{C}$ in the textbook demonstrates this.

16.27 Making changes in a nucleus requires much, much more energy than the amount produced by any chemical reaction.

16.28 The graph on page 638 of the textbook tells you that the isotope $^{56}_{26}\text{Fe}$ must have the greatest mass defect because it is the isotope with the largest binding energy per mole of nucleons. Having the greatest mass defect means $^{56}_{26}\text{Fe}$ is the most stable isotope that exists.

16.29 The factor c^2. Because c is such a large number—3.00×10^8 m/s—multiplying the mass defect by c^2 makes E tremendously large.

16.30 $^{14}_{6}C$ contains 6 protons and $14 - 6 = 8$ neutrons.

$$6 \text{ mol protons} \times \frac{1.007\,30 \text{ g}}{1 \text{ mol protons}} = 6.043\,80 \text{ g}$$

$$8 \text{ mol neutrons} \times \frac{1.008\,70 \text{ g}}{1 \text{ mol neutrons}} = 8.069\,60 \text{ g}$$

$$6 \text{ mol electrons} \times \frac{1.000\,55 \text{ g}}{1 \text{ mol electrons}} = \underline{0.003\,3 \text{ g}}$$

 14.116 7 g Theoretical molar mass

 $-14.003\,24$ g Actual molar mass

 $\underline{0.113\,5}$ g Mass defect per mole of $^{14}_{6}C$

Because you need kilojoules in your answer and the joule is defined in terms of the kilogram ($1 \text{ J} = 1 \text{ kg} \cdot \text{m}^2/\text{s}^2$), convert the mass defect to kilograms:

$$\frac{0.1135 \text{ g}}{\text{mol } ^{14}_{6}C} \times \frac{1 \text{ kg}}{1000 \text{ g}} = 1.135 \times 10^{-4} \text{ kg} / \text{mol } ^{14}_{6}C$$

Use $E = mc^2$ to determine the binding energy per mole of $^{14}_{6}C$:

$$E = \frac{0.000\,113\,5 \text{ kg}}{\text{mol } ^{14}_{6}C} \times (3.00 \times 10^8 \text{ m} / \text{s})^2$$

$$= 1.02 \times 10^{13} \frac{\text{kg} \cdot \text{m}^2 / \text{sec}^2}{\text{mol } ^{14}_{6}C} = 1.02 \times 10^{13} \text{ J} / \text{mol } ^{14}_{6}C$$

$$\frac{1.02 \times 10^{13} \text{ J}}{\text{mol } ^{14}_{6}C} \times \frac{1 \text{ kJ}}{1000 \text{ J}} = 1.02 \times 10^{10} \text{ kJ} / \text{mol } ^{14}_{6}C$$

16.31 Because the solution to Problem 16.30 is in terms of moles of $^{14}_{6}C$ but the graph in the textbook is in terms of moles of nucleons, you must convert:

$$\frac{1.02 \times 10^{10} \text{ kJ}}{\text{mol } ^{14}_{6}C} \times \frac{1 \text{ mol } ^{14}_{6}C}{14 \text{ mol nucleons}} = 7.29 \times 10^8 \text{ kJ} / \text{mol nucleons}$$

The textbook graph shows about 7.45×10^8 kJ/mol nucleons for $^{12}_{6}C$ and about 7.25×10^8 kJ/mol nucleons for $^{13}_{6}C$. Thus $^{14}_{6}C$ is less stable than $^{12}_{6}C$ and just a bit more stable than $^{13}_{6}C$.

16.32 One in which the nucleus undergoes a spontaneous change to produce an atom having a more favorable n/p ratio.

16.33 False. All atoms have a mass defect and binding energy, even radioactive ones.

16.34 Their being interspersed among the positively charged protons in the nucleus keeps the proton–proton repulsions small enough to prevent the nucleus from flying apart.

16.35 (a) The ratio increases because the number of neutrons becomes larger than the number of protons.

(b) The more protons in the nucleus, the greater the number of neutrons needed to reduce the proton–proton repulsions.

16.36 The subscript is the atomic number, which is equal to number of protons; the superscript is the mass number, which is equal to number of protons plus number of neutrons. All O atoms have eight protons, by definition, making the symbols $^{16}_{8}O$, $^{17}_{8}O$, $^{19}_{8}O$.

16.37 $^{16}_{8}O$: $8/8 = 1.00$; $^{17}_{8}O$: $9/8 = 1.12$; $^{19}_{8}O$: $11/8 = 1.38$

16.38 The band of data points, on a plot of number of neutrons per atom (vertical axis) versus number of protons per atom (horizontal axis), that represents all nonradioactive isotopes plus all radioactive isotopes having a measurable half-life.

16.39 The length of time required for exactly half the atoms in a sample of a radioactive isotope to decay.

16.40 After one half-life $10 \text{ g} \times 0.5 = 5.0 \text{ g}$ remaining
After two half-lives $5.0 \text{ g} \times 0.5 = 2.5 \text{ g}$ remaining
After three half-lives $2.5 \text{ g} \times 0.5 = 1.25 \text{ g}$ remaining
After four half-lives $1.25 \text{ g} \times 0.5 = 0.625 \text{ g}$ remaining
After five half-lives $0.625 \text{ g} \times 0.5 = 0.313 \text{ g}$ remaining
After six half-lives $0.313 \text{ g} \times 0.5 = 0.156 \text{ g}$ remaining
After seven half-lives $0.156 \text{ g} \times 0.5 = 0.078 \text{ g}$ remaining
After eight half-lives $0.078 \text{ g} \times 0.5 = 0.039 \text{ g}$ remaining

Decay to this amount takes

$$\frac{13.1 \text{ h}}{1 \text{ half-life}} \times 8 \text{ half-lives} = 105 \text{ h}$$

16.41 The textbook defines *stable* as meaning both nonradioactive atoms and radioactive atoms that have a measurable half-life. Therefore any atom lying outside the band of stability, both light brown region and dark brown central band, or outside the island of stability is unstable. To answer this question, see where the 60-proton vertical line intersects the bottom and top of the band of stability. (The 60-proton line does not intersect the island of stability, which means you don't have to worry about it here.) Where the 60-proton line intersects the bottom of the light brown region, move your finger leftward to the vertical axis and read about 67 neutrons; where the 60-proton line emerges out the top of the light brown region, move your finger leftward to the vertical axis and read about 92 neutrons. Thus an atom containing 60 protons is unstable anytime it contains fewer than 67 neutrons or more than 92 neutrons.

16.42 In a graph of number of neutrons in an atom versus number of protons, any point outside either the band of stability or the island of stability.

16.43 Because of how we define the word *stable*; for this plot, *stable* means any nonradioactive nucleus plus any radioactive nucleus having a measurable half-life.

16.44 The n/p ratio is too large for these nuclei, making them radioactive and most likely to decay by converting a neutron to a proton, so that n/p gets smaller.

16.45 The n/p ratio is too small for these nuclei, making them radioactive and most likely to decay by converting a proton to a neutron, so that n/p gets larger.

16.46 They are all radioactive; this is true because the central dark brown region of the band of stability, the region of nonradioactive nuclei, terminates at 83 protons.

16.47 The spontaneous process whereby a radioactive nucleus adjusts its n/p ratio (an effort to become more stable) by capturing or emitting subatomic particles.

16.48 The neutron and proton symbols are like symbols for atoms: subscript = number of protons, superscript = number of protons plus number of neutrons. Because a neutron "contains" no protons and one neutron, its symbol is $^{1}_{0}\text{n}$. Because a proton contains one proton and no neutrons, its symbol is $^{1}_{1}\text{p}$.

In the electron and positron symbols, the superscript is as usual number of protons plus number of neutrons. The subscript, however, indicates not number of protons but rather electrical charge. An electron contains no neutrons and no protons, making its superscript 0, and carries a charge of -1, making its subscript -1: $^{0}_{-1}\text{e}$. A positron contains no neutrons and no protons, and carries a charge of $+1$. Because a positron is nothing more than a positive electron, we use the letter *e* rather than the letter *p*: $^{0}_{+1}\text{e}$ or, because a plus sign is usually implicit, $^{0}_{1}\text{e}$.

16.49 Because it is the oppositely charged version of an electron. Whenever a positron and electron encounter each other, they instantaneously annihilate each other and create a lot of energy as they do so.

16.50 As the electrical charge carried by each particle: -1 for the electron and $+1$ for the positron.

16.51 Any nucleus below the central dark brown region of the band of stability, because the n/p ratio of such a nucleus is too low.

16.52 Any nucleus above the central dark brown region of the band of stability, because the n/p ratio of such a nucleus is too high.

16.53 True. Radioactive decay changes the number of protons in the nucleus, thus changing the identity of the element.

16.54 The nucleus loses a neutron and gains a proton because beta decay is $^1_0n \longrightarrow ^1_1p + ^{\,\,0}_{-1}e$.

16.55 When a neutron in the nucleus converts to a proton, an electron is also created and emitted. This is beta emission: $^1_0n \longrightarrow ^1_1p + ^{\,\,0}_{-1}e$. The electron created in this decay is often called a beta particle and given the symbol β^-, so that you may sometimes see the decay written $^1_0n \longrightarrow ^1_1p + \beta^-$. The symbols $^{\,\,0}_{-1}e$ and β^- are completely equivalent.

16.56 (a) Conversion of a neutron to a proton lowers the n/p ratio, which means the n/p ratio was probably too high to begin with. This puts the isotope above the central dark brown region on the band of stability.

(b) A neutron converting to a proton increases the atomic number (number of protons) by 1. The element having atomic number $73 + 1 = 74$ is tungsten, W. The number of neutrons in $^{186}_{73}$Ta is $186 - 73 = 113$. One neutron is gone because of the decay, meaning there are 112 in the daughter, giving it a mass number of $74 + 112 = 186$. The only decay process that converts a neutron to a proton also creates an electron, $^1_0n \longrightarrow ^1_1p + ^{\,\,0}_{-1}e$. The reaction is therefore $^{186}_{73}$Ta $\longrightarrow ^{186}_{74}$W $+ ^{\,\,0}_{-1}e$.

(c) Beta emission.

16.57 In positron emission, a proton converts to a neutron plus a positron, which means the nucleus loses a proton, gains a neutron, and ejects a positron.

16.58 In electron capture, a proton combines with an inner-shell electron and thereby converts to a neutron. The nucleus therefore loses a proton and gains a neutron.

16.59 (a) Conversion of a proton to a neutron increases the n/p ratio, which means the n/p ratio was probably too low to begin with. This puts the isotope below the central dark brown region on the band of stability.

(b) Conversion of a proton to a neutron means the atomic number (number of protons) decreases by 1. The daughter isotope therefore has $74 - 1 = 73$ protons, making it tantalum, Ta. The number of neutrons in the parent $^{162}_{74}$W is $162 - 74 = 88$, making the mass number of the daughter $73 + 89 = 162$: $^{162}_{73}$Ta.

Two decay processes convert a proton to a neutron, one creating a positron in addition to the neutron, the other capturing an inner-shell electron. The two reactions are therefore $^{162}_{74}$W $\longrightarrow ^{\,\,0}_{+1}e + ^{162}_{73}$Ta and $^{162}_{74}$W $+ ^{\,\,0}_{-1}e \longrightarrow ^{162}_{73}$Ta.

(c) $^{162}_{74}$W $\longrightarrow ^{\,\,0}_{+1}e + ^{162}_{73}$Ta is positron emission; $^{162}_{74}$W $+ ^{\,\,0}_{-1}e \longrightarrow ^{162}_{73}$Ta is electron capture.

16.60 Any nucleus containing more than 83 protons, which means any nucleus above bismuth in a band-of-stability graph. These nuclei are so big that they eject nucleons four at a time.

16.61 Because an alpha particle, $^4_2$He, consists of two protons and two neutrons, the atomic number (number of protons) decreases by 2 and the mass number (number of protons plus number of neutrons) decreases by 4.

16.62 (a) Above bismuth, where all nuclei are "too big" and therefore radioactive.

(b) Losing two protons changes the atomic number (number of protons) to 88, making the daughter radium, Ra. The number of neutrons in the parent is $232 - 90 = 142$.

Losing two of them means the daughter contains 140 neutrons, for a mass number of $140 + 88 = 228$: $^{228}_{88}$Ra. The combination of two protons and two neutrons is a helium nucleus, $^4_2$He, making the decay reaction $^{232}_{90}$Th $\longrightarrow$ $^4_2$He + $^{228}_{88}$Ra.

(c) Alpha decay.

16.63 As kinetic energy (energy of motion) in the emitted particle or as electromagnetic radiation, such as gamma rays.

16.64 Any of them because it is possible for any nuclear decay to produce gamma rays.

16.65 By checking superscripts and subscripts. In a balanced reaction, the sum of the superscripts on the left must equal the sum of the superscripts on the right, and the sum of the subscripts on the left must equal the sum of the subscripts on the right.

16.66 The ores must be decaying by alpha-particle emission, $^4_2$He. The particles become helium gas when they pick up two electrons each.

16.67 Mass number is number of protons plus number of neutrons and changes only when this *sum* changes.

(a) Ejection of a beta particle means the decay process is beta emission: $^1_0$n $\longrightarrow$ $^1_1$p + $^0_{-1}$e. One neutron is lost, but one proton is gained, so that the sum n + p = mass number does not change.

(b) Ejection of a positron means the decay process is positron emission: $^1_1$p $\longrightarrow$ $^1_0$n + $^0_{+1}$e. One proton is lost, but one neutron is gained, so that the sum n + p = mass number does not change.

(c) Electron capture is $^0_{-1}$e + $^1_{+1}$p $\longrightarrow$ $^1_0$n. One proton is lost, but one neutron is gained, so that the sum n + p = mass number does not change.

(d) An alpha particle is a helium nucleus—two protons plus two neutrons. Therefore ejection of an alpha particle means two neutrons and two protons lost, so that the sum n + p = mass number decreases by 4.

16.68 Atomic number equals number of protons in a nucleus and changes whenever the number of protons changes.

(a) Ejection of a beta particle means the decay process is beta emission: $^1_0$n $\longrightarrow$ $^1_1$p + $^0_{-1}$e. One proton is gained, and therefore the atomic number increases by 1.

(b) Ejection of a positron means the decay process is positron emission: $^1_1$p $\longrightarrow$ $^1_0$n + $^0_{+1}$e. One proton is lost, and therefore the atomic number decreases by 1.

(c) Electron capture is $^0_{-1}$e + $^1_{+1}$p $\longrightarrow$ $^1_0$n. One proton is lost, and therefore the atomic number decreases by 1.

(d) An alpha particle is a helium nucleus—two protons plus two neutrons. Therefore ejection of an alpha particle means two protons are lost, and the atomic number decreases by 2.

16.69 (a) You know alpha decay causes a nucleus to lose two protons (plus two neutrons), and you know number of protons in a nucleus is the same as atomic number. So moving two elements to the left of the parent in the periodic table gives you the daughter.

(b) You know beta decay creates a proton: $^1_0$n $\longrightarrow$ $^1_1$p + $^0_{-1}$e. You also know that number of protons in a nucleus is the same as atomic number. Therefore moving one element to the right of the parent in the periodic table gives you the daughter.

(c) You know that positron emission destroys a proton: $^1_1$p $\longrightarrow$ $^1_0$n + $^0_{+1}$e. You also know that number of protons in a nucleus is the same as atomic number. Therefore moving one element to the left of the parent in the periodic table gives you the daughter.

(d) You know that electron capture destroys a proton: $^0_{-1}$e + $^1_{+1}$p $\longrightarrow$ $^1_0$n. You also know that number of protons in a nucleus is the same as atomic number. Therefore moving one element to the left of the parent in the periodic table gives you the daughter.

16.70 Because gamma radiation is entirely electromagnetic radiation, which has no mass and no charge. There are no nucleons created or destroyed during gamma radiation.

16.71 Numerous answers possible. One sequence is

$$^{207}_{82}\text{Pb} \longrightarrow \ ^{203}_{80}\text{Hg} + \ ^{4}_{2}\text{He}$$

$$^{203}_{80}\text{Hg} \longrightarrow \ ^{203}_{79}\text{Au} + \ ^{0}_{+1}\text{e}$$

16.72 The superscript sum on the left must equal the superscript sum on the right, and ditto for subscripts. Because the superscript does not change, the missing particle must have a 0 superscript. Because the subscript decreases by 1, the missing element must have a −1 subscript. The particle fitting this bill is the electron, $^{0}_{-1}\text{e}$: $^{8}_{4}\text{Be} + \ ^{0}_{-1}\text{e} \longrightarrow \ ^{8}_{3}\text{Li}$. The fact that the electron appears on the left and is consumed tells you the decay process is electron capture.

16.73 The superscript sum on the left must equal the superscript sum on the right, and ditto for subscripts. Because the superscript does not change, the missing particle must have a 0 superscript. Because the subscript increases by 1, the missing particle must have a −1 subscript. The particle fitting this bill is the electron, $^{0}_{-1}\text{e}$: $^{47}_{20}\text{Ca} \longrightarrow \ ^{0}_{-1}\text{e} + \ ^{47}_{21}\text{Sc}$. The fact that the electron is created coupled with the fact that, in talking about nuclear reactions, *beta particle* is another name for the electron tells you the decay process is beta emission.

16.74 The superscript sum on the left must equal the superscript sum on the right, and ditto for subscripts. The missing particle must therefore have superscript 231 and subscript 90. The subscript tells you number of protons = atomic number; the element having atomic number 90 is thorium, Th: $^{235}_{92}\text{U} \longrightarrow \ ^{4}_{2}\text{He} + \ ^{231}_{90}\text{Th}$. The $^{4}_{2}\text{He}$ is an alpha particle, which makes the decay process alpha-particle emission.

16.75 The superscript sum on the left must equal the superscript sum on the right, and ditto for subscripts. The missing particle therefore has superscript 11 and subscript 4. The subscript tells you the number of protons = atomic number; the element having atomic number 4 is beryllium, Be: $^{11}_{4}\text{Be} \longrightarrow \ ^{11}_{5}\text{B} + \ ^{0}_{-1}\text{e}$. The fact that an electron is given off coupled with the fact that, in nuclear chemistry, *beta particle* is another name for the electron tells you the decay process is beta emission.

16.76 The superscript sum on the left must equal the superscript sum on the right, and ditto for subscripts. The missing particle must therefore have superscript 40 and subscript 19. The subscript tells you number of protons = atomic number, and the element having atomic number 19 is potassium, K: $^{0}_{-1}\text{e} + \ ^{40}_{19}\text{K} \longrightarrow \ ^{40}_{18}\text{Ar}$. The fact that an electron is consumed tells you the decay process is electron capture.

16.77 $26.2 \text{ h} \times \dfrac{1 \text{ half-life}}{13.1 \text{ h}} = 2 \text{ half-lives}$

$39.3 \text{ h} \times \dfrac{1 \text{ half-life}}{13.1 \text{ h}} = 3 \text{ half-lives}$

After 26.2 h: $100 \text{ g} \times \frac{1}{2} \times \frac{1}{2} = 25.0 \text{ g}$ or $100 \text{ g} \xrightarrow{13.1 \text{ h}} 50 \text{ g} \xrightarrow{26.2 \text{ h}} 25 \text{ g}$

After 39.3 h: $100 \text{ g} \times \frac{1}{2} \times \frac{1}{2} \times \frac{1}{2} = 12.5 \text{ g}$ or $100 \text{ g} \xrightarrow{13.1 \text{ h}} 50 \text{ g} \xrightarrow{26.2 \text{ h}} 25 \text{ g} \xrightarrow{39.3 \text{ h}} 12.5 \text{ g}$

16.78 No; because the half-life of $^{14}_{6}\text{C}$ is only 5715 years, essentially all of it would have decayed in a 120-million-year-old fossil, leaving none to use in dating the material.

16.79 Because new $^{14}_{6}\text{C}$ is constantly being produced in the upper atmosphere by incoming radiation, always replacing the 50% that disappears every 5715 years.

16.80 $\text{Age} = \dfrac{-2.303 \times \log\left(\dfrac{22.8\%}{100}\right) \times 5715 \text{ years}}{0.693} = 1.22 \times 10^4 \text{ years}$

16.81 (a) That all the $^{206}_{82}\text{Pb}$ came from the decay of $^{238}_{92}\text{U}$.

(b) $14.90 \text{ g } ^{238}_{92}\text{U} \times \dfrac{1 \text{ mol } ^{238}_{92}\text{U}}{238.029 \text{ g } ^{238}_{92}\text{U}} \times \dfrac{6.022 \times 10^{23} \text{ atoms } ^{238}_{92}\text{U}}{1 \text{ mol } ^{238}_{92}\text{U}} = 3.770 \times 10^{22} \text{ atoms } ^{238}_{92}\text{U}$

$$26.50 \text{ g } ^{206}_{82}\text{Pb} \times \frac{1 \text{ mol } ^{206}_{82}\text{Pb}}{205.974\,46 \text{ g } ^{206}_{82}\text{Pb}} \times \frac{6.022 \times 10^{23} \text{ atoms } ^{206}_{82}\text{Pb}}{1 \text{ mol } ^{206}_{82}\text{Pb}} = 7.748 \times 10^{22} \text{ atoms } ^{206}_{82}\text{Pb}$$

(c) $(3.770 \times 10^{22}) + (7.748 \times 10^{22}) = 11.518 \times 10^{22} = 1.1518 \times 10^{23}$ atoms $^{238}_{92}\text{U}$

(d) $\dfrac{3.770 \times 10^{22} \text{ atoms}}{1.1518 \times 10^{23} \text{ atoms}} \times 100\% = 32.73\%$

(e) Age $= \dfrac{-2.303 \times \log\left(\dfrac{32.73\%}{100}\right) \times (4.46 \times 10^9 \text{ years})}{0.693} = 7.19 \times 10^9$ years

16.82 The combined mass defect of the products must be greater than the combined mass defect of the reactants. This ensures that mass is lost during the reaction, and this mass is converted to energy and released, making the reaction exothermic.

16.83 To *fission* means to break up, and therefore nuclear fission is the breaking up of a large nucleus into two or more smaller ones.

16.84 To *fuse* means to meld together into one piece, and thus nuclear fusion is the combining of small nuclei into one larger nucleus.

16.85 Because each fission event produces more neutrons than it consumes. The newly formed excess neutrons are available to take part in subsequent fission events.

16.86 The superscript sum on the left must equal the superscript sum on the right, and ditto for subscripts. Therefore the missing particle must have superscript 100 (240 left − 140 right = 100) and subscript 40 (94 left − 54 right = 40). The subscript 40 is the atomic number, making the missing particle zirconium, Zr: $^{239}_{94}\text{Pu} + ^1_0\text{n} \longrightarrow ^{100}_{40}\text{Zr} + ^{140}_{54}\text{Xe}$.

16.87 The superscript sum on the left must equal the superscript sum on the right, and ditto for subscripts. Therefore the missing particle must have superscript 12 and subscript 6. The subscript is the atomic number, making the missing particle carbon, C: $^8_4\text{Be} + ^4_2\text{He} \longrightarrow ^{12}_6\text{C} + \gamma$.

16.88 The graph on page 638 of the textbook tells you that, of all the elements, $^{56}_{26}\text{Fe}$ is the most stable nucleus. Therefore fusion does not proceed any further, and iron builds up as the star burns out.

16.89 The mass of fissionable material required to keep most of the neutrons produced in a fission chain reaction in the sample. The result is a runaway reaction and an explosion.

16.90 To heat water and thereby produce steam, which is then used to power the turbines of electric generators.

16.91 Numerous answers possible. Some benefits are that electricity generated by fission lessens our dependency on fossil fuels, causes less atmospheric pollution, and may eventually be less expensive to the consumer. Two problems are what to do with nuclear waste and the potential for accidents that may release radioactive materials into the environment.

16.92 Because the speed of the fission is regulated by control rods and because all reactors are designed to operate using amounts of nuclear fuel much less than the critical-mass amount.

16.93 Because nuclei, being positively charged, repel one another, and extremely large amounts of thermal energy (in other words, extremely high temperatures) are needed to force the nuclei close enough together to fuse.

16.94 Because no one has developed a material or confinement method able to withstand the high temperatures required (up to 15 million K). Until such a material or method is created, we have no "container" to hold the fusion fuel.

16.95 Fusion fuel (heavy isotopes of hydrogen) is cheap and readily available from ocean water; fusion reactions produce no nuclear waste; no danger of an accident releasing toxic substances into the environment.

16.96 Alpha radiation is least likely to hurt you because it is not very penetrating and can be stopped by paper, clothing, or the top layer of skin. Gamma radiation is most likely to hurt you because it can penetrate most substances and therefore can go deep into your body and harm internal organs.

16.97 By ionizing the biological molecules that compose them. This ionization causes bonds in the molecules to weaken and often break, causing irreparable damage.

16.98 Because it can deposit enough energy in a molecule to knock an electron out, converting the molecule to a positive ion.

16.99 *Magnetic resonance imaging* lets doctors see deep inside the body to spot tumors and other trouble spots. *Gamma radiation from cobalt-60* destroys cancer cells. *Radiation imaging with iodine-131* lets doctors check the health of a thyroid gland. In *radioimmunoassays,* radioactive reactants are mixed with a sample of a patient's blood to determine what compounds are present in the blood. *Irradiation of foods* before they reach the supermarket cuts down on cases of food poisoning.

16.100 $_2^4$He 2p $2 \times 1.007\,30\text{ g/mol} = 2.014\,60\text{ g/mol}$

$\quad\quad\quad$ 2n $2 \times 1.008\,70\text{ g/mol} = 2.017\,40\text{ g/mol}$

$\quad\quad\quad$ 2e $2 \times 0.000\,55\text{ g/mol} = \underline{0.001\,1\ \text{ g/mol}}$

$\quad\quad\quad\quad\quad\quad\quad\quad\quad\quad\quad\quad\quad$ $4.033\,1\ \text{ g/mol}$ Theoretical mass

$\quad\quad\quad\quad\quad\quad\quad\quad\quad\quad\quad\quad\quad$ $\underline{-4.001\,50\text{ g/mol}}$ Actual mass

$\quad\quad\quad\quad\quad\quad\quad\quad\quad\quad\quad\quad\quad$ $0.031\,6\ \text{ g/mol}$ Mass defect

$$0.0316\text{ g/mol} \times \frac{1\text{ kg}}{1000\text{ g}} = 3.16 \times 10^{-5}\text{ kg/mol } _2^4\text{He}$$

Mass defect $_2^4$He (convert to kilograms because $E = mc^2$ uses kilograms)

$_3^6$Li 3p $3 \times 1.007\,30\text{ g/mol} = 3.021\,90\text{ g/mol}$

$\quad\quad\quad$ 3n $3 \times 1.008\,70\text{ g/mol} = 3.026\,10\text{ g/mol}$

$\quad\quad\quad$ 3e $3 \times 0.000\,55\text{ g/mol} = \underline{0.001\,7\ \text{ g/mol}}$

$\quad\quad\quad\quad\quad\quad\quad\quad\quad\quad\quad\quad\quad$ $6.049\,7\ \text{ g/mol}$ Theoretical mass

$\quad\quad\quad\quad\quad\quad\quad\quad\quad\quad\quad\quad\quad$ $\underline{-6.013\,48\text{ g/mol}}$ Actual mass

$\quad\quad\quad\quad\quad\quad\quad\quad\quad\quad\quad\quad\quad$ $0.036\,2\ \text{ g/mol}$ Mass defect

$$0.0362\text{ g/mol} \times \frac{1\text{ kg}}{1000\text{ g}} = 3.62 \times 10^{-5}\text{ kg/mol } _3^6\text{Li}$$ Mass defect $_3^6$Li

$_2^4$He $E = (3.16 \times 10^{-5}\text{ kg/mol } _2^4\text{He}) \times (3.00 \times 10^8\text{ m/s})^2$

$$= 2.84 \times 10^{12} \frac{\text{kg}\cdot\text{m}^2/\text{s}^2}{\text{mol } _2^4\text{He}} = 2.84 \times 10^{12}\text{ J/mol } _2^4\text{He}$$

$_3^6$Li $E = (3.62 \times 10^{-5}\text{ kg/mol } _3^6\text{Li}) \times (3.00 \times 10^8\text{ m/s})^2$

$$= 3.26 \times 10^{12} \frac{\text{kg}\cdot\text{m}^2/\text{s}^2}{\text{mol } _3^6\text{Li}} = 3.26 \times 10^{12}\text{ J/mol } _3^6\text{Li}$$

$_2^4$He contains four nucleons:

$$\frac{2.84 \times 10^{12}\text{ J}}{\text{mol } _2^4\text{He}} \times \frac{1\text{ mol } _2^4\text{He}}{4\text{ mol nucleons}} = 7.10 \times 10^{11}\text{ J/mol nucleons}$$

$^6_3$Li contains six nucleons:

$$\frac{3.26\times10^{12}\,J}{mol\ ^6_3Li}\times\frac{1\ mol\ ^6_3Li}{6\ mol\ nucleons}=5.43\times10^{11}\,J\,/\,mol\ nucleons$$

Even though each $^6_3$Li nucleus contains more binding energy than each $^4_2$He nucleus, the $^4_2$He has the larger binding energy *per mole of nucleons*.

16.101 The graph on page 638 of the textbook tells you that binding energy per nucleon is greatest for ^{56}Fe and begins a steady decrease for all atoms more massive than it. This means that fusing atoms of ^{56}Fe produces a less stable nucleus, making the reaction endothermic. Energy must be put into the reaction to make it go.

16.102 (a) The superscript sum on the left must equal the superscript sum on the right, and ditto for subscripts. Thus the missing particle must have superscript 4 and subscript 2. The subscript tells you number of protons = atomic number, making the particle helium: $^{226}_{88}$Ra $\longrightarrow$ $^{222}_{86}$Rn + $^4_2$He.

(b) Because $^4_2$He, the helium nucleus, is an alpha particle, this is alpha emission.

(c) Radium is atomic number 88, and all nuclei larger than bismuth (atomic number 83) are too large and often decay by ejecting an alpha particle, $^4_2$He.

(d) The energy all comes from the mass lost during the reaction. The reactant mass is 226.0254 g for each mole of $^{226}_{88}$Ra, but the combined product mass is only

$$
\begin{array}{lr}
1\ mol\ ^{226}_{86}Rn & 222.017\ 5 \quad\ g \\
1\ mol\ ^4_2He & \underline{4.002\ 603\ 6\ g} \\
 & 226.020\ 1 \quad\ g
\end{array}
$$

meaning the mass lost (and converted to energy) is

$$
\begin{array}{r}
226.0254\ g \\
-226.0201\ g \\
\hline
0.0053\ g
\end{array}
$$

for every mole of $^{226}_{88}$Ra consumed. Convert this mass to kilograms because $E = mc^2$ uses kilograms:

$$0.0053\ g\times\frac{1\ kg}{1000\ g}=5.3\times10^{-6}\,kg$$

$$E=\frac{5.3\times10^{-6}\,kg}{mol\ ^{226}_{88}Ra}\times(3.00\times10^8\,m\,/\,s)^2=\frac{4.8\times10^{11}\,kg\cdot m^2\,/\,s^2}{mol\ ^{226}_{88}Ra}$$

$$=\frac{4.8\times10^{11}\,J}{mol\ ^{226}_{88}Ra}\times\frac{1\ kJ}{1000\ J}=4.8\times10^8\,kJ\,/\,mol\ ^{226}_{88}Ra$$

(e) $1.00\ g\ ^{226}_{88}Ra\times\dfrac{1\ mol\ ^{226}_{88}Ra}{226.0254\ g\ ^{226}_{88}Ra}\times\dfrac{4.8\times10^8\,kJ}{mol\ ^{226}_{88}Ra}=2.1\times10^6\,kJ$

16.103 (a) The atomic number of polonium is 84, and an alpha particle is $^4_2$He. The daughter isotope must therefore have superscript 210 − 4 = 206 and subscript 84 − 2 = 82. Atomic number 82 is lead, Pb: $^{210}_{84}$Po $\longrightarrow$ $^{206}_{82}$Pb + $^4_2$He.

(b) Another way of asking this question is, "How old is the sample when it contains only 5.00% of the initial amount of ^{210}Po?" Therefore use the age formula:

$$\frac{-2.303\times\log\left(\dfrac{5.00\%}{100}\right)\times138\ days}{0.693}=597\ days$$

16.104 (a) Positron emission is $^1_1p \longrightarrow {}^1_0n + {}^0_{+1}e$; a proton in the parent nucleus becomes a neutron (and a positron is ejected). Because the parent loses a proton as it decays, it must be one place to the right of the daughter in the periodic table. Rubidium has atomic number 37, making the parent atomic number 38, strontium: $^{87}_{38}Sr \longrightarrow {}^{87}_{37}Rb + {}^0_{+1}e$.

(b) Increase:

$$^{87}_{38}Sr \quad \frac{87-38}{38} = \frac{49}{38} = 1.29 \qquad {}^{87}_{37}Rb \quad \frac{87-37}{37} = \frac{50}{37} = 1.35$$

16.105 In every nuclear decay, the superscript sum on the left must equal the superscript sum on the right, and ditto for the subscripts.

(a) $^{121}_{51}Sb + {}^4_2He \longrightarrow {}^{124}_{52}Te + {}^1_1H$

(b) $^{27}_{13}Al + {}^4_2He \longrightarrow {}^{30}_{15}P + {}^1_0n$

(c) $^{238}_{92}U + {}^1_0n \longrightarrow {}^{239}_{93}Np + {}^0_{-1}e$

16.106 Because electron capture converts a proton to a neutron and raises the n/p ratio, it is most likely in nuclei that have too low an n/p ratio.

(a) $^{13}_5B \quad \frac{n}{p} = \frac{13-5}{5} = 1.6 \qquad {}^8_5B \quad \frac{n}{p} = \frac{8-5}{5} = 0.60$

Lighter elements are most stable when n/p = 1. Therefore the ^8B ratio is too low, and this is the isotope more likely to decay via electron capture.

(b) $^{209}_{83}Bi \quad \frac{n}{p} = \frac{209-83}{83} = 1.5 \qquad {}^{194}_{83}Bi \quad \frac{n}{p} = \frac{194-83}{83} = 1.3$

As noted in the textbook, bismuth requires an n/p ratio of 1.5 to keep the nucleus stable, meaning the bismuth-194 ratio is too low, making this the isotope more likely to decay via electron capture.

16.107 Because beta emission converts a neutron to a proton and lowers the n/p ratio, it is most likely in nuclei that have too high an n/p ratio. Because positron emission converts a proton to a neutron and raises the n/p ratio, it is most likely in nuclei that have too low an n/p ratio. Fluorine nuclei are light enough to be stable with n/p = 1.

$$^{17}_9F \quad \frac{n}{p} = \frac{17-9}{9} = 0.89; \text{ too low, positron emission}$$

$$^{20}_9F \quad \frac{n}{p} = \frac{20-9}{9} = 1.2; \text{ too high, beta emission}$$

$$^{21}_9F \quad \frac{n}{p} = \frac{21-9}{9} = 1.3; \text{ too high, beta emission}$$

16.108 Three places to the left corresponds to a loss of three protons, which means the ejected particle must contain three protons and is therefore a lithium nucleus. The fact that the daughter nucleus has a mass number 7 less than the parent tells you the mass number of the ejected particle must be 7, making it ^7_3Li.

16.109 The age of the painting is

$$\frac{-2.303 \times \log\left(\frac{96.1\%}{100}\right) \times 5715 \text{ years}}{0.693} = 328 \text{ years}$$

meaning it was created in the year $2002 - 328 = 1674$, five years after Rembrandt's death. However, given the uncertainty in carbon-dating, 1674 is close enough to Rembrandt's time that the painting might indeed have been done by him.

16.110 (a) The superscripts must have the same sum on the two sides. Left: 236; right: 89 + (3 × 0) + (3 × 1) = 92; the missing product must have superscript 236 − 92 = 144.

The subscripts must have the same sum on the two sides. Left: 92; right: 37 + (3 × −1) + (3 × 0) = 34; the missing product must have subscript 92 − 34 = 58. Atomic number 58 is cerium, Ce, making the full equation $_0^1n + {}_{92}^{235}U \longrightarrow {}_{37}^{89}Rb + 3\,{}_{-1}^0e + 3\,{}_0^1n + {}_{58}^{144}Ce$.

(b) More neutrons are produced than are consumed.

(c) The energy all comes from the mass lost during the reaction. The combined mass of the reactants is

1 mol ^1n	1.008 70 g
1 mol ^{235}U	235.043 9 g
	236.052 6 g

but the combined mass of the products is only

1 mol ^{89}Rb	88.891 3 g
3 mol ^0e	0.001 7 g
3 mol ^1n	3.026 10 g
1 mol ^{144}Ce	143.881 7 g
	235.800 8 g

meaning the mass lost (and converted to energy) is

$$\begin{array}{r} 236.0526\text{ g} \\ -235.8008\text{ g} \\ \hline 0.2518\text{ g} \end{array}$$

for every mole of ^{235}U consumed. Convert this mass to kilograms because $E = mc^2$ uses kilograms:

$$\frac{0.2518\text{ g}}{\text{mol }^{235}U} \times \frac{1\text{ kg}}{1000\text{ g}} = 2.518 \times 10^{-4}\text{kg/mol }^{235}U$$

$$E = \frac{2.518 \times 10^{-4}\text{kg}}{\text{mol }^{235}U} \times (3.00 \times 10^8\text{m/s})^2 = \frac{2.27 \times 10^{13}\text{kg} \cdot \text{m}^2/\text{s}^2}{\text{mol }^{235}U} = \frac{2.27 \times 10^{13}\text{J}}{\text{mol }^{235}U}$$

$$\frac{2.27 \times 10^{13}\text{J}}{\text{mol }^{235}U} \times \frac{1\text{ kJ}}{1000\text{ J}} \times \frac{1\text{ mol }^{235}U}{235.0439\text{ g }^{235}U} = 9.66 \times 10^7\text{kJ/g }^{235}U$$

(d) $9.66 \times 10^7\text{kJ} \times \dfrac{1\text{ g TNT}}{2.76\text{ kJ}} \times \dfrac{1\text{ kg TNT}}{1000\text{ g TNT}} = 3.50 \times 10^4\text{kg} = 35{,}000\text{ kg}$

16.111 The atomic number of thorium is 90. Loss of six alpha particles, $_2^4He$, decreases mass number by 24 and the atomic number by 12. This means daughter 1 has atomic number 90 − 12 = 78 and mass number 232 − 24 = 208. Atomic number 78 is platinum, making daughter 1 $_{78}^{208}Pt$.

Loss of four beta particles, $_{-1}^0e$, has no effect on mass number but increases the atomic number by 4. This means daughter 2 has atomic number 78 + 4 = 82 and mass number 208. Atomic number 82 is lead, making daughter 2 $_{82}^{208}Pb$. The sequence is

$$_{90}^{232}Th \longrightarrow 6\,_2^4He + {}_{78}^{208}Pt$$

$$_{78}^{208}Pt \longrightarrow 4\,_{-1}^0e + {}_{82}^{208}Pb$$

16.112 Uranium. Thorium is two places to the left of uranium in the periodic table, and isotopes of uranium are alpha emitters. Alpha emission converts some of the uranium in the ore to thorium: $^{235}_{92}U \longrightarrow {}^{4}_{2}He + {}^{231}_{90}Th$, $^{238}_{92}U \longrightarrow {}^{4}_{2}He + {}^{234}_{90}Th$.

16.113 (a) The first mechanism is the correct one because it shows the colored O in the water molecule. The arrows indicate which reactant bonds must break:

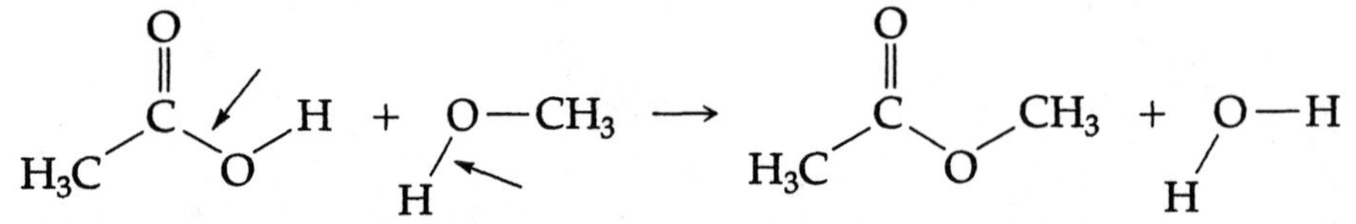

(b) If ^{18}O were radioactive, you could separate the two products from each other and use a Geiger counter to see which one was radioactive, revealing where the radioactive ^{18}O "tag" went.

16.114 (a) Tritium is the isotope of hydrogen that contains two neutrons in addition to the one proton. It has an atomic number of 1 (because it is still hydrogen) and a mass number of $2 + 1 = 3$. In beta decay, one of the neutrons converts to a proton, so that the atomic number increases by 1, making the daughter helium: $^{3}_{1}H \longrightarrow {}^{0}_{-1}e + {}^{3}_{2}He$.

(b) The superscript sums must be the same on the left and right sides, telling you the missing product must have a mass number of $15 - 3 = 12$. The subscript sums must also be the same on the two sides, meaning the missing product has an atomic number of $7 - 1 = 6$, which is carbon: $^{14}_{7}N + {}^{1}_{0}n \longrightarrow {}^{3}_{1}H + {}^{12}_{6}C$.

(c) It is constantly being produced in the upper atmosphere via the reaction shown in part (b).

16.115 The equation from Problem 16.103, $^{210}_{84}Po \longrightarrow {}^{206}_{82}Pb + {}^{4}_{2}He$, tells you that each mole of ^{210}Po yields 1 mole of ^{4}He. Thus if you know the number of moles of ^{210}Po decaying in 138.4 days, you know how much helium you have. First determine the number of moles of ^{210}Po in the initial sample:

$$1.000 \text{ g } PoO_2 \times \frac{1 \text{ mol } PoO_2}{241.981 \text{ g } PoO_2} \times \frac{1 \text{ mol } ^{210}Po}{1 \text{ mol } PoO_2} = 4.133 \times 10^{-3} \text{ mol } ^{210}Po$$

After 1 half-life, half of this amount, 2.066×10^{-3} mol, has decayed, producing 2.066×10^{-3} mole of ^{4}He. Now use the ideal gas equation to find the volume of this much $^{4}_{2}He$ gas at standard temperature (0.00°C) and pressure (1.00 atm). Remember that you must use the Kelvin temperature in your calculation.

$$V = \frac{nRT}{P} = \frac{2.066 \times 10^{-3} \text{ mol} \times 0.0821 \text{ L} \cdot \text{atm} / \text{K} \cdot \text{mol} \times 273.15 \text{ K}}{1.00 \text{ atm}}$$

$$= 0.0463 \text{ L} \times \frac{1000 \text{ mL}}{1 \text{ L}} = 46.3 \text{ mL}$$

CHAPTER
17

The Chemistry of Carbon

17.1 See solution in textbook.

17.2 (a)

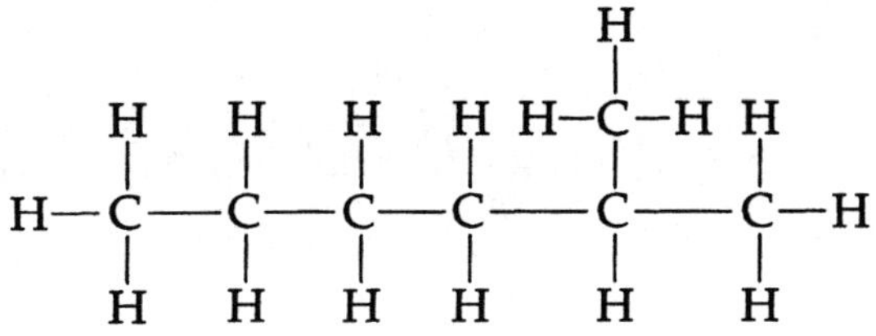

(b)

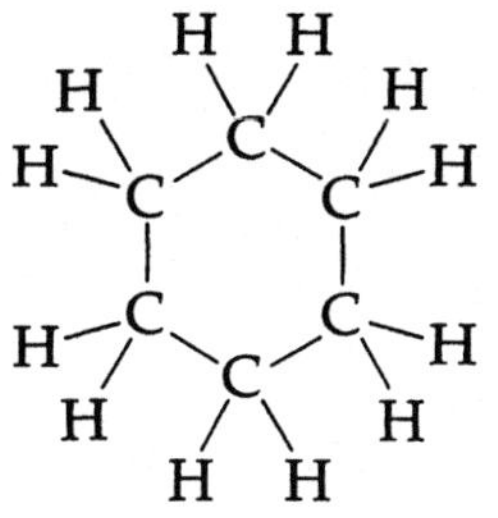

(c)

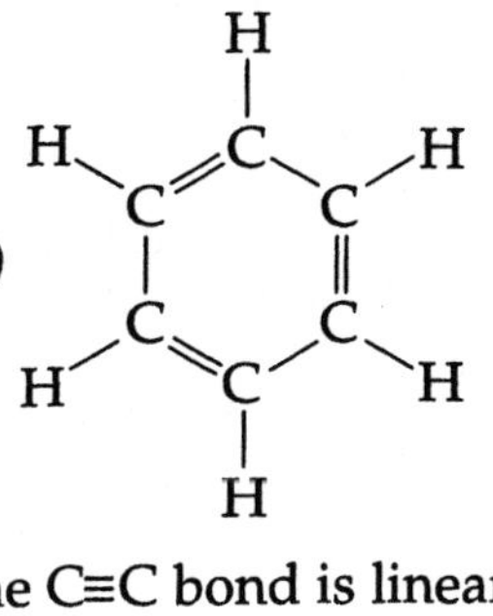

(d)

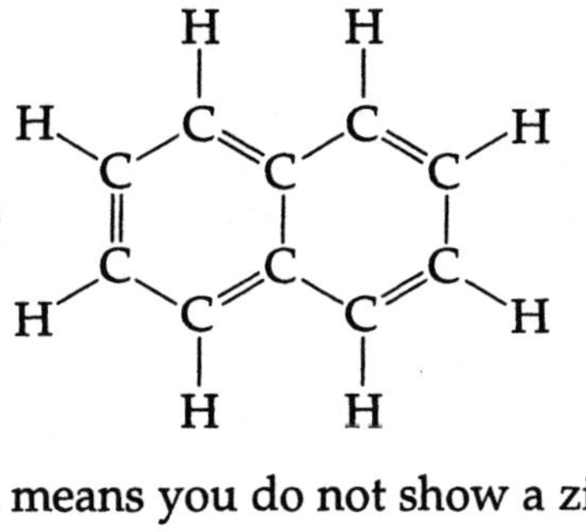

(e)

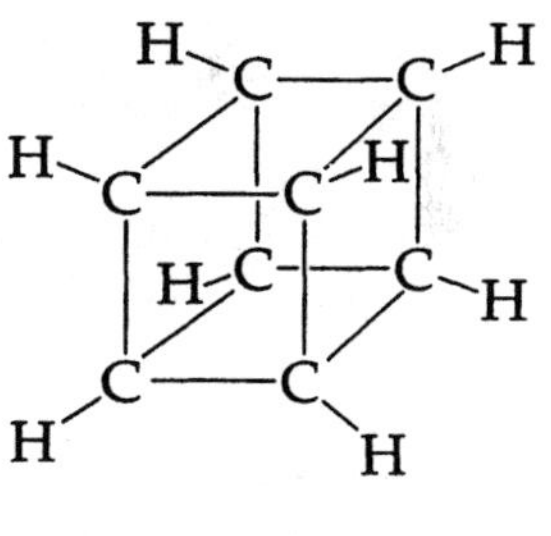

17.3 The C≡C bond is linear, which means you do not show a zigzag in that part of the molecule:

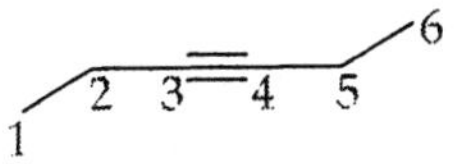

17.4 (a) The structural formula represented by this line drawing is

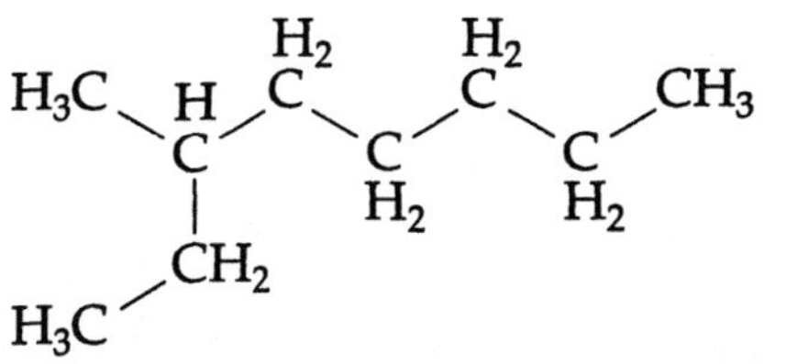

Because the second carbon from the left in the top row is attached to three carbons rather than two, the molecule is branched.

(b) The main chain is the longest one. Therefore the top row (seven carbons) is not the main chain. Instead, begin at the left bottom of the drawing and you see that the main chain is eight carbons long:

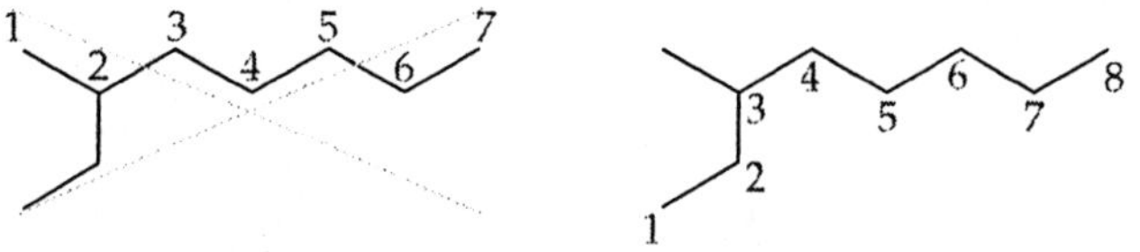

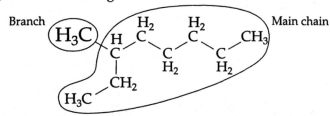

WRONG   CORRECT

(c) One carbon long:

Branch   Main chain

H_3C H $\overset{H_2}{C}$ $\overset{H_2}{C}$ CH_3

C C C

H_2 H_2

CH_2

H_3C

(d) C_9H_{20}

17.5 See solution in textbook.

17.6 The "missing" $14 - 10 = 4$ hydrogens could be the result of two double bonds or one triple bond or one double bond in a ring structure:

17.7 The more H atoms in a hydrocarbon, the less unsaturated the molecule. Thus (c) is the least unsaturated because it has eight hydrogens and the other molecules have six each:

(a) $H_3C - C \equiv C - CH_3$ (b) 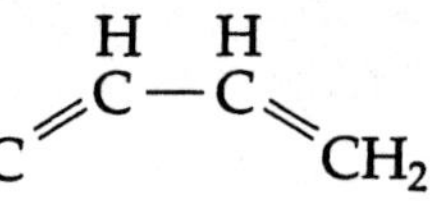 H_2C ... $\overset{H\ \ H}{C - C}$ ... CH_2 (c) H_3C ... $C = C$ ... H, H, CH_3

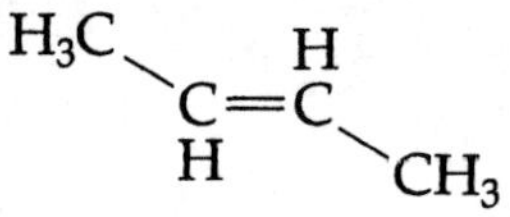

17.8 See solution in textbook.

17.9 *Oct-* means the main chain is eight C long. *2-octene* means the chain has one double bond and it begins at carbon 2. There is a methyl group, $-CH_3$, on carbon 6 of the chain and a propyl group, $-C_3H_7$, on carbon 4 of the chain:

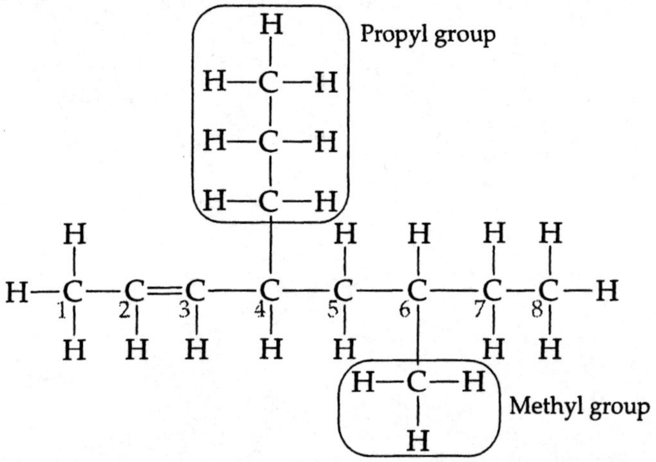

17.10 The numbering should be along the longest chain and should begin at the end that gives the double bond as low a number as possible. Thus the numbering begins correctly at the right end of the molecule but should move downward after carbon 5, along the eight-carbon chain rather than along the seven-carbon chain. The correct name is 5-ethyl-2-octene:

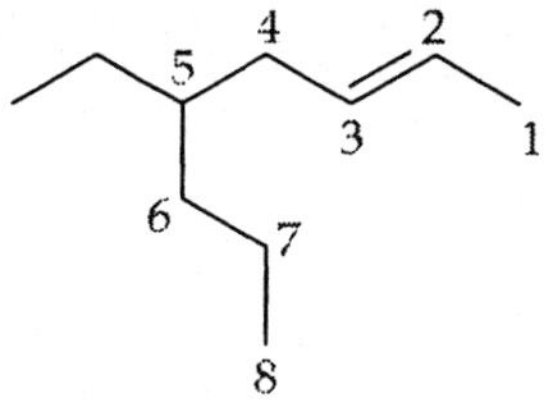

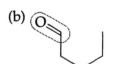

17.11 See solution in textbook.

17.12 1-Butanol. Note that when a heteroatom is present, the end of a line does *not* represent a C.

The line drawing $\diagup\!\diagdown\!\diagup\!\diagdown$ OH represents $H_3C\diagdown\underset{H_2}{C}\diagup\overset{H_2}{C}\diagdown\underset{H_2}{C}\diagup$OH,

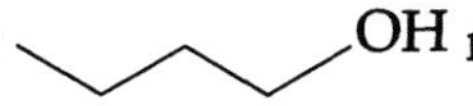

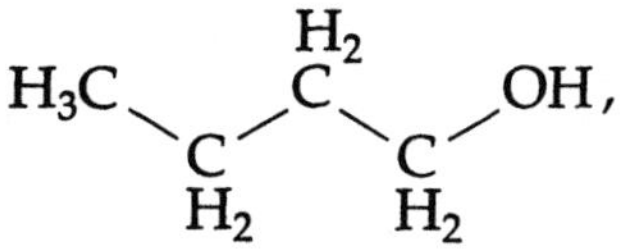

not $H_3C\diagdown\underset{H_2}{C}\diagup\overset{H_2}{C}\diagdown\underset{H_2}{C}\diagup$COH.

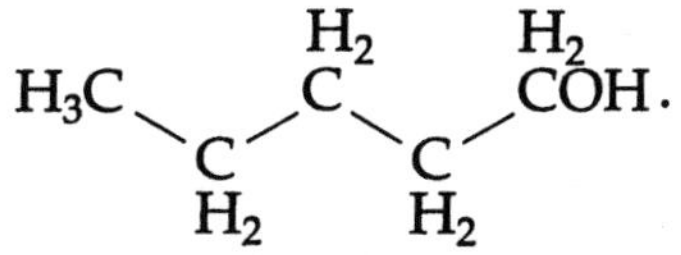

17.13 2-Aminopropane

17.14 3-Bromohexane

17.15 *Penta-* means five carbons in the main chain; 2-pentan*ol* means an alcohol group, –OH, on carbon 2; and there is a methyl group, –CH$_3$, on carbon 3:

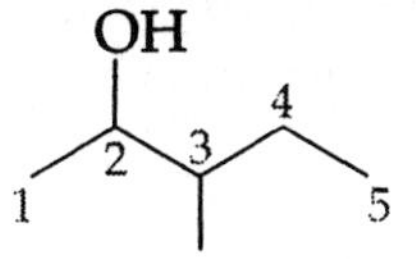

17.16 See solution in textbook.

17.17 The ending *-one* signifies a ketone, and *ethan-* means two carbons. Ethanone does not exist because the carbonyl carbon in a ketone must be connected to two other carbons. Hence, the smallest number of carbons that can exist in a ketone is 3.

17.18 (a)

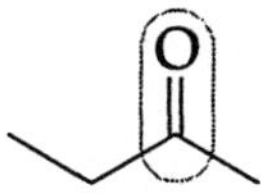

A carbon bonded to an oxygen via a double bond plus to two other carbons,

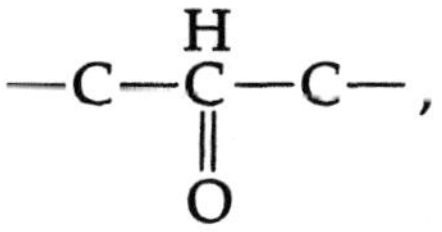

$$-C-\overset{H}{\underset{\underset{O}{\parallel}}{C}}-C-,$$ the ketone group.

(b)

A carbon bonded to an oxygen via a double bond, to one hydrogen, and to one carbon, $-C-\underset{\underset{O}{\parallel}}{C}-H$, the aldehyde group.

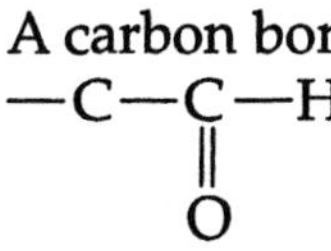

(c)

A carbon bonded to an oxygen via a double bond, to one OH group, and to one carbon,
$-C-C-OH$, the carboxylic acid group.

17.19 (a) The ending for a ketone is *-one*, and four carbons means the root name is butane. Use a number to indicate the position of the carbonyl group, and number the chain so that this number is as low as possible: 2-butanone.

(b) The aldehyde ending is *-al*, and five carbons means the root name is pentane: pentanal. No number is needed because the aldehyde functional group must be at one end of the molecule in order for the carbonyl carbon to be bonded to an H. The lowest-number-possible rule automatically makes the carbonyl carbon C 1.

(c) Carboxylic acids end with *-oic acid*, and a four-carbon main chain makes the parent butane. Use numbers to indicate positions of any branches, and number the main chain to make these numbers as low as possible: 2-methyl-butanoic acid. A 1 before *butanoic* is not needed because any carboxylic acid carbon must be a terminal carbon and the lowest-possible-number rule automatically makes the carboxylic acid carbon C 1.

17.20 Catenation refers to the ability of carbon atoms to link other carbons in long chains.

17.21 Diamond, graphite, and fullerene. Each carbon atom in diamond is tetrahedrally bound to four other carbon atoms. Graphite consists of sheets of hexagons of carbon atoms where each carbon atom is bound to three others. Fullerene consists of a sphere of carbon atoms where each carbon atom is bound to three others. The similarity in the allotropes is that, in all three of them, each carbon atom always has four bonds to it.

17.22 A carbon atom always forms four covalent bonds because it has four valence electrons and therefore needs four more to form an octet.

17.23 (a) $H-\overset{\overset{\displaystyle H}{|}}{\underset{\underset{\displaystyle H}{|}}{C}}-\overset{\overset{\displaystyle H}{|}}{\underset{\underset{\displaystyle H}{|}}{C}}-\overset{\overset{\displaystyle H}{|}}{\underset{\underset{\displaystyle H}{|}}{C}}-H$ (b) $H-C=C-\overset{\overset{\displaystyle H}{|}}{\underset{\underset{\displaystyle H}{|}}{C}}-H$ (c) $H-C\equiv C-\overset{\overset{\displaystyle H}{|}}{\underset{\underset{\displaystyle H}{|}}{C}}-H$

17.24 A hydrocarbon chain containing only one double bond is a monoalkene, meaning the general formula is C_nH_{2n}. The molecular formula is thus C_4H_8, and the possible structures are

$$H-\underset{\underset{H}{|}}{\overset{\overset{H}{|}}{C}}-C=C-\underset{\underset{H}{|}}{\overset{\overset{H}{|}}{C}}-H \quad \text{and} \quad H-\underset{\underset{H}{|}}{\overset{\overset{H}{|}}{C}}-\underset{\underset{H}{|}}{\overset{\overset{H}{|}}{C}}-C=C$$

17.25 There is no possibility of double or triple bonds in the molecule because only carbon atoms having all single bonds can have a tetrahedral geometry.

17.26 The C=H double bond is impossible; H can form only single bonds.

17.27 Organic chemistry, so called because carbon-based molecules are the major molecules found in organisms.

17.28 Because carbon atoms can bond to one another to form long chains. A few other elements are able to catenate in this way, but only carbon can form such long chains.

17.29 A compound composed solely of carbon and hydrogen.

17.30

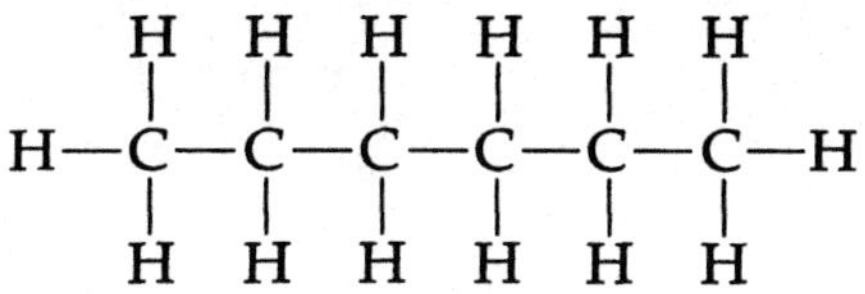

```
      H   H   H   H   H   H
      |   |   |   |   |   |
  H—C—C—C—C—C—C—H
      |   |   |   |   |   |
      H   H   H   H   H   H
```

17.31 Start with a five-carbon main chain, which means there is one branch and it contains one carbon. The branch can be on carbon 2 or carbon 3:

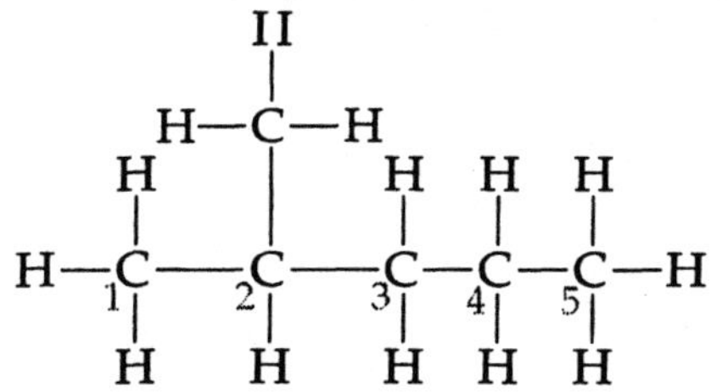

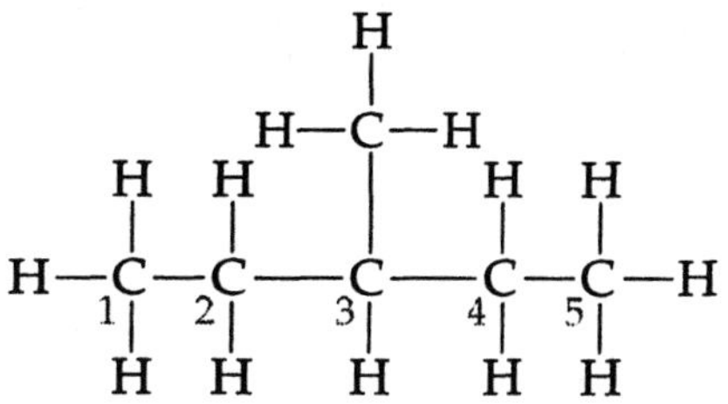

```
        II                                    H
        |                                     |
      H—C—H                                 H—C—H
  H   |    H   H   H              H   H   |    H   H
  |   |    |   |   |              |   |   |    |   |
H—C——C——C—C—C—H           H—C—C——C——C—C—H
  1|  2|  3|  4| 5|              1|  2|  3|  4| 5|
  H   H    H   H   H              H   H   H    H   H
```

Note that placing the –CH₃ on carbon 4 forms the mirror image of the structure on the left and so is not a third possibility.

Now make a four-carbon main chain, which leaves two carbons for branching, meaning two methyl groups. You may put one on carbon 2 and one on carbon 3 or both on carbon 2:

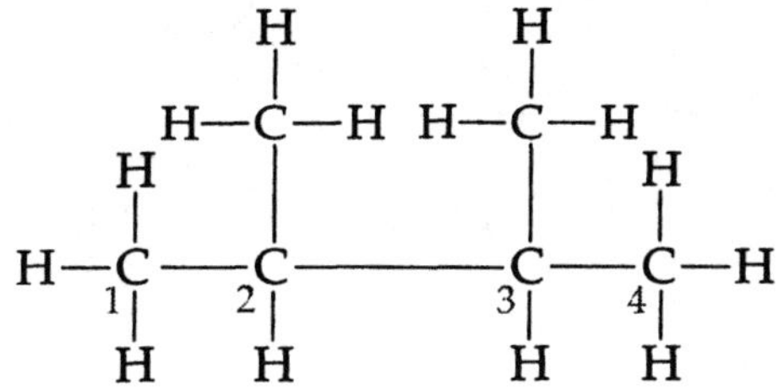

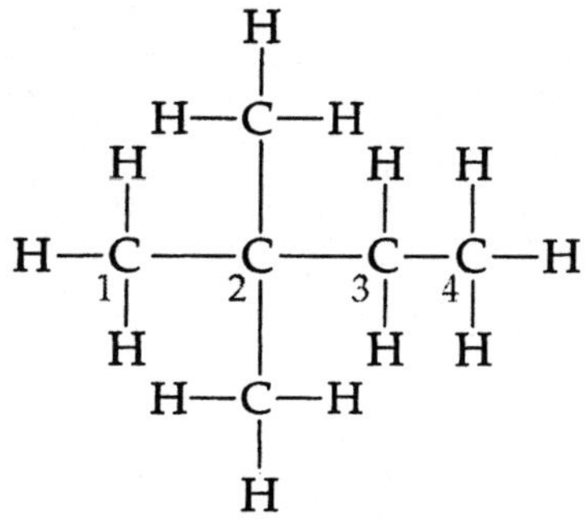

```
      H         H                             H
      |         |                             |
    H—C—H    H—C—H                          H—C—H
  H   |         |    H                  H    |    H   H
  |   |         |    |                  |    |    |   |
H—C——C————C——C—H            H—C——C——C—C—H
  1|  2|        3|  4|                  1|  2|   3|  4|
  H   H         H   H                  H    |    H   H
                                          H—C—H
                                            |
                                            H
```

You should understand why forming an ethyl group, –CH₂CH₃, from the two carbons available for branching is not a valid choice. Doing so gives this molecule,

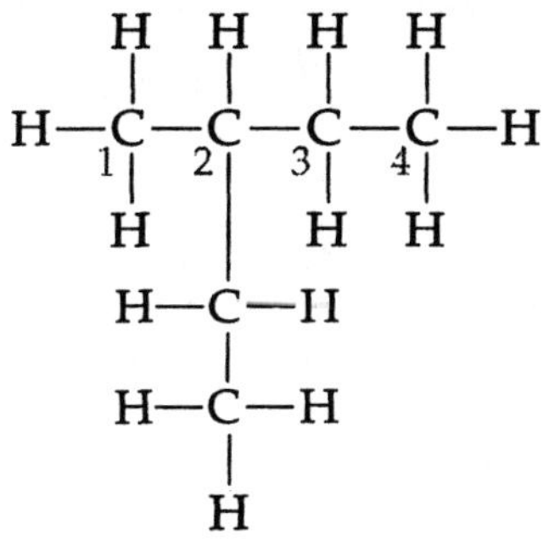

```
      H   H   H   H
      |   |   |   |
  H—C—C—C—C—H
    1|  2|  3|  4|
      H   |   H   H
        H—C—II
          |
        H—C—H
          |
          H
```

but the numbering is incorrect because the main chain is not the longest. Correctly numbered, this molecule is 3-methylpentane, which you drew earlier.

These are all the possibilities. If you go to a three-carbon main chain, any branching you add will bring you back to one of the four-carbon or five-carbon main chains already shown. Try it.

17.32 A hydrocarbon is linear if no carbon is attached to more than two other carbons. A hydrocarbon is branched if at least one carbon is attached to either three or four other carbons.

17.33 The geometry about C–C single bonds is tetrahedral, with bond angles of 109.5°. Thus a zigzag line drawing represents the true shape of the molecule more accurately than a straight-line drawing does. In a straight-line drawing, the angles appear to be 180°.

17.34 As a straight line because the geometry around C≡C triple bonds is linear, with bond angles of 180°.

17.35 Crude oil (petroleum).

17.36 Burning this cheap source of fuel with little restraint both pollutes the environment and depletes resources for future generations.

17.37 (a) Seven carbons:

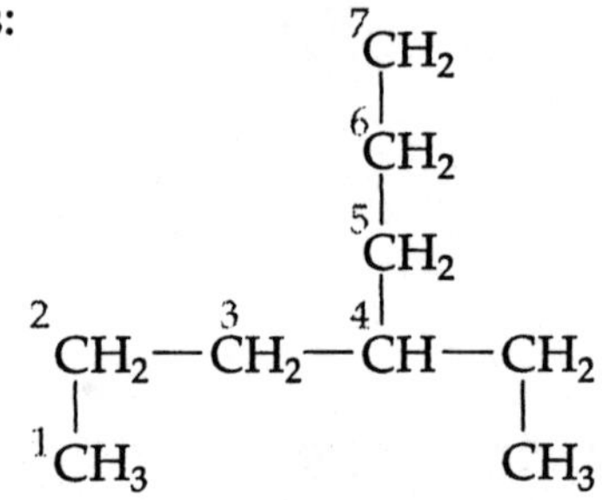

$$^7CH_2$$
$$|$$
$$^6CH_2$$
$$|$$
$$^5CH_2$$
$$|$$
$$^2CH_2 - {}^3CH_2 - {}^4CH - CH_2$$
$$\quad\quad |\quad\quad\quad\quad\quad |$$
$$\quad\quad ^1CH_3\quad\quad\quad CH_3$$

Any other counting sequence gives you a shorter main chain, and in saturated hydrocarbons the main chain is the longest one.

(b) Two carbons.

17.38 In a line drawing, a carbon atom is assumed to be anywhere a line ends or anywhere two or more lines intersect. Double bonds are indicated by double lines, and triple bonds by triple lines. The four-bond rule tells you how many hydrogens are present in the molecule. The molecular formula can be deduced by counting the number of carbons and the number of hydrogens in the molecule represented in the drawing.

17.39 (a) Each free end represents one C, and each intersection of two lines represents one C:

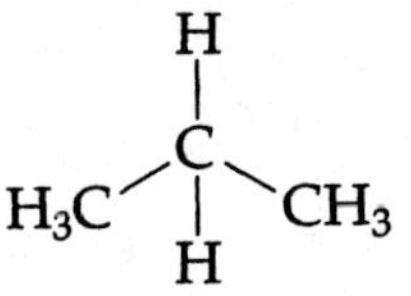

$$H$$
$$|$$
$$C$$
$$H_3C \quad | \quad CH_3$$
$$H$$

C_3H_8, linear because no C is bonded to more than two other C.

(b)

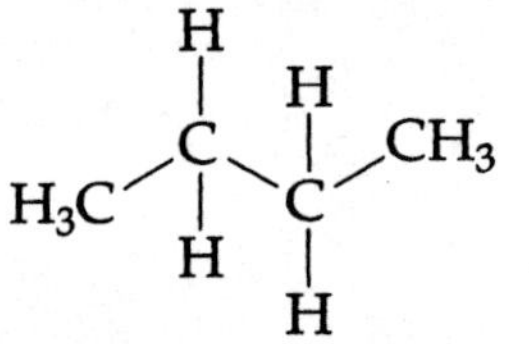

$$H$$
$$| \quad H$$
$$C \quad | \quad CH_3$$
$$H_3C \quad | \quad C$$
$$H \quad |$$
$$H$$

C_4H_{10}, linear because no C is bonded to more than two other C.

(c)

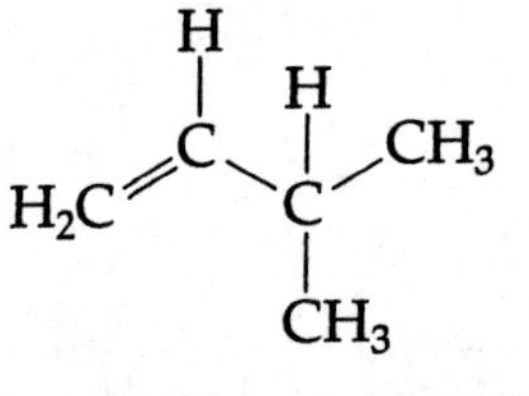

$$H$$
$$| \quad H$$
$$C \quad | \quad CH_3$$
$$H_2C \quad \quad C$$
$$\quad\quad |$$
$$\quad\quad CH_3$$

C_5H_{10}, branched because one C is bonded to three other C.

17.40 The easiest way to make a line drawing from the complex drawing of Problem 17.37 is to focus on the C atoms and ignore the H atoms. Let C1 be the point at which your pen first touches the paper, then form a zigzag while following the longest chain with your eyes. Your rendering should look something like this:

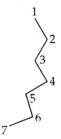

Now put your pen on the intersection representing the C to which the branch is attached (C4) and make a zigzag representing the two C of the branch:

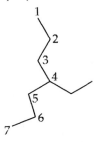

17.41 (a) $\overset{}{=}$ (b) $\overset{2\quad4\quad6}{\diagup\!\diagdown\!\diagup\!\diagdown\!\diagup}$ (c) $\overset{12}{\triangle}$
 1 2 1 3 5 3

17.42 A saturated hydrocarbon contains the most hydrogen atoms possible for its number of carbon atoms. An unsaturated hydrocarbon has fewer hydrogens than the maximum for its number of carbon atoms.

17.43 (c), because it contains a C=C double bond and therefore must contain fewer than the maximum number of H atoms.

17.44 Molecule (a) is more unsaturated because it contains two double bonds and therefore has four fewer hydrogens than the maximum allowed. Molecule (b) has only one double bond and therefore two fewer hydrogens than the maximum allowed.

17.45 (a) The structural formula corresponding to this line drawing is

$$
\begin{array}{c}
CH_2 \\
\| \\
H4\,C \\
2\,C\diagdownH6\,CH_3 \\
H_2C\overset{1}{=}3\,C=5\,C \\
HH
\end{array}
$$

C4 forms five bonds in this drawing, which is not possible.
(b) Remove an H from C2 and an H from C3 to form

$\diagup\!\!=\!\!\diagdown\!\diagup\!\diagdown$

or remove an H from C5 and an H from C6 to form

$\diagup\!\!=\!\!\diagdown\!\diagup\!\!=$

17.46 Saturated; because the general formula for saturated hydrocarbons is C_nH_{2n+2}, 12 is the maximum number of hydrogens a molecule with five carbons can have: $(2 \times 5) + 2 = 12$.

17.47 Unsaturated; the maximum number of hydrogens for a seven-carbon chain is $(2 \times 7) + 2 = 16$. This compound has two fewer than that and is therefore unsaturated.

17.48 (a) and (c), each containing four carbons and ten hydrogens; (b) and (d) are not isomers of (a) and (c) because (b) has five carbons and (d) has only eight hydrogens.

17.49 Begin with the six-carbon unbranched chain:

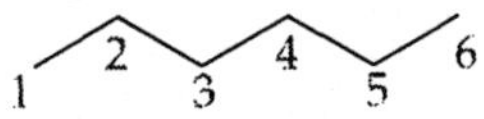

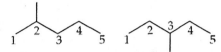

Then draw the five-carbon main chain with the one-carbon branch in all possible locations:

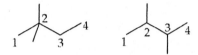

Then go to the four-carbon main chain. Here the branching possibilities are two one-carbon branches on one carbon and two one-carbon branches on different carbons:

17.50 The molecular formulas must be identical, the structural formulas must be different, and the properties are usually different.

17.51 No, because they do not have the same molecular formula.

17.52 There are too many hydrocarbons for it to be practical to assign a separate common name to each one.

17.53 Molecules 1 and 3 because they have the same molecular formula, C_8H_{16}. The molecular formula of molecule 2 is C_7H_{14}, and that of molecule 4 is C_8H_{14}.

17.54 The general formula for saturated hydrocarbons is C_nH_{2n+2}; the general formula for unsaturated hydrocarbons is either C_nH_{2n} or C_nH_{2n-2}.

17.55 Long-chain hydrocarbons. The word comes from the Greek word *aleiphas*, meaning fat.

17.56 All C–C single bonds, *-ane*: alkanes. One or more C=C double bonds, *-ene*: alkenes. One or more C≡C triple bonds, *-yne*: alkynes.

17.57 International Union of Pure and Applied Chemistry.

17.58 A homologous series is a group of compounds that all have some main feature in common. Examples include the monoalkanes, common feature only C–C single bonds; the monoalkenes, common feature one C=C double bond; and the monoalkynes, common feature one C≡C triple bond.

17.59 The general formula for alkanes is C_nH_{2n+2}, and that for alkenes is C_nH_{2n}. This means that, for a given number of carbons, an alkene contains two fewer hydrogens than an alkane.

17.60

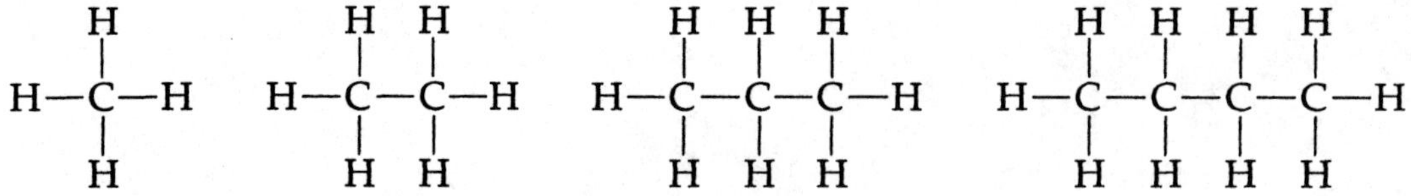

H | H—C—H | H	H H | | H—C—C—H | | H H	H H H | | | H—C—C—C—H | | | H H H	H H H H | | | | H—C—C—C—C—H | | | | H H H H
Methane	Ethane	Propane	Butane

(The first alkane to use a Greek number prefix is pentane.)

17.61 *Eth-* means two carbons, *-yne* means a C≡C triple bond: H:C:::C:H   H—C≡C—H. Ethene is a two-carbon molecule (*eth-*) containing one C=C double bond (*-ene*). Thus acetylene is more unsaturated because a triple bond is more unsaturated than a double bond.

17.62 *Meth-*, one carbon; *eth-*, two carbons; *prop-*, three carbons; *but-*, four carbons.

17.63 Alkane because it fits the general formula C_nH_{2n+2}.

17.64 Both molecules fit the general formula C_nH_{2n}, and so both are monoalkenes (one C=C double bond). Because C_3H_6 contains only three carbons, there is only one location possible for the double bond—between C1 and C2—and therefore no number indicating position is needed in the name. Because C_4H_8 contains four carbons, there are two possible positions for the double bond—between C1 and C2 or between C2 and C3. There must be a number in the name to indicate which:

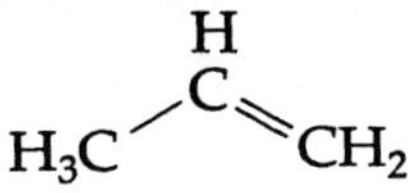

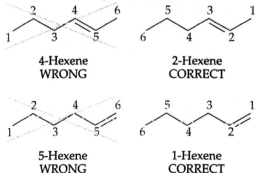

Propene 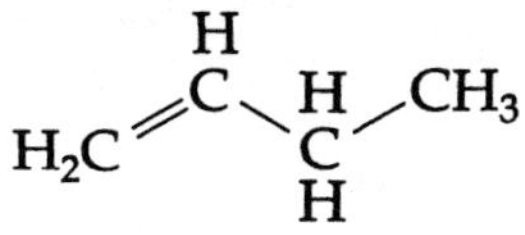   1-Butene 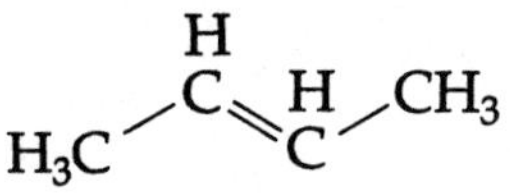   2-Butene

17.65 No; although the three compounds all have three carbons, they belong to different homologous series. Propane belongs to the alkanes, propene to the alkenes, and propyne to the alkynes.

17.66 *Hex-* means six carbons, *-ene* means a C=C double bond, and the 2 tells you this double bond is between C2 and C3:

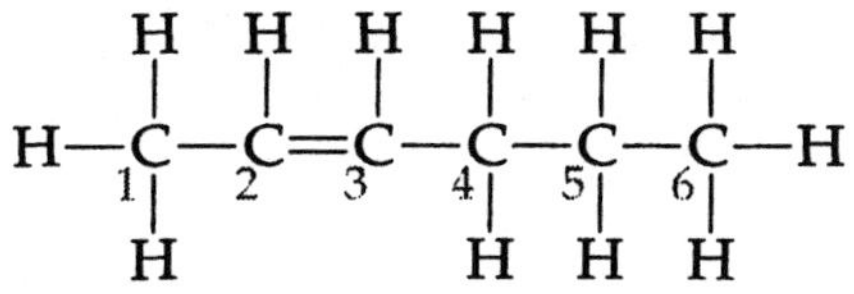

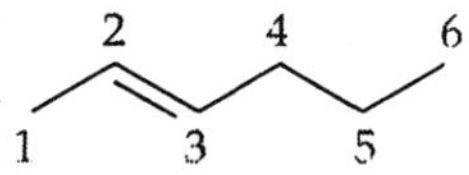

$$H-\overset{\overset{\displaystyle H}{|}}{\underset{\underset{\displaystyle H}{|}}{C}}-\overset{\overset{\displaystyle H}{|}}{C}=\overset{\overset{\displaystyle H}{|}}{C}-\overset{\overset{\displaystyle H}{|}}{\underset{\underset{\displaystyle H}{|}}{C}}-\overset{\overset{\displaystyle H}{|}}{\underset{\underset{\displaystyle H}{|}}{C}}-\overset{\overset{\displaystyle H}{|}}{\underset{\underset{\displaystyle H}{|}}{C}}-H$$

17.67 Each compound has six carbons (*hex-*) and one double bond (*-ene*). The 2 and 3 tell you the position of the double bond is different in the two compounds:

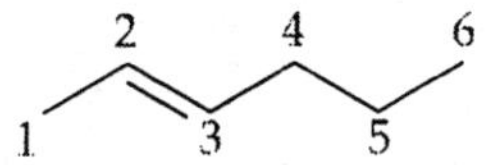

2-Hexene 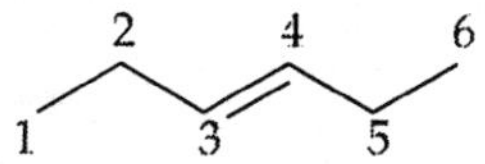   3-Hexene

Because they have the same molecular formula, C_6H_{12}, but different structural formulas, these two molecules are isomers.

17.68 1-Hexene, 2-hexene, and 3-hexene are six-carbon alkenes with the double bond in different positions. However, 4-hexene is really 2-hexene, and 5-hexene is really 1-hexene when the molecule is numbered from the correct end of the chain. The numbering must start at the chain end that gives the double bond as low a number as possible.

4-Hexene   2-Hexene
WRONG   CORRECT

5-Hexene   1-Hexene
WRONG   CORRECT

17.69 False. We number unsaturated and branched hydrocarbons from the end that is closer to the multiple bond or branch. One example is

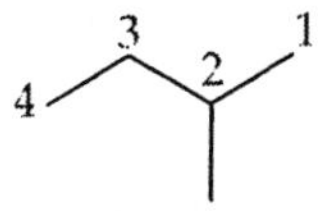

2-Methylbutane

and two more examples are the molecules drawn in the solution to Problem 17.68.

17.70 Identify and name the main chain. If the molecule is saturated, the main chain is the longest. If the molecule is unsaturated, the main chain is the longest containing the multiple bond.

17.71 Each line end represents one C, and each point where two lines intersect represents one C.

(a) $\overset{2}{\wedge}$ (1, 3), propane. (b) $\overset{2}{\diagup}\overset{4}{\diagup}\overset{6}{\diagup}$ (1, 3, 5), 1-butene.

(c) $\overset{2}{\diagup}\overset{4}{\diagup}$ (1, 3, 5), 2-hexyne. (d) $\overset{2}{\diagup}\overset{4}{\diagup}$ (1, 3), 2-pentene.

17.72 (a) *Prop-* means three carbons, *-ene* means C=C. The general formula C_nH_{2n} for mono-

alkenes tells you the molecular formula is C_3H_6; $\overset{2}{\diagup}_{1}{}_{3}$.

(b) *Oct-* means eight carbons, *-ene* means one C=C, and 1 means this bond is between C1

and C2. C_nH_{2n} gives C_8H_{16}; $\overset{2}{\diagup}\overset{4}{\diagup}\overset{6}{\diagup}\overset{8}{\diagup}$.

(c) *Hex-* means six carbons, *-ane* means all C–C bonds and the general formula C_nH_{2n+2}:

C_6H_{14}; $\overset{2}{\diagup}\overset{4}{\diagup}\overset{6}{\diagup}$.

(d) *But-* means four carbons, *-yne* means C≡C, and 2 means this bond is between C2
and C3. The general formula C_nH_{2n-2} for monoalkynes gives you the formula C_4H_6;

$1\overset{2}{-}\!\!\equiv\!\!\overset{3}{-}4$ (C≡C bonds are drawn with no zigzag).

(e) *But-* means four carbons, *-yne* means C≡C, and 1 means this bond is between C1 and C2.

The general formula C_nH_{2n-2} gives you the formula C_4H_6; $1\!\!\equiv\!\!_2{}_3\diagup^4$.

17.73 (d) and (e) because they have the same molecular formula but different structural formulas.
17.74 At the end closer to the multiple bond. Multiple bonds have priority over branches.
17.75 The numbering is incorrect. The main chain should be numbered starting at the end closer
to the double bond because multiple bonds have priority over branches.

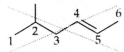

2-Methyl-4-hexene   5-Methyl-2-hexene
   WRONG   CORRECT

17.76 If there are two methyl groups on C2, as *2,2-dimethyl* indicates, there can't be a double bond
between C1 and C2 because if there were, C2 would have to form more than four bonds,
which is impossible.

Five bonds
at this C

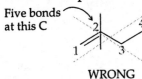

    WRONG

17.77 In each case, get the molecular formula by first drawing the longest chain, indicated by the
parent name; then adding side chains as specified; then adding H as needed to have each C
form four bonds.
(a) *Pentane* means five carbons in the main chain:

C—C—C—C—C

Add a methyl branch on C3:

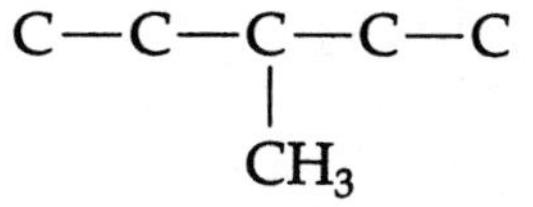

C—C—C—C—C
        |
        CH₃

Add H to C as needed:

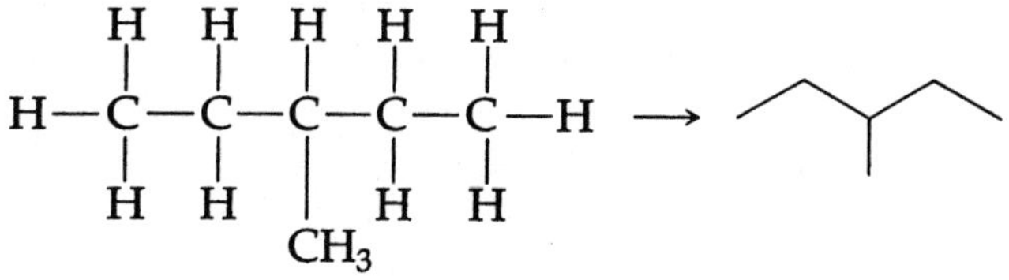

C_6H_{14}

(b) The *2-butene* means four carbons (*but-*) in the main chain and a C=C bond (*-ene*) between C2 and C3. The *2,3-dimethyl* tells you C2 and C3 each carry a methyl group:

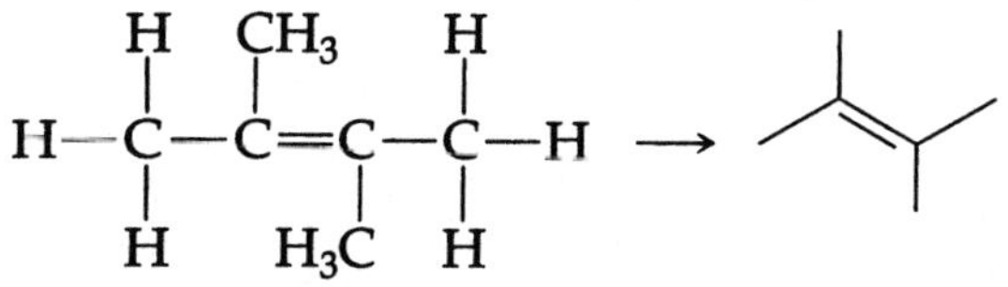

C_6H_{12}

(c) The *1-pentene* means a five-carbon (*pent-*) main chain with a C=C bond (*-ene*) between C1 and C2. The *3-methyl* tells you C3 carries a methyl group:

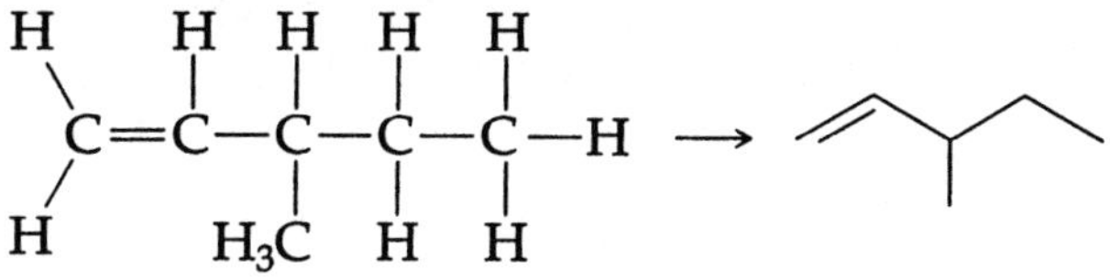

C_6H_{12}

(d) The *1-hexyne* means a six-carbon (*hex-*) main chain with a C≡C bond (*-yne*) between C1 and C2. The *5-methyl* tells you C5 carries a methyl group:

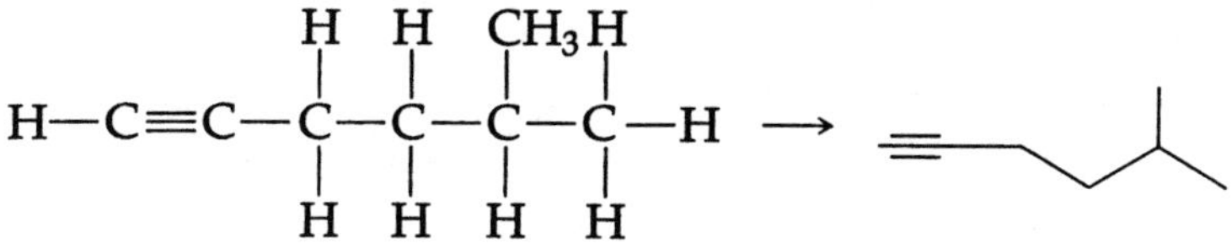

C_7H_{12}

17.78 (a) The first step is to identify the main chain. Because there are no multiple bonds, the main chain is the longest one, and six C means hexane:

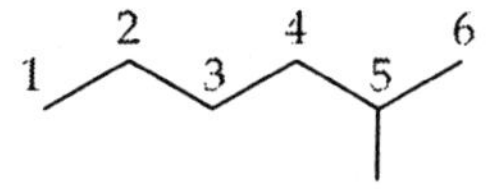

The short line off C5 is a methyl group, –CH₃, meaning the name is 5-methylhexane. The numbering is wrong, however, because it does not give as low a number as possible for the methyl group. This means you must renumber from the other end,

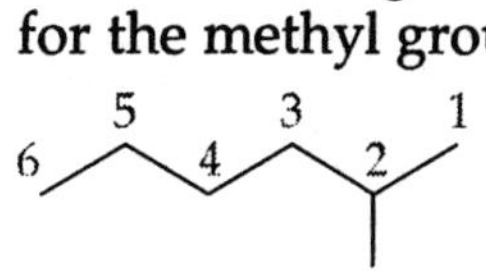

and the correct name is 2-methylhexane.

(b) The main chain must contain the double bond, and the numbering must start at the end closer to the double bond:

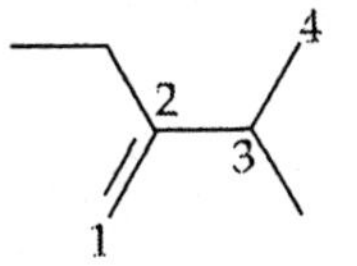

The bent line off C2 is an ethyl group, and the straight line off C3 is a methyl group: 2-ethyl-3-methyl-1-butene.

(c) The longest chain is six carbons long, the two vertical lines at the top are methyl groups, and the bent line off the bottom is an ethyl group. Number from the end that gives lower numbers to the branches, and list them alphabetically in the name, remembering to disregard *di-* when determining alphabetical order:

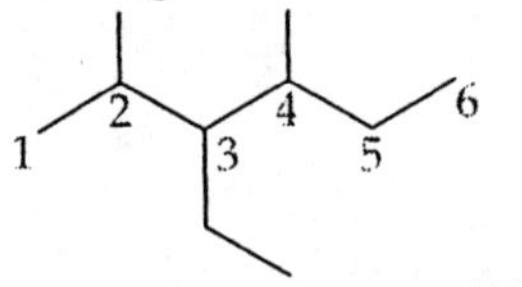

3-Ethyl-2,4-dimethylhexane

(d) Because there is a multiple bond, the main chain is not the longest one (nine carbons) but the one containing the multiple bond. Eight carbons makes it *oct-*, and the triple bond makes it *-yne*. Number from the end closer to the triple bond, and the branch has three carbons, making it *propyl*:

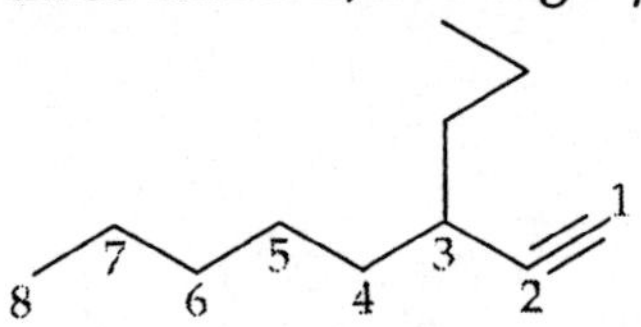

3-Propyl-1-octyne

17.79 To answer this question, you need to identify a main chain, and any way you number gives a chain three carbons long:

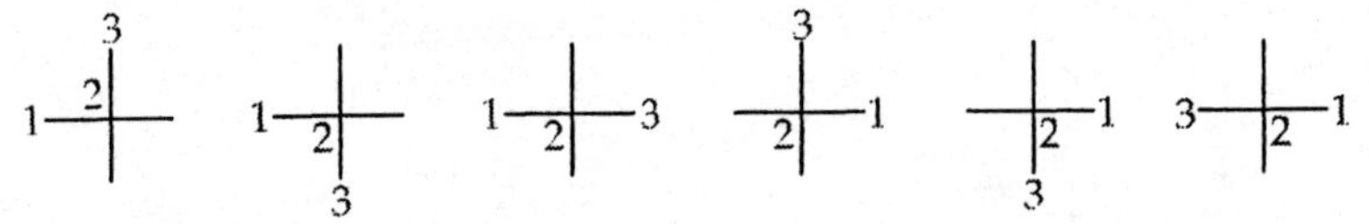

In all cases, there are two branches, both on C2, and both are methyl:

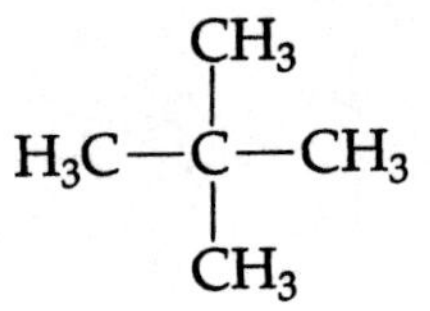

$$H_3C-\underset{\underset{CH_3}{|}}{\overset{\overset{CH_3}{|}}{C}}-CH_3$$

17.80

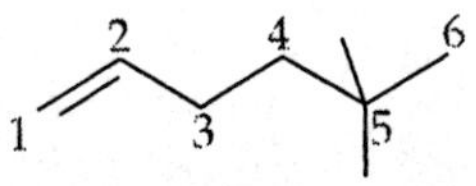

The compound can't be named 2,2,-dimethyl-5-hexene because the main chain must be numbered from the end closer to the multiple bond so that the double bond has as low a number as possible.

17.81 False. If a multiple bond is present, the longest chain that contains the multiple bond is the main chain. This may or may not be the longest chain in the molecule.

17.82 The 1 means one of the C=C bonds is between C1 and C2; the 3 means the second C=C bond is between C3 and C4; *buta-* means four carbons:  .

Determine the molecular formula by counting hydrogens, which is more easily done from a structural formula. The carbon skeleton is

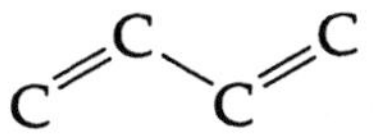

and you must add enough H to make each C form four bonds:

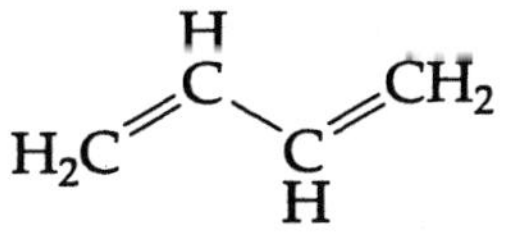

C_2H_6

17.83 As alkanes get larger, the intermolecular attractive forces get progressively stronger because there can be more and more of them in larger molecules, leading to a steady increase in boiling point.

17.84 The portion of a functionalized hydrocarbon that gives the hydrocarbon its unique properties.

17.85 By replacing the *-ine* ending of the halogen's elemental name with *-o* and then placing this prefix in front of the name of the parent hydrocarbon. When the parent contains more than two carbons, you use a number to indicate the position of the halogen. For example, CH_3I is iodomethane and $CH_3CHCH_2CH_2CH_2C{=}CH_2$ is 6-chloro-1-heptene (numbered so that the
$\quad\quad\quad\quad\quad\quad\;\;|\quad\quad\quad\quad\quad\quad\;\;H$
$\quad\quad\quad\quad\quad\quad\;Cl$
double bond has as low a number as possible; double bond takes precedence over halogen).

17.86 By putting the prefix *amino-* in front of the name of the parent hydrocarbon and, in molecules containing more than two carbons, using a number to indicate the position of the amino group. For example, $CH_3CH_2NH_2$ is aminoethane and $CH_3CH{=}CHCH_2CH_2CHCH_2CH_3$ is
$\quad\quad\quad\quad\quad\quad\quad\quad\quad\quad\quad\quad\quad\quad\quad\quad\quad\quad\quad\quad\;\;|$
$\quad\quad\quad\quad\quad\quad\quad\quad\quad\quad\quad\quad\quad\quad\quad\quad\quad\quad\quad\quad\;NH_2$
6-amino-2-octene (in numbering carbons, double bond takes precedence over amino group).

17.87 By replacing the final *-e* in the name of the parent hydrocarbon with *-ol* and, in molecules containing more than two carbons, using a number to indicate the position of the functional group. For example, $CH_3CH_2CH_2CH_2$ is 1-butanol and $CH_3CH_2CHCH_2CH_2CH_2CH_3$ is
$\quad\quad\quad\quad\quad\quad\quad\quad\quad\quad\quad\quad\quad\quad\;\;|\quad\quad\quad\quad\quad\quad\quad\quad\quad\quad\quad\;\;|$
3-heptanol.$\quad\quad\quad\quad\quad\quad\quad\quad\quad\quad OH\quad\quad\quad\quad\quad\quad\quad\quad\quad\quad\quad OH$

17.88 Number each chain to give the functional group as low a number as possible.
(a) 2-Chlorohexane
(b) 2-Bromopropane
(c) 2,4-Dichloro-3-ethylhexane (*not* 3,5-dichloro-4-ethylhexane)

17.89 Teflon is a long-chain "hydrocarbon" with all H replaced by F, generally referred to as a fluorocarbon:

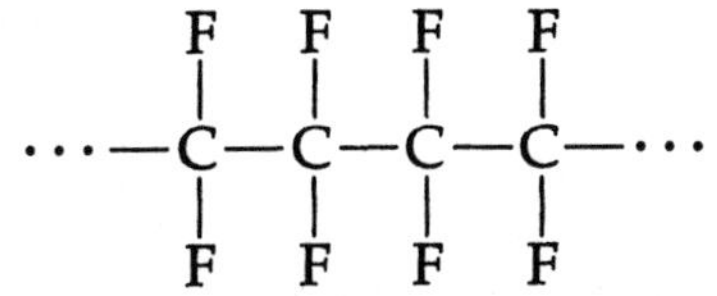

17.90 Number each chain to give the functional group as low a number as possible.
(a) 2-Hexanol　　(b) 3-Aminopentane　　(c) 3-Hexanol

17.91 Because chlorinated hydrocarbons, along with the other halogen-functionalized hydrocarbons, are often used as the starting material for synthesizing hydrocarbons containing other, nonhalogen, functional groups.

17.92 Because they destroy the ozone layer when they rise into the upper atmosphere.

17.93 Because –OH is the alcohol functional group, R–OH represents the alcohols, with R representing a hydrocarbon chain.

17.94 By reacting it with a strong base via the reaction $R\text{–}Cl + OH^- \longrightarrow R\text{–}OH + Cl^-$.

17.95 No, because 3-propanol does not exist. When the chain is numbered correctly, 3-propanol is really 1-propanol:

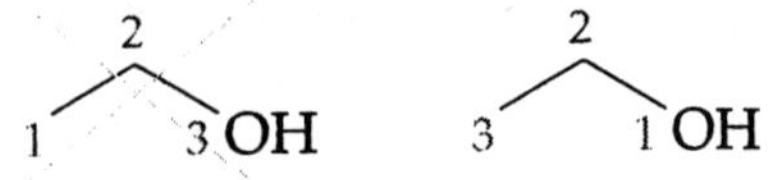

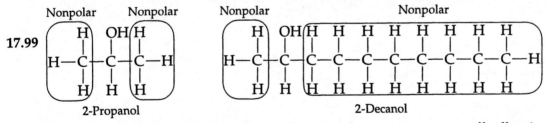

3-Propanol   1-Propanol
WRONG

17.96 One H must go with the O to form –OH, leaving nine H to bond with C atoms. This many H means no unsaturation in the hydrocarbon chain. Begin with a four-carbon chain and all possible positions for the –OH, on C1 and on C2:

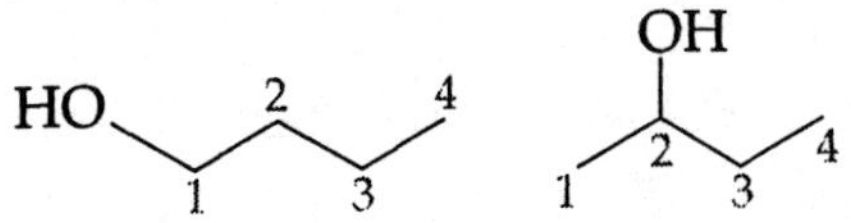

Note that when a functional group is present, the end of a line does *not* represent a C:

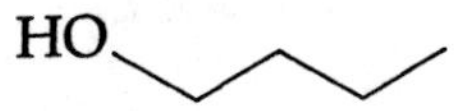

HO⟍⟋⟍⟋ is $HO\text{–}CH_2CH_2CH_2CH_3$, *not* $HO\text{–}CH_2CH_2CH_2CH_2CH_3$.

Next form a three-carbon chain and all possible positions for the –OH, on C1 and C2:

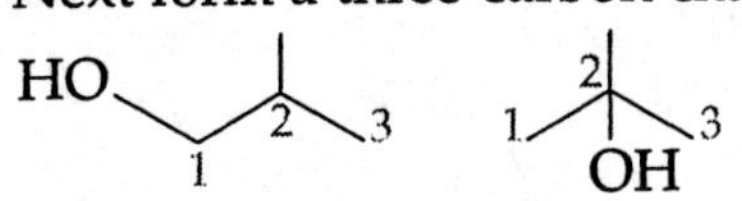

17.97 Wood alcohol is methanol. Enzymes in the human liver convert methanol to formaldehyde, which is poisonous. Horses lack this enzyme and can therefore ingest wood alcohol with no apparent ill effect.

17.98 Because large quantities of ethanol force the enzymes in the liver to metabolize the ethanol instead of the methanol. The methanol gets flushed out of the body.

17.99

2-Propanol   2-Decanol

2-Propanol is soluble in water because its nonpolar portions are small, allowing the polar –OH group, which forms hydrogen bonds, to determine the solubility properties. In 2-decanol, the large nonpolar portion "outweighs" the smaller polar –OH group, making the molecule insoluble in water.

17.100 Because there is no C at the two line endings adjacent to O, the molecular formula is $C_4H_{10}O$. Because the molecule fits the general formula R–O–R, it is an ether—diethyl ether.

17.101 (a) –CH₃ to the left of O, –CH₂CH₂CH₃ to the right: methyl propyl ether.
(b) CH₃CH₂CH₂– both left and right: dipropyl ether.
(c) CH₃CH₂– to the left, –CH₂CH₂CH₃ to the right: ethyl propyl ether.

17.102

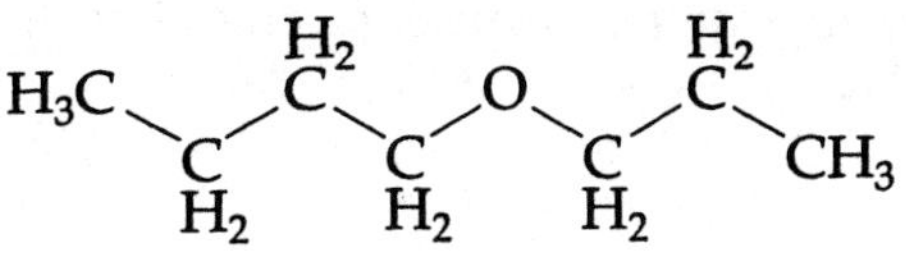

$$H_3C - \underset{\underset{H_2}{|}}{C} - \underset{\underset{H_2}{|}}{\overset{\overset{H_2}{|}}{C}} - \underset{\underset{H_2}{|}}{C} - O - \underset{\underset{H_2}{|}}{\overset{\overset{H_2}{|}}{C}} - CH_3$$

$C_7H_{16}O$

17.103 Acetic acid. *Ethan-* means two carbons, one of which is part of the carboxylic acid group, –COOH:

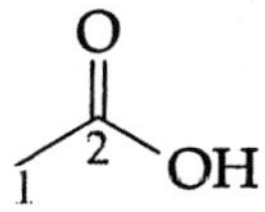

$$\underset{1}{\overset{O}{\underset{}{\|}}} \overset{2}{C} OH$$

17.104

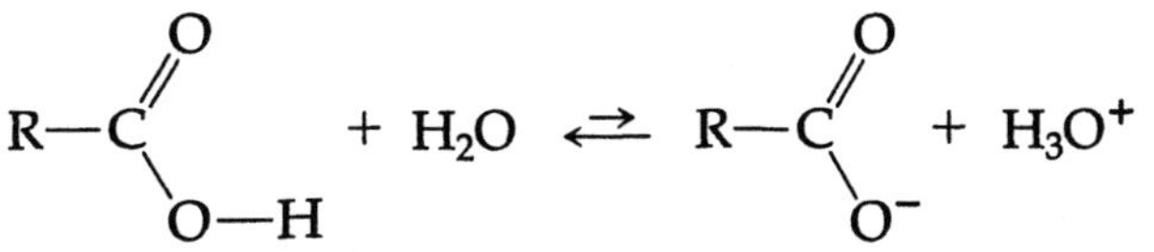

$$R - \overset{O}{\underset{O-H}{\overset{\|}{C}}} + H_2O \rightleftharpoons R - \overset{O}{\underset{O^-}{\overset{\|}{C}}} + H_3O^+$$

The equilibrium lies to the left, implying that most of the acid is undissociated and that RCOOH molecules are weak acids.

17.105 The H on the carboxylic acid group migrates to the amine and forms a covalent bond with the lone pair of electrons on N:

$$R - \overset{O}{\underset{O-H}{\overset{\|}{C}}} + \overset{}{\underset{\underset{R}{|}}{\overset{}{N}}} \overset{R}{} R \rightleftharpoons R - \overset{O}{\underset{O^-}{\overset{\|}{C}}} + \left[\overset{H}{\underset{\underset{R}{|}}{\overset{\overset{\cdot\cdot}{N}}{}}} \overset{}{} R \right]^+$$

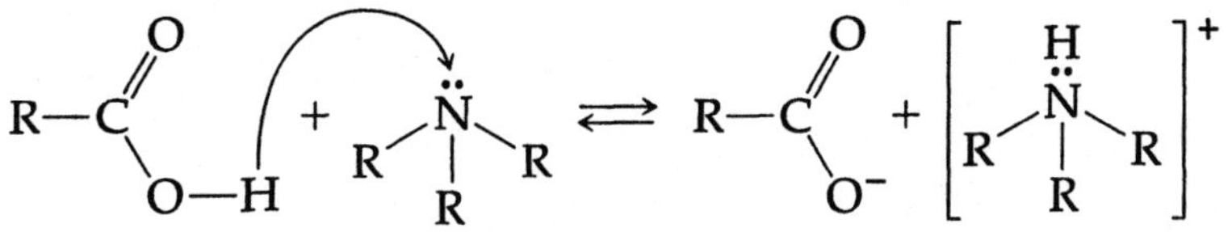

17.106 One of the H_2O hydrogens migrates to the amine and forms a covalent bond with the lone pair of electrons on N:

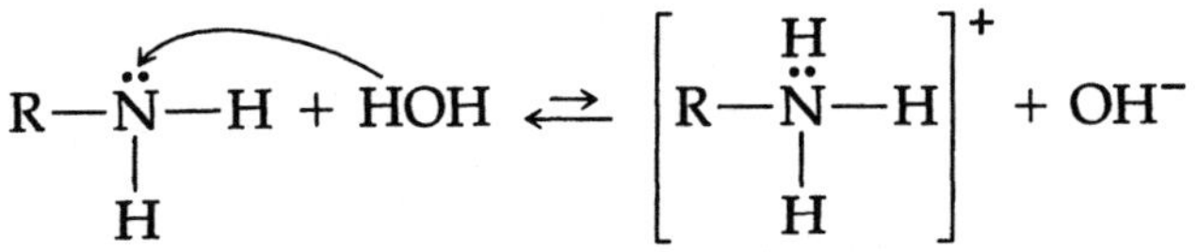

$$R - \overset{\cdot\cdot}{\underset{\underset{H}{|}}{N}} - H + HOH \rightleftharpoons \left[R - \overset{\cdot\cdot}{\underset{\underset{H}{|}}{N}} - H \right]^+ + OH^-$$

The equilibrium lies to the left, which implies that a primary amine is a weak base in water.

17.107

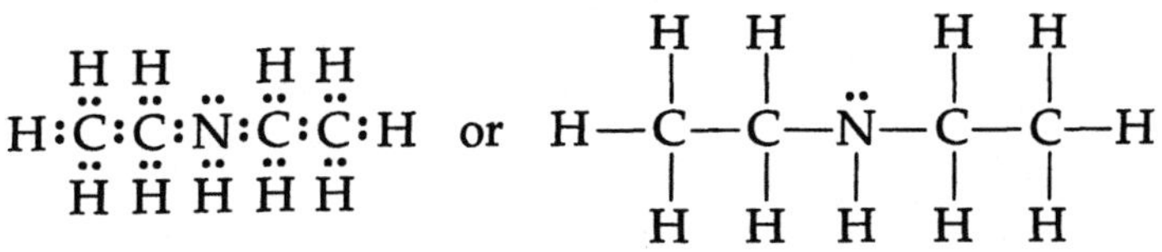

$$H\overset{\cdot\cdot}{:}\underset{\cdot\cdot}{\overset{H}{\underset{H}{C}}}\overset{\cdot\cdot}{:}\underset{}{\overset{H}{C}}\overset{\cdot\cdot}{:}\underset{\cdot\cdot}{\overset{}{N}}\overset{\cdot\cdot}{:}\underset{\cdot\cdot}{\overset{H}{\underset{H}{C}}}\overset{\cdot\cdot}{:}\underset{\cdot\cdot}{\overset{H}{\underset{H}{C}}}\overset{\cdot\cdot}{:}H \quad \text{or} \quad H - \underset{\underset{H}{|}}{\overset{\overset{H}{|}}{C}} - \underset{\underset{H}{|}}{\overset{\overset{H}{|}}{C}} - \underset{}{\overset{\cdot\cdot}{N}} - \underset{\underset{H}{|}}{\overset{\overset{H}{|}}{C}} - \underset{\underset{H}{|}}{\overset{\overset{H}{|}}{C}} - H$$

17.108

$$\underset{1}{\overset{NH_2}{\underset{}{|}}} \overset{}{\underset{2}{\diagup}} \underset{3}{\diagdown} \underset{}{\diagup} \underset{4}{\diagdown} \underset{5}{\diagup} \overset{6}{\diagdown}$$

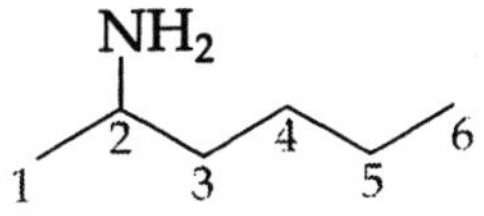

This is a primary amine because the N is bonded to two H and one R group (the hexane chain).

17.109 *Methan-* means one carbon, and *-al* means an aldehyde, which is a carbonyl group attached to at least one H:

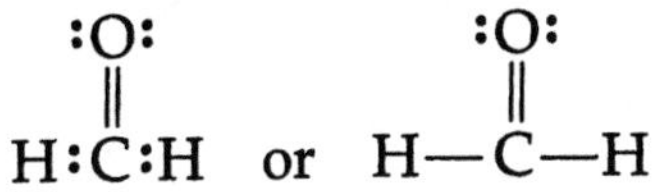

$$\overset{:O:}{\underset{}{\|}} \qquad \overset{:O:}{\underset{}{\|}}$$
$$H:C:H \quad \text{or} \quad H - C - H$$

17.110

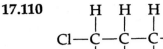

1-Chloropropane
(halogen-functionalized
hydrocarbon)

1-Propanol
(alcohol)

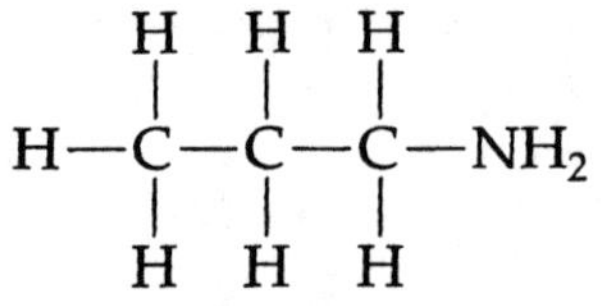

1-Aminopropane
(primary amine)

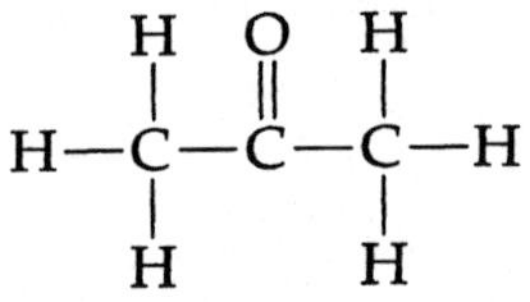

2-Propanone
(ketone)

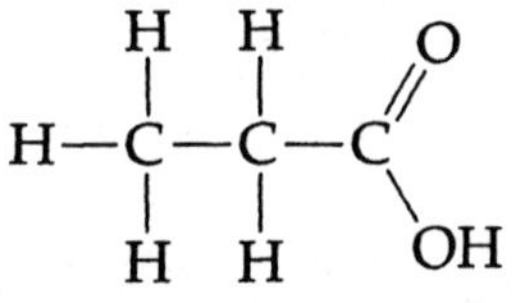

Propanoic acid
(carboxylic acid)

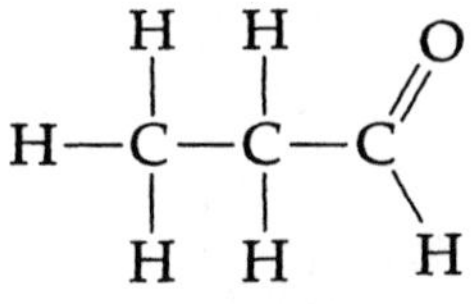

Propanal
(aldehyde)

17.111 *Propan-* means three carbons, and *-one* means a ketone, which has the general formula

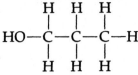

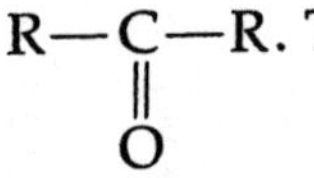

R—C—R. The 2 tells you C2 is the carboxyl carbon: 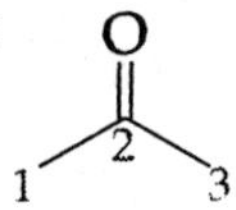 . The common name is

acetone.

17.112 Acetic acid is found in vinegar. You are likely to encounter it in any kitchen or in a salad.

17.113 (a) 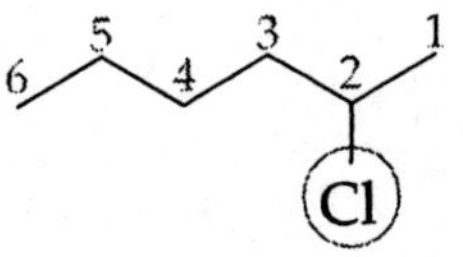 2-Chlorohexane (b) Ethyl methyl ether (c) 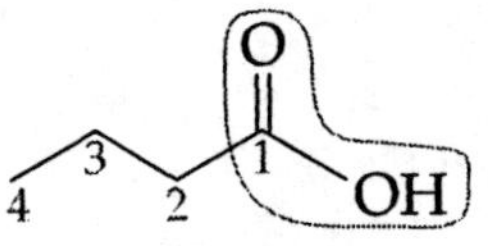 Butanoic acid (d) 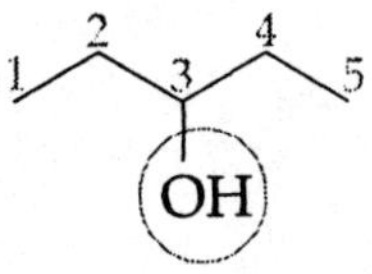 3-Pentanol

17.114 Aldehydes,

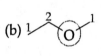

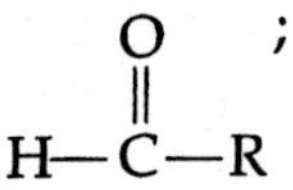

; ketones, 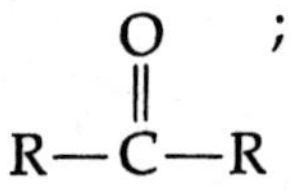 ; and carboxylic acids, .

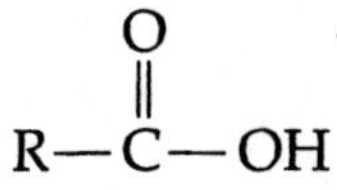

H—C—R   R—C—R   R—C—OH

17.115 (a)

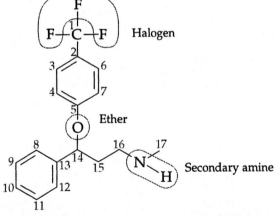

Halogen

Ether

Secondary amine

(b) $C_{17}H_{18}F_3NO$. The numbers in part (a) are shown merely to help you count the carbons. As you count, remember two things: the end of a line does *not* represent a C when a heteroatom is present, and the short line off the N represents a –CH_3 group.

17.116 Methanol dissolves readily in water because it possesses an −OH that forms a hydrogen bond to a water molecule. This helps in the solute-separation step by replacing some of the water-to-water hydrogen bonds that must be broken to create a "hole" in the water for the methanol molecules. Because hydrocarbons lack any functional group that can aid in the same way, hydrocarbons are insoluble in water.

17.117 Methyl alcohol is a molecular compound and therefore does not ionize when it dissolves in water. Some electrically charged species (ions, electrons, or protons) must be present in order for electricity to be conducted.

17.118 (a), because of the −OH group, which can hydrogen-bond with water molecules. Compound (b) is a hydrocarbon, essentially nonpolar and therefore insoluble in water. Compound (c) has an −OH group but also a large, nonpolar hydrocarbon chain. The solvent "hole" needed for this molecule is much larger than for (a) and would require breaking many more solvent–solvent hydrogen bonds.

17.119 This molecular formula fits the general formula C_nH_{2n+2}, telling you the compound is a saturated hydrocarbon. Begin with a five-carbon chain:

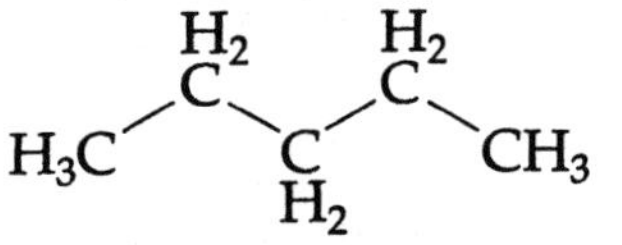

Pentane

Next do a four-carbon chain, which allows only one position for the branch:

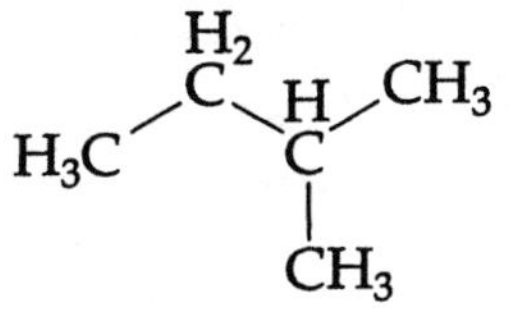

2-Methylbutane

Last is the three-carbon chain, which also allows only one position for the branches:

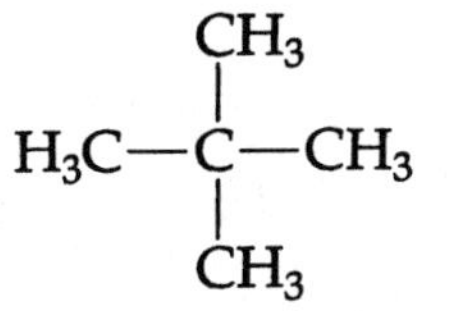

2,2-Dimethylpropane

You would expect this last isomer to have the lowest boiling point because it is the most branched of the three structures and therefore has the smallest surface area. In hydrocarbons, boiling point increases as chain length increases.

17.120 If the molecular formula were C_4H_{10}, you would recognize this as a saturated hydrocarbon fitting the general formula C_nH_{2n+2}. The Br replaced one H, which means the molecule is indeed a saturated hydrocarbon. Begin with the longest possible chain and the halogen in every possible position:

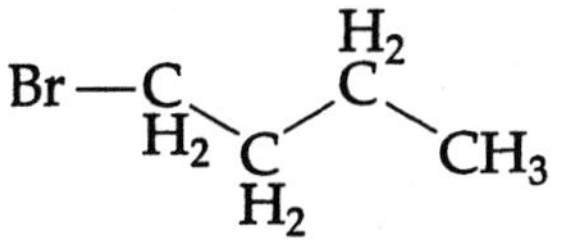

1-Bromobutane 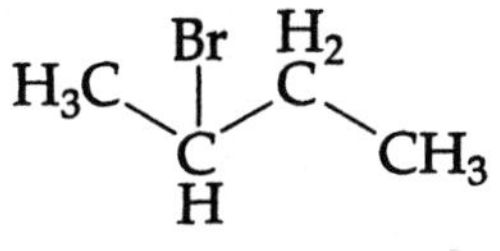   2-Bromobutane

Next do the three-carbon chain with the Br in all possible locations, listing the functional group and branch alphabetically in the name:

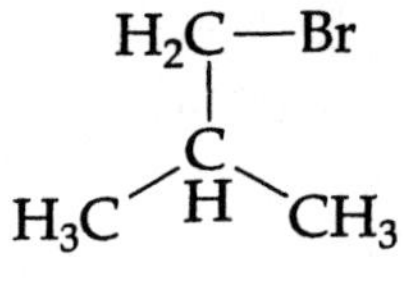

H$_2$C—Br
|
C
H$_3$C   H   CH$_3$

CH$_3$
|
C
H$_3$C | CH$_3$
        Br

1-Bromo-2-methylpropane 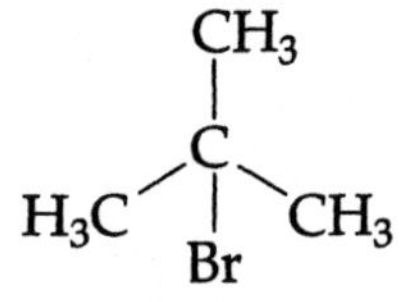   2-Bromo-2-methylpropane

17.121 Remember that a line ending where a functional group or H atom appears does *not* represent a C. The carbons are numbered in each drawing to help you count.

(a)

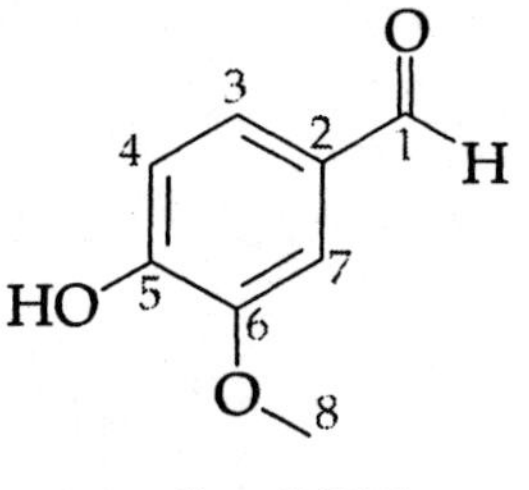

Vanillin: C$_8$H$_8$O$_3$

(b)

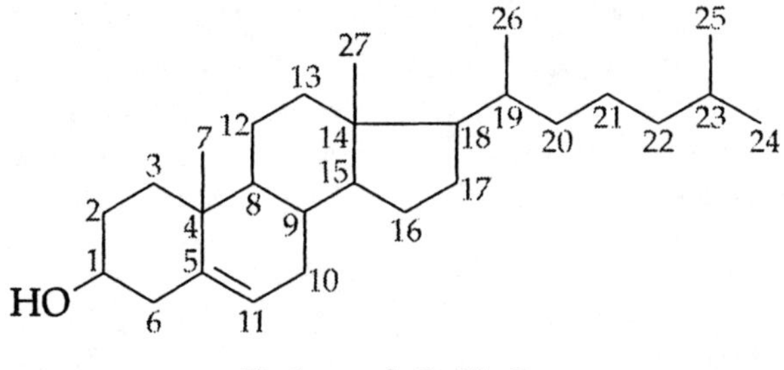

Cholesterol: C$_{27}$H$_{46}$O

(c)

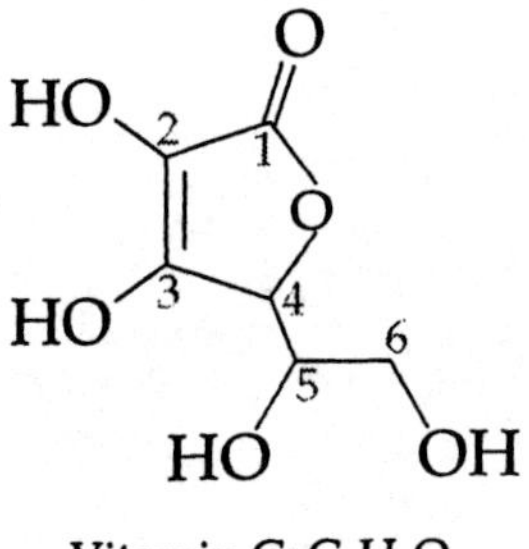

Vitamin C: C$_6$H$_8$O$_6$

(d)

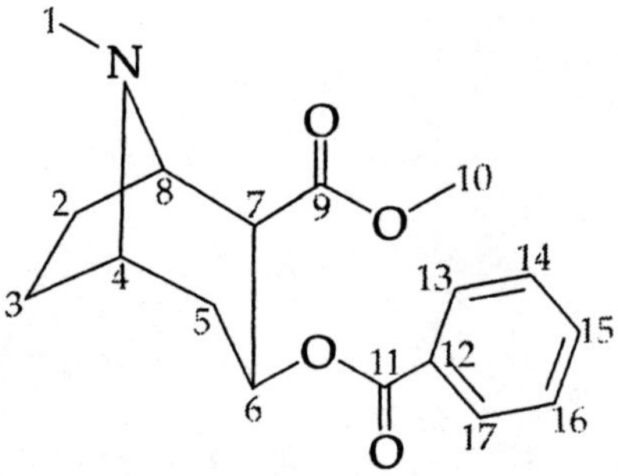

Cocaine: C$_{17}$H$_{21}$O$_4$N

17.122 (a) Isomers because they both have the molecular formula C$_3$H$_8$O.
(b) Identical. Both are the three-carbon alcohol 1-propanol.
(c) Isomers because they both have the molecular formula C$_4$H$_6$.
(d) Completely unrelated (C$_5$H$_{10}$ and C$_5$H$_{12}$).
(e) Completely unrelated (C$_6$H$_8$ and C$_5$H$_8$). Remember that, in the molecule on the left, there is a –CH$_3$ group at the end of the short line sticking off the ring.

17.123 (a) To make the molecule polar, place both electronegative Cl atoms on the same C:

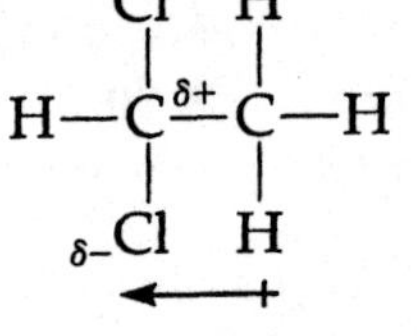

$^{\delta-}$Cl   H
| |
H—C$^{\delta+}$—C—H
| |
$_\delta$–Cl   H

(b) To make the molecule nonpolar, place the Cl atoms symmetrically so that the two δ− charges cancel each other:

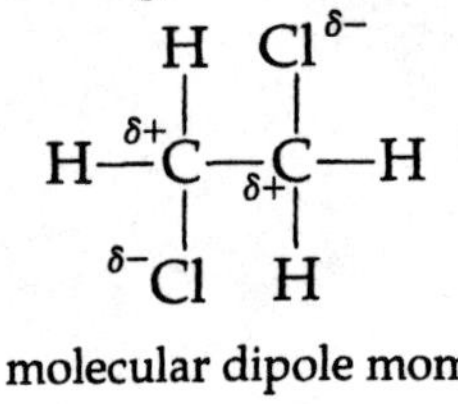

H   Cl$^{\delta-}$
| |
H—$^{\delta+}$C—$_{\delta+}$C—H
| |
$^{\delta-}$Cl   H

No molecular dipole moment

17.124 (a) To make the molecule polar, place both electronegative Cl atoms at the same end. The small number of H tells you there is unsaturation in the molecule. (Assume each Cl replaced an H, meaning original formula must have been $C_4H_8 = C_nH_{2n}$ = alkene.) Some possible polar molecules are

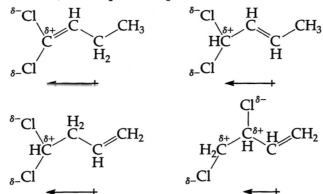

(b) To make the molecule nonpolar, draw it symmetrically. Place the Cl atoms at opposite ends so that the two $\delta-$ cancel each other, and place the double bond between C2 and C3:

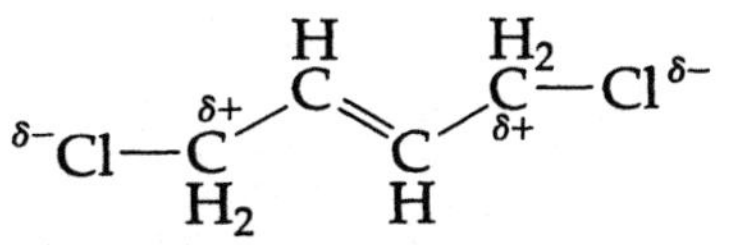

No molecular dipole moment

(c) Only in a ring structure can a molecule having this molecular formula have only single C–C bonds:

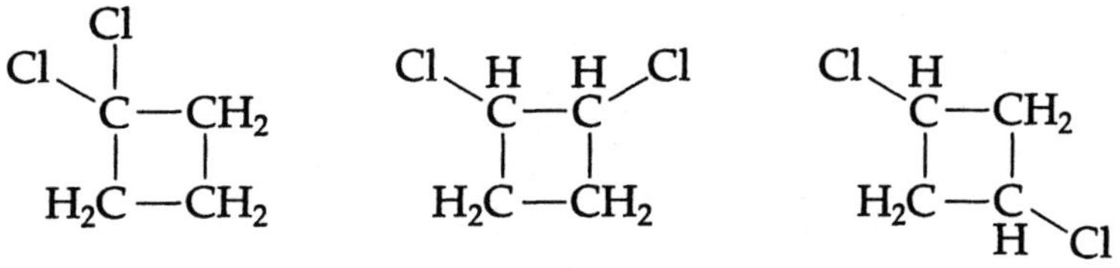

17.125

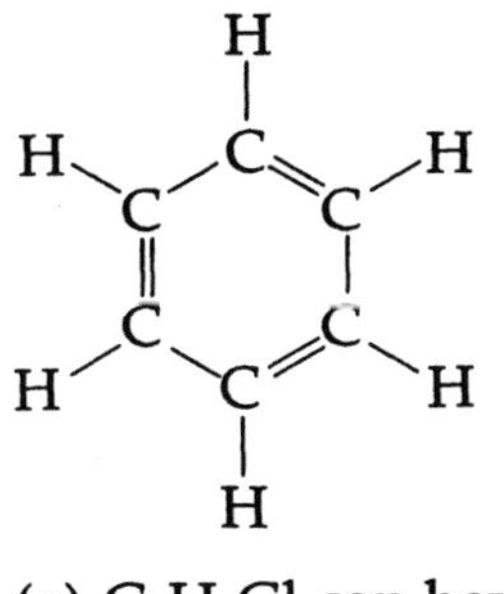

17.126 (a) C_6H_5Cl can have only one isomer because the benzene ring is planar and symmetrical. Therefore all six carbons are equivalent, and it makes no difference which one carries the Cl.

(b) $C_6H_4Cl_2$ can have three isomers:

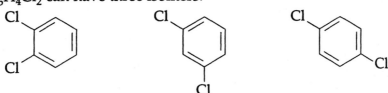

1,2-Dichlorobenzene   1,3-Dichlorobenzene   1,4-Dichlorobenzene

(There is no 1,5 or 1,6 isomer because 1,5 is the same as 1,3 and 1,6 is the same as 1,2.)

(c) $C_6H_2Cl_4$ has three isomers:

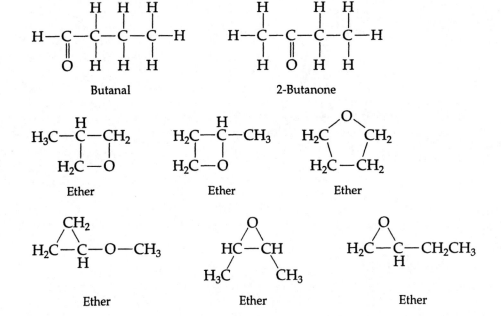

1,2,3,4-Tetrachlorobenzene   1,2,3,5-Tetrachlorobenzene   1,2,3,6-Tetrachlorobenzene

17.127 (a) Because the compound is saturated ($C_4H_{10} = C_nH_{2n+2}$), it can only be an ether or an alcohol:

Diethyl ether   Methyl propyl ether

1-Butanol   2-Butanol

(b) Because the compound is unsaturated ($C_4H_8O_2 = C_nH_{2n}O_2$), at least one of the carbons can be a carbonyl carbon, meaning an aldehyde or ketone. (It cannot be a carboxylic acid because there is only one O in the molecular formula.) If the unsaturation is caused by a ring, the compound must be an ether or alcohol:

Butanal   2-Butanone

Ether   Ether   Ether

Ether   Ether   Ether

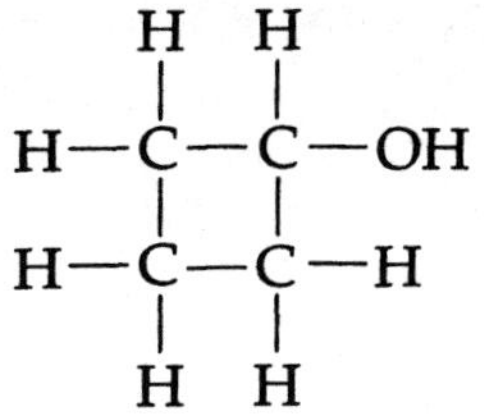

H H
| |
H—C—C—OH
| |
H—C—C—H
| |
H H

Alcohol

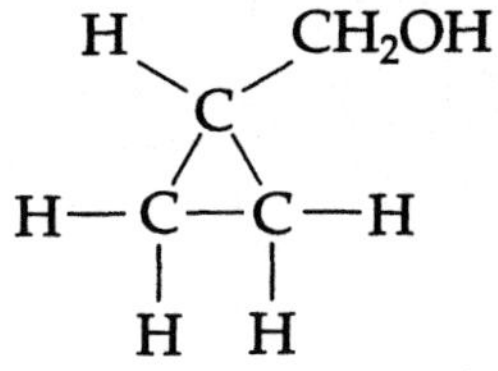

H   CH₂OH
 \   /
  C
H—C—C—H
  | |
  H   H

Alcohol

(c) Unsaturated with two oxygens can be a carboxylic acid. If the unsaturation is because of a ring, you can have a dialcohol or diether. Some possibilities are (you may have come up with others):

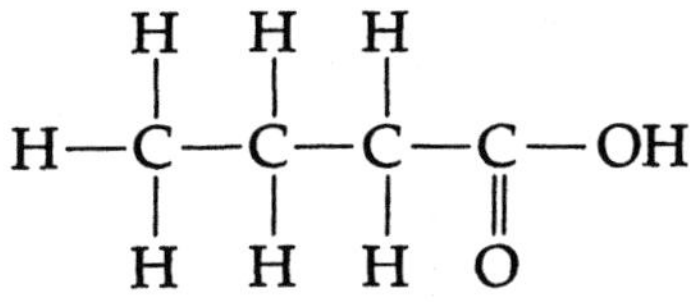

H H H
| | |
H—C—C—C—C—OH
| | | ‖
H H H O

Butanoic acid

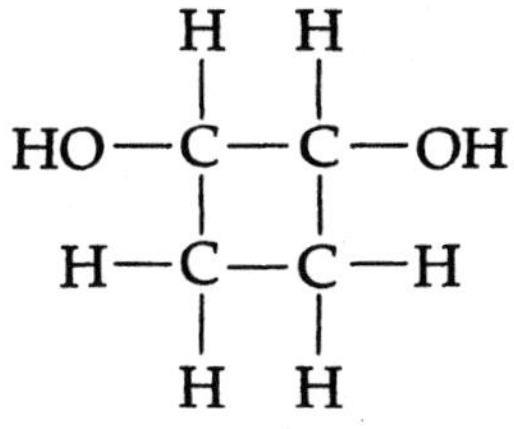

H H
| |
HO—C—C—OH
| |
H—C—C—H
| |
H H

Dialcohol

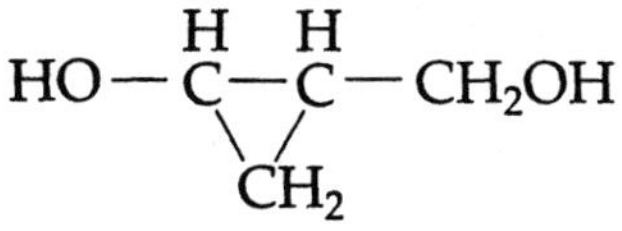

H H
| |
HO—C—C—CH₂OH
    \ /
    CH₂

Dialcohol

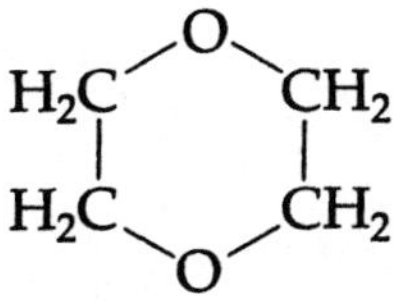

H₂C—O—CH₂
| |
H₂C—O—CH₂

Diether

O—CH₂
| |
H₂C—C—O—CH₃
    |
    H

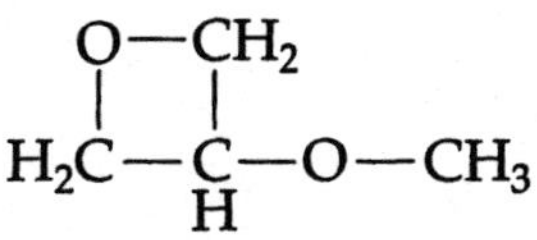

Diether

Synthetic and Biological Polymers

18.1 See solution in textbook.

18.2 (a)

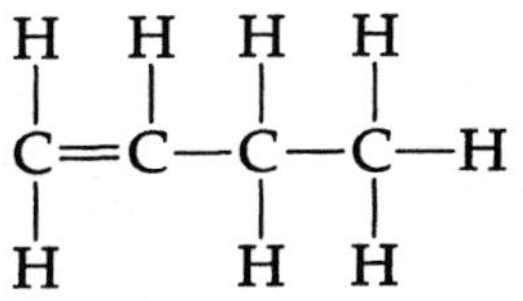

$$\underset{H}{\overset{H}{\underset{|}{C}}}=\underset{H}{\overset{H}{\underset{|}{C}}}-\underset{H}{\overset{H}{\underset{|}{C}}}-\underset{H}{\overset{H}{\underset{|}{C}}}-H$$

(b) The two electrons in one pair of the C=C bond unpair, one electron going to each C and making each available to form a C–C bond:

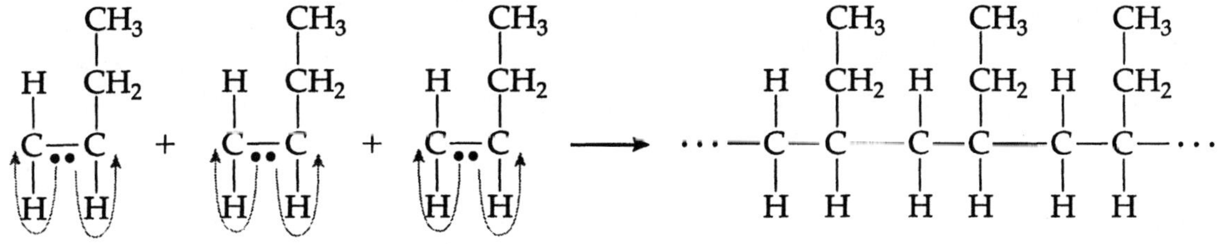

18.3 (a) H—C≡C—H

(b) The two electrons in one pair of the C≡C bond unpair, one electron going to each C and making each available to form a C–C bond:

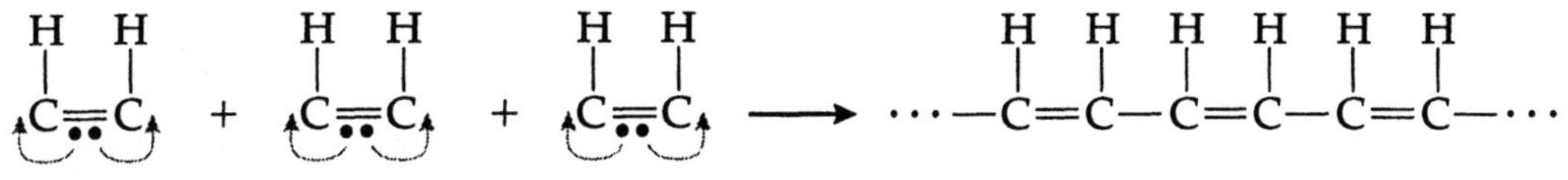

18.4 See solution in textbook.

18.5 The first amino acid named is the one that has the unreacted amino group. The second is the one that has the unreacted carboxylic acid group.

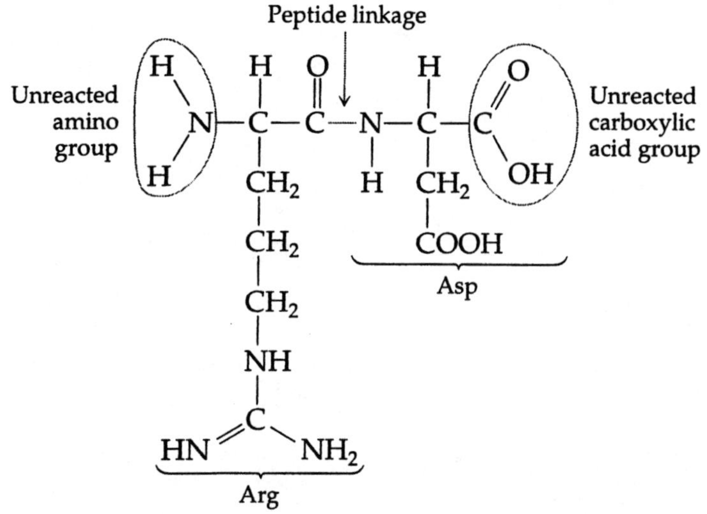

Peptide linkage

Unreacted amino group

Unreacted carboxylic acid group

Asp

Arg

18.6 Break each $\overset{\overset{\displaystyle O}{\|}}{C}$—N linkage and then identify the eight amino acids by their side chains: Asp–Arg–Val–Tyr–Ile–His–Pro–Phe.

18.7 A long-chain molecule consisting of many repeating units of some monomer.

18.8 A macromolecule is any very large molecule. Because polymers are large, they are macromolecules.

18.9 A monomer is a small molecule used to produce a polymer. A monomer unit is a monomer once it has become part of a polymer. An example of a monomer is the compound tetrafluoroethene, $F_2C=CF_2$. Its monomer unit is the molecule once two electrons of the double bond have unpaired and the unit has been incorporated into a polymer:

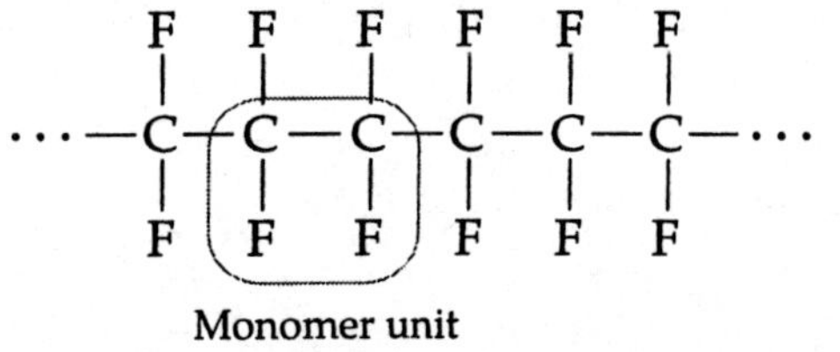

Monomer unit

18.10 Because ethylene, $H_2C=CH_2$, is the monomer from which it is made. The ethylene loses its double bond when it converts to the monomer unit

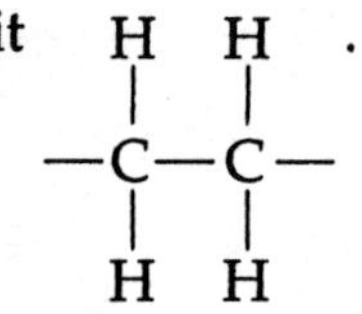

18.11 Ethylene is $H_2C=CH_2$, and two electrons from the double bond split up:

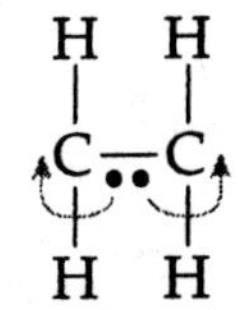

Each C now having a lone electron, it can form a covalent bond with a lone electron on another monomer:

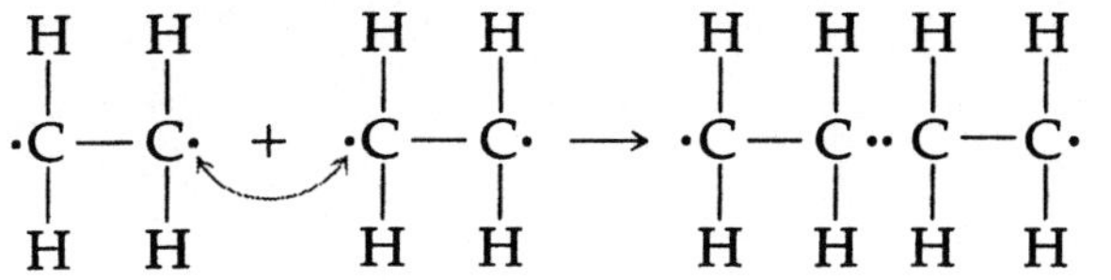

Because the dimer has a lone electron at each end, the chain can keep adding a monomer at each end.

18.12 Propene is

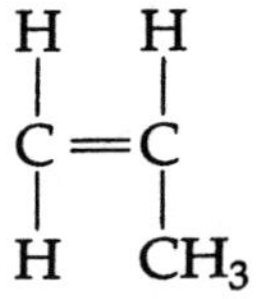

which rearranges electrons to form

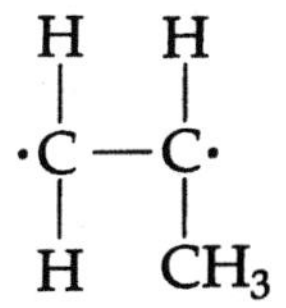

and then polymerizes to

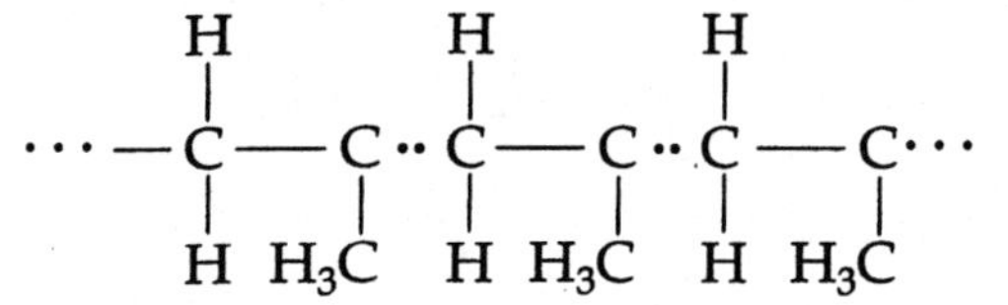

This polymer is called polypropylene.

18.13 (a) Choose an arbitrary position for the opening parenthesis:

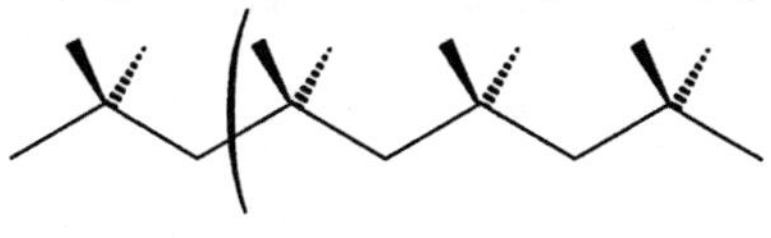

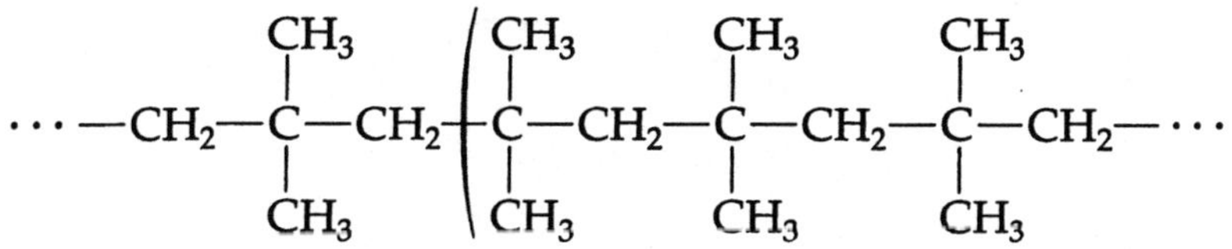

$$\cdots -CH_2-\underset{\underset{CH_3}{|}}{\overset{\overset{CH_3}{|}}{C}}-CH_2-\!\!\left(\!\!\underset{\underset{CH_3}{|}}{\overset{\overset{CH_3}{|}}{C}}-CH_2-\underset{\underset{CH_3}{|}}{\overset{\overset{CH_3}{|}}{C}}-CH_2-\underset{\underset{CH_3}{|}}{\overset{\overset{CH_3}{|}}{C}}-CH_2-\cdots\right.$$

Then position the closing parenthesis at the same location on the immediately adjacent monomer unit:

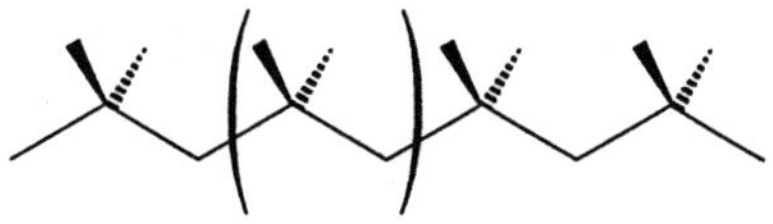

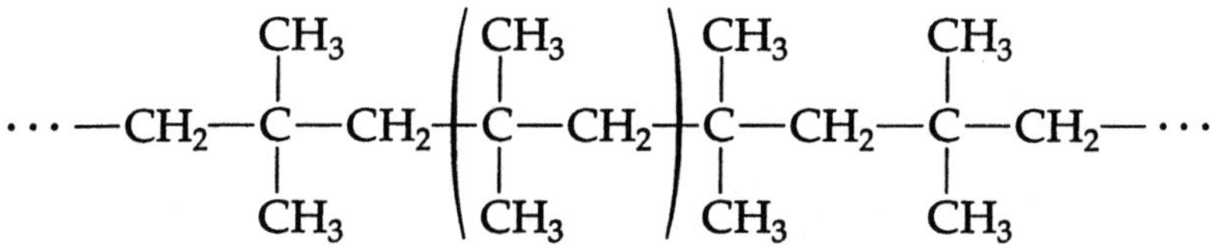

$$\cdots -CH_2-\underset{\underset{CH_3}{|}}{\overset{\overset{CH_3}{|}}{C}}-CH_2-\!\!\left(\!\!\underset{\underset{CH_3}{|}}{\overset{\overset{CH_3}{|}}{C}}-CH_2-\!\!\right)\!\!\underset{\underset{CH_3}{|}}{\overset{\overset{CH_3}{|}}{C}}-CH_2-\underset{\underset{CH_3}{|}}{\overset{\overset{CH_3}{|}}{C}}-CH_2-\cdots$$

The formula for the monomer unit is C_4H_8.

(b) The carbons in the polymer backbone are the ones that originally had a double bond, which means the monomer must have been

$$\cdot \underset{\underset{CH_3}{|}}{\overset{\overset{CH_3}{|}}{C}} \!\!\!-\!\!\! \underset{\underset{H}{|}}{\overset{\overset{H}{|}}{C}} \cdot \longrightarrow \underset{\underset{CH_3}{|}}{\overset{\overset{CH_3}{|}}{C}} \!\!=\!\! \underset{\underset{H}{|}}{\overset{\overset{H}{|}}{C}} \longrightarrow \rangle\!\!=\!\!\langle$$

(c) Monomer methylpropylene, polymer polymethylpropylene.

(d)

$$\underset{\underset{CH_3}{|}}{\overset{\overset{CH_3}{|}}{C}} \cdots \underset{\underset{H}{|}}{\overset{\overset{H}{|}}{C}} \longrightarrow \cdot \underset{\underset{CH_3}{|}}{\overset{\overset{CH_3}{|}}{C}} \!\!-\!\! \underset{\underset{H}{|}}{\overset{\overset{H}{|}}{C}} \cdot$$

18.14 Poly(vinyl chloride), PVC.

18.15 Teflon is made by the polymerization of tetrafluoroethene:

$$\cdots-\underset{\underset{F}{|}}{\overset{\overset{F}{|}}{C}}-\underset{\underset{F}{|}}{\overset{\overset{F}{|}}{C}}-\underset{\underset{F}{|}}{\overset{\overset{F}{|}}{C}}-\underset{\underset{F}{|}}{\overset{\overset{F}{|}}{C}}-\underset{\underset{F}{|}}{\overset{\overset{F}{|}}{C}}-\underset{\underset{F}{|}}{\overset{\overset{F}{|}}{C}}-\cdots \qquad \underset{\underset{F}{|}}{\overset{\overset{F}{|}}{C}}=\underset{\underset{F}{|}}{\overset{\overset{F}{|}}{C}}$$

$$\text{Polymer} \qquad\qquad\qquad \text{Monomer}$$

18.16 (a) Choose an arbitrary position for the opening parenthesis:

$$\cdots-\underset{\underset{CH_3}{|}}{\overset{\overset{CH_3}{|}}{Si}}-O\!\left(\!\underset{\underset{CH_3}{|}}{\overset{\overset{CH_3}{|}}{Si}}-O-\underset{\underset{CH_3}{|}}{\overset{\overset{CH_3}{|}}{Si}}-O-\cdots\right.$$

Now move to the right along the backbone until you come to the immediately following identical position (O on left of a bond, Si on right of same bond); this is the end of the monomer unit:

$$\cdots-\underset{\underset{CH_3}{|}}{\overset{\overset{CH_3}{|}}{Si}}-O\!\left(\!\underset{\underset{CH_3}{|}}{\overset{\overset{CH_3}{|}}{Si}}-O\!\right)\!\underset{\underset{CH_3}{|}}{\overset{\overset{CH_3}{|}}{Si}}-O-\cdots$$

(b) The monomer unit is composed of two methyl groups (dimethyl) attached to a silicon (sil) attached to an oxygen (ox); hence the name polydimethylsiloxane.

18.17 Ethylene is a small, nonpolar molecule, and therefore intermolecular attractive forces are very weak; this causes the compound to have a relatively low boiling point. Polyethylene is a huge macromolecule, and even though the molecule is nonpolar, its huge size affords many opportunities for intermolecular attractions to form, resulting in a relatively high boiling point.

18.18 The monomers have functional groups at both ends.

18.19 A bond between a carbonyl carbon and an amine nitrogen.

$$(CH_3)_2N\!-\!(H)+CH_3\overset{\overset{}{\underset{\underset{O}{\|}}{}}}{C}\!-\!(Cl) \longrightarrow (CH_3)_2N\!-\!\overset{\overset{O}{\|}}{C}\underset{CH_3}{\diagdown} \quad + \quad HCl$$

$$\underset{\text{Amide bond}}{}$$

18.20 Nylon 66 is made up of repeating units of a monomer made from hexanedioic acid chloride and 1,6-diaminohexane:

$$\underset{\substack{\text{Hexanedioic acid chloride}}}{\underbrace{\overset{\displaystyle O}{\overset{\|}{C}}-CH_2-CH_2-CH_2-CH_2-\overset{\displaystyle O}{\overset{\|}{C}}}}-\underset{\substack{\text{1,6-Diaminohexane}}}{\underbrace{\overset{\displaystyle H}{\overset{|}{N}}-CH_2-CH_2-CH_2-CH_2-CH_2-NH_2}}$$

This combination of the two molecules is *one monomer unit* in nylon 66. A chain two monomer units long is therefore

$$\underset{\substack{\text{One monomer unit}}}{\underbrace{-\overset{\displaystyle O}{\overset{\|}{C}}-(CH_2)_4-\overset{\displaystyle O}{\overset{\|}{C}}-\underset{H}{\overset{|}{N}}-(CH_2)_6-\underset{H}{\overset{|}{N}}-}}\overset{\displaystyle O}{\overset{\|}{C}}-(CH_2)_4-\overset{\displaystyle O}{\overset{\|}{C}}-\underset{H}{\overset{|}{N}}-(CH_2)_6-\underset{H}{\overset{|}{N}}-$$

18.21 From petroleum.

18.22 The aldehyde O is transformed to an –OH:

Yes, because the cyclic form has a C–O–C bond, which conforms to the general ether formula R–O–R.

18.23 A monosaccharide is a sugar consisting of only one sugar ring; glucose is an example. A disaccharide is a sugar consisting of two sugar rings bonded together; sucrose is an example. A polysaccharide is a polymer consisting of a large number of sugar rings bonded together; starch and cellulose are examples.

18.24 Glucose is a monosaccharide consisting of one glucose ring. Sucrose is a disaccharide consisting of one glucose ring and one fructose ring.

18.25 Either "hydrated carbon" or "carbon with water attached."

18.26 Yes, because most of the carbons in sugar molecules have both an H atom and an OH group attached, which together form HOH, the water molecule. Many sugars have the general formula $C_n(H_2O)_n$.

18.27 They are both polymers of glucose monomer units. They differ in the orientation of the linkage between the glucose units, a difference that makes the three-dimensional shape of cellulose very different from that of starch.

18.28 Cellulose, because wood is about 50% cellulose; carbon dioxide and water.

18.29 A compound that contains both a carboxylic acid functional group and an amine functional group.

18.30 Alanine has a methyl group in place of one of the hydrogens in glycine:

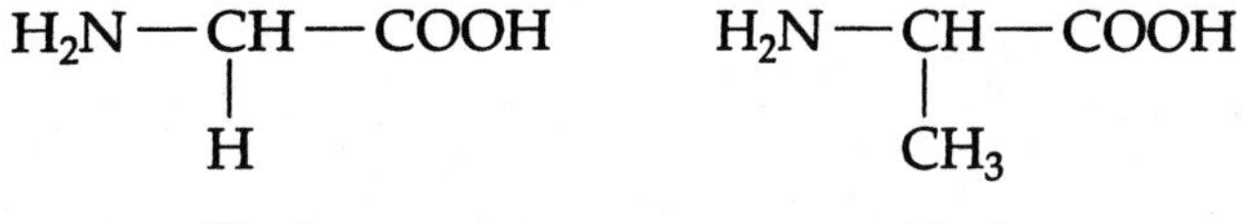

$$H_2N-CH-COOH \qquad H_2N-CH-COOH$$

with H below the first CH and CH_3 below the second CH

Glycine   Alanine

18.31 Any one of the ten amino acids the human body needs but cannot synthesize and therefore must obtain from food. See Table 18.1 of the textbook for their names.

18.32 The amide bond, $\overset{\displaystyle O}{\overset{\|}{C}}-N$, in proteins and peptides. The bond is formed when the carboxylic acid C of one amino acid bonds with the amino N of a second amino acid:

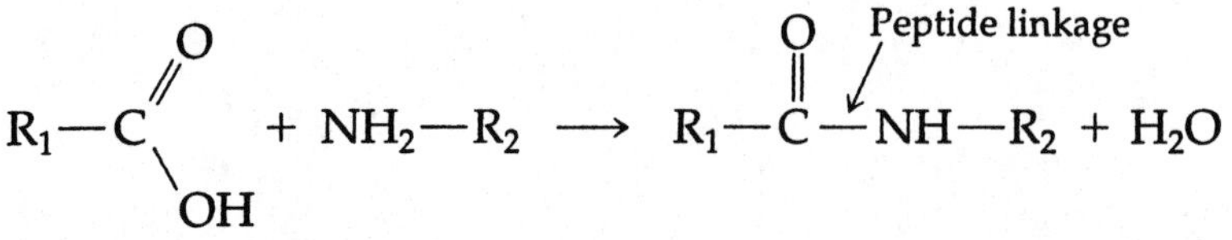

$$R_1-C\overset{\displaystyle O}{\underset{OH}{\big\backslash}} \;+\; NH_2-R_2 \;\longrightarrow\; R_1-\overset{\displaystyle O}{\overset{\|}{C}}-NH-R_2 \;+\; H_2O$$

Peptide linkage

18.33 A short or medium-length chain of amino acids. Polypeptides and proteins differ only in the length of their amino acid chains—short and medium-length chains are called polypeptides; long chains are called proteins.

18.34 The polypeptide molecule has the same amino-acid sequence as the name. The first-named amino acid contains the unreacted amino group, and the last-named amino acid contains the unreacted carboxylic acid group.

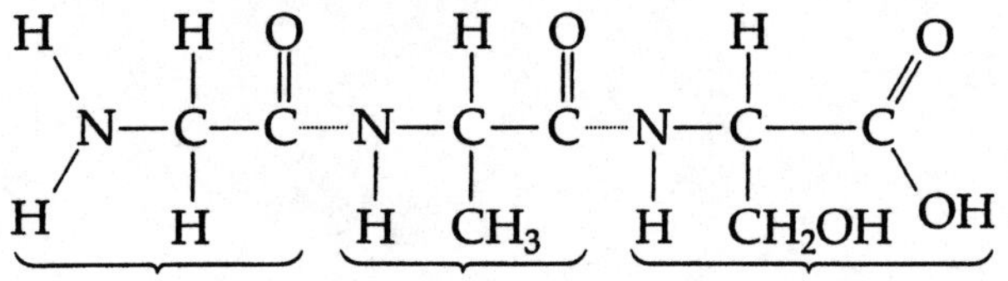

Gly   Ala   Ser

18.35 The peptide with the unreacted amino group is named first. When the amino group of alanine reacts with the carboxylic acid group of glycine, you get Gly–Ala. When the amino group of glycine reacts with the carboxylic acid group of alanine, you get Ala–Gly.

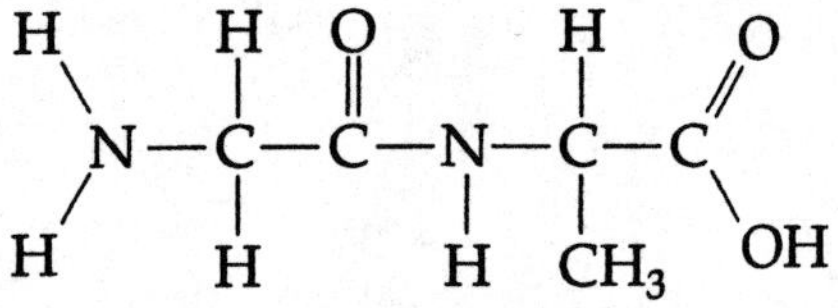

Gly–Ala 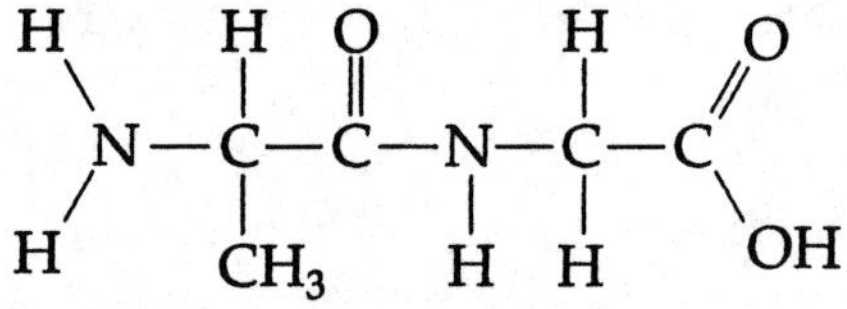   Ala–Gly

18.36 Numerous answers possible. Some functions are transport of oxygen, storage of iron, service as biological catalysts (enzymes), regulation of body processes (hormones), and formation of muscles.

18.37 The sequence of amino acids determines the three-dimensional structure of a protein, which determines how the protein functions in the body.

18.38 The sequence of bases in DNA determines the sequence of amino acids in the proteins synthesized by the body.

18.39 Alternating sugar molecules, called deoxyriboses, and phosphate groups.

One monomer unit

18.40 Hydrogen bonds. Covalent bonds would be too strong because the strands need to be able to separate when the DNA serves as a template for protein synthesis.

18.41 Four; adenine (A), guanine (G), cytosine (C), thymine (T).

18.42 Guanine–cytosine and adenine–thymine. An easy way to remember which pairs with which is to list the bases alphabetically, A C G T, and then remember that it is the two extremes, A and T, that pair, which means the other pair must be the two inner bases in the alphabetical listing, C and G.

Another memory device is to notice that C and G are both curved letters whereas A and T are combinations of straight lines. The two "curved" bases pair up, and the two "straight-line" bases pair up: C–G and A–T.

18.43 A sequence of three adjacent DNA bases; the function is to code for the incorporation of a specific amino acid into a growing protein chain.

18.44 They release their own DNA into your cells. The viral DNA then takes over each cell's protein-synthesis mechanism, causing the cell to make more virus. Eventually, there are so many virus particles that they rupture the cell, killing it. The virus particles released from the ruptured cell invade other body cells, and the process repeats at an exponential rate.

18.45 Viruses may allow physicians to incorporate portions of foreign DNA into a cell for the good of the cell. For example, once loaded into a virus cell, the gene for making human insulin might be incorporated into the cells of a diabetic patient.

18.46 (a) Yes; ···A–xx–B–A–xx–B[A–xx–B]A–xx–B–A–xx–B···

One monomer unit

You determine the monomer unit by placing an opening parenthesis at some arbitrary point along the chain (here, at a B–A bond) and then moving rightward to the next identical location (here the next B–A bond).

(b) Yes; ···A–xx–A[B–xx–B–A–xx–A]B–xx–B–A–xx–A···

One monomer unit

The monomer unit is longer here because A–B and B–A are *not* identical bonds. With the opening parenthesis at an A–B bond, you must move rightward (past the B–A bond) until you reach the next A–B bond.

18.47 In order for the interchain attractions to be stronger than those in nylon, they should be covalent bonds. Therefore design monomers that can form A–B covalent bonds even after they become monomer units in a polymer. The polymer chains will consist of A–B bonds,

A–B–A–B–A–B

but to get covalent cross-linking, each chain must also have some A and/or B free to cross-link. The two different monomers fitting this bill are

and the polymer they create is

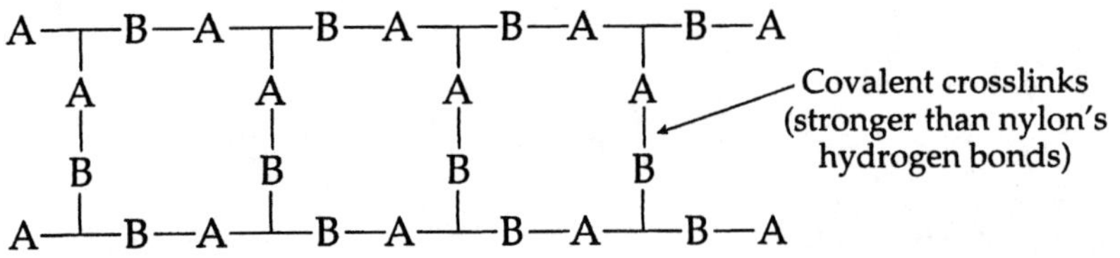

18.48 (a) Water reacts with the basic part of the alanine molecule, NH_2, as follows. When alanine is placed in water,

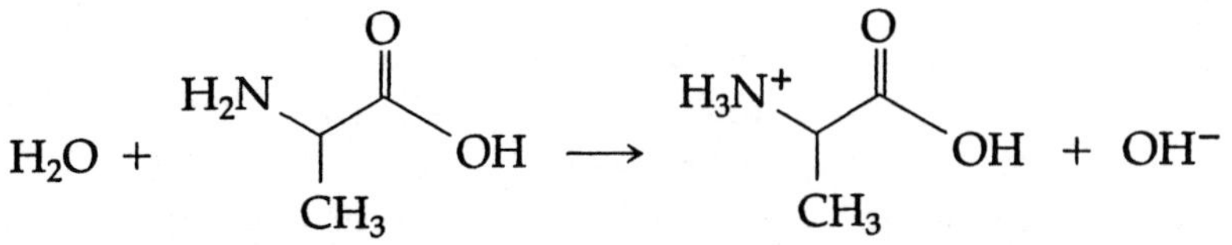

the water reacts with the acidic part, COOH, as follows:

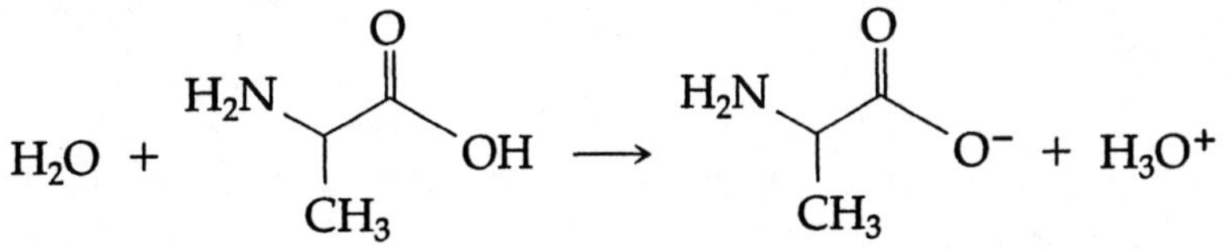

The result is an alanine carrying a positive charge at one end and a negative charge at the other. Because these two charges cancel, the net charge on the molecule is zero:

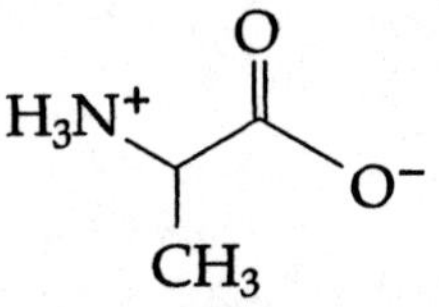

Net charge = 0

(b) The H^+ from the HCl reacts with the O^- end of the molecule to re-form OH. Now only the positive charge at N remains, giving alanine a positive charge:

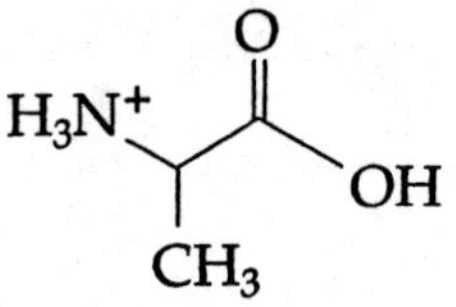

Charge = +1

(c) The OH^- from the NaOH reacts with the N^+ end of the molecule by pulling off the "extra" H^+ to form HOH. Now only the negative charge at O remains, giving alanine a negative charge:

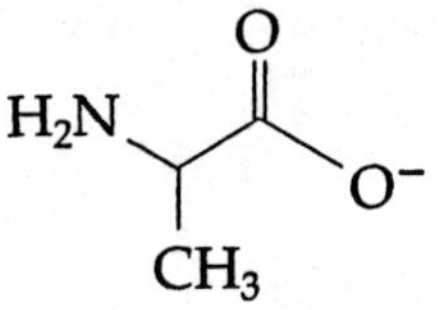

Charge = −1

18.49 (a) Deoxyribonucleic acid (DNA).

(b)  —N is the amide linkage when you are talking about nonbiological polymers and the peptide linkage when you are talking about biological polymers. The shaded boxes represent arbitrary monomer units, either hydrocarbons or amino acids. Therefore the structure represents both an amide polymer, such as nylon, and a polypeptide.

(c) Polysaccharide, because the ring structures are sugars.

18.50 (a) Ser, Arg, and Asp because in all three the side chain is polar and therefore able to react with the solvent H_2O molecules.

(b) Ala, Phe, and Ile because in all three the side chain is nonpolar.

(c) Arg because it is a basic amino acid and Asp because it is an acidic amino acid.

18.51 Aspartic acid and phenylalanine (the carboxylic acid end of which has been modified to $COOCH_3$).

18.52 You have three choices for the first amino acid: Ala–x–x, Ser–x–x, Gly–x–x. Once that choice is made, you have only two choices for the second amino acid: Ala–Ser–x, Ala–Gly–x, Ser–Ala–x, Ser–Gly–x, Gly–Ala–x, Gly–Ser–x. Then you have only one choice left for each x: Ala–Ser–Gly, Ala–Gly–Ser, Ser–Ala–Gly, Ser–Gly–Ala, Gly–Ala–Ser, Gly–Ser–Ala. The total is therefore six different tripeptides.

18.53 You have two choices for the first amino acid: Ala–x–x–x, Gly–x–x–x. Because there are two Ala to begin with, you have two choices for the second amino acid: Ala–Ala–x–x, Ala–Gly–x–x, Gly–Ala–x–x, Gly–Gly–x–x. Depending on which amino acid was used for the second one, you have these choices for the third: Ala–Ala–Gly–x, Ala–Gly–Ala–x, Ala–Gly–Gly–x, Gly–Ala–Ala–x, Gly–Ala–Gly–x, Gly–Gly–Ala–x. And the choices for the final amino acid depend on which one amino acid remains in each case: Ala–Ala–Gly–Gly, Ala–Gly–Ala–Gly, Ala–Gly–Gly–Ala, Gly–Ala–Ala–Gly, Gly–Ala–Gly–Ala, Gly–Gly–Ala–Ala. Thus six tetrapeptides can be made from two of one amino acid and two of another.

18.54 First determine the trypsin possibilities. Because there is no arginine (Arg) in either fragment, you care only that trypsin breaks peptide linkages where the COOH part of the bond comes from lysine (Lys). The trypsin fragments therefore could have come from Ala–Gly–Trp–Gly–Lys*Thr–Val–Lys, where the star indicates the broken bond, or from Thr–Val–Lys*Ala–Gly–Trp–Gly–Lys.

Whichever is the original octapeptide, it also reacted with chymotrypsin, which works on tyrosine (Tyr), phenylalanine (Phe), and tryptophan (Trp), with tryptophan being the only one of concern here. If the original peptide was the one beginning with Ala, cleavage by chymotrypsin would give Ala–Gly–Trp and Gly–Lys–Thr–Val–Lys. If the original peptide was the one beginning with Thr, cleavage by chymotrypsin would give Thr–Val–Lys–Ala–Gly–Trp and Gly–Lys. These are indeed the fragments, telling you the octapeptide was the second of the two possibilities you deduced from your trypsin information: Thr–Val–Lys–Ala–Gly–Trp–Gly–Lys.

18.55 Break all the peptide linkages to see the amino acids more easily, adding an H to the N and an OH to the carboxyl C to replace those lost when the bond formed:

Now match each side chain with Table 18.1 of the textbook to identify the amino acids.

Amino acid	Side chain	Name
First	$-CH_2OH$	Serine (Ser)
Second	$-CH_2CH_2CNH_2$ (with $\|O$ below)	Glutamine (Gln)
Third	$-CHOHCH_3$	Threonine (Thr)
Fourth	$-CH_2COH$ (with $\|O$ below)	Aspartic acid (Asp)

Note that the peptide in the textbook is drawn with the free amino end (the $-NH_2$ of the aspartic acid) on the right. As with dipeptides, however, this amino acid is named *first* when reporting the sequence. Hence the sequence is Asp–Thr–Gln–Ser.

18.56 The equation for freezing point depression is given in Section 12.9 of the textbook:

$$\Delta T_f = \frac{K_f \times \text{Moles solute particles}}{\text{Kilograms solvent}}$$

and Table 12.2 of the textbook lists 1.86 C° · kg solvent/mol solute as the value of K_f for water. Proteins do not dissociate into ions when they dissolve in water, which means moles solute particles = moles protein. Thus

$$\text{Moles solute particles} = \text{Moles protein} = \frac{\Delta T_f \times \text{Kilograms solvent}}{K_f}$$

$$= \frac{3.72 \times 10^{-4} \, C° \times 1 \, kg}{1.86 \, C° \cdot kg / \text{mol solute}} = 0.000200 \text{ mol solute}$$

$$\text{Molar mass} = \frac{10.0 \text{ g}}{2.00 \times 10^{-4} \text{ mol}} = 5.00 \times 10^4 \text{ g / mol}$$

18.57 $3.34 \text{ g } SO_2 \times \dfrac{1 \text{ mol } SO_2}{64.1 \text{ g } SO_2} \times \dfrac{1 \text{ mol } S}{1 \text{ mol } SO_2} \times \dfrac{1 \text{ mol insulin}}{6 \text{ mol } S} = 8.68 \times 10^{-3} \text{ mol insulin}$

$$\text{Molar mass} = \frac{50.0 \text{ g insulin}}{8.68 \times 10^{-3} \text{ mol}} = 5.76 \times 10^3 \text{ g / mol}$$